Reward
Management

Hay Group is a leading consultancy with some 2,000 staff in 73 offices across 38 countries focused on enabling organizations to realize their strategy through people. A strong research base and developed methodologies in reward, performance improvement, competencies, diagnostics and organization effectiveness underpin the development of innovative solutions in partnership with leading global and national organizations across all sectors.

Hay Group
33 Grosvenor Place
London SW1X 0AW
Tel: 0207 856 7000
www.haygroup.co.uk

Reward Management

A Handbook of Remuneration Strategy and Practice

5th edition

Michael Armstrong
& Helen Murlis

HayGroup
people before strategy

KOGAN PAGE

London and Philadelphia

Publisher's note

Every possible effort has been made to ensure that the information contained in this book is accurate at the time of going to press, and the publisher and authors cannot accept responsibility for any errors or omissions, however caused. No responsibility for loss or damage occasioned to any person acting, or refraining from action, as a result of the material in this publication can be accepted by the editor, the publisher or any of the authors.

First published by Kogan Page in 1988
Second edition 1991
Third edition 1994
Fourth edition 1998
Fifth edition 2004
Reprinted 2005, 2007

Apart from any fair dealing for the purposes of research or private study, or criticism or review, as permitted under the Copyright, Designs and Patents Act 1988, this publication may only be reproduced, stored or transmitted, in any form or by any means, with the prior permission in writing of the publishers, or in the case of reprographic reproduction in accordance with the terms and licences issued by the CLA. Enquiries concerning reproduction outside these terms should be sent to the publishers at the undermentioned addresses:

Kogan Page Limited
120 Pentonville Road
London N1 9JN
United Kingdom
www.kogan-page.co.uk

Kogan Page US
525 South 4th Street, #241
Philadelphia PA 19147
USA

© Michael Armstrong and Helen Murlis, 1988, 1991, 1994, 1998, 2004

The right of Michael Armstrong and Helen Murlis to be identified as the authors of this work has been asserted by them in accordance with the Copyright, Designs and Patents Act 1988.

British Library Cataloguing in Publication Data

A CIP record for this book is available from the British Library.

ISBN-10   0 7494 3984 X
ISBN-13   978 0 7494 3984 2

Typeset by Jean Cussons Typesetting, Diss, Norfolk
Printed and bound by MPG Books Ltd, Bodmin, Cornwall

Contents

Foreword

I can still recall sitting in the CIPD's library reading the 1988 edition of this book from cover to cover. So being asked now to write a foreword to the fifth edition of *Reward Management* is a bit like being invited round for a kick-about with Pele and George Best.

As the discipline has evolved from one of pay-focused administration to a strategically oriented and impacting total rewards management approach, this book has managed to combine three features that make it every bit as essential a read for reward and HR professionals, practitioners and students today as in the very first edition.

First it has profiled and promoted this shift towards strategic HR and reward management. This new edition rightly has a stronger emphasis on using reward and performance management policies and processes not just to align with business goals, but also in our more knowledge- and service-based economy, to involve and engage employees to voluntarily commit to achieving and exceeding those goals. The CIPD's latest research on the links between people and performance highlights that communication and implementation are the Achilles heels of modern HR and reward strategies.

Practice always seems to lead research in the reward field, and the second characteristic of Michael and Helen's work is that it continues to reflect leading-edge and 'hot' topics. Comparing it with the previous edition, even I am surprised at the level of change in the contents.

In the 1990s we all thought it was an inevitable progression to flexible, performance, market and cash-based rewards. Yet in this edition we rightly get a renewed emphasis on job evaluation and base pay structuring, in the wake of the strengthening impact of diversity and equal pay issues, alongside the comprehensive coverage of the many forms of contingent pay schemes, which the CIPD's latest survey shows are growing in popularity, as are flexible benefits schemes.

There would be some grounds for accusing the HR profession of being prone to adopting reward scheme 'fads' in the past. But no serious reward professional today could manage without reflecting on contemporary issues such as executive pay and the UK's pensions 'crisis', which all receive up-to-date coverage in the book. And as the 1988 edition implored, 'reward managers have to be entrepreneurs, not just administrators', an admonishment some would do well to remember in our current risk-averse times.

But thirdly, it is easy for commentators to exaggerate the level of change in reward practices. Comprehensive coverage of the full and varied range of technical 'tools' and of some of the underlying fundamentals of effective reward management and motivation still lies at the heart of this book. That's why I have always had it to refer to, be that in writing 150 job descriptions in a week at BMW early in my career, or inputting into the UN's reward strategy years later, and that is why it remains an essential reference text. Strategic vision and technical expertise, as Professor John Boudreau at Cornell University points out, are not 'either/ors' for the HR profession. They both form a 'double-barrelled driver' of the function's expanding influence and impact, and both are extensively covered in this book.

Professor Rosabeth Moss Kanter at Harvard defined reward management at its most essential core: 'when people have the opportunity to act on their own initiative, to shape their own work and feel they are rewarded for making a difference, they can do great things – that's been true throughout the ages'. It's easy to set out that reward nirvana, but fiendishly difficult to achieve and retain it. And it is precisely that mix of high challenge but potentially high returns that makes reward management such a critical component of successful HR and business strategies.

One Manager of Rewards in the recent CIPD's annual reward survey described his biggest challenge as 'controlling pensions costs, reducing the car fleet, introducing a more flexible pay structure and moving to flexible benefits, all without increasing the pay bill'. He wisely reported that he was responding to this multi-faceted agenda by proceeding 'slowly and carefully'. And no doubt with a copy of *Reward Management* on his bookshelf.

Duncan Brown
Assistant Director General
CIPD

Preface to the Fifth Edition

In this fifth edition of *Reward Management* we are incorporating much new material based on our experience, research and benchmarking activities. We have also been helped by a number of Hay Group colleagues who have made invaluable contributions based on their own extensive experience. To this we have added the considerable amount of research that has been conducted into the practice of reward management in both the UK and the United States.

In particular the developments we have observed and write about in this book include:

- the concept of total reward;
- the concept of engaged performance;
- the continuing emphasis on strategic reward and integration;
- the need to take positive action to achieve equal pay;
- the increased interest in job evaluation, partly in response to equal pay imperatives;
- the focus on career and job family structures and the reduced enthusiasm for 'broad-banded' grade and pay structures;
- the emergence of contribution-related pay as a major approach to contingent pay;
- the increased interest in flexible benefits.

OUR PHILOSOPHY

In developing and, in some areas, rethinking ideas we have expressed in earlier editions, we have continued to evolve our own philosophy about reward management, the key points of which are:

▌ It is neither possible nor desirable to be prescriptive in the sense of providing easy and superficial answers to subtle and far-reaching problems of motivation and reward. We believe absolutely that a contingency approach has to be used when dealing with this subject; ie that the right reward processes are the ones which are right for a particular organization. There is indeed such a thing as 'good practice', but it is never universally 'best practice'.

▌ The importance of understanding the culture, climate, environment and management practices of the organization before attempting any innovations cannot be overestimated.

▌ Reward policies and practices can play a significant part in change programmes, helping to achieve strategic goals and underpinning the culture. But the lead has to come from top management, which sets the direction and decides how reward management can best provide the help and support required.

▌ We are not in the business of peddling panaceas. There are no quick fixes or sudden transformations available in this field – no holy grails, only horses for courses.

▌ We do believe, however, that there are guidelines available when deciding what is the most appropriate practice. We have described the various approaches available from which a choice can be made, and their advantages and disadvantages, as they appear to us.

▌ Our approach is empirical. It is based on the experience and observations of colleagues, researchers and ourselves. It is, however, underpinned by theories about motivation, incentives and reward. But we join with Douglas McGregor[1] in the belief that 'there is nothing so practical as a good theory'; ie one which is based on practical research, experimentation and analysis of experience.

▌ We have come to the view that what we are writing about is a set of processes relating to reward management, which include the design and maintenance of pay structures as well as the fundamental processes of assessing job and role size (job evaluation) and measuring and rewarding performance (performance management, incentives and contingent pay). We have rejected the term 'reward system' because it conveys the idea of some sort of mechanism for converting inputs into outputs, and there is little that is mechanical about reward management apart from payroll operation. Of course reward management involves the application of schemes and procedures within pay structures. But what matters most is not the design, procedure or structure of the scheme, but the way it is applied, used and maintained, and these are the process issues which ultimately determine the effectiveness of an organization's reward policies and practices.

▌ We attach particular importance to sustainability – there is no point in developing elaborate 'overengineered' pay systems, however elegant they may be, if they do not carry on working well in practice with the support of line managers and employees in general.

▌ Planned and managed incremental change is easier to design, implement and sustain than quantum leaps into unknown territory.

▌ It is necessary to provide for tactical advances and retreats. We will not get it right all the time. 'L-plates' on new policies will be helpful in the context of the learning organization.

▌ Philosophy needs to precede strategy and implementation. We need to be clear about what we are paying for and why before we rush into detailed design. Strategic integrity needs to underpin technical excellence.

▌ In Voltaire's words, 'The best is the enemy of the good' – sometimes a successful future lies in agreeing what, in the short term, we can only get 'nearly right'. We follow Aristotle's teaching in the *Nichomachean Ethics* that 'It is the mark of an educated mind to rest satisfied with the degree of precision that the nature of the subject admits, and not to seek a degree of exactness when only an approximation is possible.' Practicality not perfection should be the aim. There will always be time available in the future to make improvements based on experience.

▌ It is, however, still necessary to set clear short- and longer-term objectives about what is to be achieved by reward management innovations. Some attempt must also be made to define critical success factors and performance measures and it is, of course, essential to monitor and evaluate progress in the light of these success factors and measures.

We do not expect our readers to go through this book from cover to cover. It is our experience from previous editions that users dip in principally to chapters they need to refer to. We have therefore cross-referenced chapters as far as possible, but also included an element of repetition where it is helpful to have everything in one place. That said, we hope that this text will prove useful to a wide range of specialists and non-specialists tackling the challenges of reward management at the beginning of the twenty-first century.

Acknowledgements

Thanks are due to many people who have contributed their thoughts, experience and insights to this edition.

First, we are grateful to Duncan Brown, Assistant Director General of the CIPD and leading reward thinker for our new forward.

From Hay Group we would like to thank Nick Boulter and the UK Executive for their continuing support for this book. Gratitude is also due to Hay Group colleagues for contributing new chapters and updates or improvements to existing chapters:

- Simon Barron – use of Excel spreadsheets;
- Peter Boreham – executive incentives, profit sharing, flexible benefits and pensions;
- Georgina Churchlow, Jane Phillipson and Tim Jones – equal pay;
- Philip Cohen, Mark Thompson and Julie Alderdice – job evaluation and role analysis and many of the reward chapters;
- Chris Davey – further sources of reading and information;
- Brad Hill (Hay Group Chicago) – gainsharing;
- Naomi Gill and Haydn Young – salary market information;
- Simon Garrett – boardroom pay, executive and all employee share schemes and LTIPs;
- Iola Goulton – recognition schemes and employee benefits;
- Dilum Jirasinghe – performance management;
- Ian Tinsley – mergers and acquisitions and reward policies for new and start-up organizations;
- Doris Siedentopf, Cathy Marland and Phillip Wright – international remuneration;
- Peter Smith – team rewards;
- Stephen Welch – employee opinion surveys.

We are also very grateful to Barry Rodin of Employment Conditions Abroad for his contribution to Chapter 36, to Jim Watts of the Reward Workshop for his chapter on sales force incentives, to Antony Betts and Naz Karimbhai of RSM Robson Rhodes for Chapter 34 on tax and to Pilat (UK) and Link Group for the summaries of their job evaluation methodology.

Finally we wish to record our gratitude to our partners Peggy Armstrong and John Murlis and our families for their continuing and unstinting support for the completion of this book.

Part 1

Fundamentals of Reward Management

Overview of Reward Management

The aim of this chapter is to provide a general introduction to reward management. It starts by defining reward management and its aims, which leads into a summary of the views of the main contributors to the development of the reward management concept. This is followed by descriptions of the processes and activities of reward management and the chapter concludes with an assessment of the impact that reward management can make.

REWARD MANAGEMENT DEFINED

Reward management is concerned with the formulation and implementation of strategies and policies that aim to reward people fairly, equitably and consistently in accordance with their value to the organization. It deals with the design, implementation and maintenance of reward processes and practices that are geared to the improvement of organizational, team and individual performance.

THE AIMS OF REWARD MANAGEMENT

The strategic aim of reward management is to develop and implement the reward policies, processes and practices required to support the achievement of the organization's business goals. The specific aims are to:

▌ create total reward processes that are based on beliefs about what the organization values and wants to achieve;

▌ reward people for the value they create;

▌ align reward practices with both business goals and employee values; as Duncan Brown[1] emphasizes, the 'alignment of your reward practices with employee values and needs is every bit as important as alignment with business goals, and critical to the realisation of the latter';

▌ reward the right things to convey the right message about what is important in terms of expected behaviours and outcomes;

▌ facilitate the attraction and retention of the skilled and competent people the organization needs, thus 'winning the war for talent';

▌ help in the process of motivating people and gaining their commitment and engagement;

▌ support the development of a performance culture;

▌ develop a positive employment relationship and psychological contract.

ACHIEVING THE AIMS

To achieve these aims, reward management must be strategic in the sense that it addresses longer-term issues relating to how people should be valued for what they do and what they achieve. Reward strategies and the processes that are required to implement them have to flow from the business strategy. They have to be integrated with other human resource management (HRM) strategies, especially those concerning human resource development – reward management is an integral part of an HRM approach to managing people.

Effective reward management is based on a well-articulated philosophy – a set of beliefs and guiding principles that are consistent with the values of the organization and help to enact them. It recognizes that if HRM is about investing in human capital from which a reasonable return is required, then it is proper to reward people differentially according to their contribution (ie the return on investment they generate).

Importantly, reward management adopts a 'total reward' approach, which emphasizes the importance of considering all aspects of reward as a coherent whole that is integrated with other HR initiatives designed to achieve the motivation, commitment and engagement of employees.

CONTRIBUTORS TO THE CONCEPT OF REWARD MANAGEMENT

Much of the impetus for the development of the reward management concept has come from US writers, especially Lawler with 'strategic pay'[7] and, more recently, 'Treat people right',[3] Schuster and Zingheim[4] with 'the new pay' and Flannery, Hofrichter and Platten[5] with 'dynamic pay'.

Strategic pay

Lawler emphasized that when developing reward policies it is necessary to think and act strategically about reward. Reward policies should take account of the organization's goals, value and culture and of the challenges of a more competitive global economy. New pay helps to develop the individual and organizational behaviour that a company needs if its business goals are to be met. Pay policies and practices must flow from the overall strategy and they can help to emphasize important objectives such as customer satisfaction and retention and product or service quality.

In *Treat People Right*[3] Ed Lawler stresses the importance of creating a 'virtuous spiral' in which both employers and employees win. He identifies a number of principles for achieving this, which look at the whole HRM agenda from creating the right value proposition on recruitment, through to quality of leadership. He states that: 'It is entirely possible to design a reward system that motivates people to work and satisfies them while at the same time contributing to organizational effectiveness.'

The new pay

Lawler's concept of the new pay was developed by Schuster and Zingheim who described its fundamental principles as follows:

▌ Total compensation programmes should be designed to reward results and behaviour consistent with the key goals of the organization.
▌ Pay can be a positive force for organizational change.
▌ The major thrust of new pay is in introducing variable (at risk) pay.
▌ The new pay emphasis is on team as well as individual rewards, with employees sharing financially in the organization's success.
▌ Pay is an employee relations issue – employees have the right to determine whether the values, culture and reward systems of the organization match their own.

But Lawler[6] later emphasized that the 'new pay' ideology should be regarded as a conceptual approach to payment rather than a set of prescriptions: 'The new pay is not a set of compensation practices at all, but rather a way of thinking about reward systems in a complex organisation... The new pay does not necessarily mean implementing new reward practices or abandoning traditional ones; it means identifying pay practices that enhance the organization's strategic effectiveness.'

Dynamic pay

Flannery, Hofrichter and Platten expounded the concept of 'dynamic pay' and suggested that the nine principles that support a successful pay strategy are:

1. Align compensation with the organization's culture, values and strategic business goals.
2. Link compensation to the other changes.
3. Time the compensation programme to best support other change initiatives.
4. Integrate pay with other people processes.
5. Democratize the pay process.
6. Demystify compensation.
7. Measure results.
8. Refine. Refine again. Refine some more.
9. Be selective. Don't take to heart everything you hear or read about pay.

REWARD MANAGEMENT PROCESSES AND ACTIVITIES

The processes and activities of reward management are illustrated in Figure 1.1.

The components are described below:

▌ *The business/HR strategy.* This is the starting-point; all the reward policies, processes and practices flow from here to achieve the overarching business goal of improved performance.

▌ *The reward strategy.* This determines the direction in which reward management innovations and developments should go to support the business strategy, how they should be integrated, the priority that should be given to initiatives and the pace at which they should be implemented.

▌ *Grade and pay structure policy.* This deals with the policy on the shape of the grade structure and the elements of pay within that structure, ie:

– *Base pay:* the fixed rate of pay that represents the rate for the job into which pay related to performance, competence, contribution or service may be consolidated. Policies on base pay levels will be affected by the factors discussed at the end of this chapter but,

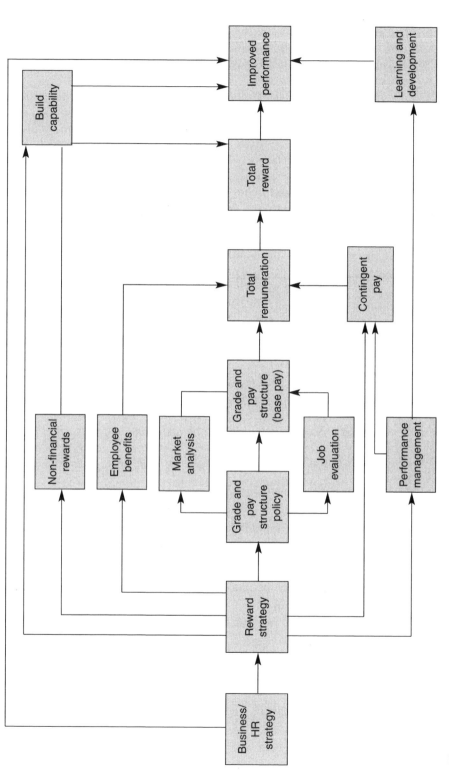

Figure 1.1 The components of reward management

importantly, they will express the intentions of the organization on the degree to which it wants pay levels to be competitive and therefore the relationship between those pay levels and market rates (its 'market stance').

- *Contingent pay:* pay for individuals that is related to performance, competence, contribution or service.
- *Variable pay:* pay in the form of bonuses or cash payments that will be contingent on individual, team or company performance.

▌ *Market analysis.* The process of identifying rates of pay in the labour market to inform decisions on levels of pay within the organization, which will be influenced by its market stance.

▌ *Job evaluation.* The systematic process of establishing the relative size of jobs and roles within the organization.

▌ *Grade structure.* The sequence or hierarchy of grades, bands or levels, which may be divided into job or career families and into which, on the basis of job evaluation, groups of jobs or roles that are broadly comparable in size are placed.

▌ *Pay structure.* The ranges of base pay that are attached to grades or levels in job or career families and the scope for pay progression related to performance, competence, contribution or service. Base pay levels will be influenced by equity and market rate considerations.

▌ *Employee benefits.* The provision for employees of pensions, sick pay, various kinds of perks such as company cars and entitlement to holidays and other leave.

▌ *Non-financial rewards.* Rewards that do not involve any direct payments and often arise from the work itself, for example achievement, autonomy, recognition, scope to use and develop skills, training, career development opportunities and high-quality leadership.

▌ *Performance management.* Processes involving managers, individuals and teams based on shared understanding, which define performance and contribution expectations, assess performance against those expectations, provide for regular constructive feedback and inform agreed plans for performance improvement, learning and personal development. Performance management will also inform contingent pay decisions.

▌ *Total remuneration.* The sum of base pay, contingent pay and the value of employee benefits.

▌ *Total reward.* The sum of total remuneration and non-financial rewards.

▌ *Building capability.* Building the capability of both the reward function and line management to understand, work with and communicate the elements of reward policy and practice and changes as they occur.

THE IMPACT OF REWARD MANAGEMENT

US writers in the 1990s such as those mentioned earlier suggested that what they call 'compensation policies' can exert a major influence on organizational cultures, processes and results. But this notion can be taken too far. The naive belief that devices such as performance-related pay can by themselves act as 'levers for change' has been responsible for many of the failures in reward innovations over the last decade. The impact of reward management on performance is not clear cut. Simplistic solutions such as performance pay working in isolation and ignoring the complexity of motivating factors won't work. As Sandra O'Neal[7] points out: 'It is simply no longer possible to create a set of rewards that is universally appealing to all employees or to address a series of complex business issues through a single set of solutions.'

Of course, reward policies and practices must respond to change and they can help to consolidate it. However, their role is to support change not to drive it. And they can play an important part in managing the psychological contract – the beliefs held by an employee and an employer of what they expect from one another. Duncan Brown[1] suggests that: 'Pay and formal reward policies are one of the most tangible symbols of a company's culture and employment offering and are inextricably interwoven with them. Therefore they are critical to demonstrating that the employer is delivering on its side of the employment bargain.'

REFERENCES

1. Brown, D (2001) *Reward Strategies: From intent to impact*, CIPD, London
2. Lawler, E E (1990) *Strategic Pay*, Jossey-Bass, San Francisco
3. Lawler, E E (2003) *Treat People Right*, Jossey-Bass, San Francisco
4. Schuster, J R and Zingheim, P K (1992) *The New Pay*, Lexington Books, New York
5. Flannery, T P, Hofrichter, D A and Platten, P E (1996) *People, Performance, and Pay*, Free Press, New York
6. Lawler, E E (1995) The new pay: a strategic approach, *Compensation & Benefits Review*, November
7. O'Neal, S (1998) The phenomenon of total rewards, *ACA Journal*, **7** (3)

2

Total Reward and Engaged Performance

The growing emphasis on employee engagement as critical to organizational performance means that the concept of total reward is exerting more and more influence on reward strategy. Pressures we have identified elsewhere in this book for organizations to recruit and keep talent in an environment where diverse and mobile employees are often more demanding and assertive about what they want from an employer will increase this influence. The messages are out there prominently and frequently for general consumption. The annual *Sunday Times* 'Best Companies to Work For' or the *Fortune* 'Most Admired Companies' spell out in articles and on Web sites why W L Gore, Microsoft and Asda for example have come high in the listings. Being an 'employer of choice' now matters in the boardroom and it matters a lot for those who manage reward. Employees and potential employees have become much more sophisticated 'customers' of total reward offerings and more questioning of what they contain. As the rising tide of literature on both sides of the Atlantic makes clear, they want options and a measure of customization to their life- and work-style decisions.

This chapter starts with a definition of the concept and explains its significance. It continues with an analysis of the constituent parts of total reward and describes in more detail the key elements of total reward using a model, 'Engaged Performance', developed by Hay Group. It concludes with an assessment of the benefits of the total reward approach and a brief description of how total reward processes can be developed.

TOTAL REWARD DEFINED

The total reward concept emphasizes the importance of considering all aspects of reward as an integrated and coherent whole. Each of the elements of total reward, namely base pay, pay contingent on performance, competence or contribution, employee benefits and non-financial rewards, which include intrinsic rewards from the employment environment and the work itself, are linked together. A total reward approach is holistic; reliance is not placed on one or two reward mechanisms or levers operating in isolation. Account is taken of all the ways in which people can be rewarded and obtain satisfaction through their work. The aim is to offer a value proposition and maximize the combined impact of a wide range of reward initiatives on motivation, commitment and job engagement. As Sandra O'Neal[1] has explained: 'Total reward embraces everything that employees value in the employment relationship.'

An equally wide definition of total reward is offered by WorldatWork,[2] who state that total rewards are 'all of the employer's available tools that may be used to attract, retain, motivate and satisfy employees'. As Paul Thompson[3] suggests: 'Definitions of total reward typically encompass not only traditional, quantifiable elements like salary, variable pay and benefits, but also more intangible non-cash elements such as scope to achieve and exercise responsibility, career opportunities, learning and development, the intrinsic motivation provided by the work itself and the quality of working life provided by the organization.'

At its best, the total reward approach embodies the organizational adoption of a more emotionally intelligent way of working. It requires the use of the key competency levers of self-management, self-awareness, social awareness and relationship management in an organizational context as part of the approach needed to secure leadership excellence in the pursuit of significantly raised performance.

The conceptual basis of total rewards is that of grouping or 'bundling', so that different reward processes are interrelated, complementary and mutually reinforcing. This is the basis of the Hay Group Model of Engaged Performance (see below). Total reward strategies are vertically integrated with business strategies, but they are also horizontally integrated with other HR strategies to achieve internal consistency.

THE SIGNIFICANCE OF TOTAL REWARD

Essentially, the notion of total reward says that there is more to rewarding people than throwing money at them, or, as Helen Murlis and Steve Watson[4] put it: 'The monetary values in the reward package still matter but they are not the only factors.' They went on to say: 'Cash is a weak tactic in the overall reward strategy; it is too easily replicated. Intrinsic reward is far more difficult to emulate.' But they also stress that total reward policies are based on 'building a much deeper under-standing of the employee agenda across all elements of reward'.

For Sandra O'Neal,[1] a total reward strategy is critical to addressing the issues created by recruitment and retention as well as providing a means of influencing behaviour: 'It can help create a work experience that meets the needs of employees and encourages them to contribute extra effort, by developing a deal that addresses a broad range of issues and by spending reward dollars where they will be most effective in addressing workers' shifting values.'

Perhaps the most powerful argument for a total rewards approach was produced by Pfeffer:[5]

> Creating a fun, challenging, and empowered work environment in which individuals are able to use their abilities to do meaningful jobs for which they are shown appreciation is likely to be a more certain way to enhance motiva-tion and performance – even though creating such an environment may be more difficult and take more time than simply turning the reward lever.

COMPONENTS OF TOTAL REWARDS

The components of total rewards are illustrated in Figure 2.1.

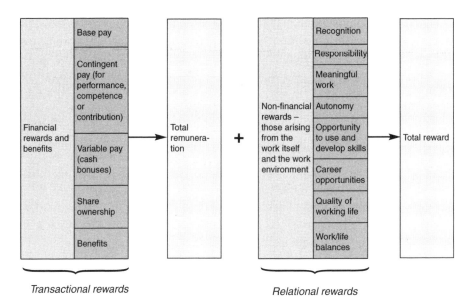

Figure 2.1 Components of total rewards

WordatWork[2] distinguish between:

▌ *Compensation* – the 'foundational' rewards that are primarily financial in nature and satisfy financial needs for income.
▌ *Benefits* – these satisfy protection needs and are unlikely to be performance-based.
▌ *The work experience* – these are the relational needs that bind workers to the organization more strongly because they satisfy an individual's needs such as personal development and fulfilment.

Most leading firms of HR and reward consultants have developed their own model of or approach to total reward with similar kinds of headings to reflect their interpretation of the idea and its links to building a healthier psychological contract or a more appealing 'employer brand'.

Duncan Brown and Michael Armstrong[6] have produced a model based on one originally developed by Duncan Brown at Towers Perrin. This distinguishes between *transactional rewards*, which are financial in nature and are essential to recruiting and retaining staff but can be easily copied by competitors, and *relational rewards*, which are concerned with learning and development and the work experience and are essential to enhancing the value of transactional rewards. The real power, as Thompson[3] states, comes when organizations combine relational and transactional rewards.

THE HAY GROUP ENGAGED PERFORMANCE MODEL

In the late 1990s Hay Group developed a model from their employee opinion and reward work, which looked not just at the transactional and relational elements of reward but focused also on what employees defined as a compelling, high-performance workplace. As Figure 2.2 shows, this model comprises six key elements.

Research by Hay Group among growing numbers of employers in the UK and elsewhere suggests that the 'Inspiration and values' cluster, followed by the 'Future growth and opportunity' cluster, is what employees value most, with tangible rewards coming third or fourth in priority – except in those organizations where a decline in salary market competitiveness has raised the level of attention on pay and taken it back to the front of people's minds.

A large part of this book inevitably focuses on the policies and processes associated with transactional or financial rewards – the tangible rewards in the Engaged Performance Model. But this does not mean that the significance of the rewards in the other five relational elements is underestimated, and the next section of this chapter there-

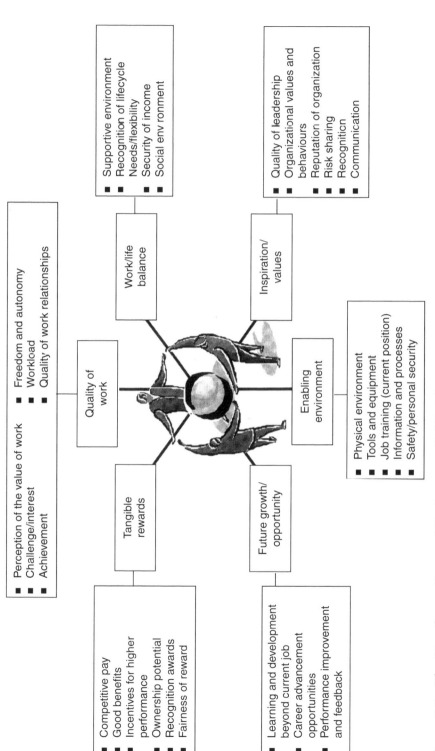

- Perception of the value of work
- Challenge/interest
- Achievement
- Freedom and autonomy
- Workload
- Quality of work relationships

Quality of work

- Supportive environment
- Recognition of lifecycle
- Needs/flexibility
- Security of income
- Social env ronment

Work/life balance

- Quality of leadership
- Organizational values and behaviours
- Reputation of organization
- Risk sharing
- Recognition
- Communication

Inspiration/values

- Competitive pay
- Good benefits
- Incentives for higher performance
- Ownership potential
- Recognition awards
- Fairness of reward

Tangible rewards

- Learning and development beyond current job
- Career advancement opportunities
- Performance improvement and feedback

Future growth/opportunity

- Physical environment
- Tools and equipment
- Job training (current position)
- Information and processes
- Safety/personal security

Enabling environment

Figure 2.2   The Hay Group Engaged Performance® Model

fore concentrates on them, relegating the discussion of financial rewards to later chapters.

RELATIONAL REWARDS

Inspiration and values

Quality of leadership

People join organizations and leave bosses. They have 'that's it' moments when they decide to stay or go either because their employer works and carries out its activities in a way they care about or because the conflict with their personal values becomes too uncomfortable to tolerate. As Goleman, Boyatzis and McKee put it:[7] 'A cranky and ruthless boss creates a toxic organization filled with negative underachievers who ignore opportunities: an inspirational, inclusive leader spawns acolytes for whom any challenge is surmountable.' The leadership styles and behaviours fostered and used in organizations have a major impact on the values of the organization and the way it behaves. Leaders play a vital role in total reward management. They exist to get things done through people, ensuring that tasks are achieved and strategies delivered, but also building and maintaining supportive and constructive relationships between themselves and the employees in their team or group. They are there to motivate people and indeed to secure engaged performance. Leaders are the sources of important rewards such as recognition through effective feedback (see Chapter 19), providing the scope to carry out meaningful work, and providing opportunities for development and learning. They are crucial to the success of performance management and to the values underpinning tangible rewards.

Organizational values and behaviours

The significance of the core values of an organization as a basis for creating a rewarding work environment was clearly identified by the research conducted by John Purcell and his colleagues.[8] The most successful companies had what the researchers call 'the big idea'. These companies had a clear vision and a set of values, which were embedded, enduring, collective, measured and managed. They were concerned with sustaining performance and flexibility. Clear evidence existed between positive attitudes towards HR policies and practices, levels of satisfaction, motivation and commitment, and operational performance.

Reputation of the organization

People want to work for a high-reputation employer. It is good to see your organization move up the 'Best Companies to Work For' league table, or attract favourable press coverage for its contribution to national life. This is often part of an employer's value proposition or 'employer brand'. Much of the public service has in the past benefited from the respect its various parts have in the community. Saying you work for a university or hospital or in overseas development places you as aligned with worthwhile organizational activity. You might be quieter about whom you worked for, however, if one of your directors had been involved in a scandal, if the organization had been caught being less than socially responsible or if it had high employee turnover and poor employment conditions.

Risk sharing

Employees have a strong sense of unfairness if they are asked to shoulder unacceptable levels of risk in an organization. On the pay front this might involve being on a highly geared incentive or commission scheme where the fixed pay element was too close to their particular 'bread line' (see also 'Security of income' below). The risks might however come rather in accountability and support for decision making – are heroic failures tolerated as part of organizational learning or are they punished in what turns out to be a 'blame culture'? This issue is fundamental to the extent to which organizations succeed with innovation and creativity.

Recognition

As we illustrate in Chapter 27, recognition is one of the most powerful methods of rewarding people. They need to know not only how well they have achieved their objectives or carried out their work, but also that their achievements are appreciated. Recognition needs are linked to the esteem needs in Maslow's[9] hierarchy of needs. These are defined by Maslow as the need to have a stable, firmly based, high evaluation of oneself (self-esteem) and to have the respect of others (prestige). These needs are classified into two subsidiary sets: first, 'the desire for achievement, for adequacy, for confidence in the face of the world, and for independence and freedom' and, second, 'the desire for reputation or status defined as respect or esteem from other people and manifested by attention, importance or appreciation'.

Recognition can be provided by positive and immediate feedback and praise where it is well deserved. Financial awards closely linked to successful delivery are, of course, financial recognition – and can be an important part of mutually reinforcing systems of recognition. And there are other forms of recognition such as public 'applause' status symbols such as representing the organization at prestigious conferences or international meetings, sales events in exotic resorts, 'employee of the year' awards and long-service awards, which are much appreciated as rewards (see Chapter 27).

Recognition is also provided by managers who listen to and act upon the suggestions of their team members and, importantly, acknowledge their contribution. Other actions that provide recognition include promotion, allocation to a high-profile project, enlargement of the job to provide scope for more interesting and rewarding work, and other forms of status or esteem symbols. Caution, however, is needed in the use of status symbols since they can be divisive. Virtually all informal rewards used without sensitivity can form a zero-sum game; one person's recognition can imply an element of non-recognition to others and the consequences of having winners and losers. Procedural justice is very important here and needs thought and careful management.

Communication

This area is not just about the quality of organizational communication, transparency and honesty (see Chapter 40). An important part of the 'respect equation' is something called 'employee voice'. As defined by Peter Boxall and John Purcell,[10] 'Employee voice is the term increasingly used to cover a whole variety of processes and structures which enable and sometimes empower employees directly and indirectly to contribute to the decision making in the firm.' Having a voice in the affairs of the firm is rewarding because it recognizes the contribution people can make to the success of the organization or their team.

Employees can have a voice as an aspect of the normal working relationships between themselves and their managers and as such it is linked closely to other reward factors discussed here such as recognition, opportunities for achievement and risk sharing. But the organization, through its policies for involvement, can provide motivation and increase commitment and engagement by putting people into situations where their views can be expressed, listened to and acted upon. This is central to Linda Gratton's concept of the 'democratic enterprise'[11] where she focuses on the importance of an adult–adult relationship that has at its heart 'the quality of openness [that] is the communication between the individual and his or her boss' as well as the involvement the individual feels in the everyday working of the organization.

Future growth and opportunity

Learning and development beyond current job

Most people want to get on. As Ed Lawler put it,[12] 'People enjoy learning – there's no doubt about it – and it touches on an important treat people right principle for both organizations and people: the value of continuous, ongoing training and development in creating a virtuous spiral.

Learning is an intrinsically satisfying and rewarding experience.' Alderfer too[13] emphasized the importance of the chance to grow as a means of rewarding people and therefore motivating them. He wrote: 'Satisfaction of growth needs depends on a person finding the opportunity to be what he or she is most fully and become what he or she can.' Employers can offer this opportunity by providing people with a sequence of experience and training that helps equip them for whatever level of responsibility they have the ability to reach. Talented individuals can be given the guidance and encouragement they need to fulfil their potential and achieve a successful career in tune with their abilities and aspirations. It helps to work within the context of a 'learning organization', and provisions can range from planned experience gathering to formal programmes. These can take the form of management and leadership programmes, team leadership development, further skills training, mentoring and one-to-one coaching. Coaching is now making a significant contribution to fast-tracking learning at senior levels where very specific behavioural issues may need tackling and where the time or inclination to go on broader leadership programmes is often lacking.

Career advancement opportunities

This element is clearly linked to the learning and development part of the talent management process. 'Will there be opportunities for me to progress?' is one of the commonest questions on recruitment. New graduates and MBAs very legitimately ask about how the organization manages and progresses talent, especially in an environment that is likely to have many fewer promotion opportunities than in the past. They want reassurance that processes are in place for identifying talent, for succession planning and for fair and reasonably transparent means of making promotion decisions. To apply this element of reward well, organizations need to be clear what the career paths are and what the criteria are for making lateral and diagonal moves as well as promotions. Competency frameworks can help a lot here since they should provide additional and welcome clarity about what matters to their

organization.

Performance improvement and feedback

Effective performance management is a powerful means of providing total reward. It is and should be the basis for developing a positive psychological contract by clarifying the mutual expectations of managers and their staff in an environment focused on success. Constructive feedback can be highly motivational. People who are allowed to claim their successes and review what they could do differently in an adult–adult context are given the opportunity to extend their range. Performance reviews should inform personal development planning and encourage self-managed learning – again support from a manager in delivering on development plans can be very motivational. Success should breed success in the creation of a high-performance culture.

This is however an area where it is possible to be very demotivational (see Chapters 18 and 19). Poorly handled feedback, arbitrary performance rating and forced distributions, lack of follow-through on performance agreements and poorly communicated recognition are all pitfalls to be avoided.

Quality of work

Perception of the value of work

People channel their discretionary effort into their work if they believe it has meaning and is worthwhile and appreciated. It can be a motivator to join a particular occupation or profession, eg fire-fighter, teacher, midwife, environmental scientist or lawyer. Or the reward can come as a consequence of the way in which leaders treat their people and their contribution. Asda, for example, have demonstrated that people working at checkouts and in other relatively unskilled basic jobs can perform well in a high-morale environment because they feel valued by their store managers and are encouraged to reach out and contribute to charity work and the life of their community.

Challenge/interest

Relatively few people in our increasingly knowledge-based economy choose to work in jobs that are repetitive and boring and where there is little challenge or interest in the work. If they have to, they tend to create interest by changing jobs more frequently than they might in a more challenging environment unless the social environment suits them (see 'Work/life balance' below). For professionals, challenge and interest are typically critical components of their intrinsic reward package and a real demotivator if missing.

To get this area right, it is important to understand the contribution of job design and role development. Job design has two aims: first, to meet the needs of the organization for operational efficiency, quality of product or service and productivity and, second, to reward individuals by satisfying their needs for meaningful work that provides for interest, challenge and accomplishment. Job design is not a static process. The roles people play at work usually develop as they respond to opportunities and changing demands, acquiring new skills and developing their competencies. Jobs and roles are, or should be, shaped over time by managers and team members to make the best of people's skills and capabilities and provide optimum levels of intrinsic reward. Ed Lawler[14] identified intrinsically motivating jobs as those where individuals received meaningful feedback about their performance in roles where they had accountability for a complete process or product, or significant part of it, and where there was scope for self-evaluation. Such roles must be perceived by individuals as requiring them to use abilities they value to perform the roles effectively and they should feel they have a high degree of autonomy over setting their own goals and defining paths to these goals.

Robertson and Smith[15] expanded on this to set out five principles for the development of rewarding jobs and roles. They identified five kinds of influence in this area:

1. *influence skill variety* – providing opportunities for people to do several tasks and to combine tasks;
2. *influence task identity* – combining tasks to form natural work units;
3. *influence task significance* – forming natural work groups and informing people of the importance of their work;
4. *influence autonomy* – giving people responsibility for determining their own working systems and making their own decisions;
5. *influence feedback* – opening and using feedback channels.

Achievement

The need to achieve applies in varying degrees to all people in all jobs, although the level at which it operates will depend on the orientation of the individual and the scope provided by the work to fulfil a need for achievement. People feel rewarded and motivated if they have the scope to achieve as well as being recognized for the achievement. University researchers, for example, want to enhance their reputation as well as making a significant contribution to their institution's research rating. Being encouraged and supported with publications helps meet this need. In industry this need might be met by assignment to participate in or lead a strategic project, or agreement on a stretching but achievable delivery target. Or it might be seeing the team succeed.

If achievement motivation is high it will result in behaviour such as taking control of situations or relationships, directing the course of events, creating and seizing opportunities, enjoying challenge, reacting swiftly and positively to new circumstances and relationships and generally 'making things happen'. People who are driven by the need to achieve are likely to be proactive, to seek opportunities and to insist on recognition. Those whose orientations are not so strongly defined can be helped to satisfy possibly latent achievement needs by being given the scope and encouragement to develop and use their abilities productively.

Achievement motivation can be supported and developed by organizations by helping develop self-confidence and self-esteem, by sound job design (see above) and by a constructive approach to performance management.

Freedom and autonomy

Less and less do people in developed economies welcome a 'parent–child'/command-and-control-based work environment. They expect to be treated as sentient adults and accorded a measure of freedom and autonomy in the way they go about their work. This goes with the high-trust workplaces more likely to achieve a real performance culture. People who feel constrained or micromanaged are very unlikely to be engaged in their work, and this climate is unlikely to be one fostering much discretionary effort. So organizations have much to gain by supporting and enabling reasonable degrees of freedom and autonomy and testing regularly that employees perceive that they exist.

Workload

This area is essentially about pace of work and manageable workloads. People working on production lines where the pace of work is not under their control and not reasonable or manageable find this stressful, and work quality as well as motivation suffers. Professionals working in a long-hours culture where there is little recognition of the pressure and relentless pressure to perform tend to feel the same. What we are talking about here is not the occasional periods of high-pressure working normal to most 21st-century businesses, but a work culture that persistently requires an excessive workload. Asked about this issue in focus groups where workload surfaces as an issue, employees often feed in comments such as 'you need to be a workaholic to work here' or talk wistfully about the last time they saw daylight during the week. Inevitably this issue links across to work/life balance and to some degree to freedom and autonomy. We see a marked trend for employees in high-pressure jobs who like the work, but not the constant pressure, to seek parallel rewards by restricting their time contract (to say 80 per cent) or to take sabbaticals or additional time off every so often to get a real break.

Quality of work relationships

Earlier in this chapter we talked about the importance of quality of leadership. But quality of colleagues matters too. Having congenial, supportive and reasonably like-minded fellow employees can make a big difference to engagement. A positive answer to 'Do I have a best friend at work?' is one of the 12 key indicators identified by Marcus Buckingham and Curt Coffman as critical to a high-performance environment.[16] This is also an area where talent management policies should pay dividends especially if the organization has recruited for behaviours such as effective teamworking and service orientation that require collaboration and are typically essential to high performance. They help good relations at work.

Enabling environment

Physical environment

Well-designed and organized offices and work areas make a significant difference to how people feel about their work. We live in a world where rising standards of interior decoration, TV shows illustrating house make-overs and a proliferation of media coverage on design mean that expectations are rising. Organizations like British Airways and Microsoft or St Luke's advertising agency, for example, have tailored the work environment to match evolving work styles and be more appealing as a place to spend working hours. Research-based organizations such as those in pharmaceuticals often ensure that their research workers feel well rewarded by providing excellent laboratory and other facilities that they can use to deliver exciting results. So a scruffy, 'down-at-heel' working environment can give some pretty depressing messages about how much the organization values employees and the standards it expects of them.

Tools and equipment

Most employees enjoy and relish the opportunity to work with state-of-the-art tools and equipment, whether it is the latest lightweight laptop, network system or mobile phone or indeed a sewing machine or forklift truck. Industrial archaeology is only appealing if you work in a museum. Word about new developments often travels fast in this area and creates demand. Employees talking to counterparts in other organizations, surfing the Web and reading the trade press very quickly learn about new developments that would make their work quicker or easier – and they want them. When costs are constrained and a move to a technology upgrade cannot be done in the short term, it is very important to explain why and what the plans for eventual change are. It is not uncommon to lose good employees tempted by this year's 'kit' unless this happens.

Job training (current position)

Many people now regard access to training as a key element in their overall package. It can be particularly important in delayered organizations where upward growth through promotion can be restricted but people can still work on effectiveness in their current role or develop laterally. As jobs and roles evolve, organizations generally need to provide training to help maintain and raise performance and learning. Such training might be skills training such as for a new piece of software, or it could be time management or team motivation, or it might be work on specific behaviours that help with effectiveness. A nice example of this is the training in emotional intelligence given by Slough Council to the professionals in its Housing Department to help them deliver more effectively in this challenging area of the council's services to residents. Effective training helps maintain motivation and engagement and is a clear sign of organizational investment in its people. It also fosters employability both within the organization and beyond, and enhanced employability is itself perceived as a reward.

Information and processes

This area covers the information provided and part of the work process and the nature and quality of the work processes themselves. There are links to communication and job design and similar imperatives apply. Most employees want to work with open, transparent information flows on issues affecting their work and they generally expect bureaucracy to be minimized as far as possible. We live in an environment where knowledge sharing is more respected than a 'knowledge is power' mindset, and people can be easily demotivated by secretiveness and the lack of trust that implies.

Safety/personal security

It is hard to expect people to be motivated if they feel their personal safety and security are at risk. The only real exceptions to this are the armed forces and related occupations where the risk is accepted as part of the contract – and even so minimized as far as possible. Employers who recognize this and, for example, provide transport for staff working late in hazardous inner-city areas, or CCTV surveillance for those working at remote sites, can actively reduce concerns about safety and security. Often this is a question of reviewing risk levels periodically and being proactive over safety – all part of an effective health and safety policy.

Work/life balance

Supportive environment

People do not leave their lives behind when they come to work. Most employers now recognize this and the best of them openly recognize needs outside work in their working practices, in the leadership styles in use and in an inclusive and supportive culture. The emphasis is on valuing people rather than mobilizing 'workers', helping employees build on their strengths and dealing swiftly with issues such as discrimination and bullying. Organizations, notably those in the public service, focused on fostering diversity and better reflecting the populations they serve, know that a supportive environment is critical to achieving their goals.

Recognition of lifecycle needs/flexibility

Since the improvements in employment rights of the 1970s, there has been a rising trend in the development of more flexible working arrangements. Maternity and paternity leave provisions are important in this, but also critical are employer attitudes to ongoing family responsibilities, notably childcare and eldercare issues. It is not uncommon now for employers to support and enable part-time working, flexible contracts and working from home. The best of them see this as an investment and talent management issue. Much depends on levels of trust and on raising these among managers who are initially sceptical. Work/life balance policies can therefore reward people by recognizing their needs outside work by providing more flexible working arrangements and making it clear that people will not be rewarded simply because they stay on after normal finishing time. It's what they deliver that counts, not how long they work.

The UK public service has certainly widened its talent pool by having family-friendly policies, tackling long-hours cultures and putting in resources to make this work. It has consequently often benefited by gaining higher levels of motivation from those for whom flexibility makes the difference at their particular stage of life.

Security of income

Highly variable income levels with a low base salary threshold, or the threat of job loss or layoff can have a severe effect on employee feelings of security and their ability to work effectively. It is hard to be committed to an employer whose levels of commitment in return are in doubt. Lack of security of income is a very real source of demotivation by employees who may feel trapped and who then try to cope by taking a second job, working evenings and weekends and destroying what work/life balance they had. Introduction of the minimum wage made some contribution to this issue, but there are still problems to address of low pay in high-cost areas and poorly designed incentive schemes that can leave people below a 'decency threshold'.

Social environment

This element recognizes the reality that work is a social institution and that employees expect, at least to some degree, to have a workplace that is some kind of community. Often this will be expressed by activities with colleagues but outside work. Or social activities may take place in working time and they may be organized by the employer or otherwise. If they are largely missing and work is seen as an impersonal and unsocial environment this will have an effect on levels of engagement. Team lunches or outings, away days and fundraising activities for charity, for example, help strengthen the social fabric of the workplace and help people feel they belong. And meeting colleagues in non-work situations can often help improve relationships and relationship management at work. Getting this element right may require some investment, if not in financial terms then in time and leadership effort to improve the social climate.

IMPLICATIONS OF THIS APPROACH FOR TALENT MANAGEMENT

Talent management is about ensuring that the organization attracts, retains, motivates and develops the talented people it needs. It is associated with a number of the other reward processes summarized above such as designing jobs and developing roles that give people opportunities to apply and grow their skills and provide them with autonomy, interest and challenge. It is also concerned with creating a working environment in which work processes and facilities enable rewarding (in the broadest sense) jobs and roles to be designed and developed.

Talent management also means developing reward processes and a working environment that ensure that the organization is one for which people want to work – an 'employer of choice'. There is a desire to join the organization and, once there, to stay. Employees are committed to the organization and engaged in the work they do. On the basis of their longitudinal research in 12 companies Purcell et al[8] concluded that:

> What seems to be happening is that successful firms are able to meet people's needs both for a good job and to work 'in a great place'. They create good work and a conducive working environment. In this way they become an 'employer of choice'. People will want to work there because their individual needs are met – for a good job with prospects linked to training, appraisal and working with a good boss who listens and gives some autonomy but helps with coaching and guidance.

Becoming an employer of choice starts with developing the image of the organization so that it is recognized as one that achieves results, delivers quality products and services, behaves ethically and provides good conditions of employment. Organizations with a clear vision and a set of integrated and enacted values are likely to project themselves as being rewarding to work for. As the Hay Group[17] explains: 'To become an "employer of choice" you have to think about the people you employ the same way as you think about customers. That means offering them a rewarding environment to work in, not just financial rewards.'

DEVELOPING A TOTAL REWARD APPROACH

Developing a total reward approach, as Manas and Graham empha-size,[18] has much in common with reward strategy development (see Chapter 3).

The most important thing to do is start by taking stock of where you are. Diagnosis should precede action. The Engaged Performance frame-work can usefully be used as the basis for this process. It provides the key headings for a 'bespoke' opinion survey (see Appendix B), for inter-view-based research or for focus groups. It helps build a real under-standing of what is going well and where the organization needs to adjust policies better to meet employee needs and expectations. As with reward strategy development the next stages involve setting and agreeing priorities and scheduling and sustaining implementation.

Making change to the transactional and tangible elements of total reward can be quite clear cut. It may not be easy to make them work well but, as explained in later chapters of this book, it is not too difficult to decide on what needs to be done. There are plenty of guidelines avail-able to help make the choice of approach and to indicate the means available for the design and implementation of tangible reward processes.

Changes to relational rewards are more difficult. By definition, they are intangible. Their introduction or provision may depend on top management providing the lead by developing what John Purcell and his colleagues call 'the big idea' – a clear vision and a set of integrated values that they ensure are embedded and enacted. It is not a matter of applying well-defined techniques.

The organization can contribute by communicating the values, giving employees a voice, setting up improved performance management processes, instituting formal recognition schemes and taking steps to improve work/life balance. It should make and focus change based on the data it has collected. A conscious effort can be made to 'bundle' reward and HR practices together, for example developing career family structures where the emphasis is on mapping career paths rather than providing a pay structure.

Importantly, the organization can ensure that line managers appre-ciate the importance of using relational rewards – exercising effective leadership, giving feedback, recognizing achievement and providing meaningful work. Ultimately, relational rewards are in the hands of line managers, and what the organization must do is to ensure as far as possible that they understand the significance of this aspect of their work and are given the training, coaching and guidance needed to acquire the skills to do it well.

The rhetoric of the total reward concept is compelling. The reality of total reward – making it work – is much more difficult. It requires a lot of effort on the part of top management, and line managers with the determined encouragement and guidance of HR.

BENEFITS OF A TOTAL REWARD APPROACH

Developing and implementing a total rewards approach may be difficult but the benefits are considerable. These are:

- *Greater impact* – the combined effect of transactional and relational rewards will make a deeper and longer-lasting impact on the motivation and commitment of people.
- *Enhancing the employment relationship* – the employment relationship created by a total rewards approach, which makes the maximum use of relational as well as transactional rewards, will appeal more to and engage individuals.
- *Increased engagement as part of the process* – involving people in their own reward package design gives them strong messages about the organization and its values. At its best, it builds relationship capital.
- *Flexibility to meet individual needs* – relational rewards may bind individuals more strongly to the organization because they recognize and can answer special individual needs.
- *Winning the war for talent* – relational rewards help to deliver a positive psychological contract and, as stated by Brown and Armstrong,[6] this can serve 'as an effective brand and differentiator in the recruitment market which is much more difficult to replicate than individual pay practices'. The organization can become an 'employer of choice' and 'a great place to work', thus attracting and retaining the talented people it needs.

REFERENCES

1. O'Neal, S (1998) The phenomenon of total rewards, *ACA Journal*, **7** (3)
2. WorldatWork (2000) *Total Rewards: From strategy to implementation*, WorldatWork, Scottsdale, AZ
3. Thompson, P (2002) *Total Reward*, CIPD, London
4. Murlis, H and Watson, S (2001) Creating employee engagement: transforming the employment deal, *Benefits and Compensation International*, **30** (8)
5. Pfeffer, J (1998) *The Human Equation: Building profits by putting people first*, Harvard Business School Press, Boston, MA
6. Brown, D and Armstrong, M (1999) *Paying for Contribution*, Kogan Page, London
7. Goleman, D, Boyatzis, R and McKee, A (2002) *Primal Leadership: The hidden driver of great performance*, p 6, Harvard Business School Press, Boston, MA

8. Purcell, J et al (2003) *Inside the Black Box: How people management impacts on organisational performance*, CIPD, London

9. Maslow, A (1954) *Motivation and Personality*, Harper & Row, New York

10. Boxall, P and Purcell, J (2003) *Strategic Human Resource Management*, Routledge, London

11. Gratton, L (2004) *The Democratic Enterprise: Liberating your business with freedom, flexibility and commitment*, FT Prentice Hall, London

12. Lawler, E E (1969) Job design and employee motivation, *Personnel Psychology*, **22**

13. Alderfer, C (1972) *Existence, Relatedness and Growth*, Free Press, New York

14. Lawler, E E, III (2003) *Treat People Right! How organizations and individuals can propel each other into a virtuous spiral of success*, Jossey-Bass, San Francisco

15. Robertson, I T and Smith, M (1985) *Motivation and Job Design*, IPM, London

16. Buckingham, M and Coffman, C (1999) *First Break All the Rules: What the world's greatest managers do differently*, Simon & Schuster, New York

17. Hay Group (2002) *Engage Employees and Boost Performance*, Hay Group, London

18. Manas, T M and Graham, M D (2003) *Creating a Total Reward Strategy: A toolkit for designing business based plans*, Amacom, New York

3

Strategic Reward

Strategic reward management is the process of looking ahead at what an organization needs to do about its reward policies and practices in the middle or relatively distant future. It is concerned with the broader business issues the organization is facing and the general directions in which reward management must go to provide help in dealing with these issues in order to achieve longer-term business goals.

Strategic reward management deals with both ends and means. As an end it describes a vision of what reward policies will look like in a few years' time. As a means, it shows how it is expected that the vision will be realized. Strategic reward management is therefore visionary management, concerned with creating and conceptualizing ideas of what the organization should be doing about valuing and rewarding its people. But it is also empirical management, which decides how in practice it is going to get there.

The foundation of strategic reward management is an understanding of the needs of the organization *and* its employees and how they can best be satisfied. It is also very much concerned with developing the values of the organization on how people should be rewarded and formulating guiding principles that will ensure that these values are enacted.

As described in this chapter, strategic reward management is about the development and implementation of reward strategies and the guiding principles that underpin them. The chapter starts with a definition of reward strategy, followed by a description of the purpose and features of reward strategies. Approaches to the development of reward strategies are then considered and the chapter ends with notes on criteria for effectiveness.

REWARD STRATEGY DEFINED

Reward strategy clarifies what the organization wants to do in the longer term to develop and implement reward policies, practices and processes that will further the achievement of its business goals. It is a declaration of intent, which establishes priorities for developing and acting on reward plans that can be aligned to business and HR strategies and to the needs of people in the organization. Brown[1] believes that: 'reward strategy is ultimately a way of thinking that you can apply to any reward issue arising in your organization, to see how you can create value from it'.

THE PURPOSE OF REWARD STRATEGY

The aim of reward strategy is to support the corporate and HR strategies and align reward policies and processes to organizational and individual needs. It provides a sense of purpose and direction and a framework for reward planning. In the words of Rosabeth Moss Kanter,[2] business strategies exist 'to elicit the present actions for the future' and to become 'action vehicles – integrating and institutionalising mechanisms for change'. This is also the case with reward strategies.

There are four powerful arguments for developing reward strategies:

1. You must have some idea where you are going, or how do you know how to get there and how do you know that you have arrived (if you ever do)?
2. Pay costs in most organizations are by far the largest item of expense; so doesn't it make sense to think about how they should be managed and invested in the longer term?
3. There can be a positive relationship between rewards, in the broadest sense, and performance, so shouldn't we think about how we can strengthen that link?
4. As Cox and Purcell[3] write, 'the real benefit in reward strategies lies in complex linkages with other human resource management policies and practices'. Isn't this a good reason for developing a reward strategic framework that clearly indicates how reward processes will be linked to other HR strategies and processes so that they are coherent and mutually supportive?

FEATURES OF REWARD STRATEGY

Reward strategy is an undertaking about what is going to be done in the future. It is concerned with the direction the organization should follow in developing the right mix and levels of financial and non-financial rewards to support the business strategy. It will set out 1) the underpinning guiding principles (the reward philosophy), 2) the intentions – this is *what* we propose to do, 3) a rationale – this is *why* we intend to do it, and 4) a plan – this is *how* we propose to do it.

However, Mintzberg, Quinn and James[4] suggest that strategy can have a number of meanings other than that of being 'a plan, or something equivalent – a direction, a guide, a course of action'. Strategy can also be:

▌ a *pattern*, that is, consistency in behaviour over time;
▌ a *perspective*, an organization's fundamental way of doing things;
▌ a *ploy*, a specific 'manoeuvre' intended to outwit an opponent or a competitor.

The reality of reward strategy

There is always a danger of reward strategy promising much but achieving little. The rhetoric contained in the guiding principles may not turn into reality. Espoused values may not become values-in-use. The things that are meant to happen may not happen.

Reward strategy can too easily be unrealistic. It may appear to offer something worthwhile but the resources (money, people and time) and capability to make it happen are not available. It may include processes such as performance management that only work if line managers want to make them work and are capable of making them work. It may be met by total opposition from the trade unions.

The characteristics of reward strategy

As Murlis[5] points out: 'Reward strategy will be characterised by diversity and conditioned both by the legacy of the past and the realities of the future.' All reward strategies are different just as all organizations are different. Of course, similar aspects of reward will be covered in the strategies of different organizations but they will be treated differently in accordance with variations between organizations in their contexts, strategies and cultures.

Reward strategy and business strategy

One of the defining features of strategic reward is that reward strategy should be aligned to (fit) the business strategy. According to this concept, reward strategy as an aspect of HR strategy exists to satisfy business needs and support the achievement of business goals. A serious objection to this notion is that it ignores the needs of the people in the organization. It can also be argued that it is simplistic in suggesting that 'fit' is easily attained. It is not. The formulation of business strategy is a complex, interactive process influenced by a variety of contextual and historical factors. In these circumstances, asks Guest:[6] 'how can there be a straightforward flow from the business strategy to the HR strategy?'. Hendry and Pettigrew[7] suggest that there are limits to the extent to which rational HR strategies can be drawn up if the process of business strategic planning is itself irrational.

Fit may be difficult to attain but reward strategy needs to take into account an important approach to business strategy that has evolved over the last decade. This is the concept of resource-based strategy, which is founded on the belief expressed by Hamel and Prahalad[8] that competitive advantage is obtained if a firm can obtain and develop human resources that enable it to learn faster and apply its learning more effectively than its rivals. Barney[9] contends that sustained competitive advantage stems from the acquisition and effective use of bundles of distinctive resources that competitors cannot imitate. The benefits arising from competitive advantage based on the effective management of people is that such a resource advantage is hard to imitate. An organization's HR and reward strategies, policies and practices are a unique blend of processes, procedures, personalities, styles, capabilities and organizational culture. One of the keys to competitive advantage is the ability to differentiate what the business supplies to its customers from what is supplied by its competitors. Such differentiation can be achieved by having HR and reward strategies that ensure that 1) the firm has higher-quality people than its competitors, 2) the unique intellectual capital possessed by the business is developed and nurtured, and 3) a culture is created that encourages commitment, engagement and continuous development.

Reward strategy and HR strategy

Reward strategy is only part – albeit an important part – of an organization's HR strategy. It is necessary to ensure that reward strategies are 'bundled' with other HR strategies so that they complement and reinforce one another. For example, job family structures as described in Chapter 16 can define career paths and thus provide the basis for planning career progression as well as producing a framework for managing performance and contribution and the delivery and management of pay. This is another argument for developing a total reward approach as a major aspect of reward strategy.

Reward strategy and line management capability

HR can initiate new policies and practices but it is the line that has the main responsibility for implementing them. In other words, 'HR proposes but the line disposes'. As pointed out by Purcell *et al*,[10] high levels of organizational performance are not achieved simply by having a range of well-conceived HR policies and practices in place. What makes the difference is how these policies and practices are implemented. That is where the role of line managers in people management is crucial: 'The way line managers implement and enact policies, show leadership in dealing with employees and in exercising control come through as a major issue' (Purcell *et al*).

The trend is, rightly, to devolve more responsibility for managing reward to line managers. Some will have the ability to respond to the challenge and opportunity; others will be incapable of carrying out this responsibility without close guidance from HR; some may never be able to cope. Managers may not always do what HR expects them to do and, if compelled to, they may be half-hearted about it. This puts a tremendous onus on HR and reward specialists to develop line management capability, to initiate processes that can readily be implemented by line managers, to promote understanding by communicating what is happening, why it is happening and how it will affect everyone, to provide guidance and help where required and to provide formal training as necessary.

Reward strategy and employees

All employees, including line managers, are stakeholders in the reward strategy. It affects their interests and, to a greater or lesser extent, meets their needs. While the reward strategy does not define the employment relationship, it plays a large part in it. The employment relationship can have a *transactional* basis – the employee provides skill and effort to the employer in return for which the employer provides the employee with a salary or a wage, the traditional economist's concept of the effort bargain. It also has a *relational* basis – intangible relationships are developed that take place within the work environment and are affected by the processes of leadership, communications and giving employees a voice, and by how jobs are designed and expectations of behaviour and performance are agreed. The psychological contract – the mutual and often implicit beliefs of employees and employers of what they expect of one another – will strongly affect the employment relationship and has both transactional and relational characteristics.

As stakeholders, employees need to be given a voice in the formulation of the reward strategy. The strategy has to take account of the mutual expectations of management and employees – who are all stakeholders in the organization alongside the owners, the customers and the community. It must also recognize both the transactional and relational aspects of the employment relationship by developing a total reward approach as described in Chapter 2.

THE STRUCTURE OF REWARD STRATEGY

There may be no such thing as a model reward strategy but there are a number of headings that can be used to provide a logical structure for the expression of the particular strategic intentions of a business. It has been suggested by Richardson and Thompson[11] that any strategy must have two key elements: there must be strategic objectives that define what the strategy is supposed to achieve, and there must be a plan of action that sets out how the objectives will be met. In other words, the two basic strategic planning questions are: 'Where are we going?' and 'How are we going to get there?'. To these could be added two more questions: 'Why do we want to get there anyhow?' and 'What values or guiding principles should we adopt in implementing the strategy?'.

The structure of a reward strategy could be built round these four questions as follows:

1. *A definition of guiding principles* – the values that it is believed should be adopted in formulating and implementing the strategy.
2. *A statement of intentions* – the reward initiatives that it is proposed should be taken.
3. *A rationale* – the reasons why the proposals are being made. The rationale should make out the business case for the proposals, indicating how they will meet business needs and setting out the costs and the benefits. It should also refer to any people issues that need to be addressed and how the strategy will deal with them.
4. *A plan* – how, when and by whom the reward initiatives will be implemented. The plan should take account of resource constraints and the need for communications, involvement and training. The priorities attached to each element of the strategy should be indicated.

GUIDING PRINCIPLES

Guiding principles define the approach an organization takes to dealing with reward. They are the basis for reward policies and provide guidelines for the actions contained in the reward strategy. They express the philosophy of the organization – its values and beliefs – about how people should be rewarded.

Members of the organization should be involved in the definition of guiding principles, which can then be communicated to everyone to increase understanding of what underpins reward policies and practices. However, employees will suspend their judgement of the principles until they experience how they are applied. What matters to them is not the philosophies themselves but the pay practices emanating from them and the messages about the employment 'deal' that they get as a consequence. It is the reality that is important, not the rhetoric.

Fundamental values

Guiding principles may incorporate or be influenced by some general beliefs about fairness, equity, consistency and transparency.

Fairness

Fairness means that reward management processes should operate fairly in accordance with the principles of distributive and procedural justice. As defined by Leventhal,[12] distributive justice refers to how rewards are distributed. People will feel that they have been treated justly (fairly) in this respect if they believe that rewards have been distributed in accordance with the value of their contribution, that they receive what was promised to them and that they get what they need. Procedural justice refers to the ways in which managerial decisions are made and HR procedures are put into practice. The five factors that affect perceptions of procedural justice as identified by Tyler and Bies[13] are:

1. The viewpoint of employees is given proper consideration.
2. Personal bias towards employees is suppressed.
3. The criteria for decisions are applied consistently to all employees.
4. Employees are provided with early feedback about the outcome of decisions.
5. Employees are provided with adequate explanations of why decisions have been made.

Equity

Equity is achieved when people are rewarded appropriately in relation to others within the organization. Equitable reward processes ensure that relativities between jobs are measured as objectively as possible and that equal pay is provided for work of equal value.

Consistency

A consistent approach to the provision of rewards means that decisions on pay should not vary arbitrarily and without due cause between different people or at different times. They should not deviate irrationally from what would be generally regarded as fair and equitable.

Transparency

Transparency means that people understand how reward processes operate and how they are affected by them. The reasons for pay decisions should be explained to them at the time they are made. Employees should have a voice in the development of reward policies and practices and should have the rights to be given explanations of decisions and to comment on how they are made.

Specific guiding principles

Reward guiding principles may be concerned with such specific matters as:

▌ developing reward policies and practices that support the achievement of business goals;
▌ providing rewards that attract, retain and motivate staff and help to develop a high-performance culture;
▌ maintaining competitive rates of pay;
▌ rewarding people according to their contribution;
▌ recognizing the value of all staff who are making an effective contribution, not just the exceptional performers;
▌ allowing a reasonable degree of flexibility in the operation of reward processes and in the choice of benefits by employees;
▌ devolving more responsibility for reward decisions to line managers.

THE CONTENT OF REWARD STRATEGY

Reward strategy may be a broad-brush affair simply indicating the general direction in which it is thought reward management should go. Additionally or alternatively, reward strategy may set out a list of specific intentions dealing with particular aspects of reward management.

Broad-brush reward strategy

A broad-brush reward strategy may commit the organization to the pursuit of a total rewards policy. The basic aim might be to achieve an appropriate balance between financial and non-financial rewards. A further aim could be to use other approaches to the development of the employment relationship and the work environment that will enhance commitment and engagement and provide more opportunities for the contribution of people to be valued and recognized.

Examples of other broad strategic aims include 1) introducing a more integrated approach to reward management – encouraging continuous personal development and spelling out career opportunities, 2) developing a more flexible approach to reward, which includes the reduction of artificial barriers as a result of overemphasis on grading and promotion, 3) generally rewarding people according to their contribution, 4) supporting the development of a performance culture and building levels of competence, and 5) clarifying what behaviours will be rewarded and why.

Specific reward initiatives

The selection of reward initiatives and the priorities attached to them will be based on an analysis of the present circumstances of the organization and an assessment of the needs of the business and its employees. The following are examples of possible specific reward initiatives, one or more of which might feature in a reward strategy:

▌ the replacement of present methods of contingent pay with a pay for contribution scheme;
▌ the introduction of a new grade and pay structure, eg a broadbanded or job family structure;
▌ the replacement of an existing decayed job evaluation scheme with a scheme that more clearly reflects organizational values and needs;
▌ the improvement of performance management processes so that they provide better support for the development of a performance culture and more clearly identify development needs;
▌ the introduction of a formal recognition scheme;
▌ the development of a flexible benefits system;
▌ the conduct of equal pay reviews with the objective of ensuring that work of equal value is paid equally;
▌ communication and training programmes designed to inform everyone of the reward policies and practices of the organization and ensure that those who conduct performance reviews or make or influence pay decisions have the necessary skills.

DEVELOPING REWARD STRATEGY

The formulation of corporate strategy can be described as a process for developing and defining a sense of direction. A logical step-by-step model for doing this is illustrated in Figure 3.1. This incorporates ample provision for consultation, involvement and communication with stakeholders; these include senior managers as the ultimate decision makers as well as employees generally and line managers in particular.

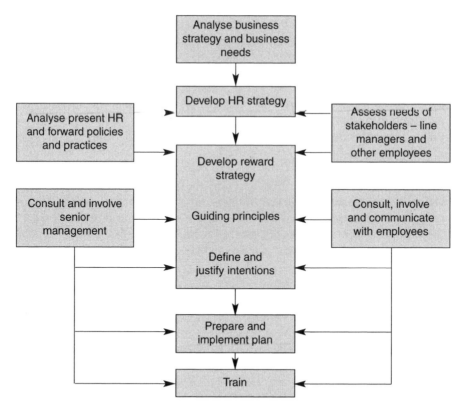

Figure 3.1 A model of the reward strategy development process

In practice, however, the formulation of reward strategy is seldom as logical and linear a process as this. Quinn[14] produced the concept of 'logical incrementalism', which states that strategy evolves in several steps rather than being perceived as a whole. This notion was developed by Mintzberg,[15] who believes that strategy formulation is not necessarily rational and continuous. In theory, he says, strategy is a systematic process: first we think, then we act; we formulate, then we implement. But we also 'act in order to think'. In practice, 'a realised strategy can emerge in response to an evolving situation' and the strategic planner is often 'a pattern organiser, a learner if you like, who manages a process in which strategies and visions can emerge as well as be deliberately conceived'. Strategy, according to Mintzberg, is best regarded as a 'pattern in a stream of activities'.

These opinions about the nature of strategy formulation suggest that, while a logical approach as shown in Figure 3.1 may provide a desirable model, the reality is different. Reward strategists do not start with a clean sheet. They have to take note and keep taking note of the changing situation in their organization, including the needs of stakeholders. They will have to take particular account of financial considerations – the concept of 'affordability' looms large in the minds of chief executives and financial directors, who will need to be convinced that an investment in rewards will pay off.

Reward strategists must also track emerging trends and may modify their views accordingly, as long as they do not leap too hastily on the latest bandwagon. It may be helpful to set out reward strategies on paper for the record and as a basis for planning and communication. But this should be regarded as no more than a piece of paper that can be torn up when needs change – as they will – not a tablet of stone. However, it is still desirable to have a clear view shared with management and other stakeholders about future intentions even if this may have to change, and there are certain criteria as set out below that can be used to judge the effectiveness of the strategy as a broad but possibly evolving statement of intent, which may usefully be recorded in writing.

CRITERIA FOR AN EFFECTIVE REWARD STRATEGY

According to Brown,[1] effective reward strategies have three components:

1. They have to have clearly defined goals and a well-defined link to business objectives.
2. There have to be well-designed pay and reward programmes, tailored to the needs of the organization and its people, and consistent and integrated with one another.
3. Perhaps most important and most neglected, there need to be effective and supportive HR and reward processes in place.

Objectives	Rating*
1 Reinforce the achievement of corporate goals.	
2 Recruit and train staff of the required calibre.	
3 Strong relationship between pay and performance.	
4 Reinforce organizational values.	
5 Motivating for our employees.	
6 Cost effective.	
7 Well communicated, supported and understood by staff.	
8 Managed effectively in practice by line managers.	
9 Efficient to operate and maintain.	
10 Flexible to react quickly to change.	

*Scale: 10 = incredible, 5 = OK, 1 = appalling

Figure 3.2   Reward strategy delivery?

A checklist for assessing the effectiveness of reward strategy delivery as drawn up by Brown[16] is shown in Figure 3.2.

REFERENCES

1. Brown, D (2001) *Reward Strategies: From intent to impact*, CIPD, London
2. Kanter, R M (1984) *The Change Masters*, Allen & Unwin, London
3. Cox, A and Purcell, J (1998) 'Searching for leverage: pay systems, trust, motivation and commitment in SMEs', in *Trust, Motivation and Commitment*, ed S J Perkins and St John Sandringham, Strategic Remuneration Centre, Faringdon
4. Mintzberg, H, Quinn, J B and James, R M (1988) *The Strategy Process: Concepts, contexts and cases*, Prentice Hall, Englewood Cliffs, NJ
5. Murlis, H (1996) *Pay at the Crossroads*, IPD, London
6. Guest, D E (1997) Human resource management and performance: a review of the research agenda, *International Journal of Human Resource Management*, **8** (3), pp 263–76
7. Hendry, C and Pettigrew, A (1986) The practice of strategic human resource management, *Personnel Review*, **15**, pp 2–8
8. Hamel, G and Prahalad, C K (1989) Strategic intent, *Harvard Business Review*, May–June, pp 63–76
9. Barney, J (1991) Firm resources and sustained competitive advantage, *Journal of Management*, **17**, pp 99–120
10. Purcell, J *et al* (2003) *People and Performance: How people management impacts on organisational performance*, CIPD, London
11. Richardson, R and Thompson, M (1999) *The Impact of People Management Practices on Business Performance: A literature review*, IPD, London
12. Leventhal, G S (1980) What should be done with equity theory?, in *Social Exchange: Advances in theory and research*, ed G K Gergen, M S Greenberg and R H Willis, Plenum, New York
13. Tyler, T R and Bies, R J (1990) Beyond formal procedures: the interpersonal context of procedural justice, in *Applied Social Psychology and Organizational Settings*, ed J S Carrol, Lawrence Earlbaum, Hillsdale, NJ
14. Quinn, J B (1980) Managing strategic change, *Sloane Management Review*, **11** (4/5), pp 3–30
15. Mintzberg, H (1987) Crafting strategy, *Harvard Business Review*, July–August, pp 66–74
16. Brown, D (2003) Presentation to CIPD Conference, Bristol

4

Reward Policies

Reward policies provide guidelines for the implementation of reward strategies and the design and management of reward processes. They will be influenced strongly by the guiding principles and reward philosophy of the organization. The reward policies will be concerned with:

- the level of rewards;
- the relative importance attached to market rates and equity;
- attraction and retention;
- the relationship of rewards to business performance;
- total reward policy;
- the scope for the use of contingent rewards related to performance, competence, contribution or skill;
- assimilation policies;
- the degree of flexibility required;
- the role of line managers;
- the need to involve employees in the design of the reward system;
- the need to communicate reward policies to employees;
- transparency – the publication of information on reward structures and processes to employees.

LEVEL OF REWARDS

The policy on the level of rewards indicates whether the company is a high payer, is content to pay median or average rates of pay or even, exceptionally, accepts that it has to pay below the average. Pay policy, which is sometimes referred to as the 'pay stance' or 'pay posture' of a organization, will depend on a number of factors. These include the extent to which the organization demands high levels of performance from its employees, the degree to which there is competition for good-quality people, the traditional stance of the company, the organization culture, and whether or not it can or should afford to be a high payer. A firm may say 'We will pay upper-quartile salaries because we want our staff to be upper-quartile performers.'

Policies on pay levels will also refer to differentials and the number of steps or grades that should exist in the pay hierarchy. This will be influenced by the structure of the company. In today's flatter organizations an extended or complex pay hierarchy may not be required on the grounds that it does not reflect the way in which work is organized and will constrain flexibility.

Policies on the level of rewards should also cover employee benefits – pensions, sick pay, health care, holidays and perks such as company cars.

MARKET RATE AND EQUITY

A policy needs to be formulated on the extent to which rewards are market driven rather than equitable. This policy will be influenced by the culture and reward philosophies of the organization and the pressures on the business to obtain and keep high-quality staff. Any organizations that have to attract and retain staff who are much in demand and where market rates are therefore high may, to a degree, have to sacrifice their ideals (if they have them) of internal equity to the realism of the market place. They will provide 'market pay'; in other words, they will be 'market driven'. The pay management process must cope as best it can when the irresistible force of market pressures meets the immovable object of internal equity. There will always be some degree of tension in these circumstances and, while no solution will ever be simple or entirely satisfactory, there is one basic principle that can enhance the likelihood of success. That principle is to make explicit and fully identifiable the compromises with internal equity that are made and have to be made in response to market pressures.

The policy may indicate that market considerations will drive levels of pay in the organization. It may, however, allow for the use of market supplements – additional payments to the rate for a job as determined by job evaluation (internal equity), which reflect market rates. The policy may lay down that these payments should be reviewed regularly and no longer offered if they are unnecessary. Market supplements for those who have them may not be withdrawn (they would not lose pay), but adjustments may be made to pay progression to bring their rates more into line with those for comparable jobs. Market pay and market supplements can lead to gender inequalities if, as is often the case, men in comparable jobs are paid more generously or more men get market supplements than women. Equal pay case law (see Chapter 11) has ruled that market pay and market supplements should be 'objectively justified' and the requirement to do this should be included in the pay policy.

ATTRACTION AND RETENTION

Market pay and market supplements are the first resort of firms wishing to attract and retain high-quality people. 'Golden hellos' and 'golden handcuffs' (recruitment and retention bonuses) may be used for this purpose. But there is more to attracting and retaining people than simply throwing money at them. A total reward policy as described in Chapter 2 is required.

Attraction policies

The overall policy should be to become an employer of choice. More specifically, an attraction strategy will need to be based on a competitive remuneration package (possibly including 'golden hellos'). In addition, the policy should be to adopt a targeted approach. This means analysing the factors for specific occupations or categories of employees that are likely to affect their decision to apply for jobs and to accept them when offered because they potentially offer higher rewards in the broadest sense than those they are getting at present or could obtain elsewhere. These factors could include career prospects, training and development opportunities, the intrinsic interest of the work, flexible working arrangements and other work/life balance policies and, especially for research workers, the facilities available to them and the scope to enhance their reputation.

Retention policies

Retention policies take into account the particular retention issues the organization is facing and sets out ways in which these issues can be dealt with. This may mean accepting the reality, as mentioned by Capelli,[1] that the market, not the company, will ultimately determine the movement of employees. Capelli believes that it may be difficult to counter the pull of the market – 'you can't shield your people from attractive opportunities and aggressive recruiters' – and suggests that: 'The old goal of HR management – to minimize overall employee turnover – needs to be replaced by a new goal: to influence who leaves and when.' This, as proposed by Bevan, Barber and Robinson,[2] could be based on risk analysis to quantify the seriousness of losing key people or of key posts becoming vacant.

Talent management policies

The overall approach to the attraction and retention of good-quality people can be described as 'talent management', which goes far beyond crude attempts to cure the problem with money. Talent management is the process of 'winning the war for talent' by ensuring that the organization attracts, retains, motivates and develops the talented people it needs. There is nothing new about the various processes that add up to talent management. What is different is the development of a more coherent view as to how these processes should mesh together with an overall objective – to acquire and nurture talent wherever it is and wherever it is needed by using a number of interdependent policies and practices. Talent management is the notion of 'bundling', ie linking HR policies and practices together so that they are mutually supportive, in action. It should not, however, be assumed that talent management is only concerned with key people – the high flyers. Everyone in an organization has talent, and talent management processes should not be limited to the favoured few, although they are likely to focus most on those with scarce skills and high potential.

The key talent management processes are:

▌ developing the organization as an 'employer of choice' – a 'great place to work';
▌ using selection and recruitment procedures that ensure that good-quality people are recruited who are likely to thrive in the organization and stay with it for a reasonable length of time (but not necessarily for life);
▌ designing jobs and developing roles that give people opportunities to apply and grow their skills and provide them with autonomy, interest and challenge;
▌ providing talented staff with opportunities for career development and growth;
▌ creating a working environment in which work processes and facilities enable rewarding (in the broadest sense) jobs and roles to be designed and developed;
▌ providing scope for achieving a reasonable balance between working in the organization and life outside work;
▌ developing a positive psychological contract;
▌ developing the leadership qualities of line managers;
▌ recognizing those with talent by rewarding excellence, enterprise and achievement;
▌ conducting talent audits that identify those with potential and those who might leave the organization.

RELATING REWARDS TO BUSINESS PERFORMANCE

This aspect of reward policy refers to the link between business performance and pay. It will cover the extent to which pay will vary according to results. Ability to pay and value for money will also be important considerations. The policy will include guidelines on how gainsharing or profit-sharing schemes should operate (see Chapters 25 and 26).

TOTAL REWARD

The total reward policy should state that although contingent rewards play an important part in the reward policies of the organization other forms of non-financial reward are regarded as being equally important.

CONTINGENT REWARDS

The policy will need to determine whether or not the organization wants to pay for performance, competence, contribution or skill and, if so, how much and under what circumstances. There may, for example, be a policy that bonuses should be paid for exceptional performance but that, to be significant, they should not be less than, say, 10 per cent of basic pay, while their upper limit should be restricted to 30 per cent or so of base pay. The policy may also indicate the approach to be used in relating pay to individual, team or organizational performance.

ASSIMILATION POLICIES

The introduction of a new or considerably revised pay structure means that policies have to be developed on how existing employees should be assimilated into it. These policies cover where they should be placed in their new grades and what happens to them if their new grade and pay range means that their existing rate is above or below the new scale for their job. The policy should therefore cover 'red-circling' (identifying and dealing with overpaid people) and 'green-circling' (identifying and dealing with underpaid people). In the case of red-circled staff, 'protection' policies may have to be formulated to safeguard their existing rates of pay. In the case of green-circled staff, the policy may have to determine when (not if) their pay should be increased to fit into the new scale. It is sometimes necessary to save costs by phasing the increase and this should be included as a possible policy. Assimilation policies are dealt with in greater detail in Chapter 17.

FLEXIBILITY

Reward policies have to take into account the extent to which reward processes should operate flexibly in response to fast-changing conditions, the adoption of a less rigid organization structure and approach to management, and changes or variations in the needs of the company or its employees. A particular aspect of this policy will be the extent to which the organization wants to introduce flexible benefits (see Chapter 32).

THE ROLE OF LINE MANAGERS

Line managers play a crucial role in administering rewards, and the policy should recognize this. The extent to which the responsibility for rewards should be devolved to line managers is a policy decision. The aim may be to devolve it as far as possible, bearing in mind the need to ensure that other reward policy guidelines are followed and that consistent decisions are made across the organization by line managers. The policy may cover the level of decisions managers can make, the guidance that should be made available to them and how consistency will be achieved. The training and ongoing support that line managers require to exercise judgements on reward and to conduct performance management reviews could also be covered by the policy.

INVOLVING EMPLOYEES

Reward policies and practices are more likely to be accepted and understood and, therefore, more effective if employees are given a voice in the design and management of reward processes. This particularly applies to job evaluation and methods of measuring and assessing performance and relating rewards to that performance (performance management and paying for performance or contribution processes).

COMMUNICATING TO EMPLOYEES

Reward processes are powerful media for conveying messages to employees about the organization's values and the contribution they are expected to make in upholding those values and achieving the organization's goals. They should not, however, be left to speak for themselves. It is essential to communicate to individuals, teams and representative bodies what reward processes are setting out to do, how they propose to do it, how they affect them, how they will benefit, and the part individuals and teams will be expected to play. It is particularly important to explain the basis of any pay-for-performance scheme and also to convey to employees how their total remuneration package of pay and other benefits is made up.

TRANSPARENCY

Traditionally, organizations in the private sector have tended to keep some information about pay policies secret. This is no longer a tenable position. Employees will only feel that the reward management processes of an organization are fair if they know what they are and how they are used to determine their level of pay and methods of pay progression. Lack of understanding breeds suspicion and hostility. One of the aims of reward management should be to enhance commitment, but there is no possibility of this being achieved if the organization is secretive about pay.

Without transparency, people will believe that the organization has something to hide, often with reason. There is no chance of building a satisfactory psychological contract unless the organization spells out its reward policies and practices and the reasons for them. Transparency is achieved through effective involvement and communication.

REFERENCES

1. Capelli, P (2000) A market-driven approach to retaining talent, *Harvard Business Review*, January–February, pp 103–11
2. Bevan, S, Barber, l and Robinson, D (1997) *Keeping the Best: A practical guide to retaining key employees*, Institute for Employment Studies, Brighton

5

The Psychological Contract

Managing reward is largely about managing expectations – what employees expect from their employers in return for their contribution and what employers expect from their employees in return for their pay and the opportunity to work and develop their skills. Expectations are built into the employment relationship, the starting-point of which, from the reward point of view, is an undertaking by an employee to provide effort and skill to the employer, in return for which the employer provides the employee with a salary or a wage.

There are two types of contracts which define the employment relationship:

1. *Transactional contracts*, which have well-described terms of exchange. These have a basis in law and are usually expressed in financial terms with specified performance requirements. They are also called 'Economic contracts'.
2. *Relational contracts*, which are less well defined or may not be defined at all. They have more abstract terms and refer to an open-ended membership of the organization. Performance requirements attached to membership may be incomplete or ambiguous.

Transactional/economic contracts are expressed in formal contracts of employment, which may be written or unwritten, and specify or indicate terms and conditions of employment. Relational contracts are expressed, in so far as they are expressed at all, in what is usually called a psychological contract, the essence of which is that it is implied rather than stated and is not subject to agreement. In a sense, the term psychological contract is an oxymoron. A contract, as defined by the *Oxford*

English Dictionary, is a written or spoken arrangement or agreement made between two or more persons, usually enforceable by law. The word 'psychological' means that the arrangement is only in the minds of those concerned – it is not agreed between them. A contract is an agreed mutual undertaking. The terms are contradictory. However, the notion of a psychological contract has now entered the vocabulary of the HR professionals and is therefore a useful way of referring to all those aspects of the employment relationship which are neither well-defined nor clearly understood. And these 'relational' aspects of employment are those which exert the greatest influence on the motivation, commitment, morale and job satisfaction of employees.

The concept of the psychological contract is an important one to anybody involved with reward management because it is concerned with defining and meeting expectations concerning pay, performance and the development and application of competence and skill. This chapter therefore starts by defining the psychological contract and its characteristics, continues by examining its significance in the employment relationship and concludes with some ideas on how HR, including reward policies and processes, can contribute to the development and maintenance of a productive and mutually satisfactory relationship.

THE PSYCHOLOGICAL CONTRACT DEFINED

Fundamentally, the psychological contract as researched by David Guest who has led UK work in this area, and others, expresses the combination of beliefs held by an individual and his or her employer about what they expect of one another. The concept is not a new one. It was first defined by Ed Schein[1] in 1965 as follows:

> The notion of a psychological contract implies that there is an unwritten set of expectations operating at all times between every member of an organization and the various managers and others in that organization.

This definition was amplified by Rousseau and Wade-Benonzi[2] more recently. They stated that:

> Psychological contracts refer to beliefs that individual hold regarding promises made, accepted and relied upon between themselves and another... Because psychological contracts represent how people *interpret* promises and commitments, both parties in the same employment relationship (employer and employee) can have different views regarding specific terms.

More succinctly, Sims[3] defined a psychological contract in 1994 as:

The set of expectations held by the individual employee that specify what the individual and organization expect to give and receive from one another in the course of their working relationship.

CHARACTERISTICS OF THE PSYCHOLOGICAL CONTRACT

A psychological contract is a system of beliefs which encompasses, on the one hand, the actions employees believe are expected of them and what response they expect in return from their employer; and, on the other, the behaviour employers expect from their employees. A psychological contract is implicit. It is also dynamic – it develops over time.

The aspects of the employment relationship covered by the psychological contract will include, from the employee's point of view:

▮ how s/he is treated in terms of fairness, equity and consistency;
▮ security of employment;
▮ scope to demonstrate competence;
▮ career expectations and the opportunity to develop skills;
▮ involvement and influence;
▮ trust in the organization to keep its promises;
▮ the expectation that s/he will be managed competently.

From the employer's point of view, the psychological contract covers such aspects of the employment relationship as:

▮ competence;
▮ effort;
▮ compliance;
▮ commitment;
▮ loyalty.

Some interesting insights into the nature of the psychological contract were provided by the IPD/Templeton/Birkbeck College research conducted in 1995. This revealed the following:

▮ 65 per cent of respondents felt that they had a lot of direct involvement in deciding how to do their jobs and organize their work.
▮ 40 per cent had a lot of loyalty to their company.
▮ 26 per cent trusted their company a good deal to keep its promises to employees.

CHANGING NATURE OF THE PSYCHOLOGICAL CONTRACT

Until fairly recently the psychological contract has not been an issue. People knew what to expect – you turned up to work, did what was required and the organization provided security and development. It was not a complicated relationship and for most organizations it worked well, providing them with a loyal, committed and dependable work-force.

Times have changed.

▌ Business organizations are neither stable nor long-lived – uncertainty prevails and job security is no longer on offer by employers who are less anxious to maintain a stable workforce – as Mirvis and Hall[4] point out, organizations are making continued employment explicitly contingent on the fit between people's competencies and business needs.

▌ Flexibility, adaptability and speed of response are all-important and individual roles may be subject to constant change – continuity and predictability are often no longer available for employees.

▌ Leaner organizations mean that careers may mainly develop laterally – expectations that progress will be made by promotion through the hierarchy are often no longer valid.

▌ Leaner organizations may make greater demands on employees and are less likely to tolerate people who no longer precisely fit their requirements.

But, more positively, many organizations are realizing that steps have to be taken to increase mutuality and to provide scope for lateral career development and improvement in knowledge and skills through opportunities for learning. They recognize that, because they can no longer guarantee long-term employment, they have the responsibility to help people continue to develop their careers if they have to move on. In other words, they take steps to improve employability. Even those which have fully embraced the 'core-periphery' concept may recognize that they still need to obtain the commitment of their core employees and pay attention to their continuous development, although in most organizations the emphasis is likely to be on self-development.

The ways in which psychological contracts are changing will, of course, vary between organizations but some of the positive and less positive developments are summarized in Table 5.1.

These trends are summarized by Hiltrop,[5] who suggests that a new psychological contract is emerging – one that is more situational and short-term and which assumes that each party is much less dependent on the other for survival and growth. He believes that in its most naked form, the new contract could be defined as follows:

There is no job security. The employee will be employed as long as he or she adds value to the organization, and is personally responsible for finding new ways to add value. In return, the employee has the right to demand interesting and important work, has the freedom and resources to perform it well, receives pay that reflects his or her contribution, and gets the experience and training needed to be employable here or elsewhere.

But this could hardly be called a balanced contract. To what extent do employees in general have 'the right to demand interesting and important work'? Employers still call the shots, except when dealing with the special cases of people who are much in demand and in short supply. In Britain, as Mant[6] points out, 'people often really are regarded as merely "resources" to be acquired or divested according to short-term economic circumstances'. It is the employer who has the power to dictate contractual terms unless they have been fixed by collective bargaining. Individuals, except when they are highly sought after, have little scope to vary the terms of the contract imposed upon them by employers.

Table 2.1   The ways in which psychological contracts are changing

From	To
Imposed relationship (compliance, command and control)	Mutual relationship (commitment, participation and involvement)
Permanent employment relationship	Variable employment relationship – people and skills only obtained or retained when required
Focus on promotion	Focus on lateral career development
Finite job duties	Multiple roles
Meet job requirements	Add value
Emphasis on job security and loyalty to company	Emphasis on employability and loyalty to own career and skills
Training provided by organization	Opportunities for self-managed learning.

THE SIGNIFICANCE OF THE PSYCHOLOGICAL CONTRACT

As suggested by Spindler:[7] 'A psychological contract creates emotions and attitudes which form and control behaviour.' The significance of the psychological contract was further explained by Sims[3] as follows:

A balanced psychological contract is necessary for a continuing, harmonious relationship between the employee and the organization. However, the violation of the psychological contract can signal to the participants that the parties no longer share (or never shared) a common set of values or goals.

The concept highlights the fact that employee/employer expectations take the form of unarticulated assumptions. Disappointments on the part of management as well as employees may therefore be inevitable. These disappointments can, however, be alleviated if managements appreciate that one of their key roles is to manage expectations. This means clarifying what they believe employees should achieve, the competencies they should possess and the values they should uphold. And this is a matter not just of articulating and stipulating these requirements, but of discussing and agreeing them with individuals and teams.

The psychological contract governs the continuing development of the employment relationship, which is constantly evolving over time. But how the contract is developing and the impact it makes may not be fully understood by any of the parties involved. As Spindler[7] comments:

> In a psychological contract the rights and obligations of the parties have not been articulated, much less agreed to. The parties do not express their expectations and, in fact, may be quite incapable of doing so.

People who have no clear idea about what they expect may, if such unexpressed expectations have not been fulfilled, have no clear idea why they have been disappointed. But they will be aware that something does not feel right. And a company staffed by 'cheated' individuals who expect more than they get is heading for trouble.

The importance of the psychological contract was emphasized by Schein[1] who suggested that the extent to which people work effectively and are committed to the organization depends on:

1. The degree to which their own expectations of what the organization will provide to them and what they owe the organization in return matches what the organization's expectations are of what it will give and get in return;
2. The nature of *what is actually to be exchanged* (assuming there is some agreement) – money in exchange for time at work; social need satisfaction and security in exchange for hard work and loyalty; opportunities for self-actualization and challenging work in exchange for high-productivity, high-quality work, and creative effort in the service of organizational goals; or various combinations of these and other things.

DEVELOPING AND MAINTAINING A PRODUCTIVE PSYCHOLOGICAL CONTRACT

General approaches

In general, the following steps can be taken to shape and define the psychological contract, develop a more productive employment relationship and increase employee commitment:

▮ During *recruitment interviews*, present the unfavourable as well as the favourable aspects of a job in a 'realistic job preview'.

▮ In *induction programmes*, communicate to new starters the organization's personnel policies and procedures and its core values, indicating to them the standards of performance expected in such areas as quality and customer service, and spelling out requirements for flexibility.

▮ Issue and update *employee handbooks and intranet entries* which reinforce the messages delivered in induction programmes.

▮ Develop *performance management* processes, which ensure that performance and competence expectations are discussed, agreed and reviewed regularly.

▮ Encourage the use of *personal development plans,* which spell out how continued improvement of performance can be achieved, mainly by self-managed learning.

▮ Use *training and management development programmes* to underpin core values and define performance expectations.

▮ Ensure through *manager and team leader training* that managers and team leaders understand their role in managing the employment relationship, through such processes as performance management and team leadership.

▮ Encourage the maximum amount of *contact* between managers and team leaders and their team members, to achieve mutual understanding of expectations and provide a means of two-way communication.

▮ Adopt a general policy of *transparency* – ensuring that on all matters which affect them, employees know what is happening, why it is happening and the impact it will make on their employment, development and prospects.

▮ Develop *personnel procedures* covering grievance handling, discipline, equal opportunities, promotion and redundancy; and ensure that they are implemented fairly and consistently.

▮ Develop and communicate *personnel policies* covering the major areas of employment, development, reward and employee relations.

Implications for reward management

Reward management policies and processes can be used to develop and support a productive psychological contract in the following ways:

▮ Pay people on the basis of their contribution to the organization, rather than relying on the carrot of promotion as a reward for loyalty and service.

▌ Reward people according to their developing competence and skills, as long as these are used to good purpose.

▌ Rely upon contingent pay more as a means of conveying messages about organizational values, critical success factors and priorities and how people are expected to contribute in specified areas, rather than as a direct motivator.

▌ Include both input (competence) and output (achievement of objectives) factors in performance management reviews so that employees can, with their managers, focus on expected behaviours.

▌ Develop team reward systems that emphasize the importance of team work, flexibility and multiskilling.

▌ Introduce gainsharing schemes which underline the propositions that 'we are all in this together' by sharing gains in added value and involving employees in analyzing performance and proposing improvement.

▌ Communicate to employees the reasons for reward innovations and how they will be affected by them.

▌ Involve employees in the development of new reward processes and structures.

▌ Provide training to *everyone* (managers and other employees alike) on the operation and implications of reward policies and practices, especially when they are being changed.

REFERENCES

1. Schein, E (1965) *Organizational Psychology*, Prentice-Hall, Englewood Cliffs, NJ
2. Rousseau, D and Wade-Benzoni, K (1994) Linking strategy and human resource practices: how employee and customer contracts are created, *Human Resource Management*, **33**, (3), pp 463–89
3. Sims, R (1994) Human resource management's role in clarifying the psychological contract, *Human Resource Management*, **33**, (3), pp 373–82
4. Mirvis, P and Hall D (1994) 'Psychological success and the boundaryless career', *Journal of Organisational Behaviour 15*, pp 361–380
5. Hiltrop, J (1995) The changing psychological contract: the human resource challenge of the 1990s, *European Management Journal*, **13**, (3), September, pp 286–94
6. Mant, A (1996) The psychological contract. Unpublished address to IPD National Conference, October
7. Spindler, G (1994) Psychological contracts in the workplace: a lawyer's point of view, *Human Resource Management*, **33**, (3), pp 325–33
8. Guest, D, Conway, N *Employee Motivtion and the Psychological Contract* IPD, London, 1997 (Issues on People Management Paper No 21).

6

Motivation and Financial and Non-financial Rewards

Increasing motivation and raising levels of commitment and engagement are key organizational imperatives. The development of reward management policies, structures and practices will be underpinned by assumptions about how people can best be motivated to deliver high levels of performances, discretionary effort and contribution. These assumptions may not be articulated but the reward philosophies and policies of an organization can be no better than the motivational theories and beliefs upon which they are based. As many HR professionals are well aware, the pay area has been dogged by simplistic 'economic man', 'effort/reward' thinking, which largely ignores psychologically based research on human motivation.

In this chapter we therefore examine motivation theory under the following headings:

▊ the process of motivation;
▊ types of motivation;
▊ the six basic concepts of motivation relating to needs, goals, reinforcement, expectations, attribution theory and self-efficacy;
▊ the implications of motivation theory for those concerned with the design and management of financial and non-financial reward policies and practices;
▊ the implications of new research on motivation, commitment, personality preferences, discretionary effort and 'flow' for performance enhancement.

THE PROCESS OF MOTIVATION

Motivation theory is concerned with what determines goal-directed behaviour. It is about:

▌ how behaviour is initiated by needs and by expectations on the achievement of goals which will satisfy those needs;
▌ how the achievement of goals and/or feedback on their achievement reinforces successful behaviour;
▌ how belief in one's ability to carry out a specific task will actuate behaviour which is expected to achieve the successful performance of that task.

The process of motivation can be initiated by someone recognizing an unsatisfied need. A goal is then established which, it is thought, will satisfy the need, and a course of action is determined which is expected to lead towards the attainment of the goal.

Alternatively, someone can be presented with a goal and if it is expected that achieving this goal will meet an unsatisfied need, action is taken to reach the goal and thus satisfy the need.

People can be motivated by rewards and incentives which will enable them to satisfy their needs or will provide them with goals to attain (as long as those goals are worthwhile *and* attainable). But the needs of individuals and the goals associated with them vary so widely that it is difficult if not impossible to predict precisely how a particular reward or incentive will affect individual behaviour.

The social context will also affect the level of motivation. This context will consist of the organization values and culture generally, but it also includes leadership and management style (the way in which individuals are managed) and the influence of the group or team in which the individual works.

TYPES OF MOTIVATION

Motivation at work can take place in two ways:

1. *Intrinsic motivation* – this is derived from the content of the job. It can be described as the process of motivation by the work itself in so far as it satisfies people's needs or at least leads them to expect that their goals will be achieved. Intrinsic motivation is self-generated in that people seek the type of work that satisfies them, but management can enhance this process through its values as well as empowerment, development and job design policies and practices. The factors affecting intrinsic motivation include responsibility (feeling the work

is important and having control over one's own resources), freedom to act, scope to use and develop skills and abilities, interesting and challenging work and opportunities for advancement. The concepts of empowerment and engagement are strongly influenced by this aspect of motivation.

2. *Extrinsic motivation* – this is what is done to and for people to motivate them. It arises when management provides such rewards as increased pay, praise, or promotion. When the motivating impact of pay-for-performance schemes is discussed, this is the type of motivation to which people are referring.

The extrinsic motivators can have an immediate and powerful effect, but this will not necessarily last for long. The intrinsic motivators, which are concerned with the quality of working life and indeed work/life balance, are likely to have a deeper and longer-term effect because they are inherent in individuals and not imposed from outside, although they may be encouraged by the organization. The effectiveness of pay as an extrinsic motivator is a matter for continuing debate, as discussed below.

BASIC CONCEPTS FOR MOTIVATION

The framework for non-financial motivators is provided by those concepts of motivation which are concerned with needs, goals, reinforcement, expectations (expectancy theory), attribution theory and self-efficacy.

Needs

Needs theory states that behaviour is motivated by unsatisfied needs. The key needs associated with work are those for achievement, recognition, responsibility, influence and personal growth.

Goals

Goal theory was developed by Latham and Locke[1] on the basis of a 14-year research programme into goal-setting as a motivational technique. They claimed that the level of production in the companies they studied was increased by an average of 19 per cent as a result of goal-setting processes with the following characteristics:

▌ the goals should be specific;
▌ they should be challenging but reachable;
▌ the goals are seen as a fair and reasonable;
▌ individuals participate fully in goal-setting;

▌ feedback ensures that people get a feeling of pride and satisfaction from the experience of achieving a challenging but fair goal;

▌ feedback is used to gain commitment to even higher goals.

Reinforcement

Reinforcement theory suggests that successes in achieving goals and rewards act as positive incentives and reinforce the successful behaviour, which is repeated the next time a similar need arises.

Expectancy theory

Expectancy theory as originally developed by Vroom[2] states that for there to be a heightened motivation to perform, individuals have to:

▌ feel able to change their behaviour;

▌ feel confident that a change in their behaviour will produce a reward;

▌ value the reward sufficiently to justify the change in behaviour.

Expectancy theory applies just as much to non-financial as to financial rewards. For example, if people want personal growth, they will only be motivated by the opportunities available to them if they know what they are, if they know what they need to do to benefit from them (and can do it) and if the opportunities are worth striving for.

Expectancy theory explains why extrinsic motivation – for example, an incentive or bonus scheme – works only if the link between effort and reward is clear and the value of the reward is worth the effort. It also explains why intrinsic motivation arising from the work itself can sometimes be more powerful than extrinsic motivation. Intrinsic motivation outcomes are more under the control of individuals, who can place greater reliance on their past experiences to indicate the extent to which positive advantageous results are likely to be obtained by their behaviour.

Attribution theory

Attribution theory is concerned with how people interpret and explain their success or failure. If they can attribute their achievement or lack of achievement to something over which they have control they are more likely either to repeat their successful behaviour (this is a form of reinforcement) or, alternatively, take steps to behave in ways they believe are more likely to succeed. Managers can do a lot to influence attributions through feedback, communication, appraisal and guidance, thus creating a social context which is more likely to foster high motivation.

Self-efficacy

Self-efficacy is the belief in one's ability to perform a specific task. Those with high self-efficacy will have the capacity to see a link between their own effort and performance and their rewards. They are therefore more likely to take action, to persist in the action and, in the face of failure, to try alternative courses of action rather than give up trying. Self-efficacy is socially learned and developed from personal experience and performance feedback, which creates a sense of competence and reinforces people's belief in themselves.

IMPLICATIONS OF MOTIVATION THEORY

Motivation theory conveys two important messages. First, there are no simplistic solutions to increasing motivation. No single lever such as performance-related pay exists which is guaranteed to act as an effective motivator. This is because motivation is a complex process. It depends on:

▮ *individual needs and aspirations,* which are almost infinitely variable;
▮ *both intrinsic and extrinsic motivating factors,* and it is impossible to generalize on what the best mix of these is likely to be;
▮ *expectations* about rewards: such expectations will vary greatly among individuals according to their previous experiences and perceptions of reward processes;
▮ *equity and fairness* – the 'felt-fair' principle applies to levels of pay in comparison with others in accordance with what people believe to be the relative size or importance of jobs and their perceptions of relative levels of performance or contribution. Pay-for-performance schemes, for example, will only be accepted as fair and may therefore only act as effective motivators if they are based on acceptable performance measures which are applied consistently. As Linda Gratton points out in *The Democratic Enterprise,*[3] 'Justice and fairness matter to companies since they are one of the key drivers of employee engagement and agility';
▮ *attributions* – the subjective and often distorted explanations people make of their successes or failures;
▮ *self-efficacy* – the differences in the degree to which people believe in themselves;
▮ *the social context* where the influences of the organization culture, managers and co-workers can produce a wide variety of motivational forces which are difficult to predict and therefore to manage.

The second key message provided by motivation theory is the significance of expectations, goal-setting, feedback and reinforcement as motivating factors. The implications of these two messages are considered below.

Creating the right climate

It is necessary in general to create a climate which will enable high motivation to flourish. This is a matter of managing the organization culture. The aims would be, first, to reinforce values concerning performance and competence; second, to emphasize norms (accepted ways of behaviour) relating to the ways in which people are managed and rewarded; and third, to demonstrate the organization's belief in empowerment – providing people with the scope and 'space' to exercise responsibility and use their abilities to the full. Without the right climate, quick fixes designed to improve motivation such as performance-related pay are unlikely to make much of an impact on overall organizational performance, although they may work with some individuals. Research from a number of sources including the CIPD and Hay Group confirms the causal link between a positive climate and organizational performance.

Flexibility

It should be remembered, in the words of McDougall,[4] that:

> attempts to apply a standardized, across-the-board system of remuneration, on the assumption of homogeneity of values and motives amongst those it is intended to reward, are unlikely to meet the needs of many of them. There appears to be a strong case for flexibility, both in terms of the mechanisms and administration of remuneration systems and in the form in which individuals receive their remuneration.

Recognizing complexity

Motivation policies should recognize the complexity of the motivation process and not attempt to adopt simplistic solutions to motivational problems. The organization should provide for a mix of various types of intrinsic and extrinsic motivation and make use of both financial and non-financial incentives. But it should be borne in mind that the social context and the ways in which these incentives are managed for individuals will be key factors influencing their effectiveness.

Goal-setting, feedback and reinforcement

Provision should be made for goal-setting, feedback and reinforcement to be major features of the management and reward processes. Performance management processes as described in Chapters 18 and 19 can fulfil this purpose well.

Managing expectations

It is necessary to manage expectations. No reward offered through an incentive, bonus or performance-related pay scheme will be effective as a motivator unless individuals believe it is worthwhile and they can reasonably expect to obtain it through their own efforts.

We discuss these implications as they affect financial and non-financial reward policies and practices below.

FINANCIAL REWARDS

Financial rewards need to be considered from three points of view:

1. the effectiveness of money as a motivator;
2. the reasons why people are satisfied or dissatisfied with their rewards;
3. the criteria which should be used when developing a financial reward system.

Money and motivation

The general theory of motivation described above has produced the following explanations of the relationship between money and motivation: the 'economic man' approach, Herzberg's two factor model, instrumental theory, equity theory and expectancy theory.

The 'economic man' approach

According to this view, which is based on reinforcement theory, people are primarily motivated by economic rewards. It assumes that they will be motivated to work if rewards and penalties are tied directly to the results they achieve. Pay awards are contingent upon effective performance.

Motivation using this approach has been and still is widely adopted and can be successful in some circumstances, eg where money and success are closely linked as in parts of the finance sector or in sales. But it is based exclusively on a system of external controls and fails to recognize a number of other human needs. It also fails to appreciate the fact that the formal control system can be seriously affected by the informal relationship existing between employees.

Herzberg's two factor model

Herzberg's[5] two factor model of motivation was developing following an analysis of anecdotes of unusually satisfying or unusually dissatisfying job events provided by 200 engineers and accountants. He claimed that money is a so-called 'hygiene factor' which serves as a potential dissatisfier if not present in appropriate amounts, but not as a potential satisfier or positive motivator. A further reason given by Herzberg for regarding salary as a 'hygiene factor', that is, a factor which prevents disease rather than promotes health, was because its impact on favourable feeling was largely short-term, while its impact on unfavourable feelings was long term extending over periods of several months.

But, as Opsahl and Dunnette[6] point out, Herzberg's argument that money acts as a potential dissatisfier is mystifying:

> In all of the definitions of unusually good job feelings, salary was mentioned as a major reason for the feelings 19 per cent of the time. Of the unusually good feelings that lasted several months, salary was reported as a causal factor 22 per cent of the time; of the short-term feelings, it was a factor 5 per cent of the time. In contrast, salary was named as a major cause of unusually bad job feelings only 13 per cent of the time. Of the unusually bad job feelings lasting several months, it was mentioned only 18 per cent of the time (in contrast with the 22 per cent of long-term good feelings mentioned above).

They concluded that,

> these data seem inconsistent with the interpretations and lend no substantial support to hypotheses of a so-called differential role for money in leading to job satisfaction or job dissatisfaction.

Herzberg's two factor model does not therefore provide a reliable basis for developing pay policies.

Instrumental theory

This theory states that money provides the means to achieve ends. It is an instrument for gaining desired outcomes and its force will depend on two factors: first, the strength of the need and, second, the degree to which people are confident that their behaviour will earn the money they want to satisfy the need. The instrumental role of money has been stressed by Gellerman,[7] who suggested that money in itself has no intrinsic meaning and acquires significant motivating power only when it comes to symbolize intangible goals. Money acts as a symbol in different ways for different persons, and for the same person at different times – a man's reaction to money 'summarizes his biography to date, his early economic environment, his competence training, the various non-financial motives he has acquired, and his current financial status'.

Money is therefore a powerful force because it is linked directly or indirectly to the satisfaction of all the basic needs. But the effectiveness of money as a motivator depends on a number of circumstances, including the values and needs of individuals and their preferences for different types of financial or non-financial rewards.

Equity theory

Equity theory, as developed by Adams,[8] argues that satisfaction with pay is related to perceptions about the ratio between what one receives from the job (outcomes in the form of pay) to what one puts into it (inputs in the form of effort and skill) compared with the ratios obtained by others.

Equity theory is related to discrepancy theory which, as stated by Lawler,[9] indicates that satisfaction with pay depends on the difference between the pay people receive and what they feel they ought to receive. Equity theory, however, emphasizes that these feelings are based on comparisons.

The significance of equity was also emphasized by Jaques.[10] He stated that: 1) there exists 'an unrecognized system of norms of fair payment for any given level of work, unconscious knowledge of these norms being shared among the population engaged in employment'; and that 2) an individual 'is unconsciously aware of his own potential capacity for work, as well as the equitable pay level for that work'. Jaques called this the 'felt-fair' principle, which states that, to be equitable, pay must be felt to match the level of work and the capacity of the individual to do it.

Application of expectancy theory

Expectancy theory, as described earlier in this chapter, states that motivation will be strong if individuals can reasonably expect that their efforts and contributions will produce worthwhile rewards.

This theory was developed by Porter and Lawler[11] into an expectancy model which suggests that there are two factors determining the effort people put into their jobs:

1. The values of the rewards to individuals in so far as they satisfy their needs for security, social esteem, autonomy, and self-actualization.
2. The probability that rewards depend on effort, as perceived by the individual – in other words, his or her expectations about the relationships between effort and reward.

Thus, the greater the value of a set of awards and the higher the probability that receiving each of these rewards depends upon effort, the greater the effort that will be put forth in a given situation.

But mere effort is not enough. It has to be effective effort if it is to produce the desired performance. The two variables additional to effort which affect task achievement are:

1. *ability* – individual characteristics such as intelligence, manual skills and know-how;
2. *role perceptions* – what the individual wants to do or thinks he or she is required to do. These are good from the viewpoint of the organization if they correspond with what it thinks the individual ought to be doing. They are poor if the views of the individual and the organization do not coincide.

Conclusions on the role of money as a motivator

Money is important to people because it is instrumental in satisfying a number of their most pressing needs. It is significant not only because of what they can buy with it but also as a highly tangible method of recognizing their worth, thus improving their self-esteem and gaining the esteem of others.

Pay can often be the key to attracting people to join an organization, although job interest, career opportunities and the reputation of the organization will also be factors. Satisfaction with pay among existing employees is mainly related to feelings about equity and fairness. External and internal comparisons will form the basis of these feelings, which will influence their desire to stay with the organization.

Pay can motivate. As a tangible means of recognizing achievement, pay can reinforce desirable behaviour. Pay can also deliver messages on what the organization believes to be important. But to be effective, a pay-for-performance system has to meet very stringent conditions as defined by expectancy theory. To achieve lasting motivation, attention has also to be paid to the non-financial motivators.

Causes of satisfaction or dissatisfaction with pay

Reactions to reward policies and practices will depend largely on the values and needs of individuals and on their employment conditions. It is therefore dangerous to generalize about the causes of satisfaction or dissatisfaction.

However, it seems reasonable to believe that, as mentioned above, feelings about external and internal equity (the 'felt-fair' principle) will strongly influence most people. Research by Porter and Lawler[11] and others has also shown that higher paid employees are likely to be more satisfied with their rewards but the satisfaction resulting from a large pay increase may be short-lived. People tend to want more. In this respect, at least, the views of Herzberg have been supported by research.

Other factors which may affect satisfaction or dissatisfaction with pay include the degree to which:

▌ individuals feel their rate of pay or increase has been determined fairly (procedural justice);

▮ rewards are commensurate with the perceptions of individuals about their ability, contribution and value to the organization (but this perception is likely to be founded on information or beliefs about what other people, inside and outside the organization, are paid);
▮ individuals are satisfied with other aspects of their employment – for example, their status, promotion prospects, opportunity to use and develop skills and relationships with their managers and colleagues.

Financial rewards criteria

The criteria for assessing the effectiveness of financial reward practices as means of motivation are that:

▮ they are, as far as possible, internally equitable as well as externally competitive (although there will always be a tension between these two criteria – paying market rates may upset internal relativities);
▮ pay-for-performance or contribution systems are created in the light of an understanding that direct motivation only takes place if the rewards are worthwhile, if they are specifically related to fair, objective and appropriate performance measures, if employees understand what they have to achieve, and if their expectations on the likelihood of receiving the reward are high;
▮ employees understand how the financial reward system operates, how they benefit from it, and how the organization will help them to develop the skills and competences they need to receive the maximum benefit.

NON-FINANCIAL REWARDS

Non-financial rewards can be focused on the needs most people have, although to different degrees, for achievement, recognition, responsibility, influence and personal growth. We also deal in greater depth with this area in Chapter 2.

Achievement

Research carried out by McClelland[12] of the needs of managerial staff resulted in the identification of three major needs, those for achievement, power and affiliation. The need for achievement is defined as the need for competitive success measured against a personal standard of excellence.

Achievement motivation can be increased by organizations through processes such as job design, performance management, and contributing skill or competency-related pay schemes.

Recognition

Recognition is one of the most powerful motivators. People need to know not only how well they have achieved their objectives or carried out their work but also that their achievements are appreciated.

Praise, however, should be given judiciously – it must be genuine and related to real achievements. And it is not the only form of recognition. Financial rewards, especially achievement bonuses awarded immediately after the event, are clearly symbols of recognition to which are attached tangible benefits, and this is an important way in which mutually reinforcing processes of financial and non-financial rewards can operate. There are other forms of recognition such as long service awards, status symbols of one kind or another, sabbaticals and work-related trips abroad, all of which can be part of the total reward process. (See also Chapter 27, 'Recognition Schemes'.)

Recognition is also provided by managers who listen to and act upon the suggestions of their team members and, importantly, acknowledge their contribution. Other actions which provide recognition include promotion, allocation to a high-profile project, enlargement of the job to provide scope for more interesting and rewarding work, and various forms of status or esteem symbols.

The recognition processes in an organization can be integrated with financial rewards through performance management and pay-for-performance schemes. The importance of recognition can be defined as a key part of the value set of the organization and this would be reinforced by education, training and performance management.

Responsibility

People can be motivated by being given more responsibility for their own work. This is essentially what empowerment is about and is in line with the concept of intrinsic motivation based on the content of the job. It is also related to the fundamental concept that individuals are motivated when they are provided with the means to achieve their goals.

The characteristics required in jobs if they are to be intrinsically motivating are that, first, individuals must receive meaningful feedback about their performance, preferably by evaluating their own performance and defining the feedback they require, second, the job must be perceived by individuals as requiring them to use abilities they value in order to perform the job effectively, and third, individuals must feel that they have a high degree of self-control over setting their own goals and over defining the paths to these goals.

Providing motivation through increased responsibility is a matter of job design and the use of performance management processes. The philosophy behind motivating through responsibility was expressed as follows in McGregor's[13] theory Y: 'The average human being learns, under proper conditions, not only to accept but also to seek responsibility.'

Influence

People can be motivated by the drive to exert influence or to exercise power. McClelland's research established that alongside the need for achievement, the need for power was a prime motivating force for managers, although the need for 'affiliation', ie warm, friendly relationships with others, was always present. The organization, through its policies for involvement, can provide motivation by putting people into situations where their views can be expressed, listened to and acted upon. This is another aspect of empowerment.

Personal growth

In Maslow's[14] hierarchy of needs, self-fulfilment or self-actualization is the highest need of all and is therefore the ultimate motivator. He defines self-fulfilment as 'the need to develop potentialities and skills, to become what one believes one is capable of becoming'.

Ambitious and determined people will seek and find these opportunities for themselves, although the organization needs to clarify the scope for growth and development it can provide (if it does not, they will go away and grow elsewhere).

Increasingly, however, individuals at all levels of organizations, whether or not they are eaten up by ambition, recognize the importance of continually upgrading their skills and of progressively developing their careers. This is the philosophy of continuous development. Many people now regard access to training as a key element in the overall reward package. The availability of learning opportunities, the selection of individuals for high-prestige training courses and programmes and the emphasis placed by the organization on the acquisition of new skills as well as the enhancement of existing ones, can all act as powerful motivators.

SOME NEW THINKING TO ADD TO THE DEBATE

Since we wrote our last edition, there has been a mass of research and literature surfacing on the whole area of motivation, commitment, the implications of raising discretionary effort, the psychological state of 'flow' associated with high performance and the implications of personality preference for the ways in which different kinds of people are motivated and rewarded.

Most reflect what Thomas describes in his book *Intrinsic Motivation at Work*[15] as 'the shift from compliance to partnership'. Academics such as

Linda Gratton at London Business School[3] and Michael O'Malley[16] also work on this theme, focusing on employee relationship management and development. This links across to the work on the use of emotional intelligence in organizations and in enhancing leadership effectiveness by Daniel Goleman, Richard Boyatzis and Annie McKee.[17] They point to the value of motivating people through more effective relationship management, not just to produce a better and more open working environment, but also to enhance the possibilities for discretionary effort.

Discretionary effort can be a key component in organizational performance. Even in fairly basic roles, Hunter, Schmidt and Judiesch[18] found that the difference in value-added discretionary performance between 'superior' and 'standard' performers was 19 per cent. For high-complexity jobs it was 48 per cent. Most organizations would consider this well worth going for.

A further critical issue in this area has been identified by Mihaly Czikzentmihalyi at Chicago University in his work on 'flow'.[19] He has looked at what is happening in the human brain when people are completely engaged and performing at their best. This is a hyperfocused state of mind in which people are remarkably unstressed even when doing challenging work. They 'lose' themselves in a task they love and 'feel out of time' (what footballers describe as being 'in the zone'). Czikzentmihalyi found that people were much more likely to be in 'flow' at work than while involved in leisure activities and that 'flow occurs most often when tasks are tightly aligned with an individual's goals'. He points out the motivational importance of building flow in organizations by providing the conditions in which flow is most likely to happen – which will vary according to the kind of work and the nature of employees themselves. Clear goals and effective feedback are central to this.

A lot of work has now been done too on meeting the motivation and recognition needs of different kinds of personality type and people with difference strengths.

Leaders familiar with the Myers–Briggs Personality Type indicator can now look at the personality preferences of their team and tailor the way in which they work on reward and retention (Hammer[20]). So rewards for someone classified as an 'ISTJ' would be about recognizing specific concrete achievements, increasing job or financial security, recognition when budgets and deadlines are met and for hard work and commitment. But for someone classified as 'ENFP', rewards would be better focused on opportunities for new learning, the provision of continual verbal and non-verbal feedback, recognition for new ideas and public recognition – preferably at a fun event.

CONCLUSIONS

Non-financial motivators are powerful in themselves but can work even more effectively if integrated with financial rewards in a total reward process. However, it is important to remember that the needs of individuals vary almost infinitely depending upon their psychological makeup, background, experience, occupation and position in the organization. It is therefore dangerous to generalize about which mix of motivators is likely to be most effective in individual cases. And this is why one cannot rely on nostrums such as performance-related pay, skill-based pay, job enrichment or performance management to work equally well for every person or in every organization. These processes need to be 'customized' to meet the needs of both the organization and the people who work there. But this customization will take place more effectively if judicious use is made of research on what people value and feel rewarded with. As Ed Lawler put it, 'Why not just ask?'[23] The most obvious way to find out what people want would be simply to ask them what rewards they value. He goes on to stress the importance of a motivational 'value proposition' as a means of effective engagement and retention.

REFERENCES

1. Latham, G and Locke, R (1979) Goal setting – a motivational technique that works, *Organizational Dynamics*, 8
2. Vroom, V (1964) *Work and Motivation*, Wiley, New York
3. Gratton, L (2004) *The Democratic Enterprise*, FT Prentice Hall, Harlow
4. McDougall, C (1973) How well do you reward your managers? *Personnel Management*, March
5. Herzberg, F, Mausner, B and Snyderman, B (1957) *The Motivation to Work*, Wiley, New York
6. Opsahl, R and Dunnette, M (1966) The role of financial compensation in industrial motivation, *Psychological Bulletin*, 66
7. Gellerman, S (1963) *Motivation and Personality*, American Management Association, New York
8. Adams, J (1965) 'Injustice in social exchange', in L Berkowitz (ed), *Advances in Experimental Psychology*, 69
9. Lawler, E (1971) *Pay and Organizational Effectiveness*, McGraw-Hill, New York
10. Jaques, E, (1961) *Equitable Payment*, Heinemann, London
11. Porter, L and Lawler, E (1968) *Management Attitudes and Behaviour*, Irwin-Dorsey, Homewood, Illinois
12. McClelland, D (1975) *Power – the Inner Experience*, Irvington, New York
13. McGregor, D (1960) *The Human Side of Enterprise*, McGraw-Hill, New York
14. Maslow, A (1954) *Motivation and Personality*, Harper & Row, New York

15. Thomas, K W (2000) *Intrinsic Motivation at Work: Building energy and commitment*, Berrett Koehler, San Francisco

16. O'Malley, M (2000) *Creating Commitment: How to attract, retain and motivate employees by building relationships that last*, John Wiley & Sons, New York

17. Goleman, D, Boyatzis, R and McKee, A (2001) Primal leadership: the hidden driver of great performance, *Harvard Business Review*, December, pp 42–51

18. Hunter, J E, Schmidt, F L and Judiesch, J (1990) Individual differences in output variability as a function of job complexity, *Journal of Applied Psychology*, **75**, pp 28–42

19. Czikzentmihalyi, M (2003) *Good Business: Leadership, flow and the making of meaning*, Hodder & Stoughton, London

20. Hammer, A L (2003) *Type and Retention: Retaining talent, leveraging type*, CPP, Palo Alto, CA

21. Lawler, E E (2002) *Treat People Right*, Jossey-Bass, San Francisco

7

Factors Affecting Levels of Pay

Reward management involves the development of pay structures of varying degrees of formality which define the rates of pay for jobs, the pay relativities between jobs and the basis upon which job holders are paid. Pay structures are designed by reference to judgements about job values as expressed by relativities with other jobs and external (market) rates of pay for comparable jobs. These judgements are made against the background of the factors which influence job values. Bearing these in mind, steps can be taken to establish internal job values by using some form of job evaluation. External values are also established by surveying and analyzing market rates, and the information gained from job evaluation and market rate surveys is combined when developing the pay structure.

This chapter deals with the factors influencing job values and relativities and the basis upon which the rates of pay for individual jobs and job holders are determined. Chapters 10–14 examine methods of providing the basic information required for job evaluation and market rate surveys.

GENERAL FACTORS INFLUENCING JOB VALUES

The general factors influencing job values are intrinsic value, internal relativities, external relativities and market practice, inflation, the circumstances of the organization and trade union pressures.

Intrinsic value

The concept of intrinsic value is based on the apparently reasonable belief that the rate for a job should be determined by reference to the amount of responsibility involved or the degree of skill or level of competence required to perform it effectively. The responsibilities of a job are the particular obligations that have to be assumed by any person who carries out the job. Responsibility is exercised when job holders are accountable for what they do. The level of responsibility is related to the outputs job holders are expected to achieve and their contribution – the impact they can make on the end results of their section, department or the organization as a whole.

Responsibility involves the exercise of discretion in making decisions which commit the use of the organization's resources. Rates of pay are therefore influenced not only by the scope of the job in terms of its impact on results but also by the size of resources controlled, the amount of authority job holders possess, the degree of freedom they have to make decisions and to act, and the extent to which they receive guidance or instruction on what they should do.

Perceptions about the intrinsic value of jobs will be influenced not only by the outputs of job holders but also by the impact they can make on the results achieved by the organization as a whole. The scope or size of jobs and their rates of pay are therefore related to the accountability of job holders for achieving results.

The intrinsic value of jobs may also be related to the input and process factors of knowledge and skills and competencies. Knowledge and skills refer to what job holders need to know and are able to do to meet the requirements of their jobs. Competencies are the behavioural character-istics which demonstrably differentiate between levels of performance in a given role.

Internal relativities

The problem with the concept of intrinsic value is that it does not take account of the other factors affecting value. It can be argued that there is no such thing as absolute value. The value of anything is always relative to something else and is affected by external economic factors as well as internal relativities.

Within an organization, job values will be determined by perceptions of the worth of one job compared with others or its position in a job or career family structure. Internal differentials reflect these perceptions, which may be based on information relating to the inputs made by job holders as reflected by the requirement to use different levels of knowl-edge or skill. Or more importance may be attached to outputs – the added value they create. Internal differentials will be strongly influ-enced by differentials established in the external market from which the organization recruits and to which existing employees may be tempted to return.

The organization structure will clearly influence differentials and methods of payment. A hierarchical structure with well-defined layers of responsibility will provide a clear indication of the pattern of differentials and produce a pay structure with fairly narrow bands. A flatter, more flexible, structure will make it hard to establish a rigid rank order and differentials will be more fluid within broader pay bands and will depend more on relative levels of competence and contribution.

External relativities

A salary or wage is a price which, like any other price, represents the value of the service to the buyer and the seller: the employer and the employed. The external value of a job – the market rate – is primarily determined by the laws of supply and demand.

However, all the market does is to allow us to assume that people occupying equal positions tend to be paid equally and as Kanter[1] puts it: 'The process is circular… we know what people are worth because that's what they cost in the job market, but we also know that what people cost in the job market is just what they're worth.'

The market rate concept is in any case an imprecise one. Market rate surveys always reveal a considerable range of rates which reflect the special circumstances of the organizations, including the level of people they employ and their policies on how they want their levels of pay to relate to market rates – their market stance or pay posture.

There will, however, be trends in market rates to which internal pay structures must respond if they are to remain competitive. Individual rates and differentials have to be adjusted in the light of changing market pressures if the organization needs good-quality staff. This will be particularly important at the intake points in a structure and in respect of individuals whose market worth is high and who are therefore vulnerable to the attractions of better paid jobs elsewhere.

It is also important to bear in mind the concept of individual market worth. In effect, this says that any employable individual has a price that is related to what other organizations are prepared to pay for his or her services. Organizations ignore at their peril the individual market worth of any employees they wish to retain whose talents are at a premium in the market place. Headhunters generally know about them and tend to keep in touch.

Inflation and market movement

Although they have reduced considerably in recent years, inflationary pressures clearly affect general trends in rates of pay and earnings. They underpin pay market movements.

Organizations have been accustomed to taking into account inflation when adjusting their pay structures although, if their managements have any sense, they have refused to commit themselves to any semblance of index linking. They have had to be prepared to increase rates by less than inflation in hard times and they have reserved the right to restrict increases to individuals to below the rate of inflation if their performance does not justify the retention of their real level of earnings. Generally, however, employers are basing pay reviews on movements in market rates, which are, in any case, responsive to the rate of inflation. In practice, it is always important to look at what is happening at national level to both prices and average earnings as the reference points employees tend to use when considering their own 'baseline' pay review expectations.

Business performance and/or financial circumstances

The business or strategic aims of the organization and its plans for achieving those aims will provide the basis for developing pay strategies and policies. The resulting business performance and/or the financial circumstances of the organization will influence the amount it can afford to pay and its pay policies on such matters as how it wants to relate pay to performance , contribution and market rates.

Trade union pressures

Depending on their bargaining power, trade unions will attempt to pressurize managements into increasing pay by at least the amount of inflation. They will press for higher rates on the grounds of the organization's ability to pay and trends in market movement and the going rate for specific jobs, and they may attempt to restore lost differentials.

FACTORS INFLUENCING PAY LEVELS FOR INDIVIDUALS

The pay levels of individual job holders will be influenced by three factors in addition to the rate for their job:

1. their market worth as mentioned above;
2. the level of skills or competence they possess – their inputs;
3. their level of performance in the job – their outputs and the overall contribution they make to organizational success.

The amount of influence these factors exert will depend on the job and the internal environment of the organization. In a non-bureaucratic and flexible firm, where the level of technology is high and a large propor-tion of the staff are knowledge workers, individual worth will be more important than position in a job hierarchy. As Kanter[1] said a decade and more ago:

> Major employing organizations are rethinking the meaning of worth itself. And as they are doing this, they are gradually changing the basis for deter-mining pay from *position* to *performance*, from *status to contribution*.

This process is largely complete in the UK private sector, but is still 'work in progress' in many parts of the public sector.

HOW RATES OF PAY FOR INDIVIDUAL JOBS AND JOB HOLDERS ARE DETERMINED

The determination of individual rates of pay is a function of a number of factors as illustrated in Figure 7.1.

Overall levels of pay will be affected by organizational goals, plans and performance, external economic and union influences, reward poli-cies and market rates.

These general considerations will, of course, affect individual rates for jobs and job holders. These rates will be determined by market relativi-ties, the 'size' of the job within the structure, as measured by job evalua-tion, and individual levels of performance. The latter will determine rates of pay above the base rate either by a performance management process or a pay-for-performance scheme.

This process of individual pay determination takes place within the framework of job and role analysis and, apart from business and market rate considerations, is largely influenced by the interrelated processes of job evaluation and performance management for those in receipt of performance-related pay. The development of job or career families has brought these two elements closer with the creation of role profiles for each level, which typically contain performance criteria.

Job evaluation is used to measure relativities and determine where the job should be placed in a pay structure (the rate for the job). Relative job size is assessed in terms of inputs (knowledge and skills), process (behavioural requirements involving the use of competences) and outputs (the level of responsibility for results and the impact the job makes on team or organizational performance).

Performance management assesses the individual's performance in the job and, in a performance-related pay environment, determines the rate of pay for that individual in the job – whether he or she is positioned within a pay range or on a pay scale. The performance management process will be based on precisely the same factors used in evaluating

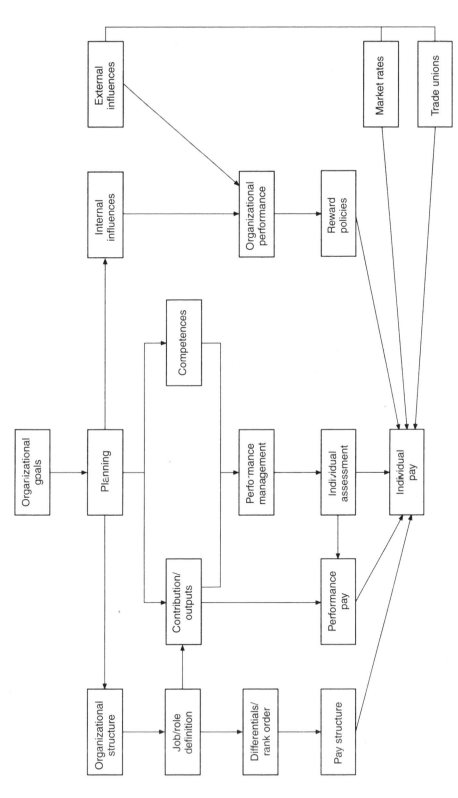

Figure 7.1 Factors affecting individual pay

the job as recorded in a job description or role definition derived from job or role analysis: namely skills, competences and results. The starting point of performance management is an agreement on skill and competence requirements (and their development) and on the principal accountabilities or main tasks of the job. This leads to agreements on specific standards of performance, targets and work plans and personal development plans, which form the criteria on which performance is reviewed and assessed.

For those on an incentive or payment by results scheme, pay in terms of total cash rewards will be determined by reference to job evaluation and the quantified results achieved by job holders.

REFERENCE

1. Kanter, R M (1989) *When Giants Learn to Dance*, Simon and Schuster, London

Part 2

The Evaluation and Development of Reward Processes

8

Evaluation of Reward Processes

The evaluation of reward processes is best carried out by a diagnostic review which, as set out below, could cover the following areas:

- basic philosophy and strategic principles;
- overall reward policies including total rewards;
- individual reward policy and practice areas;
- cost considerations;
- overall reward management;
- overall perceptions;
- communications.

The diagnostic review should be carried out by examining written strategy and policy statements, details of structures, procedures, processes and schemes, any reports and records on reward matters and discussions with managers, HR staff, employees and union representatives. It is also highly desirable to conduct an attitude survey (see Appendix B); this can be supplemented by focus group discussions with managers and employees to understand views in greater depth.

REWARD MANAGEMENT: DIAGNOSTIC CHECKLIST

Basic philosophy and strategic principles

These questions deal with the high-level, strategic issues facing organizations.

1. *Are the fundamental principles on which the system and its development is based linked to:*

    (a) the organization's current needs and goals;
    (b) HR management strategy (see also 3 below);
    (c) policy on pay levels needed to recruit, retain and engage high-quality and committed staff (see also below);
    (d) policy on assessing the pay market practice needed to achieve recruitment , retention and high levels of engagement:

    ∎ locally (for locally recruited staff);
    ∎ regionally (for regionally recruited staff);
    ∎ nationally (for nationally recruited staff);
    ∎ internationally (where the market is for specific 'world-class' individuals);

    (e) current legislation and practice on equal pay for work of equal value;
    (f) avoidance of discrimination other than differences warranted by job/role size, responsibility, complexity and valid responses to market pressures?

2. *Have these principles been developed:*

    (a) in consultation with key stakeholders (management, staff, unions);
    (b) on the basis of current and future business strategies;
    (c) by reference to any projected or needed changes in the culture of the organization?

3. *Is there a clear and articulated link between reward strategies and HR strategy on:*

    (a) organization design: the structures and processes needed to deliver organization strategy and the levels and distribution of work and differing competency profiles needed to do this;
    (b) recruitment: a reasonably attractive total package;
    (c) training: rewarding skills acquisition and use;
    (d) development: rewarding the behaviours or competences associated with good performance and continued learning;
    (e) performance improvement: delivering an effective and efficient personal contribution;
    (f) effective team/group working;
    (g) promotion: rewarding the acceptance and successful delivery of greater responsibilities;
    (h) reinforcing loyalty, integrity and commitment?

4. *Is there a strategy for ongoing reward management which:*

    (a) is based on the organization's:

- mission and values
- culture;
- current and future needs;

    (b) staff at all levels understand, at least in outline, and believe to be fair and rational;

    (c) provides for a flexible response when different parts of the organization have different needs or face different pressures?

5. *Does the strategy provide a sound basis for the development of reward policies, systems and procedures, ie:*

    (a) provision for proper responses to changing circumstances;

    (b) management of the system to protect its integrity and validity;

    (c) monitoring and management of the cost of managing the system with a focus on:

- cost effectiveness;
- avoiding duplication of effort;
- using IT to support and enable greater efficiency/improved communication?

6. *Is the strategy congruent with the culture of the organization?*

    (a) Are there any conflicts between practice and organization values, eg:

- rewarding service and experience rather than continuous improvement in performance and contribution;
- providing long-term employee benefits when shorter-term contracts are becoming more common or employees only stay in a role for a few years;
- becoming increasingly complex or cumbersome when the organization is trying to simplify the way it manages itself in other ways;
- focusing too much on equity beyond what is feasible within the fairness-based judgmental frameworks on which effective reward management depends?

Overall reward policies

These questions focus on the articulation of overall reward policies.

7. *What is the policy on levels of rewards, eg:*

   (a) the chosen place in a well-defined, surveyed and comparable pay market for different grades, levels and specialisms;
   (b) the need to attract and retain high-quality staff;
   (c) the need for stability and sustained staff commitment?

8. *What is the policy on market rates and responses to market pressure?*

   (a) Is the organization subject to skill shortages and areas of market pressure?
   (b) How are these tracked, eg through:

   ▌ analysis of retention issues through leavers or exit interviews;
   ▌ analysis of recruitment issues;
   ▌ analysis of where people come from and where they go;
   ▌ pay surveys;
   ▌ other market intelligence?

   (c) Are pay responses the only way to retain people 'at risk'?
   (d) Have other strategies, such as improved performance management and development or improved working conditions, been tried?
   (e) At what stage are specific market responses or market premiums paid?
   (f) Is it clear to staff that market premiums can go down as well as up?
   (g) Is this specifically communicated with market adjustments?
   (h) If not, how will the cost implications be managed when the market declines?

9. *Are, or should, reward levels be linked to the organization's performance?*

   (a) What are the identifiable performance measures for the organization?
   (b) Can these be tracked without undue effort?
   (c) Are they subject to external or political influences in the short, medium or long term that take sensitive handling?
   (d) Would better performance actually generate more money for rewards?
   (e) Is there scope for rewarding specific individual or team achievements?
   (f) Would this be culturally appropriate?
   (g) Who will assess and manage performance?
   (h) Are they close enough to employees – especially those out in the field – to be able to judge performance effectively?

(i) Is there trust in the current performance management processes?

(j) Are people given the training and development needed to help improve performance?

(k) Is there sufficient management capability to manage performance and motivation well? Are knowledge and experience updated and supported?

10. *What is the policy on equity?*

(a) How important is equity in the organization's culture?

(b) Is there a focus on complete equal treatment for similar jobs/jobs of the same size?

(c) Or, is there a preference for equal treatment in relation to contribution and performance?

(d) How is equity measured and tracked?

(e) Does this ensure reasonably fair and equal treatment:

▌ by location;
▌ by region;
▌ across the whole organization?

Individual reward policy and practice areas

These questions concentrate on specific areas of reward policy and practice.

Job evaluation

11. *Is a formal system of job evaluation used to determine internal relativities? If not, how are they determined?*

(a) Is this analytical?

(b) Is it related to skill sets/competences?

(c) Is it defined in terms of relevant factors?

(d) Has it been tried and proved effective elsewhere?

12. *Are the factors used for job evaluation:*

(a) relevant to the organization;

(b) relevant to the jobs they cover;

(c) unbiased in terms of sex, race or disability;

(d) relevant individually and not subject to 'double counting' (looking at the same areas from a different angle);

(e) defined in language that is clear and unambiguous?

13. *Is the scoring system:*

    (a) arithmetic or geometric; is it weighted effectively to reflect organizational values;

    (b) able to provide sensible grade breaks between distinct levels of work;

    (c) Do grade breaks fall into natural gaps in job scores?

Pay structure

14. *What is the overall policy on the pay structure?*

    (a) What is the rationale for the current pay/grade structure?

    (b) Did it/does it reflect practice in comparable organizations in terms of:

      ▌ actual levels of work performed;

      ▌ the needs of any specialist/professional groups which are different in character from the mainstream of staff, if these exist;

      ▌ union bargaining units, if relevant;

      ▌ the need to progress staff spending several years in grade to reflect experience, performance and service in grade?

    (c) Is the structure flexible enough to cater for:

      ▌ the current pattern of career development and promotion;

      ▌ changes in pay/job market conditions?

    (d) Or are there:

      ▌ too many people with no further progression or promotion opportunities, stuck on the grade maximum (even if well paid);

      ▌ many people low in range with little real prospect of progression in a low inflation/tight payroll cost control environment;

      ▌ few opportunities to respond to changes in market circumstances?

15. *What type of specific pay and grade structure or structures exist in the organization?*

    (a) Graded salary scales – general/job or career family related?

    (b) Pay spines?

    (c) Spot rates?

    (d) Pay curves?

16. *Is the pay structure relevant to the needs of the organization as a whole or the part of the organization in which it operates, ie does it:*

   (a) fit the circumstances and culture of the organization, in that it is flexible in organizations subject to rapid change or well defined and rigorously applied where order and predictability are of paramount importance;
   (b) provide a logical framework or system for enabling consistent and defensible decisions to be made on the levels of pay and differentials of all the employees to be covered by the structure;
   (c) make provision for the reasonable and sometimes inevitable fact that external market rate considerations may have to prevail over the requirements of strict internal equity, especially in the areas of skill shortage?

17. *Is the grade structure designed and administered properly?*

   (a) Are the grades or job/career families clearly defined? Do they fit the way work is currently organized (eg the number of levels in the organization, contribution)?
   (b) Are the pay ranges wide enough to allow scope for pay progression in accordance with service (where relevant), competence and performance?
   (c) Is there an adequate differential (say 15 to 20 per cent) between grades?
   (d) Is there an overlap between grades to provide some flexibility and recognize the fact that an experienced individual at the top of one grade may be of more value to the organization than a newcomer in the grade above?
   (e) Are consistent methods used to allocate jobs into grades or job/career families, including decisions on recruitment, promotion and upgrading because of greater responsibility?
   (f) Is there any evidence of inequities in the pay structure because of wrongly graded jobs?
   (g) Are pay scales regularly reviewed against external data? If not, what are the factors which are used to determine annual adjustments in pay scales? Are these factors consistent across grades?
   (h) Is there a balanced and cost-effective approach to the provision of employee benefits with status distinctions dictated only by 'good' and defensible market practice?
   (i) Is there a consistent and fair basis for allocating benefits?
   (j) Is there any evidence of salary levels falling ahead of or behind the market rates?
   (k) If so, what are the causes and are they short term or long term in nature?

18. *Is the system regularly maintained and updated:*

    (a) to take account of new jobs and roles;
    (b) to take account of structural change in the organization?

19. *Is 'grade drift' a problem (are people always trying to get jobs upgraded to improve pay levels without sufficient reason)?*

    (a) How is this controlled?
    (b) Are the controls adequate or are inconsistencies emerging?

Pay progression

These questions consider all types of pay progression schemes within a graded structure, up a pay spine or along a pay curve.

20. *Is there a consistent method of progressing pay, eg according to:*

    (a) length of service;
    (b) experience (how is this assessed?);
    (c) performance or contribution;
    (d) work level;
    (e) competency acquisition and use;
    (f) skill?

21. *Is the rate of progression based on fair and consistent methods of assessment?*

    (a) Are there effective links between performance- or contribution-based progression and the performance management and any competency framework that exists and related development planning?
    (b) Does the approval process for any service-based progression ensure that under-performers do not get undeserved increments?

22. *If a performance- or contribution-related pay system is in use:*

    (a) Is the relationship between contribution, effort and reward clearly defined and understood?
    (b) Is there a credible, well-established and managed process of performance management to support pay decisions, as well as deliver the organization's performance goals?
    (c) Is the amount of performance- or contribution-related pay sufficient to recognize the contribution not only of high-flyers but also of the reliable 'core' performers on whom most organizations depend?

(d) Do employees have a reasonable degree of control over the results which determine their reward levels?
(e) Do bonus earnings (if any) fluctuate too much or too little?
(f) Is the system easy to understand and administer?
(g) Has appropriate training in performance management and the reward process been given? Is this updated regularly?
(h) If the system or any part of it is causing problems, how are these being addressed?

Pay reviews

23. *How are pay reviews conducted?*

(a) What arrangements are made for cost of living awards?
(b) To what extent are pay levels reviewed on the basis of market-rate movements?
(c) Are there satisfactory arrangements to track market rates, both generally and for specific occupations?
(d) How much money, in terms of payroll percentage, has been and is likely to be made available for pay reviews?
(e) What arrangements are made to provide guidance on individual reviews related to contribution, performance or competence (if applicable)?
(f) How are budgets for pay reviews set and controlled?
(g) Are the budgeting arrangements satisfactory?
(h) What freedom do managers have to make their own pay decisions or recommendations at the annual pay review?
(i) How is consistency and equity achieved?

Total remuneration and employee benefits

24. *What is the policy on the structure and balance of the reward package?*

(a) What is the mix between:

▌ base salary;
▌ other cash rewards, eg bonuses (if paid);
▌ allowances of various kinds to compensate for specific circumstances;
▌ benefits, eg pensions and related relevant provisions, loans, mortgage assistance, moving allowances;
▌ sick pay and long-term disability provisions;
▌ medical provisions;
▌ leave;
▌ meals;
▌ employee advisory services;

▌ other non-cash items perceived as critical to employee engagement and total reward?

(b) Are any choices over the mix available?

▌ Why?
▌ Is this cost effective?
▌ Do staff like having a choice over individual benefits or their total package to meet personal requirements?

(c) Is the balance between different elements felt by management and staff to be:

▌ about right;
▌ in need of change?

Pensions

25. *Does the pension scheme properly reflect current:*

(a) employment patterns and demography;
(b) levels of employee mobility;
(c) comparable practice in similar organizations?

26. *Can pensions be 'topped up' where individuals have insufficient service or previous provisions?*

(a) Do the mechanisms reflect good market practice?
(b) Do they make sound financial sense for both employer and staff?

27. *Are there provisions for partners/dependants?*

(a) How do these compare against the market?
(b) Are the rules concerning their entitlements regularly reviewed?
(c) How is this communicated alongside the overall pension scheme?

28. *Is the pension scheme cost-base sound or will demographic change or changing employee profiles put pressure on affordability?*

(a) How are changes in this area being tracked?
(b) Who will decide on change and how?

Cost considerations

These questions focus on the way costs are understood and managed.

29. *What is the level of employment costs and how are costs managed?*

  (a) What proportion of operating costs are employment costs?
  (b) How does this compare to other comparable organizations in terms of magnitude?
  (c) Are equivalent costs increasing?

  ▌ Why?
  ▌ Is this acceptable and defensible in current circumstances?
  ▌ What are the options for change?

  (d) How are pay budgets for the organization and its constituent parts compiled and agreed?
  (e) Are effective costing/modelling procedures in place?
  (f) Is IT support for this good enough so that 'what ifs' can be tested speedily?
  (g) How are the costs of benefits/allowances monitored?
  (h) How are approvals given for progression/promotion?
  (i) Which elements of the system have to change with any pay adjustment?
  (j) How complex is this change process?
  (k) Could it be simplified without causing undue inequity?
  (l) How often are changes in the system required and what does the process of change cost in (if known):

  ▌ employee time;
  ▌ communications to staff?

Ongoing reward management

30. *How well is reward management carried out?*

  (a) Are responsibilities and resources for elements of the system properly distributed and managed within the pay management department?
  (b) Do the people who operate the pay system fully understand its purpose and operating principles and methodologies?
  (c) Are full records/definitions of practice kept?
  (d) Are decision-making processes about updating or changing the system straightforward and designed to produce robust and acceptable results?
  (e) Are the right checks and balances in place at top executive levels and through the organization?

(f) Is IT used effectively to increase responsiveness, accuracy and effective modelling of policy changes?

(g) Are sound cost-management processes in place for pay budgeting, monitoring spend and controlling outcomes centrally and in local offices, where needed?

(h) Could any of the processes be simplified or made more efficient?

(i) What lessons are available from improvements already achieved in comparable organizations?

(j) How well or regularly is information gathered on this? Has benchmarking been used?

(k) Is there a sensible level of information sharing between comparable organizations and reward networks (eg the CIPD Reward Forum, E-Reward)?

Overall perceptions and communications

These questions focus on perceptions and understanding.

31. *Management perceptions*

(a) Does top/operational management believe that the pay system is:

 ▮ effective;
 ▮ supporting the way people are recruited, managed, motivated and developed;
 ▮ giving the right messages to staff and potential recruits about the package on offer?

(b) If not, what changes would they want to see and why?

32. *Staff/union perceptions*

(a) Do staff and or unions like and wish to keep the current reward system?

(b) Do they find it motivational in most aspects?

(c) Has the organization tracked/measured these perceptions recently through:

 ▮ attitude surveys;
 ▮ interviews;
 ▮ focus groups;
 ▮ informal testing of views?

(d) If they do not like the current system:

- █ What do they want to change?
- █ Why?
- █ Is this realistic, given current affordability/financial circumstances?
- █ How is the organization planning to respond to acknowledge what has been learned and begin to address the issues raised?

Communications

33. *How well are reward policies communicated to employees?*

(a) How well are managers briefed on current reward practice?
(b) Are staff aware of the total value of their pay and benefits package?
(c) What improvements in communication would they like to see?

9

Development of Reward Processes

THE DEVELOPMENT PROGRAMME

The design and development of reward management processes is a matter of selecting the optimum mix of rewards and benefits within the most appropriate structure and of ensuring that the various processes fit or help to change the culture.

The problem is that the differences between the circumstances and cultures of organizations mean that there is no one right approach which suits all organizations. The concept of 'best practice' should be viewed with suspicion. What is best practice in one organization may be totally inappropriate in another. But it is still necessary to be aware of what is generally regarded as good practice and then consider how well it might apply in the context of the organization, so as to identify the options and make a choice.

It may not be desirable to lay down a set of absolute design principles. But it is possible to suggest the lines along which a development programme can be undertaken. These are as follows:

- Analyse the existing context — the work culture, circumstances and environment of the organization, the level of capability to manage reward, and the relevance and effectiveness of existing reward practices.
- Assess what changes need to be made in the light of that analysis.
- List and evaluate the options and make a choice accordingly.

The main factors to be taken into account in carrying out the analysis are:

▌ the work culture of the organization and its characteristics: type, structure, size, internal environment, external environment, business strategy and management practices;
▌ job and occupational characteristics: the number and diversity of jobs and roles;
▌ the characteristics of individual employees: their needs and expectations as expressed in the psychological contract;
▌ other internal factors, notably capability in running existing reward systems.

These factors are discussed below.

Work culture

Flannery *et al*[1] defined four forms of work culture: functional, process, time-based, and network. All four are described below, together with our analysis of the different approaches that may be adopted to reward management in each of the cultures. A single organization may, of course, contain more than one of these cultures or variations of them. Experience of working with them suggests that they are helpful to many organizations in assessing where they are or need to be.

The functional culture

In this type of culture the focus is on what the organization does and on doing it consistently. Work is specialized and integrated through deep management hierarchies. The strategic priorities in order of importance are:

▌ technology;
▌ reliability and quality;
▌ customer needs;
▌ flexibility and agility.

Reward practices in a functional culture are likely to be highly formalized with a multi-graded structure or a pay spine. There are tight job definitions, an analytical job evaluation scheme and a highly structured and well-documented performance management system linked to results and development objectives. Performance pay is governed by ratings and consolidated with base pay, with incentives confined to top management. Employee benefits are fixed or there may be flexibility with individual elements. Tight centralized control is exercised on pay determination and reviews with little devolution to line managers.

The process culture

In this type of culture work processes are designed to meet customer needs and the requirement for continuous quality improvement. The strategic priorities in order of importance are:

▌ customer needs;
▌ reliability and quality;
▌ technology;
▌ flexibility and agility.

Reward practices in a process culture will be more flexible than in the functional culture. There is still likely to be a traditional graded pay structure but this might have fewer and wider grades and there could well be job or career families. Analytical job evaluation schemes determine internal relativities, although they are used more flexibly. More attention is paid to external relativities. Performance management is much more of a joint process and rewards are related to the degree to which people sustain values such as quality and customer care and meeting time-to-market, customer response, delivery and just-in-time requirements, as well as to the achievement of quantitative targets. There is more scope for bonuses which relate to achievements or sustained high performance in the areas listed above. Partial or total flexibility in the benefits package is common.

The time-based culture

The time-based culture emphasizes speed to market and maximizing return on fixed assets. Firms with this type of culture dominate markets through technical prowess during their highly profitable phase and then use the accumulated internal competences of their people to develop market opportunities when they reach a mature, lower-return stage. They have relatively flat structures and use full-time, cross-functional project teams extensively. The strategic priorities in order of importance are:

▌ flexibility and agility;
▌ technology;
▌ customer needs;
▌ reliability and quality.

In this type of culture, reward processes are much more flexible. Job evaluation schemes are used to support decisions on relativities, not to dominate them. The focus is on flexible roles rather than jobs and, therefore, paying for the person. Job and career family-based approaches are helpful in larger organizations. Close attention is paid to keeping pace with market rates. The pay structure is likely to be broadbanded but there will probably be well-defined anchor rates and zones within the bands. Performance pay is likely to be variable – not consolidated and much more at risk. Competence-related or skill-based pay schemes may be installed at least as transitional measures. Team pay may be used for established work or project teams. A fully developed flexible benefit scheme is likely to have been introduced. A considerable amount of responsibility for pay decisions is devolved to line managers but with well-defined guidelines.

The network culture

The network culture is one in which organizations are created through ad hoc groups and temporary alliances that bring together the necessary skills to complete a specific venture. They disband after their goals are achieved. The strategic priorities in order of importance are:

▌ flexibility and agility;
▌ customer needs;
▌ technology;
▌ reliability and quality.

A completely flexible approach to pay is adopted. Pay determination is dominated by market rates. There could be a 'spot rate' structure or very broad bands without any infrastructure. The focus is on total pay, not pay increases. Variable pay in the shape of at-risk bonuses for individuals, plus some form of profit-related bonus, is the norm. Only core benefits will be provided, the emphasis being on 'clean cash'. Pay decisions are devolved to line management without firm guidelines, although strict budgetary control on overall spend is still maintained from the centre.

Culture and reward management

Reward management processes must either fit the culture of the organization as it is or be developed as a means of changing that culture in specific ways, possibly as part of a transformation programme covering such areas as performance, productivity, teamwork, organizational restructuring, competence and skills development to meet new challenges, quality and customer care. They must ensure that the organization attains its future business goals.

THE SEQUENCE FOR DEVELOPING REWARD PROCESSES

The sequence for developing reward processes is illustrated in Figure 9.1. This consists of the following phases.

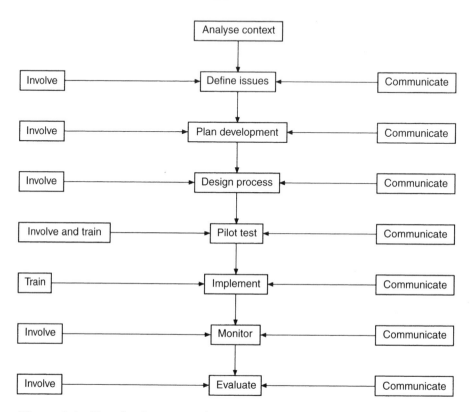

Figure 9.1 Developing reward processes

Context

∎ Analyse organization culture, structure, internal and external environment, business plans.
∎ Assess plans/need for change.
∎ Conduct diagnostic review of present reward arrangements (see Chapter 8) to determine strengths and weaknesses and areas for change.

Issues

∎ Identify issues to be addressed in the light of the contextual analysis and diagnostic review.

Plan

▌ Plan the development programme covering:

- areas for development;
- objectives to be achieved;
- resources to be used: internal/external consultants, project teams and financial budget;
- cost/benefit analysis;
- timetable;
- arrangements for communication, consultation and the training required to build capability to deliver the required change effectively.

Options

▌ List and evaluate options and select most appropriate one in the light of the context and objectives.

Development process

▌ Develop the preferred alternative, involving employees and keeping them informed.

Test the process

▌ Where possible and desirable, pilot test the process and modify as required – position the development within a 'learning organization' context to emphasize the value of joint learning.

Implement

▌ Develop and execute the implementation plan including training and capability building.

Monitor

▌ Monitor implementation and fine-tune as needed.

Evaluate

▌ Evaluate the impact of the new process and reshape and fine-tune as necessary.

Communicate and involve

∎ Communicate and involve throughout to ensure transparency and credibility.

REFERENCE

1. Flannery, T P, Hofrichter, D A and Platten, P E (1996) *People, Performance, and Pay*, Free Press, New York

Part 3

Assessing Job Size and Relativities

10

Job and Role Analysis

Job and role analysis provides the essential framework for job evaluation, as described in Chapters 11 and 12, and grade structure design (Chapter 16). It also produces crucial information for performance management (Chapters 18 and 19) and many other key HR processes such as human resource development, talent management and career planning.

JOB ANALYSIS – A DEFINITION

Job analysis is the process of collecting, analysing and organizing information about jobs. It provides the basis for a job description or role definition and data for job evaluation, organization design or review, performance management, succession planning and career management, and other human resource management purposes.

A distinction should be made between a job description and a role definition. A job description sets out the purpose of a job, where it fits in the organization structure, the context within which the job holder functions and the principal accountabilities of job holders, or the main tasks they have to carry out. A role definition additionally describes the part to be played by individuals in fulfilling their job requirements. Role definitions refer to broader aspects of behaviour, for example, working flexibly, working with others, and styles of management. They may incorporate the results of skills or competence analysis, as described below.

JOB ANALYSIS IN PRACTICE

Job analysis as defined by Pritchard and Murlis[1] is an analytical process involving gathering facts, analysing and sorting these facts and re-assembling them into whatever consistent format is chosen.

Job analysis gets the facts about a job from a job holder, the job holder's manager (preferably both) and the job holder's colleagues or team mates. It is not a matter of obtaining opinions or making judgements. What goes into a job description should be what actually happens and why, not what people would like to think happens, or what they feel people should be like to make it happen. Thus judgmental statements such as 'Carries out the highly skilled work of…' should be avoided (who is to say that the work is highly skilled and in comparison with what?).

The facts can be obtained by interviews (the best but most time-consuming way) or by asking job holders and/or their managers to write their own job descriptions in a structured format. It is helpful in both cases to provide guidance on what is needed and be quite clear about the questions to be asked and answered, and it is essential in the latter case to provide guidance on how the analysis should be carried out and expressed on either paper or on-screen.

Alternatively, questionnaires can be used – either universal questionnaires or those designed for job families.

Universal questionnaires

Universal questionnaires are designed to cover all the jobs to be analysed. They are typically used in association with computer-assisted job evaluation processes. They should be tailored to the particular organization and the range and type of jobs to be covered, and they should focus on those aspects of performance and values which are considered to be important in the organization concerned. It is usual to incorporate multiple choice questions, as in the example given in Figure 10.1, but questions may simply ask for a number to be entered to establish the dimensions of the job, for example, number of people supervised or the value of the budget controlled.

Job family questionnaires

Job family questionnaires are designed to establish the main factors which differentiate between jobs at different levels in a job family. A job family consists of jobs in a particular function or discipline such as research scientist, development engineer or personnel specialist, which are related in terms of the fundamental activities carried out but are differentiated by the levels of responsibility, skill or competence

Select the level that best describes the most common way in which the job must liaise with others.

(Internal means within the company and includes remote sites/headquarters, etc.)

1. The job involves no need for contact outside the particular work group and its management.

2. The job involves infrequent contact with others, and the contact is for the purpose of exchanging job-related information, which needs to be done accurately and effectively.

3. The job requires frequent contact with people outside the department in order to provide or obtain information. There is a need to express oneself clearly. The job requires courteous behaviour in face-to-face dealings with other employees.

4. The need to express oneself clearly is an important part of the job, and job holders will typically have had specific training in communications skills or will have been selected because they possess these skills. The importance stems from a requirement to create a favourable impression on others as well as communicate information effectively.

5. The job requires you frequently to seek cooperation from, or influence others. The job holder must develop relationships and persuade others to help resolve problems. The ability to listen to others and to develop a mutual understanding is an important requirement of the job. This level usually includes jobs which allocate, monitor and review work of other employees, or jobs which have regular and significant dealings with colleagues in a variety of different locations.

6. The job requires you to motivate subordinates or colleagues where the degree of motivation and commitment achieved will directly impact upon the result of the department.

7. The job requires highly developed communication skills for dealing with sensitive, or potentially controversial interpersonal situations. The job holder must create behaviour change in people and/or obtain the cooperation and commitment of subordinates/colleagues. This level is usually required for positions responsible for the development, motivation, assessment and reward of other employees.

Source: Pritchard, D and Murlis, H (1992) *Jobs, Roles and People: the New World of Job Evaluation*, Nicholas Brealey

Figure 10.1 Typical question from a universal questionnaire

required (job and career families and the 'ladders' used to describe changing levels of work are discussed in more detail in Chapter 15). A job family questionnaire is designed with the advice of an expert team of managers from the organization. It is based on definitions of the differentiating factors and the levels at which they may be present in a job. The questions are then structured to establish the levels for each factor in a job, as illustrated in Figure 10.2.

QUESTION 4
INFORMATION HANDLING

Please tick the box which best describes the job:

☐ 1. No responsibility for the processing of data.

☐ 2. Responsible for checking data, and referring errors for correction.

☐ 3. Responsible for maintaining, checking, updating and deleting information held in files or systems of predetermined format.

☐ 4. Responsible for extracting information from files or systems and compiling reports in standard format.

☐ 5. Responsible for gathering information from a variety of established sources and compiling reports with an agreed framework.

☐ 6. Responsible for compiling special and one-off reports, using data from a range of sources, involving non-standard information retrieval and report formats.

☐ 7. Responsible for identifying new sources of information and/or the setting up of new administrative procedures, systems and reporting formats.

Source: Pritchard, D and Murlis, H (1992) *Jobs, Roles and People: the New World of Job Evaluation*, Nicholas Brealey.

Figure 10.2   Extract from a job family questionnaire for a group of clerical and administrative jobs

Job analysis interview check lists

Elaborate check lists are not necessary. They only confuse people. The essence of the art of job analysis is to keep it simple. The points to be covered are:

▌ What is your job title?
▌ To whom are you responsible?

▌ Who is responsible to you? (An organization chart is helpful.)

▌ What is the main purpose of your job? That is, in overall terms, what are you expected to do and why?

▌ To achieve that purpose, what are your main areas of responsibility (eg principal accountabilities, key result areas or main tasks)? Describe *what* you have to do, not, in any detail, *how* you do it. Also indicate why you have to do it, ie the results you are expected to achieve by carrying out the task.

▌ What are the dimensions of your job in such terms as output or sales targets, numbers of items processed, numbers of people managed, number of customers?

▌ Is there any other information you can provide about your job to amplify the above facts, such as:

- how your job fits in with other jobs in your department or elsewhere in the company;
- flexibility requirements in terms of having to carry out a range of different tasks;
- how work is allocated to you and how your work is reviewed and approved;
- your decision-making authority;
- the contacts you make with others, inside and outside the company – the equipment, plant and tools you use;
- other features of your job such as travelling or unsocial hours or unusual physical conditions;
- the major problems you meet in carrying out your work;
- the knowledge and skills you need to do your work.

The aim is to structure the job analysis interview or questionnaire in line with these headings.

Analysing the facts

However carefully the interview or questionnaire is structured, the information is unlikely to come out neatly and succinctly in a way which can readily be translated into a job description or role definition. It is usually necessary to sort out, rearrange and sometimes rewrite the information under the headings and in the manner described below. But writing job descriptions or role definitions is not a literary exercise. All that is required is clear and simple prose.

JOB DESCRIPTIONS

The format for job descriptions will depend upon the requirements of the organization. There are many varieties but one which is commonly used consists of the following sections.

Purpose

This is a short statement of why the job exists. It should be expressed in a single sentence. When defining the purpose of a job consider:

▊ What part of the organization's/unit's total purpose is accomplished by this job?
▊ What is the unique contribution of this job which distinguishes it from other jobs?
▊ How would you summarize the overall responsibility of the job holder?

Organization

This section explains where the job fits into the organization. It sets out the job title of the person to whom the job holder is responsible and the job titles of the people who are directly responsible to the job holder. An organization chart helps illustrate the context/peer group. It should not indicate or imply relative seniority or status.

Principal accountabilities

Principal accountabilities (also known as key result areas, main tasks, main duties, major activities, key responsibilities etc) are statements of the continuing end results or outputs required of the job. They answer the question: 'What are the main areas in which the job must get results to achieve its purpose?' For most jobs between four and eight accountabilities are sufficient to cover the major result areas. Less than four probably means something is missing; more than eight may mean that individual tasks are being listed.

The main characteristics of principal accountabilities are that:

▊ taken together, they represent all the major outputs expected of the job;
▊ they focus on *what* is required (results and outputs) not *how* the job is done (detailed tasks and duties);
▊ each one is distinct from the others and describes a specific area in which results are to be achieved;
▊ they suggest (but need not state explicitly) measures or tests which could determine the extent to which the accountabilities are being fulfilled.

An accountability statement is written in the style: 'Do something in order to achieve a stated result or standard.' Each statement is made in one sentence beginning with an active verb such as prepare, produce, plan, schedule, test, maintain, develop, monitor, ensure.

Context

The context section, also called 'nature and scope' is designed to add flavour to the bare list of principal accountabilities by describing aspects of the job and the role of the job within the context of the organization.

It is usually expressed in a structured narrative which follows the questions raised at the analysis stage, namely:

▌ where the job fits in with other key aspects of the work of the organization or unit;
▌ decision-making authority;
▌ how work is assigned, reviewed and approved;
▌ the particular knowledge, skills and experience required;
▌ the degree of flexibility needed to undertake different tasks or use different skills;
▌ the particular demands of the job in such areas as total quality management, leadership, teamworking, interpersonal skills, planning, crisis management etc;
▌ the major problems job holders are likely to meet in carrying out their work;
▌ physical conditions;
▌ the plant, equipment or tools used.

Dimensions

The dimensions (sometimes called the critical dimensions) of a job include any quantitative data which indicate its size and the range of responsibilities involved. For example, output, number of items processed, sales turnover, budgets, costs controlled, numbers supervised, number of cases dealt with over a period.

ROLE PROFILES

A role profile expands the basic information contained in a job description by including more information on the skill and behavioural requirements of a job. Role profiles provide the basis for performance management, recruitment and career planning as well as the information required to develop and manage a contribution-related pay structure and develop career families.

Role profiles are based on a comprehensive analysis of a role covering:

▌ the achievements and outputs required by the organization;
▌ the skills, knowledge and expertise required in the role;
▌ the competences which defines how the outputs should be achieved.

The achievement and outputs are covered by a conventional job description in terms of purpose and principal accountabilities. Additionally, in order to obtain a full understanding of a role, it is necessary not only to analyse and describe the technical knowledge, skills and experience needed to deliver the required level of output but also the behavioural competencies that characterize the role and strongly influence how it should be performed.

It is useful to distinguish between:

▌ *skills* – learnable skills, knowledge and expertise; and
▌ *competencies* – behavioural characteristics which can be demonstrated to differentiate high performers in a given role under such headings as planning and organizing, influencing, achievement drive and concern for order.

GENERIC ROLE PROFILES

Generic role profiles cover groups or families of jobs where the nature of the tasks carried out is basically the same although there may be significant differences in the level of work undertaken.

For example, in a branch organization, the role of all branch managers will fundamentally be the same but the size of the branches, in terms of income and number of customers, and therefore the size and complexity of the role, may vary considerably. Or, in the case of design engineers working in a research and development organization, the basic role may be the same but the level at which engineers operate will vary in terms of such factors as undertaking more difficult or complex assignments, carrying out more sophisticated experiments or being involved in a wider range of projects requiring different skills and abilities.

Increasing use is being made of generic role profiles for two reasons:

▌ *Process efficiency* – there is no point in carrying out a detailed separate role analysis for every generic role in categories such as those mentioned above. All that is necessary is to produce a generic role profile covering the common ground and then identify any variations in the level at which the work is carried out. This variation analysis can be applied generically to produce a ladder of jobs differentiated by the levels at which these distinct factors apply.
▌ *Role flexibility* – the increasing requirement to build job flexibility into role profiles has encouraged the growth of generic approaches. If, for example, a group of technicians is carrying out broadly the same kind of work but on different projects, defining the role generically gives greater flexibility as people move from project to project. This avoids having to go through the unnecessary task of rewriting the job description each time, only to arrive at much the same result.

▌ *Role matching* – generic role profiles are useful when 'matching' roles to the descriptions of grades in a pay structure to enable them to be allocated to grades without having to evaluate them separately (see Chapter 11).

For roles where there are no significant differences in the levels at which the work is carried out, a conventional job description format is suitable, with only minimal amendments required.

Where, however, there are differences in the level of work, it is necessary to define a series of these levels to form a ladder or family of generic roles. This approach has been used for many years in professional and technical areas, but it is now being extended to other functions as the requirement for flexibility means that jobs have to be more generically defined, while still recognizing the need to distinguish between levels of work.

It is, however, necessary to bear in mind the importance of ensuring that generic role profiles *are* only used when posts are broadly the same. In most organizations there will always be a proportion of jobs which are individual and which should not be streamlined into generic formats.

THE SIGNIFICANCE OF JOB AND ROLE ANALYSIS

Job and role analysis can be an exacting and time-consuming process. But the effort is worthwhile. In the absence of sound job, skill and competency analysis, the processes of job evaluation, conducting market rate surveys and performance management cannot be carried out effectively. In addition, a database of properly analysed and defined jobs and roles can be an essential part of a human resource expert system used for such key activities as recruitment, training, continuous development, career planning, organization development and job design.

REFERENCE

1. Pritchard, D and Murlis, H (1992) *Jobs, Roles and People: the New World of Job Evaluation*, Nicholas Brealey Publishing, London

11

Job Evaluation: Processes and Schemes

In this chapter:

▌ job evaluation is defined;
▌ the purpose, aims and basic features of job evaluation are explained;
▌ the different types of job evaluation schemes are described;
▌ the use of IT in job evaluation is explained;
▌ consideration is given to design and process criteria and the criteria for choice;
▌ the extent to which job evaluation is used is described;
▌ the arguments for and against job evaluation are summarized;
▌ conclusions are reached about the future of job evaluation.

JOB EVALUATION DEFINED

Job evaluation is a systematic process for defining the relative worth or size of jobs within an organization in order to establish internal relativities and provide the basis for designing an equitable grade and pay structure, grading jobs in the structure and managing job and pay relativities. Job evaluation can be analytical or non-analytical, as defined below. Jobs can also be valued by reference to their market rates – 'market pricing' – and this is described later in the chapter (page 122–23).

Analytical job evaluation

Analytical job evaluation is the process of making decisions about the value or size of jobs, which are based on an analysis of the extent to which various defined factors or elements are present in a job. These factors should be present in all the jobs to be evaluated, and the different levels at which they are present indicate relative job value. The Equal Pay (Amendment) Regulations 1983 refer to 'the demands on a worker under various headings, for instance, effort, skill, decision'. The most common analytical approach is a point-factor scheme. The most popular consultants' scheme (the Hay Guide Chart Method) is also analytical but it is a factor comparison scheme, which enables understanding of the shape and balance of jobs (see Appendix E) as well as their relative size.

Non-analytical job evaluation

Non-analytical job evaluation compares whole jobs to place them in a grade or a rank order – they are not analysed by reference to their elements or factors. The most common non-analytical approach is to 'match' roles as defined in role profiles either to standardized definitions of grades, bands or levels (this is often referred to as 'job classification') or to the role profiles of jobs that have already been graded. Another approach is to rank whole jobs in order of perceived value (job ranking). The statistical technique known as 'paired comparisons' may be used to assist in the latter process. Non-analytical schemes do not meet the requirements of equal value law.

PURPOSE, AIMS AND FEATURES OF JOB EVALUATION

Purpose

Job evaluation, especially analytical job evaluation, enables a framework to be designed that underpins judgements on appropriate grading and therefore pay decisions. It is used by many employers as a value-for-money tool to ensure that their total paybill is divided appropriately in relation to the worth of jobs in the organization. Job evaluation is particularly important as a means of achieving equal pay for work of equal value. In its *Good Practice Guide on Job Evaluation Schemes Free of Sex Bias,*[1] the Equal Opportunities Commission (EOC) emphasizes that: 'Non-discriminatory job evaluation should lead to a payment system which is transparent and within which work of equal value receives equal pay regardless of sex.' This statement only refers to equal pay 'regardless of sex' but job evaluation is just as concerned with achieving equal pay regardless of race or disability or indeed age.

Aims of job evaluation

Job evaluation aims to:

▐ establish the relative value or size of jobs, ie internal relativities based on fair, sound and consistent judgements;
▐ produce the information required to design and maintain equitable and defensible grade and pay structures;
▐ provide as objective as possible a basis for grading jobs within a grade structure, thus enabling consistent decisions to be made about job grading;
▐ enable sound market comparisons with jobs or roles of equivalent complexity and size;
▐ ensure that the organization meets ethical and legal equal-pay-for-work-of-equal-value obligations.

The last aim is important – analytical job evaluation plays a crucial part in achieving equal pay for work of equal value. It is an essential ingredient in equal pay reviews or audits, as described in Chapter 13.

Features of analytical job evaluation

To meet fundamental equal-pay-for-work-of-equal-value requirements, job evaluation schemes must be analytical. Non-analytical 'job matching' methods may be used to allocate or 'slot' jobs into grades but these have to be underpinned by an analytical scheme.

The main features of analytical job evaluation as explained below are that it is systematic, judgemental, concerned with the job not the person and deals with internal relativities.

Systematic

Job evaluation is systematic in that the relative value or 'size' of jobs is determined on the basis of factual evidence on the characteristics of the jobs, which has been analysed within a structured framework of criteria or factors.

Judgemental

Human judgement has to be exercised at some points in the job evaluation process. Although job evaluations are based on factual evidence, this has to be interpreted. The information provided about jobs through job analysis can sometimes fail to provide a clear indication of the levels at which demands are present in a job. The definitions in the factor plan may not precisely indicate the level of demand that should be recorded. Judgement is required in making decisions on the level and therefore, in a point-factor or factor comparison scheme, the score. The aim is to maximize objectivity but it is difficult to eliminate a degree of subjectivity. As the EOC states in its *Good Practice Guide on Job Evaluation Schemes Free of Sex Bias*: 'it is recognised that to a certain extent any assessment of a job's total demands relative to another will always be subjective'. A fundamental aim of any process of job evaluation is to provide frameworks or approaches that ensure, as far as possible, that consistent judgements are made based on objectively assessed information. To refer to an evaluation as 'judgemental' does not necessarily mean that it is inaccurate or unsound. Correct judgements are achieved when they are made within a defined framework and are based on clear evidence and sound reasoning. This is what a job evaluation scheme can do if the scheme is properly designed and properly applied.

Concerned with the job not the person

This is the conventional principle of job evaluation. It means that when evaluating a job the only concern is the content of that job in terms of the demands made on the job holder. The performance of the individual in the job must not be taken into account. But it should be noted that while *performance* is excluded, in today's more flexible organizations the tendency is for some people, especially knowledge workers, to have flexible roles. Individuals may have the scope to enlarge or enrich their roles and this needs to be taken into account when evaluating what they do. Roles cannot necessarily be separated from the people who carry them out. It is people who create value not jobs.

It is necessary to distinguish between the concept of a job and that of a role:

▌ A *job* consists of a group of finite tasks to be performed (pieces of work) and duties to be fulfilled in order to achieve an end result. Job descriptions basically list a number of tasks or accountabilities.

▌ A *role* describes the part played by people in carrying out their work by working competently and flexibly within the context of the organization's culture, structure and processes. Role profiles, notably those used in job and career families, often set out the behavioural requirements of the role as well as the outcomes expected of those who perform it.

Concerned with internal relativities

When used within an organization, job evaluation in the true sense as defined above (ie not market pricing) can only assess the relative size of jobs in that organization. It is not concerned with external relativities, that is, the relationship between the rates of pay of jobs in the organization and the rates of pay of comparable jobs elsewhere (market rates).

TYPES OF JOB EVALUATION

The main types of job evaluation are described in this chapter as follows:

▍ *analytical schemes:* point-factor rating and factor comparison;
▍ *non-analytical schemes:* job classification, job ranking and paired comparison ranking;
▍ *non-analytical approaches* (methods of grading or valuing jobs that are not schemes in the sense of those listed above, although they may be used in conjunction with such schemes): job or role matching and market pricing.

Point-factor rating

Point-factor rating is an analytical method of job evaluation that is based on breaking down jobs into factors or key elements. It is assumed that each of the factors will contribute to job size and is an aspect of all the jobs to be evaluated but to different degrees. Using numerical scales, points are allocated to a job under each factor heading according to the extent to which it is present in the job. The separate factor scores are then added together to give a total score that represents job size. The methodology used in point-factor schemes is described below.

1 Factor selection

A number of job factors are selected or defined (usually at least 4 or 5 and often 11 or more) according to the types of jobs to be covered, the needs of the organization and what it wants to achieve from job evaluation. These are characteristics of jobs that express the demands made on job holders in such areas as decision making, problem solving, the exercise of interpersonal skills, responsibility for people and other financial or non-financial resources, emotional demands and physical demands, the inputs required from job holders in the form of knowledge, skills and competences and, sometimes, the outputs expected in the form of impact on results. Job evaluation factors break down the key components of jobs, and the set of factors as a whole represent each of the most important elements of those jobs. The different levels at which individual factors apply to jobs provide information that indicates, when considered collectively, relative job value or size.

Care has to be taken when selecting factors to ensure that they do not discriminate in favour of either sex or any racial group. It is also necessary to avoid double counting (undue repetition of job characteristics in different factors) since this would distort the results.

2 Factor plan design

The factor plan consists of the factors themselves, each of which is divided into a number of levels. The number of levels depends on the range of demands or degrees of responsibility in a particular factor that might be present in the jobs to be covered by the scheme. The number could be as few as three or as many as eight. Typically, the number tends to be between five and seven.

The levels in each factor are defined to provide guidance on deciding the degree to which they apply in a job to be evaluated. The decision on levels is made by reference to an analysis of the job in terms of the factors. It is important to ensure that each level of demand in a factor is reflected by the number of factor levels and to produce clear level descriptions that will enable consistent judgements to be made about the level of demand to be attached to jobs when they are evaluated.

A maximum points score is allocated to each factor. The scores may vary between different factors in accordance with beliefs about their relative significance. This is termed 'explicit weighting'. If the number of levels varies between factors this means that they are implicitly weighted.

The total score for a factor is divided between the levels to produce the factor scale. Progression may be arithmetic or linear, eg 50, 100, 150, 200, etc, or geometric, eg 50, 100, 175, 275, etc. In the latter case, more scope is given to recognize the more senior jobs with higher scores. Progression may also be defined in terms of percentage steps, as in Hay Guide Charts where the steps are 15 per cent.

3 Job or role analysis

As a necessary first step in job evaluation, jobs or roles are analysed systematically in terms of each of the factors. The aim is to provide factual and explicit evidence that in a conventional non-computerized job evaluation scheme will guide evaluators in selecting the level at which the factor exists in a job. The job or role analysis may be based on a paper questionnaire completed by the job holder and, usually, checked and signed off by the job holder's line manager. Alternatively, information about a job may be input direct to a PC without the need to prepare a separate paper questionnaire (see Chapter 10 on job and role analysis).

4 Evaluating jobs

In a non-computerized scheme, jobs are usually evaluated by a panel, which may, indeed should, include staff or union representatives as well as line managers and one or more members of the HR department. The panel studies the job analysis and agrees on the level and therefore the score that should be allocated for each factor and, ultimately, the total score. It is usual to start with a representative sample of 'benchmark' jobs. Job evaluation can also be conducted with the assistance of computers, as described later in this chapter (pages 123–24).

5 Grading jobs

When a job evaluation exercise is being conducted to inform the design or revision of a graded pay structure, the outcome will be a rank order of jobs according to their total scores. This rank order is then divided into grades, each of which is defined in terms of a bracket of job evaluation points. Pay ranges are then attached to each grade, which will take account of external relativities (market rates) and the need for pay progression. There is no direct relationship between job evaluation points and rates of pay – 'points don't mean pounds'. The points in a job evaluation scheme have no value in themselves. They are simply ordinal numbers that define the position of an entity in a series. All jobs within a grade will be paid within the same range of pay irrespective of their individual job evaluation scores (they are assumed to be of equal value) and pay ranges attached to grades may vary even when the job evaluation points ranges are the same.

The grading process may initially be based on the benchmark jobs. Other distinct jobs may then be evaluated and graded. This may not be necessary where there are any generic roles (ie those with basically the same range and level of responsibilities) and it is certain that the characteristics of a particular role or group of roles are virtually identical to these generic roles. In these circumstances the grading may be accomplished by matching the role to be graded with an appropriate generic role. Where there are a large number of non-benchmark individual jobs to be graded, organizations often save time by using the 'matching' process, as described below, rather than evaluating each one separately.

Once a graded pay structure has been designed, the point-factor or factor comparison job evaluation scheme can be used to determine where new or changed roles should be fitted into the structure. It can be invoked when individuals or managers believe that a job should be upgraded. However, as noted at the end of this chapter, some organizations are not using their job evaluation scheme as a matter of course and instead 'match' jobs to those that have already been graded where such comparisons can reasonably be made.

6 Reviews

The scheme should provide for a regular formal review of evaluations to ensure that they remain valid and consistent. If such an audit reveals outdated evaluations, or clear anomalies, these should be dealt with to ensure the continued relevance of the scheme and protect its credibility. It is particularly important to ensure that the scheme is not being manipulated to produce desired rather than appropriate results.

7 Appeals

Employees should be allowed to appeal against an evaluation they believe to be flawed, using an agreed and properly communicated appeals procedure.

Factor comparison

The original factor comparison method compared jobs factor by factor using a scale of money values to provide a direct indication of the rate for the job. It was developed in the United States but is not used in the UK. The two forms of factor comparison now in use, although not to any large extent, with the significant exception of the Hay Guide Chart Profile Method, are graduated factor comparison and analytical factor comparison.

Graduated factor comparison

Graduated factor comparison involves comparing jobs factor by factor with a graduated scale. The scale may have only three value levels – for example lower, equal, higher – and no factor scores are used.

It is a method often used by the independent experts engaged by Employment Tribunals to advise on an equal pay claim. Their job is simply to compare one job with one or two others, not to review internal relativities over the whole spectrum of jobs in order to produce a rank order. Independent experts may score their judgements of comparative levels, in which case graduated factor comparison resembles the point-factor method except that the number of levels and range of scores are limited, and the factors may not be weighted.

Graduated factor comparison can be used within organizations if there is a problem of comparable worth and no other analytical scheme is available. It can also be used in a benchmarking exercise to assess relativities across different categories of employees in the absence of a common analytical job evaluation scheme as long as the factors used are common to all the job categories under consideration.

Analytical factor comparison

Analytical factor comparison is also based on the analysis of a number of defined factors. Role analysis takes place to assess the extent to which each of these factors or characteristics is present in a role and this analysis is recorded in the form of a role profile. Comparisons can then be made factor by factor between roles but no scale is used. Analytical factor comparison can also be used to grade roles by comparing the role profiles with grade definitions expressed under the same factor headings. This is a form of job classification, as described later in this chapter, but with an analytical element.

In theory, analytical factor comparison could be used to produce a rank order by the process of paired comparisons (as described later). In practice, however, this is an elaborate and time-consuming procedure and is seldom used.

The Hay Guide Chart Profile Method

The Hay Guide Chart Profile Method is a factor comparison scheme. It uses three broad factors (Know-how, Problem Solving and Accountability), each of which is further divided into sub-factors, although these cannot be scored individually. Broad definitions of each level have been produced for each sub-factor to guide evaluators and ensure consistency of application. In principle, tailored Guide Charts should be produced for each organization using the method, to ensure the language is fit for the purpose although in practice there has been very substantial standardization for many years, especially in private sector companies. The method also has a unique feature – the Profile – which describes the balance in the total score between the three factors. This provides a further check on the internal consistency of each evaluation. (It has been used extensively as a tool in organizational analysis and is increasingly valued by some employers as one of the foundations of job/people matching and talent management.)

Job classification

Job classification is the process of slotting jobs into grades by comparing the whole job with a scale in the form of a hierarchy of grade definitions, which may be broken down by factor but without a numerical value attached. It is based on an initial definition of the number and characteristics of the grades into which jobs will be placed. The grade definitions may therefore refer to such job characteristics as skill, decision making and responsibility. Job descriptions may be used that include information on the presence of those characteristics but the characteristics are not assessed separately when comparing the description with the grade definition.

Job ranking

Whole job ranking is the most primitive form of job evaluation. The process involves comparing whole jobs with one another and arranging them in order of their perceived size or value to the organization. In a sense, all evaluation schemes are ranking exercises because they place jobs in a hierarchy. The difference between simple ranking and analytical methods such as point-factor rating is that job ranking does not attempt to quantify judgements. Instead, whole jobs are compared – they are not broken down into factors or elements although, explicitly or implicitly, the comparison may be based on some generalized concept such as the level of responsibility.

Paired comparison ranking

Paired comparison ranking is a statistical technique that is used to provide a more sophisticated method of whole job ranking. It is based on the assumption that it is always easier to compare one job with another than to consider a number of jobs and attempt to build up a rank order by multiple comparisons.

The technique requires the comparison of each job as a whole separately with every other job. If a job is considered to be of a higher value than the one with which it is being compared it receives two points; if it is thought to be equally important, it receives one point; if it is regarded as less important, no points are awarded. The scores are added for each job and a rank order is obtained.

A simplified version of a paired comparison ranking form is shown in Table 11.1.

Table 11.1 A paired comparison

Job reference	a	b	c	d	e	f	Total score	Ranking
A	–	0	1	0	1	0	2	5=
B	2	–	2	2	2	2	8	2
C	1	0	–	1	1	0	3	4
D	2	0	1	–	2	)	5	3
E	1	0	1	0	–	0	2	5=
F	2	2	2	2	2	–	10	1

The advantage of paired comparison ranking over normal ranking is that it is easier to compare one job with another rather than having to make multi-comparisons. But it cannot overcome the fundamental objections to any form of whole job ranking – that no defined standards for judging relative worth are provided and it is not an acceptable method of assessing equal value. There is also a limit to the number of jobs that can be compared using this method – to evaluate 50 jobs requires 1,225 comparisons.

Paired comparisons can also be used analytically to compare jobs on a factor-by-factor basis.

Job or role matching

Job or role matching, sometimes known as internal benchmarking, is what people often do intuitively when they are deciding on the value of jobs, although it has never been dignified in the job evaluation texts as a formal method of job evaluation. It simply means comparing the job under review with any internal job that is believed to be properly graded and paid and placing the job under consideration into the same grade as that job. The comparison is often made on a whole job basis without analysing the jobs factor by factor. Job matching is often based on comparisons with 'generic role profiles', ie profiles that cover groups of roles that are essentially similar.

Matching is likely to be more accurate and acceptable if it is founded on the comparison of roles against a defined set of factors, ie analytical factor comparison. This may mean matching a role profile prepared under the factor headings with a generic role profile using the same headings.

Job or role matching is perhaps the most common method of informal or semi-formal job evaluation. It can be used after an initial analytical job evaluation exercise as a means of allocating jobs into an established grade structure without going to the trouble of carrying out a separate analytical evaluation. It is frequently adopted as the normal method of grading jobs on a continuing basis. In these circumstances, the analytical job evaluation scheme has a supporting role but will be used to deal with special cases, for example new or significantly changed jobs, and to review job-matching decisions to ensure that they are valid and do not create equal value problems.

Market pricing

Market pricing is the process of assessing rates of pay by reference to the market rates for comparable jobs and is essentially external benchmarking. Strictly speaking, market pricing is not a process of job evaluation in the sense that those described above are – these only deal with internal relativities and are not directly concerned with market values although, in conjunction with a formal job evaluation scheme, establishing market rates is a necessary part of a programme for developing a pay structure.

However, the term 'market pricing' in its extreme form is used to denote a process of directly pricing jobs on the basis of external relativities with no regard to internal relativities. This approach was widely publicized in the United States in the mid-1990s and sat alongside attempts at broadbanding as originally conceived, and a disillusion with what was regarded as bureaucratic job evaluation. It is an approach that often has appeal at board level because of the focus on competitiveness in relation to the market place for talent.

The acceptability of market pricing is heavily dependent on the quality and detail of market matching as well as the availability of robust market data. It can therefore vary from analysis of data by job titles to detailed matched analysis collected through bespoke surveys focused on real market equivalence (see Chapter 14). Market pricing can produce an indication of internal relativities even if these are market driven. But it can lead to pay discrimination against women where the market has traditionally been discriminatory. It does not satisfy UK equal pay legislation.

Market pricing can be done formally by the analysis of published pay surveys, participating in 'pay clubs', conducting special surveys, obtaining the advice of recruitment consultants and agencies and, more doubtfully, studying advertisements. In its crudest form, market pricing simply means fixing the rate for a job at the level necessary to recruit or retain someone.

COMPUTER-ASSISTED JOB EVALUATION

There are a number of ways in which IT can be used to support job evaluation and simplify scheme administration. Most e-HR systems such as Peoplesoft, SAP and Rebus now provide well-developed applications that do this either for proprietary schemes such as Hay, or the bespoke schemes developed by organizations. They can make the process much more user-friendly and help ensure that the outputs from job evaluation are properly integrated with other HR processes such as recruitment, performance management, career management and succession planning.

Computer-assisted schemes can be used to help directly with the job evaluation process. The two types of IT-based systems are:

1. Schemes in which the job analysis data are either entered direct into the computer or transferred to it from a paper questionnaire. The computer software applies predetermined rules based on an algorithm that reflects the organization's evaluation standards, to convert the data into scores for each factor and produce a total score. The algorithm replicates panel judgements on both job factor levels and overall job score. It is therefore of critical importance to ensure that the algorithm constructed in the design phase is tested to ensure that it makes sense for the organization and the jobs within it. Otherwise it is all too easy to produce confusing or at worst discriminatory results. Link Consultants supply the software for such a scheme (including Hay), as described in Appendix E.

2. Interactive computer-assisted schemes using software such as that supplied by Pilat UK (see Appendix E) in which the job holder and his or her manager sit in front of a PC and are presented with a series

of logically interrelated questions, the answers to which lead to a score for each of the built-in factors in turn and a total score.

Advocates of computer-assisted job evaluation systems claim that they:

▌ provide for greater consistency – the same input information will always give the same output result because the judgemental framework on which the scheme is based (the algorithm) can be applied consistently to the input data (NB this does not absolve organizations from the need to provide high-quality, consistent and agreed input, or to ensure that the algorithms are based on rigorously tested and agreed standards);
▌ offer extensive database capabilities for sorting, analysing and reporting on the input information and system outputs;
▌ speed up the job evaluation process once the initial design is complete.

DESIGN AND PROCESS CRITERIA

It is necessary to distinguish between the design of a scheme and the process of operating it. Equal pay considerations have to be taken into account in both design and process.

Design principles

For both proprietary and tailor-made analytical schemes, the design principles are that:

▌ the scheme should be based on a thorough analysis of the jobs to be covered and the types of demands made on those jobs to determine what factors are appropriate;
▌ the scheme should facilitate impartial judgements of relative job size;
▌ the factors used in the scheme should cover the whole range of jobs to be evaluated at all levels without favouring any particular type of job or occupation and without discriminating on the grounds of gender, race, disability or for any other reason – the scheme should fairly measure features of female-dominated jobs as well as male-dominated jobs;
▌ through the use of common factors and methods of analysis and evaluation, the scheme should enable benchmarking to take place of the relativities between jobs in different functions or job families;
▌ the factors should be clearly defined and differentiated – there should be no double counting;
▌ the levels should be defined and graduated carefully;

▌ gender bias must be avoided in the choice of factors, the wording of factor and level definitions and the factor weightings – statistical checks should be carried out to identify any bias (the EOC guidelines as summarized in Chapter 13 should also be taken into account).

Process principles

The process principles are that:

▌ the scheme should be transparent and everyone concerned should know how it works – the basis upon which the evaluations are produced;

▌ appropriate proportions of women, those from ethnic minorities and people with disabilities should be involved in the process of job evaluation;

▌ the quality of role analysis should be monitored to ensure that analyses produce accurate and relevant information, which will inform the job evaluation process and will not be biased;

▌ consistency checks should be built into operating procedures;

▌ the outcomes of evaluations should be examined to ensure that gender or any other form of bias has not occurred;

▌ particular care is necessary to ensure that the outcomes of job evaluation do not simply replicate the existing hierarchy – it is to be expected that a job evaluation exercise will challenge present relativities;

▌ all those involved in role analysis and job evaluation should be thoroughly trained in the operation of the scheme and in how to avoid bias;

▌ special care should be taken in developing a grade structure following a job evaluation exercise to ensure that grade boundaries are placed appropriately and that the allocation of jobs to grades is not in itself discriminatory;

▌ there should be scope for the review of evaluations and for appeals against gradings;

▌ the scheme should be reviewed regularly to ensure that it is being operated properly and that it is still fit for its purpose.

CRITERIA FOR CHOICE

The main criteria for selecting a scheme that emerge from these principles are that it should be:

▌ *Analytical* – it should be based on the analysis and evaluation of the degree to which various defined elements or factors are present in a job.

▌ *Thorough in analysis and capable of impartial application* – the scheme should have been carefully constructed to ensure that its analytical framework is sound and appropriate in terms of all the jobs it has to cater for. It should also have been tested and trialled to check that it can be applied impartially to those jobs.

▌ *Appropriate* – it should cater for the particular demands made on all the jobs to be covered by the scheme.

▌ *Comprehensive* – the scheme should be applicable to all the jobs in the organization covering all categories of staff, and the factors should be common to all those jobs. There should therefore be a single scheme that can be used to assess relativities across different occupations or job families and to enable benchmarking to take place as required.

▌ *Transparent* – the processes used in the scheme from the initial role analysis through to the grading decision should be clear to all concerned. If computers are used, information should not be perceived as being processed in a 'black box'.

▌ *Non-discriminatory* – the scheme must meet equal-pay-for-work-of-equal-value requirements.

A summary of the various approaches to job evaluation and their advantages and disadvantages is given in Table 11.2.

THE INCIDENCE OF JOB EVALUATION

Despite considerable criticism in the 1990s, job evaluation has not diminished in use in the UK or in many other countries. In the UK, an analysis of the responses of 517 organizations to a survey of reward management policy and practice carried out by the Chartered Institute of Personnel and Development in 2004[2] established that the proportion of organizations using job evaluation was predicted to grow from 48 per cent in 2003 to 53 per cent in 2004.

A survey of job evaluation practice in the UK conducted by E-Reward Research in late 2002[3] found that 44 per cent of the 236 organizations contributing to the research had a formal job evaluation scheme, and 45 per cent of those who did not have such a scheme intended to introduce one. Analytical schemes were used by 89 per cent of the respondents. Of those, 70 per cent used point-factor rating. The most popular non-analytical approach was job classification. Schemes developed in-house ('home-grown' schemes) were used by 37 per cent of the respondents.

A 'proprietary brand', ie one provided by consultants, was used by 37 per cent of respondents, and 26 per cent used a hybrid or tailored version of a proprietary brand. The Hay Guide Chart Profile Method dominated the market (83 per cent of the proprietary brand schemes). Organizations opting for a proprietary brand did so because of its credibility and, especially with Hay, its link to a market rate database.

Organizations opting for a home-grown approach did so because they believed this would ensure that it could be shaped to meet the strategic needs of the organization and fit its technology, structure, work processes and business objectives. A minority of respondents mentioned the scope for aligning the scheme with their competency framework.

THE CASE FOR AND AGAINST JOB EVALUATION

The case for

The case for properly devised and applied job evaluation, especially analytical job evaluation, is that:

▌ it can make the criteria against which jobs are valued explicit and provide a basis for structuring the judgement process;
▌ an equitable and defensible pay structure cannot be achieved unless a structured and systematic process is used to assess job values and relativities;
▌ a logical framework is required within which consistent decisions can be made on job grades and rates of pay;
▌ analytical schemes provide the best basis for achieving equal pay for work of equal value and are the only acceptable defence in an equal pay case;
▌ a formal process of job evaluation is more likely to be accepted as fair and equitable than informal or ad hoc approaches – and the degree of acceptability will be considerably enhanced if the whole process is transparent.

The case against

The case against job evaluation has been presented vociferously. Critics emphasize that it can be bureaucratic, inflexible, time-consuming and inappropriate in today's organizations. Schemes can decay over time through use or misuse. People learn how to manipulate them to achieve a higher grade and this leads to the phenomenon known as 'grade drift' – upgradings that are not justified by a sufficiently significant increase in responsibility. Job evaluators can fall into the trap of making a priori judgements. They may judge the validity of a job evaluation exercise according to the extent to which it corresponds with their preconceptions about relative worth. The so-called 'felt-fair' test is used to assess the acceptability of job evaluations, but a rank order is felt to be fair if it reproduces their notion of what it ought to be.

These criticisms focus on the way in which job evaluation is operated rather than the concept of job evaluation itself. Like any other management techniques, job evaluation schemes can be misconceived and

Table 11.2 Comparison of approaches to job evaluation

Scheme	Characteristics	Advantages	Disadvantages
Point-factor rating	An analytical scheme in which separate factors are scored and added together to produce a total score for the job, which can be used for comparison and grading.	As long as it is based on proper job analysis, point-factor schemes provide evaluators with defined yardsticks, which help to increase the objectivity and consistency of over-simplified judgement made in non-analytical job evaluation. They provide a defence against equal value claims as along as they are not in themselves discriminatory.	Can be complex and give a spurious impression of scientific accuracy – judgement is still needed in scoring jobs. Not easy to amend the scheme as circumstances, priorities or values change.
Factor comparison	Compares jobs factor by factor, normally using a scale (or scales) intended to represent the lowest level of differences discernible to trained evaluators. Total scores for each job are determined by adding together those for each factor.	It is analytical in the sense that it compares roles to grade definitions on a factor-by-factor basis and avoids what some people believe to be the artificial precision of point-factor rating. It can also be used in benchmarking exercises – comparing roles in different job categories or families where there is no common system of analytical evaluation. In practice, a strong advantage is believed to be in the ability of evaluators to interpret or reinterpret what are generally broad factor level definitions in the light of business circumstances. These schemes should not require fundamental changes at any stage, provided they are properly maintained on a continuous basis.	Evaluators are not provided with defined yardsticks in the shape of level definitions to aid the judgement process. The natural tendency may still be to make whole job comparisons by reference to assumptions about where a job should be graded, which can too easily override the analytical data Record keeping about the rationale for individual evaluations needs to be meticulous if the integrity of the scheme is to be maintained over time.
Job classification	Non-analytical – grades are defined in a structure in terms of the level of responsibilities	Simple to operate; standards of judgement are provided in when making comparisons in the shape of the grade definitions.	Can be difficul: to fit complex jobs into a grade without using over-elaborate

Method	Description	Advantages	Disadvantages
	involved in a hierarchy. Jobs are allocated to grades by matching the job description with the grade description (job slotting).		grade definitions; the definitions tend to be so generalized that they are not much help in evaluating cases of making comparisons between individual jobs; does not provide a defence in an equal value case.
Ranking	Non-analytical – whole job comparisions are made to place them in rank order.	Easy to apply and understand.	No defined standards of judgement; differences between jobs not measured; does not provide a defence in an equal value case.
Job or role matching	Jobs or roles are compared with benchmark jobs that have been allocated into grades on the basis of ranking or job classification and placed in whatever grade provides the closest match of jobs. The job descriptions may be analytical in the sense that they cover a number of standard and defined elements	Simple to operate; facilitates direct comparisons, especially when the jobs have been analysed in terms of a set of common criteria.	Relies on a considerable amount of judgement and may simply perpetuate existing relativities; dependent on accurate job/role analysis; may not provide a defence in an equal value case.
Market pricing	Rates of pay are aligned to market rates – internal relativities are therefore determined by relativities in the market place. Not strictly a job evaluation scheme.	In line with the belief that 'a job is worth what the market says it is worth'. Ensures that pay is competitive.	Relies on accurate market rate information, which is not always available; relativities in the market may not properly reflect internal relativities; pay discrimination may be perpetuated.

misused. And the grade and pay structures developed through job evaluation seldom last for more than a few years and need to be replaced or adjusted to remedy decay or reflect new ways of working.

However, the hostility to job evaluation prevalent in the 1980s has been significantly reduced recently by the general acceptance of the importance of achieving equity through a systematic approach to valuing jobs coupled with the increased focus on equal pay and the recognition that analytical job evaluation is an essential element in achieving equality. It is these beliefs that have encouraged the recent development of new job evaluation schemes in the UK by organizations and sectors such as the National Health Service, local government, higher education and further education.

CONCLUSIONS

It could be claimed that, every time a decision is made on what a job should be paid, a form of job evaluation is required. Job evaluation is therefore unavoidable but it should not be an intuitive, subjective and potentially biased process. The issue is how best to carry it out analytically, fairly, systematically, consistently, transparently and, so far as possible, objectively, without being bureaucratic, inflexible or resource intensive. There are five ways of dealing with this issue:

1. Use a tested and relevant analytical job evaluation scheme to inform and support the processes of designing grade structures, grading jobs, managing relativities and ensuring that work of equal value is paid equally. The approach to designing a point-factor scheme is described in Chapter 12.
2. Ensure that job evaluation is introduced and managed properly along the lines suggested in Chapter 12.
3. Consider using IT to support the use and integration of job evaluation with other HR practices and to speed up processing and decision making while at the same time generating more consistent evaluations and reducing bureaucracy.
4. Recognize that thorough training and continuing guidance for evaluators is essential, as is communication about the scheme, its operation and objectives to all concerned.
5. Review the operation of the scheme regularly to ensure that it is not decaying and continues to be appropriate and trusted.

THE FUTURE OF JOB EVALUATION

The CIPD and E-Reward surveys referred to above indicated that interest in job evaluation is increasing generally. Many organizations are continuing to develop and maintain their job evaluation schemes although they may be used in a supporting rather than a driving role. This means relying on analytical job evaluation for help in designing grade structures, dealing with new or significantly changed jobs and informing equal pay reviews. On a day-to-day basis, job evaluation may not be invoked to grade jobs unless they are special cases. Grading decisions may be made by 'matching' role profiles with level definitions. But job evaluation can always be brought to the fore when needed, especially to review or investigate equal pay matters.

These approaches are helping to ensure that job evaluation is here to stay. But it still requires a lot of effort to make it work well.

REFERENCES

1. Equal Opportunities Commission (2003) *Good Practice Guide on Job Evaluation Schemes Free of Sex Bias*, EOC, Manchester
2. Chartered Institute of Personnel and Development (2004) *Survey of Reward Management Policy and Practice*, CIPD, London
3. E-Reward Research (2003) *A Survey of Job Evaluation Practice in the UK*, E-Reward, London

12

Job Evaluation: Scheme Design and Operation

In this chapter the initial focus is on the design of a points-factor analytical scheme – by far the most appropriate and popular method of job evaluation where organizations opt for a tailor-made rather than a proprietary approach such as the Hay Guide Chart profile method. The chapter then deals with the implementation of a new scheme and how job evaluation schemes should be maintained. The latter sections apply to all kinds of job evaluation schemes.

DESIGNING AN ANALYTICAL POINTS-FACTOR SCHEME

The design of an analytical job evaluation scheme is best carried out by a job evaluation panel or working group, which should include employee and line representatives as well as HR specialists. Such panels may be chaired by someone relatively senior/experienced from HR (eg the head of reward), but independent chairs such as an ACAS official, an academic or a management consultant are often used to ensure that a detached process of facilitation takes place. How panels should function is examined in the next section.

The eight steps required to design a points-factor scheme are:

1. Identify and define factors.
2. Define factor levels to produce the draft basic factor plan.

3. Analyse jobs.
4. Carry out an initial test of the draft factor plan.
5. Develop the scoring model, ie the scores for each factor and the method of progressing scores through the levels.
6. Decide on the extent to which factor scores should be 'weighted' (ie treated as being of greater or lesser importance) to produce the full factor plan.
7. Carry out a full test of the final factor plan.
8. Computerize if required.

1 Identify and define factors

Job evaluation factors are the characteristics or key elements of jobs that are used to analyse and evaluate jobs in an analytical job evaluation scheme. The factors must be capable of identifying relevant and important differences between jobs that will support the creation of a rank order of jobs to be covered by the scheme. They should apply equally well to different types of work, including specialists and generalists, lower-level and higher-level jobs, and not be biased in favour of one gender or group. Although many of the job evaluation factors used across organizations capture similar job elements (this is an area where there are some enduring truths), the task of identifying and agreeing factors can be challenging.

The choice of factors should ensure that:

▌ the whole range of jobs to be evaluated at all levels is covered without favouring any particular job or occupation;
▌ discrimination on the grounds of gender, race, disability or for any other reason should not take place – the scheme should fairly measure features of female-dominated jobs as well as male-dominated jobs;
▌ double counting is avoided, ie each factor must be independent of every other factor – the more factors (or sub-factors) in the plan, the higher the probability that double counting will take place;
▌ elision or compression of more than one significant job feature under a single factor heading should be avoided – if important factors were compressed with others it means that they would probably be undervalued;
▌ acceptable criteria for identifying differences in the size of jobs are established, provided they are understandable and written in a way that is meaningful to those who will use the scheme;
▌ they are acceptable to those who will be covered by the scheme.

The E-Reward (2003) survey[1] established that the most frequently used factors by the respondents with analytical schemes were:

1. knowledge and skills;
2. communications and contacts;
3. judgement and decision making;
4. impact;
5. people management;
6. freedom to act;
7. working environment;
8. responsibility for financial resources.

2 Define factor levels to produce the basic factor plan

The basic factor plan defines the levels within each factor and provides the framework for evaluation. A decision has to be made on the number of levels (often five, six or seven), which has to reflect the range of responsibilities and demands in the jobs covered by the scheme. The starting-points can be an analysis of what would characterize the highest or lowest level for each factor and how these should be described. For example, the highest level in a judgement and decision-making factor could be defied as: 'Deals with widely differing problems calling for extreme clarity of thought in assessing conflicting information and balancing the risks associated with possible solutions. Additionally, one of the main requirements of the role may be to develop fundamentally new strategies and approaches.' The lowest level could be defined as: 'The work is well defined and relatively few new situations are encountered. The causes of problems are readily identifiable and can be dealt with easily.' It might then be decided that there should be three levels between the highest and lowest level on the basis that this truly reflects the graduation in responsibilities or demands. The outcome would then be the definition of the factor and each of the five levels illustrated in Table 12.1. This process is repeated for each factor.

Level definitions should be carefully defined and graduated level by level to provide guidance to evaluators when they decide on the appropriate level of demand by reference to the job or role analysis – the aim should be to inform them as clearly as possible where the 'best fit' exists between the description of the type of demand in the analysis and a factor level.

Producing level definitions that are properly graduated and do not overlap with one another can be an exercise in semantics. It is certainly an art. The temptation is to differentiate by the use of comparative adjectives such as 'smaller' or 'larger', but these are meaningless in themselves. If they are used, they have to be qualified with a definition of what 'small' means. The problem is that words are often inadequate devices for conveying shades of meaning. The temptation is to produce longer and longer level definitions but this is self-defeating because it will only confuse evaluators and initiate endless arguments about the meaning of the words and which part of the definition is the most relevant.

Table 12.1 Example of factor level definitions

Judgement and decision making: The requirement to exercise judgement in making decisions and solving problems, including the degree to which the work involves choice of action or creativity.

1   The work is defined and relatively few new situations are encountered. The causes of problems are readily identifiable and can be dealt with easily.

2   Evaluation of information is required to deal with occasional new problems and situations and to decide on a course of action from known alternatives. Occasionally required to participate in the modification of existing procedures and practices.

3   Exercises discriminating judgement in dealing with relatively new or unusual problems where a wide range of information has to be considered and the courses of action are not obvious. May fairly often be involved in devising new solutions.

4   Frequently exercises independent judgement when faced with unusual problems and situations where no policy guidelines or precedents are available. May also frequently be responsible for devising new strategies and approaches that require the use of imagination and ingenuity.

5   Deals with widely differing problems calling for extreme clarity of thought in assessing conflicting information and balancing the risks associated with possible solutions. Additionally, one of the main requirements of the role may be to develop fundamentally new strategies and approaches.

Evaluators have to exercise judgement in deciding on levels. The choice is often made on the 'best fit' principle, ie an assessment of which level definition on balance fits best with the relevant characteristic of the job as indicated by the job analysis, which will have been carried out in terms of the factors in the scheme. As evaluators become more experienced they are better placed to make judgements on the basis of how the definitions fit different jobs they have already dealt with. They will be able to refer to examples in particular jobs that have already been evaluated on the meaning of a level definition. These form precedents. In job evaluation speak, they can be turned into conventions that are used to illuminate the level definitions.

In spite of the existence of carefully drafted level definitions and the availability of conventions, judgement has often to be exercised when deciding on levels. The members of a job evaluation panel have to interpret the data in the job analysis and compare these with their interpretations of the level definitions and decide where the best fit occurs. It is hardly surprising, therefore, that panels often fail to be unanimous and that the chair or facilitator has to take pains to achieve the desirable end result, that is, consensus. But a carefully thought-out factor plan, good job analyses and an experienced panel will mean that few individual judgements will vary over a range of more than two levels. The job of the facilitator in obtaining consensus is therefore not too hard.

Ensuring that level definitions are as clear and as helpful as possible is one of the main reasons for the essential process of pilot-testing a new scheme. Such tests often highlight problems in interpreting level definitions, which can then be rectified.

Guidelines for factor level definitions

The following guidelines should be used in defining levels:

1. Each level should be defined as clearly as possible as a guide to evaluators making 'best-fit' decisions.
2. The levels should cover the whole range of demands in this factor that are likely to arise in the jobs with which the evaluation scheme is concerned.
3. The link between the content of level definitions should be related specifically to the definition of the factor concerned and should not overlap with other factors.
4. There should be uniform progression in the definitions level by level from the lowest to the highest level – there should be no gaps or undefined intermediate levels that might lead to evaluators finding it difficult to be confident about the allocation of a level of demand.
5. The level definitions should not rely upon a succession of undefined comparatives, eg 'small', 'medium', 'large' – so far as possible any dimensions should be defined.
6. Each level definition should stand on its own. Level definitions should not be defined by reference to a lower or higher level, ie it is insufficient to define a level in words to the effect that it is a higher (or lower) version of an adjacent level.

3 Analyse jobs

Jobs are analysed in terms of the factors. This generally means using a questionnaire, which will ask for information about the overall purpose of the job, the main activities carried out and the demands made by the job with regard to each factor. This is often a paper exercise but it can be carried out by direct input to a computer in response to questions that have been validated for use within the context for which they have been designed.

4 Carry out an initial test of the draft factor plan

The factors should be tested on a representative sample of jobs. The aim of this initial test is to check on the extent to which the factors are appropriate, cover all aspects of the jobs to be evaluated, are non-discriminatory, avoid double counting and are not compressed unduly. A check is also made on level definitions to ensure that they are worded clearly, graduated properly and cover the whole range of demands applicable to the jobs to be evaluated so that they enable consistent evaluations to be made. A more comprehensive test should be carried out later at step 7 when the full factor plan with scoring systems and weightings has been devised.

5 Decide on scoring model

A decision needs to be made on how to set the scoring progression within each factor. There are two methods. The 'arithmetic' or linear approach assumes that there are consistent step differences between factor levels, eg a four-level factor might be scored 1,2,3,4. Alternatively, geometric scoring assumes that there are progressively larger score differences at each successive level in the hierarchy. For example, the difference between the lowest two levels for an impact factor might be between impact on own work area at the lowest factor to impact on individual customers at the next factor, whereas between the highest levels the progression may be from impact on a department to impact on the whole organization. Geometric progression assumes that this distance needs to be reflected in the scoring progression. Thus the levels may be scored 1,2,4,8 rather than 1,2,3,4. This appears to increase the scoring differentiation between higher-level jobs, although this is illusory since only the numbers in the geometric progression can actually be used. A 15 per cent difference between 100 and 115 points may look smaller than the gap between 1,000 and 1,150 points, but they are of course the same in magnitude. So in the Hay Guide Chart and Profile Method, for example, the minimum 'know-how' step difference goes from 38 to 43 points but this 15 per cent gap is between 528 and 608 points for a seasoned professional.

The rank order produced by either of these methods is unlikely to differ much, but less numerate senior managers sometimes like to think that there should be larger gaps between levels at their end of the scale.

6 Decide on the factor weighting

The aim is to design a points-factor scheme that will operate fairly and consistently to produce a rank order of jobs, based on the total points score for each job. Each level in the factor plan has to be allocated a points value. It may be decided that some factors are more significant than others and in this case they would be explicitly weighted by providing them with a higher maximum points score than other factors. Factor weighting is expressed as the maximum points available for a factor taken as a percentage of the total available points for all factors. In a scheme with six factors it may be decided that two factor such as expertise and problem solving should be weighted at 20 per cent and the remaining four factors weighted at 15 per cent. Thus, if the total score available were 800 points, the two weighted factors would have a maximum score of 160 points each and the remaining factors would each have a maximum of 120 points.

Factor weighting can be determined by the design team who discuss the relative importance of the factors and agree on how they should be weighted. This is termed 'explicit weighting'. It is essentially a judgemental process, a matter of opinion, which cannot be verified except in terms of the consensus achieved by the collective views (and prejudices) of the team. Attempts have been made to give this some validity by using the statistical technique of multiple regression analysis. But this does not produce a credible result.

Pilot testing is used to assess the results produced by the initial weighting, which can be amended if the rank order is deemed to be unsatisfactory by the design team. The criteria for deciding whether or not the results are acceptable is again judgemental. The panel has to believe that the ranking fairly represents the relative size of the pilot test jobs. The biggest problem to be overcome at this stage is the tendency of people to allow their judgements to be swayed by the existing relativities. They have to be encouraged, persuaded, even cajoled, into leaving their prejudices behind them and concentrating on the facts revealed by the job analysis and the evaluation.

In some schemes 'implicit weighting' exists rather than the explicit weighting referred to above. Implicit weighting takes place whenever factors are developed that have more levels than others and for which the same scoring progression per level exists as in the other factors. Such factors would have more points available to them because of the extra levels and would have therefore been implicitly weighted. Thus a scheme with six factors, each with the same number of six levels and a score progression of 20 points per level, would have the same maximum score of 120 points for each factor and would therefore be unweighted. If, however, two factors had an additional level and the same scoring system were used, their maximum score would be 140 points and the scheme would be implicitly weighted at 18.42 per cent of the total score for the factors with additional levels, and 15.79 per cent of the total for the remaining factors.

7 Test the full factor plan

The full factor plan incorporating a scoring scheme and weighting is tested on the same jobs used in the initial test of the draft factors. Further jobs may be added to extend the range of the test. Each test job is evaluated and scored by the panel and then ranked according to the total score. The panel should then consider the extent to which it is believed the rank order is valid. There is no single, simple test to confirm whether the ranking of roles generated by the scoring system is correct. After all, as stated in the EOC *Good Practice Guide* (2003),[2] job evaluation is in large part a social mechanism to establish agreed differentials within organizations. Therefore, the final test is whether the resulting rank order looks reasonable to all parties, and whether the appropriate tests have been made to ensure that the scheme applies fairly to the range of jobs it will cover. This is where caution must be exercised to ensure that the rank order review does not lead to weighting adjustments aimed at reverting to the previous hierarchy of roles, based on preconceptions about their relative worth, or expectations about what results the job evaluation scheme should produce. But the test may reveal a need to make further adjustments to the factor level definitions or the scoring and weighting plan. If these are revised, the validity of the rank order will need to be reconsidered. This can be an iterative process but no more than one or at most two iterations are usually required.

8 Computerize

The steps set out above will produce a paper-based scheme and this is still the most popular approach. The E-Reward 2003 survey found that only 28 per cent of respondents with job evaluation schemes used computers to aid evaluation. But full computerization as described in Chapter 11 can offer many advantages including greater consistency, speed and the elimination of much of the paperwork. There is also the possibility of using IT to help manage and support the process without using computers as a substitute for grading panels. Many HR software systems such as SAP and Peoplesoft provide for this.

Computer-assisted schemes use the software provided by suppliers but the system itself is derived from the paper-based scheme devised by the methods set out above. No job evaluation panel is required to conduct evaluations but it is necessary to set up a review panel, which can validate and agree the outcomes of the computerized process. No one likes to feel that a decision about their grade has been made by a computer on its own, and hard lessons have been learned by organizations that have ended up with fully automated but discriminatory systems.

IMPLEMENTING JOB EVALUATION

The implementation of job evaluation is carried out by selecting benchmark jobs and then evaluating them to produce a rank order as described below. When planning implementation it is important to be clear about the role of the panel, its members and its chair as also explained below.

The next stage is the design and implementation of the grade and pay structure, which is dealt with in Chapters 16 and 17, and will include the analysis of information on market rates to inform decisions on pay levels. It will be necessary to formulate assimilation policies (what to do about staff who are over- or under-graded as a result of introducing a new structure) and to estimate the costs of assimilation.

Jobs other than the benchmark jobs already evaluated are then allocated to these grades either by evaluating them separately or, more commonly and to save time, by matching them with already graded jobs. The latter approach is used for generic roles with similar responsibilities held by a number of people as there is no point in conducting separate evaluations. Where there is doubt about matching, jobs should be evaluated separately to ensure consistent and fair outcomes.

At this stage it is necessary to plot how evaluations fall into current or new grades and to calculate the cost of assimilation. It might be necessary to reconsider the grade structure if this is likely to cost too much.

A job evaluation exercise is not completed until the grade and pay structure has been designed, all jobs have been allocated to the structure, policy decisions are made and implemented on how to deal with assimilating jobs and people into the new structure, and staff have been informed of how they are affected and have the opportunity to get their gradings reviewed. The implementation programme should include the preparation of an operations manual, which will set out the basis upon which job evaluation will be managed and maintained. It will also contain details of the review and appeals procedure as described in the next section of this chapter and arrangements for training new job evaluation panel members.

Arrangements need to be made for communicating the outcome of the job evaluation exercise to employees in the shape of a new or revised grade and pay structure and information on their grading and how their pay will be affected. The usual practice is to inform individuals of their grades but not their job evaluation scores on the grounds that those are only meaningful to those who have been trained in job evaluation such as the members of the job evaluation panel who carried out the evaluation.

It will also be necessary to ensure that additional job evaluators are trained so that substitutes are available. The training should include sitting in on panel meetings. It is important to include training in what needs to be done to avoid biased evaluations. The design of grade and pay structures is dealt with in Chapter 16. A flow chart of the implementation stages mentioned above is shown in Figure 12.1.

Select benchmark jobs

When the design has been finalized, 'benchmark' jobs will need to be selected by the panel. Benchmark jobs provide the reference points for

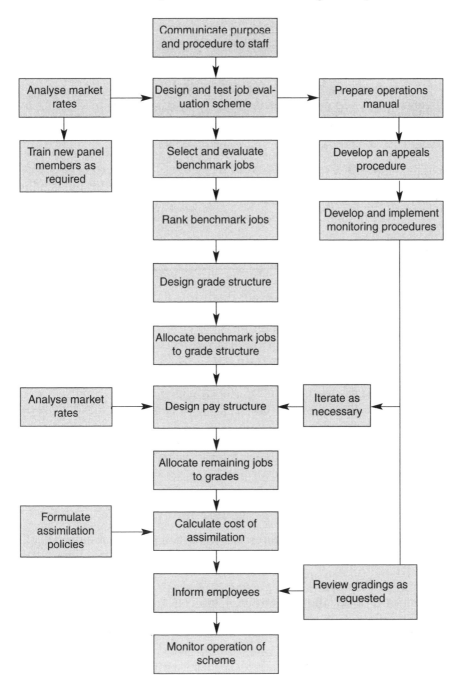

Figure 12.1 Job evaluation and grading implementation process

evaluation, bearing in mind that job evaluation is essentially a comparative process. They are the representative jobs that enable standards to be developed and refined for making judgements about comparative worth, and form the datum points that are the basis of the framework within which other jobs are evaluated.

Benchmarks will consist of the key jobs at different levels and in different functions of the organization and need to be selected whenever the total number of jobs is too large for them all to be compared with one another. As a rule of thumb, this may be the case when there are 40 jobs or more, although the number could be smaller if there are wide variations between the jobs. Normally between 15 per cent and 30 per cent of the total number of jobs may be selected, depending on the complexity of the organization, although some jobs may be carried out by a number of people (generic jobs or roles) and the percentage is therefore likely to be less than the total number employed.

The criteria for selecting benchmarks are that they should:

▌ represent the entire range of jobs according to level and function and the extent to which job holders are predominantly male or female or members of different racial groups;
▌ be well-recognized jobs with which the members of the job evaluation panel between them are familiar;
▌ be reasonably stable, ie unlikely to change much in content (although this presents difficulties in a rapidly changing organization);
▌ be precisely defined with regard to skills, responsibilities and work requirements;
▌ stand out clearly from other jobs so that they can be easily identified;
▌ include at least some jobs that can form the basis of external comparisons.

Evaluate benchmark jobs – procedure for evaluation

The best approach is for the panel to evaluate one factor at a time in all the jobs under consideration. The panel exchanges views about the factor evaluation and, under the guidance of the chair or facilitator, reaches agreement. The scores are then added up for each of the jobs and the panel examines the comparative total scores to ensure that it is happy with the result. If not, the individual factor scores may have to be reconsidered.

Experience has shown that this in-depth factor-by-factor approach rather than a job-by-job approach makes it easier to achieve consensus. It means that panel members are less likely to make decisions on total scores based on a priori judgements about the relative value of the whole jobs, which they might find it hard to change. They are more likely to focus on 'read-across' analytical judgements about the level of particular factors and it will be easier for them to refer for guidance to previous evaluations of the same factor in other benchmark jobs. It also takes less time than other methods because it is possible to concentrate on factor evaluations that are questionable relative to the levels given to other jobs.

When there are variations in factor evaluations, individual panel members are asked to give reasons for their conclusions. But the chair has to be careful not to allow them to be pressurized to change their views. If panel members have been properly trained and if there is a carefully designed, tested and understood factor plan and good information about the job, the extent to which evaluations vary is usually fairly limited, which enables consensus to be achieved more easily.

The rank order produced by the benchmark evaluations provides the basis for the design of the grade structure as described in Chapter 16. As noted above, organizations with a large number of jobs usually rely on matching the jobs not covered in the original evaluation with the grading of the benchmark jobs, especially in the case of generic roles.

The role of the panel

The role of the panel needs to be defined by reference to the following guidelines:

1. No untrained person should be allowed to take part in, nor to influence, an evaluation.
2. All evaluators should have the input information at least a week prior to the evaluation meeting (to provide the opportunity to clarify anything that is unclear and thus save time at the meeting itself).
3. No aspect of the job holder as a person should influence any aspect of the evaluation (specifically not gender or ethnic origin).
4. The evaluation is concerned with the normal content of the job as defined in a job description or role analysis. It should not be affected by the activities of any individuals that vary the standard job requirements.
5. The aim of the panel is to achieve consensus on evaluations. Voting is undesirable because it can be divisive and lead to superficial discussions.
6. A full record of the scoring decisions should be kept and, where the decision was a marginal one, the reasons why that level was determined noted (a rationale). This is particularly important if the panel found it difficult to reach consensus, as it may be relevant if a review of that evaluation is called for.
7. All evaluation scores should be treated as provisional (and not disclosed) until they have been reviewed by a review or audit panel and confirmed.

Panel members will benefit from initial training in job analysis and the principles and practice of job evaluation. It may be helpful to start with one or two dummy runs – using the scheme to evaluate two or three made-up jobs. It is essential that they should be familiar with what they must do to avoid gender or any other form of bias.

The role of the chair

Good facilitation is crucial and the overall responsibility of the chair should be to facilitate the discussion and obtain consensus on the evaluation. Consensus may be difficult to attain but experience has shown that it can always be achieved, although this may take time. In particular the chair should:

▌ make sure that the panel is well balanced and that everyone understands that all members have an equal say in the deliberations and decision making;

▌ lay down the ground rules for evaluation and agree the methodology;

▌ ensure that each job is fully understood (through examination of job information and round-table discussion) before any evaluation is attempted; the chair should have the authority to suspend an evaluation if the available information appears to be incomplete or misleading;

▌ initiate the discussion on each factor if a factor-by-factor approach is used;

▌ guide panel members through the evaluation, probing where necessary to test whether views have been properly justified on the basis of the evidence, but not giving any indication of the chair's own views – it is the panel members who carry out the evaluation, not the chair;

▌ continually reinforce the principles that it is the job and not the performance of the person that is being evaluated and the need to avoid gender or other bias;

▌ remind panel members that it is the job content as it is intended to be carried out that is evaluated, not the job as carried out by a particular job holder;

▌ actively encourage the participation of every panel member;

▌ as a facilitator, stimulate reasoned debate;

▌ ensure that people respect alternative views and, where appropriate, are prepared to change their initial stance when presented with a valid reason to do so;

▌ bear in mind that a lone voice may have a significant contribution to make; dissenters should therefore be given a reasonable chance to express their view subject to them not being allowed to dominate the discussion – most seasoned panel members will be able to recall at least one '12 Angry Men' situation where a presumed consensus for the 'obvious' conclusion was overturned by one person's persistence;

∎ be alert to, and suppress, any factions or cliques developing in the panel – one approach might be to change the seating plan each session;

∎ ensure that the consensus reached is not a 'false consensus' (one for which there is no dissenting voice only because one or more dissenters are too afraid to speak out against more dominant members) – it will be up to the chair to be particularly sensitive to this and deliberately to encourage the more reticent members to state their views;

∎ be scrupulously neutral at all times – to achieve this, chairs normally do not carry out any evaluations themselves but in their facilitator role they can when necessary challenge (gently) panel members to justify their views, press for discussion based on the evidence rather than opinion and bring to the attention of panel members any evidence or relevant facts that will help them to reach an agreed conclusion;

∎ ensure that the decisions of the panel and the rationale for those decisions are recorded;

∎ if the panel is unable to reach a true consensus within a reasonable time, not try to force the issue but have the authority to put the job to one side for further reflection or so that more information about the points at issue can be obtained.

As a last resort, chairs have been know to put panels to the vote, but this is undesirable because it divides the panel.

EVALUATION REVIEWS

There are essentially two situations where a review of the evaluation or grading of a job might properly be requested:

1. when the job is first allocated to a grade and that grade is made known to the parties concerned;
2. when the content of a job changes (or is about to change) sufficiently to place doubt on the existing grading of that job.

Requests arising under the first of these situations should be referred to as 'evaluation reviews' (often, but inappropriately, referred to as 'appeals'); requests arising under the second situation should be referred to as 're-evaluations'.

A formal 'evaluation review procedure' should be prepared, agreed and issued before any evaluation results are made known. Review should be conducted by a specially convened review panel. This might be composed of two members of the original panel plus two additional trained evaluators who were not associated with the original decision, and an independent chair. The review stages are typically as follows:

1. The employee discusses his or her concern with the line manager who will decide whether or not to support the appeal.
2. The employee, supported if appropriate by his or her line manager, submits the case for a grading review.
3. The manager responsible for job evaluation should examine the request, add notes as necessary and submit it to the review panel together with all available details of the original evaluation. If the request is based on a comparison with another job, details of that evaluation should also be provided.
4. The review panel should examine the documents and decide whether a re-evaluation is justified. If the request is based on the way job information has been interpreted rather than on matters of fact the panel should try to establish why this was not identified during the original evaluation or review.
5. The review panel should re-evaluate the job.
6. If the review panel believes that a request based on a comparison with another job is potentially valid but that it is the comparator job that was wrongly evaluated, it should re-evaluate both jobs.
7. The re-evaluation process should be the same as for the original evaluation but focusing only on the issues raised in stages 1 to 5 above.
8. The impact of any re-evaluation on the grading of the job under review should be assessed by the manager responsible for job evaluation and communicated to the employee and his or her manager as the outcome of the review panel's re-evaluation.

There should be no right of appeal to the panel but employees could be allowed to take up the case as a grievance through the normal grievance procedure.

MAINTAINING JOB EVALUATION

Job evaluation needs to be managed with care, otherwise it will decay and become discredited. Ten suggestions on what needs to be done to maintain job evaluation provided by respondents to the E-Reward survey are:

▮ 'Need to ensure that regular reviews of scheme are built in.'
▮ 'Provide adequate training for those operating the scheme.'
▮ 'Ensure trained evaluators don't get rusty.'

- 'Use IT in a smarter way.'
- 'Again, ensure better communications with employees.'
- 'More line accountability and involvement.'
- 'Find a less time-consuming way of managing it.'
- 'Have more robust process for challenging and slotting new roles.'
- 'Maintain better systems for record keeping and adopt smoother processes.'
- 'Ensure tighter policing and provide clearer rationale.'

All these are valid points but perhaps the most important one is to review the scheme regularly. As suggested by Armstrong et al:[3]

> All organizations are continually evolving, some more quickly than others. No matter how carefully the new job evaluation scheme has been developed, it can only be totally 'right' for the organization at the time of its development. Without regular review and re-tuning when necessary, it will gradually become viewed as 'yesterday's scheme', no longer valid for evaluating jobs in 'today's environment'. The review need not be time-consuming but it should be carried out on a regular basis which it is best to determine at the outset.

REFERENCES

1. E-Reward Research (2003) *A Survey of Job Evaluation Practice in the UK*, E-Reward, London
2. Equal Opportunities Commission (2003) *Good Practice Guide on Job Evaluation Schemes Free of Sex Bias*, EOC, Manchester
3. Armstrong, M *et al* (2003) *Guide to Job Evaluation*, Kogan Page, London

13

Equal Pay for Work of Equal Value

As Professor Robert Elliott of the University of Aberdeen has stated: 'Discrimination arises when equals are treated unequally.' Gender bias can apply to either men or women, but it operates mainly against women. Statistics show that the gender pay gap, in spite of 30 years of legislation, shows a difference between male and female full-time hourly pay of 18 per cent in favour of men doing identical, similar or equivalent jobs.

The gap is even more pronounced for women who work part time, with earnings on average 41 per cent less than those of their male colleagues in full-time occupation. This gap is the same as it was 25 years ago.

The Kingsmill Report[1] in December 2001 identified the main characteristics influencing the gender pay gap in the UK as:

- human capital differences such as educational qualifications, work experience and training;
- prevalent part-time working among women;
- a concentration of women in occupations that tend to attract lower pay (sales, secretarial, health, education, childcare and catering); and
- clustering of women in lower-paid, lower-status roles within a business, leading to lower pay.

Inequalities in pay exist because of prejudice, segregation and inequalities of opportunity in selection, training, development and promotion.

An attempt has been made to alleviate the latter problems through the Sex Discrimination Acts 1975 and 1986, and many firms have tried to deal with them by means of equal opportunity policies. The Equal Pay Act 1970 and the Equal Value Amendment 1983 to that Act have tackled equal pay considerations, and in 2003 the content of equal pay questionnaires was formalized through the Employment Act 2002. The EOC has been prominent recently in supporting calls for equal pay audits.

In this chapter the legal framework is considered first. The important area of job evaluation and equal value is then considered, and the chapter ends with an analysis of the considerations affecting the design of non-discriminatory pay structures.

EQUAL PAY FOR WORK OF EQUAL VALUE: THE LEGAL FRAMEWORK

The equal-pay-for-work-of-equal-value legal framework is provided by the 1970 Equal Pay Act as amended by the Equal Pay (Amendment) Regulations 1983, the Employment Act 2002 plus the case law. The Act and its Amendment are implemented through industrial tribunals, which may call for reports from 'independent experts' to carry out a job evaluation study.

The Equal Pay Act 1970

An employee in the UK can claim equal pay with an employee of the opposite sex in the same employing organization where: they are doing the same, or broadly similar, work (like work); or the work they do is work rated equivalent under a job evaluation scheme. The basis of the Act is that every contract of employment is deemed to contain an equality clause that is triggered in either of those situations. The equality clause modifies any terms in the woman's contract that are less favourable than those of the male comparator. Thus, if the woman were paid less than a man doing the same work, she would be entitled to the same rate of pay.

The three important points to note about the original Act are that:

1. Because it was confined to like work and work rated as equivalent, the scope of comparison was fairly narrow.
2. It did not make job evaluation compulsory, but did establish the important point (or made the important assumption) that, where job evaluation did exist and valued two jobs equally, there was a prima facie entitlement to equal pay.
3. The Act recognized that a job evaluation scheme could be discriminatory if it set 'different values for men and women on the same

demand under any heading'. It gave effort, skill, decision-making as examples of headings.

However, the European Commission's Equal Pay Directive of 1975 stated that the principle of equal pay should be applied to work of equal value. The EC argued successfully before the European Court of Justice in 1982 that the UK had failed to implement the Directive because the Equal Pay Act only enabled individuals to obtain equal pay for work of equal value where their employer had implemented job evaluation. As a result, the UK government had to introduce the 1983 Equal Value Amendment to the Act, which came into force in 1984.

The Equal Pay Act 1970 covered pay as well as other terms and conditions including benefits provided by the contract of employment. It did not, however, cover non-contractual arrangements, which may be covered by the Sex Discrimination Act 1975.

The Equal Value Amendment

Under the Equal Value Amendment, women are entitled to equal pay with men (and vice versa) where the work is of equal value 'in terms of the demands made on a worker under various headings, for instance, effort, skill, decision making'.

This removed the barrier built into the original Equal Pay Act that prevented women claiming equal pay because they were employed in 'women's' jobs, with no men employed in the same work. Now *any* woman could claim equal pay with *any* man and vice versa, subject to the rules about being in the same employment. Equal value claims could now be made even if there were no job evaluation arrangements, although the existence of a non-discriminatory job evaluation, which has been applied properly to indicate that the jobs in question are not of equal value, can be a defence in an equal value case.

The amendment also provided for the assignment of 'independent experts' by tribunals to assess equality of value between claimant and comparator under such headings as effort, skill and decision making, without regard to the cost or the industrial relations consequences of a successful claim.

Equal value claims can be made across sites and across employers within an umbrella organization, with potentially far-reaching consequences, provided applicant and comparator are deemed to be 'in the same employment'. This happens when they have common terms and conditions of employment. In *Leverton* v *Clwyd County Council* (1989) the House of Lords held that it was sufficient for applicants to be covered by the same 'Purple Book' agreement, despite differences in their individual terms and conditions.

Under the Equal Pay Act 1970 (Amendment) Regulations 2003 it was determined that the time limit to claim back-pay could be six years in

England and Wales and five years in Scotland and Northern Ireland. This had originally been two years.

European legislation

European legislation underpins domestic legislation. In the field of discrimination, either direct or indirect, these are primarily: Article 141, Treaty of Amsterdam (previously Article 119, Treaty of Rome); and Equal Pay Directive 75/117.

While the Equal Pay Act was limited to contractual elements of reward, Article 141 extended discrimination to non-contractual pay – though it does not confer the right to completely equal terms with a comparator, applying only to 'the ordinary basic or minimum wage or salary and any other consideration, whether in cash or kind, which the worker receives directly or indirectly, in respect of his employer or employment'. In the United Kingdom this allows cases to be brought for non-contractual rewards but under other discrimination legislation rather than under the Equal Pay Acts.

The Equal Pay Directive 75/117 aimed to eliminate discrimination on grounds of sex with regard to all aspects and conditions of remuneration. This reinforced Article 141 in those countries where equality had not yet been achieved. This Directive is to be reviewed.

Employment Act 2002

One of the biggest barriers to bringing equal pay claims has been a lack of access to information regarding other people's pay. The Equal Pay (Questions and Replies) Order 2003 of the Employment Act 2002 came into force in April 2003, and introduced the Equal Pay questionnaire (a copy of the questionnaire can be downloaded from www.womenand equalityunit.gov.uk). This completed a set of questionnaires already available under the Sex Discrimination, Disability Discrimination and Race Relations Acts. These Acts may all be used in equal pay claims.

The questionnaire is designed for use by the employee to request information from the employer about whether his or her remuneration is equal to that of named colleagues. Unions may also lodge these forms on behalf of their members. The employer has a statutory duty to respond.

The questionnaire includes:

▌ a statement of why the individual thinks he or she is not receiving equal pay, followed by a statement of who he or she believes the comparators are;
▌ factual questions to ascertain whether he or she is receiving less pay than the comparator and, if so, the reason why;

▪ a question asking whether the employer agrees that the individual and the comparator are doing equal work and a question asking whether the employer agrees that the complainant is being paid less than the comparator;

▪ guidance on issues of confidentiality and more detailed explanations of the terms 'equal work' and 'equal pay';

▪ space for the complainant's own questions.

Clearly, a key aspect of this is determination of suitable comparators. The Equal Pay Act describes comparators as follows: be employed by the same employer; *or* an associated employer; *and* either be employed at the same establishment or service; *or* at a different establishment where *common terms and conditions of employment* are laid out for the two establishments.

In addition, it is possible to select comparators who are either the predecessor or the successor to a job, and a complainant may bring a case up to six months after leaving the employer.

The employer is asked to respond within eight weeks. The response should include confirmation, or otherwise, that there is a difference in remuneration as suggested by the complainant. If a difference does exist then the employer should give reasons for this.

The Order also provides that a Tribunal may draw such inferences as are just and equitable from: a failure to reply without reasonable excuse within eight weeks of receiving a questionnaire; or responding in an evasive or equivalent manner.

The inferences that can be drawn include that a person has been unlawfully discriminated against.

The material factor defence

Once a questionnaire has been lodged, the employer has a range of defences. These include incorrect interpretation of the Act as well as genuine material factors influencing pay differences:

▪ The work being done is not rated as equivalent. This is derived from the underlying principle of the Acts. In order to bring this defence the jobs need to have been evaluated as being different using an analytical job evaluation system.

▪ The jobs have not been evaluated under a system free of sex bias. In other words there are difficulties with the job evaluation framework itself or in the method by which it is applied.

▪ There are genuine material factors other than sex, which might include:

  – The complainant is not yet operating at a satisfactory level within the job perhaps through being in a probationary period or still learning the job. The employer must be able to demonstrate that full competence has not yet been achieved.

- The complainant is operating at a lower level of performance than the comparators. The employer must be able to demonstrate that decisions on performance are based on targets and objectives understood by the participants and that the results are properly documented.
- The complainant is operating in a sector or role where there is a materially different market from that of the comparators. For example, there may be differences in pay levels due to location, such as London against Manchester, or in the nature of the job whereby the market supports a premium for the comparator. However, recent EOC guidance[2] suggests an employer cannot rely on the fact that the market rate suggests that certain jobs usually done by women are paid at less than jobs usually done by men, because the market rate may itself be based on discriminatory assumptions. What an employer has to show is not that 'that's what everybody else pays' but rather 'that's what I had to pay to get the person I needed to fill the vacancy I had'.
- The jobs are subject to different collective bargaining agreements and processes.
- The job may have been 'red-circled' for some reason such as a TUPE transfer.

If the employer depends on one of these, the employer is then required to provide evidence to support the defence. It is important to note, though, that each case should be treated on its own merits and a genuine material defence in one case may not be a solid defence elsewhere.

Discrimination includes direct, which can usually be identified, and indirect, which can generally only be identified by its results. Even where an employer has demonstrated a Genuine Material Factor (GMF) defence, a complainant can argue that the factor is indirectly discriminatory under the Sex Discrimination Act if it acts to the detriment of a considerably larger proportion of one gender than the other. For example, if the employer shows that the difference is due to length of service, the complainant may be able to argue that this indirectly discriminates against women if far fewer women than men have achieved the necessary length of service owing to their increased family or caring responsibilities. Where a case of indirect discrimination is established, the employer must show that its provision is 'objectively justifiable' – a higher standard of proof than is required with the GMF. To do this, the employer will need to demonstrate that the purpose of the provision was to meet a real business need, that the provision was a necessary and appropriate way of meeting that need and that it did not go further than was necessary. It is up to the employer, once a prima facie case of discrimination has been made, to provide cogent evidence to rebut it.

The equal pay questionnaire is the first step in a process. Should a case be demonstrated that there is bias in the system, the employer has the choice of acting to correct the inequality and ensure there is no further discrimination, or the employee can proceed through the normal grievance procedures to an Industrial Tribunal and ultimately to the ECJ. From October 2004, the complainant will be obliged to proceed through the employer's grievance procedure under the terms of the Employment Act 2002.

Equal pay case law

Case law has been built up on equal pay including:

- *Bower* v *Schroder Securities*. Julie Bower won £1.4 million, after claiming her bonus was far less than the bonuses of male colleagues doing comparable work. Schroders were unable to justify their decision to pay her a low bonus of £25,000 against the comparator who was paid £440,000, and lost the case. This case was brought under the Sex Discrimination Act 1975, as it referred to a non-contractual bonus. The main influence on the result was that Schroders could not disprove her claim of discrimination or support their view that she was a poor performer.
- *Crossley* v *ACAS*. A female employee with ACAS argued that she should be paid the same as a male comparator as she could demonstrate an equal contribution but earned significantly less only owing to shorter service. The ACAS pay scales required many years' experience to reach the top of the pay band, which, it was argued, discriminated against women who are more likely to have shorter periods of service. Although the Tribunal accepted that there was a period during which the job was being learned, it agreed the period in this case was too long. The published cost of this settlement, which eventually covered 900 staff, was in excess of £5 million.
- *Barton* v *Investec*. Ms Barton claimed that, although she had generated the same amount of revenue as a male colleague (her comparator), she had been paid only about half of the £2.1 million remuneration enjoyed by him, whom she had recruited and trained during that time. The initial Tribunal did not find in Ms Barton's favour but criticized Investec for lack of transparency in HR and remuneration policies. However, on appeal this decision was overturned on the grounds that the burden of proof was with Investec and it had not adequately proved its case.

JOB EVALUATION AND EQUAL PAY

The Equal Pay Act 1970 allows different jobs to be compared in order to determine whether they can be described as equal. The mechanism for achieving this is an analytical job evaluation system. Analytical schemes are those where jobs are broken down into components (known as 'factors') and scores for each component of the job are awarded with a final total giving an overall rank order.

Analytical job evaluation and discrimination

Many analytical schemes exist and these can be used where they are clearly described as being free of sex bias in their design. The Equal Pay Act, as amended in 1984, states that a scheme will be discriminatory if it is made on a system that discriminates on grounds of sex where a difference or coincidence between values set by that system on different demands under the same or different headings is not justifiable, irrespective of the sex of the person on whom these demands are made. The EOC[3] illustrates this with the following example: a woman may argue that, instead of 'mental concentration' (in her job) being awarded fewer points than 'physical effort' (in a man's job), it should have received the same or more points. Similarly, she may argue that the 'physical effort' (in his job) has been overrated compared with the skill her job requires for 'manual dexterity'. Even where she has received the same or more points than a man under a particular heading, she may still argue that the demands of her job under this heading have been underrated.

Although the analytical job evaluation framework selected may be free of bias, its application may not be. This arises from the need to apply judgement when evaluating any job. The risk of introducing bias at this stage can be reduced by using appropriately constructed panels. These should include a representative cross-section of employees who are trained in job evaluation. In addition, it should be clear that: it is the job that is being evaluated and not the person in the job; and the job must be fully understood before an evaluation can be undertaken.

A clear message arising from the case law is that any process should be transparent and that careful documentation of decision making is essential. This applies to all stages of the HR process including the evaluation.

EQUAL PAY AUDITS

At the time of writing there is no obligation on any organization outside the public sector to carry out equal pay audits. However, the Equal Opportunities Commission has become increasingly active in this field both in developing guidance and in publicizing the issue, and it is recommending that such audits be carried out on a voluntary basis. Its intention is that audits will only become mandatory if fewer than half of large employers, ie those with 500 or more employees, had undertaken an audit by the end of 2003, and 50 per cent of small employers by the end of 2005. In March 2003, a study by the Institute of Employment Studies[4] indicated that only 36 per cent of medium or large employers intended to carry out or had carried out an equal pay review. A CIPD survey in 2004[5] saw this figure rise to 48 per cent anticipating having reviewed by the end of 2005. Although the main area of discrimination examined was gender, employers also took the opportunity to examine race and age discrimination (age discrimination legislation is to become law in 2006).

The intention of an audit is threefold according to Jane Phillipson:[6]

1. To examine whether you pay people differently and, if so, to understand and justify the reasons behind this. This includes having the evidence to support your case.
2. To examine both the outputs (pay comparisons) and the HR processes underpinning your pay practice.
3. To agree a timescale and develop an action plan to close unjustifiable pay gaps between the genders.

It is not, according to Phillipson, about returning to the narrow pay grades of the past.

The EOC has suggested that there should be a five-step process to review equal pay:

1. *planning* – deciding the scope of the review and identifying the information required;
2. *equal work* – determining where men and women are doing equal work;
3. *equal pay gaps* – collecting data to identify equal pay gaps;
4. *analysis and recommendations* – establishing the causes of any significant pay gaps and assessing the reasons;
5. *action plan* – developing an action plan to correct gaps.

DESIGN OF NON-DISCRIMINATORY PAY SCALES

Areas of discrimination

Hay Group has described the potential equal pay risk areas under the general headings of:

▌ policies;
▌ processes; and
▌ practice.

Discrimination may be evident in any of these and it is, therefore, essential to ensure that bias of any form is avoided where possible. This will include making sure that:

▌ Any grading structure is underpinned by bias-free principles such as an analytical job evaluation system.
▌ Pay scales are supported by an unbiased grading structure, market data and full understanding of how to put together fair pay structures including progression within and between grades. Where additional qualifications or skills are needed for progression these should be equally open to all candidates irrespective of gender.
▌ There is a properly documented approach to recruitment and starting salaries, and also to promotion.
▌ Access to additional allowances is provided on an unbiased basis and is open to all relevant jobs and at equivalent levels. This will include regional allowances and market premiums for certain jobs as well as such allowances as overtime or shiftwork.
▌ Performance management processes are in place that clearly link business performance, personal performance and any performance-related pay or incentives.
▌ Bonus schemes are clearly available on an unbiased basis and the targets and objectives are transparent to all participants and decisions are properly documented.
▌ There is a policy about those roles that are treated separately or red-circled. This will include documenting the reason for the special treatment as well as how these will be dealt with in future including the period over which these will continue to be red-circled.
▌ All HR policies should be properly documented to reduce the amount of discretion within the system.
▌ All staff involved in operating any related HR policies are fully aware of how they operate and their responsibility to support any equal pay initiatives. This should include proper training on how the systems operate.
▌ There is proper documentation of all decisions made including job evaluation, promotions, pay rises, incentives, bonuses and performance management.

This is not an exhaustive list, and guidance on how to address individual issues can be found on www.eoc.org.uk/cseng/advice.

REFERENCES

1. *Kingsmill Review of Women's Employment and Pay* (2001), www.kingsmillreview.gov.uk
2. www.eoc.org.uk/cseng/advice/practical_tips_on_equal_pay.asp?SubDate =Wednesday+24+December%2C+2003
3. EOC, *Good Practice Guide: Job evaluation schemes free of sex bias*, http://www.eoc.org.uk/EOCeng/EOCcs/Advice/good_practice_guide_-_job_evaluation_schemes_free_of_sex_bias.asp
4. Neathey, F, Dench, S and Thomson, L (2003) *Monitoring Progress towards Pay Equality*, EOC Research Discussion Series
5. CIPD (2004) *Reward Management 2004: A survey of policy and practice*, Chartered Institute of Personnel and Development, London
6. Phillipson, Jane (2003) Audits will highlight problems with pay before they escalate, *Personnel Today*, 15 April

14

Market Rate Surveys and Reward Research

Competitive pay levels and salary structures can only be developed and maintained if the external market is systematically monitored by a process of external benchmarking. This can be done using a range of sources from salary and benefits information to job advertisements, companies' annual reports information, confidential contacts and other forms of market intelligence.

This chapter describes:

▌ the purpose of making market comparisons;
▌ the process of carrying out analyses of market rates;
▌ the sources of comparative remuneration data;
▌ how to conduct an organization or club survey;
▌ how market data should be used.

THE PURPOSE OF MAKING MARKET COMPARISONS

Market comparisons aim to compare external relativities, ie: 1) the rates and benefits provided for equivalent jobs in other organizations (market rates) with those provided within the organization, in order to ensure that the latter are fully competitive; and 2) the rates at which pay is increasing in other organizations (going rates) in order to provide guidance on pay reviews.

The data from market comparisons help organizations to:

▌ decide on starting rates;
▌ design and modify salary structures;
▌ determine acceptable rates of salary progression in pay structures and pay curve systems;
▌ review pay, incentives, bonuses and other forms of performance-related pay;
▌ decide on the types and levels of benefits to be provided;
▌ assess the level of increases required to salary levels generally and to the salary levels of individual employees;
▌ identify special cases where market rates have to be paid irrespective of the evaluated position of the job in the grade hierarchy.

THE PROCESS OF CARRYING OUT MARKET COMPARISONS

Sources of information

The main sources of reward information are:

▌ general published surveys and market information sourced directly from specialist electronic database providers;
▌ specialized occupational, professional, industrial or local surveys or database-sourced information;
▌ organization surveys/projects – ie those carried out by the organization, with or without the help of consultants;
▌ salary information and survey clubs – ie a group of organizations that regularly exchange information;
▌ published data in specialist or other journals, newspapers, business press, government reports and their corresponding Web sites;
▌ analyses of job advertisements;
▌ other market intelligence.

A brief description and comparative analysis of each of these is provided later in the chapter, followed by a more detailed examination of organization and club salary information projects. But before looking at these sources, it is necessary to review the basic considerations affecting market comparisons.

BASIC CONSIDERATIONS

When making market comparisons, the aims as far as possible are to:

▌ obtain accurate and representative data on market rates;

- compare like with like, in terms of data, regional and organizational variations and, importantly, type and size of job or role;
- obtain information that is as up to date as possible;
- interpret data in a way that clearly indicates the action required.

The problem of defining the market rate

People often refer to the 'market rate' but it is a much more elusive concept than it seems. There is no such thing as a definitive market rate for any job, even when comparing identically sized organizations in the same industry and location. There are local markets and there are national markets, and none of them is perfect in the economist's sense. Different market information sources of the same types of jobs produce different results because of variations in the sample, timing and job matching.

No market information source is designed or, indeed, should be designed to show that one salary level is the 'correct' market rate for any given job. It should give as clear an indication as possible of the current operating or going range for establishing salary levels or setting pay structures and define which factors affect the distribution of individual salaries within it.

Despite these points, most pay specialists and market information providers will sometimes have to put up with the reader's expectation that their survey will give a 'correct' salary for a job for any given set of conditions. Some top executives, and others needing to make policy decisions but having restricted understanding of the problems of carrying out market research, still tend to believe that it is possible to find out exactly what the precise market rate is for any given job, in any industry, at any location, for any given age or experience level – preferably to the nearest pound! But this is not a reality and is unlikely to become one. Because survey data submission is voluntary, and because decisions about pay levels tend to be pragmatic rather than strictly logical, actual salaries are less predictable than many people would like to believe. When there are few data available, salary patterns tend to be fairly anarchic. Most salary decisions in relation to market information sources are conformist, which can mean that there are regular and predictable operating ranges for jobs covered regularly by well-established information sources rather than, for instance, new or rapidly evolving jobs not yet much subject to market information analysis.

This means that, however hard you work at getting accurate results, all you will obtain is an approximation – a range of possibilities. In spite of yourself you may, where data are hard to come by, be forced into averaging averages to obtain an informed view of the derived market rate. And that is a statistically undesirable process.

It should be remembered that individuals as well as jobs have market rates. When looking at a range of market rates you have to decide two things – first, what the rate for the job should be and, second, what the range for individuals in the job should be as they enhance their marketability through experience, training and 'track record' or performance. Specialist market information sources may give some indication of the range of salaries you should offer; for example, you could set the lowest point of the range at the median (the middle point in the distribution of salary rates covered by the data source) and the highest point at the upper quartile (the value above which 25 per cent of the values in the range fall).

The more you track the actual salaries paid to people in identical jobs in similar areas, the greater the accuracy of the market rate information. But this may require a tremendous amount of effort and you may need to question the cost effectiveness of the process. That is why some people rely on published sources and other readily available data. Increased accuracy can be provided by company (do-it-yourself) and club surveys, but cost typically limits how far you can go.

However, in spite of these limitations, surveys and other market information sources are necessary to provide indications, albeit broad ones, of where the organization stands in the market place. Considerable judgement is still required to interpret results, but at least that judgement can be based on information that has been collected and analysed systematically.

Data definitions

- ▌ *Basic (or base) pay:* gross pay before deducting national insurance, tax and pension contributions. It includes merit increments or incremental payments added into salary but excludes performance-related bonuses, overtime pay, fringe benefits and most allowances. In the latter case, the only exception may be a location allowance (eg a London allowance), which may or may not be incorporated in the base salary, but whether or not it is included should be made clear.
- ▌ *Cash bonuses:* any performance-related bonus or payment under an incentive scheme, which is not part of basic pay.
- ▌ *Short-term incentives:* all short-term variable bonuses and incentives that are not guaranteed, eg all company bonus scheme, profit share or incentive payments earned over a period of less than one year.
- ▌ *On-target variable bonuses expected:* the 'on-target' of all short-term variable bonuses and incentives expected in the current year, expressed as a percentage of current base salary.
- ▌ *Long-term incentives:* incentives earned over a period of more than one year. They are not guaranteed and include share plans (share options, restricted share plans, share appreciation rights and matched purchase of shares) and cash plans (multi-year goals, deferred awards, phantom plans, performance units or shares).

▌ *Total earnings* (sometimes called 'total cash earnings'): the sum of the basic annual pay and any cash bonuses received over the previous 12 months. This figure excludes the value of employee benefits.

▌ *Employee benefits:* details of the entitlement to benefits such as pensions, company cars, private petrol, mortgage assistance, loans, permanent health insurance, medical insurance, health screening, relocation packages, holidays, other forms of leave, sick pay, etc.

▌ *Other allowances:* any cash payments made in special circumstances such as call-outs, shift- or nightwork payments, car mileage allowances.

▌ *Total remuneration:* the total value of all cash payments and benefits received by employees (note that this involves specialist knowledge and that valuing benefits depends on agreed assumptions – data should be collected and analysed carefully and the definitions both of the constituent elements included and of the rubric for the results should be clear and consistent).

▌ *Salary structure information:* the salary scale or range in the structure for particular jobs.

Regional and company variables

Market comparisons should take account of the following variables that affect the comparability and validity of the data:

▌ *Location:* whether the jobs involved need to be assessed in relation to national, regional or local markets.

▌ *Industry:* usually analysed on the basis of a simplified version of the Standard Industrial Classification (SIC).

▌ *Sector:* whether the organization belongs within the public or private sector.

▌ *Organization size:* because it can affect job size, there is often some correlation between pay levels (especially salaries for managers) and company size. The following variables are typically taken into account:

　– financial indicators, eg sales turnover, or gross deposit for many financial institutions, derived from the accounts for the annual accounting period preceding the base date of the information collected and analysed;

　– the total number of employees, analysed as necessary according to location, company, division or group.

Job matching

Market comparisons are most valid when like is compared with like. This means matching jobs as far as possible in the following respects:

- function, eg general management, marketing, production;
- sector – private or public;
- industry classification;
- location;
- size of organization;
- range of responsibilities – the tasks or duties carried out by job holders;
- level of responsibility – size or weight of the job in terms of impact on end results, resources controlled, scope for exercising discretion and judgement, and complexity.

The various methods of job matching in ascending order of accuracy are:

- *Job title:* this can be relatively misleading. Job titles by themselves give no indication of the range of duties or the level of responsibility and are sometimes even used to convey additional status to employees or their customers unrelated to the real level of work done.
- *Brief description of duties and level or zone of responsibility:* national surveys frequently limit their job-matching definitions to a two- or three-line description of duties and an indication of levels of responsibility in rank order. The latter is often limited to a one-line definition for each level or zone in a hierarchy. This approach provides some guidance on job matching, which reduces major discrepancies, but it still leaves considerable scope for discretion and can therefore provide only generalized comparisons.
- *Capsule job descriptions:* club or specialist 'bespoke' surveys frequently use capsule job descriptions that define the job and its duties in approximately 250 words. To increase the refinement of comparisons, modifying statements may be made indicating where responsibilities are higher or lower than the norm. Capsule job descriptions considerably increase the accuracy of comparisons as long as they are based on a careful analysis of actual jobs and include modifying statements. But they are not always capable of dealing with specialist jobs, and the accuracy of comparisons in relation to levels of responsibility may be limited, even when modifiers are used.
- *Full job descriptions:* full job descriptions of individual jobs, sometimes including a factor analysis of the levels of responsibility involved, may be used in special surveys when direct comparisons are made between jobs in different organizations. They can be more accurate on a one-for-one basis but their use is limited because of the time and labour involved in preparing job descriptions. A further limitation is that comparator organizations may not have available, or be prepared to make available, their own full job descriptions for comparison.

▌ *Job evaluation:* job evaluation can be used in support of capsule or full job descriptions and provides a more accurate measure of relative job size or weight. A common method of evaluation is necessary. In the UK, market information sources are created on this basis by both Hay and Watson Wyatt. This approach will further increase the accuracy of comparisons but the degree of accuracy will depend on the quality of the job evaluation process. Consistency depends on quality assurance of the evaluation process, both within organizations and across participants.

Timings of market information publication and collection

The competitiveness of current salaries can only be established by finding out what other organizations are offering and paying now. Pay data can easily become stale when the market is moving erratically, and the time lag between the collection of data and their publication is commonly three months. To mitigate this problem, market information providers sometimes offer updated results or have moved to produce information that is updated more frequently in line with client needs. The specific date for which the pay information is applicable should always be clearly indicated and any assumptions made if information has been updated should be clearly explained. Wherever possible, data providers should set out the pattern of the salary review dates of the companies included in the research.

Increases from one publication to the next – the importance of matched samples

Market comparisons involve not only assessing current market rates but also trends in pay increases in order to indicate the going rate.

The percentage rise in average pay between successive surveys will be misleading because of changes in the sample of organizations and losses, gains or replacements in the sample of job holders.

The problem can be alleviated by matching the sample of organizations so that comparisons are only made for organizations participating in both publications. But this does not cover changes in job holders, and the most refined matching process will isolate increases for individuals who have remained in the same job between consecutive base dates – referred to as 'same incumbents movements analyses'. This measure, however, may not distinguish between increases arising from general pay reviews and individual incremental, merit or performance-related payments.

Interpreting average, median and quartile increases

Since many employers review all aspects of salaries only once a year, the increase compared with a year earlier in the average earnings of a group of employees in a sample will usually approximate to the weighted average of the increases granted. The same is true of medians, with some qualifications. But rarely is the increase during a yearly timeframe in the upper or lower quartiles of an information source the same as the upper or lower quartile of the increases granted. This is because groups that have lower-than-average increases one year may often secure an above-average increase in the following year to restore their position (which may well be below the median of the market). Organizations that implement pay freezes or give below-average increases continuously over a period of years tend to end up with salaries going right through the market floor. If an organization chooses to place its salaries in the lower quartile of the market and reaches this position by awarding a lower-quartile increase for a year or two, what then? To maintain salary levels at the lower quartile of the market (or indeed at any chosen fixed relativity), it may now need to offer near-to-average increases to keep up with others in the market. Otherwise salary levels will fall below even the reduced targets that have been set and will continue to do so indefinitely.

Presentation of market information

Analysed pay data can be presented in two ways:

1. *Measures of central tendency*, ie the point about which the several values cluster. These consist of:
   - The arithmetic mean or *average* (A), which is the total of the values of the items in the set divided by the number of individual items in the set. The average, can, however, be distorted by extreme values on either side of the centre.
   - The *median* (M), which is the middle item in the distribution of individual items – 50 per cent of the sample falls above the median, 50 per cent below. This is unaffected by extremes and is generally preferred to the arithmetical mean, as long as there is a sufficient number of individual items (the median of a sample much less than 10 is suspect). Medians are often lower than arithmetic means because of the tendency in the latter case for there to be a number of high values at the top of the range.
2. *Measures of dispersion*, ie the range of values in the set, which provides guidance on the variations in the distribution of values of items around the median. These consist of:
   - *The upper quartile* (UQ): also called the 75th percentile – the value above which 25 per cent of the individual values fall.

- *The lower quartile* (LQ): also called the 25th percentile – the value below which 25 per cent of the individual values fall.
- *The interquartile range:* the difference between the upper and lower quartile values; this is a good measure of dispersion.
- *Upper and lower deciles:* also called the 90th and 10th percentiles respectively – the values above and below which 10 per cent of the individual values fall. This is less frequently used but does provide for greater refinement in the analysis of distribution.
- *Total range:* the difference between the highest and lowest values. This can be misleading if there are extreme values at either end, and is less often used than the interquartile range, except where the sample is very small.

Presentation in tabular form

Data from information sources are usually presented in tabular form. Tabular formats should identify the job, the size of the sample and, where appropriate, may include analysis criteria such the size and type of organization and its location. An example is given in Table 14.1.

Table 14.1   Presentation of market data

Job title: Marketing Executive	LQ	M	UQ	Sample
Turnover (£m) 1–10				
Base salary	33,099	38,272	45,856	27
Total earnings	33,659	40,013	47,433	
Turnover (£m) 11–50				
Base salary	33,900	39,000	46,384	31
Total earnings	34,701	42,293	48,281	

An example of a layout of results of a survey is given in Table 14.2. This quotes the average gross pay for the job and gives tabulated details by companies of salary ranges and average salaries and bonuses.

Presentation in graphical form

The significance of the information can sometimes be revealed more clearly if the tables are supplemented by graphs, which can highlight significant data or trends as in the example in Figure 14.1.

In practice, there are many variations on these forms of presentation, now often produced from computer programs available in the market place. Further information on statistical terms used in pay surveys and analysis is given in Appendix C.

Table 14.2 Presentation of survey results

Disperson	Base salary £	Total cash £	Bonus £
90th	55,400	63,420	10,357
75th	51,964	54,756	8,064
50th	44,403	49,107	6,230
25th	39,913	42,036	4,605
10th	33,570	36,810	3,218
Average	45,457	49,097	6,659
No. of incumbents	101	101	67
No. of companies	38	38	17

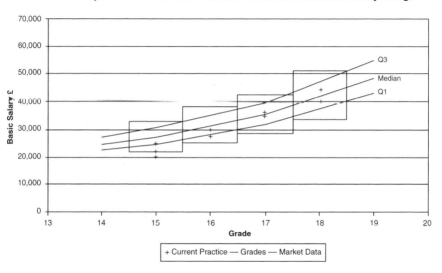

Figure 14.1 Graphical presentation of survey results

POLICY AND PRACTICE

A useful distinction to keep in mind when analysing and using market data information is that between 'policy' and 'practice'. An organization's reward policy can be defined as the various schemes, policies and rules that form the framework or guide for how an organization rewards its employees. Policy information is generally collected and analysed in questionnaire format. An organization's reward practice is the pay, benefits and other remuneration elements that each individual employee in each role within an organization receives. Practice information is generally collected in spreadsheet rather than questionnaire format.

Company and pay data commonly collected/presented

Policy

▮ company name;
▮ sector/industry type;
▮ number of employees;
▮ annual sales turnover or other financial measures;
▮ salary ranges – minimum/maximum/mid-point;
▮ salary review dates.

Practice

Data by job:

▮ job title/code;
▮ number of incumbents;
▮ modifier (+, = or _) used to indicate the relationship of the organization's job to that chosen for matching;
▮ average actual basic salary/total cash;
▮ median actual basic salary/total cash;
▮ highest actual basic salary/total cash;
▮ lowest actual basic salary/total cash;
▮ target bonus.

All surveys collect salary data, but the information collected on cash
additions to basic pay and fringe benefits varies greatly. Specialist
market data providers collect and analyse a comprehensive range of
benefits side by side with salary data. This allows a greater picture of
reward packages to be given, for example total remuneration/reward
values can be calculated and used to provide analyses that cover both
pay and benefits elements.

PUBLISHED MARKET DATA SOURCES

The impact of new technologies on market data sources

The development of IT technologies is clearly a significant contributing
factor to the increased variety of market information now available for
organizations to consider. The standard use of computer programs,
ranging from standard office programs, such as spreadsheets and databases, to the use of e-mail and the Internet as a medium for delivering
and sourcing information, is a development that has changed the ways
in which market data providers present and deliver information to organizations.

Changes to the format and delivery of market data

A key example of changes in market data format is the relative demise of the survey book format. Until recent years, the salary survey – commonly a paper-based book containing static tables and graphs of pre-chosen market information – was the most common format of published market data available. While the survey format still exists, paper publication is increasingly being replaced by electronic formats such as standard computer spreadsheet formats or pdf document formats that can be delivered directly via e-mail or published on and downloaded from Web sites.

The existence and growth of electronic and interactive data formats is clearly due to the now standard use of computer technology within reward practice. Therefore, receiving data and information in a format that is at least compatible with (if not able to link into and transmit data to and receive data from) in-house HR and other organizational systems – eg SAP and PeopleSoft – is a necessary requirement for many market data users.

Interactive market data sources

Examples of interactive market data that combine new technology in both data format and delivery are services such as Hay Group's Hay PayNet and Watson Wyatt's Reward. This generation of data sources enables participant users to access and tailor market data analyses from a large database rather than ordering pre-designed, standard analyses delivered in a static survey format. Interactive market data sources provide the user with the choice of different analysis criteria and concepts so that they can receive data outputs against their chosen criteria presented in the concepts required by their reward policy. There is also ability to choose the specific breadth and depth of the data for an analysis – from a single job, to a set of functionally specific roles to a whole family of jobs against a market defined by industry, turnover, etc – depending upon the specific contents of the database. Data can also be transferred to wider HR systems, downloaded from and input into such systems for comparison capability and stored within the interactive plat-form itself by multiple users from an organization.

The increasing interactivity of market data sources has enabled reward specialists to develop their own analytical skills in the arena of obtaining market data and in comparing their own organizational data against other data sources. In the same way that the use of specific HR systems is now a recognized skill on HR CVs, the use of leading market data sources as well as the associated analysis skills is becoming an increasingly recognized and marketable skill.

Interactive capabilities and data quality

While technology has developed the format and delivery of market data, the technological sophistication of a particular system and the interactive capabilities it possesses should not be chosen over the quality of the data that is delivered. When choosing a market data source it is vital to evaluate the interactive possibilities of the system itself but above all to focus on the suitability of the data for the purpose it will be used for. Within this changing market, principles for assessing the suitability of the market data to the organization's requirements must still be firmly established – perhaps including the additional considerations of new and improving technology and its impact on choice of format, delivery medium and ease of use and interpretation.

Evaluating market data source/survey reliability

Market information sources can be further distinguished as being either those produced by Hay Group, Computer Economics, Watson Wyatt and Towers Perrin, which are available only to participants, or those sources available 'over the counter' (eg Monks, Remuneration Economics and Reward). Whichever type is being investigated, it is advisable to ensure that they will meet your requirements for relevant information. Their potential value as a reliable information source can be evaluated with the help of the following checklist:

1. *Source*
   Who created the data source:
   - a firm of general/specialist management consultants;
   - a recognized organization specializing in salary and benefits surveys;
   - an employment agency;
   - an employers' association;
   - a professional body;
   - a trade union;
   - the government or one of its agencies;
   - a company/employer wishing to exchange salary data;
   - a specialist or other journal?
2. *Database*
   What are the data based on:
   - actual salaries paid to matched jobs or responsibility levels;
   - average salaries for jobs/grades/levels;
   - estimated market price given by employers where no direct job match has been made;
   - recruitment salaries – offered, asked or paid;
   - annual company report data based on audited earnings for the previous financial year;
   - informed opinion?

3. *Sample composition*
   Who participated:
   - other organizations similar to or competing directly with the user;
   - individual members of professional bodies or trade unions?
   Are there:
   - enough participants to provide acceptable comparisons assuming that the methods of collection and analysis are effective;
   - matched samples of participants either on the basis of the same individuals doing the same jobs or the same companies from year to year?
4. *Data collection*
   How were the data collected:
   - personal collection by the data producer to discuss job matching and current salary issues for the jobs in question;
   - postal, online or telephone questionnaires (with what response rate?);
   - from employers or job holders directly;
   - input on to a well-designed, clearly explained questionnaire?
5. *Job matching*
   How accurately are survey benchmark jobs or levels of responsibility matched:
   - against job titles;
   - against 'capsule' job descriptions or rank definitions with provisions for separating those with more or less responsibility than the core definition;
   - against full job descriptions/definitions of responsibility level;
   - by using an agreed measure of 'job size', eg the same method of job evaluation used by all participants with checks on the consistency of grading an application?
6. *Timing*
   How up to date are the salary data?
   - What is the distribution of salary review dates among participants? Are data on this provided?
   - Are data correct on a given salary date or given over a defined period, eg three months?
   - How much time has elapsed between data collection and the publication/circulation of results?
7. *Presentation*
   - Full details of sample composition and response rate;
   - tables listing average, median, upper and lower quartiles (or other quartiles such as octiles and deciles);
   - lists or bar charts/scattergrams of the raw data from which the summary analyses are calculated; coded by size/type of organization to allow more detailed analysis; giving current scales/ranges/actual salaries where not too commercially sensitive;

- analyses by company size, industry, location or other relevant factors;
- regression lines to give a 'feel' for market position; if so, is the sample or substance basis clearly explained?

8. *Increase data*

How valid is the information provided on pay increases (often hard to interpret?)?
- Is it based on matched samples of individuals in the same job year on year/organizations participating in the same research?
- Do the percentage increases quoted include performance or contribution awards, bonuses, cost of living adjustments, or a combination of these, and how well is this explained?
- Is the basis for calculation made clear?

9. *Other data*

What else do the data contain:
- details of major benefits/entitlements;
- amounts/types of incentives/profit-sharing payments;
- details of salary administration policy;
- a commentary on current developments including special areas of market pressure or other major influences, written by someone able to interpret the data effectively?

10. *Cost*

Is it worth its price in terms of:
- savings in company/personnel resources required to obtain equivalent data;
- the time/effort involved in participation?

11. *Integrity of market data producers*

Does the producer maintain consistent and professional standards? Does the market data provider:
- state when samples are too small to provide useful analysis and define the point at which this is reached;
- show ability to adapt/improve in response to changing market demands;
- include the availability of advice on the interpretation of the data, and is this available free/for a fee;
- give good value for money?

12. *Purpose*

Why were the market data collected:
- as part of the producer's sole business activity;
- as an occasional/major part of other business/consultancy activities;
- to provide other organizations/individuals with data on a particular sector of the market;
- to put forward a point of view;
- to attract press coverage?

GENERAL PUBLISHED MARKET DATA

There are many types, formats and mediums of market data, but the quality of data they provide varies enormously. Both the *Executive Compensation Review* of Incomes Data Services (IDS) and the *Pay and Benefits Bulletin* published by Industrial Relations Services (IRS) publish regular reviews of market data sources and analyses of the trend data they contain. Incomes Data Services also publishes a *Directory of Salary Surveys* every couple of years, which is essentially a consumer's guide to the whole of the survey market. IDS and IRS also analyse pay settlements and pay trends for all types of employees.

GENERAL MARKET DATA SOURCE CONTENTS

General market surveys, such as those produced by Hay Group, Remuneration Economics, Monks, PE International, Reward, Watson Wyatt and Towers Perrin are based on data collected from as large a number of participating organizations as they can attract – typically from clients and by contacting large numbers of employers. Outputs – from static survey format to interactive data analyses – can display base salary and total earnings levels paid on a given date and a certain amount of data on benefits entitlements. Most producers also provide data on annual salary movement. Sources tend to present data grouped by job title and function, and by job size or level of responsibility in relation to company size and type. The most usual company analyses are by industrial sector and size, in terms of annual sales turnover and number of employees. Interactive data sources, such as Hay Group's Hay PayNet and Mercer's Pay Monitor provide the organization with the ability to tailor analysis outputs to include a variety of analysis criteria.

Regional, local and sector considerations

Most data sources include some indication of regional variations and can be expected to add to this, given the interest in regional pay difference for jobs where local market influences are more important than national trends. Clerical and shop-floor jobs that are recruited using local sources need local salary analyses to give an acceptable picture of the market – especially among smaller organizations. National data will always be needed, however, for jobs that are recruited on a national basis. It is important to remember that, where for instance there appear to be regional differences in management pay, this will almost always turn out on deeper analysis to be related to the size of the job and nature, age and culture of the industry rather than just the location.

Traditional engineering companies tend to pay less than their high-tech counterparts and they tend to be located in different parts of the country. They may often not demand the same academic background and level of skills from the managers they employ. Nor, sadly, are some of them in a position to afford higher salaries for better-qualified managers able to improve profitability through innovation and improved financial management, other than in exceptional cases.

TAILORED MARKET DATA SOURCES

Market data providers can be asked, at a price, to extract data relating to particular firms that participated in a data source. These data are, of course, anonymous, and are only made available if a reasonable number of firms are involved. They can be very helpful if you want more specific information about your own industry. In the same vein, interactive data sources such as Hay Group's Hay PayNet allow an organization to create a 'peer group' of companies that they consistently wish to compare themselves against – defined by similarity of size, industry, location, job types alone or in combination – and then run tailored analyses for the group on an ongoing basis. By isolating the data of peer organizations, particular trends and market movements relevant to an organization can be tracked on an ongoing basis. Again, the data themselves are anonymous and are only made available if a reasonable number of firms and corresponding data exist.

SPECIALIZED PROFESSIONAL, INDUSTRIAL OR LOCAL SURVEYS

There are three basic types:

1. Analyses of members' salaries conducted by professional institutions; local or national market surveys of particular industrial groups produced by employers or trade associations.
2. Local or national market studies carried out regularly or on a one-off basis by consultants, either for a single employer or for a group of organizations that may share the cost (a multi-client study).
3. Professional institute surveys are usually more concerned with providing salary data in relation to age, qualification and membership status than they are with placing members in their organizational context. They therefore provide useful salary profiles and salary movement data, but are often of little help when it comes to looking at an individual's place in the company reporting structure in relation to particular sizes and types of organization. Some are

now including analyses by function and level of responsibility within the organization, but the relevance and clarity of the definitions should be looked at carefully. They should, therefore, mainly be used as an additional check on more specific salary data from which real job comparisons should be clearly identifiable.

These professional institute survey findings are widely read by their members, who may seek to use them either as individuals or through their unions as a negotiating base for salary improvements. If this occurs, it is essential to be familiar with the particular survey quoted and aware of any limitations in the validity of the data. If it does not correlate well with more specific salary market data, the reasons should be analysed and explained. There may be distortions caused by the inclusion, for example, of members who are high-flyers and have reached director status early in their careers, too large a proportion of members working for highly paid consultancies or multinationals, members who have moved on to more highly/lowly paid areas outside the specialism, or those who are 'blocked' within an organization because performance or unwillingness to move or take extra responsibility holds them back.

The surveys conducted by employers and trade associations deal mainly with jobs specific to their industry for which reliable outside salary data often do not exist. They cover a limited market and are useful because they can be very specific about job definitions and organization structures for the staff covered. Often they are only available to participating organizations who may then share the cost of data collection and analysis. They may be local or national and by no means all are produced regularly. It may often be worth checking with the trade association appropriate to the company whether surveys of this kind are likely to be produced before special company market surveys are undertaken.

Employers who have neither the time nor in-house expertise to conduct their own market studies are increasingly opting to commission consultants to carry out this task. The approach used is usually very similar to that outlined in the section below on company surveys, and consultants involved in this sort of exercise will need to be briefed accordingly. The choice of appropriate consultants for this type of 'one-off' study should be based on firm evidence of expertise in the field of market data provision and a good level of understanding of the personnel philosophy and market posture of the commissioning employer.

COMPANY SURVEYS

These are surveys conducted by a company approaching others to exchange comparative salary information on a 'one-off' basis. Company surveys can be conducted with or without the help of consultants. The use of consultants provides for expertise and confidentiality in the collection and analysis of data and saves time, but can, of course, be expensive.

Company surveys can be as simple or sophisticated as required. They can be as quick and cheap as simple confidential 'pricings' or exchanges of information over the telephone with established contacts willing to exchange data, or a fully fledged study of pay and benefits that is coded and circulated to all participants.

The principle advantage of the one-off company salary survey is that it is 'bespoke'. The company alone decides which jobs it needs to study and which of its local or national competitors should be invited to participate. This should, in theory, produce the best possible comparative data. The main drawback is the time it takes to complete this kind of exercise and the cost and organizational implications of taking staff away from other work while the survey is in progress.

Because of the time, effort and cost of running company surveys, there are advantages in joining or setting up a salary club. The methods used to plan and conduct a company survey are basically similar to those adopted by salary clubs, as described below. The sequence of activities is illustrated in Figure 14.2.

SALARY CLUB SURVEYS

Clubs may be administered either by management consultants or by companies themselves. Clubs tend to operate in single industries, although some cover a range of industries – a survey of 'blue-chip' companies, for instance. Many cover all managerial and professional grades, although there are those that cover only one employee category – graduates or accountants, for example, within one industry. When a single employee category is chosen, this will normally be because there is strong competition for people with skills that are in demand, eg accountants or software engineers.

Club surveys – checklist

Membership criteria

▌ Which types of company will be eligible for membership? Will they:
  - all be in the same business, ie competitors;
  - all be of similar size and type, eg all blue-chip;
  - all be in the same area;
  - all have similar parentage, eg all subsidiaries of US multinationals?

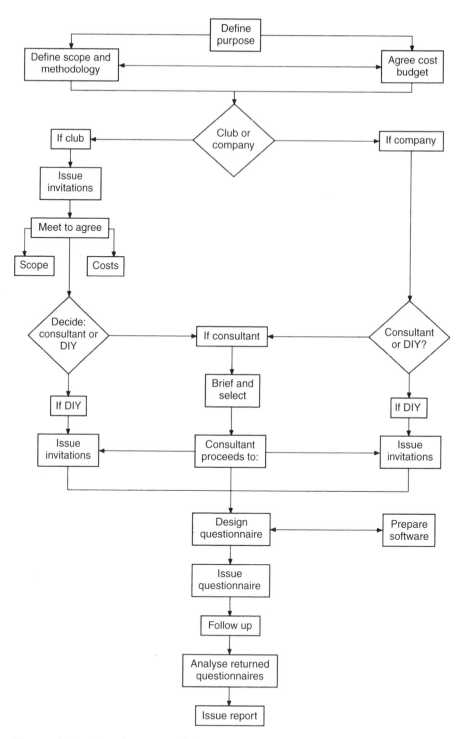

Figure 14.2 Conducting a club or company survey

▌ Will separate parts of the same company be allowed to participate or will only aggregate data be accepted? How will decentralized companies be treated?

▌ Will there be a pre-set minimum and maximum number of participants?

▌ Who will decide on requests to join the club from companies that are 'qualified' to do so? Will existing members have a veto?

▌ Will membership be restricted to companies that are able to provide data on a specified minimum number of jobs?

▌ Will it be possible to expel a club member if it transgresses club rules?

Collecting the data

▌ Who will collect the data:
  – one of the members;
  – a combinations of members;
  – a consultant?

▌ How frequently will a survey be conducted?
  – annually;
  – every six months/quarterly;
  – on a rolling basis as pay reviews happen?

▌ How will accurate jobs matching (pricing) be ensured? By:
  – using summary job descriptions/role profiles;
  – using an agreed form of job evaluation/sizing (eg Hay Group or Watson Wyatt);
  – personal visits to participants to discuss differences in job scope and other problems;
  – a 'regular audit' of job matching?

▌ Will a postal questionnaire be used to collect data, or a personal visit/interview or an e-mail containing spreadsheet and questionnaire data to be submitted via e-mail or via a secure Web site?

▌ What data will you collect:
  – basic actual salaries of individuals in post;
  – salary ranges;
  – incentive/bonus payments;
  – other cash additions to pay;
  – share options and profit-sharing payments;
  – fringe benefits including pension, death-in-service provisions, cars, medical insurance, loans etc?

▌ Will the survey be 'open' or 'closed', ie will participants be able to identify the salary ranges or the salaries paid by other members?

▌ Will all grades of employee be included in the same survey, or will separate surveys be conducted for manual, non-manual, professional and managerial grades?

▌ Is a 100 per cent response rate expected? What sanction will the club impose if members fail to provide data?

Analysing and presenting the results

▌ Which analysis format/program will be used?
▌ Which medium of distribution will be used?
▌ Will actual salaries and salary ranges be listed by company (using a simple number code) in rank order?
▌ What statistical analyses will be produced from the aggregate data:
  – averages;
  – medians;
  – quartiles (if large enough sample)?
  – interquartiles (if large enough sample).
▌ Should these be related to individuals' salaries, company averages/medians, or salary range mid-points?
▌ Will any significant regression or correlation tests be made on the statistical results?
▌ How will the results of the club survey be compared with general data on salaries, from commercial surveys etc?
▌ Will club members be charged a fee to cover the cost of analysing the results and producing the survey report

Setting up the salary club

The establishment of a salary club may start from a more informal exchange of salary information between two or more organizations that employ similar types of staff. A club may be the result of individual initiatives by one or two compensation specialists within companies. In some industries, the computer industry for example, there is more regular exchange of salary information than in others. Some consultants specialize in club survey work in certain industrial groups. If the target group is sufficiently finely defined, as for example in the international banking sector and the pharmaceutical industry, then not only is a homogeneous group of employees being surveyed, but also a very high proportion of the potential numbers of participants will probably take part.

Approaching companies

The exchange of accurate, up-to-date salary information depends on mutual trust. This will exist among established contacts but this relationship has to be carefully built up when individuals are contacted for the first time. This can be done over the telephone but, unless the person responsible for the survey has a particularly confident and persuasive telephone manner, a carefully drafted letter or email giving background material may be a better approach. Letters/emails may in any case be preferable because the recipient then has time to consider carefully whether it is worth participating and is unlikely to make a snap decision based on a single conversation. Letters/emails may be ignored, but this problem is reduced if they are worded properly, and participant rates can be boosted by following up with a telephone call. The subsequent offer of a personal visit or invitation to a forum meeting is an additional way in which relationships between organizations can be built.

In any invitation to an unknown company the messages that have to be communicated are that:

- a responsible individual/consultant is conducting the survey;
- the survey will be carried out competently and in confidence;
- the information collected and shared will be relevant, up to date and useful;
- the company will not be put to too much trouble.

Which jobs to include

The major advantage of running a club is that participants to the survey know who the other participants are and that their data are relevant. When members of the same club are in the same industrial sector they may be thought of as competitors for the same type of staff in the same salary market. This is particularly true for managers and specialists whose skills are easily transferable from one company to another in a similar line of business. At managerial level, members of the same club typically employ a rather homogeneous group of staff in terms of the experience required, the demands of the job and their qualifications. Some clubs exchange salary information only on managerial and specialist grades, eg from first-line to senior management, while others cover technical and professional grades, clerical or indeed only manual employees.

Job matching and pricing

Club surveys offer a potentially better quality of job matching than industry-wide market data research covering very heterogeneous groups. Most salary clubs take great care over this stage of their research.

A typical approach to assist the matching process is to circulate a profile job description for each job to participants. This will contain the job title, a brief description of the job's responsibilities, reporting level, supervisory responsibility (number of subordinates), together with the typical age and/or experience and qualifications an incumbent of such a job might have. An example of a profile job description used in market data analysis is given in the box below.

HR/Workforce Planning Manager

General characteristics

Develops and implements systems and programs for identifying and describing the human resource pool that is available to the organization. This position is often occupied by an individual contributor who is an expert in the design and implementation of systems. Although these systems may vary in their degree of sophistication, this incumbent must have a thorough understanding of the business, its strategy, its people requirements and its resources.

Representative activities

▌ Analyse business plan and develop forecasts of human resource requirement.
▌ Identify human resource shortages and surplus of talent to meet strategic needs.
▌ Identify data elements to be included in the human resource inventory system.
▌ Develop systems to collect and maintain current data.
▌ Develop candidate lists for vacant positions.
▌ Maintain inventory of key personnel.
▌ Monitor data input.

The key to success in any salary club survey lies in accurate job matching, a process demanding painstaking work and eternal vigilance. The wholesale regrading of a set of jobs in one or two organizations could potentially throw the results of an otherwise useful survey. The communication of changes in internal relativities is essential to the reliability of survey results. A regular audit is desirable to keep track of company regradings of jobs and to ensure they are still being matched with similar jobs in other companies.

Where individual jobs cannot be matched, organizations may be asked to price them. This involves assessing the relative worth of a job in relation to other jobs carrying similar responsibilities in areas or grades where reasonable comparisons can be made.

Salary data collection

The options for both the distribution and collection of data have expanded due to the development of IT technologies over recent years. Both standard office and specialist software and programs can be utilized to save time and smooth the process of distribution and collection. Examples include the distribution and collection of data via e-mailed spreadsheets and questionnaires and the utilization of fax and telephone interviews to collect data. Recently, the ability for organizations to input both their questionnaire and salary data via secure Web sites has been developed. Mediums and formats for distribution and collection should be chosen because of their ability to ease and speed these processes rather than because they are currently seen as the most high-tech and innovative. It is important to take into account the relationship with and the technological capabilities of the participating organizations when choosing the medium and format in which the data will be collected, analysed and distributed. In many cases opting for more than one option of distribution and collection medium and format will yield higher participation rates and work more effectively.

Collection will be made easier if clear instructions are included with any questionnaire/spreadsheet distributed, as this will provide them with a full picture of what is expected of them. It is also important to include clear indications of where guidance and assistance in completing any materials can be found. Clear, informative instructions coupled with a well-worded cover letter that clearly sets out the necessary return date and offers help with completion can greatly improve participation levels and quality.

Support is especially important when organizations are carrying out their own job matching. The need for accuracy of job matching needs to be carefully considered and monitored and the relevant and necessary support offered to all participants. It is always worth telephoning companies that have not yet returned responses a few days before the deadline to check whether or not the questionnaire has arrived safely or whether there are any problems with job matching that need to be ironed out. In these circumstances the companies may have to be visited to deliver new questionnaires and to collect the comparative data on the spot. However inconvenient this is, it should greatly improve the scope and quality of the data collected. Building time into any schedule to assist with completion and submission of data materials and for late submissions should be considered.

Club surveys, unlike many commercial surveys, collect information not only on actual salaries, but also on salary ranges. Questionnaires are used and, typically, there are number codes for each company and for each job category covered.

The calculation of benefits, and the assignment of a value to them for comparative analysis purposes, can be important in gaining accurate and appropriate results depending upon the jobs and roles being analysed. Therefore, many club surveys include at least a basic coverage of benefits in the information collected.

An example of the company information and the detailed fringe benefit data collected by one club survey is given below:

▮ *General company information:* number of employees, annual sales turnover;

▮ *Salary increases:* general increases (timing and last percentage increase), and individual increases (criteria and timing);

▮ *Graduate starting salaries:* basic salary plus bonus, projection for the next year;

▮ *Incentive/bonus schemes:* basis of payment, employees qualifying for payment, frequency and amount of payment;

▮ *Overtime premiums:* for managers, monthly and professional staff, and weekly paid staff;

▮ *Shift premiums in relation to shiftwork patterns;*

▮ *Company cars:* for business need or status, engine size (benchmark car), private petrol paid, and charges for private use;

▮ *Payment for use of employees' own cars:* mileage allowances by car engine size;

▮ *Regional and occupational allowances:* London allowances, telephone and professional institute expenses;

▮ *Relocation expenses – new employees:* disturbance, removal, temporary housing allowances plus bridging loan facilities;

▮ *Travel and accident insurance:* in the UK and overseas;

▮ *Private medical insurance:* insurer, category covered, proportion paid by the company and type of cover;

▮ *Pension scheme:* type, ie final salary or money purchase, employer and employee contribution rates, escalation of pensions in payment and ex gratia supplements;

▮ *Pension scheme – benefits:* entitlement per year of service (fraction), definition of salary used for pension calculations, contracted in or out, and life assurance provisions;

▮ *Pension scheme – additional benefits:* death in service, early retirement, partners' and dependants' pensions provisions;

▮ *Sick pay entitlements;*

▮ *Long-term disability absence:* salary continuation entitlements;

▮ *Call-out and stand-by payments and premiums;*

▮ *Holiday entitlements:* standard entitlement and additional service days;

▮ *Subsistence allowance:* for short and long stays on company business;

▮ *Overtime pay for travel:* differentials between hourly paid and salaried staff;

▮ *Share options:* entitlements by seniority;

▮ *Profit sharing:* basis, annual percentage paid (including profit-related pay under the 1987 Finance Act provisions).

Analysing and presenting the results

As survey returns come in, they should be checked carefully to ensure that acceptable matching or pricing has been given for each job. Any doubtful figures should be referred back to participants and discussed with them. Where comparisons turn out not to be close enough to be acceptable, the data should be rejected – preferably with the agreement of the participant concerned.

Salary club surveys can generally be processed very quickly and participants typically expect a report within a month of sending in their returns. Strict deadlines usually have to be set and enforced (see above) to ensure this is possible. Whoever is responsible for the survey should also ensure that the analysis can begin as soon as all returns have come in and been checked.

The methods used in the analysis and presentation of survey results will depend on the number of returns received and the degree of sophistication in salary policy of both the survey producer and the participants. It can therefore vary from simple histograms (bar charts) showing salary scales or actual ranges paid by participants and coded company by company, to complex statistical analyses that present the data in relation to a number of different variables. In selecting which forms of analysis will yield the most meaningful results and present the data in a way that helps the salary policy decision-making process, it helps to concentrate on what the data are actually based on and who will use the findings. For example, rigorous analysis techniques such as regression analysis are not appropriate for smaller data samples. However, for data based on large samples such techniques have their value and can be used to effect. What matters most is presenting the available and relevant market data in a way that shows what the actual operating salary range is for any given job – and where the extremes of practice lie as well as the mid-point – backed by a brief commentary on the underlying influences affecting the distribution.

A more detailed set of definitions of the statistical terms used in such analyses is given in Appendix C. In some data sources, the salaries for each job category are typically listed by company code, in rank order of the total cash earnings, actual base salary or salary range mid-points. Other information that might be provided is the 'compa-ratio' in each salary range for each company, matching the company average salary to the mid-point of the salary range.

Confidentiality

Although the company compensation specialist or consultant who processes the survey results will have access to the individual company codes, it is necessary for each club to decide whether all club members should have this facility or not. Knowing which code applies to which company would mean that comprehensive information about participants' salary ranges and actual salaries in payment would be available to each participant. Pay data are sensitively guarded both by individual organizations and specialist market data providers and it is now rare for newly established salary clubs to take a transparent route to publishing survey results.

Response rate

Club surveys usually expect a 100 per cent response rate. Failure to provide data normally means expulsion from the club, except in mitigating circumstances. However, it may be necessary for the club to set a minimum response rate for each job category – there is little point in a company joining a club collecting data on 60 categories if they only employ one or two of these, as they are going to lower the general response rate for particular jobs.

PUBLISHED DATA IN JOURNALS

Apart from the summaries of published market data findings that appear at various times in the business press, there are two major sources of company and public sector salary data. Both Incomes Data Services and Industrial Relations Services monitor wage and salary settlements and publish details of agreements as soon as they are made. A great deal of staff and management salary information is available because companies have shown willingness to contribute data in order to benefit from the detailed analysis of trends these organizations provide.

Both sources also comment on economic trends and analyse the effects of any government policy affecting pay. An enquiry service is part of the subscription.

Other useful sources of trend information are the government's *Labour Force Survey* and *New Earnings Survey* as well as government and union Web sites. It is also worth checking specialist information in journals such as *Taxation* to monitor the changing effects of tax on higher earnings where this might affect management remuneration policy. Newspaper coverage of surveys and major pay awards is also worth monitoring. These days few pay and benefits specialists can avoid monitoring the *Financial Times* and Sunday papers with reputable business news sections. Where resources permit, it is worth setting up press coverage files for key jobs or function and techniques, both to monitor the market and to ensure that those responsible for reward management see the same articles as the executives who may ask questions relating to them and require an immediate response on policy options.

ANALYSIS OF JOB ADVERTISEMENTS

The analysis of job advertisements seems to be an attractive approach, especially taking into account the profusion of job Web sites and recruitment agency surveys in the current market. It appeals to line managers pressing for scope to pay more money to the staff. They have a habit of collecting a biased sample of advertisements and presenting them to HR as proof that their staff are seriously underpaid and are likely to leave tomorrow. They have to be persuaded that the information is unreliable for the reasons stated below and steered in the direction of better data.

The problems include racily phrased job descriptions used in the hope of attracting high-calibre applicants that are not usually precise enough to allow accurate comparisons with real jobs. Salary levels are often 'by negotiation' (often a sign of undeveloped salary policy) or they may be overstated or inflated because the company is desperate. Even where a salary scale is quoted in full this may not be the range within which the vacancy is ultimately filled. A quick check of main national newspapers/Web sites will reveal that the salaries on offer for jobs described as 'finance director' show an enormous variation. This normally rules out useful application of the data other than as an indication of trends, though it has some value if the prospective employer is named and offers supplementary – if suspect – additions to information derived from more reliable sources.

Similar problems occur in using information provided by employment agencies. Specialist agencies may, however, have a good 'feel' for salaries in the particular areas they cover. They may therefore be worth consulting where the company is already a regular and satisfied client, and when the agencies' expertise in the area is known.

OTHER MARKET INTELLIGENCE

Setting salary levels is not, as we have shown, just about the scientific application of survey statistics. Monitoring salary markets also involves gleaning facts and opinions from personal contacts. It means building up a network of reliable people with whom trends and innovations can be discussed and insights shared, and developing a 'nose' for what currently influences pay. Job adverts for salary specialists now often specify that candidates should have a good knowledge of practice in the potential employer's industry. And most effective managers responsible for pay have built up a network of contacts to ensure they know what is going on in their sector and which factors are likely to affect pay levels for all the different types of jobs involved.

Talking to informal contacts, exchanging experience and testing out ideas are valuable supplements to the more informal activities of salary clubs. It happens over the telephone and is a common activity at conferences on pay and related issues, CIPD branch meetings and similar gatherings. Over time, the information acquired by this means can considerably sharpen an individual's 'feel' for what is going on in the salary market.

The sorts of questions you can ask are:

▌ What level are you currently paying your junior financial analyst (those with less than two years' experience)?
▌ What is the increase you believe you will have to pay to your product managers this year to keep pace with the market place?
▌ What would you need to offer in the shape of a total remuneration package to attract a really good legal executive?
▌ What rates of pay are graduate members of your profession getting two years after qualification?
▌ At what level of salary are you having to offer a company car?
▌ What do you think the trends in salary levels are likely to be for members of your profession who have executive appointments below board level in industry?
▌ What is happening to the demand for production managers in your industry sector and what impact is that having on market rates?

One of the reasons why companies employ consultants to carry out salary surveys rather than do the work in-house is because good consultants will have extensive networks of contacts, which they will use not just to get a good sample of participants but to talk to discreetly about market influences. This should enable them to explore, for instance, recruitment pressures and special inducements and incentives, and to track strategies and examples of new payment systems that might be of relevance in interpreting survey data and developing remuneration strategy.

ADVANTAGES AND DISADVANTAGES OF DATA SOURCES

The advantages and disadvantages of each source are as follows:

▌ Published market data sources
Advantages: wide coverage, readily available, continuity allows trend analyses over time.
Disadvantages: quickly out of date, risk of imprecise job matching, not specific enough.
▌ Published specialist surveys
Advantages: deal with particular categories in depth, quality of job matching better than general surveys, more sensitive to measuring key trends and hot topics.
Disadvantages: job matching not entirely precise, can quickly become out of date, only deal with particular sectors.

▮ Club surveys

Advantages: more precise job and company matching, can provide more detail on pay structure and benefits.

Disadvantages: sample size may be too small, relies on good will of participants to conduct survey.

▮ Company or 'do-it-yourself' surveys

Advantages: precise job matching, control of participants, control of analysis concepts, and acquisition of previously unavailable information.

Disadvantages: time and trouble, problem of building a large enough sample.

▮ Published data in journals

Advantages: readily accessible, good background data.

Disadvantages: not necessarily comprehensive, job matching imprecise.

▮ Analysis of job advertisements

Advantages: readily accessible, highly visible indications of market rates and trends, up to date.

Disadvantages: job matching very imprecise, salary data can be misleading.

▮ Other market intelligence

Advantages: good background.

Disadvantages: imprecise.

SELECTING DATA SOURCES

If time and budget permit, more than one source should be used to extend the range of data and provide back-up information.

General market data can be supplemented by specialist surveys covering particular jobs. A company-administered survey or a salary club can provide information on local market rates. If the quality of job matching is important, an individual survey can be conducted or a salary club can be formed. If a salary club already exists it can be joined, if there is room (some clubs are over-subscribed). Published surveys, which are readily accessible and are based on a large sample, can be used to back up individual or club surveys. But the information has to be relevant to the needs of the organization and particular attention should always be paid to the range of data and the quality of job matching.

Market intelligence and published data from journals and associated sources should always be used as back-up material and for information on going rates and trends. They can provide invaluable help with updating.

Although the analysis of job advertisements has its dangers, it can be used as further back-up, or to give an instant snapshot of current rates, but it is risky to rely on this source alone.

USING MARKET DATA

The translation of salary market data into competitive salary levels for individuals, or into an acceptable company salary structure, is a process based on judgement and compromise. The aim is to extract a derived market rate based on informed and effective estimates of the reliability of data. It means striking a reasonable balance between the competing merits of the different sources used. This is essentially an intuitive process. Once all the data available have been collected and presented in the most accessible manner possible (ie job by job for all the areas the structure is to cover), a proposed scale mid-point or 'spot' salary/rate has to be established for each level based on the place in the market the company wishes to occupy, ie its 'market posture'. The establishment of this mid-point will be based not only on assessment of current and updated salary data, but also on indications of movements in earnings and the cost of living that are likely to affect the life of the whole structure. For organizations needing to stay ahead of the market, this point will often be between the median and the upper quartile (of a significant population). For others, closer alignment with the median is adequate. Once the series of mid-points in relation to the market has been established and assessed, the principles of salary structure construction set out in Chapter 16 can be applied.

It has to be recognized that market data can rapidly become out of date. To ensure that you stay ahead of the market, or at least do not lag behind it, it may be advisable to attempt to forecast how rates will increase over the next year. This can be done by extrapolating trends and analysing economic forecasts. Inevitably, there is an element of guesswork involved and the forecasts have to be treated with caution. But they at least give you some guidance on where salaries are likely to move and what you should do about it.

Part 4

Grade and Pay Structures

15

Types of Grade and Pay Structures

Grade and pay structures provide the framework for managing pay although grade structures are increasingly used as part of non-financial reward processes by mapping career paths without any direct reference to the pay implications. The usual outcome of a formal job evaluation programme is a new or revised grade structure, which together with market rate intelligence provides the basis for designing and managing pay structures. This chapter starts by defining grade and pay structures and goes on to a discussion of their rationale and the criteria for assessing their effectiveness. The different types of grade and pay structures are then described and the choice between them and the design options are examined.

DEFINITIONS

Grade structures

A grade structure consists of a sequence or hierarchy of grades, bands or levels into which groups of jobs that are broadly comparable in size are placed. There may be a single structure with a sequence of narrow grades (often 8 to 12), or relatively few broad bands (often 4 to 5). Alternatively, the structure may consist of a number of career or job families each divided typically into 6 to 8 levels (a career or job family structure groups jobs with similar characteristics together).

The grades, bands or levels may be defined in one or other of the following ways or a combination of them:

- by means of a range of job evaluation points – jobs are allocated to a grade, band or level if their job evaluation scores fall within a range or bracket of points;
- in words that describe the characteristics of the work carried out in the jobs that are positioned in each grade or level – these grade, band or level definitions may set out the key activities and the competences or knowledge and skills required at different points in the hierarchy;
- by reference to benchmark jobs or roles that have already been placed in the grade, band or job family level.

Pay structures

Pay structures provide a framework for managing pay. A grade structure becomes a pay structure when pay ranges or brackets are defined for each grade, band or level, or when grades are attached to a pay spine. In some broadbanded structures, reference points and pay zones may be placed within the bands and these define the range of pay for jobs allocated to each band.

Graded, broadbanded or family structures:

- contain the organization's pay ranges or scales for jobs grouped into grades, bands or job family levels;
- define the different levels of pay for jobs or groups of jobs by reference to their relative internal value as determined by job evaluation, to external relativities as established by market rate surveys and, where appropriate, to negotiated rates for jobs;
- provide scope for pay progression in accordance with performance, competence, contribution or service.

Pay spines consist of a hierarchy of pay or spinal column points between which there are pay increments and to which are attached grades.

There may be a single pay structure covering the whole organization or there may be one structure for staff and another for manual workers, but this is becoming less common. There has in recent years been a trend towards 'harmonizing' terms and conditions between different groups of staff. This has been particularly evident in many public sector organizations in the UK, supported by national agreements on 'single status'. In the private sector too, it is important to consider why there may be differences between the pay arrangements for different groups of employees and to ensure that, where these exist, the risk of equal pay claims is minimized.

Executive directors are sometimes treated separately where reward policy for them is decided by a remuneration committee of non-executive directors (see Chapter 35, 'Boardroom Pay').

Spot rates

'Spot rates' may be used for some jobs, often those at senior management levels or those not covered by the pay structure. They may also be called the 'rate for the job', more typically for manual jobs where there is a defined skilled or semi-skilled market rate, eg for fitters, plasterers, cooks and cleaners.

Spot rates consist of rates that are sometimes, notably for professionals, attached to a person rather than a job. They will not be located within grades and there will be no defined scope for progression. Job holders may be eligible for incentive bonuses on top of the spot rate, but consolidated increases in pay related to performance simply result in a new spot rate for the person. Relativities between spot rates can be determined by job evaluation, but the key factor is often market relativities for the job or the market worth of the person. Spot rates are frequently used by organizations that want the maximum amount of scope to pay what they like. They have their uses in certain circumstances and are often adopted by small or start-up organizations that do not want to be constrained by a formal grade structure and prefer to retain the maximum amount of flexibility. The focus of this chapter, however, is on graded pay structures because they provide a better basis for managing grading and pay consistently within a defined framework and as such are the most typical approach.

Individual job grades

Individual job grades are, in effect, spot rates to which a defined pay range of, say, 20 per cent on either side of the rate has been attached to provide scope for pay progression based on performance, competence or contribution. Again, the mid-point of the range is fixed by reference to job evaluation and market rate comparisons.

Individual grades are attached to jobs not persons but there may be more flexibility for movement between grades than in a conventional grade structure when, for example, a person has expanded his or her role and it is considered that this growth in the level of responsibility needs to be recognized without having to upgrade the job. Individual job grades may be restricted to certain jobs, for example more senior managers, where flexibility in fixing and increasing rates of pay is felt to be desirable.

As described later in this chapter, the 'zones' that are often established in broadbanded structures have some of the characteristics of individual job grades.

RATIONALE FOR GRADE AND PAY STRUCTURES

Grade and pay structures are needed to provide a logically designed framework within which an organization's pay policies can be implemented. They enable the organization to determine where jobs should be placed in a hierarchy, define pay levels and the scope for pay progression and provide the basis upon which relativities can be managed, equal pay can be achieved and the processes of monitoring and controlling the implementation of pay practices can take place. A grade and pay structure is also a medium through which the organization can communicate the career and pay opportunities available to employees.

CRITERIA FOR GRADE AND PAY STRUCTURES

Grade and pay structures should:

▌ be appropriate to the culture, characteristics and needs of the organization and its employees;
▌ facilitate the management of relativities and the achievement of equity, fairness, consistency and transparency in managing gradings and pay;
▌ be capable of adapting to pressures arising from market rate changes and skill shortages;
▌ facilitate operational flexibility and continuous development;
▌ provide scope as required for rewarding performance, contribution and increases in skill and competence;
▌ clarify reward, lateral development and career opportunities;
▌ be constructed logically and clearly so that the basis upon which they operate can readily be communicated to employees;
▌ enable the organization to exercise control over the implementation of pay policies and budgets.

TYPES OF GRADE AND PAY STRUCTURES

The main types of structure as described below are narrow-graded, broadbanded, career family and job family.

Narrow-graded structures

Until fairly recently the almost universal type of structure in the private sector was the conventional graded pay structure as illustrated in Figure 15.1. This can be described as a single-graded structure to distinguish it from a career or job family structure, or a narrow-graded structure to distinguish it from a broadbanded structure. Single- or narrow-graded structures are still the most typical structures, but the trend is to replace them with broad bands or career or job families.

A narrow or single structure consists of a sequence of job grades into which jobs of broadly equivalent value are placed. A pay range is attached to each grade. The maximum of each range is typically between 20 per cent and 50 per cent above the minimum. For example, a '40 per cent range' could span from £20,000 to £28,000. Pay ranges are also described as a percentage of the mid-point; for example, the range could be expressed as 80 per cent to 120 per cent where the mid-point is £25,000 and the minimum and maximum are £20,000 and £30,000 respectively. The mid-point, often referred to as the 'reference point' or 'target salary', may be regarded as the rate for a fully competent individual and is usually aligned to market rates in accordance with company policies on the relationship between its pay levels and market rates for similar jobs (this is sometimes called the 'market stance').

The pay ranges provide scope for pay progression, which is usually related to performance, competence or contribution. There may be eight or more grades in a structure. Grades may be defined by job evaluation in points terms, by grade definitions or simply by the jobs that have been slotted into the grades. Differentials between pay ranges are typically around 20 per cent and there is usually an overlap between ranges, which can be as high as 50 per cent. This overlap provides more flexibility to recognize that a highly experienced individual at the top of a range may be contributing more than someone who is still in the learning curve portion of the next higher grade. What are sometimes called 'mid-point management' techniques analyse and control pay policies by comparing actual pay with the mid-point, which is regarded as the policy pay level. 'Compa-ratios' can be used to measure the relationship between actual and policy rates of pay as a percentage. If the two coincide, the compa-ratio is 100 per cent.

The advantages of narrow-graded structures are that they provide a framework for managing relativities and for ensuring that jobs of equal value are paid equally. All jobs are contained within the structure so that it is not divisive, which is a criticism levelled at job family structures (see below). Single-grade structures enable the process of the fixing of rates of pay and pay progression practices to be controlled and are easy to manage and explain to employees.

The disadvantages of narrow-graded structures are that, if there are too many grades, there will be constant pressure for upgrading, leading to grade drift. They can represent an extended hierarchy that may no longer exist in a delayered organization and can function rigidly, which is at odds with the requirement of flexibility in new team- and process-based organizations. They also reinforce the importance of promotion as a means of progression, which may run counter to the need for organizations to be more flexible and grow capability by moving people within a grade to broaden their experience and capability.

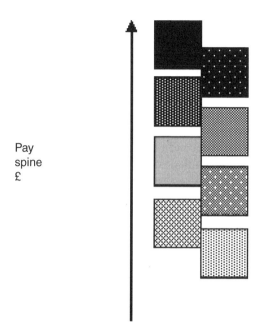

Figure 15.1   A narrow-graded structure

Broadbanded pay structures

Broadbanded structures are replacing narrow-graded structures in many organizations. 'Broadbanding' means that the number of grades is compressed into a relatively small number of much wider 'bands' in which pay is managed more flexibly than in a conventional graded structure, and increased attention is paid to market relativities. The bands can span the pay opportunities previously covered by a number of separate grade and pay ranges. The range of pay in each band is therefore wider than in a traditional graded structure, and research conducted by Armstrong and Brown[1] established that, in organizations with broad bands, 62 per cent had bands with widths between 50 per cent and 75 per cent, while the rest had bands with widths between 75 per cent and 100 per cent. Typically, there are between four and six bands in such structures. The band boundaries are often, but not always, defined by job evaluation. Jobs may be placed in the bands purely by reference to market rates or by a combination of job evaluation and market rate analysis. Bands can be described by an overall description of the jobs allocated to them (senior management, etc) or by reference to the generic roles they contain, eg technical support.

The original broadbanded concept as developed in the United States in the early 1990s was a response to overly narrow structures and allowed for unlimited progression through bands. Since then, however, many organizations have found that this lack of structure was unrealistic and unmanageable. They recognized that some method had to exist for controlling progression, otherwise costs would increase unduly, it would be difficult to ensure that rewards matched levels of contribution, and people would have unrealistic expectations of what their future earnings might be. The most common solution to this problem has been to insert 'reference points' into bands, which indicate the normal rate for a job and are aligned to market rates. Ranges for pay progression may be built round the reference point and these are often referred to as 'zones'. The erosion of the original broadbanding concept has been further advanced by the recognition in many organizations that, in the interests of equity and equal pay, job evaluation has to be used to locate reference points for jobs within bands or to define segments within bands into which zones are placed. Figure 15.2 illustrates a broadbanded structure developed for a housing association, with job evaluation segments and pay zones.

There are several main advantages claimed for broadbanding. First, it enables pay to be managed more flexibly. When asked why they have introduced broad bands, many organizations have replied that it has been in the interests of 'flexibility'. This may refer to the scope given by broadbanding to adapt rates of pay more readily to market rate increases

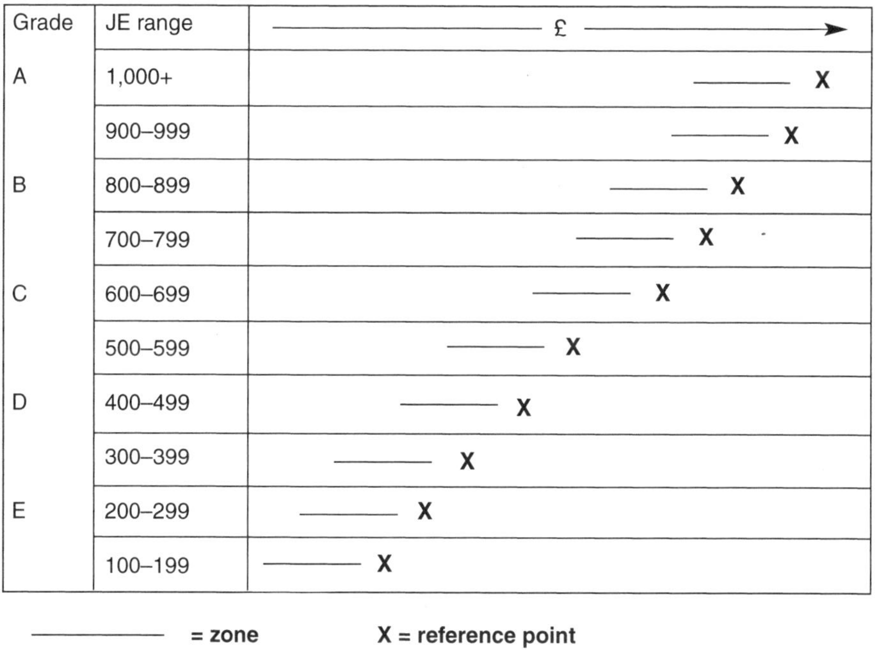

Grade	JE range	£ ⟶
A	1,000+	————— X
	900–999	————— X
B	800–899	————— X
	700–799	————— X
C	600–699	————— X
	500–599	————— X
D	400–499	————— X
	300–399	————— X
E	200–299	————— X
	100–199	————— X

————— = zone   X = reference point

Figure 15.2 A broadbanded structure with zones and reference points

or to reward lateral career development without being restricted to rigid grades. It can also mean a reduction in the costs of implementing a new pay structure because more jobs will be incorporated in the bands, with less need to increase the pay for those in jobs that might be placed below the new pay ranges in a structure with narrower grades.

Second, broadbanding provides a role-specific and performance management focus on reward, and third it dismantles the overly structured and bureaucratic approach of typical multi-graded structures. It is also claimed that broadbanding can reduce the time spent analysing and evaluating jobs because there are fewer levels between which distinctions need to be drawn.

The advantages of broadbanding may look convincing but there are a number of formidable disadvantages, some of them general and others related to equal pay considerations. In general, it has been found that broadbanded structures are harder to manage than narrower-graded structures in spite of the original claim that they would be easier – they make considerable demands on line managers as well as HR, notably in the areas of performance management and communication. Broadbanding can build employee expectations of significant pay opportunities that are doomed in many cases if proper control of the system is maintained. It can be difficult to explain to people how broadbanding works and how they will be affected, and decisions on movements within bands can be harder to justify objectively than in other types of grade and pay structures. Employees may be concerned by the apparent lack of structure and precision and they may not trust their managers to operate the policy consistently. Broadbanding can create the following equal pay problems:

▮ Reliance on external relativities (market rates) to place jobs in bands can reproduce existing inequalities in the labour market.
▮ The broader pay ranges within bands mean that they include jobs of widely different values or sizes, which may result in gender discrimination.
▮ Women may be assimilated at their present rates in the lower regions of bands and find it impossible or at least very difficult to catch up with their male colleagues who, because of longer, unbroken service and their existing higher rates of pay are assimilated in the upper reaches of bands.

These significant objections to broadbanding from an equal pay perspective have meant that greater attention is being paid to placing jobs in bands on the basis of internal relativities. Market rates are still taken into account but policy guidelines emphasize that the organization should be sensitive to market rates rather than being driven by them and should be aware of the danger of reproducing external discriminatory practices.

A further problem with broadbanding is that the introduction of bands within bands, ie zones, referred to earlier, prompts the query: 'What's the difference between a broadbanded structure with four bands, each with three zones, and a conventional graded structure with 12 grades?' The answer provided by Armstrong and Brown[1] is that zones operate more flexibly with regard to grading, pay progression and reaction to market pressures, although this does not necessarily happen. But scepticism about the broadbanding concept in its original form is increasing for this reason and because of the other difficulties mentioned above. More attention is being given to career family and job family structures.

Career family structures

In career family structures as illustrated in Figure 15.3 jobs are grouped together into 'families'. Career families consist of jobs in a function or occupation such as marketing, operations, finance, IT, administration or support services, which are related through the activities carried out and the basic knowledge and skills required, but in which the levels of responsibility, knowledge, skill or competence needed, differ. The successive levels in each career family are defined by reference to the key activities carried out and the knowledge and skills or competences required to perform them effectively. Typically, career structures have between six and eight levels, which places them somewhere between narrow-graded and broadbanded structures. The number of levels may vary between career families and certain, often higher, levels may not be divided. Within each career family there are defined career paths for progressing to higher levels and routes for pursuing careers in other families.

In effect, a career structure is a single-graded structure in which each grade has been divided into families. Jobs in the corresponding levels across each of the career families are within the same size range and, if an analytical job evaluation scheme is used, this is defined by the same range of scores. Similarly, the pay ranges in corresponding levels across the career families are the same.

An advantage of this structure is that it defines career paths within career families and so facilitates career planning. It also identifies routes for career progression between career families by clarifying what individuals have to know and be able to do if they wish to move to a new career path. It can therefore provide the foundation for personal development planning by defining the knowledge and skills required at higher levels or in different functions and what needs to be learned through experience, education or training. Furthermore, the existence of a common grading system when it is supported by job evaluation facilitates the achievement of equal pay for work of equal value. Finally, by linking pay and grade management with career development it is in accordance with good practice human resource management in the shape of 'bundling' – the belief, supported by extensive research, that HR practices will be more effective if they are interrelated and therefore complement and reinforce one another.

The disadvantages of career structures are that, whatever emphasis is placed on career development between as well as within career structures, they could be perceived as being divisive and in conflict with the principle of identical treatment for all enshrined in a single-grade structure. It may be inferred that progression can only take place in an occupational 'silo'. This has been the cause of abandoning a job or career family approach where the silos have been narrowly drawn and managed rigidly – the simpler they are the better. They may also be more difficult to manage and explain than single-grade structures.

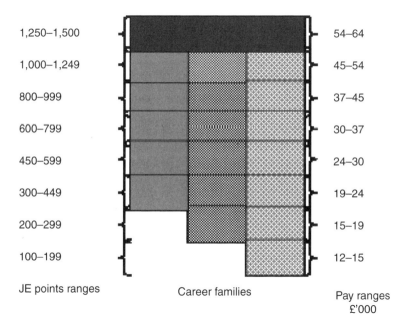

JE points ranges	Career families	Pay ranges £'000

Figure 15.3 A career family structure

Job family structures

A job family structure as illustrated in Figure 15.4 consists of separate grade and pay structures for different job or career families. Whereas career families are focused on an occupation or function, job families are typically based on common processes. For example IT, finance and HR and legal jobs would be identified as separate in a career family structure, but a job family approach might combine all these roles into a 'business support' family. This approach means that typically there are only three to five separate families although some organizations have many more. Each job family is divided into a number of levels. These can vary between job families but typically there are five to seven levels. Job families may have different numbers of levels depending on the range of responsibility they cover. The levels are usually defined as in a career family in terms of accountabilities and skills and knowledge or competence requirements – often set out as role profiles, which can then be used both for personal and career development and as one of the bases of performance management. They can also be defined by a range of job evaluation scores although this is not a universal feature. Because each job family has in effect its own grade and pay structure there may be no commonality, as in a career family structure, in terms of the ranges of pay or job evaluation points for similar levels in different families. The size of jobs in levels can vary between the same levels in different job families, as can rates of pay – there may be no read-across between them unless they are, underpinned by Hay job evaluation, linked to 'know-how' steps, as is the case of many job families. In the latter case the relationship is clear and, provided implementation has followed the guidance on equal value, there should be no real risk of unwitting discrimination. It should be stressed, however, that neither of these approaches was around when equal value legislation was passed and they have not yet been tested in tribunal – perhaps because implementation has generally been in environments that are relatively well paid, sophisticated in HR approaches and not otherwise prone to discrimination.

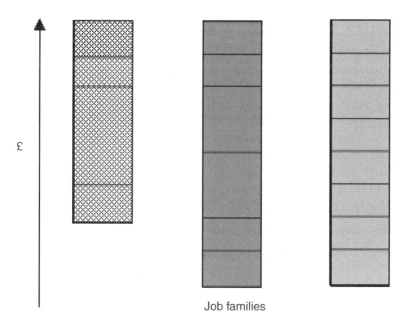

Job families

Figure 15.4 A job family structure

Table 15.1 Comparison of grade and pay structures

	Single-graded	Broadbanded	Career family	Job family	Pay spine
Features	A sequence of job grades – 10 or more. Narrow pay ranges, eg 20–40 per cent. Progression usually linked to performance.	A series of, often, five or six 'broad' bands. Wide pay bands – typically between 50 and 80 per cent. Progression linked to contribution and competence.	Career families identified and defined. Career paths defined for each family in terms of key activities and competence requirements. Same grade and pay structure for each family.	Separate grade and pay structures for job families containing similar jobs. Progression linked to competence and/or contribution.	A series of incremental pay points covering all jobs. Grades may be superimposed. Progression linked to service.
Advantages	Clearly indicate pay relativities. Facilitate control. Easy to understand.	More flexible. Rewards lateral development and growth in competence. Fits new-style organizations.	Clarifies career paths within and between families. Facilitates the achievement of equality between families and therefore equal pay.	Facilitates pay differentiation between market groups. Enable career progression against clear criteria.	Easy to manage. Pay progression not based on managerial judgement.
Disadvantages	Creates hierarchical rigidity. Prone to grade drift. Inappropriate in a delayered organization.	Creates unrealistic expectations of scope for pay rises. Seems to restrict scope for promotion. Difficult to understand. Equal pay problems.	Could be difficult to manage. May appear to be divisive if 'silos' emerge.	Can appear divisive. May inhibit lateral career development. May be difficult to maintain internal equality between job families unless underpinned by job evaluation.	

When most appropriate	In a large, bureaucratic organization with well-defined hierarchies. When close and rigid control is required. When some but not too much scope for pay progression related to performance is wanted.	In delayered, process-based, flexible organizations. Where more flexibility in pay determination is wanted. Where the focus is on continuous improvement and lateral development. Where management capability is high.	In organizations where there is a strong emphasis on career development. Where there are different career paths within and between families can be identified and defined. When robust methods of defining competences exist.	Where there are distinct groups of jobs in families. When it is believed that career paths need to be defined more clearly in terms of competence requirements. When there are distinct market groups that need to be rewarded differentially.	In a public sector or voluntary organization where there is the traditional approach and it therefore fits the culture. Where it is believed to be impossible to measure differential levels of performance fairly and consistently.

Pay spines

Pay spines are found in the public sector or in agencies and charities that have adopted a public sector approach to reward management. They consist of a series of incremental 'pay points' extending from the lowest- to the highest-paid jobs covered by the structure. Typically, pay spine increments are between 2.5 per cent and 3 per cent. They may be standardized from the top to the bottom of the spine, or the increments may be vary at different levels, sometimes widening towards the top. Job grades are aligned to the pay spine and the pay ranges for the grades are defined by the relevant scale of pay points. The width of grades can vary and job families may have different pay spines. Progression through a grade is based on service although an increasing number of organizations provide scope for accelerating increments or providing additional increments above the top of the scale for the grade to reward merit.

The advantages of pay spines are that they are easy to manage and, because pay progression is service related, it is not based on managerial judgement. For this reason they are favoured by trade unions and many managements in the public sector. The disadvantages are that: 1) relating pay almost entirely to service means that people are rewarded for 'being there' and not for the value of their contribution; 2) pay spines can be costly in organizations with low staff turnover where everyone drifts to the top of the scale; and 3) where there are a large number of incremental points in the scale, equal value complications can arise as men progress to the top while the progress of women is delayed because of career breaks. For this reason the Local Government Pay Commission in 2003 recommended a move away from service-related increments on to pay for contribution, restricting increments to the first few years in a job.

CHOICE OF STRUCTURE

Choice has always to be exercised when contemplating the design or redesign of a grade and pay structure. There is no such thing as a model structure or 'best practice' in the development process. As research by Armstrong and Brown[1] has established, there is a wide diversity of approaches; every organization adopts its own variety of structure to suit its circumstances. Generally, however, businesses and institutions with formal, hierarchical organization structures have tended to prefer conventional graded structures, which permit orderly administration and ease in managing internal relativities. Organizations that want to achieve more flexibility but within a defined framework may opt for a broadbanded structure. Those attaching considerable importance to career planning and development may opt for a career family structure. Those who believe that some job families need to be treated differently, either because career progression patterns vary or to respond to market rate pressures, may prefer a job family structure. Trade unions representing a range of professional, technical or administrative staff may favour single-graded structures while unions representing specialized professions may prefer a job family structure.

Perhaps the most important factor is the organizational context. Account needs to be taken of the organization's culture, the type and variety of people employed and the views of stakeholders – management, employees and their trade unions – bearing in mind the extent to which they are ready for change and will accept it when it comes. Additionally, the capacity of the organization to design, introduce and manage a different structure and the funds available to finance the implementation of a new structure have to be considered. The features, advantages and disadvantages and appropriateness of each type of structure are summarized in Table 15.1.

REFERENCE

1. Armstrong, M and Brown, D (2001) *Pay: The new dimensions*, CIPD, London

16

Grade and Pay Structure Design

In this chapter the design options for the main types of grade and pay structures as covered in Chapter 15 are considered. Approaches to designing single-graded, broadbanded or career/job family structures and the use of job classification as a design method are then examined and the chapter is completed with a description of approaches to the design of non-discriminatory pay structures. The importance of giving employees a voice in the design process (getting them involved) needs to be stressed from the outset.

DESIGN OPTIONS

Whichever structure is selected, there will be a number of design options. These comprise the number of grades, bands or levels, the width of the grades and pay ranges, the differentials between grades, the degree to which there should be overlap between grades, if any, and the method of pay progression within grades. In broadbanded structures there is also choice on the infrastructure (the use of reference points or zones), and in career or job family structures there are options concerning the number of families, the composition of families and the basis upon which levels should be defined. In pay spine structures there may be choice on the size of the increments.

Number of grades, levels or bands

The considerations to be taken into account when deciding on the number of grades levels or bands are:

▮ the range and types of roles to be covered by the structure;
▮ the range of pay and job evaluation points scores to be accommodated;
▮ the number of levels in the organizational hierarchy (this will be an important factor in a broadbanded structure);
▮ decisions on where grade boundaries should be placed following a job evaluation exercise that has produced a ranked order of jobs – this might identify the existence of clearly defined clusters of jobs at the various levels in the hierarchy between which there are significant differences in job size;
▮ the fact that, within a given range of pay and responsibility, the greater the number of grades the smaller their width and vice versa – this is associated with views on what is regarded as the desirable width of a range, taking into account the scope for progression, the size of increments in a pay spine and equal pay issues;
▮ the problem of 'grade drift' (unjustified upgradings in response to pressure, lack of promotion opportunities or because job evaluation has been applied laxly), which can be increased if there are too many narrow grades.

Typically, conventional graded structures tend to have between 8 and 12 grades. The structure recently developed for the NHS (in Agenda for Change) has eight common pay bands (the top one divided into four ranges) placed upon two pay spines, one for staff covered by the review body for nurses and other health professionals, the other for non-review body staff. Each pay band has a corresponding range of job evaluation scores derived from the 2003 national job evaluation scheme. There is a third pay spine for doctors and dentists.

Width of grades

The factors affecting decisions on the width of grades or bands are:

▮ views on the scope that should be allowed for performance, contribution or career progression within grade;
▮ equal pay considerations – wide grades, especially extended incremental scales, are a major cause of pay gaps between men and women simply because women, who are more likely to have career breaks than men, may not have the same opportunity as men to progress to the upper regions of the range; male jobs may therefore cluster towards the top of the range while women's may cluster towards the bottom;

- decisions on the number of grades – the greater the number the smaller the width;
- decisions on the value of increments in a pay spine – if it is believed, as in local government and as a result of the ACAS equal pay case, that the number of increments should be restricted, for equal pay or other reasons, but that the number of grades should also be limited, then it is necessary to increase the value of the increments;
- in a broadbanded structure, the range of market rates and job evaluation scores covering the jobs allocated to the band.

Differentials between pay ranges

Differentials between pay ranges should provide scope to recognize increases in job size between successive grades. If differentials are too close – less than 10 per cent – many jobs become borderline cases, which can result in a proliferation of appeals and arguments about grading. Large differentials below senior management level of more than 25 per cent can create problems for marginal or borderline cases because of the amount at stake. Experience has shown that in most organizations with conventional grade structures a differential of between 16 and 20 per cent is appropriate except, perhaps, at the highest levels.

Pay range overlap

There is a choice on whether or not pay ranges should overlap and, if so, by how much. The amount of overlap, if any, is a function of range width and differentials. Large overlaps of more than 10 per cent can create equal pay problems where, as is quite common, men are clustered at the top of their grades and women are more likely to be found at the lower end.

Pay progression

There is a choice of methods of pay progression between the fixed service-related increments common in the public sector and the other forms of contingent pay, namely performance-, competence- or contribution-related as described in Chapter 21.

THE GRADE AND PAY STRUCTURE DESIGN PROCESS

The design process will vary according to the type of structure and on the approach adopted to the use of job evaluation. The main variations are between the design of single narrow-graded structures, or broadbanded structures, or career or job family structures as described later.

An analytical job evaluation scheme is frequently the basis for designing a single-graded structure and it can be used in the initial stages of designing a broadbanded or career/job family structure. In the case of single-graded structures, decisions on the number and width of grades are generally based on an analysis of the rank order of scores produced by job evaluation.

This approach is used less often in the design of broadbanded or career/job family structures where the most common method is to make a provisional advance decision on the number of bands or career family levels, position roles in bands (often by reference to external relativities) or allocate roles into levels by a 'matching' process as described in Chapter 11. Job evaluation may only be used at a later stage to validate the positioning of roles in bands or the allocation of jobs to family levels, check on relativities and, sometimes, define the bands or levels in job evaluation score terms. The initial decision on the number of bands or levels and their definition may, however, be changed in the light of the outcome of the allocation, matching and evaluation processes.

More rarely, the grade and pay structure design is conducted by means of a non-analytical job classification exercise (see Chapter 11), which defines a number of single grades. Jobs are then slotted into the grades by reference to the grades' definition. The basic sequence of steps for designing a grade and pay structure is illustrated in Figure 16.1. Note the emphasis on involvement and communication at all stages.

NARROW-GRADE STRUCTURE DESIGN

The steps required to design a single narrow-grade and pay structure are broadly along the lines set out in Figure 16.1 as is the case for broadbanded and career/job family structure design. The particular considerations described below concern decisions on grading and pay ranges.

Grade structure decisions

An analytical job evaluation exercise will produce a rank order of jobs according to their job evaluation scores either for all jobs or by job families. A decision then has to be made on where the boundaries that will define grades should be placed in the rank order. So far as possible, boundaries should divide groups or clusters of jobs that are significantly different in size so that all the jobs placed in a grade are clearly smaller than the jobs in the next higher grade and larger than the jobs placed in the next lower grade.

Fixing grade boundaries is one of the most critical aspects of single-grade structure design following an analytical job evaluation exercise. It

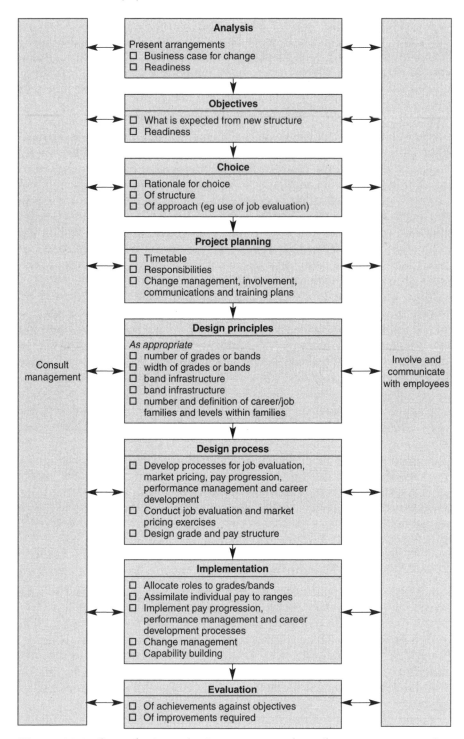

Figure 16.1 Steps for introducing a new grade and pay structure

requires judgement – the process is not scientific and it is rare to find a situation where there is one right and obvious answer. In theory, grade boundaries could be determined by deciding on the number of grades in advance and then dividing the rank order into equal parts. But this would mean drawing grade boundary lines arbitrarily and the result could be the separation of groups of jobs that should properly be placed in the same grade.

The best approach is to analyse the rank order to identify any significant gaps in the points scores between adjacent jobs. These natural breaks in points scores will then constitute the boundaries between clusters of jobs, which can be allocated to adjacent grades. A distinct gap between the highest-rated job in one grade and the lowest-rated job in the grade above will help to justify the allocation of jobs between grades. It will therefore reduce boundary problems, which lead to dissatisfaction with gradings when the distinction is less well defined. Clear grade breaks appear more naturally when job evaluation scores are based on geometric progression than when progression is arithmetic. This is because a 'step difference' principle is implicit in the former.

Provisionally, it may be decided in advance when designing a conventional graded structure that a certain number of grades is required but the gap analysis will confirm the number of grades that is appropriate, taking into account the natural divisions between jobs in the rank order. However, the existence of a number of natural breaks cannot be guaranteed, which means that judgement has to be exercised as to where boundaries should be drawn when the scores between adjacent jobs are close.

In cases where there are no obvious natural breaks the guidelines that should be considered when deciding on boundaries are as follows:

▌ Jobs with common features as indicated by the job evaluation factors are grouped together so that a distinction can be made between the characteristics of the jobs in different grades – it should be possible to demonstrate that the jobs grouped into one grade resemble each other more than they resemble jobs placed in adjacent grades.

▌ The grade hierarchy should take account of the organizational hierarchy, ie jobs in which the job holder reports to a higher-level job holder should be placed in a lower grade although this principle should not be followed slavishly when an organization is over-hierarchical with, perhaps, a series of one-over-one reporting relationships.

▌ The boundaries should not be placed between jobs mainly carried out by men and jobs mainly carried out by women.

▌ The boundaries should ideally not be placed immediately above jobs in which large numbers of people are employed.

▌ The grade width in terms of job evaluation points should represent a significant step in demands on job holders as indicated by the job evaluation scheme.

Pay range design

1. List the jobs placed within each grade on the basis of job evaluation (these might be limited to benchmark jobs that have been evaluated but there must be an adequate number of them if a proper basis for the design is to be provided).
2. Establish the actual rates of pay of the job holders.
3. For each grade, set out the range of pay for job holders and calculate their average or median rate of pay (the pay practice point). It is helpful to plot the pay practice data as illustrated in Figure 16.2, which shows pay in each grade against job evaluation scores and includes a pay practice trend line.
4. Obtain information on the market rates for benchmark jobs where available. If possible this should indicate the median rate and the upper and lower quartiles.
5. Agree policy on how the organization's pay levels should relate to market rates – its 'market stance'. This could be at the median, or above the median if it is believed that pay levels should be more competitive.
6. Calculate the average market rates for the benchmark jobs in each grade according to pay stance policy, eg the median rates. This produces the range market reference point.
7. Compare the practice and market reference points in each range and decide on the range reference point. This usually becomes the mid-point of the pay range for the grade and is regarded as the competitive rate for a fully competent job holder in that grade. This is a judgemental process, which takes into account the difference between the practice and policy points, the perceived need to be more competitive if policy rates are higher, and the likely costs of increasing rates.
8. Examine the pay differentials between reference points in adjacent grades. These should provide scope to recognize increases in job size and, so far as possible, variations between differentials should be kept to a minimum. If differentials are too close – less than 10 per cent – many jobs become borderline cases, which can result in a proliferation of appeals and arguments about grading. Large differentials below senior management level of more than 25 per cent can create problems for marginal or borderline cases because of the amount at stake. Experience has shown that in most organizations with conventional grade structures a differential of between 16 and 20 per cent is appropriate except, perhaps, at the highest levels.
9. Decide on the range of pay around the reference point. The most typical arrangement is to allow 20 per cent on either side; thus if the reference point is 100 per cent, the range is from 80 per cent to 120 per cent. The range can, however, vary in accordance with policy on

the scope for progression and if a given range of pay has to be covered by the structure, the fewer the grades the wider the ranges.

10. Decide on the extent, if any, to which pay ranges should overlap. Overlap recognizes that an experienced job holder at the top of a range may be making a greater contribution than an inexperienced job holder at the lower end of the range above. Large overlaps of more than 10 per cent can create equal pay problems where men are at the top of their grades and women are likely to be found at the lower end.

11. Review the impact of the above pay range decisions on the pay of existing staff. Establish the number of staff whose present rate of pay is above or below the pay range for the grade into which their jobs have been placed and the extent of the difference between the rate of pay of those below the minimum and the lowest point of that pay range. Calculate the costs of bringing them up to the minimum. Software such as the pay modellers produced by Link and Pilat or locally tailored Excel spreadsheets can be used for this purpose.

12. When the above steps have been completed it may be necessary to review the decisions made on the grade structure and pay reference points and ranges. Iteration is almost always necessary to obtain a satisfactory result that conforms to the criteria for grade and pay structures mentioned earlier and minimizes the cost of implementation. Alternatives can be modelled using the software mentioned above.

DESIGNING A BROADBANDED STRUCTURE

The steps required to design a broadbanded structure are set out below:

1. *Decide on objectives.* The objectives of the structure should be set out in terms of what it is expected to achieve, for example increase flexibility in the provision of rewards, reflect organization structure, provide a better base for rewarding lateral or diagonal development and growth in competence, or replace an over-complex and inappropriate grade and pay structure.

2. *Decide on number of bands.* The decision on the number of bands will be based on an analysis of the existing organization structure and hierarchy of jobs. The aim is to identify the value-adding tiers that exist in the business. An initial assessment can be made, for example, that there are six tiers comprising: 1) senior managers, 2) middle managers, 3) first-line managers and senior specialists, 4) team leaders and specialists, 5) senior administrators and support staff and 6) administrators and support staff. This structure should be regarded as provisional at this stage – it could be changed after the more detailed work in the next two stages.

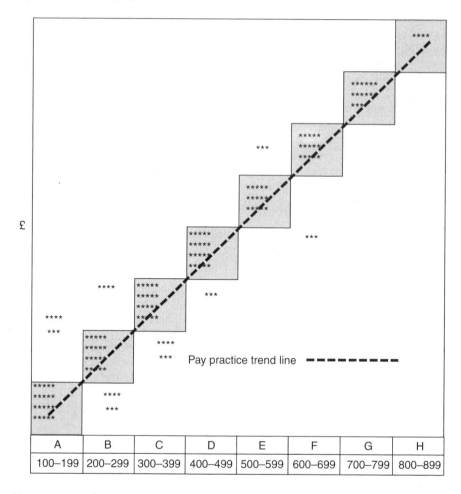

Figure 16.2 Scattergram of evaluations and pay

3. *Decide on band infrastructure.* A decision has to be made at this stage on the use of reference points and zones. If reference points are to be used, which is most often the case, the method of determining where they should be placed in bands (by market pricing, job evaluation or both) should be decided. If zones are to be used, decisions need to be made on the width of the zones and the basis upon which people should progress within and between zones. The scope for flexibility in creating special reference points and zones for individuals should also be considered.

4. *Define the bands.* Broad initial definitions are now made of each of the bands. For example, a band for senior administrators and support staff could be defined as:

Key activities:
- Provide a range of fairly complex administrative or higher-level support services.
- May have responsibility for a small section or sub-section of work.
- May prepare non-standard documentation.
- May deal with non-routine queries.
- Take action to deliver improved performance.

Performance requirements:
- Plan and prioritize own day-to-day activities in order to achieve performance objectives.
- Work under general supervision.

Relationships:
- Maintain helpful and supportive relationships with colleagues in own and other areas and with internal and external customers.
- Take a leadership role within team when appropriate.

Communications:
- Communicate orally or in writing internally and externally on non-routine matters.

People management:
- May act as instructor or mentor to more junior staff.
- May allocate work to members of section or sub-section.

5. *Prepare role profiles for benchmark jobs.* Identify benchmark jobs that are representative of different functions at the levels covered by the structure and for which market price data can probably be obtained. They should include as many of the key generic roles as possible. Role profiles for each of them are then prepared. The profiles should provide sufficient information to enable them to be matched with the band definitions and, ideally, for market comparisons.

6. *Match the benchmark roles to the bands.* The matching process should provisionally allocate each benchmark role to a band. It is best carried out by a team consisting of line managers and employee representatives facilitated by HR or an outside consultant. This initial matching may indicate that the bands need to be redefined.

7. *Obtain market prices.* Conduct surveys and/or access pay information databases to establish the market rates of the benchmark roles.

8. *Evaluate benchmark roles.* Use an analytical job evaluation method to evaluate the benchmark roles.

9. *Decide on reference points.* Assuming a decision has been made to have reference points and zones, decide on the reference points for the benchmark roles taking into account market rates and internal relativities as determined by job evaluation. This is a judgemental process because it means striking a balance between the two criteria. The weight given to either criterion will be a policy matter depending on the extent to which pay is market driven and the extent to which it is believed that internal equity is important.

10. *Decide on zones.* Assuming a decision has been made to use zones, these should now be attached to the reference points for the benchmark roles in accordance with the policy determined at stage 3.

11. *Define pay ranges of bands.* This is usually done empirically by reference to the earlier decisions on reference points and zones – the range of pay for a band will be the range of pay from the bottom of the lowest zone in the band to the top of the highest zone.

12. *Define bands in terms of job evaluation scores.* If the benchmark roles have been evaluated this will indicate the bracket of job evaluation scores that can be used to define each band, which might provide a guide to allocating non-benchmark or new roles to bands.

13. *Allocate non-benchmark roles to bands.* In theory the remaining non-benchmark jobs could be allocated to bands on the basis of job evaluation, but in practice most organizations match role profiles for such jobs (which are often generic) with the profiles of the benchmark jobs. This is more likely to work well if a reasonably representative range of benchmark jobs has been used, and if there is well-developed management capability to work on this process and deal with its implications.

14. *Communicate outcomes.* Staff should have been involved and kept informed of the progress of the design process throughout the exercise but in this final stage the way in which broadbanding works and how it will affect them must be explained in detail.

THE DESIGN OF CAREER OR JOB FAMILY GRADE STRUCTURES

The design of a career or job family structure uses the process of job family modelling. This, as developed by the Hay Group, involves:

▪ identifying groups of jobs in which the type of work is similar but it is carried out at different levels;
▪ analysing the essential nature of each of these groups of job families;
▪ stablishing the levels of work carried out in each job family;
▪ defining the differentiating factors between each level in the family in terms of job size (activities carried out) and the other differentiating factors, eg competency, knowledge and skill requirements, performance criteria;
▪ producing functional or generic role specifications or profiles;
▪ allocating roles to levels within the appropriate job family by 'matching' role profiles with job family level definitions;
▪ validating level allocations and equity across job families by the use of job evaluation processes;

▌ deciding on pay ranges for each level by reference to market rate data.

In general, there are two approaches to the design of a career or job family structure. The first is the job family modelling process described above in which analytical job evaluation is used in the design of either career or job families to validate prior decisions on grades and level and the allocation of jobs to levels by matching role profiles to level definitions. The second is to base the design on job evaluation by the grading process described in the previous section of this chapter following the use of an analytical job evaluation scheme to produce a rank order of jobs. In both approaches it is necessary to decide on the families required (usually not more than three or four) and how they should be defined.

When the design of a career family structure follows an analytical job evaluation exercise, the grades or levels determined by reference to the rank order produced by job evaluation are in effect sliced up into families. Career ladders are devised by defining the levels for each family in terms of the key activities carried out and the skills and knowledge (competences) required. Each level is also defined by reference to a range of job evaluation points. Benchmark jobs are allocated to levels according to their points scores but once the design has been confirmed many organizations allocate jobs to levels simply by matching role profiles with level definitions, although job evaluation scores can always be consulted to validate the allocation and to check that equal value considerations have been met.

If the design of a career or job family structure is based on a priori decisions on the number and definition of levels without reference to job evaluation scores, the first step is to select benchmark roles, which may be generic, and prepare role profiles defining the key activities carried out and the knowledge and skills required. The role profiles are then 'matched' with the level definitions in order to determine the allocation of the roles to levels. The role profiles may readily match one level but they often fit parts of one level definition and parts of another. In this case judgement is required to achieve the best general fit. It should be noted that, unless 'matching' is done on an analytical basis, ie against a defined set of factors, it may lead to pay discrimination and would not provide a defence in an equal pay claim.

For this reason, although analytical job evaluation is not always used by organizations that have introduced career or job family structures, it is generally accepted that it provides necessary support to the design process and rigour from an equal value perspective. An analytical job evaluation scheme will validate the level allocations, define the levels in points terms and ensure that equal pay considerations are met within and across career families. The allocation of benchmark or generic roles to levels is recorded so that at later stages role profiles prepared for the job to be graded can be matched with benchmark role profiles as well as with the level definition.

Decisions on pay levels are made by reference to market rate data and the existing levels of pay for the jobs covered by the structure.

A flow chart of the design process is shown in Figure 16.3. At each stage staff should be involved in the design process and should be kept informed of its progress.

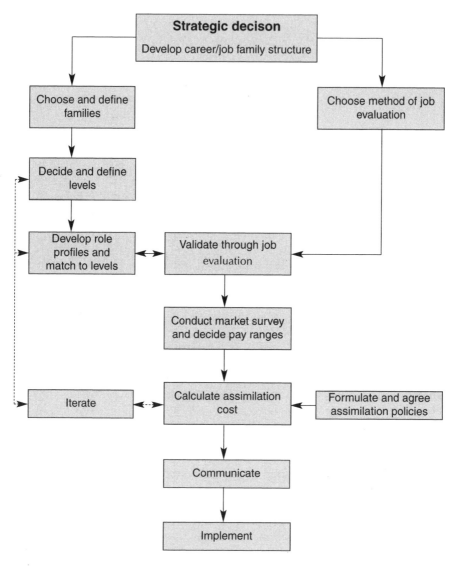

Figure 16.3 Career/job family design stages

GRADE STRUCTURE DESIGN BASED UPON JOB CLASSIFICATION

The non-analytical job classification method of job evaluation as described in Chapter 11 starts with a definition of the number and characteristics of the grades into which jobs will be placed. These a priori decisions are made without reference to job evaluation scores, as is sometimes the case when designing career or job family structures. There are therefore no problems in defining grade boundaries, as can occur when the structure is derived from the rank order produced by an analytical evaluation exercise.

When the grade definitions have been produced, jobs are slotted into the grades. This should ideally be carried out by means of a matching process that is analytical to the degree that it specifically compares the characteristics of whole jobs with the characteristics set out in the grade definitions.

Job classification is the simplest method of grade design but, when there is no analytical base, grading decisions may be arbitrary and inequitable. They may also change over time as different people become involved in the process who may not share the understanding or the values of the original team that worked on the project. Most importantly, no reliable defence will be available in the event of an equal pay claim. The solution to these problems adopted by some organizations is to use an analytical point-factor scheme to validate the gradings and check on internal equity.

DESIGNING NON-DISCRIMINATORY PAY STRUCTURES

To design a non-discriminatory pay structure it is necessary to ensure that:

▌ great care is taken over grade boundary decisions – the aim should be to avoid placing them between jobs that have been evaluated as virtually indistinguishable, bearing in mind that the problem will be most acute if grade boundaries are placed between traditionally male and female jobs (in any situation where such boundary problems exist it is good practice to re-evaluate the jobs, possibly using a direct 'comparable worth' or equal value approach that concentrates on the particular jobs);
▌ 'read-across' mechanisms exist between different job families and occupational groups if they are not all covered by the same plan;
▌ market rate comparisons are treated with caution to ensure that differentials arising from market forces can be objectively justified;

▌ care is taken over the implementation of the pay structure to ensure that female employees (indeed, any employees) are not disadvantaged by the methods used to adjust their pay following regrading;

▌ a non-discriminatory analytical job evaluation system is used to define grade boundaries and grade jobs;

▌ discriminatory job descriptions are not used as a basis for designing and managing the structure;

▌ men's jobs or women's jobs do not cluster respectively at the higher and lower levels in the grade of the hierarchy;

▌ any variation between pay levels for men and women in similarly evaluated jobs (for example, for market rate reasons) can be objectively justified;

▌ red-circling is free of sex bias;

▌ there are objectively justifiable reasons for any inconsistency in the relation of the grading of jobs in the structure to job evaluation results.

CONCLUSIONS

A major change to remuneration structures is a time-consuming and emotional business that can lead to significant additional payroll expense and, if poorly managed, can be disruptive and damaging to morale in any organization. Nevertheless, over time, the problem of 'grade drift' discussed above will lead to increasing pay costs and grading anomalies that will be perceived as unfair by employees. Systems therefore need to be developed to review grading, perhaps on an annual basis, and to ensure that jobs remain allocated to appropriate grades or bands. Such reviews might equally result in jobs being allocated a lower grade as a higher one.

This process of maintenance should be accompanied by a consideration of the continuing relevance of the grading system to organization needs. A remuneration structure is a deeply influential expression of organization culture and values. If, therefore, it is out of step with espoused values or it encourages the 'wrong' behaviours, then perhaps significant change will be required to realign the reward system to organization and people strategy. The approach to managing such change is the subject of the next chapter.

17

Implementing New Grade and Pay Structures

The implementation of new or revised grade and pay structures provides a change management challenge of considerable proportions. The scale of this challenge will be reduced if employees have a voice in its design. But it is essential to communicate the purpose and features of the new structure and how everyone will be affected. If, as is usual, the new structure follows a job evaluation programme it is necessary to manage the expectations of staff. They should be informed that, while no one will necessarily get extra pay, no one will lose. This means that assimilation and protection policies should be discussed and agreed prior to implementation. It is also necessary to ensure that training is provided for everyone concerned in administering reward.

Above all, it is important to think about how implementation is to take place and plan each aspect carefully. As Armstrong and Brown[1] comment:

> Perhaps the worst thing you can do if you are in a situation where you think your pay structures need to be redesigned is to start with the solution and to rapidly implement it. Yes, in these fast moving times, the HR function needs to be agile, responsive and results-oriented, as Ulrich[2] tells us. But in respect of such a sensitive and politically and emotionally charged issue as base pay management, this is not an area where you want to be acting first and then thinking, or perhaps regretting later.

In this chapter, consideration is first given to the general implementation issues of change management and giving employees a voice in the change process. The chapter continues with a summary of the main steps to be taken in an implementation programme and ends with a review of assimilation policies, including those concerning the protection of pay.

CHANGE MANAGEMENT

The role of HR and reward practitioners

Caldwell[3] categorizes HR practitioners as change agents in four dimensions:

1. *transformational change* – a major change that has a dramatic effect on HR policy and practice across the whole organization;
2. *incremental change* – gradual adjustments of HR policy and practices, which affect single activities or multiple functions;
3. *HR vision* – a set of values and beliefs that affirm the legitimacy of the HR function as strategic business partner;
4. *HR expertise* – the knowledge and skills that define the unique contribution the HR professional can make to effective people management.

Across these dimensions, the change agent roles that Caldwell suggests can be carried out by HR practitioners are those of change champions, change consultants and change synergists.

Linda Gratton[4] stresses the need for HR practitioners to: 'Understand the state of the company, the extent of the embedding of processes and structures throughout the organization, and the behaviour and attitudes of individual employees.' She believes that 'The challenge is to implement the ideas' and the solution is to 'build a guiding coalition by involving line managers, which means creating issue-based cross-functional action teams that will initially make recommendations and later move into action'. This approach 'builds the capacity to change'.

Approaches to change management

The following are some general prescriptions for effective change management, which apply to changes in reward structures as well as any other HR practices:

1. Mobilize commitment to change through the joint analysis of problems.
2. Develop a shared vision of how to organize and manage change to achieve agreed goals.
3. Foster consensus for the new vision, competence to enact it and cohesion to move it along.

4. Institutionalize change through formal policies, processes and practices.
5. Monitor and adjust policies and practices in response to problems emerging during the change process.

The key points emerging from these suggestions are the need for involvement (giving managers and employees a voice), and communications and training as part of a planned approach to implementation.

EMPLOYEE VOICE

As defined by Boxall and Purcell,[5] 'Employee voice is the term increasingly used to cover a whole variety of processes and structures which enable, and sometimes empower employees, directly and indirectly, to contribute to decision-making in the firm.' Employee voice can be seen as 'the ability of employees to influence the actions of the employer' (Millward, Bryn and Forth[6]).

The concept of employee voice embraces involvement and, more significantly, participation. Involvement means that management allows employees to discuss with them issues that affect them though management retains the right to manage. It is primarily a management-driven concept. Participation is about employees playing a greater part in the decision-making process. It is therefore much closer to the concept of employee voice systems – arrangements for ensuring that employees are given the opportunity to influence management decisions and to contribute to the improvement of organizational performance. The EU Information and Consultation Directive adds impetus here.

A PLANNED APPROACH TO MANAGING IMPLEMENTATION

It is essential to plan implementation. Approaches to change management and enlisting the understanding and support of stakeholders should be given close consideration at the project planning stage. As already emphasized, it is essential to provide for both involvement and participation in the design and development programme. As suggested by Armstrong and Brown[1] the implementation steps are:

1. Decide at the planning stage the overall change/transition strategy and timing.
2. Model the transition into the new structure and develop policies to manage this transition. This means formulating assimilation and protection policies as explained later in this chapter.

3. Develop detailed operating responsibilities and guidelines for the new structure including the procedures for grading or regrading jobs and managing pay progression. The authority to make pay and grading decisions and methods of budgetary control should also be covered.

4. Negotiate the introduction of the new arrangements with staff representatives and trade unions. They should have been involved throughout the process, but here the detailed 'nitty-gritty' of actual pay levels and assimilation policies and procedures needs to be thrashed out.

5. Produce and distribute communications about the new structure – how it works, who will be involved in managing it and how people will be affected (ie, answer the 'what's in it for me' questions). It is now that the benefits of regularly involving and communicating with staff throughout the design and development programme will become apparent. Broad details of the proposed changes and the reasons for them should thereby be known already. The focus at the implementation stage can then be on the detailed designs and their individual impact. It is best to use line managers as the main communicators, helping them with relevant support (booklets, question-and-answer sheets, PowerPoint presentations, etc) to get the key messages over to their staff. Information technology (the intranet) can be used to identify and address specific staff concerns.

6. Design and run training workshops for managers, and possibly all staff. In the case of broadbanded structures and some career/job family structures, managers are likely to have more freedom and discretion in positioning staff in bands or family levels and adjusting their pay. But they may well need more than an operating manual and entries on the intranet to help them manage this in an appropriate and fair manner. HR should be prepared to provide coaching to managers as well as more formal courses. They must make themselves available to give guidance, especially to the less committed or experienced managers. A cadre of line managers can be trained to coach their colleagues on managing pay in the new structure.

7. Run a pilot or simulation exercise, operating the new approach in parts of the organization, to test its workability and robustness. In one organization recently, for example, the new system was initially introduced in the IT department, where the market pressures were greatest; this assisted in estimating the HR support required for full roll-out, and also indicated the emphasis required in the staff communication and 'branding' of the changes when full implementation occurred.

8. Apply full implementation and roll-out. This will include giving all individuals information on how the new structure affects them and on their right to ask for a review of their grading if they are dissatisfied.

ASSIMILATION POLICY

The hard part of implementing arrives when the assimilation of staff to the new structure has to take place. It is necessary to have a policy on where staff will be assimilated to the new structure. This is usually at their existing salary or, in the case of a revised pay spine, on the nearest point in a new incremental scale above their existing salary. There are essentially four categories of staff to be covered by the assimilation policy:

1. those staff whose current actual pay and pay potential are both encompassed by the pay range for the new grades to which their jobs are allocated;
2. those staff whose current pay lies within the new pay range but whose existing pay potential is greater than the new maximum;
3. those staff whose current pay is below the minimum for the new grade;
4. those staff whose current pay is above the maximum for the new grade.

Current pay and pay potential both within the new pay range

In some ways this group is the easiest to deal with and the majority of staff will normally be included in it. The wider the grades the more likely that is to be the case. One point at issue is whether or not any increase should be awarded on transition and the answer should be 'no' except when, as mentioned above, the policy is to move each person's pay to the nearest higher pay point.

Good advance communications should have conveyed the fact that job evaluation and a new pay structure do not necessarily mean any increase in pay. But some people in this group may still feel disadvantaged at seeing others getting increases. This negative reaction can be decreased by introducing the new structure at the same time as any annual pay increase, so that everyone gets at least something.

It is necessary to be aware of the possibility of creating equal pay problems when assimilating staff to their new scale. For example, if two people with broadly equivalent experience and skills are on different current salaries and are assimilated into the same new grade but at the different salaries as determined by their previous salaries, it would appear that there is no equal pay problem – they are both on the same grade with the same grade and salary potential. But an equal value issue is only avoided if a lower-paid woman or man has the opportunity to catch up with the higher-paid man or woman within a reasonable period (say three or four years). However, where the difference was nothing to do with grade in the first place and can be shown to be unsustainable now that the jobs are graded equally, then an uplift in pay is required. In these circumstances the higher-paid individual may be red-circled and have his or her pay protected as suggested below. Any such salary uplifts should be reviewed and implemented only after the jobs are first assimilated into the new scales and the costs of doing so confirmed. It would be wrong to saddle the new job evaluation and grade system with the costs of rectifying past discriminatory practices.

Current pay within the new pay range but pay potential higher than new maximum

No immediate increase is necessary in this circumstance but employees should be told what will happen. If progression to the old maximum was based on service only, ie automatic annual increases to the maximum, this guarantee will have to be retained. However, once a person's pay passes the maximum for the grade, this will then become a 'red-circle' situation and should be treated as such (see below).

If progression to the old maximum was not guaranteed, but was based on performance, competencies, etc, then the new range maximum should normally be applied. Care will be needed to ensure that this does not adversely affect any specific category of staff, particularly female staff.

Current pay below the minimum for the new grade

Both justice and equity demand that, if someone has now been identified as being underpaid, the situation should be rectified as quickly as possible. Correcting this situation, by raising the pay to the minimum of the new pay range, should normally be the first call on any money allocated to the assimilation process. Each case should, however, be taken on its merits. If someone has recently been appointed to a post and given an pay increase at that time, it may be appropriate to wait until that person has completed a probationary period before awarding another pay increase.

If the total cost of rectifying underpayments is more than the organization can afford, it may be necessary, however unpalatable, to phase the necessary increases, say one portion in the current year and the rest in the next year – it is undesirable to phase increases over a longer period unless the circumstances are exceptional. The simplest approach is to place a maximum on the increase that any one person may receive. This can be in absolute terms (eg maximum of £2,000) or in percentage increase terms (eg maximum of 20 per cent of current pay). Another alternative is to use an annual 'gap reduction' approach (eg pay increase of 50 per cent of the difference between current pay and range minimum or £500, whichever is the greater).

Again, if any delay in rectifying underpayment situations is necessary and some staff have therefore to be 'green-circled', it must not disadvantage one staff group more than another. Most organizations introducing job evaluation for the first time (or replacing an outdated scheme) and using the outcome to devise a new pay structure will find that more women than men have to be green-circled. Failure to correct these would be a perpetuation of gender bias.

Current pay above the maximum for the new grade

These situations that lead to red-circling are usually the most difficult to deal with. They normally include a high proportion of people (often male) who have been in their current job a long time and who have been able to benefit from a lax approach to pay management in the past. People can take very different attitudes about what should be done about these situations and, as a result, the most protracted of the implementation negotiations are often centred on 'how to handle the red circles'.

At one end of the scale is the argument that these people are now known to be receiving more pay than the job is worth and that this should be stopped as soon as possible, especially if the organization needs that money to pay more to those people who have been (or are still) receiving less than they should. The opposite stance is that these people have become accustomed to a standard of living based on the pay that the organization has been willing to provide up to now and they should not suffer just because new standards are being applied. This is the principle that is usually adopted but there are different ways of applying it.

Any assimilation policy must set out how the 'red-circle' situations will be handled. The starting-point is normally that no one should suffer a reduction in pay – it should be 'protected' or 'safeguarded'. Thereafter, it is a matter of how quickly pay can and should be brought in line. Approaches to protection are discussed below.

Protection policies

'Indefinite protection', that is maintaining the difference between current pay and range maximum for as long as the employee remains in the job, is highly undesirable, first because it will create permanent anomalies and, second, because where there are a lot of men in this situation (which is often the case) it will perpetuate unacceptable gender gaps. The Equal Opportunities Commission in its *Good Practice Guide on Job Evaluation Schemes Free of Sex Bias*[7] states that red-circling 'should not be used on such a scale that it amounts to sex discrimination'. And, as stated by the Equal Pay Task Force:[8] 'The use of red or green circling which maintains a difference in pay between men and women over more than a phase-in period of time will be difficult to justify.'

Because of these considerations, the most common approach is now to provide for red-circled employees to receive any across-the-board (cost of living) increase awarded to staff generally for a protection period, which is usually limited to two to three years. They will no longer be entitled to general increases after the time limit has been reached (ie they will 'mark time') until their rate of pay falls within the new scale for their job. They will then be entitled to the same increases as any other staff in their grade up to the grade maximum. If a red-circled individual concerned leaves the job, the scale of pay for the job reverts to the standard range as set up following job evaluation. Where there is an incremental pay structure it is usual to allow staff to continue to earn any increments to which they are entitled under existing arrangements up to the maximum of their present scale.

If there is no limit to the protection period, red-circled staff continue to be eligible for general increases for as long as they remain in their present job. They are then on what is sometimes called a 'personal to job holder' scale.

Throughout the protection period, and particularly at the start of it, every attempt should be made to resolve the 'red-circle' cases by other means. If job holders are thought to be worth the current salary, then they may well be underused in their existing job. Attempts should be made to resolve this by either increasing the job responsibilities so that the job will justify regrading to a higher grade, or moving the person concerned to a higher-graded job as soon as an appropriate vacancy arises.

REFERENCES

1. Armstrong, M and Brown, D (2001) *Pay: The new dimensions*, CIPD, London
2. Ulrich, D (1998) A new mandate for human resources, *Harvard Business Review*, January–February, pp 124–34
3. Caldwell, R (2001) Champions, adapters, consultants and synergists: the new change agents in HRM, *Human Resource Management Journal*, 11 (3), pp 39–52
4. Gratton, L A (2000) Real step change, *People Management*, 16 March, pp 27–30
5. Boxall, P and Purcell, J (2003) *Strategic Human Resource Management*, Routledge, London
6. Millward, N, Bryn, A and Forth, J (2000) *All Change At Work?*, Routledge, London
7. Equal Opportunities Commission (2003) *Good Practice Guide on Job Evaluation Schemes Free of Sex Bias*, EOC, Manchester
8. Equal Opportunities Commission (2001) *Just Pay: Report of the Equal Pay Task Force to the Equal Opportunities Commission*, EOC, Manchester

Part 5

Performance Management

18

The Basis of Performance Management

A CHANGING PERSPECTIVE

Our understanding of performance management and how to implement it effectively has changed radically in the last few years. As recently as the early 1990s, performance management was often just another way of describing a more sophisticated performance appraisal system. This was often implemented more to provide a rating to drive a pay result than as a series of processes which enabled both organizations and individuals to focus effectively and in depth on the creation and sustained development of a high performance culture. Old ideas and concepts take time to die and appraisal is no exception. It is still part of the common parlance in many organizations and its 'top-down', 'parent–child' overtones continue to get in the way of the much more holistic approaches now being developed and used in leading organizations around the world.

Performance management acquired a new definition in the early 1990s: a process for establishing a shared understanding about what is to be achieved and how it is to be achieved; an approach to managing people that increases the probability of achieving success.

Variations on this definition come from a range of sources; from Hay Group work in the early 1990s; and from consultants and practitioners, notably Armstrong and Baron,[1] and most recently Weiss and Hartle[2] and Satterfield.[3] What they are all agreed upon are the enduring truths underlying effective performance management. These truths focus on the importance of processes over systems; the critical importance of front-end planning rather than back-end review, developing shared understanding; the importance of managing and developing people sensitively as individuals in a way which enhances their contribution, coaching; and of thinking holistically about what is needed to produce success. This is a mindset that is a long way from the preoccupation with bureaucracy, ratings and forms and the implications of (at worst) 'search, find and punish' under-performers that went with the crudest transactional view of 1980s-style performance-related pay. It recognizes the impotance of raising the use of discretionary effort and the practical application of the behaviours associated with emotional intelligence (see Chapter 2).

This chapter and the next are devoted to summaries, first of the concepts behind performance management as we now understand it, and then of the practical steps that need to be taken to ensure successful implementation. We give the bare bones here, for there are many recent pieces of research and handbooks which give greater depth on the thinking and learning in this field (see the end of this chapter and Appeneix F).

FROM ANNUAL APPRAISAL TO CHANGE INTEGRATION

There is a continuum of learning in the area of performance management. Most organizations start with annual appraisal and learn from what goes well or badly why an annual review, a well-designed set of forms and a bit of appraisal skills training doesn't get them very far. Two fundamental issues are at stake. The first of these is impact on the organization. Annual appraisal designed by personnel specialists and issued with a set of forms and a manual is, however slick the design work, not typically seen by either leaders or employees as core to the achievement of organizational goals and plans. It is seen as an additional burden in an increasingly busy working life by the majority of people in an organization and they often try to avoid doing it. Add to that the other fundamental issue – the extent to which basic appraisals skills training really enhances management capability to get into the underlying causes of performance improvement – and you have a system destined to underachieve. And that is exactly what has happened. Both the authors of this book have conducted extensive research and evaluations of how well appraisal has worked. We both conclude that organizations need to move up the line illustrated in Figure 18.1 if they are to evolve towards a high performance culture and use performance management as the means by which successful organizational performance is managed and delivered. It can then become core to HR's role as a strategic business partner in the creation of a highly engaged workforce.

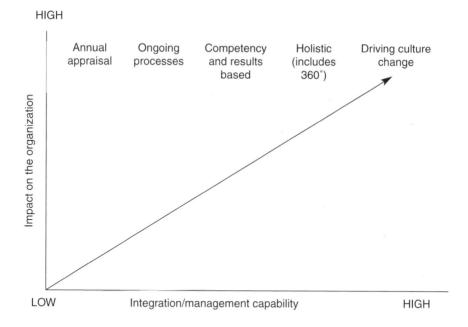

HIGH

Impact on the organization

| Annual appraisal | Ongoing processes | Competency and results based | Holistic (includes 360°) | Driving culture change |

LOW   Integration/management capability   HIGH

Figure 18.1 Evolving performance management

The message contained in this diagram is simple. If you want performance management to become a key management process for delivering the implementation of organizational strategy, then you need a much more holistic approach. To deliver this approach successfully you need to put in considerable investment in the upgrading of leadership and line management's capability to manage and develop performance both for themselves and those they work with throughout the organization.

In outline, the way organizations have gone about upgrading performance management has tended to follow the way thinking in this area has developed. First there was a realization that performance management was not much help as a once a year event – at worst it was a 'dishonest annual ritual'. The concept of continuous process became important, typically marked by provisions for more frequent review, with the focus of one of these reviews being on personal development planning, rather than just checking on progress toward the achievement of 'hard' objectives.

Since the early 1990s, many organizations have found a purely quantitative approach to performance management and measurement wanting. The understanding they began to develop of the value of competences both in setting threshold performance standards and defining behaviours associated with excellence led them to include competences in the process, typically with strong links to personal development planning. So-called 'mixed models' emerged which allowed managers and

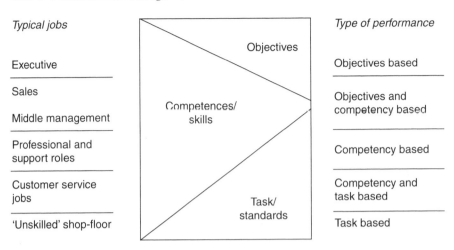

Figure 18.2 The balance of contribution required

their staff to look at the 'how' as well as the 'what' of performance and the way in which these were related. Competency frameworks joined results-focused objectives in the quest for performance improvement 'in the round'. The link with development was strengthened and the focus on the components of individual performance was sharpened. Measurement continues to remain important and indeed valued by all involved for the clarity it provides. But simply cascading down strategic objectives into bite-sized chunks through the different layers of any organization has proved problematic. There is a stage in the cascade when it is not easy always to disaggregate individual accountabilities, for objectives need to be shared and/or delivered on a collective basis. Or they need, at the customer interface, to be defined in terms of required behaviours rather than hard deliverables. As Figure 18.2 illustrates, the emphasis differs by type of role. In customer service roles, for example, competences may be much the most important element of performance; whereas at top management level the delivery of results will dominate – although how senior executives achieve their results is of increasing interest in leading organizations. Achieving outstanding results while leaving wreckage or detracting from others' ability to achieve is less and less tolerated and has resulted in senior executive severances in both public and private sectors.

At very junior, unskilled levels, in roles focused only on task completion, competences may be less important, although the quantity of such roles in the UK economy is diminishing fast.

Performance is increasingly being looked at in the round. Upward feedback, peer group review, team performance management processes and 360-degree processes are leading in many places to a more holistic approach. This implies much greater integration with the development and talent management agenda throughout an organization and, arguably, it makes strong and direct links with pay more sensitive. We will explore this in more detail later in this chapter, but it remains an important consideration when you need to ask to what degree performance management and pay processes should be separated for the better health of each.

Finally, and this is a relatively recent development born of the vicissitudes of change management initiatives, performance management is now being used by major organizations undergoing change as a key process in driving it. It is a way of ensuring that the gap between where the organization is now and where it wants to be is systematically narrowed, and that the other processes needed to make this happen (eg by using 'balanced scorecards') are implemented according to a plan which relates them to each other and the teams accountable for delivery. At this stage performance management has become *how* things get done and has truly become a core management process owned by all involved. As Satterfield says, 'Rather than performance being managed. it will occur as the natural outcome of a system characterised by effective leadership.'[3]

ORGANIZATIONAL LEVERS

The relationship between performance management as a management process and the other critical organizational levers is illustrated in Figure 18.3.

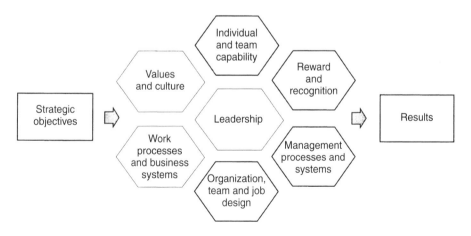

Source: Hay Group

Figure 18.3　The key organizational performance levers

This model, developed by Hay Group from the Burke Litwin model of organization change, allows organizations to look at all the elements critical to the successful management of change and diagnose where they are, what the interrelationships are and to prioritize where work needs to be done to achieve successful change and equilibrium. This model fits well with the thinking contained in this book on the place of reward management and its links with both business strategy and HR strategy and management processes. Its seven levers, focusing on the criticality of leadership, illustrate why successful performance management is dependent on foundations laid across other areas and on considered integration with them. We have never, however, seen effective performance management live and flourish without leadership in its implementation from the top. This can be the hardest element to get right. We go into more detail on this in Chapter 19.

THE INFLUENCE OF ORGANIZATION CLIMATE AND MANAGEMENT STYLE

The fundamental questions people ask in looking at performance improvement either for themselves or their organization are:

▌ What has to be achieved and how will success be judged?
▌ How am I/are we doing?
▌ How are we doing in relation to our competitors?
▌ How do our customers see us?
▌ Where do I/we stand now?
▌ Where am I/are we going?
▌ What do I/we need to work on?

The way in which these questions are addressed has a critical influence on whether performance improvement is achieved or not. We know, from research by McLelland and others, that leadership and management style and the organization climate this creates are the key dimensions in this. There are many different definitions of management style and most point to a similar range of characteristics. There is no right or wrong management style, although there are more and less appropriate styles according to people and circumstances. Perhaps the most important issues are understanding and choice – giving people the opportunity to analyse the styles they currently use and get feedback on them, so enabling them to choose which styles they can most effectively use to get results and generate the most positive organizational climate.

To illustrate the point, we have taken the Hay Group definitions of both management style and organizational climate.

Management styles

∎ *Directive* (also called 'coercive') The 'do it the way I tell you' manager who closely controls people and motivates by threats and discipline.

∎ *Visionary* (also called 'authoritative') The firm but fair manager who gives people clear direction and motivates by persuasion and feedback on both achievements and under-performance.

∎ *Affiliative* The people-first, task-second manager who emphasizes good relationships among people and motivates by trying to keep everyone happy by providing feelings of security and belonging, eg through social activities.

∎ *Participative* (also called 'democratic') The democratic manager who encourages people to provide inputs into decision making and motivates by rewarding team effort.

∎ *Pacesetting* The 'do it myself' manager who performs many tasks personally, expects people to follow his/her example and motivates by setting and demanding high standards of work.

∎ *Coaching* The developmental manager who helps and encourages people to improve their performance and motivates by providing opportunities for personal and professional development.

Most people operate with a combination of these styles, but the combination they choose affects the following six dimensions of organization climate:

∎ *Flexibility* Employee perceptions about constraints in the workplace: the degree to which they feel that there are no unnecessary rules, procedures, policies and practices that interfere with task accomplishment and that new ideas are easy to get accepted.

∎ *Standards* Employee perceptions of the emphasis management puts on improving performance and doing one's best, including the degree to which people feel that challenging but attainable goals are set for both the organization and its employees.

∎ *Rewards* Employees are recognized and rewarded for good performance and know what the organization values.

∎ *Clarity* The feeling that everyone knows what is expected of them and that they understand how those expectations relate to the large goals and objectives of the organization.

∎ *Responsibility* Employee perceptions about the authority delegated to them; the degree to which they can run their jobs/roles without having to check everything with their boss and feel fully accountable for the outcome.

∎ *Team commitment* The feeling that people are proud to belong to the organization, will provide extra effort when needed and trust that everyone is working towards the same objective.

Research among thousands of organizations around the world by Hay Group has demonstrated that there is a clear correlation between a positive organization climate and bottom line performance measures such as sales growth, productivity and customer perceptions of service quality. Such measures of employee attitude data, taken over several years, suggest in very concrete terms that if organizations manage employee engagement and satisfaction more actively they would get closer to the performance goals they strive for and they would build a better understanding of how they need to manage performance to get there.

CONTINUOUS PERFORMANCE IMPROVEMENT – BASIC CONCEPTS

Essentially, performance management has four key components:

1. planning/contracting against agreed measures/outcomes;
2. managing/coaching for performance improvement;
3. feedback and review;
4. reward and recognition.

But, before exploring these components in more detail, we would like to draw on some basic tenets which need to underpin any organization's development of its performance management processes. These focus on outcomes and on employees at all levels as the customers of performance management processes. We have summarized them from Weiss and Hartle's 1996 book as a very helpful series of reminders to keep thinking on the right track.

Tenets

1. Performance management should be a core process and a driving force, led by top management for the integration of business plans and initiatives and the delivery of continuous performance improvement.
2. There is no 'one size fits all' approach. It is not possible either to be prescriptive about the right way to design and implement performance management or to import with any real hope of success something that may have worked well somewhere else. Also, although common values matter, different processes may well be needed for different parts of an organization or for employees with needs that vary, for instance by the current stage of their career.
3. All aspects of performance matter. The 'what' as well as the 'how' of performance need both to be considered to ensure that results and the competences needed to produce performance improvement are looked at in balance.

4. Discretionary effort drives success. Raising the levels of performance is all about getting discretionary effort from people – providing an environment in which they are willing to go and rewarded for going 'the extra mile'.

5. Effective links with rewards get important messages across. This means looking at both reward and recognition and being clear about what motivates specific individuals or groups of employees. Pay systems on their own do not manage people or performance, but well-designed reward systems support performance improvement and help ensure that the performance message is a consistent one.

6. Ownership of the process is key. Line managers and employees both need to believe in the way performance is managed. Successful performance management harnesses both team and individual performance rather than concentrating on one or the other. Assessing performance should not just be a line manager's prerogative – there should be a day-to-day performance dialogue; the quality of the discussion, the focus on development and providing recognition are the real signs of a flourishing performance culture. So ownership has to be shared between line managers, teams and individuals. Very

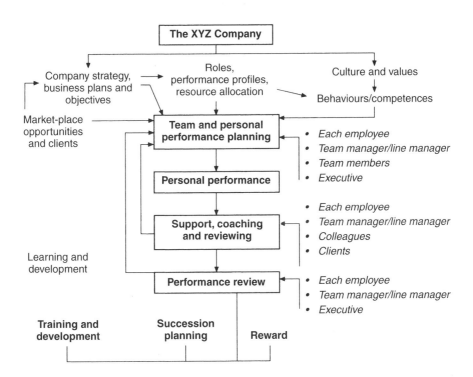

Figure 18.4 A model of performance management

importantly, the most effective and enduring performance management processes are developed with line managers and staff so that there is a proper fit between the process and real-time working practices.

7. Performance management is about relationships. People value the opinion of someone they respect and trust. Effective performance management requires rapport, candour, honesty and a genuine sense of caring. This caring creates a foundation for open dialogue where people feel their opinions can be heard and understood in a non-defensive atmosphere.

To this we would add that enhanced use of the behaviours associated with emotional intellience will improve the creation of a sustained high-performance culture. The diagram given in Figure 18.4 illustrates a typical performance management process and the elements within each phase.

Planning/contracting against agreed measures

Effective performance planning and contracting is the critical first phase of performance management. It is the basic agreement that builds clarity between individuals, managers and, increasingly, teams on what should happen over the coming year and how. It is likely to be a mixture of agreed outcomes or results and personal development goals.

Results-based objectives should be linked clearly to organizational strategies and plans in a way that makes sense to the individual or team. Often they are required to be SMART:

S	specific
M	measurable
A	achievable
R	realistic
T	time bound

And they need to be confined to those where a very specific focus is required. Development objectives should be linked to career plans, the acquisition of experience and the development of competences required either to reach defined acceptable performance levels or performance improvements. Also, part of a performance plan is an agreement as to how achievement will be tracked – be this through formal reviews; informal, sometimes team-based, reviews; or through regular progress meetings.

Performance planning is typically done in relation to an individual job/role definition or a role profile within a specific job family. (See Chapter 19 for an example.)

This also provides an opportunity to review and update job or role data to take account of significant changes that need to be agreed and recorded. It can also provide a welcome opportunity to review and discuss job design.

Team performance planning processes look across team accountabilities to ensure that everything the team is responsible for delivering is covered in terms of how responsibilities are shared and who has to contribute to ensure success. An example of such a process is given in Chapter 19. Development plans can also be shared on a team basis to help generate team coaching throughout the year both for individuals and for the team as a whole. (See Chapter 19.)

In some leading-edge organizations, performance planning is achieved by looking at organization measures derived from a balanced business scorecard (see Figure 18.5). This approach, developed by Kaplan and Norton in the early 1990s, classically looks at four dimensions or organization performance, linked to the achievement of the organization's vision:

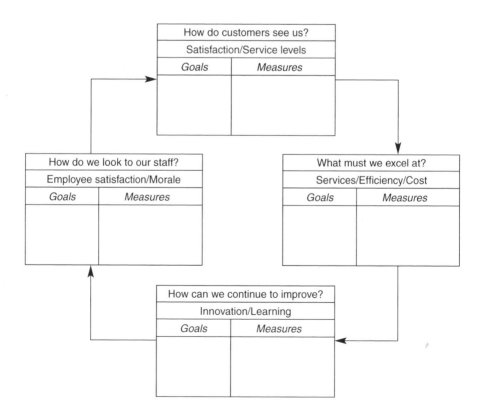

Figure 18.5 The balanced business scorecard

▊ financial;
▊ internal processes;
▊ customers;
▊ innovation and learning.

Organizational, divisional and sometimes departmental goals are set for each and individual plans are linked to this. The idea is a powerful one, focusing as it does on the growth of intellectual capital and the delivery of shareholder/stakeholder value in a way that takes account of customer/client perceptions of what it takes to meet their criteria for satisfaction. It is a move away from performance measurement driven by achievement, or otherwise, of budgetary targets – essentially a model based purely on financial control – to one focused on longer-term strategic alignment and based on measuring value.

Thinking and practice in these newer approaches to performance measurement is developing fast. They will inevitably have a profound effect on the focus of performance management and the impact will be evident first in the performance planning process.

Managing/coaching for continuous performance improvement

Attitude survey evidence from a wide range of sources indicates clearly that the quality of day-to-day management and coaching of performance improvement is where the battle for effective performance management and the creation of a high-performance culture is won or lost. You can build greater clarity about performance plans as you go if you have to in times of uncertainty. What is harder to build, or very often rebuild, is mutual confidence, respect and trust, in order to replace inappropriate management styles and a consequentially negative organizational climate with a more adult–adult, coaching-focused approach to management.

The development of good coaching skills is critical. In essence, according to Weiss and Hartle, good coaching is:

▊ *Genuine* Based on a sincere interest in helping others solve problems, learn new approaches and use new technology, develop competence and improve skills.
▊ *Empowering* Linked to the expression of positive expectations that people can do well without their manager snatching back the work as soon as there is a risk of failure. Good coaches help people identify how to solve their work problems without their manager providing all the answers. It is based on open, honest, two-way discussion while coaching.
▊ *Understanding* Being perceptive about an employee's work problems, concerns, competences and technology needs. This depends on being attentive, open-minded and not guided by pre-set assumptions about

what it is the other person needs or does not need. It reflects flexibility, adaptability and the capacity to explore ideas.

▌ *Problem solving* Diagnosing where performance is falling short of agreed and required standards. This involves offering appropriate advice and assistance which bring about performance improvements. It also involves learning to have the confidence to be an enabler rather than a controller — itself a healthy change and infinitely preferable to leading from the front all the time.

Coaching lies at the heart of effective day-to-day feedback and successful development. Our own and other research is clear that the development of effective coaching skills makes a significant difference to the quality of performance management implementation. At senior and top management levels, many leading organizations are now building in coaching from an external executive coach to help 'fast-track' improvements in leadership and delivery of required outcomes.

Feedback and review

In performance management processes that rely on regular feedback and review, the annual review should be a lighter process – a 'no surprises' summary of achievements over the year and the beginning of a new performance agreement or contract. It is a two-way process, but increasingly one that may draw on feedback from a range of sources:

▌ performance data against measurable results in the performance agreement;
▌ feedback on skills and competency development and use, related to an agreed development plan;
▌ feedback from a selected range of subordinates, peer group, managers and others affected by the individual's performance, using either a formal 360-degree feedback instrument or in terms of confidential comment against a role profile revealed only to the reviewing manager;
▌ feedback from customers/clients or other stakeholders, where this can be tracked and sampled on a fair and consistent basis;
▌ team performance feedback;
▌ a self-assessment of performance against plan and/or against a specific job/role profile – an approach which is valuable in building ownership of performance outcomes and which is particularly helpful at senior levels as part of a process of culture change focusing on greater openness and trust.

Upward/multi-rater feedback and 360-degree approaches have been an area of considerable activity in terms of various forms of computer-based instruments used to ensure both confidentiality and the use of validated approaches and performance dimensions. The growth of e-HR means that IT-assisted approaches are now often available to help individuals and teams cross-reference their contribution against objectives agreed in related parts of an organization – so enabling the process to became a real-time planning and audit tool.[4]

Performance feedback is therefore becoming both more subtle and more complex. This is creating a different environment for reward and recognition along with the realization that well-handled feedback can be a reward in its own right.

REWARD AND RECOGNITION

The efficacy of performance-related pay as a catalyst for change and producing performance improvement is dealt with elsewhere in this book. Suffice it to say here that three current developments affect the links between performance management and pay:

▌ The growing incidence of short-, medium- and long-term incentives against business performance measures is providing its own form of performance ratings, with the very direct relationship between the achievement of measurable targets and the rewards prescribed for this in the incentive plan.

▌ The concurrent reality that sustained low inflation (typically below 3 per cent) and relatively low market movement has reduced flexibility to pay aggressive performance rewards in terms of annual base salary progression. A range of increases, of 0–10 per cent from underperformers who add no value for their place in a pay range to exceptional performers, is not uncommon in 2004. In the late 1980s, a range of 0–15 per cent might have been more common against much higher inflation levels. Performance differentials in base salary now take more time to accrue and the messages in each year's pay rise feel more muted. Delivering progression and managing expectations around progression are significant challenges in both private and public sectors.

▌ The complexity and often the subtlety of the feedback from the range of sources now being tapped for each individual has, in some organizations, led to the conclusion that performance ratings should be abandoned. Although it cannot be denied that ratings become embedded in the pay culture and can, especially in the public service where pay movement has been strictly controlled, become rewards in their own right, there is a growing view that they can also be damaging. Research conducted by Hay Group on this issue in 1997 revealed a significant group of leading organizations in pharmaceuticals and the finance sector moving away from performance ratings for senior managers, because they believed ratings got in the way of rounded discussion on personal development and delivery of results. They have moved to assessments in narrative form because they believe ratings promote tunnel vision, focus on the final score and, at worst, lead to battles over the grey areas between ratings in an effort to raise the initial assessment. Critical to the move away from ratings are high levels of trust and a verbal assessment that provides a rounded appreciation of contribution as well as benchmarking against colleagues and, typically, the external market place too.

For more junior staff, however, the need for consistency among the larger number of employees involved means that the link between pay and performance management is likely to continue to rely upon ratings in some form or another. The number of ratings typically in use appears to vary between three and six, with a marked tendency towards simplification. In choosing how many ratings to go for, the following considerations are important:

▌ How many different levels of performance can actually be distinguished for the employees in question.
▌ What the ratings should be called. Numerical and alphabetical ratings tend to carry overtones of school reports. (Remember what you said to your parents when you got a B-.) Descriptors such as 'Proficient', 'Highly effective' or even 'Developing' tend to have more motivational value. 'Achievement levels' probably has more going for it as an overall term rather than 'box marking' and similar terms beloved of the public sector.
▌ How expectations need to be managed in relation to the likely distribution of ratings and how their value can be maintained. Rating drift is a besetting sin in most performance review processes, especially when money is tight. It will be important to be clear at the outset of a new approach whether absolute or relative performance is being measured. If it is absolute, there will be a presumption of drift. If performance is to be looked at on a relative basis each year, then continuous performance improvement should mean that less drift is in order. We would agree with US 'guru' Ed Lawler that this is a leadership issue and that to prevent rating inflation top management should hold line management accountable for their ratings, 'making it clear that high ratings have to be justified by operating results that are correspondingly high'.[5]

Linking rating/assessment to pay

Experience suggests that there should always be some flexibility in the way in which ratings are linked to pay. Employees are deeply suspicious of forced choice distributions and fixed relationships, because they know and see that performance is not always distributed in relation to some form of statistically normal distribution – except, perhaps, over very large populations. Managers who have had to work with forced choice distributions remember all too well the difficulties they encountered in getting the figures to come right and still give the motivational messages they wanted to – especially to the 'engine room' of good, reliable, but not exceptional, performers who may come off badly if ratings or rankings have to be manipulated. Evidence from our work in employee focus groups suggests that employees may well prefer to keep a rating they deserve when money is tight and even forgo a pay increase or accept a lower pay rise rather than have their performance devalued at the assessment or overall review stage. This may offend purists, but in our experience it is tied up with deep issues of self-esteem and reward for commitment. The same will be true of performance ranking to distribute a pay 'pot'. We return to this issue in Chapter 19.

Evaluations of performance-related pay we have conducted suggest that it may well be more productive to completely change the ratings in use than attempt to claw back 'lax' ratings and rating drift. People who were given the equivalent of a 'highly effective' rating one year do not like being called 'effective' the year after for an equivalent contribution, if this is purely linked to an attempt to reassert control over ratings.

This means that, the more line managers can be equipped and empowered to manage performance-related pay progression by taking their own view of how they will spend their allocated budget and what messages they need to give across their employee group, the less trouble there is likely to be. Provided the messages are reasonably fair, consistent and well delivered, more flexibility is likely to be more motivational for all concerned.

The importance of recognition and total rewards

Growing attention is being focused on the whole area of recognition (see Chapter 27), along with growing understanding of the importance of the psychological contract (see Chapter 5). Appreciation of the importance of recognition tends to become more acute the moment skills shortages and market pressures become part of the picture or when talent management rises in importance. When skills shortages and scaremongering about the 'demographic time bomb' were prevalent in the late 1980s boom, many employers – notably in the public sector – began to look very creatively at non-cash rewards, 'family friendly' policies and flexible working practices. Few of these were specifically performance related. In the United States, where unemployment remains very low and where market pressures are building up, there is now even greater focus on recognition programmes. As Maggi Coil, Chair of the American Compensation Association, put it at the 1998 IPD Compensation Forum conference:

❚ Any company can offer more money, stock options and bonuses.
❚ Any company can buy out the cash-based package you offer an employee.
❚ The only competitive advantage an employer can offer that is unique is the environment.
❚ Pay being equal – employees need a better reason to get up in the morning!

We dealt in detail with the implications of this in Chapter 2.

Handling the pay element

Performance rewards are normally given through a separate process from performance reviews. Although there is, and should be, a clear 'read across' between performance management and pay outcomes, the process of communicating these needs to be separated to gain maximum motivational value.

In communicating performance rewards the following considerations are critical:

❚ The amount and the rationale for the pay award should be communicated personally by the individual's manager and confirmed in a letter which reflects and provides recognition for the achievements of the year.
❚ This is part of the performance management process and another useful opportunity to get important messages across and provide motivation. Most organizations do not say 'thank you' enough.
❚ The messages given in the performance review and the pay award should always be consistent.
❚ It is helpful for individuals to know how they fared in the general run of pay awards and how issues of consistency for equivalent performance for their peer group have been addressed.
❚ This communication is also a valuable opportunity to look forward to and provide motivation for further achievement in the future.
❚ Under-performance that results in a zero pay award should be clearly signalled during the year and not left either to the performance review or the pay award. If the first an individual knows about a shortfall in performance is at the time a pay award is due, this is damaging and difficult to handle. At worst, it can be construed as constructive dismissal and lead to an Industrial Tribunal case or even legal proceedings. A zero award that comes as a surprise is perceived much more as a punishment than when it is given as a consistent message about issues that have been under discussion and remedial action for some time.

JUST-IN-TIME TRAINING/IMPLEMENTATION

When performance management was first implemented, many organizations opted for a 'Big Bang' approach. Everything was front-end loaded. All the communication and training happened when the scheme was launched and all too often interest in and commitment to embedding performance management tended to wane as the year went on. Any skills training given a good six months before it is needed tends not to be well remembered and applied. The messages tend to get mixed and lost and performance management schemes implemented this way tend to under-perform from a very early stage. As organizations have come to terms with the very profound effects performance management can have in integrating change and the embedding of a new culture, so they have been increasingly prepared to commit more resources to implementation. Performance management training is now much more commonly seen as an important part of management and staff development. The training itself is much more process than systems focused and it is commonly used to help develop feedback skills and to give individuals feedback about the way they manage and their own performance gaps in this area to coach them in improving the performance dialogue and enable them to make choices about how they improve. At its most effective, training is now phased through the first year of a new performance management process and delivered just before it is needed. This means working on understanding how and why people improve their performance (including how they learn best) and on performance planning at the beginning of the year, going through managing/coaching workshops during the year and tackling performance reviews and related pay decision processes toward the end of the year. We deal in more detail with the processes involved in Chapter 19.

REFERENCES

1. Armstrong, M and Baron, A (1998) *Performance Management: The new realities*, CIPD, London
2. Weiss, M and Hartle, E (1996) *Re-engineering Performance Management*, Kogan Page, London
3. Satterfield, T (2003) From performance management to performance leadership, *WorldatWork Journal*, First Quarter
4. Lampron, F and Koski, L (2004) Implementing Web-enabled performance management, *Workspan*, 01
5. Lawler, E (2003) *Treat People Right: How organizations and individuals can propel each other into a virtuous spiral of success*, Jossey-Bass, San Francisco

19

Performance Management in Practice

IMPLEMENTATION – RARELY A GREENFIELD SITE

For most organizations, the decision to implement performance management is not about introducing a completely new process. In Chapter 18 we illustrated the continuum along which organizations tend to upgrade what they do in this area. With the exception of start-up organizations, most have had some form of appraisal. For many organizations, this also of course means that their 'brownfield site' carries with it the bad experiences of appraisal schemes that have not lived up to their objectives and promises. In the 2004 CIPD Survey of Performance Managment, 87 per cent of the 506 participating organizations had a formal process and some 36 per cent were new systems.

Design and implementation of any new approach will therefore have to be achieved against an environment where any or all of the problems illustrated in Figure 19.1 have been encountered.

This 'vicious circle' reflects findings from a wide range of recent research, including large-scale surveys from the CIPD[1], the OECD[2] and Hay Group[3] into performance management and performance-related pay. It paints a daunting picture of the continuing problems and it is one which suggests that cosmetic changes to performance management are generally unlikely to work. In embarking upon change to performance management, serious attention will need to be paid to:

▌ diagnosis of the current situation and its causes;

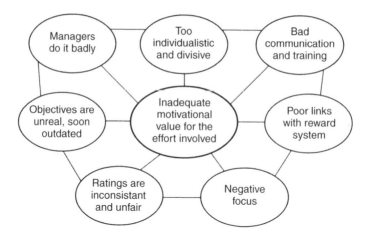

Figure 19.1 What isn't working?

▌ clarification of the objectives of performance management for the future;

▌ design – using processes to maximize leadership involvement and ownership by all those involved;

▌ training, coaching and continuing support which encourages and sustains changed behaviours, as well as explaining new systems;

▌ delivering on the promise of performance improvement and the creation of a high-performance culture, in the performance management process through evaluation and fine-tuning in relation to learning points as they emerge;

▌ realism about how long the process of change in performance management takes – at least a year for many organizations, according to the 1998 IPD and more recent research.

In this chapter we deal with each of these in turn.

Diagnosing the current situation

Successful diagnosis of the current state of performance management means looking at the systems and processes in use from a series of angles. The main approaches that will yield a real understanding of what has been happening are as follows.

The first approach is a collection of evidence from focus groups and, if possible, an opinion survey on how the scheme is viewed and the results it has produced. This means asking questions around the following themes.

Planning

▌ Are business goals clear and well understood?

▌ Are individual/team goals and the competency frameworks in place clearly linked to them – identifying the 'how' as well as the 'what'?

▌ The effectiveness of two-way performance planning and the quality and realism of the targets agreed.

▌ Is there joint agreement on what should be delivered and when?

Coaching/tracking performance

▌ Are achievements against delivery, business and development targets tracked through the year?

▌ The quality of feedback from managers/team/other stakeholders in performance.

▌ The extent of recognition and reinforcement actually occurring through the year.

▌ Is early identification of and coaching to reduce underachievement taking place?

▌ Does coaching cover required behaviours as well as positive changes in approach?

▌ Is the focus on longer-term personal development issues, longer-term business delivery issues or short- and medium-term business imperatives, ie is the balance sensible in the current business environment?

Review

▌ The extent to which there is self-assessment and reasonable preparation for each review meeting (preferably more than once a year).

▌ Are sufficient time and privacy set aside for review meetings?

▌ Is the process perceived as open and reasonably fair?

▌ The extent to which managers are using appropriate management styles to promote open discussion, agreement on outcomes and planning for the future.

▌ Are personal or environmental problems not of an individual's own making properly taken account of and dealt with on a problem-solving rather than a blame basis?

▌ The appropriateness and motivational tone of any rating scales in use, ie how well they reflect the actual range of performance differences that can be distinguished for a particular employee group.

▌ The distribution of these ratings and the consistency with which they are applied.

▌ The values underlying performance ranking in additon to or instead of rating.

▌ Consistency, fairness and speed in the handling of under-performance.

▍ The clarity of performance and development planning for the future against the current review.

▍ The way in which the guidance and performance review documentation have been used, ie whether the guidance had been read and found helpful, whether review forms have been found to be simple and straightforward or bureaucratic and cumbersome, whether they are judged to collect the right information and whether they are used through the year to help performance improvement and development. Always remember that 100 per cent compliance with the completion of performance review forms is not an indication that the process is working well, just a sign that the forms are being filled in. Confidential scrutiny of a sample of forms together with analysis of how they are used will, however, give a better idea of how well embedded the current process is and how effective the performance focus has become.

Reward and recognition

▍ The existence of clear links between delivered performance and pay increases/bonus payments or other forms of recognition.

▍ The existence of clear guidelines to ensure consistent reward practice.

▍ Personal delivery by each individual's manager of the reward messages, ie personal ownership of reward decisions.

▍ Do most employees feel reasonably well rewarded in relation to their contribution and understand how the links are made?

The quality of training and support for the process should also be scrutinized to see how helpful it has been; whether it was delivered at the right time and has helped the process of agreeing performance agreements/contracts and development plans; whether it has helped the identification and coaching of under-performance; and its contribution to consistent working of all the processes.

This activity should also be supplemented by interviews at management level to cover the same ground and assess whether, and to what extent, differences in perception exist between those who lead and operate the processes and those on the receiving end. Analysis of the findings from the diagnostic exercise can then be used to inform the assessment of needs for the future and how cautious or how radical it is possible to be in seeking to achieve change.

Clarification of objectives

Upgrading or implementing performance management is now typically achieved by setting up a working group with representation from across the organization which, with guidance from the HR function/external experts, acts as a design group. By doing this organizations can ensure that any new thinking is reality tested from the start and that new

XYZ Financial Services Group
Our Approach to Performance Management

Objectives

I. Vision
1. To underpin and support the achievement of the Group's business vision and strategy and promote flexible responses to changing business circumstances.
2. Alignment with our business planning cycle to deliver a series of linked processes that help produce business performance improvement across the range of performance measures we use.
3. To help develop and sustain a high-performance culture based on shared understanding over what is expected and commitment to achieve it, where good performance is recognized and rewarded and where poor performance is addressed fairly, constructively and speedily.
4. To provide a sound basis for performance assessments, career moves, promotions and pay decisions in which everyone involved can have confidence.

II. Guiding principles
1. To exist as a constructive and continuing dialogue through the year between managers, teams and individuals supported by a minimum of documentation. This dialogue will take account of changing business circumstances as they occur.
2. To help reinforce understanding of our business and the need for good teamwork as well as individual performance improvement.
3. To focus effort, skill and competences (ie total contribution) where they are most needed.
4. To help build the skill base of the Group to empower staff to improve their performance and so encourage and deliver continuous performance improvement and flexible responses to changing business circumstances.
5. To help build and sustain an open, honest debate about continuing performance improvement at all levels in the Group.
6. To be capable of being monitored, adapted and changed to run with the grain of the business as it evolves.

Figure 19.2   An example of a company statement of its vision and guiding principles for performance management

approaches to performance management have the best chance of gaining early 'buy-in'. We note here that the CIPD 2004 research into performance management found significantly greater emphasis on linking this process to organizational values and seeing performance as 'living the values'.

Effective changes to improve performance management depend on building clarity at the beginning on the outcomes and business benefits being sought. There needs to be a vision and strategy for performance management within HR and reward strategy. Agreement on this is the key initial task of any working group established to improve and/or implement a new approach to performance management.

Figure 19.2 illustrates a typical statement of company objectives for performance management.

These company objectives are then used to ensure that newly designed processes are a good cultural fit and set standards against which future evaluations can take place.

Design and implementation

We have stressed above the importance of a participative design process. This needs to start by:

▌ looking at the evidence on current internal practice and deciding what has gone well and should be kept and what has gone badly and should be scrapped;

▌ looking at relevant learning from elsewhere – ensuring that recent research such as the CIPD 2004 report and other recent studies and concrete examples of evolving practice are reviewed for the insights they give on the likely direction of successful change;

▌ setting the values and success criteria for the processes;

▌ taking a 'fit for purpose' view on each item the design group considers, so that flexibility and quality are automatically part of the debate.

Then the working group needs to go through the four key elements of performance management and agree what would work best and contribute most value in their own organization. We look at the key elements in turn, summarizing the kind of considerations design teams are now looking at in establishing the architecture of new processes.

Performance planning and contracting

Focus on objectives and results

First, it is important to understand how the business plans, measures and manages its performance. As far as possible any new approach to performance management should reflect this and be aligned to ensure that business objectives are met. So performance planning will need to take account of the business planning cycle. Especially at senior management level, it is of critical importance to ensure alignment of the business and performance planning cycles so that they happen and fit logically together. This avoids duplication and ensures that each reinforces the other. It also provides a better framework for looking across the organization to ensure that shared as well as individual accountabilities for delivery are taken account of setting and environment of team awareness, as well as of personal achievement. As we said in Chapter 18, this is the place for deciding how a few SMART objectives, Key Result Areas or balanced scorecard goals can best be agreed and delivery tracked through the year. A process for doing and recording this needs to be designed and tested so that it best reflects what Hartle and Wiess call 'Achievement by design'. Figure 19.3 illustrates individual and line management needs from this process.

Performance planning on 'hard' measures will generally need to vary by employee group, depending on the level of involvement and control

	Line Manager's Needs	*Individual Needs*	
Start of Year DIALOGUE	■ Understand individual's role and priorities within overall role description agreed at outset of posting. ■ Agree milestones towards overall objectives for full-term posting and date for review of 4-year norm. ■ Agree 4–6 key business objectives for year and measures of success. ■ Agree measures for tracking achievement: what, when and how. ■ Agree how job is to be performed and expected key competencies, standards and behaviours. ■ Help identify development needs to support delivery (to be done separately from setting of business (objectives).	■ Clarify on long-term expectations from role with scheduled review dates. ■ Agree four to six key business objectives and measures of success for year ahead. ■ Agreement on and support with personal development to raise performance. ■ A shared view on success over the year: what, when and how.	CONTINUING
In Year CONTINUING	■ Review progress and evidence of achievement. ■ What is going well? ■ What needs doing differently? ■ Refocus agreement if circumstances change.	■ Focus on tracking/ fine-tuning delivery against agreement for outcomes and development. ■ Understanding what is going well/less well and agreement on what to change. ■ Refocus agreement if circumstances change.	DIALOGUE
Year End	■ Review achievement of key business and development objectives. ■ Sound basis for reward recommendations and decisions. ■ Basis for next year's performance agreement.	■ Recognition for achievements against agreed work plan. ■ Honest feedback that can be used to raise performance ■ Fair rewards/base/pay bonus. ■ Basis for next year's performance agreement.	

OLD AGREEMENT	NEW AGREEMENT
———————	——————→

Figure 19.3 Building a senior management performance agreement

each group has on business outcomes. It is all too easy just to see this process from a management perspective, although in flatter and more devolved organizations there is a lot more responsibility at more junior levels. Nevertheless, there is by no means always a nice clear cascade of management objectives, and this needs to be taken account of in performance contracts that focus on quality, customer service standards and productivity, rather than seeking spuriously to identify each individual's 'bite-sized chunk' of strategic contribution.

As we stressed in Chapter 18, most organizations are increasingly also looking at the development and use of competences in performance planning. So design should take account of how competences are related to achievement. One way of doing this is to use role profiles which isolate performance themes and related competences so that the individual has a clear performance template against which to direct his or her efforts. Figure 19.4 illustrates what this looks like for a financial controller in a medium-sized service business. Recent Hay research[3] found that the provision of clear, unambiguous delivery targets raised motivation to perform because they provide much-needed clarity.

Where teamworking is important, it is important to have team performance agreements. Essentially, these need to be linked to organization measures, business unit measures and business processes as they affect specific work teams. The aim then is to look at what the team has to deliver and then break this down in terms of how individuals can contribute to this. Figure 19.5 illustrates what such an agreement might look like. It takes account of objectives that are individual, those that are shared and those where some members of the team contribute from time to time. Use of a matrix like this can then support individual performance management and development.

Personal development planning

Alongside the delivery of results, organizations now typically expect individuals to take some responsibility for developing themselves, using the internal and external development resources that are available to them, and continuously adding to their own skill base. Lifelong learning is rapidly becoming part of the vocabulary. Again this needs to be planned, agreed and coordinated to match individual and organizational needs. In designing the personal development planning process, account needs to be taken of:

▌ Current skills and competency frameworks that clarify what is needed for specific roles and for career development.
▌ The kinds of training and development activity available and needed.
▌ What can be developed through coaching and mentoring.
▌ Likely career paths in relation to where the business is going.

▌ The differing needs of individuals at various stages in their career with varying personality preferences, talents and specialisms. Current approaches to talent management recognize that a clearly different emphasis is needed for, at one extreme, a graduate trainee undertaking intensive development, as compared to an employee within 18 months of retirement, at the other.

A decision will need to be taken about whether to do all performance planning in the same meeting or process or at different times. Often, in our experience and as borne out by the 2004 CIPD research, organizations that are really serious about getting the most from the process clearly separate performance contracting from development planning to ensure that each gets the time it needs.

Managing and coaching for performance improvement

Again, the design team will need to look at what is happening now and see what can be improved and what needs to be introduced. Often they can identify places or teams within the organization where successful coaching and tracking of performance is going on. It is always worth looking for this and seeing if this can be used as a model for wider use – if possible involving the managers and team in providing an internal benchmark and spreading practices designed for the local culture that are already working well. If this does not exist, then coaching is likely to be an area where training will be needed (see below).

The following list of 'action levers' known to contribute to improved performance identifies some of the actions that can be taken to raise performance:

▌ *Top management levers:*
  – consistent messages that top management values the workforce;
  – develop a specific people management philosophy statement;
  – set an example with appropriate leadership styles;
  – decisions that recognize the importance of employee commitment to success;
  – articulate and publicize the organization's mission, guiding principles and core values;
  – regular communication to inform employees of performance results;
  – periodic communication to recognize the importance of employee efforts;
  – publicize past success stories to build pride in the organization;
  – recognize significant group, team and individual accomplishments;
  – provide technology and resources needed to meet performance expectations;

Performance themes	Key indicators	Competences
1. Management/financial information production	*What impact has the finance controller had on the quality of management and financial information and how?* ■ Quality of financial information (eg accuracy, timeliness, clarity) ■ Quality of management information (eg accuracy, timeliness, clarity) ■ Quality of reports (eg presentation, meaningfulness) ■ Effective and orderly filing system in place and maintained ■ All relevant business factors taken into account and correctly treated from an accounting perspective	■ Team leadership ■ Customer service orientation ■ Analytical thinking ■ Achievement orientation ■ Impact and influence ■ Developing others ■ Information seeking (See over for description of Competences) ■ Knowledge of business ■ Numeracy ■ Knowledge of structure and policies ■ Attention to detail/accuracy/orderliness ■ Time management/prioritization ■ Professional; qualifications ■ Communication skill (verbal, written), feedback ■ Knowledge of information systems (software systems) ■ Listening skills/patience ■ Accounting expertise and knowledge ■ Perseverance ■ Word processing/spreadsheet skills ■ Data interpretations
2. Customer support	*What impact has the finance controller had on customer service and support and how?* ■ Quality of communications with customers ■ Anticipation of, and meeting customer needs ■ Customer satisfaction with performance of the accounts team	

Figure 19.4 Performance profile: accounts–financial controller (Medium-sized service business)

Performance themes	Key indicators	Competences
3. System development	*What and how has the finance controller contributed to new systems development and utilization to meet teams' needs?* ■ Identification and prioritization of system improvements (manual and IT) ■ Implementation of system changes ■ Efficiency of process with the accounts department	(Continuation sheet – if needed)
4. Team management and development	*What and how has the finance controller contributed to team members' management and development?* ■ Team climate (eg flexibility, standards, resolving conflict, clarity, commitment) ■ Extent of accounts team integration with the consultancy ■ Identification and satisfaction of team members' training needs ■ Quality of guidance and advice for staff ■ Optimum utilization of team resources ■ Appropriate communication and discussion of relevant issues with financial director	
5. Personal development and learning	*What and how has the finance controller contributed to increase his/her own expertise value?* ■ Clarity and relevance of personal development plan ■ Progress against development goals	

Team leadership the ability to motivate a team to work together effectively; **Customer service orientation** is the desire to help or serve others, to meet their needs, focusing your efforts on discovering and meeting the customers' needs; **Analytical thinking** is understanding a situation by breaking it apart into smaller pieces, or tracking the implications of a situation in a step-by-step way. This includes organizing parts of a problem or situation in a systematic way: making systematic comparisons of different features or aspects; setting priorities on a rational basis, identifying time sequence, casual relationships or if-then relationships; **Achievement orientation** is a concern for working well or for surpassing a standard of excellence; **Impact and influence** is the ability to persuade, convince, influence or impress others in order to get them to go along with your agenda; **Developing others (including delegation)** is a genuine intent to foster the long-term learning or development of others with an appropriate level of analysis, thought or effort; **Information seeking** is the underlying curiosity and desire to know more about things, people or issues. It implies going beyond the questions that are routine and required in the job.

 - balance the importance of organization performance and employee personal goals.
∎ *Organization levers:*
 - self-managed teams;
 - employee empowerment;
 - eliminate unnecessary reporting levels and broaden span of management control;
 - minimize hierarchy and status distinctions;
 - eliminate 'silos' and create a 'boundary-less' organization;
 - effective knowledge management and knowledge sharing;
 - rely on employee task forces to solve problems.
∎ *Human resource levers:*
 - recruit for attitude and required behaviours;
 - investment in capability building at all levels;
 - enable a climate based on mutual trust and respect;
 - role/job clarity and clear career paths;
 - pay-for-contribution salary progression;
 - gain/goal-sharing incentive plans;
 - outcome-based performance management – results and development;
 - fit-for-purpose salary bands enabling flexibility;
 - competency-based HR systems to focus on employee capability.
∎ *Line management levers:*
 - job rotation and cross-training;
 - flexible work schedules;
 - use of appropriate management styles to optimize motivation and a positive work climate;
 - regular constructive feedback on employee strengths and development needs;
 - encouragement for employee skill development and learning;
 - emphasize teamwork and collaboration;
 - encourage employees to assume new responsibilities and broaden the scope of their role;
 - clearly define individual and team performance goals and measures;
 - effective performance coaching;
 - speedy, fair and effective handling of under-performance;
 - provide for ongoing employee involvement;
 - encourage risk taking and 'do whatever it takes' commitment;
 - recognize and celebrate employee accomplishments;
 - provide opportunities for fun at work;
 - consistency in decision making and, when necessary, in discipline.

Adapted from: Risher, H (2003) Refocusing performance management for high performance, *Compensation and Benefits Review*, September–October.

A business targets/senior job matrix

Business targets / names	Deryk Smith	John Graig	Christine Lutyens	Colin Groom	Emma Jones	John Evans	Stuart Philby	John Home	Ahmad Hussein
1. Net trading profit	P	P	P–C		S	S	S	S	S
2. Sales		S	P–C		S		P		
3. Manufacturing/Marketing		S	S		S	P	S	S	P
4. Output		S		S		P		P	
5. Airborne pollution equipment		S (pre-sanction)		P		S		S (post-sanction)	
6. Liquid gas plant			S	P					
7. Manpower productivity	P	S	S	S	S	S	S		S
8. Safety	S	S	S	S	S	P	S	S	P
9. ISQ 9000		S	S	S	S	P	S		P
10. Quality	P	S	S		S	S	S	S	S

Key: P = Personal accountability S = Shared responsibility C = Policy/facilitating contribution

Figure 19.5 An example of a matrix of interdependencies for a senior management team

Performance assessment and review

As we said in Chapter 18, there are many more options for performance review now, and more are emerging. Simple, top-down appraisal is being augmented and, many would say, improved by multi-source, 360-degree or multi-rater feedback and the use of a range of tools and instruments for producing clarity and consistency about individual contribution. The CIPD 2004 survey found that 14 per cent of organizations now do this.

There is an ongoing debate about performance rating and ranking.

The design process for this element of performance management needs to focus on:

▌ Who will/should be involved in the review process.
▌ What sources of performance data will be looked at.
▌ How and when these are available within the current business planning and review processes.
▌ Whether self-assessment is valuable in the preparation process – it generally is!
▌ Whether multi-source, 360-degree feedback would be helpful for development purposes; if it is to be tested, which group would it be most beneficial to start with (try to include some senior/top managers) – which group is likely to be receptive to and benefit from the insights this gives?
▌ If it is to be used, what approach should be used (eg standard instruments from an external source such as the Hay Group Organization Climate Survey, or a home-grown and tested approach)?
▌ The place of performance rating or ranking, its value in the culture needed for the future and as a mark of recognition.
▌ How the review should be recorded and the use to be made of the information collected.
▌ What managers are capable of delivering now and what training they will need to deliver good-quality, consistent performance reviews which motivate employees, including those where under-performance has been identified.
▌ How this will help the organization manage not just the extremes of performance but the motivation of their 'B' players, the majority of their people and the 'engine room' on which most organizations depend.[4]

Approaches to performance rating

Organizations should be clear that it will always be more important to raise performance that to rate it. Research from many sources including the OECD suggests that the search for a perfect and widely acceptable performance rating system appears to be a sterile one. The 2004 CIPD survey found that the use of ratings is by no means universal. While 59 per cent of participants gave an overall rating, 40 per cent did not.

Both the IPD's and recent Hay research indicate that many employees dislike rating and feel that it fails to recognize the complexity of their performance through the year. Research by Hay Group with Henley Management College did however find that within a 'measurement culture' it can be motivating. In this study of 400 individuals, 74 per cent strongly believed that using measures keeps people focused on what is important. It is also clear that rating gets in the way of the review process itself, since people wait to get their rating, prejudicing the valuable developmental aspects that should be the focus of their attention. Nevertheless, consistency of treatment in performance assessment is very important to employees and, in large organizations or where there are large groups of employees engaged in similar work, some form of rating may be helpful. Managers and teams too can find rating helpful in terms of ensuring that they apply the same values in assessing relative achievement levels. There is also, as we said in Chapter 18, the reality that performance rating systems tend to become embedded in organization culture as a form of recognition. They certainly, in our experience, have this status in much of the UK public service where they may be more important to individuals, notably high performers, as a replacement for the high bonuses or pay increases more commonly available in the private sector. The critical issue is how many different levels of performance organizations can actually identify for different groups or staff.

The main options in terms of rating systems are outlined below.

Three ratings

Essentially this approach recognizes that most people put in a good reliable contribution and that only the extremes need different attention. The performance levels are therefore:

▌ exceeded expectations;
▌ fully met agreed performance contract;
▌ did not meet contract.

The main argument for this approach is that it is both realistic in most circumstances, as well as straightforward and easy to understand. It leaves space for the subtleties of appreciating individual contribution without labelling it more than necessary. Truly outstanding performers will get the recognition they need and deserve from the 'exceeded' category. The good, reliable, core performers on whom most organizations depend will have this reality recognized in the 'fully met' category. The few under-performers most organizations have to tackle will fall into the 'did not meet' category.

The problems that arise with this approach derive from its strengths. A lack of fine performance definition can make decisions on pay links difficult. There is greater dependence on managerial judgement, flexibility and trust. It is hard to use pay/performance increase matrices. Guidance on promotion increases and on progression, notably within broader pay bands, needs to be given to ensure that the messages given are consistent.

Four ratings

An approach increasingly adopted by organizations working hard on improving their organization climate is to use a rating scale where all descriptors aim to provide positive reinforcement. This means that employees cannot be damned out of hand and the stress is on a culture of continuing improvement. If performance from any individual is totally unacceptable, this fact should have been identified as part of the processes in operation during the year and corrective action initiated at the time. It should mean that individuals are either in 'intensive care' for performance improvement or going through a disciplinary procedure.

The example given below therefore emphasizes the positive and improvable nature of individual performance:

▌ *Highly effective:* meets all the objectives of the job. Exceeds required standards and consistently performs in a thoroughly proficient manner beyond normal expectations.
▌ *Effective:* achieves required objectives and standards of performance and fully meets the agreed expectations for the job.
▌ *Developing:* a contribution that is stronger in some aspects of the job than others, where most objectives and required behaviours are met but where performance improvements are still needed to meet the full performance agreement.
▌ *Basic:* a contribution which meets some elements of the performance agreement but not others that are important and where there is room for improvement in several definable areas.

Other organizations use the term 'improvable' instead of 'basic' in this list. Yet others have created 'learner/achiever' or 'unproven/too soon to tell' categories for new entrants to a role for whom it is too early to give a realistic assessment. This is likely to be more motivational than grouping people into a 'bottom rank' as can happen with forced ranking systems.

Linking four ratings to pay is generally fairly straightforward within the context of guidelines/matrices that link pay to position in band or scale. Some 28 per cent of organizations in the 2004 CIPD survey used this approach.

Five ratings

This remains the most typical approach where ratings are in use, notably in the public service. It is used by 47 per cent of organizations in the 2004 CIPD survey. A recent example of this from a multinational is as follows:

▌ *Exceptional performance:* has exceeded expectations in the role and ALL development objectives.
▌ *High performance:* has exceeded expectations in most parts of the role as well as most development objectives.
▌ *Good all-round performance:* has fully met expectations in the role as well as the development objectives.
▌ *Fair performance:* has met some expectations in the role as well as some development objectives.
▌ *Poor performance:* has not met expectations in the role and/or development objectives.

This approach balances results, behaviours and objectives. Where performance against agreed role requirements and development objectives is different, for they are initially looked at separately, managers working with this system are asked to make an overall judgement, based on the importance and complexity of the role and development objectives and the environment in which they were completed.

Using five levels provides for two superior performance levels, a fully satisfactory level and two shades of less than effective performance. It is based on a view of the required fineness of performance definition and the extent to which managers can make sensible distinctions. It can, however, be an approach which leads to 'rating drift', ie the gradual movement of most staff into the top three ratings with significant over-population of the top rating in relation to delivered performance. Such drift devalues the recognition value of the ratings and dilutes any pay spend available to recognize outstanding performance. Experience suggests that the tendency to skew ratings upwards is generally a function of the following:

▌ the need to provide continued recognition and an impression of personal progression when there is little recognition value in the pay increases available in a cost-constrained environment (a classic public service problem that has led to 'split' ratings at the middle or middle two performance ratings);
▌ the words/letters used to define ratings which, if say C is a fully satisfactory rating, require upward movement to have motivational value, whether merited or not;
▌ the reality that it remains hard, year on year, to tell individuals that they are still only progressing at a fully satisfactory/acceptable rate when new broader banded structures and flatter/leaner organizations mean that the fillip traditionally provided by promotion is less

and less available. This can and should be counteracted by making clear that the demands on overall organizational performance rise year on year.

Six levels

In organizations where fine differences in levels of performance can be distinguished, it may be better to opt for six performance ratings, so allowing for four above the acceptable level, eg:

▍ *Exceptional performance:* meeting all objectives and requirements and contributing outstanding achievements which significantly extend the impact of the total job.
▍ *Excellent performance:* meeting all objectives and requirements and contributing some notable achievements beyond normal expectations for the job.
▍ *A well-balanced performance:* meeting objectives and requirements of the job, consistently performing in a thoroughly proficient manner.
▍ *Reasonable performance:* a contribution which is stronger in some aspect of the job than others and where most objectives are met, but with varying degrees of effectiveness.
▍ *Barely effective performance:* meeting few objectives or requirements of the job – significant performance improvements are needed.
▍ *Unacceptable performance:* failing to meet most objectives or requirements of the job and demonstrating a lack of commitment to performance improvement or a lack of capability, which has been discussed prior to the performance review.

The issue of consistency

The problem with rating scales is that it is very difficult, if not impossible without careful management, to ensure that a consistent approach is adopted by managers responsible for rating. Inevitably there are 'geese' and 'swans' in people's minds and managers interpret rating definitions in different ways. The best way to deal with this issue is to work on the development of consistent understanding before ratings are given. It is much harder to scrutinize rating distributions after the event and try to inject consistency at that stage than to build values around consistency as part of the performance management implementation process. Many organizations tackling this issue now run workshops with managers from across different departments to discuss how ratings are perceived, explore differences, test out fair assessments on case study performance reviews and, over time, build up a better common understanding and higher levels of comfort with ratings and the way they are fed back to individuals.

Peer review of assessments, whether ratings are used or not, can also be very helpful. Encouraging managers to challenge and refine each other's view of individuals, with a view to a more open and fair appreciation, can help ensure that consistent views are taken and also that the development agenda gets the attention it deserves. This approach is probably essential if the organization has moved beyond using ratings.

Another and generally effective way to support consistency in rating and performance review is to provide for a 'grandparent' or boss's boss to act as moderator on quality. Again, such an approach needs to be supported by training workshops to ensure that the different roles involved are clear and to embed understanding of common values on assessment levels. This approach is, however, difficult to implement in many of the flatter/leaner organizations currently emerging. The grandparent may be too remote or too senior and the numbers of reviews to moderate may be too great. It has also to be said that this is a rather 'low trust' option – for many organizations the objective is to build confidence in the quality and consistency of feedback and performance assessments between managers and their staff without the added bureaucracy of more checking.

Forced distributions

The requirement to ensure that performance ratings are distributed in relation to a normal curve or related distribution is something many organizations have tried (see Chapter 18). Many have abandoned this approach in the face of evidence on its demoralizing effect from employee attitude surveys and related research. In the United States, Ford and Goodyear abandoned forced ranking because of litigation about the validity of their systems.[5] Only 4 per cent of organizations in the 1998 IPD research used this approach. This was based on a broad range of organizations. Among the 400 participants from 212 organizations in the Hay/Henley survey the incidence was higher. It is a reality that over large organizations and across all employee groups there may be something like a normal distribution of performance levels. But this is hard to prove. In many organizations, and especially at senior levels where the values are around 'perform or go', then there are likely to be more high performers and relatively few examples of low contribution. In other areas, eg call centres, where the whole focus of intensive training is to produce performance at a consistent level, then the gap between high and low performance is likely to be pretty narrow.

O'Malley,[6] in a searching article on the pros and cons of forced ranking, identifies the following. Ranking might work because:

▌ it improves the pool of talent;
▌ it promotes a high-performance culture;
▌ it can heighten self-esteem in the surviving workforce.

It might not work, however:

- where it instils fear and heightens conformity;
- where it promotes 'gamesmanship' and disrupts needed cooperation;
- if it fails to recognize the organization as a dynamic system;
- because 'raising the bar' has its limits.

What all this illustrates is that there are significant conflicts between the broader objectives of performance management and performance rating. Figure 19.6 illustrates what these conflicts can look like.

Conflicts in Objectives

Performance management	Rating/pay
■ Achieving objectives	■ Marking, ranking past performance
■ Continuous performance improvement	■ Recognition for excellence
■ Personal development	■ Framework for pay increases
■ Building winners – part of the talent management process	■ Management control of distributions
■ Acquiring competences	■ Some winners/some losers
■ Enhanced employability	■ Consistency/justice
■ Recognition	■ Individual focus/Achievement
■ Looking forward to delivery of strategy	■ Prevention of 'drift'
■ Working in teams	■ Cost management

Figure 19.6 The conflicts between performance management and performance rating

Such conflicts need to be looked at in the context of individual organizations. They vary in significance. Much depends on how much of a performance culture there is. The critical issue is to ensure that, as far as possible, they are minimized in launching a new performance management process and any form of performance and achievement rating that goes with it.

Let the final word on this here be from Jack Welch, former CEO of GE, which famously ranks employees and exits the bottom 10 per cent using its 'vitality curve' forced distribution: 'Our vitality curve works because we spent over a decade building a performance culture that has candid feedback at every level. Candour and openness are the foundations of such a culture. I would not want to inject a vitality curve 'cold turkey' into an organization without a performance culture already in place.'

Handling under-performance

In tackling the tricky problem of under-performance at any level, it is always important to understand what is causing the performance shortfall. This is critical to decisions on what to do and how to deal with the issues both for the individual and for the organization.

The most usual causes of under-performance are:

█ Capability:
  – promoted beyond personal ability to develop and change (most common for senior roles);
  – insufficient development input either recently or earlier in career;
  – in the wrong role for actual or developable skills/capabilities.
█ Inappropriate attitudes or behaviours (eg resistance to change, inappropriate leadership style, 'coasting' – doing 'just enough' when there is clearly capability to make a much greater contribution.
█ Interference of background issues:
  – family (parents/children), unexpected care responsibilities;
  – marriage/relationships in difficulty.
█ Illness – medical conditions other than long-term disability that impact on presence at work, concentration and energy levels.
█ Poor management/clarity of direction:
  – being allowed to 'do the wrong things right';
  – being set unrealistic objectives.
█ Lack of support from manager/colleagues/others who should contribute to achievement levels.
█ Substance abuse – alcohol/drugs.
█ Insufficient self-confidence/self-esteem – sometimes related to discrimination, harassment or bullying.

Line managers generally need to take decisions in handling under-performance with support and advice from their HR function. They need to be aware of and use established policies (ie those for absence management, disciplinary procedures, poor performance and under-performance due to a medical condition), seeking a positive solution wherever possible.

Where an individual is genuinely in the wrong role and could perform more effectively elsewhere, potential moves should be sought. Where the problem is insufficient development – often a cause of inappropriate attitudes or leadership styles and behaviours – this needs tackling in terms of a stronger, unambiguous development plan, especially where development has been neglected in the past. This is an area where one-to-one coaching can help 'fast-track' performance improvement as the individual becomes more self-aware.

In tandem with these measures, it can often be helpful for the line manager to set up and agree a performance improvement plan – a form of short-term performance agreement where he or she works closely with the individual. This typically involves frequent meetings to review progress with the agreed actions, the provision of personal support and coaching from the line manager – it is a form of organizational 'intensive care' to help reverse a fall-off in performance before it becomes a disciplinary or severance issue.

Documentation

Although we might not go as far as Weiss and Hartle and advocate 'shred the forms', there are some very clear messages about keeping documentation simple. The increasing pressures of the current work environment mean that no one wants to get involved in unnecessary bureaucracy and spend unwarranted time in form-filling. This has to be balanced against what should be recorded by way of a performance agreement and what is needed to provide a summary appreciation of each year's contribution as a basis for moving forward. Essentially, what people need is a document or computer file that they can use through the year, gives them clarity about where they are going and records achievement in both work performance and personal development as well as isolating gaps that need to be worked on and means of tackling this. It doesn't have to be on a fixed form. If it is, this should be designed with care and an eye for presentation. Staff should get the same level of presentation as is given to customer documentation, so that it is as far as possible a pleasure to use.

Appendix F lists the key areas to be covered in either a paper- or an intranet-based system.

Training, support and sustainability

In the 1980s and 1990s far too much training in performance management tended to focus around:

▮ a brief introduction to what performance is about and the causes and remedies for under-performance;
▮ an introduction to the organization's performance management processes and the rationale behind them;
▮ video-assisted role playing to allow managers to practise giving feedback on lifelike situations, typically involving poor performance such as absenteeism, laziness and lack of commitment;
▮ a session on how to fill in the forms and what goes where.

In most cases, logical as it looks, this did not produce very good results. It was generally done at the beginning of a new scheme and not very well supported after that. Often, some 10 months had elapsed before managers had to use the appraisal skills they had been trained in and they were out of practice before they started. It is doubtful whether such a process really gives enough insight into how to produce performance improvement and motivate success in the long term.

More recently, training in performance management has been seen as much more of a developmental process that enables managers to get to the heart of how they can manage and coach people more effectively. A more typical 'leading-edge practice' approach to performance management training now is likely to focus on:

- delivering training on a 'just-in-time' basis to ensure learning is reinforced as soon as possible after it is received;
- initial focus on learning styles (eg Kolb or Honey and Mumford) because people have to learn to improve performance. Management can also gain a well-articulated idea of the way in which their own management styles impact on the organizational climate around them from style and climate feedback (see Chapter 18);
- coaching workshops for managers and team leaders to enhance coaching skills, so that the principles of coaching to achieve performance improvement are properly understood and related to the current operating environment;
- work on performance planning in relation to both the 'what' and the 'how' of performance so that a fully rounded understanding of performance against business objectives is built, together with the means of tracking performance and personal development through the year;
- workshops on performance review, to reinforce the coaching and feedback messages of earlier training and ensure that reviewers have had the chance to get some coaching and support where they need help, notably with any intractable performance problems. Some organizations find it helpful to use actors to increase the impact of this input;
- work on consistency of review, reward and recognition processes, to ensure that common values apply and to reduce the risk of patchy implementation. The relationship of performance management with both the pay system and development processes as well as business performance management needs to be clearly distinguished so that staff are clear about the purpose and nature of each.

This is a much heavier agenda than appraisal training as it used to be understood. But it is also an investment in development. It brings in many elements of management development and emphasizes their relevance. For some organizations, the opportunity to build some synergy between a variety of development initiatives means that they are prepared to spend much or even all of their development budget in a single year on performance management implementation. They may be even more willing to do so when major organizational change is under way and new values and new behaviours need to be embedded and reinforced.

In implementing performance management, it is not just management that needs training. All employees involved should receive a full briefing on the new processes and their implications for them. They need to know what to expect and how to gain the most benefit. This kind of training can often be most effectively delivered by line management, so that their own ownership of the new processes is reinforced and they are aware as early as possible of employee levels of understanding and concerns.

Evaluation and continuous improvement

Throughout this and the previous chapter we have stressed the importance of continuous performance improvement. This applies to the performance management process itself. While major change may not be needed more than every four or five years, it remains very important to review how well any new process within performance management is working and adjust and improve where this is needed. Being seen to review and change builds confidence in the process of continuous learning within organizations. Such changes might be around more sophisticated use of IT as a means of looking at team performance and other interdependencies, improved and simplified documentation, use of some focus groups to provide feedback on areas for improvement, or more effective use of competency models as they become part of the language of performance in a specific area. The important thing is to continue to monitor how the process is working and to take early and credible action if change is needed.

REFERENCES

1. Armstrong, M and Baron, A (2004) *Performance Management: Action and impact*, CIPD, London
2. OECD (1997) *Performance Pay Schemes for Public Sector Managers*, Occasional Paper No. 15
3. Houldsworth, E and Jirasinghe, D (2003) Redefining performance management realities, Paper for Hay Group April 2004 Annual Client Meeting, Vienna
4. Parus, B (2004) Recognising and rewarding worker B's, *Workspan*, 03
5. Lawler, E (2003) *Treat People Right: How organizations and individuals can propel each other into a virtuous spiral of success*, Jossey-Bass, San Francisco
6. O'Malley, M (2003) Forced ranking: proceed only with great caution, *WorldatWork Journal*, First Quarter

Part 6

Contingent Pay – Pay progression: Rewarding performance, competence and contribution

20

Contingent Pay – General Considerations

Payments in addition to the base rate can be related to performance, competence, contribution, skill or service. These are sometimes referred to as 'variable pay', but this has acquired the special meaning of payments in the form of cash bonuses which are not consolidated into basic pay. We are therefore adopting the term contingent pay to cover the various forms of additional financial rewards.

CONTINGENT PAY DEFINED

Contingent pay consists of payments related to individual performance, contribution, competence or skill or to team or organizational performance. A distinction can be made between performance (what a person achieves) and contribution (the impact made by that person on the performance of the team and the organization). The level of contribution will depend on the competence, skill and motivation of individuals, the opportunities they have to demonstrate their competence and the use they make of the guidance and leadership they receive.

TYPES OF CONTINGENT PAY

The main types of contingent pay and, in brackets, the chapters in which they are described are:

- performance-related pay (21);
- competence-related pay (21);
- contribution-related pay (21);
- skill-based pay (21);
- service-related pay (21);
- executive bonus and incentive schemes (22);
- employee and executive share schemes (23);
- team rewards (24);
- gainsharing (25);
- profit sharing (26);
- recognition schemes (27);
- shop-floor incentive and bonus schemes (28);
- salesforce incentive schemes (29);
- other cash payments (30).

This chapter concentrates on the following general considerations affecting contingent pay:

- the significance of variable pay;
- the distinction between incentives and rewards;
- the rationale for contingent pay;
- the criteria for pay related to performance, competence or skill.

THE SIGNIFICANCE OF VARIABLE PAY

Variable pay is the payment of cash to individuals in the form of performance pay or bonuses on the basis of their own performance or that of their team or organization. Variable pay has to be re-earned. It is 'pay at risk' which is awarded for specific achievements. The employee risks not being paid the bonus again unless the same, or a higher, level of performance is achieved by reaching or exceeding new targets.

Variable pay is not consolidated into base pay, as often happens with performance-related pay. The argument against consolidation is that it assumes that past performance will continue at the same level in the future and should therefore be rewarded with a permanent increase in pay. It is, in fact, a sort of gift that goes on giving – an annuity. But there is no basis for the confident assumption that past performance predicates future performance. The future does not necessarily resemble the past.

The rationale for variable pay is that the additional pay should be re-earned every year and employees have to accept the risk that they might not re-earn it.

Variable pay has always been the rule in executive pay, sales representatives' remuneration and payment-by-result schemes for manual workers. It has been less common in performance-related pay schemes, although organizations with such schemes are increasingly turning towards the use of achievement or sustained high-performance bonuses, often in the form of 'spot' payments for a particular achievement.

However, competence-related and skill-based payments are usually consolidated. This is on the assumption that the achievement of certain levels of competence or skill do predict continuing performance at those, or higher, levels. Consolidation recognizes that the acquisition of competence or skill enhances the value of individuals to the organization in the longer term and, in fact, increases their market worth.

THE DISTINCTION BETWEEN INCENTIVES AND REWARDS

When developing contingent pay policies and processes it is necessary to be clear about the extent to which a scheme is designed to provide an incentive or a reward. Incentives are forward looking while rewards are retrospective.

▌ *Financial incentives* aim to motivate people to achieve their objectives, improve their performance or enhance their competence or skills by focusing on specific targets and priorities.
▌ *Financial rewards* provide financial recognition to people for their achievements in the shape of attaining or exceeding their performance targets or reaching certain levels of competence or skill.

Financial incentives are designed to provide direct motivation – 'do this and you will get that'. A shop-floor payment-by-result scheme or a sales representative's commission system are examples of financial incentives. An achievement bonus or a team-based pay lump sum payment are examples of financial rewards. Financial rewards provide a tangible form of recognition and can therefore serve as indirect motivators, as long as people expect that further achievements will produce worthwhile rewards.

This distinction is important because it highlights the fact that schemes designed to 'incentivize' and therefore motivate people may fail to do this directly, although they could be a useful means of recognizing contribution.

THE RATIONALE FOR CONTINGENT PAY

Basic reasons

There are three basic reasons for using contingent pay:

1. *Motivation* Pay related to performance, competence or skill motivates people to achieve higher levels of performance and to increase the range and depth of their competences or skills.
2. *Message* Contingent pay delivers a general message that the organization regards performance, competence or skill as important – 'this is what we expect you to do and this is how we will reward you for doing it'. It can also deliver messages that certain values, behaviours or aspects of performance are important; for example quality, customer service, leadership and teamworking.
3. *Equity* It is right and proper that pay should be related to people's performance, contribution, competence or skill.

The first reason is probably the most popular one, but it is also the most dubious. Contingent pay can motivate but only if a number of stringent conditions are satisfied, as described later in this chapter.

Contingent pay can also deliver messages about values and expectations. It can make certain aspects of the psychological contract more explicit and it can focus attention on the things that matter. But it is not the only way of delivering such messages. There are others, namely the normal processes of management and leadership. Contingent pay can underpin and support these processes, it cannot replace them.

Impact on the organization

Contingent pay can enable an organization to do the following:

▮ establish a clear relationship between pay and performance, competence or skill;
▮ build on the benefits of performance management by recognizing achievement in a tangible way;
▮ reinforce a performance-orientated culture;
▮ demonstrate that the organization believes in the importance of developing skills and competencies;
▮ reward and therefore reinforce team as well as individual effort;
▮ concentrate effort in priority areas, clarifying key issues;
▮ attract and retain people who are confident in their ability to deliver results but expect to be rewarded accordingly;
▮ improve pay competitiveness;
▮ improve employee's commitment by enabling them to share in the success of the organization.

But contingent pay does not provide an easy answer to achieving these highly desirable objectives. It is hard to get it right and it often fails to deliver, because the process has been misconceived, badly introduced or poorly managed.

THE CRITERIA FOR PAY RELATED TO PERFORMANCE, COMPETENCE OR SKILL

Individual criteria

The criteria for a successful performance-, competence- or skill-related pay scheme are as follows:

▌ Individuals and teams know the targets and standards they are required to meet.
▌ The reward is clearly and closely linked to accomplishment or effort. People know what they will get if they achieve targets or standards and can track their performance against them.
▌ Fair and consistent means are available for measuring or assessing performance, competence or skill.
▌ People must be able to influence their performance by changing their behaviour and/or they should be able to develop their competences and skills.
▌ The rewards should be meaningful.
▌ The reward should follow as closely as possible the accomplishment that generated it.

21

Individual Contingent Pay

This chapter is mainly concerned with pay for individuals that is contingent upon their performance, competence, contribution or skill. Pay related to service is also in a sense contingent pay although pay progression that is dependent only on service in the job has nothing to do with the performance or contribution of individual employees. However, it is still a feature of the pay progression systems of many public and voluntary organizations and as such is dealt with in this chapter.

Contingent pay can take the form of executive incentive and bonus schemes (Chapter 22) and may be provided for teams, which is dealt with in Chapter 24. It also covers schemes rewarding people according to organizational performance (gainsharing, Chapter 25, and profit sharing, Chapter 26). Shop-floor and salesforce incentive schemes can also be classified as contingent pay but, because of their special nature, they are dealt with separately in Chapters 28 and 29 respectively.

This chapter deals with contingent pay under the following headings:

▌ contingent pay defined;
▌ characteristics of contingent pay;
▌ arguments for and against contingent pay;
▌ criteria for contingent pay;
▌ performance-related pay described;
▌ competence-related pay described;
▌ contribution-related pay described;
▌ skill-based pay described;
▌ service-related pay;
▌ choice of scheme;
▌ readiness for contribution pay;
▌ developing and implementing contribution pay.

CONTINGENT PAY DEFINED

Contingent pay is any form of financial reward that is added to the base rate or paid as a cash bonus and is related to (contingent upon) performance, competence, contribution, skill or service.

Contingent pay may be consolidated in base pay, in which case it forms the basis for allowances such as sick pay and for pension arrangements. Alternatively, schemes other than skill- or service-related pay may provide for awards in the form of cash lump sum bonuses. The latter arrangement is called 'variable pay'. It is sometimes referred to as 'pay at risk', which has to be re-earned, as distinct from consolidated pay, which is usually regarded as continuing as long as the person remains in the job and performs it satisfactorily.

CHARACTERISTICS OF CONTINGENT PAY

Contingent pay related to performance, competence, contribution or skill is a means of valuing people in financial terms according to their contribution. It provides an answer to the two fundamental reward management questions: 1) what do we value? and 2) what are we prepared to pay for? It is an important part of reward management but not the only part. The total reward concept as explained in Chapter 2 emphasizes the importance of non-financial rewards as an integral part of a complete package. And the concept of engaged performance as explained in Chapter 5 focuses on the ways in addition to pay through which performance and commitment can be improved.

Contingent pay is regarded by many people as the prime, even the only, method of motivating people. This view is, of course, fundamentally flawed. The relationship between motivation and rewards as explained in Chapter 7 is a complex one. It is dangerously simplistic to assume that it is only the extrinsic motivators in the form of pay that create long-term motivation. The intrinsic motivators that can arise from the work itself and the working environment may have a deeper and longer-lasting effect.

When considering contingent pay a distinction should be made between the direct motivation provided by incentives and the indirect motivation provided by rewards. Incentives are forward-looking. They encourage people to put in more effort and generate better results by defining how much they will be paid in the future when they deliver certain outputs: 'You will get this if you do that.' A shop-floor payment-by-result scheme and a sales representative's commission system are examples of financial incentives. Rewards are retrospective: 'You have achieved this; therefore we will pay you that.' The achievement may be defined by results or outcomes or it may refer to the level of competence attained. In performance-related pay (PRP) schemes the amount paid out depends on results achieved in the past. But rewards can also be prospective: 'We will pay you more now because we believe you have reached a level of competence that will produce high levels of performance in the future.' Such rewards act as indirect motivators because they provide a tangible means of recognizing achievements, as long as people expect that what they do in the future will produce something worthwhile.

Contingent pay schemes are based on processes for measuring or assessing performance, competence, contribution or skill. These may be expressed as ratings, which are converted by means of a formula to a payment. Alternatively, there may be no formal ratings, and pay decisions are based on broad assessments rather than a formula.

There are strong arguments as set out below both for and against contingent pay. Even when it is believed that the pros outweigh the cons, there are a number of exacting criteria that govern the effectiveness of contingent pay as a reward, which are also set out below.

ARGUMENTS FOR AND AGAINST CONTINGENT PAY

Arguments for

The most powerful argument for contingent pay is that it is right and proper to recognize achievement with a tangible (financial) reward rather than just paying people for 'being there' as happens in a service-related system. Pay should be related to contribution. Those who contribute more should be paid more.

The other arguments commonly used in favour of contingent pay are that:

▯ it acts as a motivator;
▯ it encourages and supports desired behaviours;
▯ it delivers the message that performance, competence, contribution and skill are important;
▯ it provides a means for defining and agreeing performance and competence expectations;
▯ it can reinforce the organization's values;
▯ it can help to achieve culture change by, for example, assisting with the development of a performance culture.

It is sometimes argued that contribution pay acts as an incentive. But the amounts typically involved and the remoteness that often exists between the effort and the reward mean that this is unlikely to be the case. Contribution pay can act as a reward and thus provide for indirect and possibly longer-term motivation. It does not provide the direct motivation that can be produced by an incentive scheme.

It has also been argued that contingent pay can act as a major lever for culture change. But this is unlikely. Culture change depends on a number of factors and pay is certainly not the major one. Contingent pay can reinforce messages about performance; it cannot by itself transform organizations.

Arguments against

The extent to which contingent pay schemes motivate is questionable. The amounts available for distribution are usually so small (typically only 2 to 3 per cent of pay) that they cannot act as an incentive. The requirements for success as set out below are exacting and difficult to achieve.

Money can assist in the motivation process but it is a mistake to believe that by itself it will result in sustained motivation. As Kohn[1] points out, money rarely acts in a crude, behaviourist, Pavlov's dog manner. People react in widely different ways to any form of motivation. The assumption that money will motivate all people equally is invalid. Money may possibly motivate those who receive it but it can demotivate those who don't. The numbers who are demotivated could be much higher than those who are motivated. Contingent pay schemes can create more dissatisfaction than satisfaction if they are perceived to be unfair, inadequate or badly managed, as they often are. If managed badly, contingent pay schemes can demotivate people. They depend on the existence of accurate and reliable methods of measuring performance, competence, contribution or skill, which might not exist. And they rely on the judgement of managers, which in the absence of reliable criteria could be partial, prejudiced, inconsistent or ill informed. They assume that performance is completely under the control of individuals when, in fact, it is affected by the system in which they work. Contingent pay, especially performance-related pay schemes, can militate against quality and teamwork.

Conclusions

A comprehensive study by Brown and Armstrong[2] into the effectiveness of contingent pay as revealed by a number of research projects produced two overall conclusions: 1) contingent pay cannot be endorsed or rejected universally as a principle; and 2) no type of contingent pay is universally successful or unsuccessful.

Performance pay has proved particularly difficult to manage. Organizations, including the civil service, rushed into performance-related pay in the 1980s without really understanding how to make it work. Inevitably problems of implementation arose. Studies such as those conducted by Bowey,[3] Kessler and Purcell,[4] Marsden and Richardson[5] and Thompson[6] have all revealed these difficulties. Failures are usually rooted in implementation and operating processes especially those concerned with performance management, the need for effective communication, involvement, and line management capability. The last factor is crucial. The success of contingent pay rests largely in the hands of line managers. They have to believe in it as something that will help them as well as the organization. They must also be good at practising the crucial skills of agreeing targets, measuring performance fairly and consistently, and providing feedback to their staff on the outcome of performance management and its impact on pay. Line managers can make or break contingent pay schemes.

Vicky Wright[7] has summed it all up: 'Even the most ardent supporters of performance-related pay recognise that it is difficult to manage well', and Oliver[8] made the point that 'performance pay is beautiful in theory but difficult in practice'. Brown and Armstrong[2] concluded their analysis of the research findings by stating that 'the research does show that the effectiveness of pay-for-performance schemes is highly context and situation-specific; and it has highlighted the practical problems which many companies have experienced with these schemes'.

What is the alternative to performance-related pay?

Most of the research and therefore the criticisms have focused on traditional approaches to performance-related pay (PRP) involving rating performance against, usually, quantitative targets and using a formula to determine the pay increase. Hostility to PRP is widespread among trade unions and academics, and doubts about the practice if not the principle are frequently expressed by line managers.

This reaction to PRP raises the question, 'What's the alternative?' One answer is to rely more on non-financial motivators. But it is still necessary to consider what should be done about pay. The reaction in the 1990s to the adverse criticisms of PRP was to develop the concept of competence-related pay, which fitted in well with the emphasis on competences (the competence industry). This approach, as described later, in theory overcame some of the cruder features of PRP but still created a number of practical difficulties and has never really taken off. In the late 1990s the idea of contribution-related pay emerged, as advocated by Brown and Armstrong.[2] This combines the output-driven approach of PRP with the input-(competence-)orientated approach of competence-related pay and has proved to be much more appealing than either performance- or competence-related pay. A CIPD survey in 2003 found that 23 per cent of respondents had PRP, only 6 per cent had competence-related pay and 63 per cent had contribution-related pay.

However, many people still have reservations about this approach from the viewpoint of achieving the fair and consistent measurement of contribution. So what are the alternatives for them? Team pay is often advocated because it removes the individualistic aspect of PRP and accords with the belief in the importance of teamwork. However, as explained in Chapter 24, team pay is often difficult to apply and it still relies on performance measurement. The CIPD 2003 survey established that only 6 per cent of respondents had team pay.

The traditional alternative is service-related pay as described later in this chapter, which was used by 12 per cent of the CIPD respondents. This certainly treats everyone equally (and therefore appeals to trade unions) but pays people simply for being there and this could be regarded as inequitable in that rewards take no account of relative levels of contribution.

The other common alternative is a spot rate system where there is a single rate for the job and no defined scope for pay progression. Spot rates are often used for senior management and, at the other end of the hierarchy, for manual workers and sales representatives. They are some-times adopted by start-up organizations and in smaller companies where pay is market driven and a matter for individual contracts rather than being determined by a company-wide system. Provision is usually made for payment by results in the form of cash bonuses (variable pay) or, for management, shares. Most people, however, want and expect a range of base pay progression, however that is determined, and spot rates are not much used in larger organizations apart from the exceptions noted above.

CRITERIA FOR CONTINGENT PAY AS A MOTIVATOR

The 'line of sight' criterion

The 'line of sight' criterion, as originated by Ed Lawler,[9] sums up the key requirement of any contingent pay scheme, especially one related to performance. This is that individuals and teams should have a clear line of sight between what they do and what they will get for doing it. A line of sight model adapted from Lawler[10] is shown in Figure 21.1.

Figure 21.1 Line of sight model

The line of sight concept expresses the essence of expectancy theory: that motivation only takes place when people expect that they will get worthwhile rewards for their effort and contribution.

Specific criteria

A contingent pay scheme is more likely to motivate people if:

1. The reward is clearly and closely linked to accomplishment or effort – people know what they will get if they achieve defined and agreed targets or standards and can track their performance against them.
2. Rewards are meaningful.
3. Fair and consistent means are available for measuring or assessing performance, competence, contribution or skill.
4. People must be able to influence their performance by changing their behaviour and/or they should be able to develop their competences and skills.
5. The reward should follow as closely as possible the accomplishment that generated it.

These are ideal requirements and few schemes meet them in full. That is why contingent pay arrangements can often promise more than they deliver.

TYPES OF CONTINGENT PAY FOR INDIVIDUALS

The following types of contingent pay schemes are described below:

▍ performance-related pay (PRP);
▍ competence-related pay;
▍ contribution-related pay;
▍ skill-based pay;
▍ service-related pay.

PERFORMANCE-RELATED PAY

Main features

Methods of operating PRP vary considerably but its typical main features are described below.

Basis of scheme

Individuals receive financial rewards in the form of increases to basic pay or cash bonuses, which are linked to an assessment of performance, usually in relation to agreed objectives.

Consolidated pay increases

Scope is provided for consolidated pay progression within pay brackets attached to grades or levels in a narrow-graded or career family structure or zones in a broadbanded structure. Such increases are permanent – they are seldom if ever withdrawn.

Cash bonuses (variable pay)

Alternatively or additionally, high levels of performance or special achievements may be rewarded by cash bonuses that are not consolidated and have to be re-earned. Individuals may be eligible for such bonuses when they have reached the top of the pay bracket for their grade, or when they are assessed as being fully competent, having completely progressed along their learning curve. The rate of pay for someone who reaches the required level of competence can be aligned to market rates according to the organization's pay policy.

Pay progression

The rate and limits of progression through the pay brackets are typically but not inevitably determined by performance ratings, which are often made at the time of the performance management review but may be made separately in a special pay review. Some organizations do not base PRP increases on formal ratings and instead rely on a general assessment of how much the pay of individuals should increase by reference to performance, potential, the pay levels of their peers and their 'market worth' (the rate of pay it is believed they could earn elsewhere).

A formula in the shape of a pay matrix as illustrated in Table 21.1 is often used to decide on the size of increases. This indicates the percentage increase payable for different performance ratings according to the position of the individual's pay in the pay range. This is sometimes referred to as an individual 'compa-ratio' (short for 'comparison ratio') and expresses pay as a percentage of the mid-point in a range. A compa-ratio of 100 per cent means that the salary would be at the midpoint.

Basis of pay progression

Pay progression in a graded structure is typically planned to deccelerate through the grade for two reasons. First, it is argued in line with learning curve theory that pay increases should be higher during the earlier

Table 21.1 PRP pay matrix

Rating	Percentage pay increase according to performance rating and position in pay range (compa-ratio) Position in pay range			
	80%–90%	91%–100%	101%–110%	111%–120%
Excellent	12%	10%	8%	6%
Very effective	10%	8%	6%	4%
Effective	6%	4%	3%	0
Developing	4%	3%	0	0
Ineligible	0	0	0	0

period in a job when learning is at its highest rate. Second, It may be assumed that the central or reference point in a grade represents the market value of fully competent people. According to the pay policy of the organization this may be at or higher than the median. Especially in the latter case, it may be believed that employees should progress quite quickly to that level but that, beyond it, they are already being paid well and their pay need not increase so rapidly. This notion may be reasonable but it can be difficult to explain to someone why they get smaller percentage increases when they are performing well at the upper end of their scale.

Amount of increases

The IPD 1998 survey of 357 organizations found that in 35 per cent of the respondents the increase was 3 per cent or less, the increase in 26 per cent of the respondents was from 6 per cent to 8 per cent, and in the remaining 39 per cent the increase was 9 per cent or more.

Conclusions on PRP

PRP has all the advantages and disadvantages listed for contingent pay. Many people feel the latter outweigh the former. It has attracted a lot of adverse comment, primarily because of the difficulties that organizations have met in managing it. Contribution-related pay schemes are becoming much more popular.

COMPETENCE-RELATED PAY

Main features

The main features of competence-related pay schemes are described:

Basis of scheme

People receive financial rewards in the shape of increases to their base pay by reference to the level of competence they demonstrate in carrying out their roles. It is a method of paying people for the ability to perform now and in the future.

Consolidated pay increases

As in the case of PRP, scope is provided for consolidated pay progression within pay brackets attached to grades or levels in a narrow-graded or career family structure or zones in a broadbanded structure (competence pay is often regarded as a feature of such structures).

Pay progression

The rate and limits of progression through the pay brackets can be based on ratings of competence using a PRP-type matrix, but they may be governed by more general assessments of competence development.

Conclusions on competence-related pay

Competence-related pay is attractive in theory because it can be part of an integrated competency-based approach to HRM. As Brown and Armstrong[2] comment: 'Increasingly, organisations are finding that success depends on a competent workforce. Paying for competence means that an organisation is looking forward, not back.' Pay based on competence avoids the overemphasis in PRP schemes on quantitative, and often unrealistic, targets. It is attractive because it rewards people for what they are capable of doing, not for results over which they might have little control.

However, the idea of competence-related pay raises two questions. The fundamental question is 'What are we paying for?' Are we are paying for competencies, ie how people behave, or competences, ie what people have to know and be able to do to perform well? If we are rewarding good behaviour (competencies) then a number of difficulties arise. It has been suggested by Sparrow[11] that these include the performance criteria on which competencies are based, the complex nature of what is being measured, the relevance of the results to the organization, and the problem of measurement. He concluded that 'we should avoid over-egging our ability to test, measure and reward competencies'.

Other fundamental objections to the behavioural approach have been raised by Ed Lawler.[12] He expresses concern about schemes that pay for an individual's personality traits and emphasizes that such plans work best 'when they are tied to the ability of an individual to perform a particular task and when there are valid measures available of how well an individual can perform a task'. He also points out that 'generic competencies are not only hard to measure, they are not necessarily related to successful task performance in a particular work assignment or work role'. Hofrichter and Spencer[13] assert that 'competency-based systems that pay for generic personality traits not clearly related to task performance are at best trivial, and at worst damaging'.

This raises the second question: 'Are we paying for the possession of competence or the use of competence?' Clearly it must be the latter. But we can only assess the effective use of competence by reference to performance. The focus is therefore on results and, if that is the case, competence-related pay begins to look suspiciously like performance-related pay. It can be said that the difference between the two in these circumstances is all 'smoke and mirrors'. Competence-related pay could be regarded as no more than a more acceptable name for PRP.

There is a strong case for rewarding the possession of competence but an even stronger one for linking the reward to outcomes (performance) as well as inputs (competence). This is the basis of the notion of contribution-related pay as described below and provides the explanation for the growing popularity of that approach compared with the more rarefied notion of competence-related pay.

CONTRIBUTION-RELATED PAY

Defined

Contribution-related pay is a process for making pay decisions that are based on assessments of both the outcomes of the work carried out by individuals and the levels of competence and competency that have influenced these outcomes. It focuses on what people in organizations are there to do, that is, to contribute by their skill and efforts to the achievement of the purpose of their organization or team.

Contribution-related pay is a holistic process, taking into account all aspects of a person's performance in accordance with the definition produced by Brumbach:[14] 'Performance means both behaviours and results. Behaviours emanate from the performer and transform performance from abstraction to action. Not just the instruments for results, behaviours are also outcomes in their own right – the product of mental and physical effort applied to tasks – and can be judged apart from results.'

It is significant that Brumbach refers to *behavioural competencies* and defines them as 'the product of mental and physical effort applied to tasks'. A defining feature of contribution-related pay is that it embraces behaviour as well as competence without falling into the competence-related pay trap of focusing entirely on competencies.

The case for contribution-related pay was made by Brown and Armstrong[2] as follows:

> Contribution captures the full scope of what people do, the level of skill and competence they apply and the results they achieve, which all contribute to the organization achieving its long-term goals. Contribution pay works by applying the mixed model of performance management: assessing inputs and outputs and coming to a conclusion on the level of pay for people in their roles and their work; both to the organization and in the market; considering both past performance and their future potential.

Main features

The main features of contribution-related pay are set out below.

Basis of scheme

Contribution-related pay rewards people for both their performance (outcomes) and their competence (inputs).

Pay awards

Pay awards can be made as consolidated pay increases but in some schemes there is also scope for cash bonuses.

Methods of deciding contribution awards

There are six basic approaches as described below:

1. *Matrix formula* – pay awards are governed by assessments of performance and competence and the amount is determined by a pay matrix such as the one illustrated in Table 21.2. This approach is somewhat mechanistic.
2. *Separate consolidated increases and bonuses* – output is the only factor that governs cash bonuses but it is treated as a subsidiary factor when considering base salary. In contrast, competence is used as the major component in determining salary.
3. *Relate consolidated increases to competence up to a reference point* – this is regarded as the rate for a fully competent person and aligned to market rates. These increases take the form of increments, which are earned as long as competence levels are judged to be progressing satisfactorily. Above that point bonuses can be earned for exceptional achievements.
   These approaches emphasize that competence determines the level of base pay as a reward for future contribution while output achievements are rewarded by cash bonuses that have to be re-earned

Table 21.2 Contribution pay matrix

Performance rating	Percentage pay increase according to performance rating and competence assessment		
	Competence assessment		
	Developing – does not yet meet all competence standards	Fully competent – meets all competence standards	Highly competent – exceeds most competence standards
Exceptional	–	8%	10%
Very effective	–	6%	7%
Effective	–	4%	5%
Developing	3%	–	–
Ineligible	0	–	–

(although they might be consolidated if high performance levels are sustained).

4. *Rewards as either consolidated increases or bonuses* – in this approach, as illustrated in Table 21.3, performers can earn a mix of base pay increase and bonus, which varies according to their position in the pay range. However, all outstanding performers receive a payment of 10 per cent of their base pay. Line managers would therefore not have to pass on the difficult message to outstanding individuals who are high in their pay range that they would be getting a smaller increase in spite of their contribution (this would be the case in a scheme using a typical PRP matrix as illustrated in Table 21.1). Here, the higher up the range individuals are, the greater the proportion of their increase that is payable as a bonus. So those high in the range who are assessed as outstanding get 8 per cent as bonus and 2 per cent addition to their base pay, while outstanding individuals low in their range and below their market rates would get an 8 per cent addition to their base pay and a 2 per cent bonus.

5. *Threshold payments* – one or two thresholds are built into pay ranges as illustrated in Figure 21.2. To cross the threshold into a higher part of the range individuals must meet contribution criteria that will define the level of competence required and indicate any performance (outcome) criteria that may be relevant.

Threshold systems are often associated with incremental scales as in the NHS where they are called 'gateways'. They may be particularly relevant where there are extended incremental scales and it is felt that progression needs to be controlled. They could be regarded as a half-way house to a full contribution pay scheme and, because they do not rely on a suspect formula and contain defined and transparent criteria, they may be more acceptable to staff and their trade

Table 21.3 Contribution matrix for base pay increases and bonuses

Position in range:		Competency assessment: Unsatisfactory	Satisfactory	Good	Excellent	Outstanding
High –	Bonus	0%	2%	3%	6%	8%
expert	Base	0%	§%	2%	21%	2%
Mid –	Bonus	0%	1%	2%	4%	6%
competent,	Base	0%	2%	3%	4%	4%
market rate	pay					
Low –	Bonus	0%	0%	0%	1%	2%
learning	Base	0%	3%	6%	7%	8%
	pay					

Adapted from: Brown, D And Armstrong, M (1999) *Paying for Contribution*, Kogan Page, London.

unions. However, their effectiveness depends on the definition of clear and assessable criteria and the willingness of all those concerned to assess contribution on the basis of evidence about the extent to which individuals meet the criteria. Judgements are still involved and this depends on the ability of managers to exercise them fairly and consistently and to be prepared to make hard decisions on the basis of objective evidence, which may mean that staff do not progress through the threshold. There is a real danger that, if managers do not have the courage of their convictions, staff will more or less automatically progress through the thresholds as happened in the time of 'merit bars', although the criteria for crossing those bars were seldom defined explicitly.

6. *Holistic assessment* – a holistic approach can be adopted to assessing the level of contribution and therefore possible awards in the shape of base pay increases or bonuses. This approach leads to a decision on the level of pay appropriate for individuals in relation to the comparative levels of contribution of their peers and their own market worth, which will include consideration of their potential and the need to retain them.

Consideration is given both to what individuals have contributed to the success of their team and to the level of competence they have achieved and deployed. Team members who are contributing at the expected level will be paid at or around the reference point for the grade or zone and this reference point will be aligned to market rates in accordance with the organization's market pay policies. If, in the

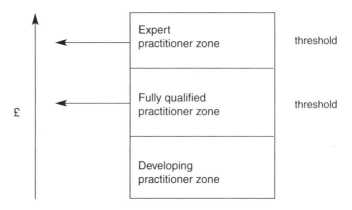

Figure 21.2 Contribution thresholds in a pay range

judgement of the line manager, individuals are achieving this level of contribution but are paid below their peers at the reference point, the pay of the individuals would be brought up to the level of their peers or towards that level if it is felt that the increase should be phased. Individuals may be paid above the reference point if they are making a particularly strong contribution or if their market worth is higher.

The policy guideline would be that the average pay of those in the grade should broadly be in line with the reference point (a compa-ratio of 100) unless there are special market rate considerations that justify a higher rate. Those at or above the reference point who are contributing well could be eligible for a cash bonus. A 'pay pot' would be made available for distribution with guidelines on how it should be used.

This approach depends largely on the judgement of line managers although they would be guided and helped in the exercise of that judgement by HR. Its acceptability to staff as a fair process depends on precise communications generally on how it operates and equally precise communications individually on why decisions have been made. The assessment of contribution should be a joint one as part of performance management and the link between that assessment and the pay decision should be clear.

Other characteristics

The other characteristics of contribution pay are that:

▌ it is concerned with people as team members contributing to team performance, not acting as individuals;

- it can operate flexibly – approaches may be varied between different groups of people;
- it is tailored to suit the business and HR strategy of the organization;
- there is a clear business-related rationale, which serves stated HR and reward purposes – individual and team contribution expectations are defined on the basis of the corporate and team business goals to be achieved and measured accordingly;
- it operates transparently – everyone understands how the scheme operates and how it affects them and staff and their representatives will have contributed to the design of the system and will take part in regular reviews of its effectiveness, leading to modifications when required.

Conclusions

Contribution pay and traditional performance pay are significantly different concepts as is shown in Table 21.4.

However, contribution-related pay decisions still ultimately depend on the judgement of line managers and contribution pay will only work if line managers are capable of making sound judgements and are willing to spend time in doing so. Training and guidance are required and HR has an important role in providing it. The requirements for success are demanding and, as explained in the last two sections of this chapter, it is essential to ensure that the organization is ready for contribution pay and to plan its introduction with great care, including ample consultation and involvement. Organizations should never rush into contribution pay – more time than is usually thought necessary is needed to plan and implement it.

SKILL-BASED PAY

Defined

Skill-based pay provides employees with a direct link between their pay progression and the skills they have acquired and can use effectively. It focuses on what skills the business wants to pay for and what employees must do to demonstrate them. It is therefore a people-based rather than a job-based approach to pay. Rewards are related to the employee's ability to apply a wider range or a higher level of skills to different jobs or tasks. It is not linked simply with the scope of a defined job or a prescribed set of tasks.

A skill may be defined broadly as a learned ability that improves with practice in time. For skill-based pay purposes the skills must be relevant to the work. Skill-based pay is also known as knowledge-based pay, but the terms are used interchangeably, knowledge being regarded loosely as the understanding of how to do a job or certain tasks.

Table 21.4 Pay for performance compared with pay for contribution

	Pay for performance	Pay for contribution
Organizing philosophy	Formulae, systems.	Processes.
HR approach	Instrumentalist, people as costs.	Commitment, people as assets.
Measure	Pay for results (the whats) – achieving individual objectives.	Multi-dimensional, pay for results and how they are achieved.
Measures	Financial goals.	Broad variety of strategic goals: financial, service, operating, etc (balanced scorecard).
Focus of measurement	Individual.	Multi-level: business, team.
Design	Uniform merit pay and/or individual bonus approach throughout the organization.	Diverse approaches using wide variety of reward methods to suit the needs of individual groups.
Timescales	Immediate past performance.	Past performance and contribution to future goals.
Performance assessment	Performance appraisal – past review and ratings focus; top-down and quantitative.	Performance management mixed model – past review and future development; partnership approach, quantitative and qualitative (possibly 360°).
Pay linkage	Fixed formula, matrix.	Looser, more flexible linkages.
Administration	Controlled by HR.	Owned/operated by users.
Communication and	Top-down, non-transparent, imposed.	Face to face, transparent, high involvement.
Evaluation of effectiveness	Act of faith.	Regular review and monitoring against clearly defined success criteria.
Change over time	All or nothing.	Regular incremental modification.

Adapted from: Brown, D and Armstrong, M (1999) *Paying for Contribution*, Kogan Page, London.

Application

Skill-based pay was originally applied mainly to operatives in manufacturing firms. But it has been extended to technicians and workers in retailing, distribution, catering and other service industries. The broad equivalent of skill-based pay for managerial, professional and administrative staff and knowledge workers is competence-related pay, which refers to expected behaviour as well as, often, to knowledge and skill requirements. There is clearly a strong family resemblance between skill and competence-related pay – each is concerned with rewarding the person as well as the job. But they can be distinguished both by the way in which they are applied, as described below, and by the criteria used.

Main features

Skill-based pay works as follows:

▌ Skill blocks or modules are defined. These incorporate individual skills or clusters of skills that workers need to use, which will be rewarded by extra pay when they have been acquired and the employee has demonstrated the ability to use them effectively.
▌ The skill blocks are arranged in a hierarchy with natural break points between clearly definable different levels of skills.
▌ The successful completion of a skill module or skill block will result in an increment in pay. This will define how the pay of individuals can progress as they gain extra skills.
▌ Methods of verifying that employees have acquired and can use the skills at defined levels are established.
▌ Arrangements for 'cross-training' are made. These will include learning modules and training programmes for each skill block.

Conclusions

Skill-based pay systems are expensive to introduce and maintain. They require a considerable investment in skill analysis, training and testing. Although in theory a skill-based scheme will pay only for necessary skills, in practice individuals will not be using them all at the same time and some may be used infrequently, if at all. Inevitably, therefore, payroll costs will rise. If this increase is added to the cost of training and certification, the total of additional costs may be considerable. The advocates of skill-based pay claim that their schemes are self-financing because of the resulting increases in productivity and operational efficiency. But there is little evidence that such is the case. For this reason, skill-based schemes have never been very popular in the UK and some companies have discontinued them.

SERVICE-RELATED PAY

Defined

Service-related pay provides fixed increments, which are usually paid annually to people on the basis of continued service in either a job or a grade in a pay spine structure. Increments may be withheld for unacceptable performance (although this is rare) and some structures have a 'merit bar', which limits increments unless a defined level of 'merit' has been achieved. This is the traditional form of contingent pay and is still common in the public and voluntary sectors and in education and the health service although it has largely been abandoned in the private sector.

Arguments for

Service-related pay is supported by many unions because they perceive it as being fair – everyone is treated equally. It is felt that linking pay to time in the job rather than performance or competence avoids the partial and ill-informed judgements about people that managers are prone to make. Some people believe that the principle of rewarding people for loyalty through continued service is a good one.

Arguments against

The arguments against service-related pay are that:

▮ it is inequitable in the sense that an equal allocation of pay increases according to service does not recognize the fact that some people will be contributing more than others and should be rewarded accordingly;
▮ it does not encourage good performance; indeed, it rewards poor performance equally;
▮ it is based on the assumption that performance improves with experience but this is not automatically the case – it has been said that a person with five years' experience may in practice only have had one year's experience repeated five times;
▮ it can be expensive – everyone may drift to the top of the scale, especially in times of low staff turnover, but the cost of their pay is not justified by the added value they provide.

The arguments against service-related pay have convinced most managements, although some are concerned about managing any other form of contingent pay schemes (incremental pay scales do not need to be managed at all). They may also have to face strong resistance from their unions and can be unsure of what exit strategy they should adopt if they want to change. They may therefore stick with the status quo.

CHOICE OF APPROACH

The first choice is whether or not to have contingent pay related to performance, competence, contribution or skill. Public or voluntary sector organizations with fixed incremental systems (pay spines) where progression is solely based on service may want to retain them because they do not depend on possibly biased judgements by managers and they are perceived as being fair – everyone gets the same – and easily managed. However, the fairness of such systems can be questioned. Is it fair for a poor performer to be paid more than a good performer simply for being there?

The alternative to fixed increments is either spot rates or some form of contingent pay. Spot rate systems in their purest form are generally only used for senior managers, shop-floor or retail workers and in smaller organizations and new businesses where the need for formal practices has not yet been recognized.

If it is decided that a more formal type of contingent pay for individuals should be adopted, the choice is between the various types of performance pay, competence-related or contribution-related pay and skill-based pay, as summarized in Table 21.5.

Although contribution-related pay shares the disadvantages of other forms of contingent pay in that it relies on managerial judgement and is difficult to manage well it is probably the best choice in most circumstances. As the CIPD survey showed, it is certainly the most popular. The last two sections of this chapter therefore concentrate on discussions of readiness for contribution pay and methods of developing and implementing it.

READINESS FOR CONTRIBUTION PAY

The 10 questions to be answered when assessing readiness for contribution pay are:

1. Is it believed that contribution pay will benefit the organization in the sense of enhancing its ability to achieve its strategic goals?
2. Are there valid and reliable means of measuring performance?
3. Is there a competence framework and are there methods of assessing levels of competence objectively (or could such a framework be readily developed)?

Table 21.5 Comparison of contingent pay schemes

Type of scheme	Main features	Advantages	Disadvantages	When appropriate
Performance-related pay	Increases to basic pay or bonuses are related to assessment of performance.	May motivate (but this is uncertain). Links rewards to objectives. Meets the need to be rewarded for achievement. Delivers message that good performance is important and will be rewarded.	May *not* motivate. Relies on judgements of performance that may be subjective. Prejudicial to teamwork. Focuses on outputs, not quality. Relies on good performance management processes. Difficult to manage well.	For people who are likely to be motivated by money. In organizations with a performance-orientated culture. When performance can be measured objectively.
Competence-related pay	Pay increases are related to the level of competence.	Focuses attention on need to achieve higher levels of competence. Encourages competence development. Can be integrated with other applications of competency-based HR management.	Assessment of competence levels may be difficult. Ignores outputs – danger of paying for competences that will not be used. Relies on well-trained and committed line managers.	As part of an integrated approach to HRM where competencies are used across a number of activities. Where competence is a key factor and it may be inappropriate or hard to measure outputs. Where well-established competency frameworks exist.
Contribution-related pay	Increases in pay or bonuses are related to inputs (competence) and outputs (performance).	Rewards people not only for what they do but for how they do it.	As for both PRP and competence-related pay – it may be hard to measure contribution and it is difficult to manage well.	When it is believed that a well-rounded approach covering both inputs and outputs is appropriate.
Skill-based pay	Increments related to the acquisition of skills.	Encourages and rewards the acquisition of skills.	Can be expensive when people are paid for skills they don't use.	On the shop floor or in retail organizations.
Service-related pay	Increments related to service in grade.	No scope for bias; easy to manage.	Fails to reward those who contribute more.	Where this is the traditional approach and trade unions oppose alternatives.

4. Are there effective performance management processes which line managers believe in and carry out conscientiously?
5. Are line managers willing to assess contribution and capable of doing so?
6. Are line managers capable of making and communicating contribution pay decisions?
7. Is the HR function capable of providing advice and guidance to line managers on managing contribution pay?
8. Can procedures be developed to ensure fairness and consistency in assessments and pay decisions?
9. Are employees and trade unions willing to accept the scheme?
10. Do employees trust management to deliver the deal?

DEVELOPING AND IMPLEMENTING CONTRIBUTION PAY

The 10 steps required to develop and implement contribution pay are:

1. Analyse culture, strategy and existing processes including the grade and pay structure, performance management and methods of progressing pay or awarding cash bonuses.
2. Set out aims, which demonstrate how contribution pay will help to achieve the organization's strategic goals.
3. Communicate aims to line managers staff and involve them in the development of the scheme.
4. Determine how the scheme will operate covering:
   - the use of performance and competence measures;
   - the performance management processes required;
   - the scope for awarding cash bonuses as well as base pay increases;
   - the approach to making decisions on awards – one of the five approaches listed on page 302 or any other suitable method of deciding on pay progression and cash payments;
   - the amount of money that will be available for contribution pay, and how that money should be distributed;
   - the guidelines and procedures needed to govern contribution pay reviews and ensure that they are carried out fairly and consistently and within available budgets;
   - the basis upon which the effectiveness of contribution pay will be evaluated.
5. Develop competence framework and role profiles.
6. Develop or improve performance management processes covering the selection of performance measures, decisions on competence requirements, methods of agreeing outcome and development objectives and the procedure for conducting joint reviews.

7. Communicate intentions to line managers and staff.
8. Pilot-test the scheme and amend as necessary.
9. Provide training to all concerned.
10. Launch the scheme and evaluate its effectiveness after the first review.

REFERENCES

1. Kohn, A (1993) Why incentive plans cannot work, *Harvard Business Review*, September–October
2. Brown, D and Armstrong, M (1999) *Paying for Contribution*, Kogan Page, London
3. Bowey, A (1982) *The Effects of Incentive Pay Systems*, Research Paper No. 36, Department of Employment, London
4. Kessler, J and Purcell, J (1992) Performance-related pay: objectives and application, *Human Resource Management Journal*, **2** (3), Spring
5. Marsden, D and Richardson, R (1994) Performing for pay?, *British Journal of Industrial Relations*, June
6. Thompson, M (1992) *Pay and Performance: The employer experience*, Report No. 218, Institute of Manpower Studies, Brighton
7. Wright, V (1991) 'Performance related pay', in E Neale (ed), *The Performance Management Handbook*, IPM, London
8. Oliver, J (1996) Cash on delivery, *Management Today*, August
9. Lawler, E E (1988) Pay for performance: making it work, *Personnel*, October
10. Lawler, E E (199) Paying for performance, Presentation at IPD Conference, Harrogate
11. Sparrow, P A (1996) Too good to be true, *People Management*, December
12. Lawler, E E (1993) Who uses skill-based pay, and why, *Compensation & Benefits Review*, March–April
13. Hofrichter, D and Spencer, S (1996) Competencies: the right foundation for effective management, *Compensation & Benefits Review*, November–December
14. Brumbach, G B (1988) Some ideas, issues and predictions about performance management, *Public Personnel Management*, Winter

22

Executive Annual Incentive Schemes

Virtually all major employers in the UK and elsewhere provide annual incentive schemes for senior executives. Typically, payments are linked to achievement of profit and/or other financial targets; there may also be elements related to achieving specific goals and to individual performance.

As rule, the payments available are significant (up to 100 per cent of salary or more for the largest UK companies) and most plans are, strictly, incentives rather than bonuses (the distinction between incentives and bonuses is discussed in Chapter 21). However, the terms 'bonus' and 'incentive' are often used interchangeably in this context.

The principal rationale for providing an annual incentive to executives is to motivate a change in behaviour and hence drive performance improvements. Other factors are:

- making executives aware of the key measures of company performance;
- the need to provide a market-competitive remuneration package;
- putting pay 'at risk' can reduce executive remuneration costs in years where performance is poor.

However, some commentators have questioned how genuine the link to performance is. For example, among FTSE 50 companies with a December 2002 year end, the median bonus for the top executive role was 64 per cent of salary (average 77 per cent) and only 7 out of 27 companies paid less than 50 per cent of salary. A detailed analysis of the bonuses paid in individual companies is beyond the scope of this book, but at first glance the general level of payments appears high given that this was generally considered to be a difficult year for most businesses.

Many UK institutional investors are starting to take a closer look at bonus payments. They are likely to review future payments in the context of the operational business results disclosed and how they compare to previous years.

In the rest of this chapter we deal with the following aspects of executive incentive and bonus schemes:

▋ the basis of the strategic decision to have executive incentives;
▋ their relationship with other components of the reward package;
▋ defining the target group;
▋ their main features;
▋ financial performance measures;
▋ non-financial targets;
▋ the target mix;
▋ the discretionary element;
▋ the link with performance management;
▋ the level of payments;
▋ treatment of windfall profits;
▋ tax planning;
▋ administering an incentive plan;
▋ executive bonus schemes;
▋ deferred bonus schemes.

This chapter covers cash-based annual incentives. It briefly covers cash long-term incentives. Chapter 27 covers share-based, longer-term incentive schemes.

THE STRATEGIC DECISION

The introduction of a new executive annual incentive scheme should be closely tied to a searching review analysis of corporate plans and objectives. It is essential to know where the enterprise is planning to go and what constitutes success before deciding how executives should be rewarded for their performance. The main question to be answered when making this strategic decision is: what do executives have to do and achieve for the company to be more successful? A good scheme will ensure that executives concentrate on business priorities.

RELATIONSHIP WITH OTHER COMPONENTS OF THE REWARD PACKAGE

It is essential to relate the incentive scheme to other elements of the reward package. This means reviewing basic salary and benefit packages to ensure that they are competitive. It also means deciding what the incentive scheme is expected to contribute in addition to other performance-related payment systems, longer-term incentives and profit-sharing arrangements. Links with performance management should also be clear.

It is particularly important to ensure that the annual incentive and any longer-term plans are complementary. As a general rule, annual incentives are used to incentivize delivery of the business strategy and plans: the longer-term plan(s) then reflect the delivery of enhanced value to the owners of the business.

If the size of incentive opportunity is being increased, by implication base salary management should be considered in parallel. For example, if the payment available for 'on-target' performance is to increase from 40 per cent to 60 per cent of salary (say), there may be a case for providing reduced (or zero) salary increases for one or two years, unless the remuneration package is already behind the market.

Anecdotal evidence suggests that many executives mentally discount the incentive payment available for on-target (not maximum) performance by up to 50 per cent. The discount is highest when the executive does not have direct influence over the performance measures being used.

DEFINING THE TARGET GROUP

For the scheme to be effective, only executives who can exert personal control over the selected performance measures as individuals or members of a team should be included in the scheme. These will certainly consist of the executive members of the board and may include the next two or three tiers of executive. Different participants may need different criteria with individual performance triggers, although incentive schemes for directors often incorporate a common measure based on overall company profitability.

Incentives for executives without board status and/or direct profit-centre accountability are often more challenging to design.

THE MAIN FEATURES OF EXECUTIVE INCENTIVE SCHEMES

When designing an incentive scheme the following features of it will need to be considered:

▌ the choice of performance measures, which lies between financial or non-financial objectives or a combination of the two;

▮ how non-financial objectives should be measured;
▮ the extent to which the scheme should be tied down to a formula or should allow an element of discretion when making payments;
▮ the link that should exist between the scheme and performance management at executive level;
▮ the level of payments that should be made according to performance – this will take account of the target level, the starting point and any limits or 'caps' that will be placed on incentive earnings;
▮ the mechanism for combining multiple performance measures;
▮ the action that should be taken over any 'windfall' profits.

These considerations should be dealt with in the following sections of this chapter. Examples of incentive schemes are given in Appendix J.

FINANCIAL PERFORMANCE MEASURES

For short-term incentives, the principal financial performance measures are:

▮ profit before tax (pre-tax profit);
▮ profit after tax (post-tax profit);
▮ earnings per share;
▮ cash flow;
▮ return on capital or assets employed;
▮ others specific to individual businesses, eg sales volume;
▮ market share.

The factors governing the choice between these measures are discussed below. The main criteria are: first, relevance to organization requirements; second, the extent to which the individual or group can influence results; and third, the existence of reliable methods of measurement – a credible management information system is a prerequisite for any scheme using financial measures. There is also a need to determine to what, if any, extent exceptional items should be included.

Profit before tax

This is the key indicator of corporate success and is therefore frequently used as the sole criterion.

Incentives are based on the profit achieved, typically above a threshold figure, the level of which is set to protect the interests of shareholders. The threshold may need adjustment after an acquisition or change in the capital structure.

Both interest and management charges are taken into account if they are within management control. This, however, may not be the case when interest rates are fluctuating widely or where the situation is complicated by overseas activities. Non-cash accounting charges such as amortization and depreciation may also be excluded. Hence many companies use an EBITDA measure (earnings before interest, tax, depreciation and amortization).

Profit after tax

This measure aligns more closely with shareholders' interests because it gives a clearer indication of the funds available for reinvestment and for payment of dividends. However, it can be significantly affected by changes in national and international tax laws and by the way in which those laws are interpreted. Profit after tax is rarely used as the chief measure in executive incentive schemes below main board level, although it is sometimes included as one of a set of criteria. The criteria for choosing before or after tax profit depends upon the degree to which managers are expected to take account of tax considerations when making business decisions.

Earnings per share

This measure relates post-tax profits to the average weighted number of ordinary shares in issue during the financial year. It is used by the City to judge company performance and has been adopted as the main measure in many directors' incentive schemes. It is, however, subject to changes in corporate taxation in the same way as post-tax profits. Before selecting this measure, the possible impact of mergers, take-overs and changes in accounting policy should be considered.

Return on capital or assets employed

This is another key measure of company performance. It can, however, be manipulated by management who could improve the ratio dramatically by the sale of assets. This criterion is, therefore, generally used in conjunction with others.

Cash flow

This measure is also focused on by the City, which will value the company by estimating the Net Present Value of future cash flow. Shareholder value techniques also put a greater emphasis on cash flow, which is not impacted by accounting policies and is therefore harder for executives to manipulate.

The importance of managing cash can be emphasized by using this criterion as one of the factors in an incentive scheme, but it is not often the sole measure of performance because it only relates to one aspect of management responsibility.

Economic Profit (EP)

Essentially, Economic Profit (EP) less is the amount of profit made by the business in a year in excess of the required return on capital. It is usually calculated as the profit after a number of accounting adjustments, less the cost of capital. The cost of capital is the weighted cost of debt plus equity. EP is growing in popularity as a measure in executive incentive schemes. To use it effectively, organizations have to use the measure as part of strategic planning, and several major organizations have gone down this road.

Advantages of EP

▌ It focuses management attention on the cost of capital.
▌ It can be adopted by a variety of companies, including subsidiaries, not just by quoted companies.
▌ It can be applied at different organizational levels from the whole company to a division to an individual plant.
▌ It may account for changes in share value and so, in theory, can assist managers in determining what needs to be done to improve share value.
▌ Some studies have shown a good correlation between EP and increases in share price. The theory is that management focus on maximizing EP will also maximize share price.

Disadvantages of EP

▌ It is complex to calculate – there are potentially over 150 adjustments that might be needed. This can bewilder and demotivate employees.
▌ The adjustments used can seem arbitrary, particularly where there is major long-term capital investment – for example, in a start-up situation, any decision on what is a realistic target EP in the early years must be wholly based on assumptions.
▌ It is based on historic information and does not take account of the positioning of the company for the future. Using EP as the prime measure of performance can lead to undue focus on short-term operating results and cost/capital reduction, particularly in industries where the payback on investments is very long-term.
▌ It is possible to achieve similar results by looking at several different financial measures in combination.

Total shareholder return

The recent trend in the UK in relation to long-term incentive plans for main board directors of quoted companies has been towards plans measuring relative total shareholder return (TSR). TSR has the great advantage of having a very clear linkage to the performance observed by shareholders. Institutional investors are themselves measured on portfolio performance relative to an index or peer group, and are generally rewarded for above-median performance. It therefore makes sense to them that company directors should be rewarded for achieving returns to shareholders above the median achieved by other companies. However, this measure is most commonly used for longer-term plans.

Use of criteria

The 2003 Hay Group Boardroom Guide Survey of Director Remuneration indicated that the criteria given in Table 22.1 are the main criteria used.

Table 22.1 Choice of criteria

Measure	% of companies
Profit	81
Earnings per share	56
Cash flow	28
Return on capital employed	19
Control of costs	13
Sales volume	9
Economic profit	9

NON-FINANCIAL TARGETS

Although it is always desirable to relate incentives to financial targets, they may not be applicable to all aspects of an executive's job, especially in functional roles such as HR director or company secretary.

To cover each key result area it may be necessary to set job-related targets which indicate what needs to be achieved to earn a specified level of reward. For example, the target may be to complete a project which meets agreed objectives within a time limit. The objectives would be defined in such terms as cost reduction, increase in productivity, or improvement in quality or customer service levels. Some schemes set a 100 per cent level for full achievement of the objectives, but provide for a partial payment if the results are less than 100 per cent but above a threshold level.

THE TARGET MIX

The mix of performance criteria between financial and non-financial measures will depend on the requirements of the business and the particular demands made on the individual executives in the scheme. At board level, the mix may be dominated by measures of corporate performance, such as earnings per share, to which all directors contribute. But a proportion of the incentive payment may be related to divisional performance (where applicable) or to individual targets. The individual targets could be defined in financial or non-financial terms and would cover each of the key result areas of the job in accordance with the contribution of job holders to overall performance. To concentrate the minds of executives on these areas and to avoid over-complicating the scheme, it is best not to have more than three or four factors.

The Hay Group Boardroom Guide Survey of Director Remuneration (2003) shows the determining factors taken into account when setting individual incentive payments: 61 per cent of companies use a number of factors.

Table 22.2 Factors used for individual incentive payments

Factor	% of companies
Individual performance	64
Team/unit/division performance	53
Company performance	92
Other factors	6

DISCRETIONARY ELEMENT

Many schemes which have a mixture of targets also allow for a discretionary element in incentive payments. This may be used by the chief executive or the remuneration committee of the board to reward a manager for exceptional performance 'beyond the line of duty', which would not be adequately recognized by the normal measures. However, UK institutional investors frown on discretionary bonuses for main board executive directors.

LINKS WITH PERFORMANCE MANAGEMENT

Discussion on the setting and achievement of targets should take place as part of the normal performance management procedure. An important feature of this process will be the review of all aspects of the results achieved by the executive, so that those factors not covered specifically by the incentive scheme are also dealt with. There is always the risk in any incentive scheme that an important aspect of the job – such as development, leadership or team-building – is neglected because the executive concentrates only on those areas where short-term rewards can be achieved. Discussions during reviews can help to put these matters into perspective.[2]

At board level it is normal to have special meetings to discuss the operation of the incentive scheme. The compensation/remuneration committee of the main board, consisting wholly or mainly of non-executive directors, is typically used for this purpose. The chairman and chief executive would normally also attend this meeting but the chief executive would withdraw when his or her own incentives were under discussion.

LEVEL OF PAYMENTS

The size of annual bonus opportunities (as a percentage of base salary) for 'threshold', 'on-target' and 'maximum' performance as revealed in the Hay Group Boardroom Guide Survey of Director Remuneration (2003) are shown in Table 22.3.

Often three decisions are required on the level of incentive payments:

1. the target level expressed as a percentage of base salary;
2. the starting-point for incentive payments ('threshold');
3. the limit, if any, to the maximum payment that can be made; with payments for intermediate levels of performance derived by interpolation.

Table 22.3 Size of annual bonus opportunity (as a percentage of base salary)

Market median (upper quartile)

Management group	Performance threshold	On target	Maximum
Chief executive	15 (2)	38 (50)	60 (100)
Main board directors	10 (21)	32 (49)	60 (80)
Other directors and senior executives	10 (15)	27 (37)	50 (60)
Senior managers	6 (9)	20 (25)	40 (50)

Source: Hay Group Boardroom Guide Survey of Director Remuneration 2003

Bonus opportunities are on the increase and many FRSE 100 companies now have a maximum bonus for the chief executive of 100 per cent of salary or more.

Target level

The level of incentive which is paid if the performance targets are reached must be meaningful. As mentioned earlier, payments of less than 10 per cent can have little motivational effect on well-paid directors. In the case of senior executives, target figures of 25–500 per cent are typical. For this level of incentive payment, however, the target, although achievable, should be tough. Indeed, the level of payment and perceived difficulty of the targets should be considered in parallel.

The payment for reaching the target level of performance should also be self-financing, ie based on profit or other financial measures after the cost of the payments. It should be based on the assumption that the company as well as the individual will benefit. Payments should be regarded as serious money, not to be handed over lightly.

Starting-point

The starting-point threshold will depend upon the extent to which demanding levels of target performance are set. If the target is reasonably difficult to attain, as it should be, then a trigger point of 90 to 95 per cent achievement of the target level of performance would be appropriate. However, percentage differences should not be used unthinkingly; because profit is the difference between two large numbers, some modelling should be carried out to ensure that the range from threshold to on-target does not cover too narrow a range of probabilities.

It is necessary, however, to provide a significant incentive to achieve the target. This can be done by making the increase in bonus for moving from threshold to target performance sufficiently large. In listed companies, shareholders are increasingly uncomfortable with payments being made to executive directors where performance is lower than that achieved in the recent past.

Upper limit

Many schemes 'cap' incentives by setting an upper limit to payments, to avoid them delivering disproportionate rewards and in the belief, which may or may not be correct, that above a certain level executives are unlikely to be able to achieve anything more by their own efforts. Some companies are also wary about offering glittering prizes that are over-enticing and therefore misdirect executives into concentrating so much on exceeding their personal targets that the needs of the business are neglected. This happened quite often in the City in the heady days before 'Black Monday' (18 October 1987). Finally, the institutional investors prefer schemes to be capped, for the reasons described above.

Where the limit, if any, is fixed depends on the circumstances, especially the level of performance that an executive could achieve. This very much depends on the nature of the business and the ability of the management to leverage. The degree of leverage will vary between industry sectors and depends on the volatility and maturity of the business.

Three notional schemes are shown in Table 22.4. Each reflects a different situation and/or aim, as follows:

▌ Scheme 1 is intended to focus participants on out-performing targets.
▌ Scheme 2 assumes targets are demanding.
▌ Scheme 3 might be appropriate for a situation in which the company is targeting a small profit after several years of making losses.

Table 22.4 Alternative approaches to incentive payment levels

Scheme	Performance	% of budgeted PBT	Bonus as % of salary
1	Threshold	95	10
	Target	100	30
	Maximum	115	100
2	Threshold	95	20
	Target	100	50
	Maximum ·	105	75
3	Threshold	25	20
	Target	100	50
	Maximum	150	75

The 2003 Hay Group Boardroom Guide Survey of Director Remuneration shows that, where performance is measured against budget, the percentages of budgeted performance shown in Table 22.5 are required to earn threshold, target and maximum incentive payments.

TREATMENT OF WINDFALL PROFITS

It may be necessary to make provisos in a scheme for the treatment of any windfall profits arising from circumstances outside the control of executives, such as the sale of company assets or favourable changes in foreign exchange or interest rates. The decision on whether or not these

Table 22.5 Percentage of budgeted performance required

Percentage of budgeted performance required	Percentage of schemes		
	Threshold	Target	Maximum
80 or less	16		
81–90	21		
91–99	46		
100	17	96	13
101–110		4	25
111–150			62
Media	95	100	115

Source: Hay Group Boardroom Guide Survey of Director Remuneration 2003

changes in strategy or 'acts of God' should generate incentive payments depends on the nature of the business and the likelihood of such windfalls occurring. This is a matter upon which the remuneration committee of the board will be expected to adjudicate.

The perceived need to curb excessive gains in these circumstances should be balanced against the demotivating effect of denying executives the incentive payment they believe they have earned. If it is decided that earnings should be 'capped' when windfall profits arise, steps should be taken to reduce possible demotivating effects by spelling out in the rules of the scheme the circumstances in which this could happen and by deciding on any changes to budgets and targets as soon as possible. In practice the degree of any adjustment will depend on circumstances.

Negative 'windfalls'

A similar, and perhaps even more difficult, problem concerns the situation when a similar change leads to under-performance against budget. If the under-performance reflects a change of strategy, such as a sale or acquisition, then it should be possible to adjust budgets before year end to allow for the impact of the change.

External shocks that reduce profits are more difficult to deal with. It is important that any policy is consistent with the approach taken to positive windfalls to avoid giving executives a one-way bet. The approach taken may also vary by role; for example, main board directors might be treated less favourably than other employees to ensure that they are aligned with shareholders.

TAX PLANNING

The main choices of payment vehicle under any incentive plan are shares, share options and cash. Since 1988 – when highest rates of capital gains and income tax were set at 40 per cent – the scope for tax planning has reduced significantly.

Periodically, tax experts will identify new loopholes that allow employers to deliver remuneration tax-effectively. Recent examples have included paying bonuses in gold bullion, coffee beans and options over gilt-edged government bonds. The risk of such approaches is that there is so much focus on tax-effectiveness that the primary objective of motivating executives to deliver enhanced business performance is forgotten. Also, the government tends to close unintended loopholes fairly quickly.

Following the 2004 Budget, any new tax minimization schemes will be required to register with the Inland Revenue. It is likely that this will further reduce the scope for any tax savings.

Unusual tax-effective ways of delivering pay tend not to be adopted by organizations whose executive pay is under close public scrutiny, for example large listed companies.

ADMINISTERING AN INCENTIVE PLAN

The incentive plan should be set up by the board. To ensure its integrity, its operation should be supervised by the remuneration committee, normally composed of non-executive directors, if they exist. They are there to ensure that the plan is run properly and that the shareholders' interests are protected.

The rules and procedures governing the plan should be set out in a short document given to all participants. From this they should be able to work out how their incentives are calculated and what they have to do to achieve certain payment levels.

The following points should be covered in the rule book and/or any annual letter setting out the terms for the coming year:

▌ scheme objectives in relation to the corporate plan;
▌ eligibility to join the scheme;
▌ timing of payments;
▌ treatment of leavers, voluntary and otherwise;
▌ accounting standards used, indicating whether the scheme is related to the audited or to the management accounts;
▌ a caveat which states that the scheme will be reviewed at regular intervals by the board and/or the remuneration committee to ensure that it is operating effectively and achieving its objectives.

EXECUTIVE BONUS SCHEMES

As an alternative to a formal, highly structured and complicated incentive plan, many companies, especially smaller ones, prefer to use the more flexible approach of an executive bonus scheme. The three main types of scheme are:

1. profit pool;
2. discretionary;
3. personal targets.

Profit pool bonus schemes

A profit pool plan sets a given percentage of pre-tax profit over an annually defined threshold. This is often distributed pro rata as a percentage of salary, as in the following example:

1. *Bonus pool:* set at 5 per cent of pre-tax profits over a 2003/4 threshold of £12 million. Its total pre-tax profits are £17.6 million; the pool is therefore £280,000.
2. *Salary cost:* the total cost of the basic salaries paid to executives in the scheme is £900,000
3. *Basis for distribution:* the proportion of the bonus pool to total salary cost applied as a percentage of basic salary.
4. *Calculations:* bonus pool (£280,000) multiplied by 100 divided by total salary cost (£900,000) = 31 per cent of salary for each participant.

This approach has the merit of simplicity. It can also be controlled from year to year by adjusting the threshold. But agreement on the formula or process to adjust the threshold can be difficult to achieve.

Discretionary bonus schemes

Some companies, especially smaller private ones, prefer to adopt a completely discretionary approach. This involves awarding bonuses simply on the basis of the opinion of the chief executive or the board, which may or may not be related to objective criteria. If there are no such criteria, there is a danger of favouritism creeping in – the link between achievement and reward is no longer clear and the scheme can have a positively demotivating effect, particularly in an autocratic culture. It can be difficult to justify large payments in such a scheme, and so the danger is that the total pay package becomes uncompetitive. On the other hand, large payments for unclear reasons tend to be discounted by employees when they calculate the total value of their package. Indeed, some companies find that these informal arrangements are becoming harder to justify as employees place more value on transparancy.

The two approaches above can be combined, with participants receiving a proportion of a bonus pool that depends on their personal performance as well as salary and/or job level.

Deferred bonus plans

Many larger companies provide deferred bonus plans to executives. In such plans, part of the annual incentive is converted into shares to be held for three years.

The deferral of bonus may be compulsory or optional. Where deferral is optional, and often when it is compulsory, the executive is provided with additional 'matching shares' proportional to the deferred element of the bonus.

Because the deferred element is part of a bonus that has already been earned, it is normally retained by the executive on leaving the company. Any retention effect comes through the matching shares, which are lost on exit. Shareholders increasingly expect matching shares to be subject to performance conditions on vesting.

The logic of deferred bonuses is that the rewards should be linked not only to operational or strategic achievements but to the value those achievements have delivered to shareholders.

23

Employee and Executive Share Schemes

THE CONTEXT

A favourable climate for employee and executive share schemes has been created as a result of the generous tax treatment of share schemes in the UK and in other tax regimes, the growth of capitalism, privatization, the success of the wider share ownership movement and the bull stock markets of the 1980s and the 1990s.

In the UK, institutional shareholders, whose interests are represented by the Investment Protection Committees (IPCs) of the Association of British Insurers (ABI) and the National Association of Pensions Funds (NAPF), have issued guidelines for share schemes of UK listed companies to operate within. They allow up to 10 per cent dilution (ie 10 per cent of the number of existing shares can be issued as new shares) through all employee schemes over any 10-year period.

Historically, using unissued shares has hidden the real cost to companies of share incentives, and the lack of any charge to reported profits has made them appear 'free'; this has also helped the growth of schemes. New international accounting rules seem likely to mean that companies will, from 1 January 2005, be obliged to charge their accounts with the value of share incentive awards over the period before they vest.

In the UK since the inception of Inland Revenue-approved all-employee schemes, it is estimated that a total of about 2.75 million employees received shares under profit-sharing schemes (now defunct) and over 2 million employees received options over shares under the savings-related scheme worth, at the outset, about £36 billion overall.

These figures exclude the substantial number of executive schemes that are not approved by the Inland Revenue, in particular most executive share option schemes and all deferred bonus and restricted share schemes. The number of employees and executives in the private sector benefiting from such arrangements is therefore huge.

WHY SHARE SCHEMES?

The rationale for executive share schemes is different from that for all-employee share schemes. Executives can be viewed as the agents of the shareholders. In order to establish a commonality of interest, it is right that they either own substantial amounts of shares themselves or that their remuneration is closely tied to movements in the company's share price.

The rationale for share schemes covering all employees is less clear; there are significant pros and cons. Also, there are alternative ways to satisfy the often quoted goals of employee involvement, participation and motivation.

Executive share schemes – a stake in the company

One of the major ways of increasing executive identification with the aims of a business is to give executives shares or share options. As share-holders or potential shareholders with the chance to benefit from the organization's success and achieve capital accrual beyond the scope of pay alone, their perception of their role can change. They can become 'owners' rather than just paid employees and this can have a beneficial effect on their commitment to the long-term future of the business. So goes the argument for executive share schemes, backed by the experience of the many organizations that have adopted this approach as a key element in executive remuneration.

Building executive commitment and loyalty

Most companies coming to the market for the first time include details of an executive share scheme in their prospectus, usually alongside an all-employee share scheme. This is a sign to potential shareholders that the organization is a well-managed company where executives have a stake in the future success of the business, with a remuneration package structured accordingly. It also shows that the top management team should be 'locked in' by the handcuffs of the share scheme as the company goes for growth. Share schemes can make beneficiaries less vulnerable to approaches from executive search consultants or at least make them very expensive to lure away. Potential employers may baulk at having to buy out existing share incentives by paying substantial 'golden hellos' to compensate for the lost awards – probably in addition to granting new share incentives to the executive in question, who will negotiate for them as an expected part of the remuneration package.

Types of schemes

This chapter considers the following schemes in turn:

▌ executive share incentive schemes;
▌ all-employee share schemes;
▌ Employee Share Ownership Plans (ESOPs).

EXECUTIVE SHARE INCENTIVE SCHEMES

Types of executive share incentive schemes

There are five principal forms of executive share incentive schemes in the UK, the first two of which are both share option schemes:

1. *Tax-favoured share option schemes* – ie the Inland Revenue-approved Company Share Option Plan (CSOP), taking advantage of the 1996 Finance Act provision (alternatively, tax-favoured Enterprise Management Incentive – EMI – options under the Finance Act 2000 are available for executives in smaller companies).
2. *Unapproved share option schemes* – often running alongside a tax-favoured scheme to provide additional potential shareholdings.
3. *Restricted share schemes* – these grant shares to executives that vest (typically in three or five years) depending upon restrictions such as continued employment and achievement of performance targets.
4. *Deferred bonus schemes* – some of the executive's annual bonus is retained, converted into shares and then released at some later date, perhaps enhanced with additional shares.
5. *Phantom share schemes* – set up in organizations where no shares or no further shares are available for distribution, now or in the future. These are essentially a form of deferred incentive based on a notional share issue and linked to the share price or notional share price of the company.

The mechanics of each of these schemes are examined below, along with some of their advantages and disadvantages, their prevalence in the UK FTSE 100 and their UK tax treatment.

Executive share option schemes

Executive share incentive schemes often take the form of share options. Essentially the rules of these schemes provide for executives to be given an option to buy shares at a future date for their market price at the time the option was granted. Provided the share price appreciates, the individual makes a profit when the option is exercised and the shares sold. The profit is the difference between the purchase price when the option was granted and the market price for which shares can be sold at the end of the option period, less any tax due on the gain. The prevailing tax regime can, and often does, have a major effect on the attractiveness of share options.

The number of share options granted is often set by reference to the executive's base salary and the value of the underlying shares at the grant date. Award levels will typically vary from year to year and between levels of executive (eg the chief executive might be granted options over shares with an underlying value of 200 per cent of salary at the grant date, whereas the rest of the board may receive options equivalent to only 150 per cent of salary).

The advantages of share options schemes are that:

▍ because they are common they are often well understood by executives and shareholders alike;
▍ they deliver no value for executives unless the share price increases between the grant and exercise dates, hence delivering value for shareholders;
▍ in some tax regimes (including, historically, the UK) they have enjoyed significant tax advantages, hence delivering greater rewards for executives at lower cost to shareholders.

The disadvantages of share option schemes are that:

▍ share options can provide the same upside as owning shares; however, there has been substantial criticism of their effectiveness as an incentive as they provide no downside risk;
▍ they are often unsuitable for established companies – modest share price volatility typically means meaningful option profits will only be delivered by inappropriately large option awards;
▍ they tend to use up shares more quickly than other types of scheme, hence creating dilution difficulties for a company with a smaller capital base;
▍ options are not affected by dividends or demergers and therefore do not reflect total shareholder return.

The other forms of executive share incentives have been developed in response to these shortcomings and to provide a better linkage with the interests of shareholders. The most common of these alternative structures is the executive restricted share scheme.

Executive restricted share schemes

Under such schemes free shares are provisionally awarded to participants. These shares do not belong to the executive until they are released or vested; hence they are 'restricted'. The number of shares actually released to the executive at the end of a defined period (usually three or, less commonly, five years) will depend on performance over that period against specific targets. Thereafter there may be a further retention period when the shares must be held although no further performance conditions apply.

As for share options, the quantum of shares awarded is often set by reference to the executive's base salary and the face value of the shares at the award date (eg 100 per cent of salary). Award levels will also typically vary from year to year and between levels of executive (eg the chief executive might be awarded restricted shares worth 100 per cent of salary at the award date, whereas the rest of the board may receive awards equivalent to only 75 per cent of salary).

The advantages of restricted share schemes are that:

▌ they are relatively simple to communicate and understand;
▌ because awards take the form of free shares, the executive shares the downside risk on the share price with shareholders;
▌ unlike share options, they can still reward executives of companies that are performing well against the backdrop of a bear market.

The disadvantages of restricted share schemes are that:

▌ they tend to be valued less highly by executives because awards are typically over fewer shares than an equivalent share option and their growth potential therefore appears lower;
▌ the combination of their unfamiliarity (compared to share options) and performance conditions that are usually measured against a comparator group can make the outcome of such schemes less transparent than share options;
▌ they generally enjoy few, if any, tax advantages.

Deferred bonus schemes

In some ways, deferred bonus schemes represent a hybrid or half-way house between short-term incentives (eg annual bonus schemes) and long-term incentives. Their starting-point is typically the annual bonus scheme, part of which is held back and converted into shares. From here on the deferred bonus scheme borrows from the restricted share scheme, as the release of the deferred shares to the executive at the end of the deferred period (often two years) will depend on his or her continued employment with the company. The release of the shares may be enhanced by 'matching' shares, perhaps depending on the company's performance during the deferral period. The 'matching' ratio sometimes varies with performance on a sliding scale.

The proportion of the executive's annual bonus that is deferred in this way can be imposed by the company, but will often be chosen by the executive within parameters outlined in the scheme (eg from 0 to 50 per cent of the bonus).

The advantages of deferred bonus schemes are that:

▌ they can significantly enhance the value and retentive impact of the annual bonus scheme;
▌ the executive shares the downside risk on share price with the shareholders during the retention period;
▌ unlike options they can still reward executives of companies that are performing well against the backdrop of a bear market.

The disadvantages of deferred bonus schemes are that:

▌ long-term pay-outs depend from the outset on good short-term performance (if there is nothing to defer there can be no deferred bonus);
▌ to encourage deferral, companies typically have to offer larger annual bonus opportunities;
▌ they generally enjoy few, if any, tax advantages.

Phantom share schemes

These can take almost any form but all have at their core the opportunity for participants to receive a cash payment that reflects in some way the value created and delivered to shareholders. For example, this could be a cash payment equal to the growth in value over three years of a notional holding of shares (ie a phantom option).

The advantages of phantom share schemes are that:

▌ they deliver a cash bonus – from the executive's perspective cash is often 'king';
▌ their use involves no issue of shares and therefore no dilution of shareholders' interests – the cash cost to the company is transparent;
▌ they are almost infinitely flexible in the sense that the scheme can be designed to fit the company's needs without the constraints imposed by the use of shares.

The disadvantages of phantom schemes are that:

▌ they adversely impact company cash flow (payments involving newly issued shares typically have a neutral or, in the case of options, positive cash flow effect);

▌ they generally enjoy few, if any, tax advantages.

Executive share scheme practice in the FTSE 100

Hay Group completed an analysis of the long-term incentive arrangements for FTSE 100 companies at January 2004 (based on published data). While share option schemes continue to be the most common form of long-term incentive at board level, companies operate a significant number of executive restricted share schemes. Below board level, however, share options remain overwhelmingly the share incentive of choice. The analysis showed:

▌ 49 companies had both restricted share schemes and share options;

▌ 13 had restricted share schemes but no share options;

▌ 32 companies had share options only;

▌ in this group cash-based long-term incentives are rare (one company only);

▌ performance measures used for executive restricted share schemes are frequently total shareholder return (TSR) measured against a comparator group. Typically no awards vest below the 50th percentile, rising to 100 per cent for upper-quartile performance (or, for larger awards, upper-decile performance). Therefore the value that the executive eventually receives will reflect both the relative performance and also the share price growth of the company.

Taxation of executive share incentives in the UK

Share options

Prior to the 1984 Finance Act, all executive share option gains were taxed as income. The 1984 Finance Act introduced the concept of 'approved' share options, which escaped any income tax liability and which were only subject to capital gains tax on gains made at the date of sale. From 1984 to 1989 approved option gains were therefore taxed at 30 per cent, whereas the highest income tax rate was 60 per cent. This huge tax bias helped drive the growth of executive share option schemes in the UK.

In 1995, income tax relief for approved executive share options was ended. At the same time the Chancellor announced a new tax relief for Company Share Option Plans (CSOPs). Under the replacement relief the employee does not incur a charge to income tax or national insurance contributions (NIC) on grant or exercise of the CSOP options, provided the aggregate CSOP options held by the employee do not exceed £30,000 and they are exercised more than three years after the date of grant. Employees are taxed on capital gains on the subsequent sale of the shares acquired through the exercise of such options. The £30,000 limit applies by reference to the value of shares under option at the time the options are granted and they must not be granted at a discount.

In 2000 a new form of tax-favoured share option called the Enterprise Management Incentive (EMI) was introduced by the government. The intention of the legislation was to help small, newly established companies offer the substantial incentives necessary to attract and retain high-quality senior talent that they would otherwise struggle to afford. EMI share options enjoy similar tax advantages to CSOPs except that the limit on options held by each employee is more generous at £100,000. EMI options can be granted by independent trading companies provided the company (or the group of which it forms part) has gross assets of no more than £30 million and has no more than £3 million of shares under EMI option at any one time.

By contrast unapproved share options are subject to income tax and NIC at exercise. The taxable amount is the difference between the value of the shares obtained and the option price paid. This income tax and NIC liability arises regardless of whether or not the executive sells the shares and has to be accounted for through the company's PAYE system. As for other options, any subsequent gains on the shares will be subject to capital gains tax.

Although today the top rates of income tax and capital gains tax are the same (40 per cent for 2003/04), gains subject to capital gains tax are eligible for reliefs (such as taper relief) that can reduce the effective rate to 10 per cent or less. Furthermore, capital gains are not subject to NIC. Hence there is still much to be gained in tax terms from tax-favoured schemes. Table 23.1 shows the extent to which companies have made use of these schemes in recent years.

Other schemes

Most executive restricted share schemes are structured so that the awards are subject to income tax and NIC when released to the participant (otherwise participants would be faced with the need to fund the tax bill some years before receiving the benefits). Thereafter any further gains on the shares held are subject to capital gains tax.

Deferred share bonus schemes can be structured so as to operate pre- or post-income tax. That is to say, if the deferred element converted into shares remains subject to forfeiture (eg in the event that the participant leaves employment) it should not be liable to income tax and NIC unless and until the risk of forfeiture falls away at the end of the deferral period. Alternatively, if the deferred shares are not subject to forfeiture (the participant merely defers receipt voluntarily) their award will be liable to income tax and NIC at the same time as the cash element of the

Table 23.1 Tax-effective executive share plans

Company share option plans (approved under Finance Act 1996)

Year	Number of employees to whom options granted during year	Initial value of shares over which options granted during year £m	Average per employee £
1999–00	240,000	1,310	5,000
2000–01	410,000	2,200	5,000
2001–02	270,000	1,900	7,000

Total number of schemes approved up to 5 April 2002: 9,581.

Enterprise Management Incentives (notified under Finance Act 2000)

Year	Number of employees to whom options granted during year	Initial value of shares over which options granted during year £m	Average per employee £
2000–01	4,582	145	31,600
2001–02	19,767	300	15,200

Up to 5 April 2003 approximately 3,500 companies had granted options over their shares.

Source: Inland Revenue

bonus. The award of any matching shares will also be subject to income tax and NIC. Any subsequent gains made on the shares would be subject to capital gains tax.

Phantom share schemes would typically be subject to income tax and NIC at payment in the same way as any other cash bonus scheme.

It is important to recognize that tax considerations have been a major influence on the choice of long-term incentive vehicles in the UK (as well as other tax regimes, such as that of the USA) and that companies need to review their arrangements when the taxation regime changes.

External controls for executive schemes

The entitlements granted under executive share incentive schemes are closely affected, in the case of listed PLCs, by the guidelines of the Investment Protection Committees (IPCs). All share schemes for directors and employees of such companies must, in the UK, be approved by shareholders in accordance with Stock Exchange rules. Furthermore, shareholders now have an annual opportunity to vote on the directors' remuneration report (as shown in the company's report and accounts), at which point they can indicate the existence of any concerns they may have over the company's existing schemes.

The IPCs represent the institutional shareholders, but also speak for the interests of shareholders as a whole. Their guidelines apply to both approved and unapproved schemes, and the principal objectives are to limit the extent to which shareholders' equity is diluted and to ensure that any dilution rewards performance that is in their long-term interests. The guidelines have not always been welcomed and have been modified many times to reflect changing company practice and evolving institutional views. It is also clear that individual companies, usually with the help of specialist advisers, have successfully negotiated variations to suit special circumstances – as long as they could convince the IPCs that this was in shareholders' interests. More recently some institutional shareholders have published their own guidelines outlining their expectations of the companies in which they invest (eg 'The Hermes Principles' published in 2002).

At the time of writing the aggregate dilution limits for employee share schemes of all types is 10 per cent over 10 years and for selective executive share schemes the limit is 5 per cent over 10 years.

Factors to be taken into account when introducing an executive share scheme

Employers considering the introduction of an executive share incentive scheme will therefore need to be sure they obtain a full understanding of:

▌ what key outcomes the company wants from the scheme (eg executive retention, motivation etc);
▌ Stock Exchange rules;
▌ the effect of current IPC guidelines on potential entitlements;
▌ the impact of any published views of a major shareholder;
▌ market practice in their industry or sector;
▌ which issues they will need to monitor to ensure that practice remains competitive;
▌ the tax position and, if applicable, requirements for gaining Inland Revenue approval.

Deciding executive share scheme entitlements and policy

For tax-favoured schemes, the Inland Revenue rules set out a maximum amount that can be granted in the form of share options; unapproved options, restricted share schemes, deferred bonuses or phantom share schemes are, of course, free of these rules. But the IPC rules also affect potential entitlements by limiting the amount of the organization's share capital that can be allocated to options or other forms of share incentive. These will, of course, not just affect the first awards under a new scheme, but will have to be complied with when schemes are extended. Companies need to ensure that they will have shares available to award when new top executives are appointed or when further awards need to be made to existing participants.

With these constraints companies therefore have to decide:

∎ whether to give the same entitlement to all directors;
∎ whether to differentiate on the basis of status, the need to retain key individuals or to recognize particular achievements;
∎ how large a differential, if any, to make between the chief executive and the rest of the board or others picked out for special recognition;
∎ whether to apply performance conditions at vesting or (very rarely) for the making of awards;
∎ whether to extend the scheme to other key executives outside the board whose services are highly valued and whose long-term commitment to the company ought to be secured in some way;
∎ the policy on death of scheme participants or severance by redundancy, retirement, takeover, liquidation or misconduct;
∎ whether to use more than one type of scheme and, if so, whether to provide different types of awards at different levels (eg restricted shares for the board and options for executives below board level);
∎ how the scheme fits in with the other elements of the executive's package (eg whether the chief executive should have a large long-term incentive and no annual bonus to reflect his or her strategic focus and avoid conflict of interest in setting the board's annual bonus performance targets).

These decisions will normally be the task of the remuneration committee – part of its role in supervising share option arrangements and safeguarding shareholders' interests. This committee will often need to take advice from pay, financial, legal and tax advisers to ensure that scheme rules comply with any regulations affecting them, are tax-efficient and reflect best practice in this complex area. In some cases the committee will feel the need to appoint its own advisers, independent of those used by the company.

An outline of the main rules to be covered by an approved share option scheme (CSOP) is given in Figure 23.1.

Outline of executive share option scheme

SCOPE	Non-transferable options to acquire shares, granted and exercised witin 10 years.

GRANT OF OPTIONS

Whom invited	Full-time directors and executives selected by board.
When	Within x weeks of announcing annual or half-yearly results.
Option price	Middle market price on the day before the date of grant (nominal value if higher) – not payable until option is exercised – subject to adjustment on fair and reasonable terms if capital is varied, eg by a scrip issue.
Fee for grant	Nominal (£1) or nil.
Individual limit	Aggregated share values, at market price at time of grant, not to exceed £30,000.
Company limit	The aggregated value of shares as above, for all options granted under this and earlier executive schemes not to exceed 5 per cent of the company's total equity, or together with all-employee share schemes, 10 per cent.

EXERCISE OF OPTIONS

General rule[1]	Not before 3 years or after 10 years from date of grant.
Performance	Options may only be exercised if the growth in the company's earnings per share exceeds inflation by at least 2% over the 3 years prior to exercise.
Death[1]	Within a year of death by deceased's nominated representative but not later than 10 years after grant.
Severance[1]	Within x months (normally less than a year) and before 10 years.
	(a) Redundancy, incapacity, retirement, takeover, liquidation.
	(b) Otherwise at board's discretion. In the event of option lapsing on loss of office, no compensation payable for loss of option rights.

SHARES

Company to keep available unissued shares (or other source, eg ESOP or Treasury) to permit exercise of options. These shares to rank equally with other shares issued by the company at time of allotment. Adjustment to be made as necessary on variation of company's capital.

ADMINISTRATION

The main features of the scheme cannot be amended without shareholders' approval. Administration in hands of board.

[1] Options exercised outside these time limits would not attract tax relief under the 1996 Finance Act.

Figure 23.1 A typical public limited company approved scheme

ALL-EMPLOYEE SHARE SCHEMES – A SHARE IN THE COMPANY'S SUCCESS

All-employee schemes are similar to executive share schemes in that they also allow employees to have a stake in the company. However, the amounts are more modest and the motivational impact is different from executive share schemes. All-employee schemes are a form of financial participation commonly implemented when executive share options are introduced and, perhaps for this reason, their use is widespread.

Executive share option schemes are selective in the choice of participant. By contrast all-employee share schemes, as the name suggests, tend to embrace the company's employee population at large. Indeed UK tax-favoured all-employee share schemes commonly require employers to allow all employees to participate on similar terms.

Types of all-employee share scheme

Unlike executive share incentive schemes, all-employee share schemes tend, almost entirely, to be driven by the tax legislation of the regime concerned. As a result the schemes listed below all stem from UK tax legislation, current as at 2003/04:

1. *Save as you earn (SAYE) share options* – which are sometimes called 'sharesave' schemes. In simple terms employees are given options over shares and enter into a monthly savings plan to provide for the option price.
2. *Share incentive plans (SIPs)* – highly flexible schemes that allow companies to offer their employees: free shares, the opportunity to buy shares out of pre-tax income, extra free shares (matched with those bought by the employee) and dividends in the form of shares. Companies can adopt one, some or all of the available mechanisms.
3. *Profit-sharing schemes* – these schemes are now defunct (though some are continuing to wind down at the time of writing) but used to allow companies to give their employees free shares. These schemes have now commonly been superseded by SIPs.

The mechanics of each of these schemes are examined below, along with their advantages and disadvantages and their UK tax treatment.

Sharesave schemes

Employees are given options over shares that are linked to a monthly interest-bearing savings plan with a bank or building society. The employee can, within limits (ie between £5 and £250 per month), choose his or her level of savings, which in turn determines the size of the option. The company can offer the option over a life of three, five or seven years and can also offer a discount of up to 20 per cent of the share price at the grant date.

When the option vests, the employee can opt to use his or her savings to exercise it or instead can take the cash fund, plus interest. Employees leaving employment usually forfeit their options but always retain their funds.

The advantages of sharesave schemes are that:

▌ employees cannot lose out – their savings are safe, regardless of share price changes;
▌ participants feel included in arrangements that are similar to those (ie executive share options) often adopted for senior managers;
▌ they create a high level of interest in the company's share price performance and can greatly reinforce success;
▌ they enjoy significant tax advantages.

The disadvantages of sharesave schemes are that:

▌ on their own most employees can have little direct impact on share price, hence the reward can be arbitrary;
▌ the level of benefit will depend on the individual's ability to save, rather than performance;
▌ they can badly affect morale when the share price falls.

Share incentive plans

Companies adopting such schemes can use a number of mechanisms to provide shares to their employees. These are:

▌ *Free shares* – the company can give employees free shares up to a personal limit of £3,000 per annum. Free shares can be allocated on similar terms (eg equally, pro rata to salary, etc) or on the basis of measurable performance (individual or team).
▌ *Partnership shares* – employees can be allowed to buy shares with money set aside from their monthly pre-tax income up to a personal limit of £1,500 per annum.
▌ *Matching shares* – if employees buy shares, the company can 'match' their purchase with free shares up to a personal limit of two free shares for each partnership share bought.
▌ *Dividend shares* – if dividends are declared on shares allocated to employees as a result of any of the mechanisms described above, they can be paid in the form of additional shares (up to a personal limit of £1,500 per annum) rather than cash.

Companies adopting such schemes do not have to incorporate all of these features; neither are they required to make use of all (or any) of the features of their scheme in any particular year.

The advantages of SIPs are that:

▮ they are hugely flexible and can be tailored to meet a wide variety of corporate objectives;
▮ employees receive real shares and therefore face the same risks as other shareholders, creating a strong identity of interest;
▮ they enjoy significant tax advantages.
The disadvantages of SIPs are that:

▮ they can be very complex to administer and for employees to understand;
▮ companies usually have to incur the costs of setting up and maintaining a trust to store employees' shares;
▮ the numbers involved per employee can be rather small and may be heavily impacted by dealing costs;
▮ because employees receive shares, rather than options, they have no protection (other than their tax savings) from falling share prices.

Profit-sharing schemes

Under such schemes companies could give their employees free shares up to a personal limit equal to the greater of £3,000 or 10 per cent of the employee's earnings, subject to a cap of £8,000 per annum. Shares had to be allocated to all employees on similar terms (eg equally or pro rata to salary). No new profit-sharing schemes can now be approved, nor can any new allocations now be made under existing schemes.

The advantages of profit-sharing schemes were that:

▮ they were simple to administer and for employees to understand;
▮ they allowed companies to share success with employees in good years in a flexible manner;
▮ they had significant tax advantages.

The disadvantages of profit sharing schemes were that:

▮ they did not allow companies to differentiate between good and bad performers;
▮ where small allocations were made, dealing costs could heavily impact the benefits.

Taxation of all-employee share schemes in the UK

Successive governments have introduced and amended (usually favourably) the taxation of all-employee share schemes. They have done this because they believe that employee share ownership should be encouraged and that it is therefore appropriate to have a tax break on these schemes.

The main tax breaks are:

- Sharesave schemes:
    - no income tax or NIC on the interest paid on the savings;
    - options can be granted at up to 20 per cent discount;
    - no income tax or NIC charge on the gain upon exercise; but these gains are subject to capital gains, where the shares are sold;
    - limit of savings of between £5 and £250 per month.
- Share incentive plans:
    - no income tax or NIC on the value of any free or matching shares, provided the employee leaves them in the plan for at least five years;
    - no income tax or NIC on the value of any dividend shares, provided the employee leaves them in the plan for at least three years;
    - no capital gains tax on any increase in value while the shares are in the plan (ie the base cost for capital gains tax purposes is their value at the date the shares leave the plan);
    - companies get corporation tax relief for set-up and running costs and the costs of acquiring shares on behalf of employees.
- Profit-sharing schemes:
    - no income tax or NIC on the value of the shares appropriated to them, provided they agreed to leave their shares with the trustees for at least two years;
    - if the shares were sold in the third year after appropriation, income tax was payable on the value of the shares at appropriation;
    - if the shares were sold in the fourth or subsequent year after appropriation, there was no income tax charge but capital gains tax could apply.

Table 23.2 shows the extent to which companies have made use of these schemes in recent years.

External controls

The IPCs have also published guidelines for all-employee share schemes. The key guideline concerns dilution of not more than 10 per cent in any 10-year period.

Factors to be taken into account when introducing an all-employee share scheme

Employers considering the introduction of an all-employee share scheme will therefore need to be sure they obtain a full understanding of:

Table 23.2   Tax-effective all-employee share schemes

Profit-sharing schemes (approved under Finance Act 1978)

Year	Number of employees to whom shares allocated during year	Initial value of shares allocated £m	Average per employee £
1999–00	850,000	650	760
2000–01	840,000	780	930
2001–02	750,000	630	840

Total number of schemes approved up to 5 April 2001: 1,584.
Note: No new profit-sharing schemes could be approved after 5 April 2001, as the scheme was withdrawn.

Savings-related share option schemes (approved under Finance Act 1980)

Year	Number of employees to whom options granted during year	Initial value of shares over which options granted during year £m	Average per employee £
1999–00	1,000,000	2,830	2,800
2000–01	1,030,000	3,460	3,400
2001–02	1,280,000	2,730	

Total number of schemes approved up to 5 april 2002: 2,359.

Share incentive plans (approved under the Finance Act 2000)

Year	Type of award	Number of companies' schemes offering shares	Initial value of shares allocated/purchased £m	Average per employee £
2000–01	Free shares	30	20	290
	Partnership shares	21	5	80
	Matching shares	16	5	80
	Dividend shares	Negligible	Negligible	Negligible
2001–02	Free shares	95	60	430
	Partnership shares	143	80	100
	Matching shares	86	50	90
	Dividend shares	24	Negligible	Negligible

The number of employees receiving awards cannot be accumulated as some receive more than one type simultaneously.
The number of schemes approved in 2001–01 (the first year the scheme was available) was 95 and, in 2001–02, 222.

Source: Inland Revenue

- why they want employees to own shares (ie what the scheme's objectives are – sharing profits, employee retention, etc);
- Stock Exchange rules;
- market practice in their industry or sector;
- the extent to which they are happy to encourage employees to invest in the company's shares (ie ideally employees should diversify their investment portfolio);
- whether the cost/benefit ratio is acceptable (ie whether employees will see the value of the share as greater than the cost);
- the tax position and, where applicable, the requirements for Inland Revenue approval (for international companies differing tax regimes can add significantly to the cost and complexity of implementing such schemes globally).

Deciding all-employee share scheme policy

Companies considering all-employee share schemes must decide:

- whether they want employees to own the shares, receive dividends and vote shares immediately;
- how much subsidy the company is willing to provide;
- whether all employees receive shares or only those who elect to join;
- whether to set the length of service requirement at the Inland Revenue maximum of five years' service or a lower figure;
- whether to exclude part-timers working fewer than 20 hours per week, or to set a lower limit;
- whether to have one scheme or two or more schemes;
- if adopting a sharesave scheme:
  - what discount, if any, to set;
  - whether to have three, five of seven years' option period;
  - what maximum savings to allow;
  - if over-subscribed, how to scale down applications;
- if adopting a SIP (because of the SIP's complexity, these are just a few of the many factors to consider):
  - which aspects of the plan to adopt;
  - how free shares should be allocated and, if performance is to be used, whether that should be on an individual or team basis;
  - if matching shares are offered what the ratio should be;
  - if partnership shares are over-subscribed, how to scale back applications.

ESOPS

An ESOP (Employee Share Ownership Plan) is an employee benefit trust linked to a share participation scheme. The trust receives contributions from the company or borrows money, and then buys shares in the company, which are allocated to employees.

A major benefit of using an ESOP, combined with employee share schemes, is that it avoids dilution. Companies that are close to the IPC limits on dilution may find an ESOP offers scope to make further grants of share options than would not otherwise be possible.

In many management buyouts the use of an ESOP has enabled the management temporarily to park a percentage of the equity, which can then be subsequently released to employees, either through purchase or through an employee share scheme or schemes. This mechanism enables all employees to share in the benefits of the buyout.

COMMUNICATING THE BENEFITS

The success of any of the mechanisms described in this chapter will depend on how well they are communicated to their participants. Effective communication will depend on:

▌ a clear understanding of the objectives the company has for the scheme (eg executive motivation, profit sharing with employees generally etc);
▌ a clear understanding of how the scheme will work (both the general rules, if a tax-favoured scheme is used, and the specifics incorporated by the company itself);
▌ timelines (ie at the launch and at the various critical points in the scheme's life);
▌ trust (employees' trust will need to be maintained over the introduction and explanation of concepts that may be unfamiliar and of which some may be wary).

Experience has shown that the communication of employee schemes greatly affects the employees' perception of the scheme and its value.

Health warning

The mechanisms described in this chapter are complex to design and operate. Companies should take appropriate professional advice before attempting to adopt or amend any of these schemes.

24

Team Rewards

INTRODUCTION

The significance of good teamwork as a key factor in achieving organizational success has directed attention to how employee reward systems can contribute to improving team effectiveness. Lateral working and collective effort have become more important, particularly as structures have been delayered and based more on a matrix. Project or programme activity has become a bigger feature of working life, both to solve specific problems and to achieve major results over the medium term. There is also a desire in some organizations to shift from individual performance-related pay (which has failed to deliver the results in terms of incentivization expected of it) to team pay and other methods of rewarding teams. In practice, it is important to decide whether the aim is to reward the outputs or outcomes of team activity, or to recognize and reward collaborative behaviour in individuals as an organizational value.

However, team rewards is one of the areas of reward policy where practical experience is still limited – it is more talked about than done. The CIPD 2003 Reward Management Survey found that only 6 per cent of respondents had team pay.

TEAM-BASED REWARD DEFINED

Team-based rewards are payments or other forms of non-financial reward provided to members of a defined team, which are linked to the performance of that team. Their purpose is to:

▌ deliver the message that one of the organization's core values is effective teamwork;

▌ help to clarify what teams are expected to achieve, by relating rewards to the attainment of agreed targets and standards of performance and behaviours or to the satisfactory completion of a project or a stage of a project;

▌ encourage group effort and cooperation by providing incentives and means of recognizing team achievements.

Typically, team-based rewards are shared among the members of teams in accordance with a published formula or on an ad hoc basis for exceptional achievements.

There are two main approaches to team-based rewards. The first is to create an incentive and a clear definition of performance, by identifying targets in advance and offering a sum of money for achieving them. A second is to reward teams retrospectively for good work done under agreed criteria, in what is effectively a recognition scheme.

A further option is to reward individuals for their contribution to team results and/or for demonstrating teamworking competencies. This is not strictly 'team based', in the sense of setting collective targets and rewarding all team members, but may help to reinforce an emphasis on teamworking.

This chapter is mainly concerned with the first, incentive-type approach, but refers to the alternatives and the circumstances in which they might be useful.

FACTORS AFFECTING TEAM REWARDS

To develop and manage team rewards – and to decide which approach to reward is most suitable – it is necessary to understand the nature of teams and how they function.

The nature of a team

Most approaches to team reward focus on small groups, taking the definition of Katzenbach and Smith:[1] 'a small number of people with complementary skills who are committed to a common purpose, performance goals and approach for which they hold themselves mutually accountable'. They assert that: 'Teams outperform individuals acting alone or in large organizational groupings, especially when performance requires multiple skills, judgements and experiences.'

There have also been some team-based reward experiments with larger groups – arguably overlapping with territory normally covered by gainsharing and profit-related pay – and we refer to these below.

Types of teams

As suggested by Gross,[2] there are four types of teams:

1. *Process or work teams:* full-time, permanent teams whose members work together to carry out a process.
2. *Parallel teams:* part-time teams that meet to solve a particular problem and then disband or meet from time to time to deal with or monitor particular issues. They are often cross-functional.
3. *Project or time-based teams:* full-time teams committed to completing a project within a given timescale and in which the membership may vary over time.
4. *Hybrid teams:* teams may have both full- and part-time or rotating members.

There are also ad hoc teams, which are formed to deal with specific issues and may be involved in troubleshooting and have, say, a 100-day agenda.

Identifying the team environment using definitions of this kind can help organizations to decide which is the most suitable approach to team reward. For example, process and project teams lend themselves to forms of incentivization and reward where the whole team benefits equally, eg through team bonuses. The more individuals are involved in brief team initiatives and are part of several teams at once, the more relevant it is to reward teamworking behaviour or the contributions individuals make to specific team results.

Team effectiveness

Four factors that influence team performance were identified by Beckhard:[3]

1. setting goals or priorities;
2. how work is allocated (roles);
3. the way the team is working (its processes);
4. the relationships between the people doing the work.

The essential characteristics of an effective team are that:

▌ it exists to attain a defined purpose and is successful in doing so;
▌ members of the team are committed collectively and individually to achieving that purpose;
▌ team members reinforce one another's intentions to pursue their team purpose irrespective of individual agendas.

Team competencies

Hay Group competency research has found that teamwork and cooperation implies the intention to work cooperatively with others and
to be part of a team, as opposed to working separately or competitively.
For this competency to be effective, the intention should be genuine. The
core question is: does the person act to facilitate the operation of a team
of which he or she is a member? The generic Hay Group competency
scale contains the following five levels:

1. *Cooperates:* participates willingly – supports team decisions, is a good
   'team player', does his or her share of work. As a member of a team,
   keeps other team members informed and up to date about the group
   process, individual actions or influencing events; shares all relevant
   or useful information.
2. *Expresses positive expectations of teams:* expresses positive expectations
   of others in terms of their abilities, expected contributions, etc; speaks
   of team members in positive terms. Shows respect for others' intelligence by appealing to reason.
3. *Solicits inputs:* genuinely values others' input and expertise; willing
   to learn from others (including subordinates and peers). Solicits ideas
   and opinions to help form specific decisions or plans. Promotes team.
4. *Encourages others:* publicly credits others who have performed well.
   Encourages and empowers others; makes them feel strong and
   important.
5. *Builds team spirit:* acts to promote a friendly climate, good morale and
   cooperation (holds parties and get-togethers, creates symbols of
   group identity). Resolves team conflicts. Protects and promotes
   group reputation with outsiders.

Gross[2] lists the following team competencies, as identified by Hay
Group:

▌ *All members:*
   – developing others;
   – customer service orientation;
   – interpersonal understanding;
   – oral communications;
   – organizational awareness;
   – organizational commitment;
   – teamwork and cooperation;
   – achievement orientation;
   – initiative;
   – analytical thinking;
   – continuous improvement.

▌ *Team leaders only:*
   – directing others;
   – empowerment;
   – team leadership;
   – self-confidence;
   – planning and organizing;
   – conceptual thinking.
▌ *Other members only:*
   – influence;
   – adaptability;
   – personal growth.

These competencies are supported by detailed definitions of the levels such as those given under 'teamwork'. Such definitions are most useful in determining rewards for the teamworking behaviour of individuals, but they can also have a role in recognition schemes that offer retrospective reward for good work by teams.

TEAM REWARD PROCESSES

The rationale for team rewards

The aim of team reward processes is to reinforce the behaviours that lead to and sustain effective teamwork. The reason for developing team rewards is the perceived need to encourage group endeavour and cooperation, rather than to concentrate only on individual performance. It is argued that pay-for-individual-performance systems prejudice team performance in two ways. First, they encourage individuals to focus on their own interests rather than those of their team. Second, they result in managers and team leaders treating their team members only as individuals, rather than relating to them in terms of what the team is there to do and what they can do for the team.

The main reasons for introducing team-based pay can be summarized as follows:

1. It is just and equitable to reward people according to the contribution they make as team members.
2. The organization demonstrates that it values high-performing teams and team members. Team pay delivers the message that teamwork is important.
3. Attention can be focused on the aspects of performance to which priority should be given and the core values to be upheld in such areas as quality, customer service, innovation and teamwork.

The basis of team rewards

In a sense, all of us do what we get rewarded for doing, whether acting as individuals or as members of a team. When considering introducing team-based rewards there are two fundamental questions to answered:

▌ Should teams be rewarded by financial means, non-financial means or a combination of the two?
▌ To what extent can we rely on extrinsic (external) rewards, whether financial or non-financial, as distinct from intrinsic (internal) rewards?

The emphasis in team reward systems is usually on team pay rather than on other forms of non-financial rewards. Pay is of course important, as a tangible means of recognition and reward and, in certain circumstances and within limits, as a motivator. This chapter therefore devotes a large portion of its contents to team pay. However, the ultimate reward for teams, especially project teams, is often the successful accomplishment of a task, as long as that is recognized. And cash is not the only means of recognition. The choice is not between financial and non-financial rewards but between financial team rewards, enhanced by non-financial rewards, and non-financial rewards alone. Worldwide research into team pay by the Motorola Corporation in 1994 found that in general their employees were more in favour of non-financial rewards than financial rewards for teamwork. It is also possible, even when using cash, to reward the group collectively rather than individuals within the group (see below, on the NHS experience).

Team pay methods

The CIPD,[4] Industrial Relations Services[5] and the Institute of Employment Studies[6] have conducted research into team pay. Each of these projects showed that the most common method of providing team pay for managerial, professional, technical and office staff was to distribute a cash sum bonus related to team performance among team members. Various formulae are used for calculating the bonus pool and there are a number of different ways in which such pools are divided between team members. There is no such thing as a typical team pay for people in these categories. This is to be expected. Their design will be contingent on the requirements and circumstances of the organization, and these will always differ.

In contrast, all shop-floor group incentive schemes tend to follow a similar pattern, bonuses being linked either to the physical output of teams or, in work-measured schemes, to the time saved on team tasks – the difference between allowed time and actual time. Because of the relatively straightforward nature of such schemes, this section concentrates on covering the formulae and methods of distribution, and on catering for individual as well as team performance.

Bonus formulae

Bonus formulae relate the amount payable to individual team members to one or more measures of team performance or to the achievement of specifically agreed team objectives. For example:

1. *Performance related to defined criteria*, as at Lloyds Bank and Norwich Union, where the criteria are sales and a measure of customer satisfaction. A Pearl Assurance scheme operating successfully for a time in the 1990s related bonuses to three performance criteria: speed of processing, accuracy, and customer service and satisfaction. In a scheme operated by Sun Life, the bonus is based on a customer service index, expressed as a percentage of the customer cases dealt with over a period. It is interesting to note that in each of these financial services companies customer service is used as a criterion.
2. *Bonus related to an overall criterion*, as at the Benefits Agency, where team bonuses are paid if there has been 'a valuable contribution to performance as determined by local unit managers'.
3. *Bonus related to the achievement of predetermined organizational and team objectives*, as at Rank Xerox, where it is linked to key organizational objectives. At Portsmouth Hospitals NHS Trust the bonus for directors and senior managers is based on an assessment of the Trust's success in meeting its corporate objectives. The finance division of the Automobile Association in Scotland operates a scheme in which teams are rewarded for their performance against productivity targets and quality measures. Dartford Borough Council pays teams according to their performance in relation to a series of targets. These are defined as tasks suitable for all or most of the team to undertake together, tasks that, if accomplished successfully, will benefit the directorate or division and, generally, tasks that are distinct from the normal duties of individual team members as set out in their job description.

Method of distributing bonuses

Bonuses can be distributed to team members in the form of either the same sum for each member, often based on a scale of payments, as at Lloyds Bank and Norwich Union; or as a percentage of base salary, as at the Benefits Agency, Dartford Borough Council, Pearl Assurance, Portsmouth Hospitals NHS Trust and Sun Life.

Payment of a bonus as a percentage of base salary is the most popular approach. The assumption behind this method is that base salary reflects the value of the individual's contribution to the team. However, there are settings (such as the NHS – see below) where offering the same flat-rate payment for all may be more culturally acceptable and may help to reinforce a message that each team member's contribution is equally important.

Team pay and individual pay

Some organizations, such as Lloyds Bank, Portsmouth Hospitals NHS Trust and Sun Life, pay team bonuses only. Others, such as the Benefits Agency, Norwich Union and Pearl Assurance, pay both team and individual bonuses.

TEAM REWARD IN PRACTICE

Basic considerations

The total team reward system is built upon the foundation of the main element of reward – basic pay. It is necessary to get this right before considering any form of team pay. As reported in the *IDS Management Pay Review*,[7] some organizations such as Ind Coope and Baxi Heating see little need for team incentives. At both companies, team members are paid simple spot basic rate salaries. Ind Coope believes that, if all team members are on the same rate, there are fewer arguments about who does what. Other companies such as The Body Shop recognize that flexible working, with team members sharing management responsibilities, implies greater pay equality. *The IDS Review* also noted that team-working is generating diverging pay strategies. On the one hand there are those that are devising a range of incentive arrangements, team bonuses being coupled with individual performance-related pay. On the other hand, other companies are flattening pay differentials and placing little or no emphasis on incentive arrangements. According to IDS, 'It is the very novelty of trying to combine cooperative behaviour, group performance and a separate emphasis on incentive arrangements that has produced these conflicting approaches.'

Referring to the Pearl Assurance team pay scheme in 1997, Gareth Trevor, then General Manager (Human Resources) at Pearl, emphasized the following:

▪ Pay is only related to performance both at an individual and a team level.
▪ Pay is only one part (and arguably a minor part at that) of the process – it reinforces the other team initiatives we have put in place but it does not lead them and, what is more, it is not even central to them.
▪ Team pay works well because staff know they have to work together but they also want to be recognized as individuals.

Research findings

A range of surveys in the past 10 years have touched on team pay, and estimates of its prevalence range from below 10 per cent to around a quarter of organizations.[8] The most detailed study remains the CIPD research[9] from the mid-1990s. This found formal team pay schemes in 24 per cent of participating organizations. The more detailed CIPD research findings and conclusions in 1996 were as follows:

▮ There are many different varieties of teams and many different types of schemes – it is not possible to prescribe a standard mode or approach to developing team pay.

▮ The conditions required for the successful introduction of team pay are stringent and many companies will not feel that they are able to meet them – this is probably a reason for the relatively small number of formal schemes.

▮ Success in the use of team pay depends more on culture, management style and working environment of the organization than the mechanics of the scheme.

▮ Improvement in team performance is dependent solely on formal reward processes – teams are capable of planning and implementing their own improvement programme or they have easy access to feedback information and they are encouraged to meet regularly to discuss how well they are performing and to decide what needs to be done.

▮ Over half the organizations with team pay are confident that it is contributing to the improvement of team performance.

▮ A fundamental and often unresolved problem with team pay is the extent to which people, including team members, are hostile to any system that does not reward individual contributions, however much they are in favour of better teamwork – bearing in mind that team pay mostly goes to individuals not teams.

▮ In a teamworking environment, some organizations are introducing or expressing interest in skill-based or competence-related pay to reward individuals for their personal contribution, while also enabling them to share in the bonus earned by their teams.

▮ Although not strictly a team pay process, organizations are increasingly including capability as a teamworker in their performance management processes as a key competency 'input' factor to strengthen collaborative behaviour.

▮ Some organizations that have adopted a 'purpose and values' approach include teamworking as a core value and assess people on the extent to which they uphold it.

▮ A number of people are expressing the view that team pay is either inadequate or inappropriate as a means of improving team performance – other forms of (non-financial) reward can and should be used instead of, or at least in conjunction with, team pay.

Finally, and importantly, improving team performance cannot be left to reward management alone. The quality of teamwork ultimately depends on the culture, values, management style, structure and operating processes of the organization, together with its performance management and employee development programmes. Reward processes, however well conceived and effective they may be, are not a substitute for good management.

Team pay experience in the NHS

There has been a great deal of interest in team pay in the public sector in recent years. This is partly as a result of the Makinson report[10] into performance rewards in government, which led directly to team pay experiments in major agencies such as the Inland Revenue and Customs and Excise.

It is partly also because of a growing concern to secure better services, allied to a recognition that outputs and outcomes derive from collective effort.

The latter motives prompted a major team pay project in the NHS, run by Hay Group and the Institute for Employment Studies from 2002 to 2004. It involved 17 team pay pilots on 15 sites, some for one year and most for two. There was a mix of team sizes, from whole hospital and primary care trusts to small specialist units. There was also a mix of payment types: equal payments to individuals in the team; an improvement fund to pay for training, equipment or improvements to working life; or a combination of the two. However, all pilots were based on the incentive principle, with performance targets, measures and rewards set out clearly in advance.

The NHS experience shows that team rewards can provide a helpful way of concentrating attention on priorities and of promoting achievement. The important caveat is that these benefits are only available if the scheme is handled in the right way. First, the organization needs to choose the right approach to team reward to suit its team types and its culture – the incentive approach (as in this project), post hoc recognition, or reward for individual teamworking behaviour. Second, the team has to be defined to include people who work together to achieve common goals. The definition has to feel coherent and logical to those within and those outside the group. Third, it is vital to have commitment to the scheme from management and staff, and cooperation from unions. Fourth, the targets must be agreed by all to be stretching but realistic, and must be seen by staff as relevant and something they can influence. Preferably the targets will be a mix of quantitative and qualitative, and will focus not just on outputs but also on outcomes. Fifth and finally, it is hard work to make a success of team bonuses. The scheme must be well managed, with good consultation and communication. If it runs for several years, it will require constant attention and reinvigoration if it is to deliver value.

The team pay pilots in the NHS have also changed or extended the picture of team rewards in three areas:

▌ While the results produced by the teams can be significant, one of the major gains is at the front end of the process, in performance planning. Work on team pay can provide far greater clarity about priorities, and this is particularly valuable in complex organizations that have a large number of targets and measures.

▌ Team reward does not have to mean payment to individuals. The creation of a common fund, which the team can spend collectively, is an alternative – particularly in an environment where personal bonuses might not be welcomed.

▌ Teams do not have to be small. It is possible to work with groups of 100 or more as long as they have a coherent identity. It is also possible to have a mix of targets, some for the broader group and some for sub-teams.

REQUIREMENTS FOR TEAM PAY

For team pay to be effective:

▌ It must be congruent with the organization's core values and management style – management must believe that good teamwork will make a significant contribution to competitive advantage and create added value, and it must act on this brief.

▌ The characteristics of the teams themselves should be appropriate for the form of team pay chosen.

Team pay works best if good teamwork is a core value of the organization, if its importance is recognized by all concerned and if active steps are taken by management to create and maintain effective teams. For specific teams the ideal requirements are that they:

▌ stand alone as performing units for which clear targets and standards can be agreed;

▌ have a considerable degree of autonomy – team pay is likely to be most effective in self-managed teams;

▌ are composed of people whose work is interdependent – it is acknowledged by members that the team will only deliver the results expected of it if they work well together and share the responsibility for success;

▌ are stable – members are used to working with one another, know what is expected of them by fellow team members and know where they stand in regard of those members (though there is an argument from the NHS experience that team pay can help to establish common identity in a new group);

▪ are mature – teams are well established, used to working flexibly to meet targets and deadlines and are capable of making good use of the complementary skills of their members;

▪ are composed of individuals who are flexible, multiskilled and good team players, while still being capable of expressing a different point of view and carrying that point if it is for the good of the team.

Advantages and disadvantages of team pay

Advantages

Team pay can:

▪ encourage teamworking and cooperative behaviour;
▪ clarify team goals and priorities and provide for the integration of organizational and team objectives;
▪ reinforce organizational change in the direction of an increased emphasis on teams in flatter and process-based organizations;
▪ act as a lever for cultural change in the direction of, for example, quality and customer focus;
▪ enhance flexible working within teams and encourage multiskilling;
▪ provide an incentive for the group collectively to improve performance and team process;
▪ encourage less effective performers to improve in order to meet team standards;
▪ serve as a means of developing self-managed or directed teams.

Disadvantages

The disadvantages of team pay are that:

▪ its effectiveness depends on the existence of well-defined teams – but they may be difficult to identify and, even if they can be, do they need to be motivated by a purely financial reward?
▪ team pay may seem inappropriate to individuals whose feelings of self-worth could be diminished – it is not always easy to get people to think of their performance in terms of how it impacts on other people;
▪ distinguishing what individual team members can contribute could be a problem – this may not be regarded as a disadvantage by a fervent believer in teams, but it might demotivate individual contributors who may still have to operate inside as well as outside a team setting;

- peer pressure that compels individuals to conform to group norms could be undesirable – insistence on conformity can be oppressive, and the way in which team leaders manage their performance needs to be monitored;
- pressure to conform, which is accentuated by team pay, could result in the team maintaining its output at lowest common denominator levels – sufficient to gain what is thought collectively to be a reasonable reward, but no more;
- it can be difficult to develop performance measures and methods of rating team performance that are seen to be fair – team pay formulae could be based on arbitrary assumptions about the correct relationship between effort and reward;
- if the team is not clearly defined, people outside the group may feel unfairly excluded if they contributed to the outputs;
- problems of uncooperative behaviour may be shifted from individuals to teams and to the relationship between teams;
- organizational flexibility may be prejudiced – people in cohesive high-performing and well-rewarded teams might be unwilling to move even to help overall organizational performance; and it could be difficult to reassign work between teams or to break up teams altogether in response to product-market or process developments or competitive pressures;
- high performers in low-performing teams may be dissatisfied and press for a transfer, especially if they believe they are being penalized on the reward front.

The case for team pay looks good in theory but there are some formidable disadvantages. It has not yet been proved that team pay for white-collar workers will inevitably be cost-effective (this is in contrast to work-measured group incentive schemes, which can produce significant increases in productivity). Perhaps this is why, in the UK, team pay has been more talked up than put into practice, as the IPD and other research projects have shown. It is the same in the United States. A 1995 survey by the Hay Group (Gross and Blair[11]) of 230 US organizations showed that only 40 per cent were pleased (8 per cent very positive and 32 per cent satisfied) with their team-based pay. The reason for failure was attributed in most cases to ill-timed communications – occurring after rather than before the event.

INTRODUCING TEAM PAY

The steps required to develop team pay are as follows:

1. Analyse situation and requirements.

2. Identify which teams should be rewarded with team pay (these can be selected – there is no need to cover the whole organization).
3. Identify the appropriate form of team pay for each group.
4. Set objectives for team pay.
5. Consult with and involve employees.
6. Design scheme in terms of the bonus formula and the methods of measurement and distribution.
7. Introduce scheme.
8. Train teams and team leaders (as part of the introduction programme).
9. Manage communications about progress against targets.
10. Monitor and evaluate scheme.

CONCLUSIONS

It was concluded by the CIPD survey in 1996 that the UK organizations they contacted that have introduced team pay are convinced that it works for them. No doubt there are many other organizations where the culture and the importance of good teamwork will make team pay an attractive proposition. Certainly the NHS experience seems to show that team rewards can be helpful in the right circumstances. The CIPD also commented that one of the limitations to the wider spread of team pay is that every scheme is unique – it is not possible to take one down from the shelf. And they are not always easy to design or manage. There is also, as the Institute for Employment Studies report[12] points out, the risk that organizational-level methods of reward (eg gainsharing) may be competing on the same ground as team-based pay. Many organizations will not venture into team pay because they are perfectly satisfied with their individual PRP scheme. It is these businesses that might consider the deliberate use of non-financial team rewards if they do want to improve teamwork. And they can assist this process if they include teamwork as a competence to be assessed in their performance management processes and rewarded accordingly.

REFERENCES

1. Kazenbach, J and Smith, D (1993) *The Magic of Teams*, Harvard Business School Press, Boston, MA
2. Gross, S (1995) *Compensation for Teams*, Hay Management Consultants/American Management Association, New York
3. Beckhard, R (1972) Optimising team-building efforts, *Journal of Contemporary Business*
4. Armstrong, M and Ryden, O (1996) *The IPD Guide to Team Reward*, IPD, London

5. Industrial Relations Services (1995) Key issues in team working, *Employee Development Bulletin*, 69, September, pp 5–15

6. Thompson, M (1995) *Team Working and Pay*, Institute of Employment Studies, Brighton

7. Incomes Data Services (1993) Managers, teams and reward, *IDS Management Pay Review*, August, pp 20–33

8. For example, Towers Perrin (2000) *Reward Challenges and Change: Survey results*, Towers Perrin, London; Industrial Relations Services (2000) Pay prospects for 2001: a survey of the private sector, *Pay and Benefits Bulletin*, 507, November; Mercer, W (2000) Employment Trends Survey 2000, CBI, London

9. CIPD (2004) *Reward Management 2004: A survey of policy and practice*, CIPD, London

10. Makinson, J (2000), *Incentives for Change: Rewarding performance in national government networks*, HM Treasury, London

11. Gross, S and Blair, J (1995) Reinforcing team effectiveness through pay, *Compensation and Benefits Review*, September–October, pp 34–38

12. Reilly, P (ed) (2003) *New Reward 1: Team, skill and competency base pay*, Institute for Employment Studies, Report 403, Brighton

25

Gainsharing – Sharing in Corporate Success

GAINSHARING DEFINED

Gainsharing can best be defined as 'a commitment to employee involvement that ties additional pay to improvements in workforce performance'. The primary components of a successful gainsharing plan are: 1) a formula to keep track of gains; 2) a link between the formula and process improvement initiatives; and 3) effective communications of how employee-generated improvements are creating gains.

Gainsharing differs from profit sharing in that profit sharing is based on more than improved productivity, and includes a number of factors outside the individual employee's control, such as depreciation procedures, bad debt expenses, taxation and economic changes. Gainsharing aims to relate its pay-outs much more specifically to productivity and performance improvements directly under the control of employees.

Gainsharing is well established in the United States, the first schemes having been introduced in the mid-1930s. They have not made such an impact in the UK. However, interest is increasing in gainsharing as a method of paying for performance that can be related to more reliable measures, encouraging teamwork and providing a basis for participation and empowerment. Based on 663 experiences in the United States, the median value of gains attributed to gainsharing plans is $2,200 per employee per year.[1] Is it any wonder that interest is rising?

Gainsharing is examined in this chapter under the headings of:

- goals;
- fundamental principles;
- formulae;
- ingredients for success;
- introducing gainsharing;
- conclusions.

GOALS

Fundamentally, the goal of gainsharing is to improve organizational performance by creating a motivated and committed workforce who want to be part of a successful company. Gainsharing is often implemented to address one of the following:

- need for a change agent, probably, and desirably, in association with other structural and process initiatives designed to achieve cultural change;
- increased competition – national or global – or declining productivity are reasons for introducing gainsharing; they have spurred managements to devise more creative pay arrangements that will stimulate both productivity and quality and keep employment costs under control.
- disillusionment with traditional incentive and bonus schemes; some organizations have abandoned piece-work or individual work-measured incentive schemes and are paying their manual workers a high basic or day rate, adding to that rate a group- or enterprise-wide incentive plan.

More specifically, the goals of gainsharing may include the following:

- focus the attention of all employees on the key issues affecting performance;
- enlist the support of all employees to ideas for improving performance;
- support programmes for empowering employees – decision making can be pushed down the organization hierarchy and employees can be given more control over their work;
- encourage teamwork and cooperation at all levels;
- promote better two-way communication about issues concerning work and productivity;
- encourage trust between employees and the company;
- share a meaningful proportion of performance gains with the employees who have collectively contributed to improvements;
- create a win–win environment in which everyone gains as productivity rises.

Certainly companies embarking on major change programmes, which often include a degree of employee empowerment, should consider whether this approach is a suitable vehicle to reinforce the changes taking place.

FUNDAMENTAL PRINCIPLES

Although the financial gain and subsequent pay-out elements are key features of gainsharing, its strength as a tool for improving performance lies equally in its other important features – ownership, involvement and communication. As Masternak and Ross[2] put it, gainsharing is 'an involvement system with teeth in it'.

Ownership

The success of gainsharing depends on creating a feeling of ownership. This feeling first applies to the gainsharing plan and then extends to the operation. When implementing gainsharing, a company should enlist the involvement of employees so that it can increase their identity with, and their commitment to, the plan, and build a core of enthusiastic supporters. Employees will own the gainsharing plan if they design it, sell it to management and communicate it to their co-workers.

Involvement

Involvement is the opportunity, which only management can give, and the responsibility, which only employees can accept, to influence the work and processes in employees' areas of competence. The increased involvement is the source of performance gains. For optimal success, employees should be heavily involved in designing a programme that will encourage the involvement of others.

Communication

The communication process is two-way: management communicates performance information to employees, who in turn communicate their ideas for improvement back to management. Employees must understand how their day-to-day activities influence the performance of the organization, and the organization must commit to providing employees with timely information on their performance and how it influenced company gains and their gainsharing payment.

FORMULAE

The traditional forms of gainsharing are the Scanlon Plan, the Rucker Plan and Improshare. Although these three plans demonstrate the roots of gainsharing, most plans today are developed with some level of employee input and can cover any of a large number of performance factors that are important to the organization. There is no such thing as a standard formula – there is always plenty of choice. Keep in mind that the formula does not define 'the plan': it simply provides the vehicle to track, or 'keep score' of, employee-generated improvement. The commitment to process improvement will, in fact, define the plan.

The Scanlon Plan

The Scanlon Plan was the first to connect employee involvement and employee-generated gains with pay. The Scanlon formula measures employment costs as a proportion of total sales. A standard ratio of employment cost/sales, say 40 per cent, is determined and, if labour costs fall below this proportion, the savings are distributed between employees and the company on the basis of a pre-established sharing formula.

The Rucker Plan

The Rucker Plan, like the Scanlon Plan, is based on employment costs, but they are calculated as a proportion of sales less the costs of materials and supplies (ie value added). Allen Rucker contended that the pay proportion of value added remains a near-constant share unless the organization suffers from severe mismanagement or a drastic change of policy. On the basis of this assumption, the Rucker Plan determines a constant share of whatever added value is created by the joint efforts of management and employees. Unlike the Scanlon Plan, Rucker offers only a formula, with little attention to an improvement means to generate gains.

Improshare

Improshare is a proprietary plan, which is based on an established standard that defines the expected hours required to produce an acceptable level of output. The standard is derived from work measurement. Any savings resulting from an increase in output in fewer than expected hours are shared between the organization and employees by means of a pre-established formula. Like the Rucker Plan, Improshare is only a formula for tracking gains, and does not offer a link to employee involvement.

Value added

Many versions of gainsharing are based on value-added elements as the key performance measures. Value added is, in effect, the wealth created by the people in the business. It can be specifically defined in many acceptable ways, but often calculated by deducting expenditure on materials and other purchased services from the income derived from sales of the product.

A manufacturing business buys materials, components, fuel and various services. The combined contribution of management and employees converts these into products that can be sold for more than the cost of the materials. In doing so, the business 'adds value' by the process of production.

In a value-added gainsharing plan, increases in value added are shared between employees and the company. Typically, the employees' share is between 25 and 35 per cent in the early years of a plan, and can exceed 50 per cent in the later years (year 5 to year 10). A value-added statement is set out in Table 25.1.

Table 25.1 A value-added statement

	£m	%
Sales income	10.0	100
Deduct: cost of goods, consumables and energy	4.0	40
Value added	6.0	60
Disposal of value added	6.0	100
Employees' share	1.8	3.0
Company's share: allocated to	4.2	70
Operating expenses	3.0	50
Operating profit	1.2	20

Value-added ratio (6.0/1.8) 3.3

A value-added gainsharing plan provides for an incentive to be paid as gains increase beyond a reference point. The fund is in deficit if the gains fall below that point. Following is an example pay-out calculation:

▌ A company has 100 employees.
▌ Average base pay per employee is £20,000 a year.
▌ Average employment cost per employee (pension, etc) is £4,000 a year.
▌ Total pay bill is therefore £2.4 million a year (£2.0 million base plus £0.4 million employment cost).
▌ Value added in a quarter increases by £200,000 from £6.0 million to £6.2 million.

▌ The increase of £200,000 is shared in the ratio of 30 per cent to employees (£60,000) and 70 per cent to the company (£140,000).

▌ Of the employees' share of £60,000, 25 per cent (£15,000) is placed in a reserve fund, leaving £45,000 available for distribution as an incentive for the quarter.

▌ The £45,000 incentive is distributed to the 100 employees in proportion to their base pay.

▌ The average incentive is therefore £225 for the quarter, or 4.5 per cent of the average base pay for the quarter of £5,000.

Developing a gainsharing formula

The following are the key considerations when developing a gainsharing formula:

▌ *How should value added be calculated?* Although it will follow normal accounting standards and principles, this can be flexible, depending on the individual company. Critical determinants are 'Do employees significantly influence this factor?' and 'Do improvements to this factor contribute to the profitability of the organization?'

▌ *What reference point or threshold should be used to trigger payments?* Determining a 'standard' or 'basis of comparison' is a critical decision. When the organization speaks of improvement, it is referring to improvement over what? Historical performance? Budget? Forecast? Plan? Industry benchmark? If value added rises above the threshold, this surplus will be shared between employees and the company.

▌ *What happens if value added falls below the reference point?* This implies that the value-added ratio (the employee share) is less than the norm. In this instance no payment is made and the company bears the 'loss'. In addition, some organizations take a portion of this loss and create a 'deficit reserve' that must be paid off with future gains before future pay-outs are made.

▌ *How can subjective factors such as quality or customer service be incorporated into the plan?* In order to be self-funded, the plan must rely on the creation of a quantifiable value-added gain. However, many organizations use qualitative factors, such as customer service, to 'modify' the share of gains that employees receive. For example, employees may receive 25 per cent of the value added if customer satisfaction remains at current levels, but 50 per cent of the gain if customer satisfaction improves dramatically, and 0 per cent of the gain if customer satisfaction falls in dramatic fashion.

▌ *How should gains be shared between employees and the company?* At first glance, a 50/50 sharing formula would seem to be the fairest to employees and the organization. However, in a loss period (poor performance) the organization takes on 100 per cent of the loss, so in a gain period it clearly deserves more than 50 per cent of the gain.

Determining the appropriate sharing formula depends on how much control employees have on the plan factors, and what measures have been taken to protect the organization from a loss (year end reserve, deficit reserves, etc). Most plans share less than 50 per cent of the gains in the early years.

▌ *What should be the performance period for the plan?* Most gainsharing plans are monthly or quarterly. The more frequent the pay-out, the more motivational the plan. However, in determining the right time-frame, the organization must also review current reporting cycles and the administrative burden of more frequent pay-outs.

▌ *What level of incentive can be achieved?* This is always an issue because it cannot be predicted. How much opportunity is there to perform above the standard? Certainly there are case studies of companies improving economic productivity by 10 per cent to 20 per cent. In the United States, it is not uncommon for Nucor Steel to have gainsharing pay-outs equal to 150 per cent to 200 per cent of base pay. There are equally examples of corporate failure. In any event, if an organization has designed a formula that it is confident will track with employee contribution, the incentive should not be capped.

▌ *What should be the basis of distribution of gains to employees?* The preferred arrangements would be an equal dollar amount to all, or in proportion to base pay. Some organizations have also elected to pay out based on attendance or seniority. This is the decision that employees will have the most emotion about. In addition to allocating gains to employees, some organizations have given a portion of gains to charity, or to employees to work on their ideas. These alternatives may serve as a bigger motivator to employees than cash.

Choice of formula

There is no such thing as a standard gainsharing formula that can be applied in any organization. Every gainsharing plan is unique because it has to fit the particular needs and characteristics of the company and its employees. There is always a choice, and companies will inevitably be faced with a dilemma – should they select a relatively simple but crude value-added plan or go for a more complex set of criteria? In general, for each factor you add to a plan, you make it 10 times more difficult to understand. Do your best to keep it simple.

Ingredients for success

The potential benefits of gainsharing are considerable, but the commitment is enormous. There are a number of demanding requirements for success. The main ingredients are the following:

▌ *Management style and commitment* – the management team must believe in shared decision making. They must be willing to go out and talk to employees and to listen to and act on their suggestions. A 'command and control' organization is not likely to succeed with gainsharing.

▌ *Culture* – the norms and values of the organization should support the thrust for performance improvement, teamwork and cooperation. Gainsharing can be a lever for developing a more performance-orientated and cooperative culture but it will not work if it starts from scratch.

▌ *Climate* – employee relations should be reasonably stable and there generally should be a working atmosphere of mutual trust between management and employees. Again, gainsharing can help to develop trust, but it cannot do it alone.

▌ *Involvement* – the underlying philosophy of gainsharing is that organizational members want to be involved in their work, employees have something worthwhile to say, employee suggestions can save money and improve corporate performance, and all contributors should share in the gains generated by these improvements. Employee involvement in a gainsharing plan can be said to be the most critical factor in its success. Employees must be encouraged to assume their new and expanded role because no gainsharing plan will work without employee enthusiasm, support and trust. It is necessary to believe not only that people actually carrying out the work have the best ideas about how it should be done but also that they will be most receptive to their own ideas.

▌ *Communications* – management must be prepared to communicate information on organizational goals, projects and problems that have previously been in their private domain. This information can include news about orders, customer reactions, quality initiatives, new market developments, changes in product mix and plans for introducing new technology. Management must also be prepared to listen to the reactions and comments of employees about the information. Gainsharing is more likely to be successful if effective systems for communication are already in place, but its introduction can stimulate all-round improvements – an important benefit.

▌ *Corporate strategy* – one of the most important criteria for the successful implementation of gainsharing is that it should be an integral part of corporate strategy. It must therefore be congruent not only with corporate culture but also with the organization's goals and objectives. It may have to be recognized that developments in corporate strategy may influence the way in which gainsharing operates.

▌ *Scope for improvement* – there must be scope for improvement in performance by means of the joint efforts of management and employees. Clearly, there is no point in introducing gainsharing if the chances of increasing value added are slim. It is dangerous to make any promises on financial outcomes, but there should be some basis for a shared belief that performance can be improved and that, as a result, there will be financial gains.

▌ *Nature of the organization and its technology* – a delayered organization relying largely on teamwork will be more likely to benefit from gainsharing. The size of the organization or plant working under a plan should not be so huge that employees cannot understand the work going on elsewhere and how the efforts of each area interrelate. Gainsharing can work well when jobs are highly interdependent, as in flexible manufacturing systems, when just-in-time is in operation, and in cellular manufacturing operations. A full computer-integrated manufacturing (CIM) system would be an ideal environment for gainsharing.

INTRODUCING GAINSHARING

The initial steps to take when considering the introduction of gainsharing are the following:

▌ Define as clearly as possible the reasons for introducing the new culture and its objectives.
▌ Review the organization's culture, climate, structure, processes, technology, and strategies for growth. Specifically, gather input on the five enablers of gainsharing success:
  – *business focus:* the extent to which the organization has a clear focus and consistent goals and directions;
  – *team dependence:* the degree to which accomplishments depend on integrated efforts among employees and departments;
  – *empowerment:* the extent to which employees are encouraged to take risks and suggest improvements;
  – *willingness and ability to change:* the degree to which employees: a) trust supervision, and b) are more motivated to get the job done than by fear of making a mistake;
  – *human resource programmes:* the extent to which: a) the current HR programmes effectively measure job performance, and b) the compensation system is perceived as equitable and motivational.
▌ Sound out the views of line managers, other employees and, if appropriate, union representatives, on their attitudes to gainsharing – an attitude survey may usefully be conducted for this purpose, or 'focus group' discussions can be held.

It is highly desirable for the design to be done in consultation with line managers and employees. Gainsharing is about involvement, and those concerned should participate as fully as possible in the design of the plan and in discussing the arrangements for future communication and involvement. A project team may be set up consisting of management and employee representatives but it is also essential during the design phase to communicate to all employees what is happening and why.

Once the initial design of the plan has been completed, it should be communicated to all employees by a team-briefing process. The brief should explain the philosophy of the programme, the basis upon which the formula will operate and be revised, how they will be involved and how they may benefit. There should be no doubt in anyone's mind at this stage about the purpose and components of the plan. It is also advisable to build in a review stage after, say, six months' operation, rather than wait for a whole year. The briefing should have emphasized that the reference point in the basic formula could be amended as necessary at the end of each financial year and it is desirable to make provision for such an amendment within the established rules. It is essential to validate the scheme. The organization should have a clear idea of the intended results and track the programme's performance against those expectations.

CONCLUSIONS

Gainsharing is a potentially valuable component in an organization's overall reward strategy. However, it must be developed and maintained as part of an integrated process of business communications, process improvement, employee involvement and reward management – it cannot work in isolation. It should also be remembered that gainsharing is essentially a participative process. It is not, like most profit-sharing schemes, simply a method of handing out money for reasons that are beyond the ken and control of employees. The success of gainsharing depends largely on the opportunities it presents for involvement so that employees can establish a clear link between their performance and their rewards – an essential requirement for success in any pay-for-performance scheme.

REFERENCES

1. American Compensation Association and Center for Alternative Reward Studies (1994) Survey of 663 Organizations
2. Masternak, R and Ross, T (1992) Gainsharing: bonus plan or employee involvement?, *Compensation & Benefits Review*, January–February, pp 46–54

26

Profit Sharing

Profit sharing is a plan under which an employer pays to eligible employees, as an addition to their normal remuneration, additional sums in the form of cash or shares in the company related to the profits of the business. The amount shared is determined either by an established formula, which may be published, or entirely at the discretion of management. Profit-sharing schemes are generally extended to all employees of the company.

OBJECTIVES OF PROFIT SHARING

Most companies which operate profit-sharing schemes have one or more of the following objectives in mind:

- to encourage employees to identify themselves more closely with the company by developing a common concern for its progress;
- to stimulate a greater interest among employees in the affairs of the company as a whole;
- to encourage better cooperation between management and employees;
- to recognize that employees of the company have a moral right to share in the profits they have helped to produce;
- to demonstrate in practical terms the goodwill of the company towards its employees;
- to reward success in businesses where profitability is cyclical.

Schemes which share profits according to some universal formula among all or most employees may not provide any direct incentive because they fail to satisfy the three basic requirements of an incentive scheme, namely:

1. that the reward should bear a direct relation to the effort;
2. that the payment should follow immediately or soon after the effort;
3. that the method of calculation should be simple and easily understood.

They can, however, be a very useful means of fostering commitment and business understanding. In companies where there is a strong profit-sharing ethos, such as John Lewis, they can, in good years, be large enough to be a significant reward (ie 15 per cent or more).

TYPES OF SCHEMES

The main types of profit-sharing schemes are:

1. *Cash* – a proportion of profits is paid in cash direct to employees. This is the traditional and still the most popular approach.
2. *Stock* – a proportion of profits is paid in shares. This has the further benefit of facilitating employee share ownership, which increases employee alignment with business performance.

Until recently, the UK government encouraged companies to set up approved profit-sharing scheme schemes. These were share based and had tax advantages. These plans have now been phased out and replaced by share incentive plans (SIPs) (see Chapter 23).

Cash schemes

The main characteristics of typical cash schemes can be analysed under the following headings, which are discussed below:

▌ eligibility;
▌ formulae for calculating profit shares;
▌ methods of distributing profit shares;
▌ amount distributed;
▌ timing of distribution.

Eligibility

In most schemes all employees are eligible. The normal practice is to require one year's service (say) to be completed before a share in profits can be received. Profit shares are then usually paid in relation to the pay earned. Payments may be recued pro rata to the time served between the date on which one year's service was completed and the end of the financial period in question.

Formulae for calculating profit shares

There are three basic approaches to calculating profit shares. The first is to use a predetermined formula for distributing a fixed percentage of profits. The formula may be published to staff so that the company is committed to using it. The advantages of this approach are that it clarifies the relationship between company profits and the amount distributed and demonstrates the good faith of management. The disadvantages are that it lacks flexibility and the amount paid out may fluctuate widely in response to temporary changes in profitability.

The second approach is for the board to determine profit shares entirely at its own discretion without the use of any predetermined or published formula. The decision is based on a number of considerations, including the profitability of the company, the proportion of profits that it is felt should reasonably be distributed to employees, estimates of the expectations of employees about the amount of cash they are going to receive and the general climate of industrial relations in the company. This is the more common approach and its advantages are that it allows the board some flexibility in deciding the amount to be distributed and does not commit it to expenditure over which it has no control. Random fluctuations can be smoothed out and the profit-sharing element of remuneration can be adjusted easily in relation to other movements in pay within the company. This approach is, in some ways, analogous to a dividend declaration to shareholders. The disadvantage is that a secret formula or the absence of a formula appears to contradict one of the basic reasons for profit sharing: the development among employees of a firmer commitment to the company because they can identify themselves more clearly with its successes and appreciate the reasons for its setbacks. The scheme is no longer a completely realistic profit-sharing device if employees feel that they are insufficiently rewarded for improved performance or insulated from reverses. These arguments against flexibility are powerful ones but, on balance, a flexible approach is to be preferred because it does not commit the company to distributing unrealistically high sums when profits are shared out.

The third approach is a combination of the first and second methods. A formula exists in the sense that a company profit threshold is set, below which no profits will be distributed. A maximum limit is set on the proportion of profits that will be distributed, for example, 5 per cent and/or that percentage of salary that will be distributed as a profit share, for example, 10 per cent.

Finally, schemes can be run on an explicitly smoothed basis. Each year, the profit share formula produces a sum, which is added to the profit share pool. A fixed fraction (perhaps half or a third) is distributed, with the balance being carried forward. This has the effect of smoothing out the payments to staff. An example of this approach is given in Table 26.1. In this example, each year 7 per cent of profit above £10 million is added to the pool. One third is paid out and the balance carried forward. It may be seen that there is much less volatility in the distribution than in the profit achieved.

Table 26.1 Profit share with smoothing

Year	Pool brought forward £m	Profit £m	Addition to pool £m	New pool £m	Amount distributed £m	Pool carried forward £m
1	1.1	20	0.7	1.8	0.6	1.2
2	1.2	25	1.05	2.25	0.75	1.5
3	1.5	15	0.35	1.85	0.62	1.23

Methods of distributing profit shares

The main ways of distributing profit shares in cash schemes are to:

▌ Distribute profits as a percentage of basic pay with no increments for service. This is a fairly common arrangement and those who adopt it do so because they feel that profit shares should be related to the individual contribution of the employee, which is best measured to pay. Service increments are rejected because the level of pay received by an individual should already take into account the experience he or she has gained in the company.

▌ Distribute profits as a percentage of earnings with payments related to length of service. This approach is also frequently used and its advocates argue that it will ensure that loyalty to the company will be suitably encouraged and rewarded. They claim that to rely on pay as the sole arbiter of profit shares would be unjust because many valuable employees have, through no fault of their own, limited opportunities for promotion or significant pay progression. However, equal pay legislation may make this approach harder to sustain in future (see Chapter 13).

▌ Distribute profits in proportion to pay and some measure of individual performance. This approach is rare below board level because of the difficulty of measuring the relationship between profits and performance and because it is considered that individual effort should be rewarded directly by performance-related pay or promotion.

▌ Distribute profits as a fixed sum irrespective of earnings or service. This is completely egalitarian but rare because the felt impact of the scheme is unequal.

Amount distributed

The amount to be distributed in profit shares tends to be at 'directors' discretion'. Some organizations provide limits within which the directors decide. A maximum of 5 per cent of profits is typical, but this maximum may be linked to profits reaching a defined level.

The proportion of pay shared out can, however, vary from as little as 2 per cent to 20 per cent or more. Ideally the share should be somewhere between 5 and 10 per cent of pay in order to be meaningful without building up too much reliance on the amount to be distributed.

Timing of distribution

Most schemes distribute profits annually, although a few share out profits twice or even four times a year. Distribution is usually arranged to fall in good time for either the summer holidays or Christmas.

EMPLOYEES' ATTITUDES

The Involvement and Participation Association (IPA) questioned 2,700 employees in 12 companies about their attitudes to profit sharing. Table 26.2 shows extracts from the survey.

The IPA believes that the survey 'suggests that profit sharing does significantly improve employee attitudes and employee views of their company'. The IPA reaches this view essentially by adding together the percentages recorded under 'Agree strongly' and 'Agree'.

Of course, employees like the cash but their gratitude to the company is probably short-lived. Company profits can be remote figures to people in the offices and on the shop-floor. They will express some interest in their size, because it affects the hand-out, but the idea of working harder to generate more profit has to be grown and depends on employee commitment in an environment where staff feel valued.

BENEFITS OF PROFIT SHARING

Profit sharing and profitability

A survey carried out by Wallace Bell and Charles Hanson in 1985–86 sought to establish a correlation between profit sharing and profitability.

Table 26.2 Attitudes to profit sharing – Industrial Participation Association

	Agree strongly	Agree	Don't know	Disagree	Disagree strongly
	%	%	%	%	%
1 Profit sharing created a better attitude in the firm	10	55	16	18	1
2 It is popular because people like to have the bonus	24	69	4	3	–
3 It strengthens people's loyalty to the firm	6	41	12	34	2
4 It makes people try to work more effectively so as to help the firm to be more successful	6	45	15	31	3
5 It is good for the company and its employees	14	72	11	3	–

They surveyed 113 profit-sharing companies and 301 non-profit sharing companies and compared their performance on the basis of nine economic ratios over a period of eight years. Taking the composite results of all 414 companies, the average performance of the profit sharers over the eight years was better than that of the non-profit sharers in every one of the nine economic ratios used. And taking an average of averages, the average or ratios of the profit sharers was 27 per cent higher than those of the non-profit sharers. Of course, as Bell and Hanson say, the profit-sharing companies were not better just because they had profit sharing. It was because they were good companies that introduced profit sharing.

The particular features of how these companies achieved success were that managers:

█ had clear and defined objectives and the ability to harness the resources needed to achieve them;
█ recognized that their most important resource is people;
█ saw employees not in terms of 'them and us', as adversaries, but as part of a team that should be working together for the success of the enterprise and sharing in its success;
█ were able to generate a reciprocal attitude among the employees and thus overcome the 'them and us' feelings that are found equally, and sometimes more strongly, among employees towards management;
█ were able to generate a commitment to success.

Similar evidence linking profit sharing and business performance has been identified in research by Martin Conyon and Richard Freeman. This shows strong correlation between the now defunct approved profit-sharing schemes and both productivity and share price performance.

Profit sharing and industrial relations

A Glasgow University Centre for Research into Industrial Democracy and Participation survey referred to earlier expressed the more pessimistic view that the influence of profit sharing on industrial relations is marginal. The researchers concluded that profit sharing was used by employers as an effort–reward operation and not as an attempt to involve employees more closely in the decision-making apparatus. Yet, the evidence that profit sharing does increase effort hardly exists at all and that is simply because, as was mentioned earlier, the link between effort and reward is so tenuous. What, therefore, is the point of having a profit-sharing scheme if it is not used to increase productivity by means of involving employees and mounting a communications campaign pointing out how they benefit from increased output and profitability?

CONCLUSIONS

It is worth noting that a number of companies have introduced profit sharing primarily because they feel that it is their duty to share their prosperity with their employees. If this view is held, then any uncertainty about the benefits arising from profit sharing is not an argument against its introduction. It is, of course, possible to take the opposite view: that profits are the wages of capital and that a company is not under any moral obligation to share profits with its employees, although it has the duty of treating them fairly and providing them with the rewards, benefits and conditions of employment that are appropriate to the contribution they make.

For anyone contemplating the introduction of profit sharing, or wondering whether to continue an existing scheme, the fundamental question is, 'do you consider that, in addition to all the benefits already provided by the company to its employees, it has a moral obligation to share its prosperity with them?' If the answer to this question is 'yes', a profit-sharing scheme is what you want. If the answer is 'no', there may still be good reasons for considering profit sharing. But alternative means of rewarding employees and increasing their identification with the company (as described elsewhere in this book) may well deserve attention.

27

Recognition Schemes

DEFINITION

The 'total reward' concept discussed in Chapter 2 is based on under-standing the needs and expectations of employees in order to motivate them and obtain their total cooperation and engagement, on the basis that this leads to financial success for the organization and personal fulfilment for employees. Appropriate recognition of employees plays a vital role in this. As stressed by Michael Rose,[1] schemes are about saying 'thank you' for a job well done,[1] and thereby motivating the recipient (and their colleagues) to continue to do those things that benefit the organization. Recognition will not motivate the unmotivated employee, but it can reinforce the motivated and encourage and reassure those who are trying to succeed.

At the most basic level, recognition is free. It does not cost the organization or its managers anything except the two minutes it takes to say 'well done and thanks', in person or by e-mail, or the 15 minutes to write a brief note of appreciation, yet it speaks volumes. More complex recognition programmes – those organization-wide schemes that offer a fat cheque or generous prize – can work well if well designed, but they can all to easily miss the boat as by focusing on the few they may alienate the many.

BACKGROUND

As more organizations begin to understand that not all or even the majority of employees are motivated by money, they are seeking alternative ways to motivate and encourage employees. Ongoing survey research conducted by MORI on behalf of the GMB[2] shows that, for most employees, money is not the prime motivator in employment. In fact, tangible benefits rank fourth, behind 'interesting and enjoyable work', 'job satisfaction' and 'a feeling of accomplishment'. Appropriate recognition contributes towards both job satisfaction and a feeling of accomplishment.

A recent study into recruitment and retention in the public sector[3] found that the feeling of being valued was an important factor in people's decisions to stay in or leave a job. This is exacerbated with public sector employees by the need to be valued by external stakeholders such as government, citizens and the media, rather than simply by line managers. Surveys such as these lend further credence to the extensive array of management theory that supports the role of recognition in the workplace.

If money is not the main motivator (see Chapter 6) then it stands to reason that throwing money at recruitment, retention and motivation issues will have only limited success. In fact, this response harks back to Taylor's[4] 'economic man', which was current management thinking in 1912. Within a very few years it was recognized that this was only a part of the story. Hawthorne (in his research at Western Electric Company of America) illustrated the social concept of motivation through informal processes and social contact rather than 'carrot and stick' (which is how commentators such as Alfie Kohn[5] describe most pay-for-performance schemes). Dale Carnegie,[6] author of *How to Win Friends and Influence People*, taught that the single most important thing was to make people feel important.

The 1940s saw Maslow[7] developing his famed hierarchy of needs – five stages that individuals move through culminating in the fulfilment of their own potential. The fourth level of need was esteem, a combination of self-respect and the need for the esteem and appreciation of others. Others such as Hertzberg[8] and McClelland[9] were also concerned with motivation. Perhaps the most telling work has been from Locke,[10] who stated: 'People's goals or intentions play an important part in determining behaviour.' If an organization can harness the behaviours of its employees through understanding and acting on their personal goals and intentions then it will have a significant impact on organizational success.

Recognition schemes seek to put this body of theory to positive use, aligning personal and organizational goals by encouraging and rewarding actions and behaviours that positively impact on organizational success.

TYPES OF RECOGNITION SCHEME

Recognition schemes may be formal or informal, financial or non-financial, private or public. The most important aspect is that the recognition is meaningful to the individual recipient (and colleagues), as this is how it will most positively impact on motivation.

Day-to-day recognition

At the most simple level, recognition is private, non-financial and takes place on a day-to-day basis. This is through (what should be) the normal process of good management – giving genuinely felt (people can spot when they are being manipulated insincerely), positive feedback to individuals, teams or groups of employees for work well done, either orally (for preference) or in a short note. This costs nothing, encourages people and should be done frequently, not just as part of the annual performance review process.

The most effective recognition is given directly by the immediate manager, not some far-off company-wide scheme (McCormick and Ilgen, quoted in La Motta).[11] This study found that the most effective recognition schemes were manager led, as opposed to company initiated, and they recognized performance rather than mere presence.

Day-to-day recognition of employees and colleagues should be a natural part of the routine of work, not the subject of a scheme, process or system. Such recognition should be a part of the organizational culture. If it is not, it needs to be before any more structured scheme will pay dividends.

Informal recognition

In an organization with a large proportion of relatively low-paid employees, it is important to have a relatively informal recognition scheme, with a greater number of recipients of moderate to low-cost awards being made frequently. Julian Richer, founder of hi-fi chain Richer Sounds, believes 'it is always better to give 1,000 people £10, than one person £10,000'.[12] Other retailers offer instant awards (of £10 or less) to employees who catch a shoplifter, spot a forged banknote at the till or (in the case of John Lewis) help them to be 'never knowingly undersold' by advising them when another retailer offers the same product for less.

Informal recognition schemes are not competitive (and nor should they be). Every person, team or group who meets the standard or who does an excellent job should benefit. Kohn argues strongly against any system that creates 'winners' because, 'for each person who wins, there are many others who... have lost'.[5] The schemes aim 'not to compensate employees for their extra effort on the job; it is a small token for a large amount of thanks and gratitude for our teammates'.[13]

These recognition schemes may also involve some form of public recognition, such as through an intranet, house journal, notice board or 'Employee of the Month' scheme. Approaches such as these tell everyone about particular achievements or effective contribution. The only proviso is to avoid the perception of 'Jane's turn' – awards should always be based on merit.

Formal recognition

Formal recognition schemes are more highly structured, with fewer, higher-value awards. Schemes provide individuals (and importantly, through them, their partners) with tangible means of recognition in the forms of gifts, vouchers, holidays or trips in the UK or abroad, days or weekends at health spas, or meals out. Team awards may be through outings, parties and meals. Such schemes may be centrally driven (with a formal nomination process and regular award ceremonies) or devolved to line managers, providing them with the authority and an associated budget to recognize individuals or teams in accordance with guidelines.

Winners of formal awards report that the benefits last longer than the actual prize, as they are offered the opportunity to meet people and take part in projects they would not have previously been considered for, as well as improving their promotion prospects.[14]

The key with formal schemes is to ensure that the award fits the achievement, that it is made to the right people and that it is 'felt fair'. While it is highly motivating to be formally recognized for a major achievement (eg for successful completion of a project or finalizing a major sale), it may be demoralizing and demotivating to see 'someone else recognized for an accomplishment that I contributed towards, or when I consider my latest success to be at least equal to the one being recognized'.

Financial recognition schemes

Some organizations may say, 'We have recognition schemes. We recognize good performance through our team productivity incentive and performance-related pay.' This may satisfy the minority of employees for whom financial well-being is utmost. Yet the research suggests that, for most employees, this is not the case, so an undue reliance on financial recognition (or incentives) may not have the desired impact. In addition, cash awards are quickly spent and forgotten and can make employees question 'Is this enough for the effort I put in?' They may need to be increased to have the same effect (£100 this year has less impact if I got £100 last year as well).

If an organization does choose to use financial awards (of any size), the award will have considerably more impact if it is delivered in person by the manager (or director), in the form of cash, cheque or a voucher. It is a reality that a higher-than-usual direct payment to the bank account may not even be noticed. Rose[1] offers additional advantages to non-financial reward – they differentiate the award from pay, they have longer 'memory value', the perceived value can be higher than the actual cost, and awards can be tailored to the recipient.

EXAMPLES

One of the difficulties of any corporate recognition scheme is that the award needs to be appropriate to the individual. For instance, a bottle of champagne to each member of the top-performing team (including the support staff) is a nice gesture, but loses some of the effect if any of the recipients are non-drinkers. Similar faux pas would include meat packs or Christmas turkeys to vegetarians, food hampers that transgress dietary rules to those who follow strict halal or kosher diets, tiepins or cufflinks to women, tickets to the football for a non-sports fan... the list could go on. Most employees will at least appreciate the gesture, but how much more meaningful it would be to personalize the gift appropriately to the recipient (and, of course, appropriate gifts are far better value for money).

Some ideas for non-cash awards include:

▌ air miles;
▌ airline tickets or hotel packages;
▌ balloons or flowers (delivered to the workplace) – a variation on this theme is where the main recipient is encouraged to give a flower to each individual who contributed towards the achievement;
▌ basket of fruit;
▌ books;
▌ bottle of champagne (have a calligrapher personalize the label with the name and date);
▌ car parking for six months;
▌ charity donation;
▌ chauffer-driven car for a month;
▌ cinema vouchers;
▌ conference attendance fee;
▌ dinner out for two (include a taxi and organize a babysitter);
▌ experience days (eg rally driving, hot air balloon ride, or a day at a health and beauty spa – now offered by many retailers);
▌ food hamper;
▌ Fridays off for a month;
▌ gift certificates;
▌ gold coffee mug (with a 'gold star service' motif);
▌ house cleaning for a year;

- jewellery (eg watch, tiepin or brooch);
- joke/funny gifts;
- logo merchandise (T-shirt, mug, cap, mouse mat, etc);
- magazine subscription;
- pen and pencil sets (monogrammed?);
- personalized items;
- plaques or certificates;
- points-based catalogue gifts that the individual can select;
- priority car park for a month;
- retail shopping vouchers;
- small gift (eg mug with appropriate cartoon);
- small number of company shares or options;
- tickets to a concert, theatre or sports event;
- trophy (passed from one person to another);
- T-shirt;
- write a letter to the person (and copy to their manager) – personal letters from the chairman or chief executive can mean a lot.

Lastly, with any award, remember to say 'well done and thank you' and make sure that the individual feels really valued for what he or she has contributed.

DESIGNING A RECOGNITION SCHEME

There are some key principles involved in designing a successful recognition scheme, most of which are true for incentive schemes in general (see Chapter 22 for more detail on the design of incentive schemes). These include the points discussed in the following sections.

Keep it simple

Recognition, as with any reward scheme, should follow the 'KISS' principle (keep it simple, stupid). If employees cannot explain the scheme to their partner (or teenage son/daughter), the likelihood is that they don't understand it and will be unable consciously to demonstrate the values or exhibit the behaviours that will be rewarded under it.

For example, as part of a wider cultural change programme, a major UK utility company introduced a recognition programme called 'Values in Practice'. The scheme attempted to embed the six stated corporate values through a recognition scheme that offered a quarterly £1,000 award to an employee (nominated by a colleague) for exemplary demonstration of the company values. Yet a later research project found that one-third of the focus group could not name any of the values they were supposed to espouse.[15]

Align awards with culture

There is a danger that organizations may seek to introduce incentive or recognition schemes to disguise or hide management failures. It should not be necessary to have a formal 'scheme' in order to 'make' managers recognize good work, exceptional customer service or extra effort. Saying 'thank you' for a job well done should be a normal part of good management practices. Sadly, it isn't always. There is a truism that 'employees leave managers, not organizations'. Lack of recognition is often a key reason why people will leave. Sometimes that is a fault of the line manager ('they are only doing what is expected; why should I thank them?'); in other cases the behaviour is accepted practice within the organization and the expectations are unreal.

There may be a hierarchy of recognition, such that, if an organization does not practise 'lower-order' forms of recognition (such as the simple day-to-day recognition of saying 'thank you'), employees may react negatively to formal or informal schemes. The story of the professional staff within a law firm viewing dinner for two as 'food parcels' is, sadly, not apocryphal. Nor is the view that 'organizations "do" recognition so they can get away with paying less'. Sincerity matters.

Make it happen

In many ways, designing a recognition scheme is the easy part. The difficulties come when the scheme has to be integrated with other business initiatives, both within human resources and in other areas of the business. Sound implementation is vital.

First, it is important that everyone knows about the scheme, whether it is so that they can work towards an award under the scheme or so that they know how to nominate colleagues – and what to nominate them for. With a formal scheme that relies on colleagues noticing and nominating their peers, it may be worth considering entering all nominees into a draw to win a prize.

It is also important to keep the impetus up. An all-singing, all-dancing launch has not made the point if 6 or 12 months later no one is getting awards because everyone has forgotten about the scheme (or worse, been disillusioned when they or their nominee didn't 'win'). Most of us have seen the 'Employee of the Month' photo boards that haven't been updated since April and it's now December. The scheme should be built into the induction programme for new employees, and should be refreshed at appropriate intervals.

Pay the tax

Finally, try to avoid giving employees a nasty surprise when they complete their tax return by paying the tax on a financial award or taxable benefit at the time the award is made (and don't forget to budget for tax). And tell employees that the award is tax-paid so the organization gets the credit for effective scheme design.

REFERENCES

1. Rose, Michael (2001) *Recognising Performance*, CIPD, London
2. Edmonds, John (2003) Is money a good motivator? A trades union perspective, Presentation by John Edmonds, ex-General Secretary of the GMB, at Hay Group Reward Conference, 24 September
3. Audit Commission (2002) *Recruitment and Retention: A public service workforce for the twenty-first century*, Audit Commission, London
4. Taylor, F W (1911) *Principles of Scientific Management*, Harper & Brothers, New York
5. Kohn, Alfie (1993) Why incentive plans cannot work, *Harvard Business Review*, September–October, pp 1–7
6. Carnegie, Dale (1937) *How to Win Friends and Influence People*, Simon & Schuster, New York
7. Maslow, A H (1943) A theory of human motivation, *Psychological Review*, **50** (4), July, pp 370–96
8. Hertzberg, F W, Mausner, B and Snyderman, B B (1959) *The Motivation to Work*, 2nd edn, Chapman & Hall, London
9. McClelland, D C (1988) *Human Motivation*, Cambridge University Press, Cambridge
10. Locke, E A (1975) Personal attitudes and motivation, *Annual Review of Psychology*, **26**, pp 457–80
11. La Motta, T (1995) *Recognition: The quality way*, Quality Resources, New York
12. Richer, Julian (1996) *The Richer Way*, Emap Business Communications, London
13. Handel, J (2001) Recognition: pats on the back motivate employees, Workspan, December
14. Trapp, Roger (2001) Main attraction, *People Management*, 25 October
15. Murphy, Michael G and Mackenzie Davey, Kate (2002), Ambiguity, ambivalence and indifference in organisational values', *Human Resource Management Journal*, **12** (1), pp 17–32

28

Shop-floor Incentive and Bonus Schemes

Incentive or bonus schemes relate the pay or part of the pay received by employees to the number of items they produce or process, the time they take to do a certain amount of work and/or some other aspects of their performance. They usually provide for pay to fluctuate with performance in the short term, but they can, as in measured day work, provide for a long-term relationship. They are often referred to as payment-by-result schemes.

We examine in this chapter:

▌ the main types of incentive schemes – individual piece-work, work-measured individual schemes, measured day work and group incentive schemes;
▌ alternative approaches – high day rates, performance-related pay, productivity bonuses and the use of other criteria in bonus schemes;
▌ bonus schemes in different environments;
▌ the considerations affecting the design of incentive schemes;
▌ the process of selecting an incentive scheme;
▌ how to introduce an incentive scheme.

INDIVIDUAL PIECE-WORK

In individual or straight piece-work a uniform price is paid per unit of production. Operators are therefore rewarded according to the number of pieces they produce or process, so pay is directly proportioned to results.

Most piece-work schemes provide a fall-back rate or minimum earnings level. It is common for the minimum rate to be set at 70–80 per cent of average earnings, although some companies set it as low as 30 per cent and others set it equal to the minimum time rate. Companies may also provide guaranteed payments for downtime due to machine failure, maintenance work or waiting for materials.

Advantages of piece-work

The advantage to employers of piece-work is that the system is easy to operate, simple to understand and can be left to run by itself, provided there is adequate supervision to ensure that quality does not suffer. Piece-work can also enable employers to estimate and control manufacturing costs effectively.

The advantage to employees is that they can predict their earnings in the short term and regulate their pace of work in accordance with the level of pay they want to attain.

Disadvantages

Employers can find that they lose control over the level of production, which depends largely on the self-motivation of the workforce. Quality can suffer if close supervision is not exercised and the negotiation of piece-rates for new work can be time consuming and fractious.

For employees, it may be difficult to predict longer-term earnings as work fluctuates from week to week. The intensity of work required in this system may cause undue stress or lead to repetitive strain injury (RSI).

Piece-work has become more inappropriate as an incentive method as new technology has changed work arrangements. In larger-scale manufacturing it has largely been replaced by work-measured schemes or some other form of incentive or bonus payment.

WORK-MEASURED SCHEMES

In a work-measured scheme, the job, or its component tasks, is timed and the incentive payment is related to performance above the standard time allowed for the job. The amount of incentive pay received depends on the difference between the actual time taken to perform the task and the standard time allowed. If a task is done in less than the standard time, then there is a time saving, which means that the operator's output will increase.

Methods of measurement

Work measurement involves working out standard values or times for a complete task, which can, however, be broken down into components requiring simple human motions, to each of which standard minute values can be allocated. Work study or industrial engineers can measure the time taken for each component with the help of a stop-watch. A large number of timings will be made in each task to ensure that the variety of conditions under which an operator works are included so as to minimize distortions. Measurements may therefore be taken at different times of the day, and a number of operators may be timed on the same task to extend the range of timings and reduce the risk of errors.

The work study engineer who measures the job will be entirely objective about the stop-watch timing but a subjective assessment will also have to be made of the operator's speed, or effectiveness. This is known as the operator's effort rating. The performance of a qualified worker, if motivated, without over-exertion, is known as standard performance. Industrial engineers sometimes relate this to walking at a reasonably brisk pace, say four miles an hour. All operators who have been timed are given an effort rating relative to this standard and this is taken into account when deciding on standard times.

A refinement of individual work measurement is to adopt a predetermined motion time system such as methods time measurement (MTM). Such a system can be used when a mass of data has been assembled over a period of time, which can lead to the production of 'synthetics' – standard times which can be applied to a particular task or operation. If these synthetics are based on reliable data they can eliminate the need for expensive and time-consuming work measurement and avoid disagreements about the accuracy of standards (especially when individual standards have involved the use of subjective effort rating).

When calculating standard values or times, allowances can be made to cover a reasonable amount of relaxation, personal needs, fatigue, and contingencies associated with the work, such as machine adjustments and maintenance.

Performance scales

When standard values have been calculated, a performance scale can be drawn up against which an operator's performance can be rated. Common scales include the British Standards Institute (BSI) 100/133, on which 100 represents the performance of an average operator working conscientiously without financial motivation, and 133 represents the same worker's performance with financial motivation. Other scales are the BSI 75/100 or the 60/80 scale, which all work on the same principle, ie that the performance for a motivated worker will be set at one-third more than the performance of an operator working without an incentive.

Payment scales

Incentive payments are made when performance exceeds the standard. The relationship between pay and performance usually follows either the proportional or regressive pattern as explained in Chapter 16.

When proportional payments are made, the incentive payment increases in direct proportion to performance. Thus on the BSI 100/133 scale the incentive may be 1 per cent of basic pay for every point above BSI 100. If, for example, the operator works at BSI 110, the incentive payment is 10 per cent of base pay.

In a regressive payment system (the old Halsey/Weir or Rowan schemes) the incentive payment increases proportionately less than output. For example, a performance of BSI 110 may produce a payment of 8 per cent of basic pay, while one of BSI 120 may result in a payment of 14 per cent.

The proportionate payment method is the most equitable one, but a regressive system has the advantage for employers of making mistakes in rate fixing less costly and lowering unit wage costs for output above standard performance. For obvious reasons, however, the latter approach is viewed with suspicion by trade unions and workers.

It is usual, and advisable, to establish a ceiling to the amount of incentive pay which can be earned to avoid excessive amounts being paid out because of loose rates, or some other form of degeneration (this is sometimes called capping). Typically, the upper limit is set at 133 points in a BSI 100/133 scheme, resulting in a maximum payment of 33 per cent of base pay in a proportional payment system or less – for example, 20 per cent – in a regressive system.

The problem of degeneration

Incentive schemes degenerate. The consultants and work study engineers who install them say they should not degenerate but they do. In an ideal world they would not: managers and supervisors would be able to exercise the degree of control the consultants advise. But the latter do not always live in the real world where there are numerous opportunities for workers to gain more from an incentive scheme than they have earned. Both individual and group incentive schemes are prone to this type of degeneration, which is often called wage or earnings drift.

The main causes of degeneration are:

▌ *Special allowances*. All schemes have allowances for the payment of shop-average earnings or some other figure which includes a premium over the base rate in certain circumstances. The most common are for unmeasured work or waiting time. Clearly, the higher the proportion of the time when pay is unrelated to effort, the more the scheme degenerates. Allowances are in theory controlled by management, but supervisors closer to the shop-floor have been known to make their life easier by granting allowances too readily. This can be done on an hour-to-hour basis and in small increments, which can all too easily be missed by more senior managers. Allowances can also be manipulated by, for example, workers booking in waiting time rather than time on a more difficult job that earns a less than average bonus.

▌ *Erosion of standards.* The type of work or the work mix can change almost imperceptibly over a period of time. It may not be possible to point to a change in method sufficient enough to justify a retiming of the job under the rules of the scheme. The original ratings, although not slack, may not have been particularly tight; the workers and their representatives will have seen to that. As time goes on, workers learn how to take short cuts, sometimes risky ones, which increase or maintain earnings for less effort.

▌ *Cross-booking.* Workers may cross-book from difficult tasks on which it is hard to earn a good bonus to easier ones. Work measurement is not an exact science, whatever work study engineers may say, and some ratings are easier than others. The ability of work people to get round a scheme should never be underestimated. For example, if there is a reasonably generous fall-back rate, as there often is, employees may work more slowly on the more difficult jobs, thus saving their effort but still earning a reasonable standard rate, while working hard and fast on the easier jobs to achieve the bonus earnings they want. Research studies have frequently shown that workers set the level of bonus earnings they want to achieve and adjust their efforts accordingly. They can sometimes be under pressure from their fellow workers not to work too hard and thus 'bust' the rate, or at least inspire management to launch a rate-cutting exercise.

To prevent management from becoming aware that some jobs are easier than others, workers may not record all their time on these jobs, thus keeping earnings down. Workers then allocate their time to other jobs to raise them into the bonus-earning range, or simply take it easy. They operate, as it were, on borrowed time.

Preventing degeneration

To avoid degeneration, it is advisable only to introduce a payment-by-result scheme when the following conditions apply:

▌ short-cycle, repetitive work;
▌ changes in work mix, tasks or methods are infrequent;
▌ shop-floor hold-ups are rare and not prolonged;
▌ management and supervision are capable of controlling the scheme, not only technically, but also to prevent manipulation;

▌ productivity is so low that the stimulus of a bonus scheme, even when it might cause problems later, is still worthwhile.

It is also necessary when introducing a scheme to use the best work study engineers available to ensure that accurate and even standards are obtained.

Recording systems and rules for booking time on non-bonus-earning activities should be instituted which minimize the risk of allowance manipulation and cross-booking. Incentive earnings and performance rates should be monitored continuously and immediate action should be taken to crack down on drift. New jobs need to be timed properly and the implications of any changes in methods or work mix should be understood and reflected in altered standards – it is essential to agree initially with trade unions that changes can be made in these circumstances and when there has been an error in the original bonus calculation.

Importantly, managers, supervisors and industrial engineers should be trained in how to manage and control the scheme. It should be impressed upon them that they will be held accountable for productivity and ensuring that the scheme will not degenerate.

MEASURED DAY WORK

Measured day-work schemes became popular in large batch or mass production factories in the 1950s and 1960s when it became evident that, in spite of all efforts, it was impossible to control wage drift.

In measured day work, the pay of employees is fixed on the understanding that they will maintain a specified level of performance, but pay does not fluctuate in the short term with their performance. The arrangement depends on work measurement to define the required level of performance and to monitor the actual level. The fundamental principles of measured day work are that there is an incentive level of performance and that the incentive payment is guaranteed in advance, thereby putting employees under an obligation to perform at the effort level required. In contrast, a conventional work-measured incentive scheme allows employees discretion on their effort level but relates their pay directly to the results they achieve. Between these two extremes there is a variety of alternatives, including banded incentives, stepping schemes and various forms of high day rate.

Measured day work seeks to produce an effort–reward bargain in which enhanced and stable earnings are exchanged for an incentive level of performance. Its disadvantage is that the set performance target can become an easily attainable norm and may be difficult to change, even after extensive renegotiation.

The criteria for success in operating measured day work are:

- total commitment of management, employees and trade unions, which can only be achieved by careful planning, joint consultation and a staged introduction of the scheme;
- effective work measurement and efficient production planning and control and inventory control systems;
- the establishment of a logical pay structure with appropriate differentials from the beginning of the scheme's operation – the structure should be developed by job evaluation and in consultation with employees;
- the maintenance of good control systems so that swift action can be taken to correct any shortfalls on targets.

These are exacting requirements and this is one reason why measured day work is relatively rare and has been abandoned by a number of organizations in favour of a high day-rate system topped up with team or factory-wide bonuses.

GROUP OR TEAM INCENTIVE SCHEMES

Group or team incentive schemes provide for the payment of a bonus either equally or proportionately to individuals within a group or team. The bonus is related to the output achieved by the group in relation to defined targets or to the time saved on jobs – the difference between allowed time and actual time.

Group bonus schemes are in a sense individual incentive schemes writ large – they have the same advantages and disadvantages as any payment-by-results system. The particular advantages of a group scheme are that it develops teamworking, breaks down demarcation lines and encourages the group to monitor its own performance and discipline itself in achieving targets – an essential characteristic of a high-performance work group. In addition, job satisfaction may be enhanced by relating the team more closely to the complete operation. Group bonuses may be particularly appropriate when teams of workers are carrying out interdependent tasks and have to operate flexibly in a just-in-time or cellular manufacturing environment. These requirements may be prejudiced by incentive schemes which emphasize the link between individual pay and performance. Individual schemes might also be invidious because workers have only limited scope to control the level of their own output and are expected to support others, to the detriment of their personal bonus.

The potential disadvantage of a group incentive scheme is that in some manufacturing or operational systems, management is less in control of production – the group can decide what earnings are to be achieved and can restrict output. Thus the scheme fails to provide an incentive. Some opponents of group schemes object to the elimination of individual incentive, but this objection is only valid if it were always possible to operate a satisfactory individual payment-by-results scheme.

Group or team incentive schemes are most appropriate where people have to work together and teamwork has to be encouraged (see also Chapter 24). They are most effective if they are based on a system of measured work where targets and standards are agreed by the team, which is provided with the control information it needs to monitor its own performance. A variety of measured day work or a high day-rate system topped up with achievement bonuses related to quality, delivery to time or cost targets may function well.

ALTERNATIVE APPROACHES

Piece-work and other forms of traditional incentive schemes are in decline. In 1983 the proportion of male manual workers receiving incentive payments was 47 per cent. In 1990 the proportion was 37 per cent. There are a number of reasons for this. Traditional doubts about the unfairness and ineffectiveness of incentive schemes have come to the fore over the last decade as the manufacturing sector in the UK declined and the need to control pay costs became more crucial in the recession of the early 1990s. Incentive schemes were perceived by many organizations as being difficult to control (they seemed inevitably to create wage drift) and costly to maintain.

The other reasons for this decline have been:

▌ *The nature of the work* – individual incentive schemes can function well when workers are engaged on simple, repetitive tasks and/or can control the pace of the work themselves. However, they are inappropriate in process industries and in assembly line production where the pace is controlled by the machine. More jobs now involve the operation of complex machines or the delivery of services requiring the integrated work of many individuals. Cellular manufacture places more emphasis on teamworking than individual effort. Knowledge work in high-technology plants is not amenable to direct payment for results. Rapid changes in technology militate against the stability which is necessary for the successful operation of an incentive scheme.

▌ *Increased emphasis on quality* – incentive schemes emphasize speed, often at the expense of quality.

▌ *Shorter runs penalize workers* – because of the shorter runs required in much of today's manufacturing, operatives may lose incentive pay because they have less opportunity to maintain top speed on one job before being switched to another.

▌ *Health and safety problems* – there is growing evidence that in the types of short cycle and repetitive operations associated with piece-work, workers who perform a single operation for most of the time are susceptible to repetitive strain injuries.

The alternative approaches include the use of high day rates, performance-related pay and schemes designed to increase productivity as described below. There are also a number of new developments in bonus schemes in different work environments as discussed in the next section of this chapter.

High day rates

In the face of these pressures, managements have often reverted to the payment of time rates, although in many cases the policy has been deliberately to adopt a 'high day-rate' policy which involves paying above the going rate but requires workers to meet specified standards of output and quality. This high day-rate policy has often been accompanied by the introduction of a bonus scheme which is related to some general measure of productivity or quality and is paid out on a group or a factory-wide basis.

Performance-related pay

Performance-related pay (PRP) schemes for manual workers relate a proportion of pay to indicators of performance such as quality, flexibility, contribution to team work and ability to hit targets. They are, in fact, based on the same principles as the PRP schemes for managerial, professional, technical and office staff described in Chapter 21 – namely, a system of assessment which leads to pay progression through a range.

PRP for manual workers has been in existence for a long time but its popularity has increased over the last decade because of the general pressure to introduce performance-related pay, increased disenchantment with traditional incentive schemes, and the belief that PRP is more appropriate in high technology, multi-skilled environments where payment-by-result systems are likely to be ineffective.

Companies introducing PRP for manual workers claim that they increase the commitment and capability of their employees. As Kinnie and Lowe[1] comment on the basis of their research into PRP on the shop-floor, the firms they contacted wanted to get 'better value' from their employees but not necessarily in a way that resulted in an immediate reduction in costs or increases in profits. Their objective, more broadly, was to bring about a longer-term improvement in the motivation and performance of the workforce as a whole, rather than simply paying a chosen few more.

It is established by Kinnie and Lowe that PRP in these firms often formed part of an overall approach aimed at focusing attention on their individual employees. It could be used as a key component in a wide-ranging attempt to change the management style or even the whole culture of an organization. The specific benefits achieved by the firms contacted were considered to be:

▌ Improvement in the quality of relationships between team leaders and the members of their teams – this arose because of the need to clarify performance requirements and discuss results against agreed expectations.
▌ Employees gained increased awareness of critical factors affecting performance such as quality, delivery and costs.
▌ Employees gained more information about their company and what it was trying to achieve.
▌ The commitment and capability of employees were improved.

But PRP for manual workers suffers from the same problems as in the office, namely, subjectivity, lack of ability or commitment on the part of supervisors to review performance, and the difficulty of translating assessments fairly and consistently into pay awards. In addition, it can arouse the hostility of trade unions, who object to what they believe to be a potentially unfair dependence on the judgement of supervisors on pay increases for their subordinates. These problems have to be considered carefully before introducing PRP for manual workers, and it should always be remembered that performance-related pay is only one of the factors affecting performance.

Productivity-based schemes

Productivity payments fell into disrepute during the 1960s and 1970s when an outbreak of 'productivity bargaining' took place that aimed to counter pay freezes by producing self-financing bonus schemes. Sadly, many of these schemes depended on specious measures. They were therefore not self-financed and melted away when the pay thaw arrived in 1979.

But productivity, if it is correctly measured, is a perfectly proper basis for the payment of a bonus, usually for a department or a factory. Productivity can broadly be defined as a ratio of inputs to outputs, for example, direct hours worked to units produced, cost per unit of output or, in a more general sense, an added value ratio (employment or direct labour costs as a proportion of total sales value less the cost of bought-in parts and materials). One of the best ways of paying for productivity is to develop a gainsharing plan, as described in Chapter 25. Such a plan is not just about bonus payouts. It also focuses on employee involvement in improving productivity through work teams, improvement groups or quality circles.

Use of other criteria in bonus schemes

The other criteria for use in bonus schemes are quality (in terms of meeting quality standards, delivery to time and waste control), cost reduction, and service delivery (the level of service generally to customers). These are discussed in more detail below when we consider bonus payments systems in a number of different environments, including that of total quality management.

BONUS SCHEMES IN DIFFERENT ENVIRONMENTS

Traditional incentive schemes tend to be concerned only with output and unit costs. However, significant changes have been taking place in the working environment in recent years. To maintain competitive advantage in the face of global competition, organizations have had to introduce new systems of work and technology. These have led to the development of alternative approaches to paying for performance, particularly in total quality management, just-in-time and cellular manufacturing environments. These approaches generally take the form of bonus rather than incentive schemes.

Total quality management

Total quality management (TQM) is a systematic way of guaranteeing that all activities within an organization happen the way they have been planned in order to meet the defined needs of customers and clients. The emphasis is on involving everyone in the organization in activities which provide for continuous improvement and for achieving sustained high levels of quality performance.

The TQM approach is about gaining commitment to quality. Everyone at every level in the organization has genuinely to believe in quality and to act on that belief. Total quality can be described as an attitude of mind which leads to appropriate behaviour and actions.

For manual workers, a quality bonus can be paid on a plant-wide basis as a specific part of a bonus scheme, or it may be incorporated in a gainsharing plan. One approach is to set a standard of quality (this could be zero defects) and pay a quarterly bonus of, say, 10 per cent of pay, if this standard is achieved. The bonus would be reduced on a sliding scale related to any decline from the zero defects target.

Alternative bases for measuring quality can be used, as was the case at British Steel, Strip Products, where in some works, the quality measure is the amount of prime (top quality) product produced as a percentage of the liquid steel used in the manufacturing process. The higher the percentage of prime product, the less non-prime product has been made and the less liquid steel has been wasted in the various stages of production. As the prime percentage increases, so does the bonus.

Quality in manufacturing companies can also be measured simply in terms of waste – the percentage of output rejected or downgraded. As the volume or proportion of wastage falls, the quality bonus rises.

Another quality measure is delivery to time – the bonus increases on a sliding scale as the percentage of deliveries made on time increases.

A delivery-to-time criterion is, of course, an important element in setting customer service levels and 3M includes this factor (the percentage of deliveries completed on time) as one of the elements in its West Midlands plant bonus scheme – the other elements are productivity (goods packed output per attendant hour) and waste improvements (waste being defined as the percentage of waste on all product lines).

Just-in-time

Just-in-time (JIT) is a programme designed to enable the right quantities to be purchased or manufactured at the right time without waste. It provides for the required flow of production to be maintained with zero inventory (no buffer stocks) at each stage of the supply/manufacturing chain.

The overriding feature of JIT is that materials or parts are generated in the exact quantity required and just at the time they are needed. A classic JIT system consists of a series of manufacturing units each delivering to one another in successive stages of production. The amount delivered by each unit to the next unit is exactly what the latter needs for the next production period (usually one day). There are no safety margins in the form of buffer stocks, live storage or work in progress.

Bonus payments in a JIT environment can be based on performance in relation to the critical success factors for JIT. These are:

∎ *Productivity* – output in relation to the cost of producing it.
∎ *Inventory and work in progress* – the aim of JIT is to minimize inventory and work in progress. A bonus can be related to inventory and WIP targets.
∎ *Delivery* – JIT demands the achievement of high levels of delivery standards, to internal as well as external customers. Delivery-on-time standards can be set for different stages in the manufacturing process and for despatch to customers.

▮ *Quality* – JIT is based on a zero-defects philosophy. Bonuses can therefore be related to quality performance as described earlier.

▮ Set-up times – JIT depends on speed in setting and resetting machine tools and manufacturing systems. Set-up targets can be fixed and bonuses paid on achievements in relation to target.

▮ *Flexibility* – JIT requires flexibility in the use of plant, machinery and, it follows, people. The ability to apply a number of skills (multi-skilling) in setting up, operating and maintaining plant and machinery is needed by employees in a JIT environment. A skill-based pay system as described in Chapter 21 can reward employees for enlarging their range of skills to cope with the variety of tasks they may be required to carry out.

▮ *Team work* – JIT systems are often based on cellular manufacturing processes. These require team work as described below, and the bonus payment system will almost inevitably have to be related to group or factory-wide performance rather than to individual output.

Cellular manufacturing

A manufacturing cell consists of a small number of closely cooperating machines. Within a manufacturing system a cell can be regarded as the smallest autonomous unit capable of sustained production.

Cellular manufacturing involves the logical arrangement of numerically controlled equipment into groups or clusters of machines to process families of parts. By definition, processing parts in a manufacturing cell includes completing as much of the workplace processing as possible within the cell before moving it to the next sequential processing, assembly or stock-holding station. Cells are staffed by teams of interdependent and multiskilled workers.

Cellular manufacturing systems demand team work and flexibility. Within the system, high-performance work groups will be functioning that are to a large extent responsible for their own planning, operations, quality and production control. Cellular manufacturing systems require multiskilled people and are therefore possible environments for skill-based pay systems, although such systems are not always cost effective.

It will, however, be important to ensure that a team incentive or bonus system operates in which team members are given the maximum opportunity to monitor their own performance and take action to improve it, and are rewarded accordingly.

CONSIDERATIONS AFFECTING THE DESIGN OF INCENTIVE SCHEMES

As Bowey and Thorpe[2] have commented: 'Many managers still believe that as long as an incentive scheme is designed, maintained and operated correctly, higher performances will follow automatically.' But managers often admit that decay is inevitable and seem prepared to live with that uncomfortable fact.

Both these assumptions can be challenged. A payment-by-results scheme will only work if it fits the requirements and situation of the organization and if full consultation has taken place during its introduction. Degeneration *can* be controlled, as described earlier in this chapter, but it is hard work.

When considering the introduction of a new scheme or the revision of an existing one, it is first necessary to understand the criteria for success.

Criteria for success

The criteria for the success of an incentive scheme are that:

▌ it should be appropriate to the type of work carried out and the workers employed;
▌ the reward should be clearly linked to the efforts of the individual or team;
▌ individuals or teams should be able to calculate the reward they get at each of the levels of output they are capable of achieving;
▌ individuals or teams should have a reasonable amount of control over their efforts and therefore their rewards;
▌ the scheme should operate by means of a defined and easily understood formula;
▌ the scheme must be carefully installed and maintained;
▌ provision should be made for controlling the amounts paid to ensure that they are commensurate with effort;
▌ provision should be made for amending rates in defined circumstances.

These are demanding criteria and they need to be kept in mind throughout the selection process as described below.

SELECTING AN INCENTIVE SCHEME

The steps required to select an incentive scheme are:

▌ define objectives and assumptions;
▌ analyse the existing situation;
▌ evaluate alternative systems.

Define objectives and assumptions

Everyone takes for granted that the prime purpose of an incentive scheme is to provide a means of motivating employees that will improve their performance and levels of productivity in the organization. Other objectives which need to be considered when reviewing existing schemes or considering introducing a new scheme are to:

▌ obtain consistency in performance;
▌ reduce or at least contain labour costs per unit of output;
▌ improve product quality and the level of customer service;
▌ reduce waste;
▌ obtain a lower level of rejects;
▌ improve delivery times;
▌ gain better control over pay to eliminate wage drift, and thereby get value for money;
▌ reduce the levels of inventory and work in progress;
▌ improve labour flexibility;
▌ improve equipment utilization;
▌ reduce pay disputes;
▌ expand the skill base;
▌ generally convince all employees that the incentive pay arrangements are fair and equitable.

The definition of objectives should lead to an assessment of the extent to which they are being achieved by existing incentive schemes. But it is also necessary to examine and if appropriate challenge the assumptions held by management about pay and rewards. These can include assertions such as: 'the workers in this plant are only interested in money', 'the existing system is the best one we've got so why change it?', 'all we need to do is to tighten up the loose rates' (rather than find out why the rates were loose in the first place), 'that's the way the workers want it', 'you can't rely on the so and so's to work without a fairly juicy carrot' (as well as a big stick), and so on and so forth.

Analyse the existing situation

The existing situation should be analysed by obtaining answers to the following questions:

▌ What is the system of work – batch, mass production or process?
▌ What manufacturing, operational and quality control processes are in operation (eg FMS, CIM, cellular manufacturing, TQM)?
▌ How much new technology is involved in the shape of computerized production control and scheduling systems (eg MRPII), robotics and numerical control (CNC or DNC)?

▊ To what extent does the work require highly developed technical skills?

▊ To what extent is multiskilling an important feature of the work?

▊ To what extent can the work be described as skilled, semi-skilled, unskilled, repetitive or varied?

▊ Is the work flow or cycle steady or intermittent and are the work methods constant or varied?

▊ How long are the typical work runs?

▊ What is the average lot size?

▊ How frequently are operators required to reset their machines?

▊ How often are methods changed?

▊ Does the work mix change much?

▊ Are product designs and specifications frequently modified?

▊ How tight are the tolerances to which operators have to work?

▊ What is the underlying attitude to product quality? To what extent is this of real concern or is only lip service being paid to it?

▊ What is the incidence of waste and rejects?

▊ How much waiting time is there?

▊ To what extent is the machine work paced? How much control do workers have over their output levels?

▊ What level of productivity is being achieved? Is that high enough?

▊ What is the scope for increasing work rates?

▊ To what extent is the work carried out on an individual, team or production line basis?

▊ What proportion of workers are able to participate individually or in teams in a payment-by-results scheme?

▊ If productivity needs to be increased, to what extent is that a matter of improving work organization, systems of work (including computerization and automation) or the quality of management and supervision rather than relying on an incentive scheme to work miracles?

▊ What is the climate of employee relations?

▊ To what extent have employees been involved in the design and operation of incentive schemes?

▊ What is the union's attitude to incentive schemes?

▊ How likely are employees to respond positively to a new or revised incentive scheme?

▊ Are managers and supervisors capable of controlling an incentive scheme?

▊ Has the firm the industrial engineering resources required to install and maintain an incentive scheme?

▊ Is there adequate management information available to enable the scheme to be monitored and controlled?

Evaluate alternatives

The alternative arrangements should be evaluated against the criteria listed above and the following points concerning each approach:

Time rates

The first point to consider is whether or not an incentive scheme of any type is suitable. The alternative of using time or day rates may be preferable where:

- individual or team effort does not determine output;
- achieving a fair and consistent relationship between performance or skill levels and reward is difficult;
- it is not easy to establish accurate standards by means of work measurement;
- there are numerous product or product mix changes;
- design changes or modifications are frequent;
- work runs are short, and new set-ups for machines are frequent;
- quality is a prime consideration;
- job stoppages are numerous and downtime is considerable;
- there is a history of unsatisfactory shop-floor relations;
- it is believed that the time and cost involved in operating an incentive scheme outweigh its (dubious) benefits;
- the company is confident that performance can be improved and high levels of productivity maintained better by other means, including more effective operational systems, better management and supervision, non-financial incentives and job design.

Work-measured individual incentive schemes

This type of scheme may be appropriate when individual effort clearly determines output and:

- the work requires purely manual skills and/or only single/purpose hand tools or simple machine tools are used;
- a high proportion of task content is specified;
- work measurement can readily be applied to the tasks and an effective system of work measurement is in use;
- product changes or modifications are limited;
- job stoppages are small;
- a stable climate of employee relations exists.

Measured day work

Measured day work may be appropriate when individual effort largely determines output and:

- conditions are unsuitable for a work-measured scheme;
- operations are of the process type or assembly line;
- accurate work measurement of operations is possible so that acceptable standards can be achieved;
- the unions are responsive to the benefits of the system;
- high-calibre management negotiators are available.

Group incentive schemes

These may be suitable if collective effort clearly determines output and the other features necessary for individual incentive schemes are present.

Performance-related pay

Performance-related pay may be considered when:

- the company wants to focus the attention of employees on such critical success factors as quality, delivery and costs, as well as output;
- it is believed that team leaders and supervisors are fully committed to the system and can learn new performance management skills;
- a consistent and fair relationship between performance and reward can be achieved;
- the company has PRP for non-manual staff and wants to move towards an integrated pay structure;
- employees and trade unions are likely to support the scheme.

INTRODUCING AN INCENTIVE SCHEME

Prerequisites

Following research into payments systems and productivity, the Pay and Rewards Research Centre of Strathclyde University concluded that the three essential prerequisites for introducing a successful scheme were as follows:

- the top of the organization is committed to a programme of change;
- a team of managers is developed which knows what is required of it and has the enthusiasm to make it work;
- the rest of the workforce is convinced that the project is worthy of their support and is shown how to make it work.

The importance of the last of these prerequisites – a participative approach – was emphasized by Bowey and Thorpe[2]. There is no point in introducing a scheme which aims to increase productivity without involving employees in discussing how to obtain improvements and how they will benefit financially from them. It is equally necessary to discuss at each development stage the design of the scheme and how it will operate.

In a work-measured scheme, work measurement techniques should be demonstrated; many companies train selected employee representatives in these techniques so that they can agree timings and, importantly, retimings. Any agreement should spell out the circumstances in which retiming will take place and how such retimings will be conducted, in consultation with employees and their representatives. Management must be completely open about the scheme while making it clear that it will not be allowed to deteriorate.

REFERENCES

1. Kinnie, N and Lowe, D (1990) Performance-related pay on the shop floor, *Personnel Management*, September
2. Bowey, A and Thorpe, R (1986) *Payment Systems and Productivity*, Macmillan, London

29

Salesforce Incentive Schemes

The design of a salesforce pay plan is often a sensitive issue. This is because, for many organizations, the motivation of the salesforce has an immediate, strong impact on business results. Designing an effective pay plan is also a challenging task because of the immense variation in custom and practice and the frequently ill-informed assumptions that are made about how to motivate salespeople. The array of choices includes bonus schemes, incentive pay, commission and competitions. This chapter will review these. The motivational theory issue is really beyond the scope of this chapter. However, it cannot be ignored since, within any particular salesforce, it is likely that there are views held by influential individuals which range from Tayloresque 'carrot and stick' notions to more enlightened principles, taking in Maslow, Herzberg and others along the way. The reality is that a salesforce can include the same range of individual styles and preferences as any other occupational group. However, it is just as likely that a particular salesforce will have become focused on a behavioural style and it is crucial that one understands what this is and whether it is appropriate.

The design of sales incentives has been traditionally the preserve of the top sales manager. This sometimes leads to the development of arrangements which are at odds with remuneration policies for other employees. This might arise because of custom and practice (for example, commission pay is typical in some industries) or because there is a real difference between the cultures of different parts of the same organization. The authors' experience suggests that sales directors are now ever more likely to seek professional input, from their personnel function or from external consultants. In many companies the traditional functional boundaries between sales and other employees are becoming blurred. This can mean that the rationale for differences in remuneration policy has to be carefully thought out and communicated to avoid the risk of divisiveness.

CORE DESIGN ISSUES

In designing a sales pay plan, the following questions have to be answered:

- How will the different elements of remuneration reward performance?
- Is an incentive plan appropriate?
- How much of total pay should be through incentives?
- What performance measures should be used?
- Should the plan reward individuals or recognize a team?
- Are there potential sources of inequity in the allocation of sales territories or customer base?
- What will be the impact of any new scheme on the earnings of your highest performers? Will some be penalized by and others benefit from changes which are necessary (for example, the inclusion of new measures of sales performance)?

Changes in sales pay are often stimulated by a change in business strategy and/or evidence that some element of the existing plan is dysfunctional.

THE REWARD MIX

The blend of reward mechanisms used and how much can be earned through each of them should be a strategic choice, to create a reward policy which is geared to the nature and culture of the business. The following commentary suggests a framework for evaluating the options open to you. However, for some sectors of the economy, such as financial services, there is well-established custom and practice. While to the outsider some aspects of such custom and practice appear to defy common sense, it can be difficult to break with these traditions. The most important issue in these circumstances is that the detailed design of the scheme should provide an effective management tool to channel sales behaviour in an appropriate direction.

Salary

Salary is a market-driven 'rate for the job'. In some situations it may be appropriate to pay salary only, with no bonus or commission. For example, in some forms of high-value capital goods sales, there is a whole organization system selling the product or project to the customer. While an individual may have the tag of account manager, a sales incentive could be highly divisive. In some situations the use of sales incentives could be construed as unethical (eg pharmaceuticals).

These same issues may lead to a choice to pay mainly by salary, but with a small incentive pay opportunity. The main function of the incentive payment in these situations is to provide a motivational vehicle for clarifying and communicating the key performance issues.

Salary management follows the same principles as for any other group of employees. It is important to clarify the extent to which salary should be a rate for the job or reflect achievement of results and/or competences. If both a sales incentive plan and a performance-based salary review system are used by an organization, it may be felt that there is double counting unless the salary review looks at broader issues than sales results.

It is often argued that pay by salary attracts people with high security needs at the expense of attracting those with high achievement motivation. There is little evidence on this issue, but one observes many achievement-focused people working in salaried salesforces. Perhaps the root issue is that pay by salary represents a fixed selling cost; incentive or commission pay is variable. A 'salary-only' approach brings with it a need to ensure that the organization recruits high-quality people. Under a commission pay structure, only the good performers survive.

Incentive pay

Incentive pay is geared to the achievement of specified results and is paid in addition to salary. The principles which govern effective incentive scheme design are generic and therefore not repeated here. In relation to sales schemes, there are several issues which are especially important.

'You get what you pay for' is a well-established truism. The measures used in a sales incentive scheme design are potentially a matter of corporate success and failure. There are two sets of factors to be taken into account. First, what does successful sales performance look like? In most cases this will not simply be a case of sales volume or revenue. If your organization's future depends on repeat business from a customer base, then customer satisfaction and retention are important measures of sales success. Achieving sales is all very well, but how important is it to you to receive cash? If you have several product lines, it may well be that customer profitability can be dramatically improved by increasing the range of products sold to each of them. The first important thing to clarify is the range of quantitative and qualitative factors which define sales success.

The second set of factors is concerned with *how* the salesperson influences sales success. Taking the end-to-end process of acquiring customers and making sales to them, how does the salesperson influence the result and how much impact do their actions have? Practical experience of designing such schemes indicates that it is often helpful to work directly with salespeople and not rely on job descriptions or what sales managers tell you, since these often represent an idealized view of what happens. The reality is sometimes very different. This analysis will lead to a set of sales success factors in which you know the salesperson can have a strong influence.

These factors should then be refined to a few key measures:

▮ *Team or individual?* When people use the term 'the sales team', they sometimes mean nothing more than the individuals reporting to the same sales manager. The key question is the extent to which salespeople are dependent on one another to achieve success. In some cases this is unambiguous, for example in the case of the major account team who all focus on one customer. It may be that teamworking is both essential to success and crosses functional boundaries. An obvious example is the relationship in many organizations between field salespeople and telesales. Yet it is surprising how often incentive plans for these different functional groups are designed independently from each other.

▮ *Yesterday's heroes* can become today's sinners because the rules of the game have been changed. It is most likely that a newly developed sales pay plan will replace an existing scheme. In such a case it is probable that the performance criteria will include new measures and that these will lead to some salespeople earning less than they previously did for the same performance. This does not make the new plan inappropriate but does emphasize the need to carefully model the effect of the new pay plan so that the effect on earnings is known in advance.

▮ *Equality of opportunity* is an important reward principle. In relation to sales incentives, the central issue in this regard is how sales territories or customer portfolios are determined. If, for example, a carelessly drawn line on a map can make a substantial difference to the sales potential of a territory, the incentive plan is likely to fall into disrepute.

▮ *Target ratcheting* can be a major source of dispute. If targets are based on past performance and incentive pay is based on achieving those targets, the effect can be to penalize success by making it progressively harder for the top salespeople to earn incentive pay.

▮ *Accelerators and decelerators* are often used to modify the relationship between performance and reward. Accelerators may be appropriate to increase the incentive to perform above a given level. Decelerators are sometimes used to reduce the impact of windfalls on earnings.

▌ *Management by incentive* is a major risk. It is very tempting to design an incentive plan which covers all the angles by including every conceivable performance measure and rules to cover all possible situations. Such plans are ineffective for three reasons. The complexity of the scheme which results from this is so great that few people understand it properly. This same complexity makes the plan time consuming and expensive to administer and creates risk of mistakes and disputes. The incentive plan may become a management security blanket or disempower line managers. It is important that the sales incentive plan is designed to support effective management, not to substitute for this.

Commission

This term is often used loosely in describing sales incentives. Here we define commission pay as payment of a percentage of the sales result. The simplest commission schemes pay a percentage of sales revenue, so that earnings vary directly in proportion to results. All of the issues discussed under 'Incentives' are equally relevant in relation to commission. A commission scheme will typically have the following features:

▌ *On Target Earnings* (OTE) represents the commission earned for 'standard' performance. Opinions vary, but we suggest that the performance standard for OTE should be set at a level where at least 50 per cent of the sales team will achieve it.
▌ *Salary* is often included in a commission scheme. However, what is normally meant in this context is a payment 'on account'. If performance falls short of the level needed to earn the 'salary', the deficit may be rolled into the next performance period.
▌ *Pensionable earnings* are sometimes defined. If the salespeople are self-employed then this will not apply. The most appropriate way of providing a pension for commission-paid employees would be a money purchase arrangement. However, some organizations which operate a defined benefit scheme choose to make all commission earnings pensionable up to a defined limit (normally OTE).

Commission schemes typically treat the salesperson as a self-standing profit unit. The commission plan is structured to share the gross margin of sales between the organization and the salesperson. If the organization provides selling tools such as a car, mobile phone or portable computer, these costs may be explicitly taken into account.

The design issues which may need to be considered include:

▌ *Definition of a sale.* It is common practice to pay commissions at the point in time when the goods have been invoiced to the customer. However, there are further issues to consider. It may be appropriate to apply a 'claw-back' of commission in the case of product returns and bad debts.

▮ *Long-term sales.* It may happen that the salesperson sets up a deal with a customer in which the initial order is part of a much larger contract, or the start of a longer-term business relationship with the prospect of repeat business. It may be appropriate to apply a different commission rate to the initial and subsequent orders if the sales role is clearly focused on gaining new business and the ongoing maintenance of customer relationships is handled by others.

▮ *Split commissions.* In certain circumstances, more than one salesperson may be involved in a particular sale. It is important that the ground rules for commission splitting are clearly set out in advance.

▮ *House accounts.* Certain major accounts may be designated 'house accounts', where the business relationship is managed by the sales director or by a major accounts team. If there is a requirement for field-based salespeople to service the account it may be appropriate to pay them commission at a reduced rate.

The main risk inherent in commission schemes is that the salesperson will be motivated only by personal gain. The interests of the organization or the customer may not predominate. Previous mis-selling is a good example of what can go wrong. It is wise to ensure that the rules of the commission scheme, as well as the performance measures it uses, are designed to pay only for outcomes which are acceptable to the organization. This risk can be further reduced by paying true salary, which is related to wider issues than financial performance.

A further issue which often arises is that of career progression. A commission pay scheme might not give any recognition to levels of competence or performance except through the level of earnings. In these circumstances salespeople often ask for a career structure. The most common way of providing this is to define a number of levels of sales role. Progression through these is governed by a set of criteria which could include performance levels and competence standards.

Competitions

Competitions are typically used in addition to salary, incentive or commission pay to provide a focus for a short-term sales campaign. This might include a new product launch or a drive for customers in a new market sector, for example. The rewards from a competition could be cash, although it is commonplace for such schemes to take the form of non-cash incentives, such as:

▮ *luxury consumer goods* available either directly or through catalogues which offer a choice of alternatives in exchange for points earned through performance;

▋ *holidays* of varying length and location to reward different levels of achievement;

▋ *car schemes* to recognize exceptional performance by allowing top performers to have a more prestigious car;

▋ *premium clubs* to provide special rewards for a given number of high achievers at the end of a sales contest. Membership can be marked by symbols such as a special tie or an upgraded car and would typically include attendance at a special 'sales conference' in an exotic place.

The issues which may need to be considered include the following:

▋ *Motivation* of the whole salesforce may prove difficult if there is only one winner or a very small number of winners. The majority may simply not attempt to win. It is often helpful to have different levels of award for different levels of performance.

▋ *Prize hunters* may pursue competition rewards to the detriment of their broader objectives.

▋ *Income tax* has to be paid. It is normal practice for non-cash incentives to be made tax paid. It can be very demotivating to find that tax is due on the purchase value of a performance award with no company provision to cover the liability.

▋ *Administration* can be very time consuming. The motivational impact of a non-cash scheme can be severely damaged by poor administration.

Non-cash incentives should not overshadow the continuing need to have competitive salaries and cash incentives. Consumer goods should not replace pay to any serious extent. Their role should be to provide additional recognition and a focus for generating excitement around a sales campaign.

The reward mechanisms outlined here could be used in any combination. Each of them can be used to reinforce different elements of performance. The choice of which to use and the detailed design must be governed by a clear understanding of the sales behaviours which are to be reinforced.

CONCLUSIONS

The main issues in the development, implementation and ongoing maintenance of a sales scheme may be summarized as follows:

▋ Blurring of the functional boundaries between sales and other roles in organizations is leading to a requirement to be very clear about the rationale for any differences in reward policy. Additionally, it is important that sales rewards are developed in an holistic manner and not thought of independently from other groups.

▋ The design of sales reward schemes will have a strong impact on how salespeople act. It is therefore essential that the scheme reinforces the kinds of behaviours that you really want.

▋ Sales reward schemes often have a short shelf-life. Any such scheme should be continuously reviewed to ensure that it fully supports your business aims.

▋ Changes to a sales reward scheme should be carefully modelled to make sure that the effects on individuals' earnings are both predictable and appropriate.

▋ Custom and practice can constrain an organization from implementing a sales reward structure which is objectively wholly appropriate.

▋ A mediocre design which is well communicated, managed and administered is preferable to a technically excellent scheme which few people understand.

30

Other Cash Payments and Allowances

To ensure a balanced set of remuneration policies, organizations often have to use one or more of a number of different additional payments to meet market needs. These can be divided into two categories:

1. payments in response to market pressure – the need to attract and retain talent;
2. payments to reward special circumstances or working practices.

In times past when there was a formal incomes policy, or nowadays to get special, subtle market advantage, payments in the latter category can be, and certainly have been, used as responses to the market.

MARKET PRESSURES RESPONSES

These are essentially lump sum payments or continuing allowances used to obtain competitive advantage in a tight labour market. They are used on recruitment and as 'top ups', often called 'market premia', to basic salary – paid only to employees in scarce categories, whose basic salary will otherwise be contained within the organization's normal salary structure. They are now in widespread use in the UK both in the private and the public sector, but most of the thinking behind them has come from the United States.

The following are the most common forms of payment in this category:

1. *Golden hellos:* also called recruitment bonuses, 'up-front' or 'front-end' bonuses. These are payments to entice sought-after individuals to join a particular employer. They can be paid as a lump sum on joining or as a phased bonus, sometimes over as much as a couple of years. Such payments have been used for graduates with rare specialisms (sometimes in the form of generous relocation allowances – repayable if the graduate leaves within a year or two), computer specialists, researchers, financial specialists and top executives likely to make an exceptional contribution to the business.

    There are no set formulae for determining these payments – they can run from quite large amounts, say, a year's salary, down to a few hundred pounds. At senior level, the offer of shares is also common.

    'Up-front' market premium payments can also be given as benefits: perhaps a larger or more exotic company car than is normal for the grade, a second car, special pension arrangements, housing assistance, additional relocation assistance etc. In conceding to demands for additional benefits, organizations need to think hard about the effects this may have on others who have the same rare specialisms, but have been in the job well before market pressure built up. Otherwise there is the risk of a 'dual market', which could have equal value implications if the existing population is largely female, say, and the new recruits earning more are male. Some adjustment to their reward package may have to be considered, therefore, to keep the team together. In addition, the tax implications of golden hellos should always be explored.

2. *Golden handcuffs:* these are payments given to staff to lock them into the organization and prevent them being 'attracted away' by the competition. Again, they are being used in both the public and the private sector in the UK. They are used both as 'retention payments' for staff subject to severe market pressure and, more rarely, for keeping staff in departments that have been cut back by redundancy – to ensure that a core of the best people stays. Golden handcuffs can take the form of phased lump sum payments, sometimes in the form of guaranteed bonuses, which may then be phased out if the market eases or circumstances change. They may be tied to performance or delivery criteria, notably when used at times of major organizational change as retention bonuses, or to keep people until a plant or site closes. They also commonly take the form of shares – especially at executive level – on the basis that equity participation breeds additional commitment to the business. Again, the tax implications of these provisions should be fully explored.

3. *London and large town allowances:* these are paid because of housing and other cost-of-living differentials. Many London employers either have a separate London allowance for more junior staff, which is reviewed annually and paid as an addition to basic salary or, alternatively, they expect to pay extra on basic salary in response to local

market pressure. Both Incomes Data Services and Industrial Relations Services report regularly on changing company practice in this area. Reward reports in detail – through local cost-of-living surveys – on the effects of changes in living costs including house prices.

REWARDS FOR SPECIAL CIRCUMSTANCES OR WORKING PRACTICES

Golden handshakes/termination or severance payments

Golden handshakes are also discussed in the context of redundancy (see Chapter 31), and are essentially termination payments – usually substantial ones – paid typically to top executives to ensure that they leave with a financial cushion and without making any fuss. They are commonly negotiated as part of the 'compromise agreements' used to enable senior executives who may 'no longer fit' to depart with dignity 'to pursue other interests' or even 'spend more time with their family'. In size they tend to bear some notional relation to the unexpired period of the executive's contract, where there is one. Where there is no fixed term contract, or where the company feels that, in addition to its statutory redundancy obligations it only needs to tide the individual over until a new job is found (enshrined in the legal concept of obligation to mitigate loss) – then a year's salary tends to be the maximum. But again there are no set rules. Lawyers are quite often involved in top executive 'separations' and the good ones are familiar with current practice as it is likely to apply to the case in question. Advice on the tax treatment of such 'compensation for loss of office' payments should always be sought before they are paid. Payments to directors show up eventually in the accounts of public companies – something in which the press and shareholders usually take great interest. There is growing public distaste for 'rewards for failure'. This should be borne in mind at the time the details of a separation are negotiated – a case for making any large payment should be prepared and it should be one that holds water for shareholders as well as curious journalists. Part of the separation 'handshake' package commonly involves outplacement counselling to enable executives to decide what to do next, with professional assistance and support.

Overtime payments

Overtime payments are typically made wherever the standard working week is exceeded on a regular basis for employees at supervisory level and below. In some union negotiated environments and in other special circumstances it may be extended to the lower levels of management. But it is usually implicit if not explicit in most management contracts that managers and professionals will work whatever hours can be reasonably required to ensure the fulfilment of their responsibilities. Sometimes exceptional management overtime (eg in business start-ups or during special projects) is rewarded by one-off bonuses.

For staff working overtime and being paid for it, the levels of payment vary in relation to whether the work is done on weekdays, at the weekends or on national holidays. Payments currently vary from time to time-and-a-half (sometimes after a minimum threshold of overtime working, say, eight hours a month) on weekdays to time-and-a-half on Saturdays and higher multiples for Sundays and national holidays. People who maintain essential services on Christmas Day expect very high rewards – as high as four times the normal rate – as compensation for being away from their families and sometimes in addition to time off in lieu.

The payment of overtime pay is generally held to be reasonable as long as the nature and amount of overtime working is strictly controlled. People do not work well and consistently if excessive overtime is worked and they should never be allowed to take on too much to supplement what may be, or is perceived to be, an inadequate basic salary. Overtime practices are also continuing to change with the use of annual hours agreements, which exchange flexibility for overtime over a given working year, but provide for additional pay beyond this. Incomes Data Services, IRS and other survey producers report regularly on developments in this area.

Shift pay and unsocial hours payments

These are given where the pattern of working hours differs from the typical working day, typically to computer staff, production employees, various medical staff, broadcasting employees and others where 24-hour cover for services is essential. Payments relate to the shift patterns worked, to associated time-off arrangements and to market practice in the sector in question. As with overtime, care should be taken to ensure that working practices are sensible and not geared to propping up otherwise uncompetitive pay rates. Buying out practices that have got out of hand is both difficult and expensive.

Attendance bonuses

Attendance bonuses are generally paid to categories of staff where absenteeism is a problem and the organization wishes to encourage more consistent attendance. They can be useful where the work itself or the environment is unpleasant and it is not within the employer's power to improve this. Many employers reject the idea because they consider it is a payment for what is already a contractual obligation which merely gives employees the opportunity to earn a bit more 'by getting out of bed earlier'. Such employers have not always been so scathing however, in the face of severe market pressure during times of national incomes policy in the 1970s; or indeed in the face of a very tight local market where they need to resort to payments of this kind to get the edge.

Honoraria

These are essentially lump sum payments in recognition of specific expertise and contribution. They have been used effectively in the public service as a form of performance reward that is psychologically more appealing than straight 'merit pay'. They can also be used to reflect rotating membership of specific management or other committees/task forces to reflect the additional responsibility involved.

Clothing allowances

Clothing allowances are paid to staff who need to buy special clothing for work where the company does not provide uniforms. Such payments are market related and should be reviewed for tax implications. Dry cleaning vouchers are sometimes also provided as part of the policy.

Christmas bonuses and 13th-month payments

These are normally paid as a matter of tradition in some sectors. Christmas bonuses tend to be relatively small unless they contain a performance element. The essential purpose is generally to reward loyalty and recognize this by helping with the extra costs of the season. Their use appears to be declining. Thirteenth- or even 14th-month payments have come to the UK from Europe. They are found among some organizations with European parents where home country policy has been translated into local practice. Such payments tend to be given as 'double month' salaries paid either at Christmas or in the summer or sometimes divided between the two. A UK variation is the payment of an annual salary on a four-weekly basis, giving 13 equal payments in the year.

Payments for qualifications

These are used by companies to reward success such as passing accounting, actuarial, legal, managerial or other professional and technical examinations and MBAs to recognize their added value to the organization. Such payments are generally given as lump sum payments, but can be given as pay increases – sometimes as part of a reward system linked to competency development. Where these payments are made to people who have recently left full-time education, they can fill a useful motivational 'gap'. The wait between annual reviews can seem a long time to someone in their teens (which is one of the reasons why increases for junior staff are often paid on a six-monthly basis).The idea has also translated into payment for skills and competences, which is covered in Chapter 21.

Part 7

Employee Benefits and Pensions

31

Employee Benefits

DEFINITION

Employee benefits are elements of remuneration given in addition to the various forms of cash pay. They provide a quantifiable value for individual employees, which may be deferred or contingent like a pension scheme, insurance cover or sick pay, or may provide an immediate benefit like a company car. Employee benefits also include elements which are not strictly remuneration, such as annual holidays.

The terms 'fringe benefits' and 'perks' (perquisites) are sometimes used derogatively, but should be reserved for those employee benefits which are not fundamentally catering for personal security and personal needs.

OBJECTIVES

The objectives of the employee benefits policies and practices of an organization might be:

- to increase the commitment of employees to the organization;
- to provide for the actual or perceived personal needs of employees, including those concerning security, financial assistance and the provision of assets in addition to pay, such as company cars and petrol;
- to demonstrate that the company cares for the needs of its employees;
- to ensure that an attractive and competitive total remuneration package is provided which both attracts and retains high-quality staff;

▌ to provide a tax-efficient method of remuneration which reduces tax liabilities compared with those related to equivalent cash payments.

Note that these objectives do not include 'to motivate employees'. This is because benefits seldom have a direct and immediate effect on performance unless they are awarded as an incentive; for example, presenting a sales representative with a superior car (eg a BMW) for a year if he or she meets a particularly demanding target. Benefits can, however, create more favourable attitudes toward the company leading to increased long-term commitment and better performance.

BENEFITS POLICIES

Policies on employee benefits need to be formulated in the following areas:

▌ *Range of benefits provided:* some benefits, such as pensions and holidays, are expected, others, such as permanent health insurance, are optional extras.

▌ *Scale of benefits provided:* the size of each benefit, taking into account its cost to the company and its perceived value to employees. Note that the perceived value of some benefits such as company cars or pension schemes (particularly in the case of older employees), can be very different from their actual cash value.

▌ *Proportion of benefits to total remuneration:* in cash terms, a benefit such as a pension scheme can cost the company between approximately 5 and 15 per cent of an employee's salary. A decision has to be made on the proportion of total remuneration to be allocated to other benefits which incur expenditure of cash by the company. This policy decision is, of course, related to decisions on the range and scale of benefits provided, and it can be affected by decisions on allowing choice of benefits and on the distribution of benefits. Some companies try to move towards a 'clean cash' policy which minimizes the number and scale of fringe benefits.

▌ *Allowing choice:* benefits will be most effective in the process of attracting and retaining employees if they satisfy individual needs. But individual needs vary so much that no benefits package or single item within the package will satisfy all employees equally. Younger employees may be more interested in housing assistance than a company pension plan. Some employees have ethical or political objections to medical insurance schemes. Not everyone wants a company car – especially if they live in an inner city area and have a spouse with a better car entitlement. Many people may prefer cash to an automatic benefit which is not precisely what they want. Methods of providing employees with choice are discussed in Chapter 32.

▌ *Allocation of benefits:* policy on the allocation of benefits determines the extent to which it is decided that a single status organization should be created. If the policy is to have a hierarchy of benefits, then the allocation of these at different levels has to be determined, usually in terms of broad bands of entitlements – typically called benefit grades.

▌ *Harmonization:* in the new flatter organizations, where multiskilling is prevalent and new technology is eliminating the old distinction between white- and blue-collared workers, harmonization of benefit packages is increasingly taking place. The objective is to increase unity of purpose and improve team work by abolishing invidious distinctions between benefits, rewarding different levels of responsibility and contribution by pay alone. Single status companies are becoming much more common. Full harmonization means that there are no distinctions at any level in the hierarchy between the benefits provided, which may vary only with length of service or specific market practice.

Partial harmonization may provide the same basic benefits in some areas such as pensions, holidays, sick pay and redundancy for white- and blue-collared staff, but have a hierarchy of benefits above this base according to job grades. These benefits could include company cars, topped-up pension schemes or medical insurance.

▌ *Market considerations:* whatever degree of choice or harmonization is decided upon, the precise arrangements will always be affected by market considerations. It may only be possible to attract and retain some key staff by, for example, offering a company car in line with what other organizations are doing for similar jobs. To attract a senior executive, it may be necessary to offer him or her a special pension arrangement – especially if he or she is earning over the Finance Act 1989 'earnings cap' (£102,000 for the 2004/05 tax year). As in all aspects of pay, market considerations and the need to offer competitive packages may have to override the principle of equity.

▌ *Government policy:* it is essential, when reviewing benefit policies, to monitor tax legislation in order to assess the relative tax efficiency of benefits and to keep employees informed of the implications for them. For example, since 2001 the government has substantially changed the basis of company car taxation to encourage individuals to drive more environmentally friendly cars and to discourage the provision of free private fuel.

▌ *Trade unions:* trade unions are increasingly concerned with the whole remuneration package and therefore may be involved or ask to be involved in negotiating the provision and level of benefits. Many companies, however, resist negotiating such items as pensions, although they will be prepared to consult unions or staff associations on benefit arrangements and do sometimes have trade unionists as trustees of the pension scheme.

BENEFITS PRACTICE

All employers provide benefits in some form or another to employees, but practice varies according to:

▮ *Employee status:* typically, the more senior the employee, the more benefits provided. But this is not always the picture. A growing number of organizations, especially in high technology and other sectors requiring rapid growth and employee flexibility, have opted for harmonized benefits and conditions for core benefits.

▮ *Local 'national' sector practice:* there are marked differences in benefits entitlements between the finance sector and the rest of the private sector, between organizations where workforce costs form a small part of corporate expenditure and those which are labour intensive, and between profitable and progressive organizations and those which have to keep a tight control on workforce costs to survive. Differences by job function may also exist.

▮ *Private or public sector status:* differences were much greater in the early 1980s than in the new millenium. Apart from generous, index-linked pension schemes and longer holidays, the public sector enjoy comparatively few fringe benefits and they very rarely have company cars – recently market competition for scarce skills has changed that for many public servants, notably in local authorities, non-departmental public bodies and the new Executive Agencies hived off from the core of the Civil Service.

▮ *Employers' views on the advisability of providing benefits:* the extent to which they wish to use benefits to attract and retain staff – some organizations take a much more generous line than others or simply prefer to pay more in 'clean cash' than in benefits.

So the emphasis now in the UK is predominantly on cash payments rather than benefits. Most employers have therefore concentrated on providing a competitive set of 'core' benefits to supplement cash remuneration. The wilder extremes of tax-efficient 'beyond the fringe' benefits only exist in areas where extremely high pay is given in response to severe market pressure and for directors/owners of private companies where shareholder pressure is not an issue.

A BALANCED APPROACH

Benefit entitlements are an area which employees watch closely and where perceived injustice can rapidly cause problems. They are also a major component of employee costs, particularly at management level where keeping up with 'best practice' can add 40 per cent or more to basic salary costs for a fairly average group of executives. The costs can rise sharply above that level where special pension provisions have to be made for older directors, eg those who are earning over the pensions 'cap', and who have been newly recruited with little by way of preserved pension entitlements and expectations of retiring on two-thirds salary in line with Inland Revenue limits. Luxury cars are also a major cost item and other benefit costs can sometimes rise rapidly and unpredictably, such as medical insurance in the UK.

In this chapter we look first at all the major benefits currently provided by UK employers to give an overview of the options available. We then discuss:

- intangible benefits as an important part of the total benefits package;
- the development of employee benefit strategies;
- how to recognize the need to review benefits;
- the steps to take when modifying the benefits package;
- the important subject of communications.

PRINCIPAL TYPES OF BENEFITS

Benefits can be divided into the following categories:

1. *Pension schemes:* these are generally regarded as the most important employee benefit. In the UK they are typically financed during the employees' working lifetime to provide a guaranteed income for them or their dependants on retirement or death. Pension schemes are so important that they are dealt with separately in Chapter 33.
2. *Personal security:* these are benefits which enhance the individual's personal and family security with regard to illness, health, accident, redundancy or life assurance.
3. *Financial assistance:* loans, house purchase assistance, relocation assistance, discounts etc.
4. *Personal needs:* entitlements which recognize the interface between work and domestic needs or responsibilities, eg holidays and other forms of leave, child care, career breaks, retirement, counselling, financial counselling, personal counselling in time of crisis, fitness and recreational facilities.
5. *Company cars and petrol.*
6. *Other benefits* which improve the standard of living of employees such as subsidized meals, clothing allowances, refunds of telephone costs and credit card facilities.
7. *Intangible benefits:* characteristics of the organization which make it an attractive and worthwhile work place (see also Chapter 2).

PERSONAL SECURITY

Death-in-service benefits

Provided either as part of the pension scheme or as a separate life assurance cover, this benefit provides for a multiple of salary to be paid to an employee's dependants should he or she die before retirement. The range of multiples of salary payable generally ranges from one to four times (currently the limit set by the Inland Revenue). Entitlements may be dependent on employee status or they may be the same for all employees in organizations with harmonized or single status benefit provisions. This is not a particularly expensive benefit to provide and is usually appreciated by employees because it saves on the personal life insurance cover needed to provide for their liabilities if they die prematurely and benefits can generally be paid free of income or inheritance tax. Death-in-service benefits are also discussed in Chapter 33.

Personal accident cover

This insurance cover provides for compensation should an employee be involved in an accident causing serious injury or death. It is a very common benefit, particularly where there is a great deal of travel involved or where the work can be hazardous for environmental and sometimes political reasons.

Permanent health insurance

Also called long-term disability cover, this form of insurance provides for continued income once the provisions of the company sick pay scheme are exhausted. It is therefore used to provide security of income for those struck down with chronic or terminal illnesses, normally payable after the first six months of sick leave and continuing until death or retirement, when the employee's pension becomes payable. Cover can be provided either through a separate insurance or through the ill-health early retirement provisions in the pension scheme. The income provided under permanent health insurance schemes typically ranges from between one-half to two-thirds of salary at the time illness occurred, usually with some provision for escalating payments in relation to rises in the cost of living and a deduction to allow for state benefits. This benefit is not particularly expensive to provide as a percentage of payroll for a group of employees. It is certainly much cheaper than any cover available to individuals. The cost will vary in relation to the age profile of employees and any special health risks involved in employment. It is a much-appreciated benefit – the dependants of an employee with terminal cancer or multiple sclerosis can be saved from financial hardship by the scheme's payments. This is a common benefit for employees at all levels among major employers. Employees are only taxed on benefits which are paid and not on the insurance premiums paid by the employer.

Business travel insurance

Arguably a benefit, business travel insurance is normally provided as a matter of course for all employees who have to travel extensively on company business. The insurance cover may be more generous than that obtainable by individuals and it will be offered at advantageous rates.

Given the generosity of some provisions it is not surprising that benefits experts occasionally amuse themselves by working out how much an employee would be worth dead if he or she died in service (four times salary), in a plane crash (personal accident cover pays out in full), while travelling abroad on company business (business travel insurance pays out too), with an entitlement to dependants' pensions (typically due for the spouse and children under the age of 18).

Medical insurance

There are two basic forms of medical insurance available in the UK:

1. schemes which cover the costs of private hospital treatment at rates which vary with the location and status of hospital selected by the employer (BUPA, PPP, WPA, etc);
2. schemes which pay out cash to those being treated under the National Health Service, eg Hospital Savings Association (HSA).

The former type of scheme may also pay out if the employee chooses to be treated under the National Health Service. Cover for private medical insurance may be taken out by employers either:

▌ on a group discount basis, so that employees can obtain cover more cheaply for themselves and their families than they could as individuals; or
▌ at no cost to employees. In this case free cover may only be extended to employees, with the possibility of covering families under group discount arrangements – or it may cover spouses and often dependent children too; or
▌ somewhere in between the above.

Apart from the obvious comforts of private health care, the real benefit to employers of medical insurance is the freedom it provides for employees to be treated at times that suit their work commitments. For as long as the National Health Service has to run long waiting-lists for non-emergency surgery, then medical insurance is a desirable benefit. It can prevent months of performance below par. Private medical treatment also has connotations of status which can increase premium costs. If employees go for minor surgery in unforeseen numbers, partly at least to say they have received private treatment, such costs can escalate rapidly. Some organizations have had to resort to requiring employees to pay, for instance, the first £50 of any treatment costs to keep their schemes within reasonable limits. Medical insurance is an increasingly competitive market. Apart from the three main organizations providing private medical cover mentioned earlier, there is a growing number of other insurers competing for business. It is always worth negotiating with insurance companies and provident associations to see if they can come up with a more appealing quote – or getting brokers or advisers to do this for you.

Health screening

Looking after employee health by providing screening can mean anything from providing for mass X-rays to screen for chest ailments, to cervical smears for female employees, to the full panoply of total health checks. Full screening is often provided for executives, especially for those over 40 or subject to particular stresses and hazards. At its most sophisticated, screening will look not just at an employee's current state of health but analyse his or her lifestyle and diet to provide advice on the prevention of future problems and the management of stress. Such screening may be far more appreciated than more expensive benefits, particularly if it picks up a health problem early and facilitates immediate treatment before the condition has got out of hand.

Extra-statutory sick pay

Although all employees are covered by statutory sick pay provisions, most major employers supplement these provisions by continuing sick pay for longer than the statutory period. Typically they provide for a given period at full pay and then a further period at half pay until the scheme's provisions are exhausted, sometimes after six months or more. Sick pay entitlements are generally service related. Entitlements may vary with status or be harmonized, depending on the employment philosophy prevailing in particular sectors. Generous sick pay provisions are usually much appreciated, but absenteeism often needs to be strictly monitored and controlled to prevent abuse of the system.

Extra-statutory redundancy pay

Although the statutory redundancy payments available in the UK provide some cushion for longer-serving employees losing their jobs, they are not very helpful to shorter service and indeed higher-paid employees made redundant through no fault of their own. Trade union agreements therefore frequently cover both redundancy policy and extra-statutory redundancy entitlements to provide additional job security or at least compensation for those covered by them. Many organizations too, faced with a redundancy arising from restructuring or change of business direction, are more generous with redundancy provisions. This normally takes one or more of the following forms:

▌ extra notice compensation;
▌ additional service-related payments – these vary considerably, two weeks per year of service being fairly common and one month per year of service not being uncommon, and many ignore the statutory weekly pay limit;
▌ *ex-gratia* payments given as compensation for loss of office (golden handshakes, see also Chapter 30).

Policy on redundancy is obviously influenced by what the organization can afford, but account should be taken of the fact that the relative generosity of treatment may well affect the morale of those whose jobs are safe. Redundancy exercises are very unsettling for everyone concerned. They need very careful planning and handling to ensure that the minimum disruption and hardship are caused.

Information on the severance package

When employees are told that they are to be made redundant, they should also be given precise details of the severance package. Preparing this is a major task for company pay specialists – one which often has to be performed in secret and at great speed. The information to be given to newly redundant employees typically comprises the following:

▌ actual date of redundancy;
▌ notice payments and additional notice payments due;
▌ statutory and extra-statutory service-related redundancy payments;
▌ any ex-gratia payments included in the package;
▌ accrued pension rights and any augmented rights given on redundancy (eg early retirement provisions where it is technically possible to turn redundancy into compulsory or voluntary early retirement);
▌ the position on other benefits, eg continued medical insurance or retention of the company car for a limited period to provide protection and continued mobility while a new job is found;
▌ when and how payments of all kinds are to be made;
▌ provisions to deal with special cases of hardship;
▌ sources of information and advice both within the organization and outside.

The humanity and consideration shown for individuals when the package is explained can do much to ease their shock and sense of loss on being made redundant. This is always a situation that needs to be dealt with on a one-to-one basis and for which training in counselling skills is helpful.

It is probably worth emphasizing – even in a chapter such as this – that redundancies should never be announced on Fridays – an early or mid-week breaking of the news provides time for advice to be given and for personal adjustment to the trauma before employees have to face the weekend, and often their social life, without any form of support.

Outplacement advice (career counselling)

One of the benefits which an increasing number of employers are offering to redundant employees is professional help in sorting out what it is they really want to do next and in showing how to apply effectively for the jobs they want. This service can be called outplacement, career counselling or one of a variety of other names dreamed up by the consultants who provide it. It can be given on a one-to-one basis for managerial staff leaving in mid/late career or as a series of lectures and advisory sessions for more junior employees. Good outplacement consultants or career counsellors have a high success rate in helping people replan their lives, build on their strengths and present themselves effectively to potential employers. The provision of career counselling does of course have wider spin-off benefits and a positive effect on the morale of those still in post in the organization who see their ex-colleagues learning to survive the trauma of redundancy.

As with any consultancy work, it is always wise to see several outplacement consultants or career counsellors, review their track record and see who provides the most appropriate service for the employees in question.

FINANCIAL ASSISTANCE

Company loans

Loan schemes either provide for modest sums to be lent interest free or for more substantial sums to be loaned at favourable interest rates. Small sums tend only to be loaned on a compassionate basis where there is personal hardship. Larger loans tend to be for defined purposes such as home improvements or car purchase, but may come without any strings attached at all. Repayments are normally made by regular deductions from salary on a basis specified or agreed between employer and employee. The benefit is more common in the finance sector. The taxable threshold for loan benefits should be monitored (see Chapter 34).

Season ticket loans

The high cost of commuting in to London and other major conurbations has led many employers to offer interest-free loans for annual season tickets. Such loans normally fall below the taxable threshold for loan benefits (see Chapter 34) and are repaid in instalments over the year.

Mortgage assistance

Subsidized mortgages are a very substantial benefit, especially for those who have to buy property in high-cost housing areas. The benefit is mainly confined to the finance sector and is usually provided by subsidizing interest payments on mortgages up to a given price threshold – often a multiple of salary. Where given, this benefit tends to be provided for all employees subject to age, grade and service requirements. Service requirements may, however, have to be dispensed with if they cause recruitment difficulties for staff categories already likely to have subsidized mortgages with other employers. The amounts available for subsidy normally rise either with seniority or salary level.

Housing assistance can also be given in the form of bridging loans and a guaranteed selling price (usually based on averaging of current valuations), especially for employees who move at company request and who cannot sell one house before they have to move into the house they buy near their new place of work.

Relocation packages

Companies recruiting managers and specialists from other parts of the country, or requiring employees to move, normally expect to pay the costs of removal. They also expect to compensate to some extent for the personal upheaval involved as well as paying for legal and agents' fees and the costs of moving their possessions, buying new carpets and curtains and even school uniforms. Following the March 1993 Budget, the Inland Revenue limits tax-free relocation assistance to £8,000. Companies can use this to the full or exceed it on a taxable basis if they believe this is necessary to induce an employee to make a move essential to business needs to an area not of their choice. Packages can either be drawn up individually or be controlled by set guidelines. Several specialist consultants offer assistance with the property side of relocation.

Company discounts

Where a company has products or services which can be offered to employees at a favourable discount, this is normally much appreciated. Such schemes can run from free sweets or a fixed weekly allowance to employees in sweet factories, to low-cost second and third cars for people working in car manufacturing. Some organizations, unable to give discounts on their own products, negotiate discounts for their employees from suppliers. These 'affinity benefits' are growing into a substantial industry. Trade unions are also active in the area of negotiating discounts as a means of attracting and retaining membership.

Fees to professional bodies

Fees for recognized professional bodies such as the Institute of Chartered Accountants or the Chartered Institute of Personnel and Development may be refunded.

PERSONAL NEEDS

Holidays

Annual leave entitlements are a major benefit. Until the introduction of the European Working Time Directive in 1998, there was no statutory obligation to offer any paid holiday except for the standard bank holidays. Employers are now obliged to offer a minimum of 20 days' paid holiday per year, including bank holidays. The entitlement for holiday begins to accrue on the first day at work.

In practice, most organizations have always offered annual leave well in excess of this minimum, with very few UK companies giving less than four weeks to employees at any level. Basic holiday entitlements are typically five weeks plus bank holidays, with some organizations offering up to six weeks for senior executives (who in practice may rarely have time to take full benefit of the provision) or on a service-related basis to more junior staff (although this may change as the government moves to outlaw age discrimination in the workplace, to comply with EU regulations).

Long entitlements may also be given in recognition of working unsociable hours or agreeing to flexible working practices. Some organizations specify minimum as well as maximum holidays, requiring employees to take one break of two weeks from their entitlement to ensure that they get away from work for at least one reasonably lengthy period a year. Many employers also need to specify when holidays can be taken, either to ensure that everybody is not off work at the same time when continuous working has to be maintained, or to ensure that everybody is off during an annual shutdown.

Compassionate leave

Granted when close relatives are ill, or die, or to deal with other unforeseen events, compassionate leave is normally the subject of formal policy in larger employers. It is usually paid leave for a limited period and unpaid for longer periods. This provision gives the opportunity for the organization to show concern for the individual and recognition of the importance of family responsibilities at times of personal hardship. Sensitivity in dealing with requests for compassionate leave, or offering it when it is clearly necessary, can do much for employee morale – not just for the employee concerned, but for the immediate work group who see that a colleague has been well treated at a time of personal crisis.

Maternity leave

More women are active in the workforce, and a growing number of women choose to or have to return to work (either full or part time) after their babies are born. This reflects changing demographic patterns: the requirement for both partners to work to make ends meet where housing costs are high, the growing number of single-parent families and the fact that more women (particularly professionals) are starting families later with no intention of breaking their career. Recent surveys show that just over half of all women with pre-school children are in some form of paid employment. The nuclear family with a wife at home is a reality for only a small proportion of the population and, for better or worse, a diminishing one.

All female employees are entitled to 26 weeks' 'ordinary' maternity leave, with the right to return to work on the same terms and conditions that applied before the leave, irrespective of service, hours worked, status of employment and size of the workforce. Female employees with at least 26 weeks of continuous employment by the beginning of the 14th week before the expected week of childbirth (EWC) are entitled to 26 weeks' additional maternity leave, which begins at the end of ordinary maternity leave.

Women entitled to additional maternity leave are also entitled to receive Statutory Maternity Pay (SMP) during ordinary maternity leave, providing average weekly earnings are equal to the lower earnings limit for national insurance contributions and that sufficient notice is given. SMP is paid by the employer for 6 weeks at 90 per cent of average weekly earnings and 20 weeks at the lesser of the SMP standard rate (£100 per week as at April 2003) and 90 per cent of average weekly earnings. Women not eligible for SMP may qualify for the Maternity Allowance paid by the social security office. SMP is paid whether or not the employee intends to return to work after the birth.

A woman has the statutory right to continue to benefit from all contractual terms and conditions of employment during the period of ordinary maternity leave, except for wages or salary. Contractual benefits could include annual leave, public holidays missed (where the contract states that public holidays are additional to the basic leave allocation), company car and mobile phone (unless for business use only), professional subscriptions, participation in share schemes, medical, life and disability insurance and company contributions to pension schemes (which must be calculated as if the employee was working normally).

There remains an area of uncertainty around profit share, bonus, incentive and commission payments. Whether payments should be made under such schemes will depend on the type of scheme, whether the scheme is included in the employment contract, and the terms and conditions of the specific scheme. Whatever the conclusion regarding a particular scheme, organizations should take care to ensure a consistent approach between employees taking the various kinds of leave – maternity, paternity, parental and adoption leave.

There is no statutory right for these benefits to continue during additional maternity leave, with the exception of annual leave. This must continue to accrue as per the Working Time Directive, which entitles employees to four weeks' paid leave each year.

It should be noted that these are the current statutory minimum requirements. Many organizations offer enhanced maternity arrangements, such as offering full wages or salary for longer than the first 6 weeks (one engineering company has been reported as offering 52 weeks on full pay, in an effort to attract more female employees), full benefits for the period of additional maternity leave or the right to add parental leave to the end of the maternity leave period.

Where employers find that they employ large numbers of women and are dependent on their skills, generous maternity leave provisions can help with long-term recruitment and retention. It can also be a very useful and cost-effective policy in areas of professional skill shortage, enabling employers to attract qualified women (providing this is achieved without infringing the sex discrimination legislation).

Paternity leave

In April 2003, the UK introduced a statutory right to paid paternity leave. An employee is eligible for paternity leave if he expects to have responsibility for the upbringing of the baby, and is either the baby's biological father and/or the mother's husband or partner (someone who lives with the mother in an enduring family relationship). It should be noted that a female in a same-sex relationship may be eligible for paternity leave, and terms such as 'father', 'he', 'him' and 'his' should be taken as including those females who qualify.

Fathers who have been continuously employed within an organization for at least 26 weeks ending with the 15th week before the EWC are eligible for 2 weeks' paid leave on the birth or adoption of a child. Paternity leave can be taken as a two-week block, or in two one-week blocks, and has to be completed within a period of 56 days beginning on the date on which the child is born or placed for adoption.

To be eligible for Statutory Paternity Pay (SPP), the father must have average weekly earnings that are at least equal to the lower earnings limit for national insurance contributions. SPP is paid for two weeks, and is the same as the standard rate of SMP (the lesser of £100 per week (as at April 2003) and 90 per cent of average weekly earnings). As with ordinary maternity leave, all contractual terms and conditions of employment continue through paternity leave.

Again, many employers offer more generous paternity leave provisions. The 2003 Hay Group Survey of Employee Benefits found that over 60 per cent of organizations grant between 1 and 10 days' fully paid paternity leave, with most offering 3 or 5 days. IDS surveys have drawn similar conclusions.

Parental leave

The Parental and Maternity Leave Regulations came into force on 15 December 1999. All parents of children under the age of five with more than one year's service are entitled to 13 weeks of unpaid 'parental leave' for each child (so parents of twins get 26 weeks), or 18 weeks for parents of disabled children. A parent with less than one year's service becomes entitled to parental leave after one year's service has been completed. The leave must be taken before the child's fifth birthday, unless the child is disabled or adopted. Parents of disabled children have until the 18th birthday to take the leave, while parents of adopted children must take the leave within five years of adoption or before the 18th birthday, if earlier.

Employees are guaranteed to get the same job back if they take a block of leave of four weeks or less, or the same or a similar job for longer blocks of leave. A similar job must offer the same or better terms and conditions (including pay). Employers report low levels of take-up of parental leave, primarily because it is unpaid.

There is a 'default agreement', which covers all companies that do not have their own leave arrangements. Under this default scheme, parents must give 21 days' notice of their intention to take parental leave (except when it is to be taken immediately after the birth or at the end of maternity leave), can take up to four weeks' leave per year, and the employer can postpone the leave, once, for up to six months (again, except when it is to be taken immediately after the birth or at the end of maternity leave).

Adoption leave

New regulations have also made adoption leave available from April 2003, to an adoptive parent (whether married or not) who is matched with a child under the age of 18 by an approved adoption agency that provides the employee with a certificate supporting the entitlement to leave. Leave periods and payments are similar to maternity leave, except that all paid leave will be at the standard rate of SMP, being the lower of £100 per week (as at April 2003) and 90 per cent of average weekly earnings.

Career breaks

A growing number of major UK employers are providing for employees (both men and women) to take up to five years off to rear children. People taking breaks are usually brought in regularly to keep up to date with developments both in their skills area and the organization in general and are entitled to return full or part time to work with no loss of job status.

Sabbaticals

Although sabbaticals are a comparatively rare benefit in the UK, they can be a useful retention factor for professionals able to use the time to travel and update their knowledge. They may also be granted to long serving employees either as straight leave or as time to get involved in something of value to the community. There is no set pattern to the length of leave given – it varies from a few weeks up to a year.

Other leave

Some UK organizations have been highly imaginative in offering leave to suit employees' changing needs. For example:

∎ *IVF leave:* five days' paid leave for women undergoing IVF treatment, and one and a half days for their partners;
∎ *Benidorm* leave: up to three months' unpaid leave, with no loss of service, for employees who wish to take advantage of long 'winter-sun' holidays;
∎ *finance leave:* employees can take one day per year to manage personal finances, through an intranet site and in-house seminars, or by visiting their financial planner, bank or building society;
∎ *Christmas leave:* a half-day to 'chill out' in the pre-Christmas rush (or do the Christmas shopping); or
∎ *volunteer leave:* six days' paid leave to work on charitable community ventures.

Childcare

In order to attract or retain employees with young dependent children, employers can offer financial or practical childcare provisions. For example, companies such as the HSBC are providing workplace nurseries or crèches. Although expensive to provide, such arrangements work well where travel with a child to the workplace is relatively easy. They can pose problems where parents reject the idea of commuting with a toddler in the rush hour. Cash payments or childcare vouchers are also now being offered by a growing number of organizations to offset employee costs for childminders, nannies, or after-school babysitters.

Practical or financial help in finding, recruiting and retaining childcare providers may be welcomed. For instance, arranging a 'nanny share' for two or three employees; retainer payments for childminders for part-time workers.

Other types of provision, such as flexible hours or help with transport, can ease practical problems for employee and employer, and be perceived as a benefit.

Pre-retirement counselling

Many larger employers now provide a series of lectures and an information pack for employees nearing retirement. The areas typically covered are:

▌ personal financial planning;
▌ managing increased leisure time;
▌ health in retirement;
▌ local sources of information and advice.

Personal financial counselling

Top executives and other higher rate tax payers are not always as effective as they might be in organizing their own personal financial planning. Even finance directors able to work wonders with corporate financial policy may have little time or inclination to deal properly with family financial matters. To help with this problem and provide the necessary specialist advice, many major employers offer senior executives the chance to go to independent advisers for personal financial counselling. This should be provided by fee-charging advisers who are not going to benefit from the sale of particular financial products, ie those who typically return commissions to either the company or the individual executive where commission-earning products are bought on recommendation. The advice given usually covers areas such as:

▌ making a will;
▌ inheritance and other planning;

- required insurance cover;
- provisions for dependants;
- savings and investment strategy;
- finance and property;
- planning for school fees;
- trusts and covenants;
- tax planning.

Advice is generally provided on a one-to-one basis once the executive has produced an inventory of his or her personal financial situation under guidance. The position is usually reviewed regularly to take account of changed personal circumstances. Companies may also offer this service to widows and widowers of employees to help them plan how best to make use of death-in-service benefits and take stock of the financial situation in which they have been left. Given that many widows of an older generation may have little idea about financial management, this can be a valuable and much-needed benefit.

Personal counselling

Traditionally provided as part of company 'welfare' services, a new generation of personal counselling services (EAPs or Employee Assistance Programmes) has grown up among major employers. Their purpose is to help employees deal with the traumas of bereavement, divorce, elder care, alcoholism and the spectre of AIDS. Larger employers typically provide specially trained 'in-house' counsellors on a confidential basis or an outsourced counselling service. Others provide a referral service to counsellors in the community, eg Relate, Alcoholics Anonymous, etc.

Sports and social facilities

Most employers recognize that work is also a social institution. They therefore try to provide at least some leisure activities so that colleagues can meet together outside working hours. Depending on the size, location and culture of the organization, provisions vary considerably. It may be entirely appropriate to negotiate favourable membership terms at nearby health and sports clubs. Whatever the circumstances, providing a social focus can have beneficial effects on the organization's culture (eg assisting team building) and should therefore be regularly reviewed as part of the remuneration package. It can certainly be a retention factor where staff are difficult to find and keep.

COMPANY CARS

Few other countries in the world provide company cars to the same extent as the UK. Foreign parent companies setting up in the UK often experience difficulty in persuading head office that such generous provisions are necessary to compete in the salary market. Employees seldom move from a job where they have a car to a non-car job, even if it carries a much higher basic salary. This is because in the private sector, and now in parts of the public sector too, cars are a mark of managerial status. Company cars are normally taxed, insured and maintained at company expense. They are, therefore, a large benefit and create a major differential and, some would say, distortion at the point in a salary structure where they are given on the basis of status alone.

The cash value to an employee of a company car can be as much as £5,000 to £10,000 a year (or more) depending on the model. The gap in a reward structure between the 'haves' and 'have nots' in company car terms is therefore considerable and can and does frequently cause heartache.

Until the mid-1990s, company cars were a tax-efficient benefit. A series of tax increases means that this is no longer the case; successive governments have changed the taxation of company cars with the aim of reducing the number of company cars on the road. Between 1994 and 2002, cars were taxed based on the number of business miles driven each year, with tax payable reducing as mileage increased over certain thresholds. This produced driver behaviours that were exactly opposite to those aimed for, as company car drivers abandoned trains and planes in order to reach the magical 18,000-mile barrier at which tax was minimized. Taxation is now based on carbon dioxide (CO_2) emissions produced by the particular vehicle, with lower levels of tax payable on more environmentally friendly cars. The government's stated intention is that the changes should be 'revenue neutral'. However, a neutral position inevitably creates winners and losers – the winners are those who have the opportunity to select a vehicle with low emissions, while the losers are those who drive over 18,000 business miles per annum.

Company car policies are often a benefit 'trouble spot' and can take an inordinate amount of top executive time to get right. Car fleet management is not an area for amateurs. Most large organizations have a fleet manager in charge of the acquisition and maintenance of the company car fleet, leaving the details of allocation policy and the way in which cars fit into remuneration policy as the main problems of the compensation and benefits specialists. Here a number of problems arise. People who are not entitled to them often try to get cars on the basis of business need, or to get their jobs regraded to a level where car provision is automatic. When they eventually get cars there may still be problems about the model, the permitted extras or the replacement cycle. In devising the remuneration policy element of company car policies, the following areas have to be dealt with in relation to what the company can afford in the face of competitive practice:

1. *Allocation policy:* this deals with who is to get cars on the basis of status, and what the annual mileage threshold is, before cars are given in response to business needs (this is typically around 10,000 miles but may vary based on the position).
2. *Car model entitlements:* when deciding car model entitlements the choice is between setting them rigidly in relation to a small number of models at each status level or, as is now more common, in relation to a benchmark price or lease cost, allowing varying degrees of freedom of choice. Few companies allow open sports cars, while others restrict the choice to models manufactured in EC or Scandinavian countries or even to models manufactured in Britain. The market trend is to allow as wide a choice as possible within a given cost framework.

   Organizations may also choose to allow some flexibility either on the additional extras that may be added to the car at employees' expense or, indeed, over whether they can make a contribution out of salary to either the lease cost or the purchase price of a more expensive car if they want one. In either of these cases, strict limits must be set because there is a strong tendency to stretch allowances to their limits and indeed beyond! A typical example of the problem is the organization which leases cars and sets an absolute lease cost limit of, say, £350 a month, and finds that a remarkably high proportion of employees will passionately want metallic paint on this model, which takes the leasing cost to £375. If they are then told that the limit is £350, they may complain bitterly that the company can surely afford an extra £25 a month.

   An increasingly common response is to let employees pay the extra – typically with a cost ceiling that might be 20 per cent about the monthly lease cost or purchase price. Some organizations set no ceilings on additions, typically those with a high proportion of young professionals who can then at least try having a Porsche for three years before moving on to a less personally costly family Volvo. If ceilings are imposed it is critical to stick to them *without* exception.

   Most car fleet managers know that if they allow themselves to be swayed by these specious arguments, the level will creep up incrementally and the allocation policy will be in tatters. It can however be very hard to hold the line in times of severe market pressure. Chief executives can, and sometimes do, intervene to ensure a favoured candidate gets the car he or she wants. As we have already said, car policy demands far more boardroom time than it should. Getting top executive commitment to the imposition of firm limits each time they are reviewed can help contain abuse of policy by directors with 'special cases'.

3. *Replacement cycles:* cars are commonly replaced every three to four years, or 60,000 to 80,000 miles, but this varies with the use and durability of the cars involved. Three years is the the most common replacement period. Salesforce cars suffer more wear and tear and therefore tend to be replaced more frequently than top executive cars, especially where annual mileages for the latter are relatively low.
4. *Eligibility to drive:* the policy on who may drive the car, eg employees/spouse/family/named drivers, is usually determined by the provisions agreed under the insurance cover negotiated. Flexibility in this area is often appreciated – especially in dual career families where the nanny or au pair needs to be insured to drive the car to get children to school and ferry them around, or where children under 25 are drivers.
5. *Permitted fuels:* All UK employers now specify that all new company cars run on unleaded petrol – for both environmental and (as the UK government intended when it reduced the tax) cost reasons. The use of alternative fuels such as compressed natural gas (CNG) for fleets is also growing – again encouraged by the government.
6. *Fleet management:* the management of the car fleet involves not only selecting purchasing and disposal of cars, but also encouraging drivers to treat their cars properly so that their resale value holds up when they fall due for replacement. Fleet management may be done 'in house' or be outsourced.

Company car policies are normally set out in a paper or intranet based manual for drivers that is regularly updated.

Company cars – the future

Now that cars are no longer tax effective in general, an increasingly common solution is to offer employees a cash alternative to their car entitlement. Employees can then choose the combination of cash and car which best meets their personal and business needs and which is most sensible from a tax point of view. Cash alternatives also go some of the way to removing status differences and irregular jumps in employees' packages between the 'haves' and the 'have nots'.

The 2003 Hay Group Benefits Survey shows that 72 per cent of organizations allow employees to take a cash alternative to a job-status vehicle, and 31 per cent allow cash in lieu of a job-requirement vehicle. There is also increasing flexibility around the choice of car, with 90 per cent of organizations permitting employees to take a smaller car (either for no benefit or taking the difference as cash), and 69 per cent allowing employees to take a bigger car and pay the difference.

Some employers are now offering 'car ownership schemes', either instead of company cars or to employees who are not eligible for a company car. Under such schemes the employer allows the employee to buy or lease his or her own car, by providing employee loans or taxable cash allowances. As it is classed as the employee's car there is no benefit-in-kind tax paid on the car. Instead, tax is paid on the loan or allowance. This may be operated as part of a larger flexible benefits scheme (see Chapter 32).

Private petrol

Free private fuel remains a top and senior management benefit. It is taxable, with tax again being based on the CO_2 emissions of the vehicle in question. For many company car drivers, the tax charge on free private fuel may well be higher than the value of fuel provided, and this has led to many organizations reviewing their policies.

Car allowances

Where cars are not provided but are used regularly for business purposes, many employers pay car allowances. These should be designed to make a sensible contribution to the cost of depreciation, maintenance and other running costs. A car used on business will inevitably need replacement earlier than one used more occasionally. Organizations such as the Automobile Association provide guidelines on running costs as a basis for setting allowances.

Mileage allowances

The cost of fuel used on business journeys is normally reimbursed. For company cars this will be on a mileage rate which reflects the actual cost of petrol or diesel. For employees' own cars, there will be an addition to compensate for wear and tear. These rates vary both in relation to the price of fuel and market practice. They may also vary in relation to total annual business mileage. The full allowance may be payable for short journeys, but a lower allowance can apply for much longer journeys. Again, the Automobile Association figures are often used in setting the level of allowances.

OTHER BENEFITS

Other benefits incude:

▌ subsidized meals in staff restaurants;
▌ luncheon vouchers – especially where employers have sites in large towns/cities;

- clothing allowances/cleaning tokens for employees who have to wear company uniforms;
- the refund of telephone rentals and the whole or part of the cost of calls – for those required to work at home or from home on occasions;
- educational allowances for expatriates – to ensure continuity of education for their children;
- credit card facilities for petrol or other purchases – especially for those who do a lot of travelling;
- mobile telephone/fax machines and laptop computers – typically job-need related but perceived as a reward too;
- funding of non-job-related evening classes/training to encourage employees to broaden their interests and skills – an area where 'leading edge' employers such as Asda have taken major initiatives.

INTANGIBLE BENEFITS

It should already be clear from much of this book that the authors do not believe that people work for money alone. As we said in Chapter 2, there are many determinants of the decision to work for, and stay with, a particular employer. Throwing money at recruitment and retention problems may be the worst possible strategy because this only deals with one aspect of what may be a complex problem. It is also, of course, self-limiting, because there has to be an ultimate ceiling on employment costs. Engaged performance, the psychological contract and motivation were discussed in Chapters 5 and 6. What we want to emphasize here is the simple fact that employees weigh up a number of tangible and intangible factors when looking at what employers have on offer. The list below sets out in more detail the main items involved. Most of them are strongly related to the need for personal recognition and the desire to go on learning and developing as a career goes through different stages. Recognition of the overlap between private and working life is also important. Most people prefer to work for an employer who is caring and supportive as well as challenging and successful.

The principal items that form part of the 'psychological contract' are:

- Status – recognition of seniority and professional excellence.
- Power – the opportunity to influence the course of the business and take responsibility for a growing number of functions and people.
- Recognition for achievement – a culture in which managers praise and reinforce individual success.
- Training opportunities – the chance to acquire a wider range of skills in preparation for promotion and to function more effectively and confidently.

▌ Career progression – the prospect of promotion, preferably in relation to a properly designed succession plan, to ensure that the right experience is acquired at the right time to enable new responsibilities to be taken on when the individual has been properly prepared for them.

▌ Good working conditions – pleasant, spacious and well-designed offices and other work environments which facilitate effective working both for individuals and teams.

▌ A well-managed organization – an appropriate organization structure infused with a sense of purpose and commitment. The reputation for running a 'rough shop' spreads quickly and prevents successful recruitment of all but those who believe they can change it – until they give up!

▌ Recognition of the need to balance work and family responsibilities – employees knowing that they are treated as responsible individuals whose family commitments are important to them. This means not developing a culture where becoming a workaholic and risking family breakdown is a key means to promotion. It also means taking a reasonable view on attendance, for instance, at school functions and other family occasions. Organizations seeking to recruit women returners are finding that they have to pay greater heed to the family responsibilities of their men to enable women to feel free to take up employment with adequate partner support. One is mindful of Rosabeth Moss Kanter's paradox – 'succeed, succeed, succeed and raise terrific children' (*When Giants Learn to Dance*, p 21).

▌ Flexibility – a willingness to tailor conditions to the particular needs of individuals. Companies can rapidly develop this when they have to attract staff in great demand, but there may also be benefits to be gained, in terms of commitment and stability, from using the principle in other areas.

DEVELOPING EMPLOYEE BENEFIT STRATEGIES – KEY FACTORS

The key factors to be taken into account in developing employee benefit strategies are that they should:

▌ be an integral part of the total reward management strategy of the organization, which in turn should specifically support the achievement of its business objectives;

▌ add value to basic remuneration and performance-related pay policies by extending the purely financial provisions of these policies into areas where the company will benefit from providing additional rewards and which will support the achievement of employees' specific needs;

- be in line and supportive of the culture of the organization and its value system;
- demonstrate to employees that they are members of a caring and enabling organization which is concerned in highly practical terms with meeting their needs for security, support and other forms of help so that they are able really to give of their best;
- meet the needs of the organization to increase the commitment of its members, to develop their identification with its objectives and to increase unity of purpose;
- meet the real needs of individual employees rather than those needs which management believes they should have;
- help the organization to recruit and retain high-quality and well-motivated staff by being competitive in the market place;
- ensure that benefits are cost effective in the sense that the increase they produce in commitment and improvement in recruitment and retention rates justify their cost;
- take account of relative tax efficiencies in structuring the package;
- establish an appropriate degree of flexibility in operating the benefit package;
- provide a measure of individual choice to employees;
- aim to avoid an over-divisive approach which places employees into clearly defined 'have' and 'have not' categories;
- bear in mind the importance of the non-tangible benefits as well as those which provide extra remuneration or financial assistance;
- be creative – not simply offering what competitors offer but devising new approaches to structuring the package and to providing individual benefits which are tailored to the strategic needs of the organization (like giving secretaries having to cope in poor, if temporary, office conditions, fresh flowers on their desk every week in recognition of their commitment and tolerance of the environment).

RECOGNIZING THE NEED TO REVIEW BENEFITS

The impact and effectiveness of the benefits package should be kept under constant review to identify its impact and effectiveness. The symptoms that might indicate the need for attention include:

- problems in managing the expectations of prospective employees on their benefits package (the 'every other employer I'm talking to provides mobile phones/laptops' syndrome);
- problems in retaining staff because of dissatisfaction with the package (as established at leaving interviews);
- discontent expressed by management on the extent to which the benefits package provides value for money;

- general information on trends in the provision of benefits which indicates that the level of benefits provided by the company is out of line with good practice elsewhere;
- discontent expressed by staff on the scale of benefits provided by the company or the basis upon which they are allocated;
- pressure from staff to be allowed more choice in the benefits they get;
- changes in fiscal law which reduce the tax efficiency of individual benefits;
- problems in administering benefit policies, for example company cars.

MODIFYING THE BENEFITS PACKAGE

The steps required to modify or redesign the benefits package are as follows:

1. Analyse trends in the market place using survey and other data for the provision of benefits, and assess what is regarded as the best practice in each area.
2. Analyse trends in the recruitment and retention of staff to assess, in the light of the market survey, any areas where it is believed that improvements in the benefits package and/or the way it is applied might improve the ability of the organization to attract and retain staff.
3. Assess in discussions with management what it wants the employee benefits, strategies and policies of the organization to achieve and the extent to which the present arrangements satisfy these objectives.
4. Consult employees on their needs (consider using an attitude survey for this purpose).
5. Obtain the views of relevant trade unions or staff associations.
6. Assess the tax implications of current and projected government policies.
7. In the light of these processes of analysis and consultation:
   (a) conduct an overall review of employee benefits strategies under the headings listed above;
   (b) review each of the main policy areas as set out in the key dimensions part of this section;
   (c) decide, on the basis of these reviews, any changes required to strategies and policies and the steps required to get these changes formulated, agreed and introduced.
8. In the light of revised strategies and policies and by reference to the analytical and consultative steps taken earlier (stages 1 to 5):
   (a) subject each benefit to careful scrutiny to determine any changes required to content or application;

(b) examine the costs of each benefit and assess whether it is providing value for money (this involves comparing the cost of providing and administering the benefit with an assessment of the extent to which it is meeting the needs of the company and its employees – clearly low cost to employer/high value to employee items will be the most attractive);

(c) decide if any additional items should be included in the package and assess their likely contributions to meeting organizational and individual needs and their overall cost effectiveness;

(d) decide if any items should be eliminated on cost-effectiveness grounds – but beware of taking away traditional benefits if the timing is poor and the change is the wrong symbolic act;

(e) plan the steps required to make the changes, including the design of the benefit, consultation with staff and methods of communicating information on the changes to all those affected (including tax implications).

9. Introduce the changes, ensuring that the supporting administrative systems are properly installed and that the communication programme takes place as planned.

COMMUNICATING THE BENEFITS PACKAGE

Employee benefits can easily be taken for granted by staff, and it is therefore important to tell them about what they are getting and its value. This can be done in company newsletters or, better still, by means of employee benefits statements which set out in full the scale and cost of the benefits for each individual employee.

TRENDS IN EMPLOYEE BENEFITS POLICY

The Hay Survey of Employee Benefits was first published 30 years ago, in 1974. Since then, the survey has highlighted significant changes in benefits provision in UK organizations, driven by a combination of legislative and environmental changes. For instance:

▮ The rising prevalence of the mobile telephone has seen the proportion of employers offering some form of home telephone rental subsidy dropping from 84 per cent in 1990 to 28 per cent in 2003.

▮ In 1970, 59 per cent of organizations offered a defined benefit pension scheme based on 1/60th of final pay for each year of service. This figure increased to over 90 per cent during the 1980s and 1990s, but is now falling as organizations close defined benefit schemes to new entrants and offer defined contribution schemes instead.

∎ Only 2 per cent of organizations reported offering any form of child-care facilities or contribution to childcare costs in 1990. This has risen to 16 per cent, with childcare vouchers being a popular benefit to include in flexible benefit schemes.

Perhaps the greatest change has been in company car provision. The median level at which status cars are provided has fallen steadily from 800 Hay units in 1974 to just over 500 Hay units in 2003. There is also greater flexibility around the choice of car, as evidenced by the 2003 Hay Benefits Survey, which reported that 67 per cent of status company car drivers can pay to 'trade up' to a more expensive vehicle and 90 per cent can 'trade down', with 52 per cent receiving a cash payment in compensation. In 1994, only 30 per cent of respondents allowed employees to 'trade up', and just 11 per cent offered a cash payment to employees who elected to take a cheaper car. However, not everything changes. New car prices remained static between 2000 and 2003, resulting in little movement in either typical lease prices or car allowances during this time.

The main trends in benefits policy are:

∎ continued simplification of benefit packages;
∎ increased emphasis on individual need and individual choice, particularly evidenced by flexible and voluntary benefit schemes (see also Chapter 32);
∎ more attention paid to communicating the benefits available to employees.

32

Flexible Benefits

'Flexible benefits' is a blanket term for employers giving employees more control over their reward packages without the employer incurring extra cost. In reality, the approaches different employers have taken to flexible benefits have varied considerably, including:

- introducing new 'voluntary' or discounted benefits funded by the employee out of post-tax income or by salary sacrifice;
- varying up or down the level of existing benefits (eg holidays or cars) with a compensating adjustment to cash pay;
- redefining the benefits package in terms of a 'flex fund' to be spent as the employee determines.

The business case (see below) for these flexible approaches is well established, and HR professionals have long advocated greater flexibility in benefits provision. However, the UK has lagged behind the USA in the introduction of plans: until the mid to late 1990s flexible benefits plans remained very much the exception and it has only been in the last few years that they have become widespread.

The recent growth in the prevalence of flexible benefits plans has been driven by the success of some high-profile plans, improvements in administration technology and an increasing focus on the employee as consumer.

The prevalence of such schemes in the private sector may be seen in Table 32.1. The public sector has generally been much slower to embrace flexible benefits. Prevalence also varies by industry sector; for example, most banks operate formal schemes. The proportion of organizations with formal schemes is likely to increase substantially over the next three to five years.

Table 32.1 Prevalance of flexible benefits plans in the private sector

Type of plan	Percentage of organizations
Formal plan	16
Flexibility for certain benefits only	82
Individual flexibility at management discretion	10

Source: Hay Group Benefits Database

This chapter covers:

▌ the business case for flexible benefits;
▌ plan architecture;
▌ flexing existing benefits;
▌ designing and implementing a plan;
▌ practicalities (including tax);
▌ possible barriers – administration and communications;
▌ sources of further information.

THE BUSINESS CASE FOR FLEXIBLE BENEFITS

The main business drivers for flexible benefits are to:

▌ meet the increasingly varied needs of today's diverse workforce;
▌ increase the perceived value of the package by targeting expenditure into areas selected by employees;
▌ aid recruitment and retention (flexible benefits will normally be preferred by employees to fixed benefits of equivalent value);
▌ reinforce culture change – for example, flexible benefits can reduce status divisions between grades or be used to encourage greater personal responsibility among employees;
▌ position the employer as flexible and forward-looking in its approach to managing people;
▌ tie in with a range of other people initiatives designed to make HR processes more flexible, for example: performance-related salary increments; broadbanding, job families, flexible working hours;
▌ provide leverage to the employer's purchasing power to benefit employees and thus secure their loyalty;
▌ highlight the aggregate value of the package;
▌ respond to employee demand;
▌ take advantage of tax/NI advantages for certain benefits (see below).

In the specific situation of a major merger – or for businesses that are, by their nature, acquisitive – flexible benefits can be a relatively inexpensive way of harmonizing terms and conditions.

Flexible benefits can also be used to control costs by providing employees with a fund to spend rather than promising a particular level of benefits (see below). Hence, if the cost of a particular benefit increases, the employee can choose whether to spend the extra on the benefit. Many US employers have used this approach to contain health-care costs.

PLAN ARCHITECTURE

There are various ways that a flexible benefits plan can be set up. Some of these differences are substantive and others are mainly of consequence in terms of communication and/or administration.

Sometimes simple solutions can be the most effective. The key objective is to find a design that meets the business need, is attractive to staff, can be understood by them and that the organization has the resources to operate.

The four main plan architectures are as follows:

▌ individual plans operating independently;
▌ umbrella plan;
▌ flex fund approach;
▌ voluntary ('affinity') benefits.

These are considered in more detail below.

Individual plans operating independently

In this approach, there is a series of individual flexible benefits and the choices in each benefit impact cash earnings (only). For example, a company might operate:

▌ a flexible car scheme with choices made on recruitment/replacement;
▌ a flexible holiday plan with choices made at the beginning of the holiday year; and
▌ a flexible pension plan where contributions can be varied quarterly (say).

This is a simple, pragmatic and common approach, which is easy to introduce and administer. The disadvantage is that the impact may be limited.

Variation around existing entitlement

Under this approach, the benefits offer is still defined in terms of a particular level of entitlement to each benefit (eg 25 days' holiday, a 10 per cent employer pension contribution and a car worth £15,000). However, employees may choose to trade up/down/out from their current entitlements and select new benefits from the menu provided. The value of the benefits bought and sold is then aggregated and the net amount added to or deducted from pay.

A simplified example of how this might look for an employee whose salary is £30,000 per annum is shown in Table 32.2.

Table 32.2 Simple example of variation around existing entitlement

Benefit	Standard entitlement	Selected entitlement	Monthly cost saving (extra cost)
Holidays	25 days	22 days	£35
Car	Lease cost £300 per month	£240 per month	£60
Company pension contribution	10% of salary	10% of salary	nil
Private medical insurance	Cover for self	Cover for self, partner and child	(£45)
Dental insurance	nil	nil	nil
Childcare vouchers	nil	£200 per month	(£200)
Total monthly adjustment			(£150)

In the most simple arrangements, only two or three benefits might be flexible, with flexibility under each benefit being operated fairly independently. In more sophisticated plans, there is a unified approach to communication and to making choices under the plan.

Flex fund approach

In this approach, the employee has a fund of money to 'spend' on benefits. This is sometimes described as the 'cafeteria' approach. The fund might comprise:

▌ total remuneration;
▌ total benefits value;
▌ a specific flex fund related to grade and/or salary;
▌ a percentage of salary or total remuneration.

The flex fund may be presented in terms of points or pounds. Choice will depend on ease of communications, the emphasis of the plan, the overall benefits strategy and the degree of pricing flexibility required.

Generally, certain 'core' compulsory benefits need to be maintained, for example a minimum level of life insurance. Core benefits might be provided independently or be purchased from the flex fund.

It is usually necessary to constitute the flex fund in such a way that, as a minimum, staff can replicate their existing package without additional cost. This is typically achieved by giving a big enough fund to 'buy' the existing benefits.

A simplified example of a flex fund benefits choice menu for someone with a salary of £30,000 with a flex fund of £12,000 is shown in Table 32.3.

Table 32.3 Simple example of variation around existing entitlement

Benefit	Minimum choice	Maximum choice	Price
Holidays	20 days	30 days	0.4% of salary per day
Lease car	£300 per month (£3,600 per annum)	£500 per month (£6,000 per annum)	Annual lease times 1.25 (to allow for insurance and maintenance)
Company pension contribution	5% of salary	25% of salary	Face value less 10%*
Private medical insurance	Cover for self only	Cover for self, partner and children	£500 each per adult: £200 for one or more children
Dental insurance	n/a	Level 3 cover for self, partner and children	£40, £100, £180 per individual for Level 1, 2 or 3 cover respectively
Childcare vouchers	n/a	50% of salary	Face value less 5%

*The adjustment reflects the fact that employer NICs (12.8% for 2004/05) are not payable on these benefits. The adjustment for childcare vouchers is lower to allow for the charge payable to the provider.

The impact of the choices made is shown in Table 32.4. The overspend would be funded by salary sacrifice. Had less than £12,000 been spent, the unspent flex fund would be paid as a monthly, non-consolidated cash sum.

Table 32.4 Example of impact of flex fund choices made (shown in Table 32.3)

Benefit	Choice	Cost
Holidays	25 days	£3,000
Lease care	£350 per month	£5,250
Company pension contribution	10% of salary	£3,000
Private medical insurance	Cover for self and partner	£1,000
Dental insurance	Level 2 cover for self and partner	£200
Childcare vouchers	nil	nil
Total		**£12,450**
Flex fund		£12,000
Over- (under-) spend		£450

Voluntary ('affinity') benefits

Some 'flexible benefits' plans do not introduce flexibility to existing benefits provision. This may be because existing benefits are very limited, are already well targeted or are hard to flex. Instead, employees can be provided with access to a range of new or uprated benefits, which may be available at an advantageous cost to purchase out of their post-tax salary or, in some cases, by salary sacrifice.

The advantages of this approach are that:

▌ leverage is provided by employees to the purchasing power of the employer and/or supplier;
▌ new benefits may be introduced at minimal extra cost;
▌ third-party suppliers can often provide an 'off-the-shelf' solution;
▌ administration will often be relatively easy and may be handled by the third parties;
▌ employees will save time as well as money if the providers are well chosen.

The disadvantages are that this approach may:

▌ not meet employee needs for flexibility in existing benefits;
▌ potentially offer less good deals than are available elsewhere;
▌ offer insufficient employer control where the process is outsourced;
▌ leave the employer exposed if the products offered (especially investment or insurance products) prove to be unsuccessful.

Voluntary benefits may be combined with any of the approaches described above. Popular voluntary benefits include:

- *health:* private medical insurance, dental insurance, health screening, healthcare cash plans, eyecare;
- *protection:* critical illness insurance, life insurance, income protection insurance, personal accident insurance;
- *leisure:* holidays, days out, travel insurance, computer leasing, bicycle leasing, pet insurance, gym membership;
- *financial:* additional pension contributions, season ticket loans, employee share plans;
- *vouchers:* childcare vouchers, retail vouchers;
- *home:* household goods, online shopping.

Some voluntary benefits schemes have more in common with an online shopping portal than traditional employee benefits.

FLEXING EXISTING BENEFITS

Approaches to flexing some of the main traditional benefits, ie cars, holidays, pensions, private medical insurance and insurance benefits, are considered below.

Flexing company cars

Flexible car schemes are extremely common, and offering employee choice is the norm in many sectors. However, some employers operate a flexible car scheme independently of their other flexible benefits because car replacement does not coincide with the flex plan renewal cycle and because most staff are not eligible for a car.

The main types of flexibility that can be introduced are as follows:

- *Trading up.* Employees are able to obtain a more expensive vehicle by making a personal contribution (or by declining other benefits).
- *Trading down.* Employees are able to trade down to a cheaper car and receive additional cash and/or benefits.
- *Trading out.* Employees are able to decline a car and receive cash or other benefits in lieu.
- *Personal leasing.* Employees are given access to a personal contract purchasing (PCP) arrangement. Access may be targeted towards employees who have traded out of the company car arrangement and/or individuals who are not entitled to a company car. (To avoid a lease car becoming taxable as a benefit in kind, arrangements with the leasing company may need to be kept to an arm's length relationship.)

Typically, companies will place limits on the extent of trading up or down. Employees who trade out will normally be required to have a car insured for business purposes, and the employer may impose conditions on its age, specification and maintenance.

A major practical issue concerns what happens when the employee leaves. For example, if he or she has traded up then, to the extent the employer's extra costs have not been fully recouped, these may be deducted from the final salary payment.

Flexible holidays

Offering buying and selling of holidays is relatively straightforward and is a part of many flex plans. Some employers may offer only one choice of buying or selling, reflecting existing entitlements and their business circumstances. For example, in some public sector organizations, where holiday entitlement is already 30–35 days, only trading down is allowed.

There are cost implications to allowing the buying and selling of leave, as follows:

▌ Employees who buy extra time off save payroll costs (including national insurance). However, this needs to be considered in the light of any consequential increase in overtime or temp costs.
▌ Offering holiday selling generates a cash cost in terms of extra pay and employer's NICs. This may be offset by higher productivity and/or lower overtime or temp costs, assuming that employees are currently taking all their leave.
▌ Most employers impose limits on flexibility and many require line manager sign-off. There is normally a lower limit of at least 20 days and an upper limit of 30–35 days.

It is important that flexible holidays dovetail effectively with other HR policies, for example flexitime. Care is also needed to ensure that employees who sell holidays do not abuse the sick pay system.

Flexible pensions – defined contribution

It is relatively easy to flex defined contribution or 'money purchase' plans (including group personal pensions and stakeholder pensions) because the employer contribution is a clearly denominated sum of money. The following approaches are available:

▌ *Trade-up.* The employee has the option to receive a higher employer contribution in lieu of salary or other benefits.
▌ *Trade-down/out.* The employee has the option to sacrifice some or all of the employer contribution and receive cash or other benefits instead.

▌ *Personal pensions and stakeholder pensions.* The employee has the option to have the employer contribution paid into his or her private pension plan.

Employer pension contributions are not subject to employer or employee national insurance contributions. Hence, taking an additional employer contribution in lieu of salary is more NI effective than the employee making additional voluntary contributions (AVCs).

Flexible pensions – final salary

Most organizations choose not to flex final salary pension schemes. This is partly due to pricing complications and partly due to the communications challenge. Pricing is complicated because the cost of final salary pension provision depends on:

▌ individual factors such as age, sex, health and rate of career advancement;
▌ macroeconomic elements such as investment returns, salary inflation, etc;
▌ how long the employee stays with the organization and the reason for leaving.

Notwithstanding the above, a number of organizations have flexed final salary schemes with varying degrees of success. Often a fairly simple approach is taken with a fixed cost being associated with a particular accrual rate. This is easy to explain and is intuitively fair. Nevertheless, this approach will lead to winners and losers and may impact on long-term company costs.

Flexible private medical insurance

Flexibility may be provided by allowing employees to:

▌ sell cover for family members;
▌ sell cover for themselves;
▌ buy cover for themselves (if not already provided);
▌ buy cover for family members (if not already provided).

Many employers do not allow selling of cover for the employee unless he or she is covered under another policy. This reflects: 1) the need for employees to receive prompt treatment and return to work, and 2) a need to restrain flexibility to avoid 'selection' risks and cost increases (see below).

Flexing insurance benefits

When flexing insurance benefits, it is important to recognize that offering flexibility can push up premiums due to 'adverse selection'. Selection is the process whereby people who expect to claim on insurance policies are more likely to take out cover than others. In a traditional group insurance policy where all eligible employees are covered, the risk of selection is quite low; if, however, employees are given a choice of cover, the risk of selection increases.

Selection is a particular problem where there are cross-subsidies. For example, in a healthcare scheme the insurer will consider the demographic make-up of the population and the claims history to date, but for a large population will normally charge premiums on a per-head basis. However, older or less healthy employees are more likely to claim than others and hence for them the policy is arguably more valuable. Consequently, if employees are given a choice over their cover, healthier employees may opt out and older and/or less healthy employees remain in the scheme. This will, over time, drive up costs.

Selection is a potential problem for flexible benefits plans and can apply to all forms of insurance. If an insurer judges the selection risk to be high, it may push up the premiums, impose restrictions on cover or even refuse to cover a scheme. Therefore most flex schemes impose limits on the frequency and extent of choices.

DESIGNING AND IMPLEMENTING A PLAN

Like any other major initiative, the design and implementation of a flexible benefits project needs appropriate and professional project management. Specific points to note include:

▮ the need to liaise with interested third parties such as the pension plan trustees;
▮ realistic deadlines – as a guide, the time to implementation is normally around 9–18 months;
▮ the need for a high-level sponsor;
▮ the need, if possible, to involve staff in the process – this implies skilled facilitation to avoid raising expectations too far.

Depending on the size of the organization and the size, make-up and capability of the HR function, it is often useful to set up one or more flexible benefits working parties. These might include representatives from functions such as finance, IT, payroll, communications, pensions, purchasing and line management as well as trade union or staff association representatives.

Approaches to projects vary between organizations. Although some firms design and implement their own plans with minimal outside assistance, others rely extensively on outside advisers on the basis that the development of flexible benefit plans is a complex process with many financial and tax considerations to be taken into account. Outside advisers might include one or more of the following:

▌ *Consultants:* May offer a start-to-finish service or may specialize in certain areas such as design and communication.
▌ *Benefits providers and brokers:* Some of the largest firms have the capability to offer a start-to-finish service including administration while others may be weak in elements outside their main areas of expertise, for example the link from reward strategy to design. Several offer off-the-shelf voluntary benefits products.
▌ *Administration providers:* Some providers offer a start-to-finish service while others concentrate on administration. Some offer an IT solution only while others offer full outsourcing.
▌ *Tax accountants and lawyers:* May be focused on tax/NI issues or offer a full design service.

An outline work plan for developing a flexible benefits plan is shown in Figure 32.1.

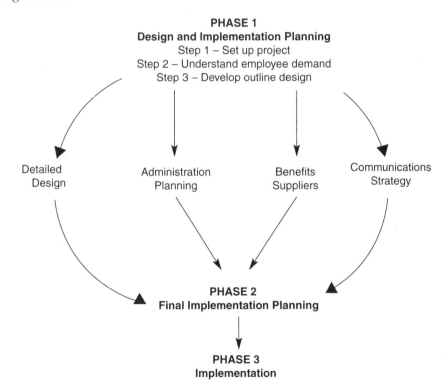

Figure 32.1 A work plan for developing flexible benefits

PRACTICALITIES

Tax and NI Implications

Under some old case law (*Heaton v Bell*, 1969) where there is a cash alternative to a benefit, tax may be payable on the cash amount. The strict, theoretical position is that:

▮ if the employer offers pay and the employee chooses the form in which this is delivered, tax is payable on the cash amount;
▮ if the employer and the employee negotiate package changes, then tax is based on the actual cash and benefits received.

In most flexible benefits plans tax (and if appropriate NI) is payable on the actual cash and benefits received. This is easily achievable, provided the plan is set up correctly.

At one time the opportunities for tax and NI savings through flex plans were material but this is no longer a major input to plan design. At the time of writing, some benefits have income tax and/or NI privileges, including pensions, some forms of childcare assistance and computer leasing.

Employment law

Offering flexible benefits does not suspend the normal implications of employment law. In general, flex does not, of itself, introduce new issues beyond those normally faced in operating pay and benefits programmes. Specific points to note are as follows:

▮ If changes are made to terms and conditions of employment, these must either be an unambiguous improvement or will require the consent of employees.
▮ Under TUPE, any pre-existing rights to flexible benefits are transferred along with other contractual rights.
▮ Where deductions are being made to the earnings of individuals, written consent should be obtained to these deductions.
▮ The employer should reserve the right to make alterations to the flex plan in the future (some changes might be forced by reasons beyond its control).

Pensions

The part pensions can play in a flexible benefits programme was considered earlier in this chapter. However, where the flex plan leads to an individual's cash earnings changing, this can have knock-on pensions implications.

The normal approach taken is to base pensions on notional salaries. In other words, any impact on earnings caused by trading up/down is ignored for pensions purposes. However, this will require careful communications, changes to pension scheme rules and possibly changes to insurance policies.

Similar issues apply to life assurance, permanent health insurance (long-term disability income schemes) and other programmes linked to salary.

POSSIBLE BARRIERS – ADMINISTRATION AND COMMUNICATIONS

By far the biggest concerns for companies planning a flexible benefits plan are administration and communications. These elements were identified as major disadvantages of flexible benefits by 76 per cent and 55 per cent of employers respectively in a recent survey (Employee Benefits/MX Financial Solutions Flexible Benefits research 2003). These issues are considered below.

Administration

It is imperative for the credibility of the flex plan that administration is carried out effectively. However, this is true of all benefits programme administration, and flexible benefits administration is not necessarily more complicated than (for example) pensions administration.

When considering flexible benefits administration, before examining factors such as what software package to use, methods of capturing preferences, etc, it is instructive to think through the fundamentals of what administration is trying to achieve.

The flexible benefits administration system effectively sits in the middle of a process that involves flows of information and money between a number of different parties and systems, as shown in Figure 32.2.

Possible IT approaches include:

▌ a bolt-on to existing payroll, benefits or HR software;
▌ an off-the-shelf package from a software supplier or consultancy – in reality some tailoring will be built in to the system;
▌ a newly written system from an external supplier;
▌ an approach developed in-house – this is most likely to be relevant for employers whose organizational competence is in this area, for example firms in the IT or banking sectors;
▌ a spreadsheet or database using proprietary software – this can be effective for a simple plan or a small population.

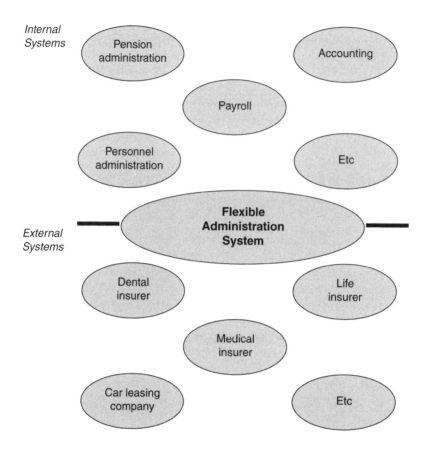

Figure 32.2   A flexible benefits administration system

There are consultancy and software firms that will provide an outsourced approach to administration. This can be an effective approach and costs have been reducing recently.

Communications

A communication strategy is a vital component to the successful implementation of a flex plan. A clear communications strategy should be developed as the design is clarified covering the types of message, timing and media. The main stages of communications are as follows:

▌ *Consultation.* Any staff consultation undertaken as part of the design work can be a useful way of highlighting that a plan is coming, providing expectations are managed appropriately.

▌ *Building awareness.* The idea here is to let staff know a plan is coming, familiarize them with the idea of flexibility and build a brand for the flex plan.

▌ *Principal initial communication.* The purpose here is firmly to embed in participants' minds that they will have the opportunity to participate in the plan. They should be given an outline of plan basics such as which benefits are covered and how to make choices. Approaches might include: workshops/road shows; a video; e-mail/intranet; briefings via line managers or a large conference.

▌ *Back-up materials.* These materials are the reference sources that participants will use to understand the plan details. There is a need to balance readability and comprehensiveness, and the balance between these elements may be influenced by the extent to which 'live' approaches to questions are available (see below). These materials may be delivered in the form of a booklet or online.

▌ *Dealing with queries.* Methods here will be very dependent on the size of the plan, and possible approaches will include: an internal or outsourced telephone or e-mail help line; group meetings (eg at lunchtime); one-to-one clinics; or appointing a local 'expert' for each department or site.

▌ *Reminders.* Reminders may be issued to coincide with the renewal or regularly throughout the year.

SOURCES OF FURTHER INFORMATION

▌ IDS Studies Plus – Flexible Benefits (Summer 2001 and Autumn 2003). These useful publications include background information on designing and implementing a plan and a number of very detailed case studies.

▌ *Employee Benefits Magazine* (Centaur Communications Limited). This magazine is published monthly and includes a useful range of articles on benefits issues, including flexible benefits. It publishes an annual survey on flexible benefits.

33

Pension Schemes

INTRODUCTION

Pensions have always been a significant and valuable part of the remuneration package. However, the technical complexity of pensions provision and the slow rate of change meant that, historically, HR and reward professionals often had little involvement in pensions issues.

Over the last 10 years or so, there has been an explosion of activity in the pensions field. As a result, pensions have moved up the agenda both in the boardroom and in HR. Over this period the majority of private sector organizations have reviewed their pensions provision and many have made significant changes.

In this chapter consideration is given to:

- pension scheme design – including the major changes that have occurred in recent years;
- pension scheme governance;
- pensions and change – for example, purchase/sale situations;
- executive pensions; and
- the future – ie the key pensions policy questions that will be addressed over the next few years.

PENSION SCHEME DESIGN

Why provide pensions?

Historically, leading employers in the UK and elsewhere have provided pension arrangements for the following reasons:

1. There is a perceived moral obligation to provide a reasonable standard of post-retirement living for employees, especially those with long service. A similar logic extends to providing pensions for dependants on a current or retired employee's death. This obligation is less apparent in countries where state pension provision is at a higher level than in the UK.
2. A good pension scheme demonstrates that the employer has the long-term interest of employees at heart.
3. A good scheme may help to retain and attract high-quality staff.
4. Pensions can be a tax-efficient form of remuneration. This was a particularly significant issue in the past when personal rates of income tax were higher than now and when other tax-efficient vehicles (eg ISAs or offsetting mortgages) were not widely available.

However, in recent years many employers have questioned the level and volatility of pensions cost and this has caused them to review scheme designs.

Main scheme types

The two main approaches that have been adopted for pension provision in the UK are described below. Recently, some employers have begun to adopt other designs and these are discussed further later in this chapter.

▮ *Defined benefit (final salary) schemes.* The employer's pension promise to the employee is expressed by means of a formula specified in the scheme rules. The pension is typically proportional to service and (some definition of) salary. Traditionally, the salary used has been that paid over the last year (or sometimes three years) before retirement, which is why they are often known as 'final salary' schemes. A typical design is shown in the section 'Final salary scheme design' below.
▮ *Defined contribution (money purchase) schemes.* Here the employer's pension promise to the employee is expressed as a contribution formula, typically expressed as a percentage of salary. The contributions are invested and the money used at retirement to purchase a regular income, usually via an annuity contract from an insurance company. The employer's contribution as a percentage of salary may be fixed, age related or linked to what the employee pays – see below.

In both types of scheme, employer and employee typically contribute to a fund. In a defined contribution scheme, members have individual shares of the fund, which represent their personal entitlements and which will directly determine the pensions they receive. In a defined benefit scheme, all employee and employer contributions are paid into a combined fund and there is no direct link between fund size and the pensions paid.

Apportioning risk

Pension provision is an extremely long-term and unpredictable business. Consider a female employee currently aged 25. It is not possible to predict the future trajectory of her salary, how long she will stay in employment, her age of retirement, how long she will live after retirement and whether she will have a partner or other dependant(s) when she dies.

Because of these uncertainties, there are risks attaching to pensions provision for the employer and/or the employee. The apportionment of this risk varies considerably, depending on the type of pension scheme provided.

Final salary risks

Because the pension is based on a guaranteed formula, there is a risk that the cost of providing this guaranteed benefit will be higher than expected. Typically employee contributions are fixed and those of the employer vary based on specialist advice from the scheme actuary. Hence, the risk of higher-than-expected costs falls on the employer. Costs might exceed expectation if, for example:

▌ salaries grow faster than expected;
▌ longevity increases;
▌ the fund investments perform less well than expected.

Defined contribution risks

Under a defined contribution scheme, the cost of employer contributions is predictable but there is a risk that the resulting pension falls short of expectations. This risk normally falls on the employee. For example, the pension may not meet expectations if:

▌ the fund investments perform poorly, either in the long term or in the period immediately preceding retirement;
▌ the annuity rate (ie the conversion rate from lump sum to regular pension) is unfavourable – for example, because interest rates are low.

From the above discussion, it can be seen that there is a huge philosophical difference between final salary (guaranteed pension, variable cost) and defined contribution (uncertain pension, fixed cost).

Typical provision in the UK

The design of final salary schemes, the reasons behind the recent widespread move to defined contribution schemes, and the design of such schemes and some of the new hybrid designs emerging, are discussed below. More detailed design elements such as member contributions, contracting out, protection benefits and leaving-service benefits are then examined.

Final salary scheme design

The final salary pension scheme has been the mainstay of occupation pensions in the UK for many years. Until around the earliest years of the 21st century, designs were relatively standardized, as in the following examples of typical private sector and public sector final salary schemes:

▌ *Typical private sector final salary scheme:*
  - a pension of 1/60th of final-year basic salary per year of service;
  - payable from age 60 or 65;
  - pension in payment guaranteed to increase in line with inflation (up to 5 per cent per annum);
  - part of pension may be exchanged for a tax-free lump sum;
  - fixed employee contribution of 0 to 5 per cent of salary.
▌ *Typical public sector final salary scheme:*
  - pension of 1/80th of final-year basic salary per year of service, plus lump sum of 3/80th of basic salary per year of service;
  - pension in payment guaranteed to increase in line with inflation;
  - fixed employee contribution of 1.5 per cent to 6 per cent of salary.

The protection benefits payable on death or in the case of serious ill health are considered below.

Because final salary schemes provide a high level of certainty for the participant (provided the scheme is adequately funded), they tend to be favoured by employees and unions. In addition, because of modest employer contribution rates, many defined contribution schemes are expected to produce lower pensions for most members than a typical final salary scheme, although defined contribution schemes may be better for younger, mobile employees.

The move towards defined contribution schemes

As discussed above, cost fluctuations under final salary schemes are typically the employer's responsibility. The scheme actuary compares the scheme's assets with the estimated fund required to underpin the benefits earned to date. The actuary also calculates the estimated cost of the future benefits being earned (normally expressed as a percentage of payroll).

In the recent past, schemes often had surplus assets that could be used to fund the cost of the benefits being earned. Many employers could therefore suspend contributions for several years (a 'contribution holiday').

More recently, many schemes have moved into a funding deficit, whereby the scheme's assets are less than the estimated fund required to underpin the benefits earned to date. These deficits have resulted from stock market falls, increased longevity and changes in the way these assessments are carried out. As a result, employer contribution rates have risen sharply as employers have needed to make up the deficit in addition to paying the cost of the benefits being earned. As well as being painful in its own right this contribution increase has highlighted the potential cost volatility of this type of scheme.

In itself, a funding deficit might not be enough to provoke an employer to review of pension provision. However, there have been other financial change drivers including:

▌ a new accounting standard, FRS17, which sharpened the focus on pension scheme funding just as many schemes moved into deficit;
▌ moves by the Thatcher and Major governments (and some individual schemes) to guarantee benefits that were previously discretionary (eg pension increases), thereby removing a possible cost-saving safety valve;
▌ the abolition by the Chancellor of the Exchequer (Gordon Brown) of advanced corporation tax relief on equity dividends for pension schemes.

As a result of the cost increases, many leading companies have questioned the financial wisdom of final salary provision. Other factors in this trend have been as follows:

▌ Final salary schemes provide much more value to older and longer-serving employees. However, greater labour mobility has led many employers to question this emphasis, particularly in newer industries with young, high-turnover workforces.
▌ The increasing use of flexible benefits. Because defined contribution schemes involve a personal fund there is no cross-subsidy; they are therefore easier to incorporate into a flexible benefits plan.
▌ A 'snowball' effect, with the increasing popularity of defined contribution schemes encouraging other employers to review provision.
▌ Employees have often underestimated the employer's pension costs in final salary schemes.

All of these factors have led to many private sector employers closing their final salary schemes to new entrants and setting up defined contribution schemes with more predictable costs. This trend has been particularly pronounced in labour-intensive sectors.

The public sector has so far mostly retained its final salary schemes. This reflects:

▌ the need to offer a competitive remuneration package in an environment where many private sector reward tools are practically or politically undeliverable (eg large bonuses, share schemes, private healthcare and generous car policies);
▌ strong union support for final salary schemes;
▌ a lack of political will to tackle a complex and long-term issue – in particular, because many such schemes pay pensions from government revenue rather than from a fund, cost increases are not felt for many years;
▌ lower turnover in some parts of the public sector.

Defined contribution scheme design

There is a very wide variety of defined contribution design models available, as follows:

▌ Employer contribution is a fixed percentage of salary. For example, the employer pays 8 per cent of salary for all members. This is easy to understand and explain.
▌ Employer contribution is a percentage of salary that increases with age (or service). For example, the employer pays 6 per cent of salary for all members, increasing to 9 per cent at age 40 and 12 per cent at age 50. This design partly mirrors the way final salary schemes work and may be targeted to deliver a benefit equal to a certain percentage of final or average salary.
▌ Employer contribution is a multiple of that paid by the employee. For example, the employer will pay double what the employee contributes up to a maximum employer contribution of 10 per cent of salary. This design ensures that employer spend is targeted on those who most value it.

All three approaches are fairly common, and are often used in combination. For example, the employer may pay a fixed contribution of 3 per cent of salary and then match what the employee pays up to 5 per cent of salary. Hence, the maximum employer contribution is 8 per cent of salary.

There is also considerable variation in the maximum available employer contribution rates. Typically, for staff and middle managers these range from 3 per cent to 15 per cent with a median of around 8 per cent (source: Hay Group Survey of Employee Benefits 2003).

It is evident that the lower levels of contribution are highly unlikely to deliver an adequate retirement income unless the employee makes substantial contributions and/or has other forms of saving. For example, a pension contribution of 3 per cent of salary made from age 20 to age 60 might be expected, using conservative assumptions, to provide a pension of only around 10 per cent of final salary.

At retirement, the employee may take up to a quarter of the fund as a tax-free lump sum. The remainder of the accumulated fund is used to purchase a regular pension ('annuity') from an insurance company. The member typically determines the form of annuity chosen, subject to some government-imposed restrictions. The decisions required include:

▮ the rate at which the annuity should increase in payment;
▮ the benefits payable to a surviving partner on death;
▮ whether the annuity should be guaranteed or on an investment-linked basis (for example, a 'with profits' annuity).

There is also the option not to take an annuity initially and instead 'draw down' an income from the pension account. (This approach is used mainly by more financially sophisticated members and/or those with larger individual funds.)

Hybrid schemes

The major philosophical difference between a defined benefit (final salary) scheme and a defined contribution (money purchase) was mentioned earlier. Moving from final salary to defined contribution provision shifts all of the risk from the employer to the employees.

For this reason, many commentators now advocate 'hybrid schemes' that seek to split the risk between both parties. Some employers have started to adopt such designs, and examples include the following:

▮ *Career revalued average salary scheme.* This is a type of defined benefit scheme. Instead of pension being based on final salary, the employee receives a pension proportional to service and career average salary, with salary from earlier years revalued by RPI (say).
▮ *Combined final salary/defined contribution scheme.* Under this approach, both types of scheme are in operation. A final salary scheme might be provided for staff who meet an age and/or service qualification, with defined contribution provision applying to other staff. For example, membership of the final salary scheme might be limited to staff aged 40 or more, with no backdating of service; pension in respect of previous service would be provided on a defined contribution basis.
▮ *Cash balance scheme.* Employees are provided with a guaranteed individual retirement fund proportional to service and final or average salary. As in a defined contribution scheme, a proportion may be taken as cash with the balance being used to buy an annuity.
▮ *Schemes with an element of discretion.* Low-level guaranteed benefits are provided, perhaps on a final salary or career average basis.

However, there is discretion to provide enhanced pensions as and when the scheme's funding position allows it. A variant of this approach is to operate a defined contribution scheme with a modest final salary (or career average salary) guarantee.

█ *Capped final salary.* A self-imposed cap is applied to pensionable salary with defined contribution provision on the excess salary. The logic here is that it is reasonable to transfer some risk to the employee once a basic level of guaranteed retirement income has been built up.

█ *Reduced cost final salary.* This is not strictly a hybrid scheme, but has been adopted in a number of companies. This approach involves retaining final salary provision but with some benefits scaled back to restrain costs. For example, some have reduced the accrual rate from 1/60th per year of service to 1/80th or, more commonly, have increased employee contributions. Often employees and unions prefer this to a move towards defined contribution provision.

Member contributions

With the exception of employers in the financial services sector, the norm for final salary schemes has always been to require member contributions. Some formerly non-contributory schemes have recently introduced member contributions on the grounds of affordability. A majority of defined contribution and hybrid schemes also have member contributions. The arguments for and against member contributions are summarized in Table 33.1.

Table 33.1 Arguments for and against member contributions

Arguments in favour of requiring member contributions	Arguments against requiring member contributions
● Reduces cost to employer of a particular level of pension provision. ● Targets employer pension spend on employees who will appreciate it. ● Reduces employee take-up and hence total cost. ● Can increase employee engagement. ● Aligned with market practice. ● In contracted-out (see 'Contracting out') final salary schemes, the employee is benefiting from reduced NI contributions – allowing for this and tax relief means that the net impact on take-home pay can be very small.	● Easy-to-explain competitive advantage. ● Employer contributions are more NI effective than employee contributions – some employers are moving towards replacing employee contributions with employer contributions funded through salary sacrifice. ● Non-contributory scheme likely to have 100% take-up, thus ensuring employees have adequate retirement provision.

Pension schemes have, for a long time, offered the opportunity for the member to top up pension by making additional voluntary contributions ('AVCs'), which normally work in a similar way to defined contribution schemes with the member having an individual fund.

The regime for employees to top up their pensions has become increasingly liberal, and the level of freedom is set to increase further from April 2006.

Contracting out

For many years, the government has allowed contracting out from the second-tier state pension – S2P (formerly SERPS). Under contracting out, benefits are provided by a private pension scheme in lieu of the state benefit. As a general rule, this works as follows:

▌ *Final salary schemes.* Both employer and employee pay reduced NI contributions subject to the pension scheme providing a minimum level of benefits.
▌ *Group personal pensions and stakeholder schemes* (see below). If the employee elects to contract out, a portion of the NI contributions is rebated into his or her pension account.

Protection benefits

The main protection benefits in final salary schemes normally include:

▌ pensions to partners and/or dependent children on death in service or following retirement;
▌ a lump sum (often four times salary) on death in service;
▌ a pension on premature retirement due to ill health.

In a defined contribution scheme, the benefits available are similar, but may be provided differently, for example:

▌ lump sum benefit on death in service of up to four times salary;
▌ dependant's pension on death in service purchased with accumulated fund and/or provided through insurance policy;
▌ the benefits (if any) on death after retirement are selected by the individual when an annuity is purchased;
▌ ill-health benefits are typically provided by means of a 'permanent heath insurance' policy, which pays an income of 50–75 per cent of salary for employees on long-term sick leave (some final salary schemes also take this approach).

Leaving service

When an employee leaves an employer (or withdraws from the pension scheme), the normal entitlement is to:

▌ *final salary* – subject to two years' service, a deferred pension based on salary at and service to date of leaving and payable from retirement date: the link to final salary is lost, but the pension must be revalued to retirement in line with inflation (or 5 per cent per annum compound, if less);
▌ *defined contribution* – the fund built up to date: this will continue to accrue investment returns up to retirement.

In both cases, the employee may also request that the value of the pension be transferred to a new employer's scheme or an individual pension contract.

In the public sector, employees can often change employer with little change to their accrued pension.

PENSION SCHEME GOVERNANCE

The governance of pension schemes is extremely (and increasingly) complex. In this section we give a brief introduction to how pension schemes are governed, the tax regime, legislation/regulation and the various parties involved.

How pension schemes are established

The two main ways of establishing tax-approved pension schemes in the UK are under trust and under contract.

Trust-based schemes

Historically, most UK occupational pension schemes have been set up via trusts. Trusts are, in some ways, quite anachronistic, and the law governing them is mostly older case law. They are also notoriously difficult to define; however, one possible definition is that 'a trust is an equitable obligation binding a person (who is called a trustee) to deal with property over which he has control (which is called the trust property) for the benefit of persons (who are called the beneficiaries) of whom he may himself be one and any of whom may enforce the obligation' (Hewitt Bacon and Woodrow Pocket Book 2004, NTC).

However, trust law has, with a few exceptions, functioned well for many years. The reasons for using a trust are:

▌ to ensure tax approval by the Inland Revenue;
▌ to keep the scheme assets separate from those of the employer, thereby providing security;
▌ to provide legal rights to beneficiaries who are not and have not been employees, such as partners and dependants.

Trust-based schemes are governed by a scheme trust deed and rules detailing benefit entitlements and the rights and responsibilities of the members, the sponsoring employer(s) and the trustees. It will also govern what is permissible under the scheme, including any powers of amendment.

Trustees may be individuals and/or the directors of a trustee company. They may or may not be members of the plan. A proportion must be member nominated and elected, with others typically nominated by the employer. Over the years, the importance role of the trustees has been emphasized at the expense of the sponsoring employer(s). For example, the trustees are now primarily responsible for investment strategy and appointing advisers.

The trust deed and rules and the trustees are an important consideration when considering change – there have been cases of employers taking strategic decisions on pensions that could not be delivered under the scheme rules or else required consent from the trustees.

Contract-based schemes

Approved defined benefit schemes (at least in the private sector) are invariably set up as trusts. However, defined contribution schemes may be set up as trusts ('occupational money purchase schemes') or on the basis of a contract with an external provider, such as an insurance company. These contract-based schemes include group personal pension schemes, stakeholder schemes and retirement annuity contracts (now largely superseded).

Stakeholder schemes are a new, highly regulated, form of defined contribution schemes with very low provider charges. All employers with five or more employees must offer a stakeholder scheme unless they have another scheme with wide employee access and that meets certain criteria. There is no obligation on employers to contribute to a stakeholder arrangement.

The pensions tax regime

In simple terms, the tax regime for approved UK pension schemes is as follows:

▌ Employee contributions attract income tax relief.
▌ Employer contributions are deductible for corporation tax purposes.

- Employer contributions are not taxable as a benefit-in-kind.
- Employer contributions are not subject to employer or employee NICs.
- Income and capital gains on scheme investments are not subject to tax (although schemes can no longer reclaim advanced corporation tax on equity dividends).
- Pensions in payment (including those paid to dependants) are taxed as earned income and do not attract NICs.
- A proportion of the pension may be taken in the form of a tax-free lump sum at retirement.
- A tax-free lump sum may be paid to dependants on death in service.

Because of these tax privileges, there are restrictions on what may be provided from a tax-approved scheme. These are discussed below (see 'Executive pensions').

Pension scheme regulation

The UK pensions field has to operate within a bewildering framework of legislation, regulation and case law. The complexity partly reflects the fact that pension schemes have to deal not just with pension law but with trust law, employment law, tax and social security laws, financial services law and EU law. It also reflects frequent government-imposed changes, which may or may not be retrospective.

It should also be noted that the interaction between regulation and the pension scheme's own governing documents can be complex.

Interested parties

One of the many complications of pension provision is the sheer variety of interested parties. In a final salary scheme, these will typically include most of the following:

- the employee;
- the employee's dependants;
- the sponsoring employer(s);
- the employer's pensions manager;
- the trustees;
- the actuary (who gives advice on funding);
- consultants who may give advice on design, communication, etc;
- administrators (may be in-house or third party);
- lawyers (responsible for drafting the scheme rules and other advice, as required);
- the scheme auditors;
- the investment manager(s);

▌ investment consultants (giving advice on which managers to select);
▌ the Inland Revenue;
▌ the Occupational Pension Regulatory Authority (OPRA);
▌ the Pensions Ombudsman.

Some of the above roles may be combined. For example, a firm of consulting actuaries may provide actuarial, consultancy, administration, legal and investment consultancy advice.

PENSIONS AND CHANGE

Purchase/sale and transfer of undertakings

When businesses are bought and sold, this raises pensions issues. If a company with its own pension scheme is purchased as a whole, then the pension scheme including its assets and accrued liabilities will effectively be acquired along with the company. The acquirer will then need to consider whether it wishes to amend the scheme going forward, in much the same way that it will consider changes to other aspects of reward. It should be noted that in some transactions the funding position of the pension scheme could be a factor in determining the price paid.

If only some employees from a scheme are part of the transaction (for example, because a division or site is being sold), then the situation is different. In law, the vendor's only obligation is to provide leaving-service benefits. However, in practice, for the transaction to be successful, it will be necessary to secure the goodwill of the transferring staff. In this case, a 'bulk transfer' will occur and the terms (ie the monies transferred and the benefits provided) will be a matter of negotiation.

In situations where public sector staff are transferred to the private sector, for example as part of an outsourcing process, there are detailed regulations about what must be provided by the new private sector employer.

The government's 2004 Pensions Bill proposes certain future service pensions obligations on a new employer when a TUPE-protected transfer of undertakings takes place.

Closing a final salary scheme

When an employer moves away from final salary provision, it has a number of options regarding the final salary scheme, as follows:

▌ Close the scheme to new entrants only, with existing members continuing to earn benefits as their service increases. This is the most common method, but it takes a considerable time for the employer's financial exposure to be materially reduced.

▮ The scheme stops benefit accrual: members receive a pension based on accrual to date of closure and salary at retirement; hence there still remains the potential liability arising from unknown future salary increases.

▮ The scheme stops benefit accrual with all employees being provided with discontinuance (typically leaving-service) benefits – normally these are based on accrual to and salary at closure with revaluation to retirement in line with inflation (or 5 per cent per annum compound, if less).

EXECUTIVE PENSIONS

The design of executive final salary schemes

Historically, most executive pensions in larger companies have been provided on a final salary basis. However, today, around a quarter of FTSE 100 provide their chief executives with defined contribution pensions.

In the private sector, final salary executive pensions have tended to involve accelerated accrual compared to that for other staff. Instead of providing a maximum two-thirds pension after 40 years of service (an accrual rate of 1/60th per year of service), a full pension is normally subject to just 20 or 30 years' service (equivalent to an accrual rate of 1/30th or 1/45th). The two-thirds pension provided is normally inclusive of any pensions from previous employments.

The theory behind accelerated accrual is that executives typically experience rapid salary growth throughout their careers and hence any job change would otherwise constrain their pensions expectations (expressed as a percentage of final salary). This issue is less of a problem in the public sector where the final salary link is often retained when transferring employment.

Recently, commentators have started to question the need to provide executives with a guaranteed pension of two-thirds of final salary because:

▮ the final salary may be a short-term peak earned for just a few years;
▮ since most executive pension schemes were set up, executive salaries have risen significantly in real terms, income tax rates have fallen and incentive opportunities have multiplied: hence executives now have more opportunities to save in other ways;
▮ the cost of this type of provision can be very high indeed.

For these reasons and to limit the tax concessions available, successive governments have limited the amount of pension that may be delivered through tax-approved pension schemes.

Limits on pension provision

Traditionally, the pensions available from occupational schemes have been subject to complex limits on the benefits payable, proportional to service and earnings. For personal pensions, stakeholder schemes and some other defined contribution schemes, age-related limits on contributions have applied instead.

In 1989, the earnings cap was introduced. This applied to individuals joining tax-approved pension schemes after 1 June 1989. The cap limited the salary that could be taken into account for pension purposes to £60,000. This figure was indexed to RPI (only) and stands at £102,000 for tax year 2004/05. The earnings cap did not have a profound impact on the level of pension provided to executives, with most large private sector firms providing compensation in the form of one or more of the following ways:

▌ funded unapproved pension schemes (FURBS) – a funded pension scheme that lacks most of the tax privileges of an approved scheme;
▌ unfunded unapproved pension promises (UURBS) – effectively a promise from the employer to pay a particular level of pension;
▌ cash allowances.

From 2006, the government will replace the cap with a 'lifetime limit' on tax-effective pension savings of £1,500,000 (equivalent to a retirement pension of £75,000 per annum). Unlike the earnings cap, this limit applies to everyone, but any existing accrued benefits above this figure will be protected.

There will also be a limit on the pension earned in any year of £215,000. Both the lifetime and annual limits will increase annually.

In future, where pensions exceed the lifetime limit, companies will be able to offer FURBS, UURBS or cash (as above). A further (new) option will be to provide a bigger pension in the tax-approved scheme but to pay a tax 'recovery charge' of 25 per cent on the excess funds: this levy is in addition to income tax, giving a composite rate of 55 per cent.

The future of executive pensions

Executive final salary schemes have been very expensive to provide, particularly on an unapproved basis. Many investors and remuneration committees would now prefer a more modest, fixed-cost approach to be adopted. This might involve a pension allowance of perhaps 20–50 per cent of salary payable in cash or to a pension vehicle selected by the executive. There are signs of this happening, but the executive final salary scheme is unlikely to die completely for some decades.

THE FUTURE

Looking at the medium-term future of UK occupational pension provision, a number of key questions arise, as considered in the following sections.

Does the final salary scheme have a future?

It remains to be seen whether the final salary occupational scheme has a long-term future. Its obituary has been written many times before. However, this time there is significant evidence of a move away, with more than 50 per cent of such schemes now closed to new entrants.

Where final salary provision is surviving in the private sector, one or more of the following factors may apply:

▌ The scheme is still in surplus.
▌ Providing a guaranteed, final salary pension is a component of a very caring and paternalistic people strategy.
▌ The employer has deep pockets and/or people costs are low compare to turnover.
▌ The scheme has been modified to reduce employer cost.

Will the public sector move towards defined contribution schemes?

Given the huge (and rising) costs of its current schemes, this is a possibility. However, doing so would remove a significant retention lever and would cause major industrial relations problems. Any such change would probably imply a need to increase other elements of pay.

Will defined contribution schemes provide adequate retirement incomes?

There is a significant risk that many defined contribution schemes will fail to deliver the standard of retirement living expected by their members. A previous generation of defined contribution schemes failed for just this reason.

Tackling this issue implies increasing employer contributions and/or providing education to employees to allow them to increase their own saving. For example, some employers pay for financial advice or offer online pension modelling through the company intranet.

There are also strong arguments for considering some of the hybrid design options outlined above. These generally involve providing at least some pension guarantees to employees, but should avoid the degree of cost fluctuation associated with traditional final salary schemes.

Can two-tier pensions be sustained in one employer?

Where an employer has scaled back pension for new employees, this creates inequalities with longer-serving staff. Some commentators have suggested a compensating increase to another part of the package. However, unless this is as part of a flexible benefits scheme, such an approach can fall foul of equal pay legislation, where comparisons are made for each element of pay separately.

Another factor to consider here is that staff in the final salary scheme, particularly any who are nearing retirement, will be unlikely to leave. This is especially true if alternative employers have also moved to defined contribution provision.

Can pensions be communicated effectively?

A key and long-standing problem in the pensions field is communications. The difficulties arise because:

▌ pensions are intrinsically complicated;
▌ retirement feels a long way off to many people;
▌ there can be a tension between effective design and ease of communication – for example, providing employees with choice may be desirable, but requires clear communication;
▌ some of the language used around pensions is not always helpful to the layperson;
▌ pension scandals have reduced employee confidence.

This is a field where HR, marketing and communications professionals can add value. Sadly, many pensions booklets and annual benefits statements are virtually indecipherable for most employees. In addition, communications are often very dependent on the written word.

To ensure employee engagement, pensions communications should:

▌ give a clear, easily assimilated overview of the main scheme provisions;
▌ allow employees to understand the likely level of pension payable;
▌ encourage additional saving, where appropriate;
▌ highlight where advice and clarification are available from;
▌ in final salary schemes, identify how much the employer is spending on the employee's behalf.

A variety of media should be used, perhaps involving booklets, annual statements, frequently asked question sheets, workshops and interactive pension-modelling tools. Written materials should be tested on non-experts to ensure readability.

Issues and opportunities arising from tax simplification

The government's tax simplification proposals (see above, 'Executive pensions') and other changes have created some challenges and opportunities for people management looking forward, as follows:

▌ Many of the restrictions on scheme design that currently exist will fall away. This should allow some more creative designs to emerge.
▌ It will become possible to draw a pension while still working for the same employer. This will allow a phased approach to retirement that may suit some employees and employers.
▌ Compulsory retirement on the grounds of age will disappear. This will probably mean more active performance management and a more creative approach to career management for older workers.
▌ The minimum retirement age (other than on grounds of ill health) will increase from 50 to 55. Schemes will be given discretion on how to achieve this.
▌ Employers may wish to help employees to make the best of the very liberal regulations for making extra voluntary contributions.

Are final salary schemes well enough funded?

The security of final salary pensions in a closed scheme is a complicated question well beyond the scope of this book. However, the latest government proposals are set to:

▌ considerably bolster the level of financial obligation on solvent employers in respect of closed schemes;
▌ introduce a levy-based scheme to fund a minimum level of benefits from under-funded schemes where the sponsoring employer is insolvent.

CONCLUSIONS

As noted at the beginning of the chapter, pensions are now changing very quickly. It is to be hoped that companies will be inspired to find solutions that balance the requirement for financial affordability and predictability with a desire to provide employees with a decent standard of retirement living.

Of course, there is no reason why an employer needs to provide a pension at all, let alone a 'gold-plated' arrangement. However, it is crucial to the employer brand that the pension benefits provided are part of a coherent overall remuneration package and are communicated clearly and realistically. This implies that, if pension provision is modest, employees should have the opportunity to provide for themselves, perhaps by means of employer-funded access to financial planning advice and from above-market salaries.

34

Tax Considerations

WHY DO TAX CONSIDERATIONS MATTER?

Tax efficiency

Given the global environment in which many companies now operate, the value and importance attached to remuneration packages and often their cost have increased over the past few years. Companies have often found that, in order to get the best people, they need to offer competitive and sophisticated packages, particularly for senior positions.

In devising these packages it is useful to ensure that they are designed in the most tax-efficient way possible. This benefits both the company, as costs associated with providing the reward or benefit element may be reduced, and the employee, who has the opportunity to receive enhanced benefits. However, legislative changes can mean that the life-span of any tax-efficient scheme may be limited. This is an important factor to bear in mind when designing compensation arrangements based on tax efficiency.

Tax-efficient reward elements and benefits can be described as those for which the tax payable on the provision of the benefit is less than the tax that would be payable by the employer and employee on the equivalent cash sum. The UK government has consistently tightened up the rules on the provision of tax-efficient benefits since the 1980s and as a result they have become less prolific. The tax breaks associated with company cars, for example, have significantly diminished in recent years.

Generally, the announcements made in the Budget each year lead to the publication of the Finance Act and ultimately to new tax legislation being published. In 2003, there was a comprehensive rewrite of the tax legislation on income tax on earnings and pensions. This resulted in the publication of the Income Tax (Earnings and Pensions) Act 2003.

The Inland Revenue may also announce changes during the course of the tax year, confirming their interpretation of the tax legislation. Furthermore, the judgments made in tax cases are also relevant in determining the interpretation of tax law. The interpretation of the tax legislation in these cases normally takes effect immediately.

In this environment of frequent change it is important that advice is sought on tax issues from a tax specialist and/or the Inland Revenue prior to the introduction of, or change to, any benefits that might be affected. Furthermore, it is advisable to review benefits after each Budget to assess the implications of any tax changes.

In addition to income tax, benefits are also liable to employer's National Insurance contributions. Class 1A National Insurance contributions are payable on the provision of most benefits, at a level of currently (2004) 12.8 per cent.

THE BASICS OF TAX LAW

In general, employees used to be taxed under Schedule E set out in the Income and Corporation Taxes Act 1988. In 2003, a new Act was introduced, the Income Tax (Earnings and Pensions) Act (ITEPA) 2003. This Act primarily restates the elements of income tax legislation relating to employment income, pension income and social security income. Income from sources other than employment will continue to be taxed under the various schedules set out in the Income and Corporation Taxes Act 1988.

Income tax was introduced in the UK as a temporary measure to finance the war against Napoleon, and to this day it remains a temporary tax that must be re-enacted each year or lapse. The schedular system of tax in the UK has its roots in the earliest days of income tax when it was necessary to allocate each specific source of income received to a particular schedule; rental income from land is assessed under Schedule A, income from woodlands was assessed under Schedule B and income from government securities under Schedule C. As mentioned above, employment income was taxed under Schedule E; however, it is now taxable under ITEPA 2003.

Under ITEPA 2003, tax is charged on 'employment income'. Employment income is split into 'general earnings' and 'specific employment income'. The term 'specific employment income' includes amounts that count as employment income and in particular refer to payments made to and benefits received from a pension scheme, payments and benefits on termination of employment and share-related income.

The term 'emoluments' has generally been replaced by the term 'earnings', which is defined by section 62 ITEPA 2003. This defines earnings in connection with an employment as:

- any salary, wages or fees;
- any gratuity or other profit or incidental benefit of any kind obtained by the employee for money or money's worth;
- anything else that constitutes an emolument of the employment.

To a great extent, the new definition of earnings is based on the old definition of emoluments. There are, however, some changes. Now, the use of the words 'any gratuity or other profit or incidental benefit of any kind' refers to the more familiar 'perquisites and profits whatsoever'.

However, the addition of the term 'money or money's worth' is new and reflects that the Revenue recognizes the fact that only money or money's worth falls within the provisions of the new legislation. The concept of money or money's worth is something that is of direct monetary value to the employee or capable of being converted into money or direct monetary value to the employee. There have been a number of tax cases that discuss this very point. In Tennant v Smith HL 1892 3 TC 158 an individual was an agent for the bank and, as part of his duty, he was required to reside in a house provided by the bank. If the individual was ever absent, another bank official was deputed in his place. There was an argument put forward by the Crown to include the annual value of the house occupied rent free in the taxable income of the individual. It was held that the value of the house was not an emolument of office, as the benefit could not be converted into money. Therefore it was established that, if a benefit is conferred upon an employee that cannot be converted into money (or money's worth), that benefit should not be taxable in the hands of the employee. These are the general principles; however, a number of statutory exceptions to these principles have since been established most notably in a separate benefits code. This code taxes certain benefits without specifically linking it to its realisable value.

General earnings relate to the net taxable earnings from employment for a particular tax year. The charge to tax for general earnings does depend upon the residence status of the employee.

Residency

If an employee is resident, ordinarily resident and domiciled in the UK, the entire amount of his or her earnings that are received are taxable in the tax year of receipt. Prior to ITEPA 2003, these earnings were taxable under Schedule E, Case I. If, however, an employee is either resident, ordinarily resident or domiciled outside the UK, the basis on which his or her earnings are chargeable to tax differs.

If an employee is resident, ordinarily resident but not domiciled in the UK, any earnings arising for 'duties performed in the UK' are taxable in the UK. If, however, the earnings are 'chargeable overseas earnings', they are only chargeable to UK tax to the extent to which they are remitted to the UK. Chargeable overseas earnings are earnings from an employment with an employer based overseas where the duties relating to this employment are performed wholly outside the UK. Prior to ITEPA 2003, chargeable overseas earnings were taxable under Schedule E, Case III.

Generally, if the earnings relate to a UK employment or UK duties, they are liable to UK income tax. Therefore an individual who is not resident in the UK can still be liable to UK income tax.

Allowable deductions

The legislation governing allowable deductions has substantially been rewritten in ITEPA 2003, with the aim of achieving consistency. In general, a deduction is usually allowable for expenses incurred 'wholly, exclusively and necessarily' for the purposes of employment. In addition, it is necessary that expenses reimbursed cannot exceed earnings from employment.

Expenses are deductible from either general earnings or specific employment income. Expenses are deductible for the year in which the income is assessed.

If an individual has two different income sources, one taxable as employment income and the other under Schedule D, for example business profits from a trade or profession, expenses incurred in connection with income from one source cannot be deducted from income of another source. The reason for this is that there are different rules governing the taxation of income from different sources.

PAYE obligations

The Inland Revenue does depend on the employer to provide it with details of employment income earned by the employee. The operation of PAYE requires that the employer deducts tax at source from employment income paid to the employee in a tax month. A tax month runs from the 6th of the month to the 5th of the following month. The employer is then required to account for this tax directly to the Inland Revenue, by the 19th of each month.

The scope of PAYE has gradually increased over recent years with more and more elements of remuneration coming within its ambit. In addition to withholding tax on pay and other cash remuneration, employers have a number of other withholding obligations. In particular there is an ever-growing list of non-cash benefits provided to employees that are treated as 'notional payments' and in respect of which PAYE must be operated. The list includes such things as cash and non-cash vouchers, credit cards and 'readily convertible assets'.

The concept of 'readily convertible asset' (and its forerunner 'tradeable asset') was first introduced in 1994 and substantially enhanced in 1998 and 2003. If an employee is given an asset that is 'readily convertible', the employer has an obligation to account for PAYE on this as if the employee had received cash. The PAYE due is normally based on the best estimate that can be reasonably made of the amount of the assessable income. It is therefore possible that even after PAYE has been operated there will be a residual liability to income tax, if the 'best estimate' turns out to be less than the total liability to income tax, when this is determined. A readily convertible asset for these purposes includes a trade debt, gold bullion and any other asset that is capable of being sold on a recognized investment exchange. It will therefore catch listed shares and securities among other things. The list of readily convertible assets also extends to assets where trading arrangements exist or where there is an understanding that such arrangements may exist. For example, this could catch certain shares in private companies, perhaps where a share dealing service is set up to allow employees to realise the value of their holding.

Other arrangements now brought within the scope of PAYE include enhancements to assets held by employees and gains made from the exercise of certain share options and other share-related benefits.

A number of other benefits, although taxable, are not subject to PAYE. Strictly the tax on these benefits should be collected by self-assessment. However, in many cases the tax on these benefits is also collected through PAYE by an adjustment to an individual's PAYE Coding Notice. The Inland Revenue gives this Notice to the employer and through this, the correct withholding tax should be applied through PAYE. In short, the PAYE Coding Notice specifies the amount of income that can be paid tax-free and reflects reliefs available to the individual as well as taxable benefits.

Table 34.1 shows how the rate of tax increases from the lower rate of 10 per cent through the basic rate of 22 per cent to the higher rate band of 40 per cent for the 2004/05 tax year. All income earned above £31,400 is taxable at 40 per cent.

Table 34.1 Income tax rates, 2004/05

Rate %	Taxable bands £	Tax payable £
10	1–2,020	202
22	2,021–31,400	6,464
40	31,400 upwards	

Taxable income is determined as the income received by the individual after the deduction of all reliefs and other tax-deductible expenses.

In general, prior to Finance Act 1989, the taxable amount was based on amounts earned by an employee in a tax year irrespective of whether these amounts had actually been paid. After Finance Act 1989, this was changed so that an employee was taxed on the total amount received in a tax year rather than an amount earned. In the case of directors, the amount taxable in any one tax year is based on when the director becomes entitled to the sum. Directors in large public companies are likely to be treated in the same way as senior employees in that they will receive a regular monthly salary and an annual bonus.

There are five points at which director's earnings may be treated as having been paid for the purposes of PAYE. The five occasions are listed as follows and the earliest of these occasions is considered to be the tax point:

1. the time when the payment is made;
2. the time when the person becomes entitled to the payment;
3. the time when sums on account are credited in the company's accounts;
4. where the amount of income is determined before the period ends, when the period ends;
5. where the amount of income for a period is not known until after the period has ended, the time at which the amount is determined.

Occasions stipulated in (1) and (2) apply to all employees whereas (3), (4) and (5) only apply to directors.

Reporting

In addition to the obligation to account for tax under PAYE, employers are also required to submit a number of different returns to the Inland Revenue listing payments made and benefits provided to employees. The most well-known return is that for employees with earnings in excess of £8,500 in any year (formerly known as 'higher paid' employees but since the limit has not been raised since 1979 the 'higher paid' tag has long since been dropped). This return, referred to as a P11D, is required for every employee to whom an employer provides expenses and benefits, unless the Revenue has given a specific dispensation.

If an employer grants share options to individuals or makes any share awards, whether under an Inland Revenue approved scheme or not, during the course of the tax year, the employer is required to notify the Inland Revenue by 7 July of details of the option grants/share awards made.

At the end of each tax year, the employer needs to send the Inland Revenue an end of year return (P14) and a declaration on form P35. The

P14 records details of earnings paid to the employee together with details of deductions of tax and National Insurance contributions, among other details.

NATIONAL INSURANCE

Class 1 National Insurance is payable by employees and employers. This accounted for 95 per cent of the total National Insurance fund in 2003/04. Class 1 contributions are payable by the employee (primary) and the employer (secondary). The liability to Class 1 National Insurance arises to the extent that earnings are paid to an individual, not earned. Also, unlike income tax, which is an annual charge, National Insurance is calculated on the earnings paid in an earnings period.

For 2004/05 the employer's rate of National Insurance is 12.8 per cent and the employee's rate is 11 per cent up to the upper earnings limit of £31,720 and 1 per cent above that.

Class 1A National Insurance contributions are payable by the employer on the provision of benefits in kind. This is payable at 12.8 per cent.

All benefits or facilities provided to an employee by reason of employment are generally taxable based on the cash equivalent value of the benefit or facility. In ITEPA 2003, the legislation on the taxation of benefits is contained within the benefits code. This covers in particular, expenses payments, vouchers and credit tokens, living accommodation, cars, vans and related benefits and loans.

There are special tax rules that apply to provision of benefits to directors and also to employees who earn more than £8,500. For those individuals who earn less than £8,500 (including benefits), there is no need to submit a P11D form with details of all benefits provided, to the Inland Revenue. This limit of £8,500 has remained for well over 25 years, resulting in the vast majority of employees exceeding the limit. The value of the benefit used to be taxable based on the cost to the employer. However, this has changed and now the value of the benefit is taxed upon the cash equivalent or monetary value.

NON-TAXABLE BENEFITS

There are certain benefits that are not taxable. These include (at the present time, 2004) the benefits discussed in the following sections:

▌ Accommodation – if it is wholly, exclusively and necessarily for the purposes of the job, this is a non-taxable benefit.
▌ Meals – provided they are served to employees in general.

▌ Car parking space – provided this is close to or at work.

▌ Subscriptions – to approved professional institutions/bodies.

▌ Christmas parties and other annual functions – these are not taxable provided the aggregate cost does not exceed £150 in the tax year.

▌ Gifts from third parties are exempt where the cost does not exceed £250.

▌ Long-service awards – a tax-free award can be made to employees with a minimum of 20 years' service.

▌ Counselling services to redundant employees.

▌ Mobile phones are also exempt, even when available for personal use by the employee.

▌ Costs relating to employee liability insurance, professional indemnity insurance and work-related uninsured liabilities are not a taxable benefit if paid by the employer. If they are paid by the employee, they are allowable as a deduction against earnings.

▌ If an employee is relocated, qualifying removal expenses and benefits from the time of the job change to the end of the tax year are exempt up to a maximum of £8,000 per move. If expenses exceed £8,000, they do attract a withholding obligation but the amount does need to be reported on the year-end return.

▌ Payments given as compensation for loss of office – these are taxable if they exceed £30,000, subject to current tax legislation.

▌ Loans – an interest-free loan up to the value £5,000 is not taxable on the employee.

▌ Workplace nurseries – these are not considered to be taxable benefits in kind provided they are places that are made available by the employer.

▌ Miscellaneous others – these include the provision of computer equipment, a tax allowance to cover expenses incurred by homeworkers, over night expenses and work-related training.

Approved pension schemes

There are essentially two types of pension scheme:

1. *Personal pension schemes*: Personal pensions are designed for people who work and who are not members of an employer's occupational scheme. There may be a number of reasons for this, eg the individual is self-employed, the employer does not offer a pension scheme or the employee is not eligible or chooses not to join the employer's scheme. A personal pension operates by building a 'pension pot', which is used to purchase an annuity at retirement. Employee contributions attract tax relief at the highest rate that tax is paid by the individual. The tax relief is claimed through the self-assessment tax return.

2. *Occupational schemes*: As described in Chapter 33, there are different types of employer pension scheme: final salary scheme and a money purchase scheme. A final salary scheme pays a pension based on an individual's salary at retirement and the number of years of service. A money purchase scheme is used to build up a pot of money, which is used to buy an annuity. Employers are able to make contributions to an approved pension scheme for the employee without attaching a tax charge, provided certain criteria are satisfied.

Contributions made by all employees are also tax deductible from earnings for the employee. The relief available is based on the employee's age. Income accruing within a pension fund does so on a tax-free basis, and employees are able to receive part of their pension fund as a tax-free lump sum at the time of retirement, the remainder being subject to income tax.

There is a pensionable earnings cap of £102,000 for the 2004/05 tax year. For those individuals earning above the cap, employee contributions made in respect of earnings above the cap do not attract tax relief. For these individuals, unapproved pension arrangements may be suitable – although as we explain in Chapter 33 this environment is set to change in 2006 (see also below).

Unapproved pension schemes

The imposition of the earnings cap has meant that 'high earners', ie those earning above the earnings cap, may desire to make alternative arrangements for their pension fund.

Funded unapproved schemes

An employer makes contributions to a trust with the view that the assets grow in value for the benefit of the employee. An employee is chargeable to income tax on the value of the contributions paid into the trust. The employer is entitled to a corporation tax deduction for the contributions made to the trust. When the benefits are taken at retirement, they can either be taken as a lump sum or be used to buy an annuity tax free.

The government has proposed that the UK pension system is changed to simplify it. The proposed changes are described in Chapter 33 and briefly described as follows. From April 2006, the pension regime in the UK will undergo significant reform. There will be a lifetime allowance of £1.5 million and funds in excess of this will be taxed at either 25 per cent or 55 per cent. Personal contributions will be restricted to 100 per cent of earnings for tax relief purposes and employer contributions will be unrestricted, but taxed if they exceed £200,000. Pension scheme members who have funds in excess of £1.5 million at 6 April 2006 will be able to register and protect their funds from a tax charge. The minimum age of taking retirement benefits will be increased from 50 to 55 by 2010. The new proposals widen the current investment rules with regard to pension fund investments.

SPECIAL BENEFITS

Company cars

If a car is made available to a director or employee who is paid more than £8,500 a year, the employee will be liable to tax based on the value of the benefit. This value is calculated by reference to the list price of the car and the level of CO_2 (carbon dioxide) emissions. Until 6 April 2002 the car benefit was calculated on the list price of the car, with deductions available for the amount of business mileage and the age of the car. There are now no discounts available for higher levels of business mileage or for older cars. Furthermore, the emissions criteria become stricter over the initial three-year period. Cars that are made available to employees or to their families are considered to be derived from employment and taxed as employment income accordingly.

The cash equivalent for the car benefit is reduced for any periods of 30 days or more when the car is unavailable. This also applies to the provision of fuel benefit. If the employee is required to contribute to the cost of the car, the cash equivalent is reduced accordingly.

If employees use their own car for business purposes, they can claim a deduction for a business proportion of their running costs, eg insurance, road tax, petrol, etc. Mileage allowances paid are taxable if they exceed the tax-free allowance. These limits vary with the kind of vehicle.

Fuel benefit

From 6 April 2003, the new car fuel benefit regime is linked to the level of the car's CO_2 emissions. The CO_2 emissions' percentages that apply to determine the company car benefit are also used in the car fuel calculation. However, instead of applying the percentage to the list price of the car, the percentage is applied to a specified amount. For the 2004/05 tax year, the specified amount is £14,400. However, the Treasury do have the power to change the defined specified amount.

The benefit of fuel has been eroded over the past few years due to the increase in the scale charges. It is necessary for an employee to cover significant private mileage in a year to realize the value of fuel benefit.

Living accommodation

Generally, if living accommodation is provided for employees that is not wholly, exclusively and necessarily provided for them to perform their job, this is treated as earnings assessable under ITEPA 2003. Tax is charged on the cost of providing the benefit. The charge to tax arises if living accommodation is provided for 1) the employee, or 2) a member of his or her family or household.

The method for calculating the amount of earnings depends on the cost of providing the accommodation. Briefly, where the cost is less than £75,000 the cash equivalent is the rental value of the accommodation less any sum made good by the employee. Where the cost exceeds £75,000 the cash equivalent increases to include a notional interest charge on the excess. The charge for living accommodation applies to higher and lower-paid employees.

Loans

Generally if an employee or his relative is provided with a cheap loan the employee is taxable on the cash equivalent of the loan. A cheap loan is one that carries a low rate of interest or is interest-free. In this case the amount of earnings is calculated by reference to the Inland Revenue's official rate of interest less any amount of interest actually paid by the employee on the loan. The official rate of interest is set by the Inland Revenue and generally moves in line with bank rates, although has been set at 5 per cent since January 2002.

Share schemes for directors and employees

As described in Chapter 23, organizations introduce share schemes for a number of reasons such as:

▌ to provide an incentive for key members of the management team based on performance; and
▌ to encourage employees generally by giving them a stake in the company.

The Inland Revenue has specific provisions for a number of tax-efficient share schemes. There are the approved Save As You Earn (SAYE) share option scheme and the Share Incentive Plan (SIP), both of which are all-employee plans, which are regarded by employers and employees as important ways in which to achieve loyalty and commitment. In addition there are Company Share Option Plans and Enterprise Management Incentives.

Inland Revenue approved plans

- *SIP:* This is an all-employee scheme. Employees participate by purchasing shares out of their pre-tax salary (partnership shares), which may be matched with free shares. In addition, employees can simply be awarded free shares. These shares, once purchased or awarded, are held on behalf of participants. The employee can receive the shares after five years tax free.
- *SAYE Plan:* This is an all-employee plan that enables employees to save between £5 and £250 a month under an approved contract. Individuals are granted options to buy shares in the company, which they can exercise after a period of three, five or seven years. These savings and also a tax-free bonus can be used to exercise their options. Under this plan, a discount of up to 20 per cent can be set on the option price. When the option is exercised there is generally no charge to income tax. On sale of the shares, any rise in value is subject to capital gains tax.
- *Company Share Option Plan:* This is a discretionary share scheme so the company is able to decide which of its directors/employees should participate. Under this plan, the maximum market value of the shares at the time of grant is subject to a limit of £30,000. There is no tax payable at the time of grant. At exercise, there is generally no income tax payable. When the individual sells the shares, the growth in value from exercise to sale is subject to capital gains tax.
- *Enterprise Management Incentive (EMI):* The EMI was introduced in 2000 and is specifically aimed at smaller companies. The EMI is very flexible and allows an employer to grant options to the value of £100,000 to each employee. There are a number of qualifying conditions that companies and employees have to fulfil. Provided the conditions are not breached when the employee exercises the option, no income tax or National Insurance liability arises. On the eventual sale of the shares, capital gains tax is payable on the difference between the sales proceeds and the option exercise price. The employee can claim the relief from the date the option was granted.

Generally, a corporation tax deduction is available for an employing company in respect of the opportunity cost of providing shares to employees. This will broadly be based on the market value of the shares when they are acquired. The tax relief will be calculated based on the difference between the market value of the shares when they are acquired and any amounts payable for the share, ie the 'profit' to the employee. The corporation tax deduction is not available until the employee becomes taxable on the receipt of the shares. This change was introduced in the Finance Act 2003.

Set-up and administration costs relating to approved share schemes will continue to be tax deductible.

TAXABLE BENEFITS

There are a number of employee benefits offered by companies that are taxable on the employee as a benefit in kind. These include:

- private medical insurance;
- payments for expenses that have not been wholly, exclusively and necessarily incurred in the performance of relevant duties of the employee;
- payment of telephone rental charges and private telephone calls;
- the cost of luncheon vouchers above 15 pence per day.

We emphasize that the basic principles of benefit taxation are not clear cut and that it is always advisable to get a ruling from the Inland Revenue on any specific new benefit under consideration. In addition, it is important to ensure that employees are fully aware of the tax liabilities on their benefits in kind.

TAX AND THE SELF-EMPLOYED

The income tax position for individuals depends largely on whether they are employees and their income is taxable as employment income or whether they are taxable under Schedule D. (Some employees, eg professionals who teach and write for fees but have either a full- or a part-time contract, may be both.) It is now very difficult to have a contract with a 'self-employed person' if he or she works more or less full time for one 'client'. There are a number of tax cases that have debated this point. However, the basis of being self-employed is generally dependent upon a number of factors. Guidance is available from the Inland Revenue to help decide whether an individual is an employee or is self-employed.

USING OUTSIDE ADVISERS

The changing nature of taxation makes it vital for organizations to keep up to date with developments in law and Inland Revenue practice. Most human resource departments and reward specialists use a number of annually updated publications and Web sites as well as consulting external tax advisers to assist with both tax compliance and tax planning advice.

Authors' health warning: This chapter was completed in summer 2004. It is intended as an overview and guide and will need to be updated with each Budget and as any new tax legislation or tax judgments change the UK tax regime.

Part 8

Special Aspects of
Reward Management

35

Boardroom Pay

SETTING THE STYLE OF REMUNERATION POLICY

The principles affecting boardroom pay are generally the same as those described elsewhere in this book for all employees. What is different is the public visibility of pay decisions and the fact that salary policy for directors is usually an indication of corporate culture. Statements in many company annual reports confirm this, especially when an organization decides to change, and usually sharpen, rewards at the top. The press has always reacted badly to major pay hikes – playing on the politics of envy and the so-called 'fat cats' syndrome. More recently, major institutional shareholders have taken considerable interest in the link between executive rewards and corporate success and the press in the UK is alays prepared to make adverse comments on what are perceived to be excessive pay increases for boards, when increases for the rank and file have been kept at a minimum in times of low inflation.

The way in which boards of directors are paid tends to reflect the pay philosophy of the organization as a whole. Boards that have adopted and believe in the value of incentives, for instance, will push the concept of performance-related pay down through the whole organization. Those who choose to reinforce other values such as loyalty and commitment may place more emphasis on these – but they may, of course, offer performance rewards too.

Critical to the success of the remuneration policies for more junior staff is the level at which boardroom pay is set in relation to the competition. Boards, especially in family companies where remuneration does not come from basic salary alone, do not always appreciate that the level of their basic pay sets the ceiling below which all other salaries generally have to fit. Failing to recognize this or allowing for necessary exceptions can create 'headroom' problems, which have an impact on both recruitment and retention.

Also potentially damaging are salary levels which employees perceive as excessive in relation to their own rewards. High boardroom pay can and should be an outward sign of corporate achievement. But the taste can go sour if employees perceive that their pay is 'just a cost to be controlled' and that there is no potential share for them in the organization's success. It is no coincidence that many companies that have gone for generous bonus or incentive schemes or executive share options at the top have also opted to introduce performance-related pay further down, perhaps in addition to some form of all-employee profit sharing or share scheme. Such actions have not just tempered possible accusations of executive greed but have given everyone a potential share in success. They may also reassure shareholders that good and competitive remuneration practice has been introduced at all levels. It is, after all, in the interests of shareholders that the employees and the board are motivated to achieve the same goals and to deliver corporate success.

CORPORATE GOVERNANCE AND BOARDROOM PAY IN THE UK

Reward management in the UK boardroom is complicated by the way that UK companies are run and has to be set against the backdrop of the many reviews of directors' pay and related corporate governance issues that have taken place here in the past decade or so.

Corporate governance

In simple terms, a UK company is owned by its shareholders, but the power and responsibility for almost all decisions concerning its business operations are devolved to its board of directors, including most decisions about pay. Public company shareholders in particular are usually far removed from any day-to-day or even strategic decision making. In the UK (as in the USA) the board of directors is a single or 'unitary' structure, responsible for corporate governance as well as business decision making. While some other countries use two-tier board structures that separate the two, the 'unitary' board structure relies on an internal division of responsibility, typically between non-executive (corporate governance) and executive (business decision making) directors.

UK reviews of corporate governance and directors' pay

A number of reviews have taken place in the UK into corporate governance processes and directors' pay. They were each undertaken in response to a different set of factors but all included recognition (implicit or explicit) of the potential for conflicts of interest arising as a result of the 'unitary' board structure. The sequence started with the Cadbury Report, was furthered by Greenbury and tied together by Hampel. Subsequently, Turnbull and then Higgs examined how boards work together, including a review of the structures and processes by which directors' rewards are set. The stated objectives of these reviews were various but at their hearts was often the concern of the government of the day that directors' pay might, at best, be out of control and, at worst, include aspects that might be encouraging behaviour contrary to shareholders' interests. The outcome of these reviews (and other government initiatives) is the current system of corporate governance, disclosure and shareholder rights that is outlined in Appendix I, along with references to the underlying laws, regulations and codes.

PAY MANAGEMENT PROCESSES IN UK COMPANIES

In broad terms, the UK 'unitary' board typically manages its own pay along the following lines:

▌ Responsibility for the pay of the executive directors is delegated to the remuneration committee (to be formed of at least three independent, non-executive directors), which will make its annual recommendations to the board.
▌ The pay of the non-executive directors is usually managed by the chairman, perhaps in conjunction with the chief executive, who will also make recommendations to the board (often less frequently than annually).
▌ The board as a whole votes on these pay recommendations but no director is able to vote on his or her own pay.
▌ Shareholders have the opportunity annually to vote on the acceptability of the remuneration committee's report on boardroom pay in the company's report and accounts and to vote to approve (or otherwise) any new long-term incentive schemes for the board or that involve the issue of new shares or the transfer of treasury shares.

The impact of the annual vote of the remuneration committee's report is purely advisory but most boards seek to achieve high levels of shareholder approval – the disapproval of a small but significant minority of shareholders can be very damaging to the company's reputation and, if not addressed, can jeopardize the remuneration committee chairman's position.

Executive directors' pay

The principles (outlined in the Greenbury Report) that should underpin the recommendations of remuneration committees concerning executive directors' pay are that:

- basic salaries should be maintained at a level that allows the company to compete effectively for good-calibre executives;
- annual pay increases (if any) should be awarded in relation to performance and an assessment of market competitiveness from one or more reputable sources;
- the basis, targets and payments from executive incentive schemes should serve the needs of the business and be satisfactory to shareholders in both the short and the longer term;
- the balance between the elements of pay and benefits should be maintained on a sensible, competitive and defensible basis;
- relationships between boardroom pay and that of employees at a more junior level should remain consistent and sensible;
- in addition, directors contracts should be reviewed from time to time to ensure they remain up to date and defensible (eg notice periods should be 12 months or less).

In applying these principles the remuneration committee should seek proper, professional and, where appropriate, independent external advice. Some of the consequences of these principles are examined in more detail later in this chapter.

The 2003 Higgs Review suggested that boards should adopt a process whereby the performance of individual directors, as well as the board as a whole, should be assessed each year. The results of this process clearly should be used to support the work of the remuneration committee.

Non-executive directors' pay

The pay for non-executive directors (again from Greenbury) should:

- provide a reasonable recompense for the time and commitment a non-executive director contributes to board meetings (ie reflecting the role undertaken, time commitment required, committee and other responsibilities taken on, the company's size and the individual's unique skills/reputation);
- not be so large or so structured (eg by participating in any incentive scheme or having a company car) as to jeopardize the non-executive director's independence.

In response to the second condition, many companies pay non-executive directors purely in cash but now some allow or even require their non-executive directors to take some or all of their fees in the form of the company's shares.

In the introduction to his 2003 review, Sir Derek Higgs observed that, 'Too often the governance discussion has been shrill and narrowly focused on executive pay with insufficient attention to the real drivers of corporate success. It would represent progress if this Review were to open a richer seam of discussion, one with board performance and effectiveness at the core.' Although the spotlight seems very unlikely to move away from directors' pay, it does seem that the press and boards themselves increasingly recognize the need for a clear link between pay and performance at board level and that 'payments for failure' (large pay-offs to directors leaving as a result of poor performance) will be much more difficult to make in the future.

OUTSIDE THE UK

In the rest of Europe the level of detailed disclosure of boardroom pay is currently lower than in the UK and the USA and, perhaps as a result, debate is less heated. Even so the UK review process has been echoed in other countries such as Germany (the Cromme Code), France (the Bouton Report) and the USA (the Sarbanes-Oxley legislation). The last of these was in direct response to the high-profile failures of US corporations apparently due, in part, to inappropriate reward structures, and the focus in the USA is now on value for money from boardroom pay as never before.

THE BALANCE BETWEEN BASIC SALARY AND INCENTIVES FOR FULL-TIME DIRECTORS

Basic salary differentials

Differentials in basic salary exist in the UK between directors in different functions and between the board as a whole and the chief executive. Differences between directors by function are normally market related – based on survey and other evidence of competitive remuneration practice.

To set the basic salary differential between the managing director or chief executive and other directors, survey evidence should also be sought. Evidence from a number of sources suggests that board salaries are, on average, some 60–70 per cent of chief executive's pay. The earnings differential with sales directors may sometimes be lower, or even the reverse (ie higher than the chief executive), where special incentive arrangements exist. It may also be narrower for other directors in response to market forces or where recent recruitment has dictated a higher basic salary that has not, as it often does, yet triggered a general review of boardroom pay.

As we have already shown in Chapter 26, the majority of major UK employers operate executive incentive schemes and the payments involved continue to grow as a proportion of basic salary. In more aggressive and performance-orientated organizations, incentive payments which exceed 100 per cent of basic salary are being made, sometimes with no 'cap' when profits rise unexpectedly. In good times such payments are, as we have already said, an outward visible sign of company and indeed executive success – the 'applause' given to those who perform well.

The credibility of this approach, however, probably depends in the long term on whether the beneficiaries are prepared to take the decline in payments as inevitable when profits fall, or when the country faces an economic recession from which even they cannot escape. (A recent review of chief executives' bonus payments at the top of the FTSE 100 would suggest this is not happening and that annual bonuses may be being held at high levels to compensate for poor returns from long-term incentives.)

Such considerations inevitably affect the decision on where to set basic, pensionable salary and what to provide as performance reward. If basic salaries are set competitively, there will be less temptation to 'fudge' the incentive payments in lean years because executives have become more dependent than they should on 'risk' payments. Provision of the benefit of independent personal financial counselling, to help directors plan their incentive payments sensibly in 'good' years, is worth considering (see Chapter 34).

Before a board decides to implement change in its current salary and incentive arrangements, it needs to consider how this will affect salary policy for staff lower down. A particular concern should be the differential within the level of management just below. The basic salary differential should provide for sensible progression and a reasonable jump on promotion to the legal responsibilities of a full-time directorship.

ENSURING LONG-TERM COMMITMENT

The use of fixed-term service agreements used to be perceived as a benefit as well as a legally required written contract of employment. Such agreements were thought of as status symbols – signs of company commitment to its top executives. There is now concerted pressure to limit the terms of such contracts fo 12 months or less; hence it is now necessary to look for other methods of ensuring directors' long-term commitment.

Share options, deferred bonuses or other long-term incentives are the three main ways in which remuneration policy can provide messages on the need for loyalty and commitment to the organization.

Their design (see Chapter 23) will reflect the different emphasis the company may wish to place on attraction, retention and motivation. Some examples are illustrated below.

Deferred bonus schemes

Some companies have adopted deferred bonus schemes under which part of the executive's annual bonus is deferred for, say, two years. The deferred element is converted into shares, each of which is matched with an extra, free share on condition the executive remains employed by the company at the end of the deferral period. Such a scheme is designed to reward: 1) annual (sometimes personal) performance, and 2) loyalty to the company, but does not differentiate on the basis of long-term performance (other than that reflected in the share price).

Share option schemes

Some companies have adopted share option schemes under which options are awarded to executives that may be exercised if long-term performance conditions are met. Typical conditions may be that the company's earnings per share (EPS) growth should exceed inflation by a set amount over three years and that the executive remains employed by the company at the exercise date. Such a scheme emphasizes: 1) share price growth (the option has no final value to the executive unless the share price increases), 2) loyalty to the company, 3) real earnings per share growth (which the executive may be able to influence by profit maximization, cost control, etc), and 4) share capital stability or reduction (eg through the buy-back of shares).

Performance share schemes

Some companies adopt performance share schemes under which executives are provisionally awarded shares. The release of the shares is subject to the company's performance, typically determined on a sliding scale by reference to the company's total shareholder return (a combination of share price growth and dividend yield) ranking against its chosen peer companies over a three-year period. Release is also conditional on the executive remaining employed by the company at the vesting date. Such a scheme emphasizes: 1) relative share price and dividend performance (hence even if the company's share price falls the scheme can deliver rewards to participants, provided the company's peers have done worse), 2) loyalty to the company, 3) value delivered to share-holders (in the form of share price performance and dividends), but does not link directly to business performance.

Economic factors

Although share option schemes remain extremely common for a variety of reasons (see Chapter 23), the historically typical economic 'boom-bust' cycle means that they periodically fail when stock market values are low. During the last recession, Hay Group found that 70 per cent of companies in the FTSE 100 had executive options in issue that were 'deep underwater' (ie the share price was less than 80 per cent of the option price). During such times the popularity of other arrangements, such as performance share schemes, tends to grow. When the bull market returns, however, options become fashionable again as companies and their executives see the possibility of large option gains returns.

INDIVIDUAL REMUNERATION PACKAGES

Over the last 15 years or so, a lot has been written about the concept of 'cafeteria' or 'flexible' remuneration packages. Most of the work, and the practice, originated in the United States and other countries such as Australia where the tax regime is helpful to this approach. The idea essentially is that employees should be offered the chance to select how they wish to be paid in terms of cash and benefits and so have their remuneration tailored to their personal ambitions and lifestyle.

For executives in particular, the story does not end there. Many remuneration packages are individually negotiated and tailored at the time of recruitment to a board level appointment. As companies find that they cannot always promote to board level from within, they face increasingly tough negotiations on remuneration packages from those they seek to recruit from outside. In some cases the demand may not be for a package which is only nationally competitive, but for a globally competitive one, especially at the top of major multinationals. There are a number of reasons for this:

1. Directors, perhaps comfortably in post somewhere else and approached by executive search consultants, often feel they are in a good position to negotiate major improvements for themselves as an 'incentive' to move (they might be being enticed into a volatile and precarious environment where job security cannot be guaranteed, or one which is much more publicly exposed).
2. People are more aware than ever of market rates for top executives and see a move as an opportunity to 'catch up' to a more realistic level. People at board level usually expect a substantial improvement

in earnings to make it worth their while to move. This can make recruiting top calibre directors from outside very expensive, unless they are working in a sector or organization where they are currently underpriced.

3. Directors may employ their own specialist remuneration and sometimes pension advisers to make sure they get a good deal.

4. Being an effective director generally goes with having an ambitious and assertive personality – it is unreal to expect such people not to be shrewd negotiators and to look after their own interests, especially if they perceive that they are being brought in to wake up a 'sleepy' organization. In such circumstances they will often see a shake-up on the pay front (which usually means moving to the more competitive end of market practice), as part of a necessary process of change.

HR directors, company secretaries and indeed chief executives increasingly therefore often need to be flexible when faced with demands from an executive they may have spent a long time trying to entice and will need to have:

▌ a willingness to tailor the remuneration package to fit individual requirements;
▌ a clear idea of which items of pay they are prepared to negotiate on;
▌ the ability to cost out alternatives quickly;
▌ a maximum total earnings cost they are prepared to go to to get the executive they are after;
▌ a prepared case to defend a package which other directors or even shareholders may initially perceive as an anomaly.

GUIDING PRINCIPLES FOR BOARDROOM REMUNERATION

The following guiding principles on boardroom remuneration have been developed by Hay Group:

1. Pay policies and practices for executive directors can and should be used to attract and retain top executives of outstanding ability and to help focus and reward performance which results in increased shareholder value.

2. The pay of executive directors should be determined on the basis of an explicit pay philosophy and strategy which has been consciously developed to support the organization's business strategy, structure and approach to human resource management.

3. The pay of executive directors should be tailored to the organization's particular culture, management style and competitive environment. Pay can help to reinforce a distinctive culture and management

style. The degree to which there is a clearly agreed set of values at board level can help to foster a desired culture throughout the organization.

4. The pay of executive directors should foster a pay-for-performance orientation and top-management focus on sustained performance and the creation of shareholder value.

5. Executive directors' pay processes should become part of the overall management process. Performance objectives and measures should be consistent with the organization's decision-making processes and management information systems. If it is not the right measure for the incentive scheme, it is probably not the right measure for making decisions.

6. The design of executive director pay packages should consider the needs of individual directors but not at the expense of underlying goals and objectives. Too many pay schemes in the UK have been developed on the basis of tax efficiency alone with little or no regard for fundamental business objectives.

7. The pay of executive directors should be determined and monitored in a manner which safeguards against self-interest and avoids impropriety. Pay philosophy, scheme design and pay levels should be approved and monitored by independent non-executive directors.

8. While the design of top pay systems can be complex, schemes should be easily understood and clearly communicated. The objective is to influence behaviour and focus efforts, not to strain for over-precise measurements. If directors do not understand the scheme, it will not work.

36

International Remuneration

The continuing development of emerging markets, the consolidation within many industry sectors to produce a smaller number of larger, international companies and improved global communications have made it essential for UK companies to compete within an international market in order to survive. This internationalization of the market place has prompted a number of situations where remuneration must be considered on an international basis:

▌ UK-based organizations will find it necessary to send some staff abroad to further the development of their overseas interests or as part of the career development of the employee.

▌ Non-UK-based international companies will send staff to the UK to address specific business requirements or for them to gain international experience as part of their management development programme. While some organizations will choose to treat staff covered by either of these two situations on an expatriate basis, some may consider that the duration or the developmental purpose of any such assignment makes an expatriate assignment inappropriate and would look to some other basis for remuneration.

▌ There will be those UK companies that recognize that a proportion of their staff could be recruited from outside the UK and/or that such staff could be lost to companies based outside the UK. In this instance, it would be necessary for the organization to consider remuneration for such roles on an international basis in order to judge and manage the competitiveness of their remuneration.

▌ The employee may be required to work across a number of other countries (any of which may serve as his or her base), which may or may not include the UK. Maybe such roles are truly pan-European, with the job holders able to reside anywhere, within reason, across Europe. As such, the remuneration of the individual could be driven by practice/policy of the home or host country or some 'basket' of countries. The latter may be particularly appropriate if a team of staff is engaged in such work and some level of equity of treatment is desirable.

Thus, while the subject of international remuneration meant expatriate remuneration in the past, today it can mean a range of situations that needs to be addressed and managed in a variety of ways. Indeed, it is becoming increasingly apparent that the 'one size fits all' approach to expatriate remuneration is not necessarily the most effective. In recent years the rapid growth of emerging markets and the need to develop employees for management roles across 'global' organizations has highlighted many of the shortcomings of adhering to remuneration methods with colonial roots. In short, managing an increasing number of nationalities, from both developed and less developed countries, at different stages of their careers, highlights the difficulty of imposing a single remuneration system across the 'overseas' workforce.

This chapter deals with expatriate pay under the following headings:

▌ types of overseas employment;
▌ expatriate remuneration;
▌ main benefits associated with expatriate assignments;
▌ less common benefits associated with expatriate assignments;
▌ taxation;
▌ employees coming into the UK;
▌ international job market;
▌ pan-European roles.

TYPES OF OVERSEAS EMPLOYMENT

The terms and conditions of employment while abroad typically depend upon the nature of the work and its likely duration:

▌ *Feasibility studies:* Where an employee, or team of employees, visits a territory to assess the potential market for the introduction or development of the company's goods or services. These visits rarely last longer than a month and the method of payment is usually no more sophisticated than a reimbursement of expenses.
▌ *Commuter assignments:* Such assignments have grown in popularity for two quite different reasons: first, in response to the growing unwillingness of employees to disrupt their children's education or the career of a spouse for the sake of a full expatriate assignment; second, where the organization does not wish to enter into the cost or

commitment of a full expatriate assignment. Further, it may believe that the employee(s) concerned would be willing and able to travel to the work location on a Monday morning (or Sunday evening!) and return home on the Friday evening without detriment to the work or themselves. Such assignments are usually confined to European countries where the relative ease of travel and work permits makes such patterns of work manageable both for the organization and for the employee. Although it is not uncommon for 'Eurocommuters' to sustain this pattern of work indefinitely, it inevitably puts a strain on family life and can make it difficult for the employee to feel truly integrated into the work environment. However, one of the main advantages for the employer is that it can be more flexible and significantly cheaper than a full expatriate assignment. Small, serviced apartments can be rented instead of larger, more costly family houses and the added cost of moving children to international schools, etc, is avoided. The company would pay all reasonable out-of-pocket expenses plus the cost of travel, with the employee continuing to be paid in the UK where he or she would continue to pay income tax, national insurance, etc. Sometimes, the employer recognizes the inconvenience to the employee of such assignments and pays some form of lump sum, probably linked to the delivery of the project the employee was sent overseas to work on. This type of assignment can also be employed usefully at the start of an expatriation to ensure that both employer and the employee have a 'probationary period' during which arrangements can be undone without too much difficulty.

- *Contract work:* Construction and civil engineering companies typically recruit contract staff for specific projects. Food and accommodation are often provided on site, in which case there might be no local currency payment. A lump sum or series of lump sums for the contract, agreed in advance, is then paid in the UK.
- *Short-term assignments:* The definition of a short-term assignment varies from company to company but often refers to a period that does not exceed six months. Some companies choose to make the break point at three months, others at the point where the employee becomes liable for tax in the host country. Such situations might describe the presence of headquarters staff in the offices of a subsidiary when newly acquired or when such staff are sent in to address poor business results at one of their overseas locations. Such an arrangement is not dissimilar to the commuter assignment in the sense that employees on short-term assignments would typically continue to be paid in the UK, and pay tax in the UK, but would receive some allowance paid in the local currency to cover out-of-pocket expenses, hotels, etc. As with the commuter assignment, it is unusual for the assignee to be accompanied by family in the host location. As such, it is not uncommon for the employer to pay for a certain number of flights home over the period of the assignment,

which can be used by the employee or the employee's family. Any additional tax liability arising from the assignment is usually met by the employer.

▍ *Expatriate status:* Employing local nationals is usually much cheaper and has distinct local political advantages (eg in the Middle East, where localization is a strong national imperative for many countries) by comparison with expatriation, but many UK organizations continue to mix the local workforce with at least some management from the UK headquarters. Whether these UK managers are still employees of the parent company, whether they are kept on the UK payroll or whether they are transferred to the local company and local payroll would tend to be dependent upon who wants the manager there and the anticipated duration of the posting. If it is the country organization that is driving the posting, then the country might be expected to pay and be more obviously responsible for the assignee and, hence, have him or her on the books and pay his or her remuneration directly. If it is the UK headquarters that wishes to have the manager spend time in the host organization, then the costs of the assignee may be split between the host country and the headquarters or even fully funded by the headquarters. If the assignment is expected to be relatively short, it may be considered inappropriate to go through the administration of transferring the individual to the host country's payroll and changing the employee employment/contract status. If the individual concerned is employed by the host country company rather than the parent company and the source of remuneration is local, it is generally accepted that the employee's status is a *secondee* and not an *assignee*.

EXPATRIATE REMUNERATION

Of those types of overseas employment described above, the one that most obviously prompts special treatment of the employee is the expatriate assignment. How much expatriates are paid depends upon their job and status, personal commitments, the territory to which they are assigned and other variables.

An expression commonly found in the policy documents of multinational companies runs approximately thus: 'the aim of the expatriate remuneration policy is to ensure that individuals are "neither better nor worse off" as a result of their overseas tour of duty'. However, more and more companies are now increasingly unwilling to commit to such statements, faced with the spiralling cost of expatriate assignments and an increased focus on the real value to the company of sending employees abroad. It is often only possible to maintain an expatriate's home standard of living at significant cost to the company, particularly if the spouse is working as well.

The cost of sending an employee abroad far exceeds the salary outlay. In addition, the company must consider the air fares to and from the destination, which are not insignificant when individuals are accompanied by their families and may return once or twice a year for leave, or need to go to a holiday resort for rest and recuperation. Accommodation costs, relocation expenses, language training and UK boarding school fees are further financial burdens to be carried by the employer. Clearly, it is an expensive exercise and one that should not be undertaken without some obvious benefit to the employer. It is now generally accepted that the most common reason for assignment failure is the inability of the expatriate or partner, or both, to adapt to the local culture. Yet despite the importance of the spouse's contribution to a successful assignment, few organizations include the spouse in the selection process. A pre-assignment trip to the host location to allow the expatriate and any accompanying family to decide whether they can live in the host location, as well as a cultural briefing before going, is recognized as a way of minimizing assignment failure. Language tuition and independent financial counselling are often arranged for expatriates at this stage and are recognized as diminishing anxiety quite considerably.

Companies should remember that this anxiety and sense of displacement recur when the individuals are repatriated. The problems of re-entry have been researched in some detail in recent years and good employers now recognize that the assignment does not end with the expatriate's return to the home country. If appropriate, employees should be made aware that practical assistance and counselling are available to them, should they require them.

There are three main expatriate remuneration systems in current use as described below:

1. balance sheet or build-up (home based);
2. local market rate (host based);
3. hybrid (usually a combination of home- and host-based pay systems).

The choice of the most appropriate method is dependent on a number of factors, which would normally include:

1. reason for the assignment (developmental, management function, skills transfer);
2. nationality of expatriates and the countries to which they are sent (developed, developing, etc);
3. length of the assignment (short-term, long-term, permanent);
4. need for equity between certain groups of employees (eg other expatriates, local peer group).

Executive, married with two children; non-contributory pension fund

| Index for Hong Kong | UK = 100.0 |
| | Hong Kong = 124.9 |

Exchange rate UK£1 = HK$12.33

UK salary	£70,000
Net	£48,307
Spendable income	£30,278
Housing and savings	£18,029

Local spending component = UK spendable income – index/100 – exchange rate

$$= 30,278 - 1.249 - 12.33$$
$$= HK\$466,286$$

Home	Housing and savings	£18,029
component	Expatriate	£10,500
	Location expenses (i)	£7,000
	expenses (ii)	
	Class 1 contributions (iii)	£2,536
	contracted out	
	Total home	£38,065
	component	
		= HK$469,341

Notes

(i) Given as an incentive to be expatriated – 15% of UK notional salary.

(ii) Specific to location of assignment ranging from 0% to 30% of UK notional salary = 10% for Hong Kong.

(iii) Assume UK social security contributions. After first year, Class 1 contributions will cease and Class 3 contributions will be paid.

Total Hong Kong dollar requirement = HK$935,627 net.

This figure assumes that the expatriate receives free accommodation.
Therefore the following options exist:

a) provide free accommodation and gross the salary up to give the expatriate sufficient to cover the extra tax liability;

b) give an accommdation allowance in addition to the guaranteed net salary and gross this up for Hong Kong tax.

Assume cost of accommodation = HK¢800,000 (3-bedroom flat – Hong Kong Island mid-levels).

a) Free accommodation – taxable value 10% of gross salary
Gross	= HK$1,141,877
Tax (including tax on local accommodation, schools)	= HK$206,250
Net	= HK$935,627

b) Accommodation allowance of HK$800,000 (full rental cost)

Net	= HK$935,627
Plus acocmmodation allowance	= HK$935,627
Plus accommodation allowance	= HK$800,000
Gross (including tax on local education)	= HK$2,083,210
Tax	= HK$347,583

Two children, one of whom will remain in a boarding school in the UK, with the other at school in Hong Kong.

The first calculation represents the ongoing costs of a successful assignment using a build-up approach to determine the assignment salary.

One can see from this that the extra cost of providing an accommodation allowance is:

HK$2,083,210 – HK$800,000 – HK$1,141,877   = HK$141,333
                                                    = £11,463

Additional ongoing costs to company (other than salary):

Company car	= HK$72,039
Utilities	= HK$34,003
Local education (one child)	= HK$89,185
Home education (one child)	= HK$128,600
Club	= HK$20,400
Medical insurance	= HK$34,721
Furniture storage	= HK$16,000
Air fares (economy)	= HK$59,000
Accommodation	= HK$800,000
Total additional ongoing costs	= HK$1,253,948

Total ongoing costs, including gross cash salary
(based on providing 'free housing')   = HK$2,395,825

                                        = £194,309

NB: Those costs, which have been incurred in sterling, have been equated to HK$ at a rate of UK£1 = HK$12.330

Source: ECA International, March 2004

Figure 36.1   Example of a build-up calculation for an assignment to Hong Kong

Balance sheet ('build-up') approach

The home-based balance sheet is still the most commonly used expatriate remuneration method. Despite being administratively complex, relying as it does on data from providers of cost-of-living and tax information, it is favoured because it is easy to communicate and transparent to the expatriate. It is also considered to be the most appropriate method of pay for short- to medium-term assignments, after which the expatriate will return to the home country. Based on the home 'notional' salary, the employee remains tied into the home country salary scale, thus making it much easier to slot back into the home country salary structure. Repatriation can be difficult if the expatriate has been receiving a local market rate salary significantly higher than the UK rates.

The three components of the balance sheet system – notional home salary, spendable income and the main allowances – are described below and illustrated in Figure 36.1. On pages 508 and 509.

Notional home salary

The notional home salary is the equivalent salary paid in the home country of the job abroad. The expression 'home base' salary implies an element of reality whereas this component is, in almost all organizations, hypothetical.

Its purpose is to serve as the foundation upon which the other components are built. It is used as the basis for pension contributions and is expressed in terms of the salary that the expatriate will receive upon return. It should be updated annually in line with salary increases for home-based 'peer' group staff.

Spendable income

The expression 'spendable income' is so phrased as to distinguish it from deductible income and is sometimes known as 'net disposable income'. It refers to the portion of income that remains after tax, social security, pension and, sometimes, housing and personal savings obligations have been met. It is used as a measure of expenditure levels and is a vital yardstick when ensuring that the expatriate will be 'no worse off' abroad than at home. Certain companies deduct housing costs from the gross income as a contribution to the provision of host country accommodation. However, housing has proven such an emotive issue over the years, especially if individuals are committed to ongoing home country mortgage payments, that many companies have removed it from the balance sheet altogether and treat it separately.

Allowances

Companies calculate a number of allowances in arriving at the total expatriate remuneration package. These are designed to compensate for disruption and to make the assignment attractive to the employee, if that is deemed to be necessary. Most are applied to the notional home salary but one of them, the cost-of-living allowance, is based on spendable income.

Cost-of-living-allowance

The cost-of-living allowance is reached by applying an index to the home country spendable income. The index measures the relative cost, in the host country, of purchasing conventional 'shopping basket' items, such as food and clothing. In an effort to ensure that the expatriate maintains his or her home standard of living, indices inevitably include the pricing of items peculiar to the home country. The shopping basket is also weighted to reflect home country purchasing patterns. Indices can of course be negative as well as positive, though the majority of companies still rarely make a deduction from the expatriate's salary to account for cheaper living costs even though this gives rise to a windfall for the employee.

Cost-of-living information can be obtained from sources such as Employment Conditions Abroad, the EIU, and ORC Worldwide and UBS (see Appendix A). There is a choice of the type of index that can be used. It is now quite common for organizations to favour the 'efficient purchaser' index over a standard index. The efficient purchaser index makes the assumption (probably quite justifiably) that the expatriate will quickly adapt to local shopping patterns. This can result in significant savings to the company. Like all indices, these should be treated with some caution. Some cover diplomatic rather than commercial centres and are, therefore, based on a diplomatic lifestyle, which may be very different from that adopted by an expatriate employed by an industrial concern.

Incentive premium

The incentive, or foreign, premium is intended to offer the expatriate a financial inducement to accept the assignment. It was originally designed to recognize and compensate for the disruption to family life and separation from family and friends. An increasing number of companies are either reducing this premium or doing away with it altogether, particularly for intra-European assignments. They are questioning why an employee should receive 10–15 per cent of gross salary for simply moving from one culturally similar country to another when no such allowance would be payable in the case of a relocation within the UK. The incentive premium is also considered to be at odds with domestic reward systems, which are increasingly focused on pay linked to performance and results.

Hardship allowance

This allowance constitutes a financial recognition of potential discomfort and difficulty in the host country. Some of the factors usually taken into account are:

▌ an excessively hot or cold climate;

▮ health hazards;
▮ poor communications;
▮ isolation;
▮ language difficulties;
▮ daily possibility of burglary, kidnap, mugging, etc;
▮ scarcities of food;
▮ poor amenities;
▮ political risk;
▮ *force majeure*, floods, typhoons, earthquakes, etc.

As distinct from the incentive premium, the hardship allowance is variable and, for places such as North America, Australia and parts of western Europe, a zero percentage is common (although companies that build an incentive premium into their hardship allowance may have a minimum allowance of 10 per cent at home gross salary – paid net). Hardship allowances are usually expressed as a percentage of notional home salary. The maximum, for locations of extreme difficulty, rarely exceeds 30 per cent.

Other allowances

There is a variety of other allowances that are peculiar to locations, companies or individual circumstances. Some will be used instead of one of those listed above and some in addition. Some examples are as follows:

▮ *Separation allowance* – if personal circumstances or unpleasant conditions in the host country prevent expatriates from taking their family abroad, a separation allowance may be paid. Alternatively, additional trips home may be permitted.
▮ *Clothing allowance* – a one-off payment for clothing and accessories that expatriates need to buy on account of the particular territory to which they are assigned. Tropical countries requiring light clothing are the obvious examples where clothing allowances might be payable.
▮ *Added responsibility allowance* (position allowance) – occasionally applicable when the overseas job carries greater responsibility than the notional job in the home country. It is a difficult allowance to manage and, in practice, many expatriations are seen as promotions so the notional home salary is increased accordingly. The added responsibility allowance, therefore, is seldom found.
▮ *Relocation allowance* – this payment is intended to cover the cost of incidental expenses arising when moving from one country to another. For example, it might cover the cost of new electrical appliances. It is usually in the order of one month's salary, normally tax free, and is paid before the assignment begins. It might also be paid at the end of the assignment before the expatriate returns home.

Make-up of the 'balance sheet'

The 'balance sheet' is usually built up in two parts: the 'local' or 'host country' component and the 'home' or 'base country' component.

The home component consists of any other allowances added to that portion of the notional home salary that remains after deductions for home country tax, social security, pension contributions and other expenses. Also, employee pension contributions would continue to be paid by the employer into a home-based scheme for a defined contribution approach – in a defined benefit scheme, contributions could lapse during the assignment without any deduction from the benefit. Where spendable income is distinct from commitments such as housing costs and savings, this, too, will be deducted. The remainder tends to represent 25–30 per cent of the notional home salary and is converted at the same exchange rate used for the local component and the two, combined, form the total net pay, which is then grossed up for host country tax and social security.

The local component is calculated by applying the cost-of-living index to the net (home country) spendable income and converting the result at an appropriate exchange rate. This position is usually delivered in the host country in the local currency. Thus any exchange rate fluctuations are borne by the company rather than the employee.

Companies that transfer senior employees often allow them to stipulate a portion of their salary that they would like to have paid in home currency consistent with their normal investment/savings requirements in the home country.

Method of payment

When the total earnings have been calculated and expressed in local currency, the company will opt for one of several methods of payment. Many elect to split the salary between home country and host country, particularly in situations where the home country currency is more stable than that of the host country or where the local remittance facilities are limited. The expatriate thus has the opportunity of building up some capital and is assured of a lump sum in the home country for the servicing of continuing domestic commitments such as mortgage and insurance payments.

A split salary also has political advantages in countries where the market rate is low and where marked contrasts in income and expenditure patterns would be demotivating for the local workforce. Many host organizations, particularly joint venture operations in emerging markets, simply refuse to bear the cost of (by local standards) inflated expatriate packages. In such cases it is not unusual for the host company to pay a salary that equates to local rates and for the sending company to bear the cost of additional payments, usually offshore.

Most multinationals quote and pay a gross salary, especially in developed countries, but a few guarantee net emoluments to their expatriates. Paying net throughout the world is extremely costly but it does mean that the employer rather than the employee benefits from any exchange rate fluctuations in favour of sterling. The employer can also benefit from any tax planning.

Market rate approach

Paying the local going rate is usually favoured when it is important for the expatriate to be paid on a par with the local peer group. This can be desirable in high-paying countries such as the United States or Switzerland, where a balance sheet approach might yield an uncompetitive salary by local standards and the company therefore risks losing the employee to local competitors. The market rate is also preferred when the assignment is likely to be long-term or permanent.

The main advantage of this method of payment is that it is administratively simpler than the balance sheet. The main disadvantage is that it can rarely be applied if the employee is moving from a high- to a lower-paying country, as might be the case with a Swiss moving to the UK. It also discourages repatriation, in that expatriates may find it more financially advantageous to remain in the host country rather than returning to employment at home.

Hybrid approach

The hybrid method is usually a compromise between a home-based balance sheet and the local market rate. A typical hybrid approach might be a variation of the greater of home or host system where a balance sheet is compared to the local market rate equivalent. Another approach is to pay the expatriate an amount in the host country that equates to the spendable income of his or her peers, but continue to pay an amount in the home country that allows the employee to maintain home country expenditure on house and savings.

MAIN BENEFITS ASSOCIATED WITH EXPATRIATE ASSIGNMENTS

Housing

Housing allowances, where paid, are sometimes built into the balance sheet method of remuneration but it is more common for them to be treated as separate items. Although there are some employers who provide free accommodation for expatriates up to a certain ceiling, there is now an increase in those who require the employee to make a contribution to housing costs in the form of a 'housing norm deduction'. The level of contribution varies, but is usually around 10-15 per cent of gross notional salary. As this obliges the employee to rent out the home property, the company will usually meet the cost of a property management company to handle home-base rental formalities. The majority of employers strongly recommend that the expatriate retain the home property rather than sell, thus avoiding the risk of re-entering the property market during a boom period. Letting property, of course, is not without risk but this seems to be the preferred practice of a growing number of companies.

Utilities

The cost of utilities can be exorbitant in certain overseas locations – particularly in hot climates where the electricity bill is distorted by the constant use of air-conditioning. Most companies accept that it is their responsibility to make bottled gas, water, electricity and telephones available to their employees abroad but some exact a contribution from the expatriate – usually no more than 20 per cent – to discourage them from wasting power or making too many extravagant international telephone calls. Other companies put a ceiling on the total cost of reimbursing rental and utility costs.

Pensions

Many organizations aim – for as long as legally possible – to retain their expatriates in the home country pension scheme, often based on a notional salary, with the rationale that the expatriate is likely to spend his or her retirement in the home country. Once the maximum period of 'temporary absence' is exceeded, organizations typically operate offshore umbrella schemes or provide an overall guarantee of target benefits. Not only is this approach potentially expensive, but it is also based on traditional pension provision in the shape of defined benefit pension schemes and little scope of cross-border transferability of pensions.

Both these premises are no longer fully applicable in the current environment where defined contribution pension provision is becoming the norm, where – at least within the EU – cross-border pension transferability is eased and where the concept of lifetime employment and the resulting implication of adequate pension provision being the responsibility of a caring employer has largely disappeared. In addition, limitations of tax-approved and therefore tax-favourable pension provision by employees in many countries means that the previous cost advantage for companies to deliver a large part of remunerations as pension is no longer as significant. A model for the future, which should be considered, is therefore to decide on a competitive overall level of remuneration (including the value of pensions) but to deliver this value in a different mix, for example through shorter-term savings vehicles or stock-based reward.

Car

Cars are a common prerequisite for expatriate staff of all grades. In many countries, for status or security reasons, a chauffeur/guard is provided by the company in addition to the car. In certain European locations, however, the company car is not as tax-efficient as a benefit as it is in the UK and it is not, therefore, local custom to provide any but the most senior employees with a car – or those whose job demands it, such as salespeople. Sensible multinational companies fall in line with market practice in such territories. Likewise, although expatriates may be entitled to a car in, for instance, Hong Kong or Tokyo, they may elect to waive the benefit on the grounds that driving in such over-populated cities is more difficult and more frustrating than using the public transport system.

Educational expenses

Most companies will pay for the children of expatriates to be educated in the host country. The cost is rarely as high as subsidizing home country (boarding) school fees. In many overseas territories, there may be a limited choice of foreign language schools. Where the method of instruction is, for instance, American, it may be appropriate for the children of UK expatriates to attend only for primary education, owing to UK university entrance requirements.

Many companies will take the view that it is unreasonable to expect students following one syllabus, such as GCSE, to be interrupted by a transfer to the US curriculum and will assist with UK school fees. The level of assistance varies but is commonly a percentage (such as 75 per cent) of basic boarding and tuition expenses up to a set annual maximum. It is most uncommon for companies to finance 'extras' such as fencing, tap dancing or scuba diving!

Some companies place a financial ceiling on their school fee assistance, while others apply age or year minima and maxima. A few make provisions for kindergarten in the host country. In general, it is fair to say that global policies are a thing of the past. Cost-conscious multinationals are now careful not to pay for UK boarding school fees unnecessarily but aim to take a flexible country-by-country approach, simultaneously assessing the individual requirements of each expatriate family.

Health insurance

It is essential that all overseas personnel are adequately covered for private treatment by health insurance; few countries have national health services as sophisticated or generous as that of the UK. The cost of private medical care in the United States, for instance, is exorbitant and the national provisions are almost non-existent. The major UK schemes such as BUPA and PPP have international plans for which the premium rates will vary, depending on the country assignment and the cost of medical treatment there.

Holidays

Annual leave

Holiday entitlement is usually in line with or slightly above home country practice, 25 or 30 working days being the norm. Comparatively ungenerous host country practice – such as the standard fortnight in the USA – tends to be overridden. Particularly high hardship regions may encourage companies to allow for holidays in excess of 30 working days.

Public holidays

Host country practice is usually followed with respect to public holidays although, in non-Christian countries, certain UK public holidays such as Christmas Day and Easter Day may be allowed in addition to the local festivals.

Home leave

If a norm had to be quoted, it would probably be a fair generalization to suggest that companies will pay for expatriates and their families to fly back to their home country once per year. However, the variations on this practice are too numerous to mention and are increasing all the time as the issue of home leave becomes more emotive and a matter of as much heated negotiation as the annual pay review.

Location affects the frequency of home leave; areas of extreme hardship often merit a second home trip, while areas of low hardship, separated from the home country by a prohibitive air fare, such as Australia, might not even qualify for an annual return trip. Indeed, it is quite common for one home trip per tour (usually three years) to be provided from the Antipodes.

Marital status, however, has the most profound effect upon the regularity of home trips. Employees on married accompanied status, particularly those with children, will, as a rule, be provided with the minimum (ie, one return trip per annum). Not surprisingly, single status or married unaccompanied personnel fare rather better. Where companies distinguish between those two latter categories, the single-status staff tend to be provided with one extra trip per year on the grounds that it is cheaper for the employer to pay for two single fares than one family trip. In a company where this distinction is understood by the staff, it acts as an incentive for single-status employees to volunteer themselves for expatriate posts. Married unaccompanied personnel, by contrast, would be likely to benefit from three return trips per annum in an effort, on the part of the employer, to minimize their separation from their families. In addition, employers would typically be very flexible over how travel is arranged, up to the same cost as the agreed package. So the expatriate might be able to exchange one home trip using business class for economy-class tickets for his or her partner/family to visit the host country. In some organizations a maximum travel budget for family visits either way is agreed.

LESS COMMON BENEFITS ASSOCIATED WITH EXPATRIATE ASSIGNMENTS

Servants

Although the employment of servants may sound like a relic of a bygone century, there are still many countries in the world where it represents affluence, power and status. In such locations, expatriates – and the companies that they represent – are expected by the local populace to conform to best market practice and it is probably not unreasonable to infer that the esteem in which they are held will increase in proportion to the number of servants they employ. They will also, in many cases, be providing much-needed employment and so be contributing to the wealth of the community.

In addition, there are locations, notably parts of Africa and Central America, where security poses a real threat to anyone whose affluence is notable. In such places, merely being foreign might be enough to trigger thoughts of theft, kidnap or brutality in the minds of the local criminal fraternity. It therefore goes without saying that security guards are an essential part of these remuneration packages.

Club subscription

Club membership fees and subscriptions are usually paid for by an expatriate's employer if there is a good business case. The social environment is seen as an important part of the settling-in process as well as a useful source of business contacts, particularly in developing countries.

Sports clubs are the commonest form of benefit and, in some areas, it may be necessary to provide access to more than one club – for instance where a golf club does not have separate facilities for squash and swimming. This benefit is not to be underestimated since, in many expatriate communities, the waiting list for club membership is long and the cost of joining correspondingly high.

Rest and recuperation

'R&R' is usually a feature of a remuneration package for an expatriate in a high-hardship territory. The intention of the employer is to fly the expatriate (plus family if appropriate) to the nearest non-hardship location where decent meals, temperate climate and good communications may be enjoyed. R&R visits rarely exceed one week and are often no more than long weekends. The advantages to the employer are twofold: the trip is relatively cheap and the employee returns to work refreshed, with minimum disruption to the work schedule. R&R leave also often doubles as a shopping trip to allow the expatriate to stock up on essential items.

TAXATION

UK expatriates working abroad for a full financial year are not liable for UK tax unless their salary is paid in the UK as long as they do not fall foul of the 183-day rule. This rule, which means that UK taxation is incurred at least on some income, applies if an expatriate visits the UK for more than 183 days in any one tax year or for on average more than 90 days per year for the period of the whole assignment.

Local taxation rates in host countries, however, are enormously variable. True to the policy of 'keeping the expatriate whole' (ie ensuring that they are 'no worse off' in the host country), companies may elect to safeguard them from fiscal penalization by one of the following methods:

▌ *Tax protection.* When an expatriate is paid a gross salary and working in a location where the tax rates are low, the employer need make no adjustment, but when the host country tax rates are higher than in the employee's home country, the difference is reimbursed, usually in the home country.

▌ *Tax equalization.* The system of tax equalization is more equitable than that of tax protection and is therefore favoured by multinationals with large numbers of overseas employees. An expatriate who has benefited from a tax 'windfall' through the protection system, having, for instance, worked in a zero-tax country such as Saudi Arabia, may, justifiably, be reluctant to be transferred to a country with rates similar to the UK where 'windfalls' and reimbursements will be equally negligible. The tax equalization system offers a fairer global policy in that it reimburses tax excesses to those in high tax areas but makes a deduction from the total remuneration of those in low- or zero-rated countries. Thus, all staff are maintained on a tax standard that reflects that of the home country.

▐ *Net payments.* The payment of a net salary not only ensures expatriates throughout the world of fiscal equity but removes the onus of tax administration from the employee in countries that have no equivalent of the PAYE system. However, as mentioned above, it is extremely expensive to operate a net payment system.

EMPLOYEES COMING INTO THE UK

Clearly, those employees coming to the UK from overseas would be treated in a broadly analogous way to those employees going overseas from the UK. In this situation, if the employee is to be an expatriate, the policy applied will be that relevant to the home country and not necessarily that defined by the host country. If the posting is defined as a secondment, and thus the employee's contract and terms of employment are with the host company, remuneration will be driven by the host company's policies and practices.

The question of internal remuneration equity between this employee and his or her direct peers within the host organization is an issue that needs to be considered. If the employee is coming from a 'cheaper' country, with respect to relative levels of remuneration, it is tempting to set his or her remuneration towards the lower end of any relevant local pay range. Conversely, an employee coming from an 'expensive' country may be paid towards the higher end of, or even above, any relevant local pay range. There may be sound reasons for adopting either approach (eg control of costs, ease of transition, etc). However, one must consider how the employee or his or her colleagues will feel when salary/remuneration disparities become common knowledge. If such differences in individual pay are driven by differences in anticipated performance, then such differences would be more easily defended by the employer and understood by the employees. Where someone is brought in to provide high-value skills or contribution, a higher remuneration would seem to be appropriate. Conversely, an employee who is there on a development secondment, or who has been promoted into this new role, would be expected to perform below a fully acceptable standard for some time and, hence, would be remunerated at below the fully acceptable level at least for an initial period of time.

Thus, while it may be tempting to do so, great care must be taken if one is going to take the employee's previous absolute remuneration in his or her home country into direct account when setting remuneration in the UK.

INTERNATIONAL JOB MARKET

In most international organizations based in the UK, there is the recognition that certain of their jobs could be filled by non-UK nationals. Indeed, there may be an advantage to doing so, either to gain from a different set of cultural values or ways of working, to demonstrate one's international credentials or to optimize labour costs. It is not uncommon for menial, domestic jobs or other very low-paid jobs, such as cleaning, to be filled by people coming in from lower-paying countries. More recently, there has been the targeted recruitment of software developers from countries such as India by some companies to meet both skills shortages here in the UK and to combat the high remuneration levels commanded by local software developers. The nursing profession would be a further example where nurses from the Philippines and elsewhere have been deliberately targeted by UK employers. However, the comments made already concerning pay equity among those carrying out similar or even identical work would need to be addressed, so employment cost advantages may be achieved or maintained.

Where jobs have a clear international dimension and multi-country scope, it is recognized that potential employees could come from an international market place. Indeed, one should also recognize that existing 'international' employees could be recruited by organizations not based here in the UK. As such, one would need to accept that the remuneration market place is international and that remuneration policies and practices need, for some employees or roles, to reflect a broader set of countries than just the UK. In such circumstances, it is not uncommon for organizations to select those countries that they might expect to recruit from or lose staff to and consider their approach to remuneration against this 'basket' of country practices, social arrangements, legislation, etc.

PAN-EUROPEAN ROLES

Some organizations, notably consultancies and IT systems development and/or implementation companies, recognize that some of their staff spend so much of their time outside of their country that they could live anywhere within the region without additional detriment to either themselves or their employers. In such circumstances, the employer should decide which home locations would be acceptable to it and limit the freedom of location of employees to those locations, should the employees decide to move from the present home country location of their own volition. The company should be clear about the circumstances in which it would make any contribution to any moving expenses – clearly, if the employer gained no benefit from any such relocation, it might be considered inappropriate for it to contribute anything to such costs. Indeed, the company might even be slightly disadvantaged by any relocation and might wish to pass on, or at least share, the cost penalties incurred to the employee, eg the additional cost of local IT support, additional transportation costs, higher employer tax or social insurance payments, higher administration costs, etc. For certain consultancy and IT client-project-based organizations, this situation can be further complicated by the observation that members of the same client project team could come from a variety of different home countries. The fact that they may be working side by side doing similar work raises the question of how equitable their base remuneration should be. This would be of even greater significance if the same team tended to go from client location to client location over a protracted period.

An additional complication might come from the payment of any project-related bonuses. If such bonuses were paid as a percentage of home country base salary, any inequity in base salary would simply be magnified by these bonus payments. When one considers that the eligibility for such a bonus might stem from an individual's or team's performance on the project, relating the size of the payment to where the person lives at weekends would seem potentially unfair. At the other extreme, of course, the payment of a bonus based upon an equal slice of the project bonus pool might result in very different relative bonuses being paid out, in terms of purchasing power in the country of residence, ie what the employee might be able to buy in the home country with the money paid out.

The precise approach chosen will depend on a number of factors such as:

▌ recruitment and retention pressures;
▌ view of internal equity;
▌ stretch of targets relating to achievement of bonuses;
▌ link of remuneration elements to performance objectives (what are we paying for?).

37

Mergers and Acquisitions

The implications of a merger or acquisition on pay and conditions of employment do not seem to be considered seriously enough in most most take-over battles. Executives and employees are too often pawns in a game of chess played by remote grandmasters. However, acquisitions or mergers do not always live up to expectations and one of the principal reasons for failure is the demotivation of managers and staff. This is inevitable if insufficient attention is paid to their needs and fears as well as any existing imbalances between the reward strategies and remuneration levels of the organizations set to merge. This issue has assumed increasing significance as globalization leads to mega-mergers between organizations starting from very different places in the reward philosophy spectrum.

The degree to which staff are affected by a merger or acquisition does, of course, vary. At one extreme the holding company adopts a completely 'hands-off' approach, leaving the acquired company to run its own business, in its own way, and with its own terms and conditions of employment, as long as it delivers the goods. At the other extreme, the acquisition is merged entirely into the parent company and all terms and conditions of employment are 'harmonized'. The employees affected, however, might have different views about the extent to which the process is harmonious.

Between these two extremes there is a measure of choice. In some cases it is only the pension scheme that is merged. In others, it is the pension scheme and all the other benefits that are harmonized, leaving separate pay structures. In making decisions about what should be done and how, the points on the following check-list should be considered jointly and in advance by the parties concerned.

MERGER AND ACQUISITION CHECK-LIST

Executive rewards

1. *What should be the approach to executive remuneration?*

   Typically in merger or acquisition situations, the proposed remuneration of the chief executive and other key members of the top team is agreed in advance or very early on. It will often be subject to external advice and will take account of market practice, previous remuneration arrangements and issues of governance, most importantly the scrutiny of such arrangements exercised by the main institutional investors. All elements of the remuneration package will be considered, including base salaries, annual bonus arrangements, share option and other long-term incentive arrangements and service contracts.

   Once the shape of remuneration at the very top of the organization has been determined, this is likely to cascade through the organization, first to other members of the senior executive population, then to management and ultimately to employees in general. So far as senior executives are concerned, it is often the case that remuneration for this group will be dealt with on a common basis, extending in the largest merged organizations to the top 50 or 100 job holders.

   Where the merged organization focuses essentially on a single business or a related set of businesses, executive remuneration beneath the top levels of the organization will typically be defined within a common framework. However, where the new organization contains a highly diverse range of businesses, in which remuneration arrangements have been and continue to need to be different, different remuneration packages may well continue, particularly so far as salaries and bonus arrangements are concerned. However, even in these circumstances, service contracts, benefits arrangements, pension entitlement and access to long-term reward, for example through share options or restricted shares, may well be applied on a common basis.

   Generally, the pressure to confirm executive remuneration arrangements rapidly in the new circumstances will be high, as the alignment and motivation of the top management team and the executives who support them are typically regarded as critical, both internally and externally, in beginning to reap the benefits of the merger or acquisition.

Salary structure

Once the approach to executive remuneration has been set, attention then typically turns to reward arrangements for management and other employees. At this stage, key questions include:

2. *To what extent, if at all, should a common salary structure be introduced?* To answer this question information will be needed, first, on the economics and strategy of each business unit to see how far they conform. Then, if the business case emerges, details will be needed on:
   (a) existing salary structures;
   (b) organization structures, with salaries and grades for each job;
   (c) the distribution of salaries within each grade;
   (d) the method of job evaluation used;
   (e) policies and procedures for grading or regrading jobs and for fixing salaries on appointment or promotion;
   (f) any terms and conditions negotiated with trade unions or staff associations;
   (g) the similarities and differences between the work carried out in each company and, therefore, the type of people employed.

3. *What are the advantages and disadvantages of merging salary structures?* The advantages seem obvious. A common basis is established throughout the group which facilitates movement and a consistent approach to salary administration. The disadvantage is the disturbance and potential cost of merging, bearing in mind the regradings and salary increases that might be necessary as well as the expense of job evaluation. Why go to all this trouble if the operations in the respective companies are dissimilar and they are located in entirely different parts of the country? It could even be damaging.

4. *If salary structures have to be merged, how should this be done?* The choice is between:
   (a) a full job evaluation exercise involving rebenchmarking, which may be disturbing, time consuming and expensive but may now have to be looked at in the light of recent equal values cases; or
   (b) the arbitrary slotting of jobs into the new structure using existing job descriptions (if any). This could result in gross inequities unless full job descriptions are available or there is already a good fit between the two salary structures; or
   (c) a compromise between (a) and (b), slotting in jobs without a full evaluation if the fit is obvious, but evaluating doubtful or marginal cases. Note that if pay is negotiated with a trade union or staff association they would have to be involved and they will obviously fight against any detrimental changes.
   (d) using this as an opportunity to adopt a new structure based on job family models/generics and broader pay bands.

5. *When the merger takes place, should action be limited to the creation of a common grade structure, defining benefit levels but allowing different salary scales to reflect regional or separately negotiated variations in rates?* It is possible to have common grade structures with different salary

levels as long as the differences can be justified by reference to market rates.

6. *What should be done about staff whose grade or salary range is changed as a result of merging pay structures?*
   To regrade people and adjust their salaries to higher levels could be prohibitively expensive. To reduce salaries could be impossible, especially if there are trade unions in existence who carry any weight at all. It might then be necessary to 'red circle' staff affected by grade changes, that is, give them 'personal to job holder' gradings and salary brackets which they retain as long as they are in the same job.

General salary reviews

7. *Should general salary reviews be centralized and take place simultaneously in all locations?*
   The answer is clearly yes if a common salary structure exists or pay is negotiated centrally. If structures or pay levels vary or if site negotiations continue, then it may be best to maintain local arrangements.

Performance management

8. *How should performance management be tackled in the new situation?*
   There are two central questions to consider here, namely:
   (a) To what extent are there well-established and effective performance management policies and processes and what is the desirability of standardizing them, as opposed to allowing different systems to continue?
   (b) What is the capability of executives and managers to manage performance effectively? (After all, the presumed benefits of the merger or acquisition will rely, to a very large degree, on how effective the organization is at implementing its declared strategy – and good performance management is key to achieving this.)
   For the practitioner, an important first step here will be to examine the policies, processes and capability that already exist, from whichever part of the merged or acquired organization they come. If the operating model for the new organization is a fairly centralized one, it will then be important to shape an approach to performance management that can apply across the whole organization, ideally building on the best that already exists, bringing in best practice from outside and creatively shaping an approach to performance management that can best underpin the declared business strategy (eg balanced scorecard approaches, which concentrate not merely on the financial performance and other quantitative outputs

required, but also the capabilities, behaviours, innovation and other practices required to deliver performance). Where, by contrast, divisions and business units are to be allowed to function on a largely decentralized basis, the challenge may be to promulgate and apply principles of performance management and some kind of governance process that ensures that performance management is effectively undertaken but in a way that best reflects the needs of the different parts of the organization.

Salary administration procedures

9. *Should standardized procedures operate throughout the new group?*
   The answer to this question depends in part on the degree of centralization or decentralization to be adopted. It may be that divisions and business units can undertake the processes of salary administration perfectly well without the need for some group-based approach. However, a significant shift that is taking place in many, particularly large, organizations at present is the introduction of a 'shared services' approach to HR (and, for that matter, to other support functions, such as finance). At a transactional level, therefore, a centralized approach to salary administration may well be desirable on the basis that it is the most efficient and cost-effective means of managing the process. It has the added benefit that management information regarding salaries and payroll costs is accessible centrally, thereby providing an additional management control tool.

   On the other hand, another shift that is taking place in some organizations is the increasing devolution of salary administration/ management to line managers, with HR playing a more reduced role, ensuring that the relevant data are available in user-friendly form at one level and providing decision support to line managers at another. These key questions of cost efficiency on the one hand and line management empowerment on the other are therefore central to the approach taken in this area.

Bonus schemes

10. *Should different arrangements for bonuses be allowed to continue?*
    To a large extent, the answer to this question derives directly from the view taken concerning executive remuneration (see above). Particularly in a situation where there are divisions and business units focused on different market places and customer segments, and where this is reflected in the executive remuneration arrangements established, there is much to be said for retaining effective local bonus schemes that have an immediate link to performance and support achievement of the merger/acquisition strategy. From

a group perspective, the issue then becomes one of defining the design principles on which bonus arrangements are determined and following up with appropriate processes of governance, which enable the group to confirm that bonus arrangements are being designed and applied in an appropriate manner.

Profit-sharing schemes

11. *What should be done about profit sharing, assuming a scheme exists in one or other or both of the companies?*
    Clearly, if there has been a complete take-over and the merged company loses its status as a separate profit centre or can no longer issue shares under arrangements such as profit sharing share schemes, then the scheme in the company which has been taken over must be discontinued and employees moved into the take-over company's scheme, if one exists. If there is no scheme in that company, consideration would have to be given to some form of compensation, which could be as high as three times the average of the last three years' payments. It is worth noting that the more progressive organizations in the UK have introduced highly successful sharesave schemes in recent years, to the point where the existence of such schemes is often viewed as a hallmark of the best employers in the private sector. It may be that a merger or acquisition creates the opportunity for the introduction of such an arrangement to be considered.

Pension schemes

12. *What should be the approach to pension arrangements?*
    In the last few years, the question of pensions strategy and the arrangements deriving from this have become a critical issue, particularly in the private sector. It is no exaggeration to say that this is one of the most important issues that arises when a merger or acquisition takes place and that resolution of the pensions issue can be a 'make-or-break' consideration. For this reason, pensions cannot be considered as simply one element in the overall remuneration approach but must be treated as a major concern in its own right. Almost always, the merged organization or the acquirer will be faced with additional pension arrangements that do not easily align with the established policy and approach. In any event, it may well be that a fundamental review of pensions would have been required anyway, whether the merger or acquisition had taken place or not. For these reasons, it is often the case, in a merger or acquisition, that harmonization or alignment of all the other elements of remuneration is resolved, say within 12 to 24 months of the merger or acquisition taking place, while leaving pensions

as a distinct issue to be addressed and (hopefully) resolved in a longer timeframe. Expert technical advice (actuarial and legal) will almost certainly be required, taking into account existing and impending pensions legislation. Recent experience has also demonstrated that getting it right on the pensions front is a critical public relations issue: many large organizations have been damaged by taking ill-thought-through decisions in this area (for that matter, others have benefited from developing creative solutions), and time and resource must be made available to arrive at the right solution in this area. Chapter 33 deals in depth with the issues arising.

Other benefits

13. *To what extent should employee benefits be harmonized, for example:*
    (a) company cars;
    (b) free petrol for company cars;
    (c) life insurance;
    (d) sick pay;
    (e) private medical insurance;
    (f) mortgage subsidy;
    (g) season ticket and other staff loans;
    (h) lunch arrangements, including luncheon vouchers;
    (i) leave entitlements;
    (j) discount facilities?

The degree to which benefits should be harmonized is, like other areas of reward management, a policy question, the answer to which depends first on the philosophy of the controlling company (the extent to which it believes in centralization and absolute consistency in the treatment of employees) and second, on the circumstances in each company (the degree to which their operations and their geographical locations are linked or adjacent). Considerable variations in benefits between employees in different parts of a group are undesirable, especially if there is any interaction or interchange between establishments. Any approach to harmonization must clearly draw an appropriate balance between cost on the one hand and motivation (or avoidance of demotivation) on the other. Although it has taken some while to develop in the UK, a key consideration is the opportunity to introduce a flexible benefits approach, which allows employees choice in which benefits they take within an overall level of cost and can often provide the basis for achieving effective harmonization in a merger or acquisition. Key considerations regarding flexible benefits are dealt with in Chapter 32.

Trade unions or staff associations

14. *If a trade union or staff association has negotiating rights, how should they be involved?*

Trade unions and staff associations will inevitably be suspicious of any merger or acquisition, on the grounds that this is likely to cause a reduction in jobs and, quite possibly, deterioration in the terms of employment. It is therefore vital, at the earliest possible stage following merger or acquisition, that a strategy be developed for dealing with any trade union or staff association involved, particularly where negotiating rights exist. It is always, of course, possible to appeal over the heads of the trade union or staff association to employees. This may seem particularly attractive in a situation where the acquirer or predominant party to the merger has no trade union or staff association and the other does. However, experience demonstrates that trade unions and staff associations can cause damage in such situations unless effectively handled and can do so both inside the organization and externally. Shaping the strategy and initiating an early approach so that communication is established is therefore usually vital. Often, the trade union or staff association will press for early reassurances that no employees will lose their job. Clearly, it may not be feasible to give any such reassurance, and defining the messages (what can and cannot be said) up-front is therefore a critical part of shaping the necessary approach.

Communication strategy

15. *What should be the approach to employee communications?*

Experience in mergers and acquisitions demonstrates that this is one of the most important things to get right. If the organization itself does not communicate effectively, a communication vacuum will be created that will inevitably be filled with all sorts of rumour, almost all of it negative and potentially damaging. The critical issue, therefore, as soon as possible following announcement of the merger or acquisition, is to determine and then manage communications in the most effective manner. Of course, this is not restricted to the question of remuneration (although this will be a critical concern on many people's minds), but is to do with the totality of the way in which employees are to be managed in the new situation. Accountability for leading on communication may rest with the HR function or may be a shared accountability with line management. Either way, it is impossible to overstate the significance of successful communications – however good policies for managing employees are in a technical sense, this will mean very little if communication is badly handled.

38

Reward Policies for New, Start-up and High-growth Organizations

KEY CHARACTERISTICS AND INFLUENCES

Genuine 'start-up' organizations originate with entrepreneurs, either individuals or a very small group, for whom issues of reward tend to be low on the priority list. Typically, there is little order or system in such reward arrangements as exist: these tend to be chaotic, personalized and often reflective of the fact that those concerned are more interested in the creation of long-term wealth than in anything that could be considered an immediate salary. Where some semblance of a systematic approach to reward exists, it is often heavily influenced by the previous experience and prejudices of those involved. In this context, the thinking of the founders of the business will typically be based on:

- reward systems from previous employers (bringing the staff handbook/salary policy with you);
- throwing out the bits of these that they found demotivating;
- 'cherry picking' from reward policies they have known or liked the sound of from other employers;
- selection of benefits (notably pensions) provided on a basis that suits a small high-powered cadre but can't easily be extended to a more balanced group of employees in a maturing organization;

▌ failure to understand the underlying pluralism of employment – that inevitably not all employees will be fired with the same enthusiasm as top management. They are in it for different reasons, like having a job just round the corner from home, rather than wanting to make their first £1 million by 30.

WHERE TO START

The objectives of a reward system designed to meet the needs of a business start-up are to:

▌ Attract and keep people anxious to make the organization grow and flourish.
▌ Reward the risk of coming into a new venture with high rewards and generally a share in the business if the risk pays off – for those who have real control over development. It is more difficult and probably unrealistic to reward support and more junior staff on a 'high-risk' basis.
▌ Provide a sensible basic salary that is reasonably competitive with the market for most staff and highly competitive if rare skills have to be brought in. This is one time to pay at the top of the market.
▌ Lock people in to give business stability – typically with generous share schemes for senior executives and an all-employee SAYE share scheme SIP or profit sharing for everyone else. (see Chapter 23)
▌ Minimize overheads by keeping benefits to a decent basic core until there is some 'fat' in the system or where competitive pressure indicates additions to the various benefits.
▌ Pay out bonuses or provide non-cash rewards (have a party!) when key milestones in the business plan are successfully achieved
▌ Recognize that in the early days office accommodation may be at best basic and demonstrate willingness to improve conditions as soon as practicable (fresh flowers in an aged but clean reception area – or even in the staff lavatories – can have a significant effect on the way the company is perceived).

PREPARING FOR GROWTH

Whatever the basic components of the reward system in a 'start-up' they should be developed with an eye to appropriateness in a larger organization. Particular attention will be needed in these areas:

▌ *Pensions:* schemes for small partnerships/groups of professionals or the self-employed will not easily adapt to cover 140 to 200 employees after three years. Professional advice will be needed to achieve this.

- *Pay relativities:* starting on a 'spot salary' basis is logical, but internal relativities should always be defensible as the organization grows.
- *Executive share options/employee share schemes:* should be capable of extension – again an area for good professional advice.
- *Performance rewards:* need to relate to the milestones in the business plan and be based on achievement of agreed objectives/performance standards. Chief executive-driven discretionary bonuses are typically suspect unless the boss really is in the 'tough but fair' (or preferably just the fair) category.

THE INVOLVEMENT OF INVESTORS/AUDITORS/OTHER ADVISERS

If the business is promising and set to grow then sooner rather than later investment will be sought from providers of venture capital. Such organizations typically take a very robust view of reward systems, requiring introduction of long-term share schemes and highly geared incentives to ensure that the top management group they have entrusted with their money really are fully committed to the business. Clear and well-constructed contracts will be required and the high-risk/high-reward approach mentioned earlier will be what counts.

If the company decides to float it will have to ensure that its financial house is in order. Auditors, lawyers and others providing advice at this stage will again, as part of 'due diligence', go over the elements of executive reward policy and the structure of payroll costs with a fine tooth-comb. This is the time when 'beyond the fringe' benefits (company yacht, etc) come under scrutiny to potential institutional shareholders.

Such advisers may, or may not always, be mindful of the rationale for pay systems and the messages the individual elements can give. Sad to say, while some are very helpful and constructive, others may have a perspective that is sometimes narrow and confined to their specialism and its accomplishing prejudices – be it over-zealous cost control or a desire to pin down every last detail in fine print. This can come as a shock to a free-wheeling entrepreneurial organization. Faced with criticism about 'unorthodox' approaches to pay from such sources the important questions to ask are:

- Is what we are doing illegal in any way (in terms of employment law)?
- Are there tax implications we don't know about?
- Is it uncompetitive for any reason?
- What messages will the symbolic act of taking it away give?
- Are you mistaking 'unorthodox' on our part for real creativity in finding rewards that match our developing culture?

▌ What culture *should* we be aiming for as a larger/listed organization?
▌ Where can we get advice about putting our house in order if necessary?

REINFORCING THE CULTURE OF SUCCESS

Much of the success of a growing organization depends on close and effective teamwork. Reward systems need to support this. This means that as organizations grow they have much to gain from implementing:

▌ performance rewards which reflect team as well as individual achievement;
▌ consistent and as far as possible harmonized benefits;
▌ the beginnings of a formal approach to setting internal relativities so that a defensible 'pecking order' emerges;
▌ effective performance management as part of the way the business is run;
▌ management of the reward system by an individual who is a wise custodian of both policy and implementation until the organization is large enough to have a personnel/HR/remuneration professional to do the job and has grown/improved the management capability in reward issues.

This last point is, in fact, critical. Experience shows that most of the mistakes made by new business in the reward area are because the wrong person had accountability for it. If he or she perceives reward management as merely an administrative system, fails to take a broad view of its purpose or (at worst) incompetently develops policies that divide and cause dissent, then the business is at risk. Good and promising businesses have foundered on disagreements over pay. Sensible pay policies are the oil in the works of any organization. In a small, growing organization oil can turn to grit very fast indeed.

A NOTE ON JOINT VENTURES

There is a further category of 'start-up', different in nature to the entrepreneurial model described above, but which also needs to be considered and will frequently be encountered by the reward practitioner. This category relates to joint ventures or like arrangements set up by two established organizations and often designed to leverage a new technology, break into a new market and so on. Such situations can give rise to a complex reward challenge, for the following reasons:

▮ The joint venture may be staffed, at least in part, by executives from both partners. In all likelihood, as in a merger or acquisition, the existing reward arrangements on which these executives are employed may be very different and the question then arises as to whether these individuals are secondees, whose entitlements are to be retained, or whether a new reward policy needs to be developed as a basis for new contracts.

▮ The joint venture may need to attract expertise from outside for whom the remuneration package needs to look very different to anything that currently exists in either partner organization.

▮ As for the 'genuine' start-up described above, joint ventures are often inherently more risky than employment within the established partner organizations. The business potential for growth may also be significantly greater. In these circumstances, aggressive reward arrangements, designed to offer high earnings opportunities in both the short and medium term, often need to be created. A key consideration here is whether or not long-term rewards should relate exclusively to the performance of the joint venture or, in part, to the performance of the parent organizations. The reward practitioner is often key to resolving these issues at an early stage and allowing the joint venture to proceed on an agreed basis.

Part 9

Managing Reward Processes

39

Reward Management Procedures

Reward management procedures are required to achieve and monitor the implementation of reward management policies and to budget for and control payroll costs.

The procedures will be concerned with:

- generally monitoring the implementation of pay policies concerning the pay structure and internal and external relativities;
- conducting pay reviews;
- dealing with specific procedures for fixing pay on appointment or promotion;
- dealing with anomalies;
- controlling payroll costs;
- controlling the implementation of pay policies and budgets.

Many of the procedures required are now operated much more effectively with the aid of computer software and spreadsheets (see Appendix H).

MONITORING THE IMPLEMENTATION OF PAY POLICIES AND PRACTICES

The following pay policies and practices need to be monitored:

▌ the operation of the pay structure from the point of view of internal and external relativities, the incidence of grade drift and the degree to which the structure is appropriate as a framework for managing rewards;

▌ the application and impact of performance management and pay-for-performance processes and systems;

▌ the implementation of pay progression policies.

The check-list set out in Chapter 6 contains questions on all these aspects of reward management, and further criteria for evaluating the effectiveness of pay practices are included in the relevant chapters of this book on job evaluation, pay structures, performance management and performance pay.

There are, however, two additional methods of monitoring – compa-ratio analysis and attrition analysis – which are described below. We also discuss below approaches to monitoring internal and external relativities.

COMPA-RATIO ANALYSIS

A compa-ratio (short for comparative ratio) measures the relationship in a graded pay structure between actual and policy rates of pay as a percentage.

The policy value used is the reference point in the grade structure which represents the target rate for a fully competent individual in any job in the grade. This reference point is aligned to market rates in accordance with the organization's market stance policy. The reference point may be at the mid-point in a symmetrical range (say 100 per cent in a 80–120 per cent range), or the top of the scale in an incremental pay structure. Reference points need not necessarily be placed at the mid-point; organizations are increasingly positioning them at other points in the range.

Compa-ratios provide a shorthand way of answering the question: 'how high, or low, is an organization paying its employees (individually, in groups or in total) relative to its policies on pay levels?' Compa-ratios are calculated as follows:

$$\frac{\text{actual rate of pay}}{\text{reference point rate of pay}} \times 100$$

A compa-ratio of 100 per cent means that actual and policy pay are the same; less than 100 per cent means that pay is below the reference point and greater than 100 per cent means that pay exceeds the reference point.

Types of compa-ratios

There are three types of compa-ratios:

1. *The individual compa-ratio,* which describes the individual's position in the pay range against the pay policy reference point for the range and can be used to reposition an individual's pay in the range if it is too high or low.
2. *The group compa-ratio,* which quantifies the relationship between practice and policy for the whole organization or a defined population group (function, department, occupation or job family). It is a calculation of the sum of actual pay as a percentage of the sum of job reference point rates. This ratio has an important part to play in the overall pay management process. It can be used to establish how pay policy has been implemented overall and identify differences between parts of the organization which may indicate problems in the policy itself or in the way it has been implemented by managers. It can also be used to plan and control pay budgets.
3. *The average compa-ratio,* which is the sum of each individual's compa-ratio divided by the number of individuals. It is therefore not the same as a group compa-ratio which is based on the relationship between the sums of actual rates of pay and the sums of job reference points of pay. The average compa-ratio can therefore differ from the group compa-ratio according to the spread of individual compa-ratios at different job sizes. The group ratio is more frequently used.

Interpretation of compa-ratios

Compa-ratios establish differences between policy and practice. The reasons for such differences need to be established. They may be attributable to one or more of the following factors:

▌ differences in aggregate performance levels or performance ratings;
▌ differences in average job tenure – average tenure may be short when people leave the job through promotion, transfer or resignation before they have moved far through the range and this would result in a lower compa-ratio. Or a higher ratio may result if people tend to remain in the job for some time;
▌ the payment of higher rates within the range to people for market reasons, which might require recruits to start some way up the range;
▌ the existence of anomalies after implementing a new pay structure;
▌ the rate of growth of the organization – fast-growing organization might recruit more people towards the bottom of the range or, conversely, may be forced to recruit people at high points in the range because of market forces. In a more stable or stagnant organization,

however, people may generally have progressed further up their ranges because of a lack of promotion opportunities.

Some differences may be entirely justified, others may need action such as accelerating or decelerating increases or exercising greater control over ratings and pay reviews.

ATTRITION

Attrition or slippage takes place when employees enter jobs at lower rates of pay then the previous incumbents. If this happens, payroll costs will go down given an even flow of starters and leavers and a consistent approach to the determination of rates of pay. In theory, attrition can help to finance pay increases within a range. It has been claimed that fixed incremental systems can be entirely self-financing because of attrition, but the conditions under which this can be attained are so exceptional that it probably never happens.

Attrition can be calculated by the formula: *total percentage increase to payroll arising from general or individual pay increases minus total percentage increase in average rates of pay*. If it can be proved that attrition is going to take place the amount involved can be taken into account as a means of at least partly financing individual pay increases. Attrition in a pay system with regular progression through ranges and a fairly even flow of starters and leavers is typically between 2 and 3 per cent, but this should not be regarded as a norm.

MONITORING INTERNAL RELATIVITIES

Internal relativities can be monitored by carrying out periodical studies of the differentials that exist vertically within departments or between categories of employees. The study should examine the differentials built into the pay structure and also analyse the differences between the average rates of pay at different levels. If it is revealed that because of changes in roles or the impact of pay reviews differentials no longer properly reflect increases in job size and/or are no longer 'felt-fair', then further investigations to establish the reasons for this situation can be conducted and, if necessary, corrective action taken.

It is also useful to analyse trends in key pay ratios, eg between the pay of the chief executive and that of the lowest-paid category of employee. If, for example, this ratio has changed from 7:1 to 6:1 the implications will need to be considered not only for those at either end of the spectrum but also for intermediate jobs in the hierarchy.

MONITORING EXTERNAL RELATIVITIES

One of the most important pay policy decisions an organization must make is its competitive stance – how it wants its pay levels to relate to the market. Its stance may be to pay above the market, to match the market or to pay less than the market.

Information on competitive rates and trends can be obtained by means of pay surveys, as described in Chapter 12. These can be used to establish the extent to which pay levels are generally keeping pace with the market or whether any particular groups of employees are out of line. The information can be obtained from published, specialized or 'club' surveys and databases. Attention should be paid to trends as well as the distribution of market rates for individual jobs. Care should be taken to include in the selection of benchmark jobs chosen for comparison purposes any occupations or market groups which are particularly sensitive to competitive forces.

The information on external relativities together with general data on current pay practices can be summarized and charted as illustrated in Figure 39.1. This shows:

▌ the pay practice line – the average of the actual pay of job holders in each grade;
▌ the pay policy line – the line joining the reference points in each grade;
▌ the median and upper quartile market rate trend lines applicable to the benchmark jobs which are used for pay comparisons.

Particular attention should be paid to the market relativities of key jobs in the various occupations or job families.

This analysis will indicate any need for general market rate increases or a case for looking at the competitive position of particular job families or individual jobs.

Whenever any action is taken to deal with market forces by, eg setting up separate market groups, paying market rate premia or deliberately paying high in the range for some market-sensitive jobs, the aim should be to make explicit and identifiable any compromises with internal equity that have been made in response to market pressures.

Market-place matching

A decision has to be made on the point in the review period when the aim will be to achieve the chosen competitive stance. An organization is most competitive at the start of the review period and gradually loses ground as pay inflation inevitably takes place in the market. It is necessary for the organization to project the point in the review period where it wants to achieve its competitive position.

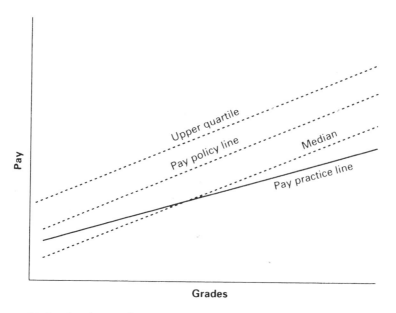

Figure 39.1 Analysis of pay structure policy and practice in relation to market rates

There are three basic approaches to making this projection:

1. *Lead/lag* – project the position to half-way through the review period, which means that the organization will lead the projected market for the first six months and lag the projected market for the next six months.
2. *Lag/lag* – select the start of the review period, in which case the organization will lag the projected market for the whole of the review period as the market pulls ahead of the policy.
3. *Lead/lead* – project the position to the end of the review period so that the organization will lead the market for the full review year as the market gradually catches up with the policy.

Clearly, the lead/lead approach is the most competitive but also the most expensive.

PAY REVIEWS

Objectives

Pay reviews are a major means of implementing the organization's reward policies for improving performance and ensuring the continued motivation and retention of employees. They are also the manifestation to employees of these reward policies.

It is important, therefore, that the way in which reviews are conducted and the outcome for employees reflect these policies and the organization's culture. So far as employees are concerned, the review should, within reason, meet the expectations the organization has created among them as to how they will be rewarded in relation to their performance and contribution. However, the extent to which this can be achieved in practice may be limited by budgetary constraints on the amount of money available for pay increases, which will ultimately be derived from the business performance of the organization, or, in the public sector, government guidelines on pay increases. The review policy and practice will also be affected if pay is negotiated with trade unions.

When planning and conducting a pay review, consideration should be given to the need to:

▌ provide general 'across-the-board increases' in response to market trends, increases in the cost of living or negotiated pay settlements;
▌ conduct a review of the pay structure to reflect the need to respond to external pay market forces or to change differentials;
▌ provide individuals with performance-related pay increases;
▌ deal with increases in market rates affecting particular occupations or job families.

An integrated approach

We discuss these aspects of the review separately in the next four sections of this chapter. But this does not imply that they should necessarily be treated as discrete activities. There is an increasing tendency for organizations to relate pay increases entirely to the combined impact of individual performance and any changes in the individual's market worth (sometimes called performance-only or merit-only increases). Market worth is affected by movements in the market rate applicable to the individual's job and by the fact that the value of individuals to other organizations will increase as they gain experience and achieve higher levels of performance and competence.

An integrated approach means typically that there are no general increases, either for market rate movements or for increases in the cost of living. Everything is done on an individual basis. Clearly, this is more appropriate where the type or level of jobs and the culture of the organization are in accord with the concept of individual contracts and, therefore, pay reviews. An integrated approach may be adopted for senior or highly specialized roles where performance is very much related to individual abilities and competence and more account has to be taken of market forces. It may also be appropriate in smaller and rapidly growing organizations that rely on individual endeavour and contribution. But many larger and more bureaucratic organizations are adopting this approach because it does provide them with greater flexibility in targeting pay increases where they are most likely to produce a marked impact on organizational performance.

GENERAL REVIEWS

General reviews take place when an across-the board increase is given to employees in response to general market rate movements, increases in the cost of living or union negotiations. The review may take place at the same time as individual reviews, in which case employees would be informed of the elements of their pay rise attributable either to general increases and/or to their performance, assuming that there is a PRP scheme.

Alternatively, the general review may be conducted separately because the organization believes that employees will be more motivated by distinct performance-related payments at a different time or because it is thought that better control can be exercised over such payments if they are dealt with separately.

Many organizations, however, have reacted against cost-of-living reviews on the grounds that the main priority is to keep their competitive position and this means responding to market rate increases. And, of course, there is no sense in giving both cost-of-living and market rate increases because movements in market rates inevitably reflect any increases that have taken place in the cost of living. So why pay twice?

A further argument against cost-of-living increases is that the organization is not in the business of protecting its employees against inflation. When rates are low this presents no problem, but no organization can cope with inflation rates such as those prevalent in the 1970s, and it would be a hostage to fortune if any indication was made that there was a possibility of doing so in the future (inflation can go up as well as down). Yet another argument in favour of combined increases based on market rate movements and individual performance is that it provides for more flexibility to target increases, especially when financial resources are limited. Increases can be flexed more within budgets according to individual performance and market worth. High achievers can be given more and poor performers may find that their real rate of pay (ie allowing for inflation) has gone down. And there is no reason for this not to happen – why should anyone in a contribution or performance-related pay system be given the right to retain their present rate of pay irrespective of actual delivery?

STRUCTURAL REVIEWS

Structural reviews take place when it is necessary to make changes to pay ranges following increases in market rates or the cost of living (assuming the latter is accepted as a reason for structural changes, which we believe to be a doubtful proposition). In a graded structure a general market rate increase means that there has been a change in the pay policy line which could be represented by the percentage difference between the old and new range reference points. If existing differentials are to be maintained, this would mean the same percentage increase for all grades.

A structural review may also follow a policy decision to change the pattern of differentials to respond to changes in the organization structure or levels of responsibility. The opportunity to adjust differentials may be taken during a general market-driven structural review but care will have to be taken to avoid too much conflict between the desired pattern of internal relativities and the need to respond to market forces generally.

If it is considered that the existing range sizes should be retained the range minima and maxima would be increased by the same percentage as the reference point. The range size could be altered by increasing or decreasing the percentage change to range maxima or minima as appropriate and this would affect the scope for pay progression within a range to reflect a decision to provide more or less room for such movement.

A structural review does not mean that individual pay increases should necessarily correspond with any general increases to range reference points or maxima.

INDIVIDUAL REVIEWS

Individual reviews determine contribution or performance-related pay increases or special achievement or sustained good performance bonuses if they are allowed as additions or alternatives to base pay rate increases. They also take into account the position to which performance pay progression has brought individuals in their pay ranges or curves – this may influence the size of the performance award or a decision to give a lump sum bonus rather than a pay increase.

The reviews are conducted by reference to performance reviews and/or ratings as described in Chapters 18 and 19. The four main issues concerning individual reviews are timing, budgeting, guidelines for reviewing managers, and control.

Timing of individual reviews

As mentioned above, individual reviews can be integrated with general reviews or conducted separately. In either case they may take place at a fixed date, typically once a year, although fast-moving organizations may prefer more frequent reviews, say twice a year. The review date can be varied to suit the circumstances of the organization. This approach can be used to advantage in rapidly growing organizations but it can also be adopted in periods of high inflation or when employee turnover is excessively high. Some organizations like to hold rolling reviews for individuals based on their birthday or starting/promotion date in order to allow more attention to be given to the individual's review. But this system is more difficult to budget for and control and it is particularly hard to give individual attention to ensuring that their pay increases reflect relevant movements in market rates.

Individual review budget

The individual performance review budget should be expressed overall in terms of the percentage increase to the payroll that can be allowed for performance-related increases. The size of the budget will be affected by the following considerations:

∎ The amount the organization believes it can afford to pay on the basis of budgeted revenue, profit, and payroll costs.

∎ What the organization thinks it ought to do to address a discrepancy between pay practice and pay policy. For example, group compa-ratio analysis may reveal that the total of actual rates of pay is less or more than the average of reference point rates of pay. If average actual rates are too low (and this is not because of a high influx of new starters) allowance may have to be made in the budget to redress the difference in full or in part, depending on how much the organization can afford to spend. Conversely, if the average of actual pay is above the policy level, the budget may be restricted.

∎ The organization's policies on pay progression – the size and range of performance-related increases. These policies will have influenced the design of the pay structure (see Chapter 16), and the factors affecting their development and application (see Chapter 21). Account should clearly be taken, when budgeting, of fundamental considerations concerning how much the organization should be prepared to pay to make performance-related pay a worthwhile basis for motivating employees and awarding them according to their con-tribution. There is no point in having PRP unless the organization truly regards performance payments as an investment to provide for increased prosperity in the future. To skimp on them unduly in periods of temporary recession could be short-termism at its worst.

The basic budget would be set for the organization as a whole but, within that figure, departmental budgets could be flexed to reflect differences in compa-ratios or any other special circumstances.

Individual review guidelines

Guidelines for managers are necessary on how they should distribute their pay increase budget among their staff. The aim is to achieve as much consistency and equity as possible between departments while still allowing managers a reasonable degree of freedom to manage the distribution of rewards within their departments. The latter principle is in accordance with one of the fundamental tenets of human resource management (HRM) philosophy – that the performance and delivery of HRM is a line management responsibility. How can they exercise this responsibility if their freedom to act in one of the most important aspects of human resource management is unduly constrained?

There will, however, always have to be some limits to freedom, and managers generally prefer some guidance on how to distribute performance awards.

The guidance should start with rating practices – methods of helping managers to rate fairly and to achieve consistency in reviews and ratings are discussed in Chapter 19.

The main guidelines on linking pay increases to ratings are described below. In each case, ultimate control would be exercised by imposing an overall budget limit on the increase in the departmental payroll arising from performance-related payments.

Average and min/max guidelines

These indicate the average performance award – say 5 per cent (when market movement is 4–5 per cent), with restrictions on the maximum and minimum pay increases that can be awarded, eg 3 per cent minimum and 10 per cent maximum. This is the simplest form of guideline and gives a fair degree of freedom to managers. It can work well, especially in the absence of an elaborate performance rating system.

Reward/rating guidelines

These relate performance pay increases or bonuses, if they are given, to ratings by the use of a scale such as the one set out in Table 39.1.

The guidelines would also emphasize that anyone whose performance is rated as ineffective should not be eligible for an increase and, in fact, should be going through the disciplinary procedure.

This form of guideline is more directive than the min/max approach. It can help managers to achieve a more consistent relationship between the rating and the reward but it does not achieve any control over the distribution of awards between the guideline increases.

It must also be accepted that managers can and do decide in advance what increases they want to award and adjust their ratings accordingly. It is in recognition of this phenomenon that some organizations conduct pay reviews quite separately from performance reviews and use the ratings purely as a means of indicating pay increases. The ratings can simply signal an exceptional, above average, average or below average increase or no increase at all.

The problem with this approach is ensuring that pay decisions are properly and fairly linked to performance; it is, after all, a process of paying according to performance and not according to managerial whim. It is necessary to emphasize to managers that there should be a proper read-across from their performance review and they should be required to justify their recommended pay increases on this basis.

Table 39.1   Scale for relating reward to ratings

Rating	% Increase
Outstanding	10
Very effective	7–8
Effective	5
Developing	3

Table 39.2   Forced choice performance pay review guidelines

Rating	% Distribution	% Increase
Outstanding	5	10
Very effective	15	7–8
Effective	60	5
Developing	15	3
Ineffective	5	0

Forced choice distribution guidelines

These, as the name implies, indicate the way in which different performance ratings and awards should be distributed among employees by defining the percentage who should be rated at each level (see Table 39.2).

This distribution would produce an average award of about 5 per cent. It is based on the normal distribution (see Appendix C) and this could be challenged as being an unjustifiable assumption. It is certainly one that has attracted a lot of criticism when exposed in PRP evaluations. Intelligence may be distributed normally in large populations (although even that is not universally accepted) but there is no reason for assuming that the distribution of people according to the way in which they apply their intelligence follows the same pattern. In any case, can anyone be confident that the population of any single organization, let alone a department within that organization, conforms to this shape?

In recognition of this situation, organizations often skew their recommended distribution by increasing the proportion at higher levels on the assumption, which may or may not be correct, that they employ higher than average people. Another approach, possibly with more justification, is to avoid forcing ratings into a nil award category and simply indicate that the lowest rating category should apply to, say, 10 per cent of the population. The awards in that category can be 3 per cent for developing or below average employees while ineffective employees should get nothing. The distribution between the two categories would not be forced.

Forced distribution provides the most rigid guidelines and is the easiest to control if the objective is to achieve the greatest degree of conformity. But we cannot favour an approach which puts managers in straitjackets and ducks the issue of managing diversity, which is a challenge to which those responsible for reward management policies have to respond positively. (We return to this issue in Chapter 42.)

Performance matrices

Performance matrices, as described in Chapter 21, can be used to define performance-related increases according to ratings and position in the pay range. Control can be exercised over performance review costs by analysing the distribution of ratings first (usually with the help of a computer) and then adjusting the figures in the matrix to ensure that the increase to the payroll would be within the budget. Software is available which can adopt an iterative or 'what if' approach to calculating the cost implications of different configurations of the matrix in the shape of variations in the amount and distribution of awards and/or variations in rating distributions.

Ranking

As described in Chapter 21, this is a form of forced distribution. Managers are asked to rank staff in comparable categories in order of merit (this approach is often associated with an old-fashioned system of merit rating which allocates points according to the assessed level of merit). The rank order is divided into groups and the percentage increase is dependent on the group in which individuals are placed. Thus someone in the top 10 per cent of the rank order might get a 10 per cent increase while someone in the next 10 per cent might get a 7 per cent increase and so on.

Pay modelling

The use of software packages for modelling pay systems has enabled organizations such as government agencies and insurance companies with formal pay structures and performance or merit rating procedures to relate pay increases precisely to the ratings they use.

Choice of method

The choice between these methods depends on the degree to which the organization believes that the benefits of uniformity and consistency are more important than the benefits of giving a reasonable degree of choice to line managers. It is a matter of opinion. But as we have made plain earlier, our view is that forced distribution systems, if they are operated rigidly (and if that is not the case, the process can hardly be called one of forced distribution), go too far in the direction of constraining the rightful responsibility of managers in this important area. It is better to produce guidelines on appropriate increases for different ratings which can be varied at the discretion of managers as long as (a) total increases are within the pay review budget, (b) an upper limit for increases is not exceeded unless the circumstances are exceptional, in which case the proposed increase has to be justified, and (c) the distribution of awards looks sensible overall, ie it is not skewed unreasonably in either direction.

PLANNING AND IMPLEMENTING PAY REVIEWS

Non-negotiated pay reviews

The steps required to plan and implement a non-negotiated pay review are:

1. Agree budget.
2. Obtain and analyse data – market rates of pay, market pay increase trends, distribution of existing levels of pay in relation to pay policies, compa-ratios, attrition, performance ratings, etc.
3. Prepare and obtain agreement to review guidelines – budget, distribution of variable pay awards, dealing with anomalies, use of market rate and other data, dates for completion, procedure for reviewing and agreeing proposals, etc.

4. Issue budgets, data, guidelines and timetable to reviewing managers.
5. Provide advice and support.
6. Set up peer review processes.
7. Iterate to achieve acceptable proposals in relation to budget, pay policies and review guidelines.
8. Summarize and cost proposals.
9. Obtain approval.
10. Update payroll.
11. Generate letters from managers to employees.
12. Inform employees.

Negotiated pay reviews

1. Obtain and analyse data on pay settlements and movements in market rates.
2. Agree target settlement, taking into account affordability; comparability; effect, if any, on other units, divisions or employee groups in the company; and the balance of power between management and trade unions.
3. Prepare negotiating brief.
4. Negotiate to achieve best settlement in accordance with targets.
5. Reach agreement.
6. Implement.

PROCEDURES FOR GRADING JOBS AND FIXING RATES OF PAY

Job grading

The procedures for grading new jobs or regrading existing ones should lay down that grading or regrading can only take place after a proper job evaluation study conducted by a member of the personnel department or a job evaluation panel advised and assisted by a specialist. An appeal system should be built into the procedure.

The steps which can be taken to control grade drift are discussed later in this chapter.

Fixing rates of pay on appointment

Managers should have a major say in pay offers and some freedom to negotiate when necessary but they have to take account of relevant pay policies, and the amounts should normally be confirmed by a member of the personnel function and/or a higher authority.

Policy guidelines should set out the circumstances in which pay offers above the minimum of the range can be made. It is customary to allow a reasonable degree of freedom to make offers up to a certain point, eg the 90 per cent level in an 80–120 per cent pay range. Most pay systems allow offers to be made up to the reference point depending on the extent to which the recruit has the necessary experience, skills and competences. Offers above the reference point should be exceptional because this would leave relatively little room for expansion. They are sometimes made because of market pressures, but they need to be very carefully considered because of the inevitability of grade drift unless the individual is promoted fairly soon.

Promotion increases

Promotion increases should be meaningful, say a minimum of 5 per cent but often 10 per cent or more. They should not normally take the promoted employee above the reference point in the pay range for his or her new job so that there is adequate scope for performance-related increases. One good reason for having reasonably wide differentials is to provide space for promotions.

DEALING WITH ANOMALIES

Within any pay structure, however carefully monitored and maintained, anomalies will occur and they need to be addressed during a pay review. Correction of anomalies will require higher-level increases for those who are under-paid relative to their performance and time in the job, and lower levels of increase for those who are correspondingly over-paid. It is worth noting that over-payment anomalies cannot be easily corrected in fixed incremental structures, and this is a major disadvantage of such systems.

The cost of anomaly correction should not be huge in normal circumstances if at every review managers are encouraged to 'fine-tune' their pay recommendations to ensure that individuals are on the right track within their grade according to their level of performance, competence and time in the job. It is important, therefore, that managers should be given the scope to carry out such fine-tuning by making adjustments to the rate of progression as necessary. Of course, they may need guidance on what they can and should do, and they also need clear information on the relative positions of their staff in the pay structure in relation to policy guidelines as a basis for decision making. The conduct of pay reviews can make a major impact, not only on motivation and commitment, but also on the perceptions of employees about the fairness of the whole process of reward management. It should not, therefore, be carried out mechanistically.

In a severely anomalous situation, which may be found at the implementation stage of a new structure or at major review, a longer-term correction programme may be necessary either to mitigate the demotivating effects of reducing relative rates of pay or to spread costs over a number of years.

As well as individual anomaly correction there may be a need to correct an historical tendency to over-pay or under-pay whole departments, divisions or functions by applying higher or lower levels of increases over a period of time. This would involve adjustments to pay review budgets and guidelines and, obviously, it would have to be handled with great care.

CONTROLLING PAYROLL COSTS

Pay review budgets

Pay review budgets for managers set out the overall increase in their payroll that they are allowed to recommend for their departments to cover the cost of competence and/or performance-related awards. This is the basic control mechanism, and managers should be required to keep strictly within their budgets and own the financial consequences of so doing.

In Bass Brewers, for example, control is exercised mainly through the pay review budget but managers are also expected to use their judgement in controlling progression by reference to a pay policy line based on market rate comparisons and the rates of pay for people carrying out similar jobs in their departments.

Review budgets restrict the scope for managers to make excessive awards leading to unjustifiable grade or band drift. But by themselves they will not prevent drift. Additional control is required by careful monitoring of the distribution of pay in grades or bands to ensure that anomalies and drift do not occur. Peer reviews or moderating processes can be used which enable out-of-line payments to be identified and thus provide for consistency. These involve getting groups of budget centre managers together to exchange information about their proposals and, if challenged by one of their colleagues, justify them. Such reviews should specifically check that the levels of pay for people in similar roles are consistent with the levels of competence and contribution demonstrated by them.

Some companies, such as Zeneca, give managers a pay review budget at the beginning of the year and get them to plan how they can use this most effectively to help them to achieve their business plans. For example, if a manager is controlling a number of key development projects, he or she might reserve some money for awards to project teams when they complete their project satisfactorily or at predefined milestones.

Pay review budgets are usually only concerned with performance or competence/skill-related awards. They may not therefore control the payroll costs arising from new appointments, transfers and promotions. Some companies set budgets which control increases arising from promotions and upgradings as well as variable pay. Others aim to achieve complete control through total payroll budgeting.

Total payroll budgeting

The problem with pay review budgets is that they do not control total payroll costs within departments. These are, of course, dependent on the number of people employed in different roles and their rates of pay. Payroll costs vary as a result of changes in those numbers and increases in pay arising from general and individual pay reviews; the amount of pay offered to new, promoted or transferred staff (which, if they replace existing staff, could be higher or lower than the rates paid to those replaced); and the extra pay earned by staff on promotion or upgrading.

A total payroll budget is based on present payroll costs adjusted for forecast changes in the number and mix of those employed in the budget centre and the forecast cost of general and individual pay increases. When budget centre managers are held accountable for their total payroll costs this means that they have to justify the numbers and types of staff they employ and any increases to payroll costs they believe are required to cover pay reviews, promotions and additional costs arising from recruitment or transfers.

When preparing their budgets, managers are issued with guidelines on what they should allow for general and individual pay review increases and they will be expected to keep within these guidelines when preparing the budget and conducting their pay review. If the financial performance of the organization means that more money can be made available to fund competence- or performance-related increases, then these budget guidelines may state the extent to which extra pay costs arising from such increases can be included in the budget.

When submitting their payroll budget proposals, budget centre managers can make out a case for an increase in their budget above the guidelines to cover anticipated extra staff, promotions or increases in responsibility (role enlargements). But they would have to justify these increases in added-value terms; in other words, they would have to prove that the income generated by these additions will exceed the cost of them. Increases must be self-financing. Conversely, if they are able to plan the maintenance or increase of present activity levels and outputs by reducing staff numbers, they can make out a case for using the extra cash thus released to fund competence-related, performance-related or career development increases. These can be used to reward staff for the additional contributions they deliver against rising expectations.

This approach means that some budget centre managers might have more cash than others to reward their staff. This could result in inequities unless the awards are fully justified. Such proposals would therefore need to be subjected to rigorous assessment. Subsequent rewards would also need to be monitored carefully. Payroll budgets can be flexed during the year in response to changes in activity levels or new projects. Many companies have interim reforecasts once or twice a year which require managers to review their original budget in the light of experience to date and amend it as necessary.

Control is exercised over budget expenditures by regular reports analysing variances, which budget managers may be required to explain and deal with.

This type of budgeting procedure can enable effective control to be maintained over payroll costs *and* restrain managers in a relatively unstructured pay system from overpaying staff. But full control still requires monitoring and peer review (moderating) processes.

The critical pay budgeting issue is the quality of understanding and ownership line managers have of their budgets. For many, this is an area where considerable support from personnel is still needed – a role in which the consultancy skills of HR professionals are increasingly called upon.

CONTROL

Control over the implementation of pay policies generally and payroll costs in particular will be easier if it is based on:

- a clearly defined and understood pay structure;
- clearly defined pay review guidelines and budgets;
- well-defined procedures for grading jobs and fixing rates of pay;
- clear statements of the degree of authority managers have at each level to decide on rates of pay and increases;
- a personnel (HR) function which is capable of monitoring the implementation of pay policies and providing the information and guidance managers require and has the authority and resources (including computer software) to do so;
- a systematic process for monitoring the implementation of pay policies and costs against budgets.

These aspects of control have been covered elsewhere in this book, but there are three further features of a control system which need to be considered; namely, the control of grade drift, the problem of devolving authority to managers to develop 'ownership' of the reward management processes in their departments while still retaining control, and the provision of control information.

Control of grade drift

Grade drift – the tendency for people to be upgraded without a justifiable increase in their job size – can be controlled by the following methods:

▌ using a strong evaluation panel trained in the job measurement methodology on a formal basis and advised as necessary by an independent expert;

▌ insisting on rigorous comparisons with well-established benchmark jobs – the re-evaluation of such jobs should be a major exercise;

▌ ensuring that panels ask pertinent questions on any claims that an increase in responsibility justifies regrading – among these questions it is useful to ask, not only what the increased responsibilities are, but also how they have arisen and what effect this will have on another job if it has lost those responsibilities;

▌ requiring a sponsoring manager to provide supporting justification;

▌ resisting demands from managers for jobs to be regraded simply because of market rate pressures, difficulties in recruitment or threats to leave to get more money. If these concerns are genuine there are better ways of dealing with them than upgrading by, for example, reconsidering market stance policies, market rate premiums or creating special market groups. What must not be allowed to happen is upgrading someone simply in response to threats.

Developing ownership without losing control

We have frequently referred in this book to the concept that line managers should take ownership of reward practice. This is an aspect of empowerment – devolving down the line the responsibility for making decisions on key management issues – and pay is definitely one of these issues.

Devolution does not mean abdication, and the following steps are required to ensure that freedom is exercised within the framework of generally understood guidelines on corporate pay policies and how they should be implemented:

▌ Discuss and agree with managers, team leaders and staff the key reward processes which will maintain standards throughout the organization – these will include processes for job evaluation, tracking market rates, performance management, performance rating and paying for performance, skill or competence.

▌ Ensure that all concerned thoroughly understand and appreciate the new freedoms and their associated responsibilities.

▌ Train managers and team leaders so that they have the level of knowledge required to make informed, business-led decisions about reward – the aim is to ensure that they are 'pay literate'.

▌ Develop computerized personnel information systems that reduce all the bureaucratic reporting which has been necessary in the past. As Clive Wright, then Manager, Corporate Remuneration, ICL, said at the Compensation Forum in January 1993:

> Recording and reviewing the key business numbers at the centre, without involvement of the line operations, is essential, if you want to convince people that empowerment and reduced bureaucracy is actually happening. As long as we keep asking people to send in reports, fill out forms, and sign off changes at detailed levels, no one will believe anything has really changed.

▌ Ensure that the central remuneration specialists change from a controlling to a guidance and support role.

▌ Spell out to all concerned that in providing this guidance and support the HR function has a duty to audit reward management processes departmentally to ensure that they are being used in the most effective way. It must be emphasized that the organization has every right to see that proper procedures are being followed and that, where appropriate, consistent policies are being applied.

▌ Ensure that managers understand and accept the principle that while they may have a fair degree of independence they are still interdependent with other operating units. They must therefore consider the implications of what they are doing on other parts of the business.

▌ Achieve, as far as possible, a reasonable balance between empowerment and control. The aim must be to give managers the maximum space and freedom to act. But it is still necessary to ensure that their actions do not contravene fundamental reward management policies and guidelines, or prejudice the overall impact of reward processes as a means of helping the organization as a whole to move forward in accordance with its strategic plans.

Pay review documentation

The pay review documentation for line managers is best dealt with by a spreadsheet (see Appendix H). The information should consist of:

▌ name, job title and present salary of job holder;
▌ details of last pay increase – amount, date and reason;
▌ performance rating;
▌ proposed increase – amount and percentage.

The individual details on this spreadsheet should be totalled so that the percentage increase to payroll overall can be calculated and compared with the budgeted figure.

PAY PLANNING

In any pay system where progression rates vary according to performance there will be anomalies. These can arise when performance suddenly improves or gets worse and staff are either under- or over-paid because it is not possible, using the normal guidelines, to place them on the right curve immediately. In this situation these people would have to be treated individually and their salary increases adjusted to accelerate or decelerate their progression through the range, so bringing them back in line.

It is in these circumstances that managing reward processes requires judgement and a sensitive approach. Inevitably, this book has largely been about systems and procedures. But ultimately we are dealing with people who want and deserve to be treated as individuals, and this applies as equally to those who manage as to those who are being managed. Mechanistic systems of salary administration may make life easier for the personnel department but that is not the object of the exercise. No members of an organization can be really happy, well motivated and committed if they feel they are part of a machine which pays no attention to their individual needs.

Salary planning and administration must adopt the stance of thinking first of what is right for individuals in terms of their aptitudes, abilities, skills, performance and needs. Of course, this approach must always be tempered with the knowledge that the organization also has needs which demand satisfaction. But an integrated approach to reward management can optimize the needs of the organization and those of the individuals, and these should be seen as complementary, not opposed.

Salary planning therefore has to treat people as individuals who are pursuing a career. This means looking at how that career is developing and ensuring that the incentives and rewards for increasing competences and improving contribution and performance go hand in hand with progress within and through the organization.

40

Communicating the Benefits

WHY COMMUNICATE?

One of the prime objectives of the reward system should be to motivate people and so ensure their commitment. Hence the theme of paying for performance and contribution which has run throughout this book. But how can the system motivate if left to its own devices – if people are unsure why the system was developed, suspect that it is unfair, or are unsure about how their pay will be linked to performance, or what their future rewards are going to be as they take on greater responsibility? And how can the organization get any mileage out of its logical, equitable, competitive and even creative reward system, its high level of rewards or its generous employee benefits package if it does not tell its employees all about them?

Payment systems can sometimes demotivate even more effectively than they motivate, even if introduced with the best intentions. This is because they often seem to be unfair. Pay is perceived as being either inequitable or not commensurate with performance. Elliott Jacques called this the felt-fair principle. He suggested on the basis of extensive research that people feel their pay ought to be fair in relation to their personal contribution, to what other people are being paid within the organization, and to what is being paid by other organizations for similar jobs. If management wants to motivate its employees, these expectations must be satisfied. It is worth remembering that the most respected theory of motivation – the expectancy theory – states that it is what people expect to get, if it is worth having, which will motivate them most effectively, rather than what they have already got.

So it is important to motivate people by telling them that what they have got is worth having – if that is the case – and even more important to tell them what they can expect. This starts with the recruitment process and ends with the way in which retirement or indeed severance is handled. If they have been rewarded for doing well, that has to be communicated to them. If they are going to get higher rewards for doing even better in the future, that must also be communicated, but more clearly and attractively.

WHAT TO COMMUNICATE

The following is what you should communicate to staff in general and to individual employees.

Staff in general

1. *The organization's salary policy:* This will set out the principles followed in setting pay and benefit levels.
2. *The pay and benefits structure:* This will define the salary ranges for each grade and the benefits available, including details of the pension scheme and the approach to total rewards.
3. *Methods of grading and regrading jobs:* Where job evaluation exists, details will be given of the job evaluation scheme, including how evaluations are carried out and the right to appeal against gradings.
4. *Salary progression:* The method by which salaries are progressed within grades or individually.
5. *Incentive/bonus schemes:* Details of any incentive, bonus, profit-sharing or share purchase schemes including how bonuses or profit shares are calculated and distributed and the procedures for purchasing shares.
6. *Reward systems and organizational change:* How remuneration policy will be affected by mergers/take-overs, change in corporate direction and indeed the bad news of liquidation and closures.

Individual employees

1. *Job grade or job or career family:* What this is and how it has been determined.
2. *Salary progression:* The limit to which their salary can go in their present grade and the means by which they can progress through the grade or pay bands, depending on performance or contribution.
3. *Potential:* Their potential for higher salaries following promotion, subject to meeting defined performance criteria and the availability of suitable positions. In other words, this information, plus that

contained under the heading of salary progression, should create expectations of what staff can get and define the action or behaviour they have to do to get there.

4. *Performance management:* How performance and potential are focused, managed and assessed, including details of the criteria used, the method of assessment and the right of the employee to know what his or her assessment is and why it has taken that form.

5. *Salary levels:* The reasons for the level of reward they are getting or the salary increase at the last review and what the employee must do to get more.

6. *Benefit statement:* The value of the benefits the individual employee receives so that he or she appreciates the level of his or her total remuneration. An example of a total remuneration statement is given in Figure 40.2.

7. *Total rewards:* Wherever possible, it helps to outline what is in the 'value proposition' for employees – linked to organizational values.

In summary, the aim must be to manage the individual's expectations about the range of factors that affect his or her pay and avoid a situation where she or he is overly focused on one factor alone.

Figure 40.1 Get the balance right

As Figure 40.1 illustrates, the right balance needs to be struck to ensure that everyone understands what affects their pay. In most organizations this tends to be:

▌ job/role size – grade/level in job family;
▌ pay markets – for the function by location/industry sector;
▌ individual performance – the performance, contribution and capability of the individual;
▌ ability to pay – the ability of the organization/sector to pay premium or closer to average rates of reward.

Statement of
Pay and Benefits for
John Smith
Smith Jones Ltd
1 April 2004

As part of our ongoing research into the competitiveness of Smith Jones Ltd's employee benefits, we have prepared this personal statement for you. Our company values relate to the link between performance and reward, and in line with this we wanted to show you how competitive your total benefits package is when compared with other companies. This statement summarizes your pay and the value of your personal benefits. Hay Group, a major provider of market salary and benefits information, have prepared this statement using information provided by Smith Jones and information from their comprehensive databases.

Your Total Package

The graph below shows how your total remuneration package is made up:

- ■ Base Salary
- ■ Other Cash
- □ Potential Bonus
- ⊞ Pension
- □ Holiday
- ⊞ Car
- □ Other Benefits

Pay and Benefits

Your basic annual salary as at 1 April 2004 is: £ 30,000 p.a.

Other Cash Payment
(such as shift payments or a substitution allowance): £ 3,500 p.a.

Potential Bonus:
(actual 2003 payment was £2,000) £ 4,500 p.a.

Potential Earnings: **£38,000 p.a.**

The table below sets out the cost to Smith Jones of the benefits you are entitled to receive, as valued by Hay:

Retirement, Death and Ill-health benefits:

Holidays: £ 4,500 p.a.

£ 700 p.a.

Company Car: £ 5,200 p.a.

Other Fringe Benefits
(see below for more details): £ 1,500 p.a.

Total Cost of Benefits: **£11,900 p.a.**

Total Package Value: **£49,900 p.a.**

Other Benefits included above:

- Meals at subsidized cost or lunch allowances;
- Gifts, awards, advice and counselling (including pre-retirement and financial counselling);
- Professional subscriptions, where relevant to job;
- Free products;
- Sports and social facilities;
- Personal and accident insurance;
- Private health care.

In addition, you are currently eligible to receive the following benefits, which have not been included in the above valuation:

- Further education assistance, where relevant to job;
- Free car parking facilities;
- Site facilities.

Figure 40.2 Example of a total remuneration statement

Comparison with Other Employers

We have commissioned Hay Group to conduct an independent assessment of the benefits offered by us compared with other UK companies in our market sector. The chart below compares the benefits package provided by Smith Jones to those provided for similar jobs by other employers. The chart shows that the total benefits package provided by Smith Jones is higher than that provided by most other organizations.

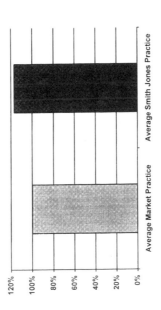

| Average Market Practice | Average Smith Jones Practice |

The Market Practice on this graph is based on the typical (median) figures from the Hay database of companies in our market sector.

Conclusion

We hope this Statement aids your understanding of your Total Remuneration Package. If you have any questions regarding this statement, please contact the Human Resources department, on 0207 1555 1234.

N Graham

Neville Graham
Human Resource Manager

Notes

The base salary figure shown above is your base salary as at 1 April 2004. However, the other figures are based on the payments achieved and benefits you were eligible to receive during the 2003 calendar year (1 January to 31 December). National Insurance Contributions payable by us on your behalf have been excluded.

Your package has been valued by Hay based on annual pension costs over an average career (using Hay's method) and using typical costs for other benefits (as advised by Hay). The figures (such as the one for Retirement, Death and Ill-health benefits) may therefore be different to information previously provided to you by Smith Jones Ltd.

Although there is no legal requirement in the UK for a minimum holiday allocation, employers typically offer a minimum of 20 days' leave (excluding bank holidays). This statement therefore values the amount paid for any holidays over this 20-day minimum.

Every effort has been made to ensure the accuracy of this statement as at 1 April 2004. If this statement is not consistent with your actual package, as outlined in your contract of employment, then the terms and conditions stated in that contract will prevail.

If you have joined Smith Jones within the last year, you may not have been eligible to receive all of the payments and benefits detailed above. However, it is expected that such benefits will be offered to you during 1998, subject to your performance as an employee of Smith Jones.

The valuation of your benefits (other than pay) is intended to illustrate the total value of your package and to allow comparisons with those provided by other employers; the figures should not be used for any other purpose. This statement does not take into account your individual family or financial circumstances or your health, and is not a recommendation for you to follow any particular course of action.

HOW TO COMMUNICATE – GENERAL INFORMATION

The best way to communicate general information about salaries and benefits is to include the details in a staff handbook which is issued to all employees on joining the company and is updated regularly. In many organizations this is now available on the intranet where it can easily be consulted at work. This can be supplemented by brochures specially written for employees describing, for instance, the pension scheme and other profit-sharing or share ownership schemes. In these publications discrete emphasis should be placed on the scale of benefits that employees enjoy and the scope provided for rewarding improved performance and loyalty to the company. Many large companies such as IBM mount continuing internal PR campaigns using e-mail or paper communication to explain the system and its benefits.

The written statement should be supplemented by initial briefings during the induction period. Whenever major changes are made, the information should be disseminated widely through the intranet, staff newspapers and bulletin boards, and joint consultative committees and by means of team briefing (face-to-face briefings made by managers or supervisors to their staff).

HOW TO COMMUNICATE – INDIVIDUAL INFORMATION

Individual members of staff will, of course, receive letters of appointment, which should tell them their grade and refer them to a staff handbook and/or site on the intranet which gives details of the grading and performance schemes. Whenever they are upgraded or promoted they should receive another letter congratulating them on the event and providing encouragement for the future. Considerable attention should be given to the wording of these letters to ensure that they come over as warm and sincere rather than cold and bureaucratic or, worse, patronizing. They should always be handed over personally by the manager to ensure that the opportunity to get needed messages across is taken.

Face to face

The best way to communicate personal information is face to face. Employees should be seen regularly by their manager for discussions and coaching on their performance. Personal explanations should be given to them of the reasons for the employee's rate of salary progression or most recent increase. These meetings should focus on recognition and coaching as well as discuss what actions the employee has to take to progress faster or to get more next time.

Potential for promotion, lateral moves and salary progression in the longer term should also be discussed at these meetings. Ideally, employees should be given the opportunity to talk to their immediate supervisor's manager in order to get a broader view. People with strong potential should also meet a career planning adviser who can act as a mentor in discussing future career steps, the further training or experience they need and the glittering prizes that await them if they do really well.

IMPLEMENTING COMMUNICATIONS

Considerable care will be needed in preparing handbooks, brochures and letter and text for the organization's intranet. They need to be clear and informative and, while they should emphasize the scale of benefits employees receive, they should not overdo it. Experts' help in preparing and presenting this information can be useful.

Individual managers and supervisors should be trained both in how to coach and review the performance of their staff and in how to convey information about assessments and rewards in a way which will motivate them. Their performance in doing this should be monitored.

AUDITING COMMUNICATIONS ON REWARD SYSTEMS

Whoever is responsible for the reward system, and the messages which communications about them should convey, should regularly audit their quality, consistency and effectiveness. The key items that usually need looking at and the main questions to ask are:

▌ Job advertisements/recruitment literature/Web site job ads – do descriptions of the remuneration package do justice to what is on offer and what the organization is seeking to pay for?
▌ Offer letters/contracts – is as much attention paid to highlighting the attractiveness of all elements of the package as stating the bald elements of entitlements? Do they convey and confirm organizational values?
▌ Staff handbooks/intranet sections on specific reward elements – is layout clear and unambiguous and is the style one that will have immediacy and meaning to the groups of employees covered? Is the information sensibly grouped?

(*Do not* use complicated language if most of the readers left school at 16, respond better to visual presentations and have reading habits that centre on the *Sun* and *Hello!*. Remember that it is possible to describe share options without using arcane legal terminology and that if the way in which incentive measures are described is impenetrable this will hardly focus motivation.)

▮ Salary increase letters – do they properly thank people for their efforts and contribution? Is delivery made an occasion of and done personally?

▮ Policy changes – are these communicated to convey the logic and the benefits?

▮ Severance (retirement/redundancy) – is the approach perceived as caring and concerned? If not, what is the likely effect on remaining employees?

▮ Company videos communicating change – do these come across as sincere and provide helpful information or do they look hastily assembled and have too high a 'cringe factor' to be useful?

Regular employee research should be undertaken to understand employees' expectations and assess the impact of current reward arrangements. See Appendix B, which describes how to conduct such surveys.

MAJOR CHANGES TO REWARD SYSTEMS

Most employers now recognize, or have learned the hard way, that major changes to reward policy not only take time to implement but that implementation has to be a carefully planned campaign. Communication is the key. The quality of communications will largely determine the acceptability of the proposed changes.

RULES FOR COMMUNICATION

In the 1985 IDS/IPM publication 'The Merit Factor – Rewarding Individual Performance', 12 rules for internal communications were reproduced. As background to any communication plans we believe they have enduring value and list them below:

1. There is no such thing as a stone-cold certainty in business decisions and it is important everyone in a business realizes this.
2. If a board cannot or will not clearly spell out its business strategy, employees are entitled to assume it does not have one.

3. Assume that in an information vacuum, people will believe the worst.
4. Never take it for granted that people know what you are talking about.
5. Always take it for granted that people doing a job know more about it than you do.
6. Telling people something once is not much better than not telling them at all.
7. Never assume that people will tell you anything that reflects unfavourably upon themselves.
8. Remember that employees read newspapers, magazines and books, listen to the radio, watch television, and surf the Internet.
9. Do not be afraid to admit you were wrong; it gives people confidence that you know what you are doing.
10. Asking for help, taking advice, consulting and listening to others are signs of great strength.
11. Communicating good news is easy but even this is not often done by management; bad news is all too often left to rumours and the grapevine.
12. Changing attitudes in order to change behaviour takes years – changing behaviour changes attitudes in weeks.

COMMUNICATIONS MEDIA

Bearing these in mind (and some of the cynical, if realistic, perceptions they contain), the following means of communications media can be used to draw from, together with some of their more appropriate uses:

▪ poster campaigns – for creating expectations for, say, a new pay or performance management system;
▪ staff newsletters – for explaining new policies or providing updates on how a new policy (job evaluation for instance) is being implemented;
▪ E-mail – to alert staff to policy changes and new reward options, which they can then discuss with their manager or HR;
▪ personal letters – to explain the personal impact of policy developments;
▪ brochures/intranet entries – where a major policy has to be explained, eg a PRP contribution-related pay system or a new pension scheme;
▪ individual meetings – where a personal, confidential or difficult message has to be got across and maximum impact is needed;
▪ videos – where a large number of staff in distributed sites have to be reached – good if a charismatic chief executive can convey his or her commitment to policy changes or development;

▌ team briefings – to inform groups of employees, consult with them and ensure they properly understand change (eg to an incentive scheme).

Whatever the chosen media, the presentation should be as professional as possible. Ill-conceived, hasty and scruffy presentations will always give employees the impression that the organization does not really care about them and that it is doing as little as it can get away with. This is not the area for penny pinching – the price in terms of justifiable resistance and cynicism is too high.

41

Developing and Introducing Reward Management Processes – The Use of Consultants

WHY USE CONSULTANTS?

There are four possible reasons for using management consultants:

1. They bring expertise in solving problems based on their understanding of relevant techniques and their experience in analysing similar situations.
2. They can open closed doors, releasing ideas already developed within the organization that have been stifled by the universal habit of resisting change. The saying: 'A prophet is not without honour save in his own country and in his own house' (Matthew 5:7) is as true today as it was in New Testament times. Consultants can play the role of catalysts or change agents as well as coaches in strategy implementation.
3. Consultants can act in an independent and disinterested way, unaffected by local politics and pressure groups.
4. Consultants have the time to concentrate on the problem they have been set. They can act as an extra pair of hands, leaving management more time to get on with the day-to-day task of running the business.

HOW CAN THEY HELP?

In reward management, the areas in which management consultants can help are:

- advising on reward strategy, eg following a merger or change in corporate direction;
- helping build 'reward literacy' at senior management level at times of strategic change;
- developing improved links between reward and performance management and career development;
- developing/implementing improved approaches to job evaluation;
- designing and reviewing pay structures to fit business needs;
- conducting salary surveys and employee opinion surveys;
- advising on salary levels for individual jobs; for example, non-executive directors seeking information on the right remuneration for a managing director or newly appointed board members;
- designing incentive/bonus schemes;
- developing gainsharing or profit-sharing plans, including share ownership schemes;
- advising on pension schemes;
- developing total reward packages covering the whole range of benefits and non-cash rewards;
- advising on the personal tax implications of remuneration policies.

HOW TO CHOOSE A CONSULTANT

The golden rule in selecting consultants is to be absolutely clear in advance about what you want them to do. Objectives and terms of reference need to be defined as a basis for briefing any firms pitching for the assignment and, later, for monitoring progress. If there is a need but objectives need clarifying, commission a small 'scoping' project to set the direction more clearly.

To identify possible consultancies, look at professional registers (eg the Management Consultancies Association, CIPD, the Institute of Management Consultants) and talk to recent clients if you can. The comparative advantages of large or small firms needs to be considered. A large firm will have ample resources and back-up facilities. It will be able to tap a reservoir of experience and expertise. A smaller firm may be able to provide exactly the type of advice you need because it specializes in a particular area. It may also provide you with more individual attention.

Unless you are absolutely certain from personal knowledge that one firm is exactly right for you, it is always advisable to approach three or four different consultancies and get them to pitch for the job. Select firms on the basis of recommendations you can trust.

Give the consultants your terms of reference and any further information they need to prepare a proposal. Meet them to discuss the brief – you can get some measure of their ability by the speed and accuracy with which they size up your situation and the quality of the questions they ask. 'Chemistry' is also important; you can begin to assess whether you could work with them at this stage.

Always ask them to submit a written proposal which should set out:

(a) the terms of reference;
(b) their understanding of your situation and requirements;
(c) how they would carry out the assignment;
(d) what they would achieve: the benefits for your organization;
(e) how the assignment would be staffed;
(f) the proposed programme of work and who would do it;
(g) the cost of their fees quoted as daily or hourly rates and as a total based on their estimate of the length of the assignment. Make sure that this specifically includes or excludes fee increases in the pipeline and ask for an estimate of expenses.

In coming to your decision on which firm to select, the following points should be taken into account:

1. The reputation of the firm – methodologies, ability to innovate.
2. The initial impression they made, ie quality of consultants and 'chemistry'.
3. The quality of their proposal with particular reference to:
   – the relevance of their proposed solutions;
   – the practicality of their proposals from the view of implementation;
   – the realism of the programme.
4. The cost of the proposals in relation to their value.

When you have made your choice, confirm it in writing by reference to the proposal, subject to any modifications that have been agreed. If you want to be certain about the costs of the assignment and if you believe that the length of time estimated for completing it is reasonable, it may be worth agreeing a fixed price.

USING CONSULTANTS

A responsible firm of management consultants will work in partnership with clients and stick to its brief, but it is natural for people with enquiring minds – and if consultants don't have those, they are in the wrong business – to identify new problems and to offer solutions to them. It is up to you to make sure that these really do add value and that no extra time is spent on the assignment unless you agree that it is worthwhile and unless the costs are also agreed.

You should expect consultants to complete their programme within their own estimate of time and costs. They could take longer if they come up against unforeseen snags and this is a joint problem if the delay has adverse effects on your business. But unless you have caused delays or misled the consultants in your brief, it is their responsibility to overcome the problems and to carry the burden of any extra costs they may have incurred.

Ensure that working arrangements with consultants are agreed at the outset. There should be regular progress or 'milestone' meetings when you can check how the assignment is going and deal with any problems as they arise. You should expect the consultants to discuss their preliminary findings with you and to present their interim conclusions and initial recommendations. It is in everyone's interest that alternative proposals should be evaluated jointly and that the feasibility of the implementation programme should be reviewed.

The final report and presentation (where these are involved) should include a convincing analysis of the situation and any problems that have been identified. Recommendations should be derived logically from this analysis and they should include an assessment of costs and benefits and a plan for implementation which sets out precisely who does what and when to achieve specific outcomes.

Working effectively with consultants is about building good working relationships, based on confidence and trust. Often this boils down to 'chemistry' – whether you believe and observe that the consultants who work with you are in sympathy with your organization and understanding what change it is able to achieve.

The best consultants rapidly build partnerships with their clients so that they can test the validity of what they are doing at several levels – from technical experts to the HR director, and as far as the chief executive and board when major change appears necessary. Their concern will be the overall 'health' of the organization and enabling it, and the people within it, to achieve their potential. In the reward area this will mean that technical excellence must be matched by an understanding of the business and HR strategy implications of proposed changes or improvements. Strong process consulting skills are almost always required. Reward consultants increasingly need to be able to:

▌ have highly developed interviewing skills, especially at the diagnostic stage of strategy/policy development work;
▌ be able to run effective focus groups with staff of all kinds/levels;
▌ be able to present their diagnosis and recommendations to audiences of many kinds;

- recognize when the presenting issue is more about, for example, performance management than reward, and have skills in that area too;
- undertake thorough 'technology transfer' to ensure that any solutions they help develop are fully understood and owned by their clients;
- work in partnership with internal or other consultant project teams working, for example, on major change initiatives.

CONTACTS

The Management Consultancies Association can be contacted at 49 Whitehall, London SW1A 2BX (tel: 020 7321 3994; Web site: www.mca.org.uk). CIPD can be contacted at www.cipd.co.uk. The Institute of Management Consultants can be contacted at www.imc.co.uk.

Part 10

Questions and Trends

42

Reward Management
Questions

1. *Is there any substance behind the rhetoric that a strategic approach to reward management is important?*

   It is easy to say that a strategic approach to reward management is a good thing. All writers on this subject, including ourselves, do so. But it is much more difficult to be specific about what reward strategies look like, how they are derived from business strategies and, importantly, what impact they make.

   A reward strategy is by definition a broad-brush affair. It indicates intentions without necessarily specifying just how these intentions are to be realized. This comes later when more detailed reward plans are prepared and implemented to achieve strategic aims.

   Ed Lawler[1] has made a positive and clear case for linking business and reward strategy. His essential message is that business strategy sets out what businesses have to do – how they must perform and behave – to be effective. Reward management processes help to drive performance by influencing individual and therefore organizational behaviours.

   Reward strategies may be broad but they have to be explicit. They have to state, in effect: this is what the business intends to do, and this, therefore, is how reward policies and processes can help the business to do it. The reward strategy must support the implementation of corporate transformation programmes; help to achieve cultural change; focus attention on the things that matter if the business is to succeed; and do whatever can be done to ensure that the

organization has the competent, skilled, well-motivated and committed workforce it needs to achieve its business targets.

It should always be remembered, however, that a strategy can
promise much but deliver little. Strategy is only as good as what it
achieves. It is an undertaking about the future but it must lead to
action and must therefore spell out:

▌ an intention – to do something;
▌ a purpose – to achieve something;
▌ a measure – to establish what has been achieved.

2. *How can we reconcile the often conflicting needs for our pay structures and
levels to be equitable, both internally and externally?*
For employees, a 'felt-fair' pay structure is one in which they believe
that they are paid appropriately for what they do in comparison
with others. Initial comparisons will be internal and they will be
aggrieved if they feel that, without justification, they are being paid
less than others who are doing the same or even less demanding
work or contributing less effectively. Internal equity also means, of
course, paying equal salaries or wages for work of equal value. It is
important as a means of achieving both job satisfaction and meeting
legal requirements.

To get and to keep the right people, organizations have to pay
competitively. And the 'felt-fair principle' applies just as much to
external as internal equity. Employees will be unhappy if they know
or think that they are being paid less than the going rate, even if they
have no intention of leaving or little chance of getting work elsewhere.

The importance of being competitive depends partly on the
degree to which the organization relies on the external as distinct
from the internal labour market. And the need to be competitive
may only apply to certain jobs where the demand exceeds the
supply. Organizations which have to use the external market in
these circumstances may well find that they have to offer people
more to join than the job is worth according to their internal job
evaluation. This situation is commonly dealt with by paying a
market premium on top of the normal rate for the grade in which
the job holder is placed, according to the rules of internal equity.
When this is a recurring problem for a category of employees, the
solution may be to form special market pay groups for the job
family concerned, with different pay scales, thus sacrificing the
principle of internal equity to the imperative of external competitiveness. The extent to which this approach is adopted depends on
the strength of the market forces and of the needs of the organization for an individual or a category of employee. If these are both
strong then there may be no alternative but to accept that competitiveness must be given priority.

Problems can occur if an organization has to respond to market pressures for recruits but fails to increase the pay of those in the same jobs within the organization in line with market rate increases. People will complain if they find that newcomers doing the same work are paid more than those who have been in those jobs for some time. And they will find this out, even when the pay structure is not published. Managements should never underestimate the propensity for employees to exchange information among themselves on what they are paid. Discrepancies can be justified if they result from a decision to pay recruits according to their market worth where this reflects higher levels of competence and experience. The problem would not exist in an ideal situation when internal rates keep pace with market rates. But in the real world this frequently does not happen, either because the organization cannot afford it or because it is unaware that its pay levels are lagging behind market rates.

The only way to respond to reasonable complaints from employees that newcomers are being paid more than they are is to state, honestly and openly, that the organization needs these people, that they were only available from outside and could not be attracted for less. An undertaking could be made that the problem will be addressed in future pay reviews in line with the company's policy to do its best to maintain a balance between the demands for internal equity and external competitiveness.

This answer may not satisfy anyone, but it is the only possible one to give if the company has to recruit at a higher rate and if it cannot afford to bring everyone into line with the new rates immediately.

Employees who are very dissatisfied may threaten to leave if they do not get an immediate increase to restore the balance. This process of 'putting a pistol at an employer's head' can, of course, happen at any time when employees feel that they have a strong case (eg when they have received a firm offer from another employer – people sometimes test the market by applying for jobs) or when they are just trying it on, possibly on the strength of one or two job advertisements.

The theoretical answer to this sort of approach is to reject it on the grounds that the organization is not going to respond to blackmail – 'if once you start doing this you'll never be able to stop'. Some organizations insist on a policy of refusing to bow to such demands, which is easier when the person concerned is not vital to the business and substitutes can easily be obtained. The decision may be much tougher in the case of someone who is crucial to the organization and cannot readily be replaced, and in exceptional circumstances businesses have been known, reluctantly, to abandon their policy line. Organizations without a clear policy on this issue have to decide on the merits of the case, but this is one decision which should not be left entirely in the hands of line managers. They should be required to seek approval for any action they take from higher authority and/or the HR department. Sometimes, in our experience, it is an issue which requires decision at board level, especially for senior or significant contributor posts.

3. *We believe that conventional job evaluation schemes are rigid, bureaucratic and expensive. But what do we put in their place, if anything?*
The way in which job evaluation schemes are operated can be all these things. But this results from how the scheme is being used rather than being a fault in its design.

Organizations cannot choose whether or not to evaluate jobs. They must make decisions on the rate for jobs and about relativities, and, if they do have a formal pay structure, where jobs are placed in that structure. There is, however, a choice of method and it is inevitable that an analytical scheme will be more complex to administer than a non-analytical one. Exposure to equal value issues must also be considered.

The recent CIPD and E-Reward surveys have found that the majority of organizations are not abandoning job evaluation, but as Murlis[2] comments:

> They are jettisoning old, cumbersome approaches and learning to use the new approaches. Job family models which reflect the levels at which work is done in a specific area, the key elements of work and the corresponding competences, are, for example, often underpinned by some form of measurement of the size of each level – both to inform understanding of the 'shape' of the family and to assist with matching the levels to the market data being used.

Even organizations with broadbanded structures – which have often been promoted as obviating the need for job evaluation – frequently retain it in the background as a management tool to define the band boundaries and to assist in making borderline decisions on allocating jobs to bands. But this is essentially a support role. Grading decisions are no longer dominated by job evaluation and the expensive panoply of panel procedures becomes a thing of the past.

4. *Must we have an analytical job evaluation scheme to ensure that equal pay for work of equal value requirements are met?*
While analytical job evaluation schemes can never be completely objective, they still provide the most reliable means of making valid comparisons between jobs. This is simply because they are structured and are, or should be, founded on systematic job analysis. The outcome of evaluation using an analytical scheme without built-in gender bias is the best method of defending an equal value claim before an industrial tribunal.

But many organizations do not have analytical schemes for this purpose, or indeed any other purpose. This may be because they don't care, they can't be bothered, they are satisfied (rightly or wrongly) that they don't have a problem or, as one HR director of a large organization said to us: 'We refuse to be obsessed by equal pay.'

There is no doubt that equal pay for work of equal value is achievable without the aid of analytical job evaluation, although it might be difficult to prove that this is the case. And some organizations, especially those with broadbanded structures, keep an analytical scheme in reserve to deal with equal value questions as they arise, or to audit pay levels from time to time. This is good, although not essential, practice. But if there is no such scheme, extra care needs to be taken over pay and grading decisions for jobs held by men and women in the interests of justice and equity as well as to avoid legal difficulties.

5. *How can pay relativities be managed when roles are flexible and pay is individual?*
   Finely graded pay structures containing carefully defined, fixed jobs are a thing of the past in many organizations. Many organizations never had them to start with. The traditional world of job evaluation and the strict control of conformity was not for them. But most learn that it is still necessary to analyse and monitor the distribution of rates of pay to identify and deal with anomalies.

6. *How can I be satisfied that the market rate data I am getting is valid and reliable?*
   The validity and reliability of market rate data depends mainly on three factors:

   ▌ *The sample frame* – the data collected should be fully representative of the organizations with which comparisons need to be made.
   ▌ *Job or role matching* – the extent to which good job matching has taken place, so that it can be said with some confidence that like is being compared with like.
   ▌ *Timing* – the degree to which the information is up to date or can be updated reliably.

   But it is most unlikely that a perfect sample, precise job matching and the complete coincidence of timing will always be achieved. This is why it is usually advisable to obtain data from more than one source. It also underlines the point that, ultimately, a judgement has to be made about the level of pay in the market place, which should be used as the reference point for decisions on rates of pay within the organization.

7. *How can we prevent grade drift?*
   Grade drift takes place when unjustifiable upgradings take place, often because of pressure by managers or employees, and some-

times by manipulation of the job evaluation scheme. Manipulation is more likely with decayed job evaluation schemes and when people are allowed to get away with creative job descriptions. Often, the problem is pay, not grading.

Grade drift is a larger problem in finely graded pay structures, which increase the likelihood of boundary problems. When designing such structures, it is desirable to minimize these problems as far as possible by creating a distinct gap between the highest-rated jobs in one grade and the lowest-rated jobs in the grade above.

In reviewing upgrading proposals in a finebanded structure it is necessary to ensure that a proper case is made, supported by a realistic job analysis.

Grade drift can also be managed by instituting and maintaining a rigorous pay review and budgeting system which forces managers to control pay movements in their departments and provides the basis for monitoring upgradings.

8. *Broadbanding sounds good in theory, but in practice isn't it a much more difficult system to control than a normal finegraded structure?*

The answer to this question is 'no and yes'. Broadbanding, once established, is easier to run than a multi-graded structure because it can operate more flexibly, grading decisions are easier and it relies less on the continuous application of job evaluation. But it does need more 'hands-on' care than a conventional scheme, which can be controlled more or less mechanically. More data on market rates has to be made available and line managers need careful guidance and training on how to exercise the responsibilities that are likely to be devolved to them to manage pay. They will also need more information. You cannot remove traditional grade structures and leave a vacuum.

Individual employees will have to be briefed carefully on how broadbanding affects them and the basis upon which they can progress laterally through bands, rather than vertically through a hierarchy. Particular care has to be taken in setting up and managing competence profiles and assessments if, as is likely, competence development is a major factor governing progression. This extra work may or may not be balanced by the savings in effort that broadbanding may provide, but converts to this approach are generally convinced that the effort is worthwhile.

9. *How do I get everyone to buy in to a new contingent pay process?*

To the HR specialist, the case for contingent pay is often irresistible, especially if its developmental purposes are emphasized and it is regarded as a framework for a continuing dialogue between managers and those they manage throughout the year, rather than an annual and threatening (to both parties) event.

Line managers who carry out performance reviews and the same line managers or employees who are on the receiving end may, however, see things differently. Line managers frequently don't want to do it because they believe it is unnecessary, time consuming or both. They may feel that they have other, much stronger priorities. Even when they conduct a review, they may do it badly, either because they are going through the motions or because they have not been given essential and thorough training in such skills as providing feedback.

Employees may react defensively against performance reviews for all sorts of reasons, for example: they don't like negative feedback, even when it is justified; they are dubious about performance rating; they see them as perfunctory affairs; or they are concerned that the performance data will be used as a stick to beat them with in subsequent disciplinary procedures.

Getting people to buy in to performance management is a matter of:

▌ Ownership – both parties must feel that this is their process, not something which has been forced upon them by the HR department.

▌ Understanding – of how they can both benefit from it, which means emphasizing the positive developmental aspect of performance management. If it is just seen as a means of generating ratings for PRP purposes, it is more likely to be rejected by those concerned.

▌ Skill – developed by training managers and other employees in conducting performance management processes. These skills include: agreeing objectives; defining competence profiles; reviewing performance and competence levels; giving and receiving feedback; coaching; and preparing and implementing personal development plans.

10. *What are the implications for reward management of the delayered or lean organization?*
   The reduction of hierarchies after delayering means that multi-graded pay structures are no longer appropriate. This is one of the main reasons for broadbanding.

   Lean organizations offer fewer opportunities for promotion or upgrading. This is another reason for broadbanding, which facilitates rewards for lateral career moves within wider pay ranges and for the development and effective use of competences. This is an environment which fosters self-managed career progression and requires the provision of tools such as competency models and career maps to enable the process.

11. *What are the implications for reward management of the 'flexible firm'?*
   The two main characteristics of the flexible firm are role flexibility and the 'core/periphery' approach to resourcing the organization.

Role flexibility arises because, in a constantly changing business environment, jobs also change. People have to expand their roles by taking on new responsibilities and roles can develop in line with the capability of the person carrying them out. In other words, both roles and the people in them grow. To keep pace with change and the varied demands made on people individually or in teams, workers have to become multiskilled. Flexible roles require flexible pay processes. Traditional grade structures, which constrain people into narrowly defined jobs, and job evaluation and pay schemes which result in people being rewarded for non-adaptive behaviour, are no longer appropriate.

The focus has increasingly to be on competence and skill development and rewards for growing roles (lateral growth) and flexibility. Both for individual roles in broadbanded structures and job families, templates and role profiles can be produced jointly with employees, which help to clarify expectations of what is required while not constraining flexibility when it is needed.

Core structures retain a relatively small number of key workers on continuous and long-term contracts, while relying on a peripheral workforce of part timers and temporary or contract workers to enable the firm to adapt rapidly to increases or decreases in activity levels. Special care has to be taken over the reward packages and development of the key core workers. But tension may be created if the differences between the ways in which core and peripheral workers are treated become too large. Peripheral workers are an important part of the firm and should not be neglected or taken for granted. As far as possible, values and practices should be shared with the core.

12. *How can we motivate the bulk of our employees on whose efforts we depend when there is not much money available in the pay-for-performance kitty?*
Much of the thinking that went into the early performance-related pay schemes centred on rewarding 'key players' and ensuring that high performance produced significant rewards.

In some organizations the overall results achieved depend crucially on the effective performance of a small number of people, who are directing the enterprise or who are responsible for innovation, marketing and sales. In such cases, it makes business sense to reward these people highly and put a large proportion of pay at risk. Most organizations, however, depend on the efficient performance of employees at all levels. In these circumstances, a pay system that siphons off resources to a few 'star' performers would be at best irrelevant and at worst counter-productive in motivating the 'engine room' of the organization.

But when performance pay budgets are tight, the range of performance awards on offer is limited. A few high performers may get one-off bonuses of 10 per cent or so. However, the majority of employees have recently been getting overall increases in pay covering both individual performance pay and across-the-board awards of 3 to 5 per cent. This is in line with the general movement in earnings or what they would expect in any case.

A performance-related increase of, in effect, 1 or 2 per cent is not going to provide much of an incentive at all. PRP in these circumstances will not directly motivate. But this does not destroy the validity of the concept that people should be valued according to their contribution.

The good, reliable 'core' performers should be rewarded according to their market worth and this should increase as they gain experience. Even if they cannot be given large performance-related increases, they should at least be eligible for an achievement bonus if they make a special contribution, or for a special sustained performance bonus if they consistently deliver a fully competent level of performance. There may be scope for including them in team bonus schemes and there is certainly much merit in their participating in organization-wide gainsharing, profit sharing or share schemes.

Motivating the 'engine room' – the good, reliable core performers – is not just a matter of pay. There are other ways of ensuring that employees feel valued, including scope to demonstrate their growing competence, recognition through performance management processes, and opportunities to increase their employability.

13. *Performance-related pay has had a bad press over the last few years. Why is this so?*

The concept of performance-related pay (PRP) suffered from over-marketing and crude approaches in the 1980s. That was the decade in which most private sector organizations got rid of their expensive fixed incremental pay systems and, under the influence of the entrepreneurial/finance/economic/transactional ethos of the time, believed that PRP could be a major lever for culture change as well as a powerful motivator. The government of the day joined in and fervently believed in the miracle-working powers of PRP as a means of converting its own departments/agencies, etc, into commercial enterprises overnight.

Performance-related pay was viewed simplistically as an instrument for producing high levels of individual and organizational performance. This asks too much and there has been no evidence that PRP is guaranteed to deliver this result. Research has also shown that PRP can demotivate people if it is managed badly and, consequently, is felt to be unfair. Vicky Wright[3] has pointed out that: 'Even the most ardent supporters of performance-related pay recognize that it is extraordinarily difficult to manage well ... it is a part of managing people which requires constant attention and improvement.'

In spite of the perceived problems of managing PRP effectively, most people still believe that it is right to reward employees according to their contribution and competence and that, directly or indirectly, this will motivate them to improve their performance and develop their competences. But some are seeking alternatives to the crude model of output-based schemes for individuals and many are reconsidering how they measure contribution and competence.

14. *Is competence-related pay no more than a 'flavour of the month'?*
    Interest in competence-related pay was generated by writers such as Ed Lawler,[4] who advocated people-based as distinct from job-based pay – paying people according to their value in the market and in relation to their knowledge, skills and competence. Interest was also created by the drive for organizational and role flexibility resulting in moves from narrowly defined jobs and job standards to broader generic roles, where the importance of competence development and continuous improvement is fully recognized. Other factors have been dissatisfaction with conventional performance-related pay and a belief that, having established competence frameworks and profiles for recruiting and developmental purposes, it is logical to extend this to reward, thus providing an integrated approach to human resource management.

    However, pay schemes based purely on competence have never really caught on. Only 6 per cent of the respondents to the 2003 CIPD reward survey had such schemes. The three main reasons for this lack of enthusiasm have been 1) the difficulty of measuring competency levels in the form of behaviour, 2) the problem of converting impressionistic assessments into hard pay figures and 3) importantly, the reluctance of managers and others to accept that levels of competency are all that matters. Surely they say, with some reason, it's no use people behaving well unless it results in high performance. But the need to consider competence as well as performance has not been ignored on the grounds that if performance management is about improving performance it is necessary to consider how the results were achieved as well as the results themselves. This need has been more generally recognized in contribution-related pay schemes where both inputs in the form of competence and outputs in the form of results are considered.

15. *Is the use of forced distribution to control the distribution of pay increases a good idea?*
    Forced distribution means that the distribution of ratings by managers and therefore the distribution of pay increases is 'forced' to conform to a predetermined pattern, which may follow the normal distribution curve. For example, managers could be required to distribute their ratings as follows:

A (excellent) 10 per cent
B (above average) 20 per cent
C (average) 40 per cent
D (below average) 20 per cent
E (poor) 10 per cent

This pattern could be varied to skew the distribution positively so that, for example, 50 per cent must be rated C and 10 per cent rated D, the other proportions remaining the same.

Forced distribution may appeal to managements that want to exercise complete, albeit arbitrary, control over pay distribution. But line managers hate it. They feel that it shows lack of trust by senior management and, reasonably enough, they refuse to accept that the distribution of performance is identical in each part of the organization. Staff also dislike being forced into categories without, seemingly, any proper consideration being given to their individual characteristics and the variations in performance in different areas that they know to exist. Because of these objections a very small proportion of organizations use it – only 8 per cent of the respondents to the survey of performance management carried out by the CIPD in 2004.

A variation of the use of forced distribution was given a lot of publicity recently. This was at GE, where Jack Welch in effect used it as a means of identifying and removing under-performers so that the bottom 10 per cent in the distribution of assessments were liable to be dismissed. However, he pointed out that: 'Our vitality curve [the GE forced choice distribution] works because we spent over a decade building a performance culture that has candid feedback at every level. Candour and openness are the foundations of such a culture. I wouldn't want to inject a vitality curve cold turkey into an organization without a performance culture already in place.'

Even if forced distribution were desirable, which it isn't, it could never work unless such a performance culture already exists.

16. *Why should we move to variable pay?*
Variable pay is pay that varies with performance. It is 'at risk' pay, in the sense that people may receive a lump sum bonus one year but risk not getting it next year if their performance, or that of their team or organization, does not justify it. The argument for variable pay is that, because it is not consolidated into base pay, people will not go on receiving the benefit of a previous increase which is not justified by their present performance. In addition, awards can be more focused on specific attainments and can be made at any time as a spot bonus to recognize a major achievement. The acceptability of variable pay depends on a number of factors, including a reasonable level of base pay, shared values regarding risk, and clarity on the relationship between risk and reward.

17. *How can we introduce a more flexible and performance or contribution-related pay scheme to replace our present fixed incremental system?*
    The decision to move to performance- or competence-related pay is often made as part of a cultural change programme – moving from an environment in which people are rewarded just for being there and carrying out the same old job to one in which they have to earn their increases. Another reason is simply to save money. In an organization with low staff turnover there is nothing to stop staff moving inexorably to the top of the scale, with the likelihood that a proportion of them will be paid more than they are worth.

    The first thing to recognize is the need to think very hard about how the change is to be managed. Clearly, a proposal to abolish a deeply embedded fixed incremental system will be resisted by any people who think they are going to lose by it or who believe that to adjust pay on the basis of managerial judgement is likely to be intrinsically unfair. Trade unions are often vociferously against performance-related pay.

    This means paying attention to the following guidelines on change management.

    ▌ 'People support what they help to create' – commitment to change, or at least its acceptance, is improved if those affected by change participate in planning and implementing it.
    ▌ Hard evidence and data on the need for change are the most powerful tools for its achievement, eg attitude survey findings.
    ▌ Identify people who can act as champions of change.
    ▌ Remember that resistance to change is inevitable if the individuals concerned feel that they are going to be worse off. Therefore take steps to remove or at least diminish those fears by explaining how the change will work and how it will affect them.

    Tinkering with a pay spine by allowing extra increments to be earned on the basis of the ratings produced by an existing performance appraisal scheme is generally doomed to failure, as the Inland Revenue found. It could be adopted as a transitional policy but this needs to be explicit. PRP will only work and will only be acceptable if it is based on a fully developed performance management process, as described in Chapters 18 and 19. And it is essential to provide training in face-to-face briefing for all concerned in how the process works and the part they play. Reliance should not be placed on written material alone.

    It is also necessary to monitor the introduction of PRP very carefully to ensure that it is operating fairly. Attitude surveys and focus groups can be used to obtain reactions from managers and other employees and action taken to deal with any weaknesses these identify.

18. *To what extent, if at all, should we provide rewards for individual performance or competence to those taking part in a team-based pay scheme?*
    A few team-based pay purists assert that the whole ethos underpinning team pay will be destroyed if there is any variation in the rewards paid to individual members of the team. But team pay enthusiasts are more likely to concede that team bonuses should be a percentage of the basic pay of team members which, they assume, will reflect the value of the individual to the team.

    Others point out that the difficulties of managing the performance of individuals within a team cannot be ignored. Vicky Wright and Liz Brading[5] comment that:

    > Leaving team dynamics to manage performance by such things as team pressure can be dangerous and unfair. Managing team performance is important, but it is not a substitute for managing individual performance.

    This suggests that there might be a case for providing individual rewards to team members, but how can this be done in a cohesive work team in which there is a high degree of interdependence among team members? Would it not be invidious to single out individuals?

    An answer to this dilemma can be provided by the use of competence-related pay. This is necessarily always orientated to individuals and it is reasonable to assume that as competence increases (including competence as a team worker) the contribution of the individual to team results will increase correspondingly.

19. *Flexible benefits sound a good idea, but aren't they very complicated to operate in practice?*
    Flexible benefits schemes can be relatively simple, with a choice among only two or three benefits; or they can cover the whole range of benefits apart from core pensions, sick pay and holiday benefit entitlements.

    There may be some fairly complex analytical processes in designing a flexible benefits scheme, eg costing the various benefits and considering entitlement and tax implications. Having designed the scheme, it is not difficult, even when it is a fairly complex scheme, to drive it through a computerized payroll system which has been adjusted to take account of flexible benefits. Such a system is described in Chapter 32. With this in place, the administrative burden is unlikely to be much more than the work required to run the existing benefits scheme.

20. *How can we reconcile the pressure to devolve more responsibility for pay decisions to line managers with the need to achieve a reasonable degree of equity, fairness and consistency in managing rewards?*
    While it is highly desirable for line managers to be given the

maximum scope to manage pay within their departments, this does not mean that the HR department can abdicate its responsibility for monitoring pay decisions.

But the HR department is not there to police line managers in order to impose total uniformity. There has to be some scope for diversity, because of the range of factors which have to be taken into account at departmental level. What the HR function must do is provide guidelines and information to line managers, which will help them to be equitable, fair and consistent. This will include the basis for progressing pay; the relationship between the level of competence required in a role and the payment for someone in that role; the distribution of the pay of people carrying out similar roles; and the market rates of pay for those roles.

In addition, it is still necessary for the HR department to monitor proposed pay increases or gradings and question either the pattern of increases generally or unusual individual awards. But the members of the HR department carrying out this role must be prepared to recognize that there will be differences between departments and accept those differences as long as they are justified. They must also be prepared to act as coaches and consultants who are focused on building pay literacy and sound judgements.

21. *How can we improve line management capability in dealing with reward matters?*
We have frequently mentioned the issue of line management capability. If, rightly, more responsibility for managing pay should be devolved to them, how can we be sure that they will do it properly? Some will be excellent, some very poor (which would make their position as line managers questionable) and the majority will do the work fairly well but not well enough.

Training and the availability of good guidance notes are important but they are not enough. The personal touch is what counts.

We spoke to one senior reward manager about introducing a new reward system and he told us that he had to spend a lot of time 'holding the hands of line managers'. By this he meant sitting down with them and going through what they had to think about and say to their people about the annual individual pay review, and giving them on-the-spot help and guidance. It is a common story in public and private sectors and essential to ensuring that the right messages get across. Line managers still do not think ahead enough about how individuals will feel and respond and how to give effective recognition, the context for the pay review, or indeed confirmation in the pay award that performance needs to improve.

Dealing direct with line managers is an important part of the role of reward specialists, indeed anyone in HR. Those concerned with reward should not spend their time in their offices manipulating figures, issuing instructions and checking up on people. They should be out there, talking to line managers, as informally and regularly as possible. The aim should be to see each manager accountable for pay decisions before the pay review, to discuss the guidelines and processes involved and to deal with queries and problems. Managers who are responsible for operating the performance management process should be seen regularly to review how they are getting on and coach them on any issues they are facing. This is a time-consuming but essential process.

REFERENCES

1. Lawler, E (1995) The new pay: a strategic approach, *Compensation & Benefits Review*, July–August, pp 14–22
2. Murlis, H (1996) 'Managing the paradoxes,' in H Murlis (ed) *Pay at the Crossroads*, IPD, London
3. Wright, V (1991) 'Performance-related pay', in F Neale (ed) *The Performance Management Handbook*, IPD, London
4. Lawler, E (1990) *Strategic Pay*, Jossey-Bass, San Fransisco
5. Wright, V and Brading, L (1998) A balanced performance, *Total Quality Review*, October

43

Trends In Reward Management

It has often been said that the field of reward management suffers from a tendency to follow the latest fashion – sometimes referred to as 'fad surfing' – without due consideration of organization context or culture. Those who have approached their senior management boards or committees with recommendations to change the reward system will invariably receive the question, 'That sounds sensible enough, but what do others – especially our competitors – do?' If they can be convinced that a recommendation is in line with 'best practice' then approval is likely to be given. There are, however, signs in the first decade of the 21st century that this traditional approach to reward, which can lead to organizations implementing reward systems that are out of line with their business objectives or culture, is finally in decline.

One of the principal drivers of this change is the approach known as 'total reward', which was the subject of Chapter 2 of this book and is considered below.

The major recent trends in reward management that we have observed through our consultancy practices, research and study of the latest literature are summarized in this final chapter under the following headings:

- total reward;
- engaged performance;
- the new realism;
- job evaluation;
- equal pay for work of equal value;

▋ broadbanding;
▋ career family structures;
▋ contribution-related pay;
▋ flexible benefits;
▋ line manager capability.

TOTAL REWARD

The total reward concept emphasizes the importance of considering all aspects of reward as an integrated and coherent whole. It emerged during the late 1990s as a means of maximizing the combined impact of the whole range of reward initiatives on motivation, commitment and job engagement. It addresses the crucial issues of recruitment, retention and talent management. It has encouraged organizations to consider much more carefully the role of non-financial rewards, including recognition schemes, and to rely less on money as the sole motivator.

This concept encourages organizations to consider their 'employee proposition' in broad terms, taking into account the myriad reasons why people seek to join and stay with them. The traditional elements of reward management such as pay and benefits do, of course, play a part, but total reward considers the impact of other aspects of work too – intangibles such as leadership style and environmental factors such as location and workplace facilities.

In order, therefore, to achieve the much-coveted prize of 'employer of choice', all elements of the employment experience need to be aligned and consistently applied. This requires coordinated management across the organization. For the reward specialist, for example, it means closer understanding and cooperation with colleagues in HR specializing in people development, resourcing and employee relations.

In concert with this more holistic approach to employee motivation is an increasing realization that reward systems must be flexible if they are to motivate effectively the diverse workforce of the 21st century. This may manifest itself at the most basic level through the removal of the bottle of champagne as a universal token of recognition, as it is one that does not take account of the impact on non-drinkers, particularly those who avoid alcohol for religious reasons.

ENGAGED PERFORMANCE

The focus on the factors creating engaged performance, which again started in the late 1990s, has attached increasing importance to the relational rewards that are associated with the work environment and learning and development rather than the transactional rewards, which are about pay and employee benefits. This highlights issues about what employees value most in the shape of rewards. These include matters such as inspiration and values (the quality of leadership, organizational values and behaviour, the reputation of the organization, recognition and communication), and growth and opportunity (learning and development, career advancement opportunities and performance feedback).

GREATER REALISM ABOUT THE ROLE OF REWARD

There was a tendency for writers on reward management during the 1990s to exaggerate the role of reward management as a lever for change – press the lever called performance-related pay and, lo and behold, you get superior organizational performance without, seemingly, having to do anything else. This naive belief in the power of reward created expectations about reward initiatives that could never be met. Marc Thompson[1] wrote that 'Reward management is a job of short-term damage limitation not the strategic lever for change that appears so seductive in the writings of American commentators.' This is probably going too far. Reward management can certainly support cultural change even if it cannot drive it, especially if it is treated as an integrated part of a range of organizational and HR initiatives.

JOB EVALUATION

Job evaluation was more or less written off in the 1990s by many people on the grounds that, apart from being time consuming and bureaucratic, it was no longer relevant in the days when 'the market rules, OK?' But in the 2000s research has shown that job evaluation is flourishing, although it is more often used in a support role rather than as a driver for grading decisions.

The trend in favour of job evaluation has emerged partly because organizations have recognized that internal equity is important but also because of the increased prominence of equal pay considerations.

EQUAL PAY

The focus on equal pay in the early 2000s epitomized by the Kingsmill Report of 2001[2] and the work of the Equal Opportunities Commission has created increased pressure not only to introduce analytical job evaluation but also to conduct equal pay reviews or audits. Public sector organizations are required to conduct equal pay reviews. Private sector organizations appear to be reluctant but the pressure to do so will no doubt increase.

BROADBANDING

Broadbanding has been one of the most prominent ideas in reward management for some time. But many organizations have jumped on the bandwagon without fully appreciating what they were getting into. The two questions that emerged from the experience of developing broad bands in the 1990s and early 2000s were: 1) What's the point of unstructured broad bands if, in effect, they simply consist of spot rates? 2) What's the difference between, say, a four-banded structure with three zones in each band and a 12-graded structure? The answer given by broadband devotees to the first question was that at least there was some overall structure within which spot rates could be managed. In reply to the second question, the usual answer was that, as roles develop, movements between zones could be dealt with more flexibly. Neither of these responses is particularly convincing.

Apart from these fundamental flaws, disillusionment with broadbanding has increased for the following reasons (see also Armstrong, 'What's happening to broad-banding?'[3]). In general, it has been found that broadbanded structures are harder to manage than narrower-graded structures in spite of the original claim that they would be easier – they make considerable demands on line managers as well as HR. Broadbanding can build employee expectations of significant pay opportunities, which are doomed in many cases if proper control of the system is maintained. It can be difficult to explain to people how broadbanding works and how they will be affected, and they may be concerned by the apparent lack of structure and precision. Decisions on movements within bands can be harder to justify objectively than in other types of grade and pay structures. And they create equal pay problems.

The trend is therefore for organizations to develop broad-graded structures, ie structures with 6 to 10 grades, which are managed in the same way as traditional narrow-graded structures using reference points, zones and compa-ratios. These are often associated with the other development in grade and pay structures, namely career family structures.

CAREER AND JOB FAMILY STRUCTURES

Possibly the most significant recent development is the use of career and job families. A career family structure is one in which separate job families are identified and defined but a common grade and pay structure applies to all the families. They can be distinguished from job families, which may contain separate 'market groups' (eg, business support roles) each with its own graded pay structure.

In effect, a typical career family structure simply slices up a broad-graded structure into a number of families each of which contains levels that are defined by reference to key activities and competence or knowledge and skill requirements. Thus they define career paths within and between families and, because this can be treated as part of an integrated approach to human resource management, it is perhaps their most important feature. Continuous development, not pay considerations, comes first, and career families in broad-graded structures may well be the most likely direction the development of grade and pay structures will take. Career families are currently being introduced in universities as part of the pay modernization programme. They tend to use broad grades; for example, at Southampton University there are four families with common grades and a maximum of seven levels.

Of course, career and job families are not new. In one form or another they have been around a long time. They do not therefore constitute 'the next big thing' in reward management practice. But it seems a natural evolution, which clarifies how grade and pay structures can work as part of integrated HR policies in a way that broadbanding has failed to do.

CONTRIBUTION-RELATED PAY

The concept of contribution-related pay was only introduced as an alternative to performance-related or competence-related pay in 1999 by Duncan Brown and Michael Armstrong.[4] Since then it has burgeoned to the extent that in its 2003 survey of reward management the CIPD found that 63 per cent of respondents stated that they had contribution-related pay compared with 23 per cent with performance pay and only 6 per cent with competence pay.

Contribution-related pay rewards people for both their inputs (competence) and their outputs (performance). In a sense it is a combination of performance and competence pay. The attraction of contribution-related pay is that it is a holistic process, taking into account all aspects of a person's performance. It does not simply concern itself with the achievement of objectives without considering how they were achieved and therefore how performance could be improved. Neither is it focused on competence with the implication that it is competence that matters not performance. A further reason for its increasing popularity is that the term 'contribution' resonates with people. They feel that this is what working in organizations is all about – we are there to *contribute* to the achievement of organizational and team objectives, not just to perform or to display competence.

FLEXIBLE BENEFITS

There is nothing new about the notion of flexible benefits as described in Chapter 32. What is happening is that the notion is being taken up – the Hay benefits database indicates that 16 per cent of organizations have formal schemes and 82 per cent flex at least some of their benefits. The two main arguments in favour of flexible benefit schemes – that 1) they meet the increasingly varied needs of today's diverse workforce and 2) they increase the perceived value of the package by targeting expenditure into areas selected by employees – are convincing more and more people. Concerns about the cost of introduction and administration have largely been allayed by the development of systematic approaches to the provision of flexible benefits supported by software.

For reward managers the question now with respect to flexible reward systems is not 'should we or shouldn't we?' but 'what should it look like for us?'. The theory of flex is to find out what employees want through surveys or online 'employee relationship management' systems and then to tailor the reward offer accordingly. In practice, however, it is not always in the best interests of an employer simply to provide whatever people want: there needs to be a balance to ensure that employee needs are met while reinforcing the values of the employer through reward. Most employers and employees believe, for example, that there should be a cash alternative to a car and that the use of car provision to underline hierarchical status is no longer appropriate to these less deferential times. Employers and employees are not always in such accord, however. This is certainly true with respect to the pension benefit, which is rarely highly valued among young people. From their point of view, it would be more advantageous to receive a higher level of pay with which to secure access to a higher mortgage loan than to put money into a rather abstract benefit. This analysis is supported by numerous employee surveys (including a recent one at the Department for Work and Pensions!), which indicate a lack of interest in pensions. Nevertheless, for most organizations the pension remains a 'core benefit' with no cash alternative for those who wish to opt out because the message it gives is one of a responsible employer thinking of the future welfare of its people.

LINE MANAGEMENT CAPABILITY

It is now generally accepted that more responsibility for pay decisions should be devolved to line managers. But in doing so, the issue of the capacity of line managers to make such decisions fairly, consistently and in accordance with policy guidelines has been questioned. Too often, they have been thrown in at the deep end. Some have swum away without difficulty; others have floundered. This means that in planning the implementation of reward initiatives it is essential to devote time in the programme for educating and training line managers and to ensure that continuing guidance and help are provided by HR as required.

REFERENCES

1. Thompson, M (1992) *Pay and Performance: The employer experience*, Institute of Manpower Studies, Brighton
2. Kingsmill, D (2001) *Review of Women's Employment and Pay*, HMSO, Norwich
3. Armstrong, M (2004) What's happening to broad-banding?, *IDS Executive Compensation Review*, June
4. Brown, D and Armstrong, M (1999) *Paying for Contribution*, Kogan Page, London

Appendices

Appendix A

Further Sources of Reading and Information

There is a very large body of literature published around reward management. This section is intended as a guide to the main sources and a limited selection of the key recent literature. It is certainly not exhaustive. The fact that a particular source or organization is listed here does not imply the authors' recommendation.

REWARD MANAGEMENT AND STRATEGY

Books and reports

Armstrong, M (2002) *Employee Reward*, 3rd edn, Chartered Institute of Personnel and Development, London

Armstrong, M and Brown, D (2001) *New Dimensions in Pay Management*, Chartered Institute of Personnel and Development, London

Berger, L A and Berger, D R (eds) (1999) *The Compensation Handbook*, 4th edn, McGraw-Hill, New York

Brown, D (2001) *Reward Strategies: From intent to impact*, Chartered Institute of Personnel and Development, London

Chartered Institute of Personnel and Development (2001) *Reward Determination in the UK*, CIPD, London

Chartered Institute of Personnel and Development (2001) *The Future of Reward*, CIPD, London

Druker, J and White, G (2000) *Reward Management: A critical text*, Routledge, London

Harvard Business Review (2001) *Harvard Business Review on Compensation*, Harvard Business School Press, Cambridge, MA

Heneman, R L (ed) (2002) *Strategic Reward Management: Design, implementation, and evaluation*, Information Age Publishing, Greenwich, CT

Homan, G and Thorpe, R (2000) *Strategic Reward Systems*, FT Prentice Hall, London

Kanter, R M and Wilson, T B (2002) *Innovative Reward Systems for the Changing Workplace*, 2nd edn, McGraw-Hill, New York

Lawler, E E (2000) *Rewarding Excellence: Pay strategies for the new economy*, Jossey-Bass Wiley, San Francisco

Martocchio, J (2003) *Strategic Compensation: A human resource*, 3rd edn, Prentice Hall, London

Schuster, J R and Zingheim, P K (2000) *Pay People Right!: Breakthrough reward strategies to create great companies*, Jossey-Bass Wiley, San Francisco

Suff, P (2001) *The New Reward Agenda*, IRS Management Review 22, Industrial Relations Service – Eclipse Group, London

Journal articles

Case, J (2001) When salaries aren't secret, *Harvard Business Review*, **79** (5), May, pp 37–49

Gherson, D J (2000) Getting the pay thing right, *Workspan*, **43** (6), June, pp 47–51

Giles, P (2001) Building a foundation for effective pay programs, *Workspan*, **44** (9), September, pp 28–32

Lawler, E E (2000) Pay strategy: new thinking for the new millennium, *Compensation and Benefits Review*, **32** (1), January–February, pp 7–12

Watson, S (2002) Heart stoppers: creating change with harming performance, *Workspan*, **45** (5), May, pp 58–62

TOTAL REWARD AND MOTIVATION

Books and reports

Bowen, R B (2000) *Recognizing and Rewarding Employees*, McGraw-Hill, New York

Chartered Institute of Personnel and Development (2002) *Total Reward*, CIPD, London

Graham, M D and Manas, T M (2002) *Creating a Total Rewards Strategy: A toolkit for designing business-based plans*, Amacom, New York

Herriot, P (2000) *The Employment Relationship: A psychological perspective*, Routledge, London

Kazenbach, J R (2000) *Peak Performance: Aligning the hearts and minds of your employees*, Harvard Business School Press, Cambridge, MA

Lawler, E E (2003) *Treat People Right: How organizations and individuals can propel each other into a virtuous spiral of success*, Jossey-Bass, San Francisco

Thomas, K W (2003) *Intrinsic Motivation At Work: Building energy and commitment*, Berrett Koehler, San Francisco

Journal articles

Ben-Ora, D and Lyons, F H (2002) Total rewards strategy: the best foundation of pay for performance, *Compensation and Benefits Review*, **34** (2), April, pp 34–40

Herzberg, F (2003) One more time: how do you motivate employees?, Classic reprint, *Harvard Business Review*, **81** (1), January, pp 87–96

Hollyforde, S and Whiddett, S (2002) How to nurture motivation, *People Management*, **8** (14), 11 July, pp 52–53

Murlis, H (2004) Making executive coaching part of total reward, *IDS Executive Compensation Review*, July, pp. 21–23.

Murlis, H and Watson, S (2001) Creating employee engagement – transforming the employment deal, *Benefits and Compensation International*, **30** (8), April, pp 25–29

Watson, S (2003) Total rewards: building a better employment deal, *Workspan*, **46** (12), December, pp 48–51

EQUAL PAY AND JOB EVALUATION

Books and reports

Advisory, Conciliation and Arbitration Service (2003) *Job Evaluation: An introduction*, Acas, London

Armstrong, M *et al* (2003) *Job Evaluation: A guide to achieving equal pay*, Kogan Page, London

Chartered Institute of Personnel and Development (2001) *Equal Pay Guide*, CIPD, London

Equal Pay Task Force (2001) *Just Pay*, Equal Opportunities Commission, Manchester

Falconer, H (2003) *One Stop Guide: Equal pay reviews*, Personnel Today Management Resources, Reed Business Information, Sutton

Incomes Data Services (2003) *IDS Studies Plus: Job evaluation*, Incomes Data Services, London

Kingsmill, B (2001) *Review of Women's Employment and Pay*, HMSO, Norwich

Journal articles

Heneman, R L (2001) Work evaluation: current state of the art and future prospects, *World atWork Journal*, **10** (3), Third quarter, pp 65–70

IRS Employment Review (2003) Chasing progress on equal pay, *IRS Employment Review*, **774**, 18 April, pp 19–22

Paddison, L (2001) How to conduct an equal pay review, *People Management*, **7** (12), 14 June, pp 58–59

GRADE AND PAY STRUCTURES

Books and reports

Armstong, M and Brown, D (2001) *New Dimensions in Pay Management*, Chartered Institute of Personnel and Development, London

Gilbert, D and Abosch, K S (1996) *Improving Organizational Effectiveness through Broad-banding*, ACA, Scotsdale, Ill

Journal articles

Armstrong, M (2000) Feel the width, *People Management*, 3 February, pp 34–38

Armstrong, M (2004) What's happening to broad-banding?, *IDS Executive Compensation Review*, June

LeBlanc, P V and Ellkis, M E (1995) The many faces of broad-banding, *ACA Journal*, Winter, pp 52–56

Richter, A S (1998) Paying the people in black at the big blue, *Compensation and Benefits Review*, May–June, pp 51–59

PERFORMANCE MANAGEMENT

Books and reports

Armstrong, M and Baron, A (1998) *Performance Management: The new realities*, Chartered Institute of Personnel and Development, London

Armstrong, M and Baron, A (2004) *Performance Management: Action and impact*, Chartered Institute of Personnel and Development, London

Baguley, P (2002) *Performance Management in a Week*, 2nd edn, Hodder Arnold, London

Incomes Data Services (2003) *IDS Studies: Performance management*, Incomes Data Services, London

Personnel Today and PeopleSoft (2004) *Performance Management Survey*, Personnel Today Management Resources, Reed Business Information, Sutton

Suff, P (2001) *Performance Management – Revisited*, IRS Management Review 21, Industrial Relations Service – Eclipse Group, London

Journal articles

Lawler, E E and McDermott, M (2003) Current performance management practices: examining the varying impacts, *WorldatWork Journal*, **12** (2), Second quarter, pp 49–60

Morris, E and Sparrow, T (2001) Transforming appraisals with emotional intelligence, *Competency and Emotional Intelligence Quarterly*, **9** (1), Autumn, pp 28–32

Peiperl, M A (2001) Getting 360 degree feedback right, *Harvard Business Review*, **79** (1), January, pp 142–47

Williams, V (2001) Making performance management relevant, *Compensation and Benefits Review*, **33** (4), July–August, pp 47–51

CONTINGENT PAY

Books and reports

Armstrong, M (2000) *Rewarding Teams*, Chartered Institute of Personnel and Development, London

Armstrong, M and Brown, D (1999) *Paying for Contribution: Real performance-related pay strategies*, Kogan Page, London

Chartered Institute of Personnel and Development (2002) *Guide to Bonus and Incentive Plans*, CIPD, London

Geldman, A, Holroyd, K and Suff, P (eds) (2003) *Restructuring Performance-related Pay*, Managing Best Practice No. 105, Work Foundation, London

Incomes Data Services (2003) *IDS Studies Plus: Employee recognition schemes*, Incomes Data Services, London

Parker, G, McAdams, J and Zielinski, D (2000) *Rewarding Teams: Lessons from the trenches*, Jossey-Bass Wiley, San Francisco

Reilly, P (ed) (2003) *New Reward: Team, skill and competency based pay*, Institute for Employment Studies, Brighton

Rose, M (2001) *Recognising Performance: Non-cash rewards*, Chartered Institute of Personnel and Development, London

Thompson, M (1992) *Pay and Performance: The employer experience*, Institute of Manpower Studies, Brighton

Trevor, J (2003) *An exploration of the determinants of reward management approach, design and operation*, Judge Institute of Management Studies.

WorldatWork (2001) *The Best of Variable Pay: Incentives, recognition and rewards*, WorldatWork, Scottsdale, AZ

Journal articles

Fisher, J (2001) How to design incentive schemes, *People Management*, **7** (1), 11 January, pp 38–39

Freeman, R (2001) Upping the stakes, Employee share ownership feature, *People Management*, **7** (3), 8 February, pp 25–29

Keegan, B P (2002) Incentive programs boost employee morale and productivity, *Workspan*, **45** (3), March, pp 30–33

Luo, S (2003) Does your sales incentive plan pay for performance?, *Compensation and Benefits Review*, **35** (1), January–February, pp 18–24

EMPLOYEE BENEFITS

Books and reports

Chartered Institute of Personnel and Development (2004) *Flexible Benefits*, CIPD, London

Daugherty, C (2002) How to introduce flexible benefits, *People Management*, **8** (1), 10 January, pp 42–43

House of Commons Work and Pensions Committee (2003) *The Future of UK Pensions, Third Report of Session 2002-03*, Stationery Office, Norwich

Hutchinson, P (2002) *Flexible Benefits: A practical guide*, Butterworths Tolley, Croydon

Journal articles

IRS Employment Review (2003) Benefits and allowances, Annual survey, *IRS Employment Review*, Part 1, No. 776, 23 May, pp 29–34; Part 2, No. 777, 6 June, pp 30–35; Part 3, No. 778, 20 June, pp 28–34

Lewin, C (2003) Pension developments in the UK, *Benefits and Compensation International*, **32** (9), May, pp 19–21

JOURNALS AND PERIODICALS

Benefits and Compensation International, Pension Publications
http://www.benecompintl.com

Compensation and Benefits Review, Sage Publications
http://www.sagepub.com

Employee Benefits, Centaur Communications
http://www.employeebenefits.co.uk

E-Reward Research Reports, e-reward.co.uk
http://www.e-reward.co.uk

IDS Executive Compensation Review, Incomes Data Services
http://www.incomesdata.co.uk

IDS HR Studies, Incomes Data Services
http://www.incomesdata.co.uk

IDS Report, Incomes Data Services
http://www.incomesdata.co.uk

IRS Employment Review, IRS Lexis Nexis
http://www.irsemploymentreview.com

Managing Best Practice Reports, Work Foundation
http://www.theworkfoundation.com

Pay Magazine, Gee Publishing
http://www.paymagazine.com

Pay and Reward, Centaur Communications
http://www.payandreward.co.uk

People Management, Personnel Publications
http://www.peoplemanagement.co.uk

Personnel Today, Reed Business Information
http://www.personneltoday.com

Workspan, WorldatWork
http://www.worldatwork.org

WorldatWork Journal, WorldatWork
http://www.worldatwork.org

ORGANIZATIONS

Advisory, Conciliation and Arbitration Service (Acas)
Brandon House
180 Borough High Street
London SE1 1LW
Tel: (020) 7210 3613
http://www.acas.org.uk

Chartered Institute of Personnel and Development (CIPD)
CIPD House
Camp Road
London SW19 4UX
Tel: (020) 8971 9000
http://www.cipd.co.uk (includes CIPD special interest reward forum
http://www.cipd.co.uk/communities/forums/rwrd/)

Chartered Management Institute (CMI)
Management House
Cottingham Road
Corby
Northants NN17 1TT
Tel: (01536) 204222
http://www.managers.org.uk

Equal Opportunities Commission (EOC)
Arndale House
Arndale Centre
Manchester M4 3EQ
Tel: 0845 601 5901
http://www.eoc.org.uk

e-reward.co.uk
33 Denby Lane
Heaton Chapel
Stockport
Cheshire SK4 2RA
Tel: (0161) 432 2584
http://www.e-reward.co.uk

Incomes Data Services (IDS)
77 Bastwick Street
London EC1V 3TT
Tel: (020) 7250 3434
http://www.incomesdata.co.uk

Institute for Employment Studies (IES)
Mantell Building
Falmer
Brighton BN1 9RF
Tel: (01273) 686751
http://www.employment-studies.co.uk

Management Consultancies Association (MCA)
49 Whitehall
London SW1A 2BX
Tel: (020) 7321 3990
http://www.mca.org.uk

National Association of Pension Funds (NAPF)
NIOC House
4, Victoria Street
London SW1H 0NX
Tel: (020) 7808 1300
http://www.napf.co.uk

Roffey Park Institute
Forest Road
Horsham
West Sussex RH12 4TD
Tel: (01293) 854059
http://www.roffeypark.com

The Work Foundation
Peter Runge House
3 Carlton House Terrace
London SW1Y 5DG
Tel: 0870 165 6700
http://www.theworkfoundation.com

MARKET RATE SURVEYS

Incomes Data Services (IDS) regularly publish the *Directory of Salary Surveys*, http://www.salarysurveys.info
UK survey coverage at national and local level, specialist benefits surveys, overseas and expatriate surveys and databases.

For general guidance on how to read market rate data:
Incomes Data Services (2002) *Understanding Salary Surveys*, IDS, London

HAY GROUP SURVEYS

Main online publications:
Boardroom Remuneration Guide
Compensation Reports Subscription Service
Employee Benefits Subscription Service

HR4IT
Managing People in Contact Centres
Offshore Financial Organizations: Guernsey, Jersey, Isle of Man (members only)
Periodical Publishers' Association (members only)
Retail Survey
UK HayOil (participants only)

Hay Group
33 Grosvenor Place
London SW1X 7HG
Tel: (020) 7856 7000
http://www.haygroup.co.uk

INTERNATIONAL COST-OF-LIVING DATA

ECA International (Employment Conditions Abroad)
Cost-of-living reports:
Anchor House
15 Britten Street
London SW3 3TY
Tel: (020) 7351 5000
http://www.eca-international.com

Economist Intelligence Unit (EIU)
Worldwide cost-of-living service:
15 Regent Street
London SW1Y 4LR
Tel: (020) 7830 1007
http://www.eiu.com

ORC Worldwide
Liscartan House
127/131 Sloane Street
London SW1X 9BA
Tel: (020) 7591 5600
http://www.orcworldwide.co.uk

UBS AG
Prices and earnings – a comparison of purchasing power around the globe:
1 Curzon Street
London W1J 5UB
Tel: (020) 7567 5757
http://www.ubs.com

Appendix B

Using Employee Surveys to Inform Reward Decisions

More and more organizations in the private and public sectors and internationally are using employee research inputs to help them create effective reward strategies. These can help create a multidimensional total reward strategy, specifically tailored to the organization and its people.

Employee surveys provide the 'customer perspective' on reward strategy. The first part of this appendix outlines how they can be used to inform reward decisions. The second looks at the changing face of employee surveys and how to run them effectively so that they become an essential business tool.

REWARD DECISIONS: OLD WAY

Early attempts at using employee surveys to help develop reward strategy were crude and rude. Take the example of the major UK company (11,000 people, eight locations around the country), which put a question on its employee survey: 'How satisfied are you with your levels of pay?' Overall the results weren't too bad: the typical company surveyed by Hay Group gets around 35–40 per cent positive answers to this question. This company achieved a bit above that. So far so good. But these results were used as a justification for not giving much of a pay rise in the next union negotiations. This was not bad in itself, but the error was compounded by a lack of understanding about why the scores were quite good, and a clumsy way of communicating the pay decision: 'you told us you were happy with pay, so we are not giving you a pay rise'. This approach has undermined not just negotiations, but also people's faith in future surveys.

REWARD DECISIONS: NEW WAY

Some current approaches take a holistic view of what makes employees feel rewarded or motivated. These more sophisticated reward surveys (eg the Hay Group Engaged Performance survey (see Chapter 2) and related tailored versions) cover the following areas:

- *Tangible rewards:* actual and perceived fairness, the balance of the different elements and how they knit together. (Consumer market researchers use very complicated statistical tools such as trade-off and conjoint analysis to help design product features to appeal to consumers. But these approaches are hardly used in the design of reward packages. Perhaps this is the next step of evolution.)
- *Opportunities for personal and professional growth.* In an era when people are changing jobs more and more frequently, the average employee is also looking to develop his or her skills for the next job, whether it is a promotion within the current organization or a more senior role elsewhere.
- *The degree to which the work environment is an enabling one,* ie enables people to do their best with the most appropriate degree of autonomy and leadership.
- *How work is measured, valued and has intellectual challenge.* What are the 'non-tangible rewards'? Several years ago, this author was doing some work for a large insurance broker who had an attrition problem. 'Lots of people are leaving for more highly paid jobs', they said, 'but we've benchmarked our pay rates and we are about average in the market.' After a quick lesson in mathematics, where it was explained that average meant that (by definition) there would be several companies paying more, we conducted some research among employees. The problem wasn't tangible rewards (which were perceived to be OK), but lack of non-tangible rewards, such as managers saying 'thank you' and people feeling valued. These were much easier and cheaper to resolve than a rethink of reward strategy and a blanket pay rise.
- *Work/life balance.* Is there flexibility and scope for people to manage their work within the context of other things in their life?
- *Inspiration/values.* Does the 'brand' or the purpose of the organization excite people and make them feel part of something special? Charities are a good example: most of them have two types of employees – those who want a job and those who want to support the cause. This second is worth a lot: many people volunteer their

time free of charge because they are rewarded in other ways. That is obviously the extreme: but perhaps companies with stronger, sexier images use this strength to attract and keep better people within reasonable cost. Initial research by Hay Group suggests that companies among the Fortune magazine listing of the World's Most Admired Companies in 2004 paid on average 5 per cent less than their less admired counterparts.

Overall, researching the balance between these six things provides a much wider perspective on what motivates and rewards employees to contribute at their best and put in the discretionary effort that creates success. By looking at the relative impact of these items, organizations will be helped to create a reward strategy better aligned to their overall strategy – including talent retention.

EMPLOYEE SURVEYS: A NEW AGENDA

As with many reward tools, surveys are becoming more sophisticated and more focused on the links between business and HR strategies. They are no longer the 'happy sheets' of the past. The new agenda says that surveys should:

- map views on pay, benefits and the total reward agenda;
- identify the big issues around performance and growth;
- provide evidence for the business case for engaged employees, whether through customer satisfaction, operational measures or improved financial performance;
- help to identify triggers for attrition and improve retention rates;
- support change efforts, or new developments such as a change in strategy, new initiatives, assessing the impact of corporate restructuring, etc; and, of course,
- support benchmarking and external comparisons, not just on pay, but on all the other issues.

These factors mean that a survey becomes a business tool for the organization to measure performance. Many organizations now adopt a 'balanced scorecard' approach to performance management, looking not just at financial data, but also at customer and employee feedback and the internal processes such as knowledge management. For employee surveys to add value on this ground, they need to be structured, systematic and serious – and preferably longitudinal so that trends can be monitored and acted upon. So the modern survey is one that is part of the lifeblood of the organization, not just some kind of 'annual attitude audit'.

'DOUBLE OR NOTHING'

Conducting surveys without communicating and acting on the results is both unwise and risky. The difficulty is that the mere asking of questions raises expectations that the organization will act on the results. It is also important that all of senior management are committed to a survey and what it can do for the organization (and for them if they handle the findings well). As Tennyson would have said, 'tis worse to have asked and not acted than never to have asked at all'. This 'double or nothing' outcome means that surveys need to be handled professionally and properly.

OVERVIEW OF THE SURVEY PROCESS

Experience from Hay Insight and other leading survey consultancies suggests that there are nine key steps in conducting a successful employee survey, which can be used to measure reward:

1. initial planning;
2. securing management and employee buy-in via interviews and focus groups;
3. survey design, development and testing;
4. pre-survey communications;
5. survey administration;
6. data analysis and results presentation;
7. distribution of local results, training, local feedback and action planning;
8. post-survey communication;
9. action implementation.

As this list makes clear, the survey itself (steps 3, 5, 6, 7) represents less than half of the whole exercise. The way in which the steps work in detail is explained below.

1 Initial planning

As the first step, this is one of the most critical to get right – setting the scene for the whole survey and making decisions that will impact the rest of the process.

Typically, a project team is formed, which includes the following:

▌ project sponsor – the top executive/figurehead who will champion the survey (not much time required);

▌ project manager – responsible for project delivery (a lot of time required);
▌ internal communications manager – responsible for internal communications;
▌ technical manager – responsible for design, set-up and administration of Internet or paper questionnaires;
▌ translations manager – responsible for the translation of questionnaire/other survey materials where the survey covers several geographies and/or languages.

To start the process and secure support from key stakeholders, an initial planning meeting is essential with the project team and chosen suppliers/consultants to confirm the goals and objectives of the survey, define respective roles and responsibilities, plan for data analysis (eg types of demographic comparisons) and finalize a project schedule. This session should also begin to develop a communication strategy for the whole process.

Key responsibilities of project manager role

▌ Agree on the objectives of the employee survey with senior management.
▌ Establish any critical issues that need to be addressed by the employee survey.
▌ Agree the project plan and timeline that needs to be adhered to.
▌ Brief local management on the survey process and project.
▌ Promote the survey internally; get buy-in from key stakeholders.
▌ Set up communication strategy and coordination of all communication materials before, during and after the survey administration period.
▌ Collect data on the number of employees to be covered by the survey (online or paper questionnaire).
▌ Determine language requirements and organize translations if necessary.
▌ Collect information on the organizational structure to enable demographic and team analysis of the results.
▌ Review and sign off the questionnaire content and layout.
▌ Agree survey methodology (ie online or paper, or both).
▌ Arrange for managers to be trained in how to interpret and communicate their data and how to develop and implement action plans (train-the-trainer or manager training).
▌ Provide managers with ongoing advice and support.
▌ Coordinate post-survey communications (eg results, progress on action plans, etc).

2 Management and employee buy-in through interviews and focus groups

Experience shows that meeting with senior managers to review the proposed process, clarify objectives and deliverables, identify information of practical use to management and develop an initial plan for management action based on the survey results significantly helps gain buy-in from those who will be accountable for using the survey information and can avoid points of resistance at later stages.

It is important to engage senior management in a discussion of what they hope to gain from the employee survey and how they can use the results to help accomplish their goals and enhance their effectiveness. This will help ensure support for potential actions and avoid the 'double or nothing' issue mentioned above. Often, these senior management interviews use scenario-planning techniques to sketch out possible reactions to various results outcomes. (How do we respond if most people say they are planning to leave within two years, or they don't think appraisals and performance reward are fair?)

It is also wise to conduct focus groups with a cross-section of employees to understand their issues and concerns, and to give them input into survey design. Our experience has shown that employee involvement at this stage stimulates interest and helps instil a sense of 'ownership' in the project.

3 Survey design, development and pre-testing

In addition to the obvious – ie the questions – the questionnaire should include the following:

▌ An introduction explaining the purpose of the survey and any relevant background information (eg previous surveys, etc). It should emphasize confidentiality, encourage employees to participate and advise them of the questionnaire submission date.
▌ Instructions on how to complete the survey and definitions of the terminology used (eg immediate manager, senior management, etc).
▌ A coding section (organization and demographic questions to get background information about the respondents). Without such codes it is impossible to understand how the views and opinions of different groups of employees vary.

The core questionnaire and any associated materials such as covering letters, e-mail invitations, respondent instructions, etc, will need to be translated into the respondents' first language. It is important that the integrity of any translation is secure. Only those who are expert in the discipline, with the necessary cultural sensitivity, should handle the translation.

Although it is more common to randomize the order of questions in the questionnaire, the following sample questions, which can be linked to the Engaged Performance Model, are listed by overall category to show how the structure fits together. In general, each question would take a five-point Likert 'agree/disagree' scale, with a preface such as 'How strongly do you agree or disagree with each of these statements?'

█ *Tangible pay and reward:*
   – Individual performance is adequately rewarded.
   – Team performance is adequately rewarded.
   – I am satisfied with the company's flexible benefits programme.
   – My benefits package is competitive.
█ *Personal and professional growth:*
   – I am kept informed about what is required of me to advance.
   – The current appraisal system clearly differentiates on performance levels.
   – I receive enough feedback on how I am performing.
   – I have a good understanding of the potential career moves in the company.
█ *Enabling environment:*
   – I have relevant skills and abilities that are not used in my present job.
   – This company encourages and rewards innovation.
   – Management are receptive to employees' ideas and opinions.
█ *Being valued and challenged:*
   – Poor performance is not tolerated here.
   – Employees are held accountable for the quality of work they do.
   – My supervisor provides me with recognition or praise for good work.
█ *Work/life balance:*
   – This company takes a genuine interest in the well-being of employees.
   – My supervisor is flexible when I have a personal or family matter to attend to.
   – Stress in my job is a real problem.
█ *Inspiration/organizational values:*
   – I am proud to work for this company.
   – I understand the company's business strategy and values.
   - Employees are expected to behave in a way that is consistent with the company's values.

Questionnaire design is a complicated subject. Leading questions need to be avoided and bias prevented and it is generally wise to seek professional guidance to help ensure that the results are meaningful and that data from individual questions can be linked to specific actions.

4 Pre-survey communications

Communication is a critical part of the survey process and should never be neglected. The absence of a communications plan or the deployment of a weak plan can result in low employee awareness of and commitment to the project, which will result in low response rates.

All survey participants need to be briefed on the company's rationale for conducting a survey, and on practical logistics for completing the questionnaire. Senior managers should be briefed initially, followed by communications to all employees.

Survey communications should include:

▮ An initial announcement of the survey. This should explain the aims of the survey, the process, practical logistics for completing the questionnaire and timeline, and should commit to open communication of results.
▮ A 'cover' communication from the managing director/chairman, distributed with the questionnaire itself, reiterating the above points and guaranteeing the confidentiality and anonymity of individual replies.
▮ Reminder communications to employees during the course of administration, to advise them of the response rate to date and to underline the importance of the survey results reflecting the views of as many employees as possible.
▮ A 'thank you' communication, straight after the administration phase of the survey has been completed, which thanks employees for their participation, advising them of the overall response rate and highlights the next steps in the survey process.
▮ Post-survey communications of results (both company-wide and local) to all employees and regular updates on the progress of follow-up activities and action plans.

By far the most effective means of communicating to employees is face to face, ie having line managers carry out briefing sessions with their teams. As well as ensuring all employees hear a consistent message about the survey, this will provide them with an opportunity to raise and discuss issues directly with their line managers.

Communication plays a key role in achieving a high response rate. Other factors that affect the response rate include:

▮ a clear, concise, user-friendly questionnaire;
▮ effective planning, resourcing and coordination of the survey development process;
▮ well-explained linkage of the survey with other existing/developing performance measurement systems;

▪ visible commitment of senior management to feed back survey results openly and honestly, and to follow up on key issues wherever possible;

▪ if second or subsequent survey, clear evidence of successfully implemented improvement actions as a result of employee input from the previous survey.

5 Survey administration

There are some key general principles that make the difference between effective and ineffective surveys:

▪ Employees should be given the opportunity to complete the questionnaire in work time.

▪ Each employees should be given sufficient time (around 30 minutes) in which to complete the questionnaire.

▪ Consideration should be given to those not working in an office environment for whom it will be more difficult to physically complete the questionnaire.

▪ Do not forget about people who might be on leave.

▪ Consideration should be given to shift patterns, where relevant.

▪ Participation must remain voluntary.

▪ The administration method(s) should target every single member of staff.

Growing numbers of organizations are using the Internet to survey their employees. Very few have gone entirely to electronic survey tools – a mix of paper and online is the most common. However, when using an electronic method, there are several other considerations to take into account in the process design:

▪ Has the online questionnaire been proofread?

▪ Are the organization codes and demographic codes correctly presented?

▪ Will the system capture the information submitted by respondents in a secure and usable format?

▪ Will the system be confidential and secure? Is the system password protected? Can unauthorized others access respondent data?

▪ Will the respondent interface be easy to use? Is the questionnaire formatted so that the design and appearance won't impact how employees respond?

▪ Will the system allow respondents to save part-completed surveys and return to them later?

▪ Will the system permit branching and filtering, ie using the employees' responses to direct them to the section relevant to them?

▌ Will the system allow you to identify non-respondents so that they can be sent reminders?

▌ Will the system have the capacity to allow a large number of employees to log on at the same time?

▌ Will the system handle non-European script (if applicable)?

▌ Will the system allow respondents to choose a preferred language version (if applicable)?

▌ Will the system be able to cater for survey branding (eg graphics and image files)?

▌ Will the Web survey templates be thoroughly checked prior to launch to ensure that questions are correctly aligned and displayed and all other content is as it should be?

And, for those people completing a paper version, it is essential to set up a secure method of distribution and return, and to assure people about the confidentiality. Paper questionnaires also require additional analysis resources for data entry and, if applicable, merging with the online data set. Only once this has been done and the data have been edited or verified can analysis take place.

6 Data analysis and results presentation

One of the keys to successful reward surveys is to make a link back to corporate strategy and plans. This means that the way in which the data are analysed and presented to senior management is crucial. Traditionally, employee surveys are presented as a big pack of PowerPoint slides, which often put the audience to sleep. Sometimes, if the results are poor (ie too challenging), the survey itself is humanely put to sleep.

Analysing the survey through a lens of the business plan or reward strategy is the first step. This can often mean reorganizing the findings to tell a story, rather than a question-by-question exposition of the percentage who agree, are neutral or disagree to each one. Often, multivariate statistical analysis will help to identify the key drivers of motivation and make it easier to understand what is making people respond in a certain way.

The second step is to ensure that the results are communicated in a clear and convincing way. There are many, many publications that talk about presenting results, but here are some general guidelines:

▌ Focus on the story, not the data.

▌ Think about your aim from the communication; how will you use the data to support your goals?

▌ Use visual aids (such as PowerPoint) in a way that supports your argument visually. Do not use them if they do not add to the story.

▌ Rehearse, especially if you are presenting to senior management.

7 Distribution of local results, training, local feedback and action planning

Managers should be provided with detailed information and guidelines on understanding and interpretation of the data that helps them: 1) identify their local strengths and weaknesses; 2) benchmark to put the results into context (for example, questions relating to teamwork tend to draw more positive responses from employees than questions dealing with compensation) and highlight internal best practice.

Managers should communicate the results to their own team (with support from local HR/the consultants/the steering group), as it is important that they take ownership of the results in terms both of communicating them and of using them to drive improvements. This helps local teams identify their own specific actions and builds employee commitment to action planning.

8 Post-survey communication

In addition to local communication of results, organization-wide communication of the overall findings can demonstrate powerfully that management is listening and taking the results seriously. It can often be a challenge to communicate the results to employees effectively. It is important to:

- manage expectations;
- be honest: talk about the good and not-so-good results;
- provide clear information in simple terms;
- not over-commit with an unachievable action plan;
- target only a few areas (not a laundry list) to address in any one period;
- follow up on any actions and commitments that were made;
- provide managers with the support and tools they need to deliver action plans;
- emulate and promote best practice;
- celebrate success.

9 Action implementation

The action planning process is an important but not sufficient conclusion to an effective survey process. Clear accountability for implementation and achievement of improvement identified by the survey as priorities is necessary. This typically includes setting objectives based on survey findings for managers in their performance plan. At more senior levels, these objectives are now often included in incentive plans, as part of a 'balanced scorecard' performance measurement and management scheme, linking back to their own personal reward strategy.

Appendix C

Statistical Terms Used in Pay Surveys and Analyses

PAY DATA

Most commonly used statistical methods and computer packages assume that the data under analysis are normally distributed. In such a distribution the individual items are more likely to be close to the average than far from it but are evenly distributed above and below the average. There are very few instances of data being exactly 'normal' but many are close enough to make no real difference. An example would be the heights of children at a given age; most would cluster around the average with a few extremes. Figure C.1 illustrates a normal distribution.

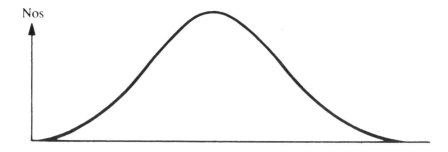

Figure C.1   Normal distribution

Pay data, however, tend not to be symmetrically distributed; typically there is a greater spread above the average than below it. Overall, this reflects the fact that there are more people in lower-paid jobs and the differences in pay between lower-paid jobs is less. Pay data therefore tends to have a skewed distribution similar to that illustrated in Figure C.2. The distribution which pay typically has is known as 'lognormal'. Technically this means that the logarithm of pay is normally distributed – in simple terms it reflects the fact that an additional £1,000 has a much greater impact on a salary of £10,000 than on a salary of £50,000.

Because pay is not normally distributed, most statistical methods should only be used with care.

SALARY SURVEYS

Salary and benefits surveys collect together a mass of useful, and not so useful, information. Rather than just presenting listings of the data collected, most surveys present summaries or analyses of the data. This section provides explanations of the more usual terms used in salary surveys.

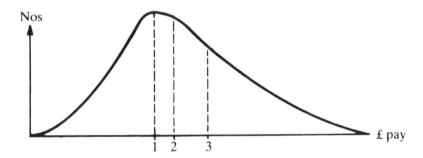

Figure C.2   Lognormal distribution (eg pay)

Measures of central tendency

There are three statistics that are commonly used to describe the middle or centre of a set of data, the average or mean, the median, and the mode.

Average or mean

The arithmetical average, or mean, is calculated by adding all the reported salaries together and dividing by the number reported. In salary survey data the mean can be unduly influenced by one or two extremely high (or low) values. Some surveys, therefore, also quote averages with the two highest and lowest values omitted, which reduces the likelihood of the answer being distorted. If the data is lognormally distributed as in Figure C.2, the mean will be at position 3; the higher values at the top pull the mean up more than the low values pull it down.

Median

The median is the middle-ranking salary, ie that which 50 per cent of the reported salaries are equal to or above and 50 per cent equal to or below. This measure is less influenced by outlying values than the average or mean and is therefore used widely in salary surveys as a measure of central tendency. In Figure C.2 it would be at position 2; this divides the area under the curve into two equal parts.

Mode

The mode is that value which appears most frequently in a given set of data. This is not always a central value and indeed in some sets of data there can be more than one modal value. Where data is clustered around a centre it can be useful to show which value(s) occur most frequently.

As salaries can vary by small amounts, they are usually grouped into ranges before a mode is derived and the range with the most reported salaries is known as the modal range. However, this is only useful if the ranges are of consistent widths. In Figure C.2 the mode is at position 1, the point where the curve is at its highest.

The mode is more commonly used in describing benefit provisions where there are often only a limited number of possible alternatives.

Relationship of mean, median and mode

As already mentioned, pay is usually lognormally distributed as in Figure C.2. If this is so then the mean will be higher than the median and the median higher than the mode. In a normal distribution as in Figure C.1, the mean, median and mode all coincide at position 1.

Measures of spread

Most surveys give some indication of the relative spread of the data as well as statistics describing its centre. The relative spread shows whether the reported salaries are close together or whether there is great variability.

Range

The range is the total spread from the highest value to the lowest value and is shown in most surveys by actually quoting the highest and lowest values. Although this is a very simple measure it can be misleading if the extremes are unrepresentative of the data as a whole.

Standard deviation

The standard deviation is of great importance in many branches of statistics, especially those linked to experiments, but has little relevance in the field of reward management. It requires a relatively complex calculation, and the main reason for its use in salary surveys is that it is available on statistical packages. Technically it is the square root of the average of the sum of the squares of the difference from the mean for each observation. If the data is normally distributed then roughly 95 per cent of all data lie within two standard deviations each side of the mean. However, as already mentioned, pay data tends not to be normally distributed, so this approximation does not always hold good.

Quartiles

There is great confusion as to whether a quartile is a point or a range. Quartiles, in the original statistical definition, were the three points which divided the data into four equal parts; the upper quartile, the median and the lower quartile. However, in recent years it has been used increasingly to mean a range – one of the four equal parts. Indeed the confusion has spread so far that recent editions of the Oxford dictionary give both definitions.

Where salary surveys refer to upper and lower quartiles they are using the original technical sense of a point. The upper quartile is that value which 25 per cent of values exceed and 75 per cent are less than. The lower quartile is that value which 75 per cent of values exceed and 25 per cent are below. As with medians and other quantiles discussed below, the quartiles can be (and often are) equal to one or more of the values.

The quartiles, unlike the standard deviation or the range, are little influenced by one or two outlying values.

Inter–quartile range

This is a measure of spread between the upper and lower quartiles. It is therefore the range which covers the middle 50 per cent of values; 25 per cent of values lie below and 25 per cent above the inter-quartile range.

Deciles, percentiles and other quantiles

Other quantiles are similar to quartiles. For example the ninth decile is that value where 10 per cent of values exceed and 90 per cent are less than; the 99th percentile is that value which 1 per cent exceed and 99 per cent are below. These other quantiles are sometimes used in salary surveys but are more frequently used by companies to set their salary policy.

Calculation of medians, quartiles and other quantiles

When calculating quartiles and other measures the critical point is whether the sample is sufficient to support the results. In broad terms it is usually accepted that for a measure to have any validity there should be at least three observations in each part in which the sample of data is divided, and preferably more. For example, medians should not be defined on less than six observations and even this can be misleading if the data included in the sample are in any way unrepresentative.

There are various formulae for calculating quantiles. The following are the most commonly used. If there are N observations and the observations are ranked in descending order:

median $\dfrac{N+1}{2}$ observations from the top

(If there are 20 values this gives 10.5, ie the average of the 10th and 11th observations)

upper quartile $\dfrac{N+3}{4}$ observations from the top

(If there are 20 values this gives 5.75, ie a weighted average of the 5th and 6th observations calculated by taking three times the 6th value and one times the 5th and dividing by 4)

lower quartile $\dfrac{3N+1}{4}$ value from the top

ninth decile $\dfrac{N+9}{10}$ value from the top

first decile $\dfrac{9N+1}{10}$ value from the top

PAY ANALYSES

There are three other common statistical techniques used in analysing pay data.

Correlation

Correlation measures how closely two variables are related, for example salary and company size. Correlation coefficients vary from +1 to –1 and typically assume a straight line relationship. A value close to +1 indicates that a high value in one variable will be reflected by a high value in the other. A value close to –1 indicates that a high value in one variable will be reflected in a low value in the other, and near 0 indicates that there is no correlation and so a high value in one variable can reflect any value in the other.

For example, in low-level jobs there is little correlation between pay and company size and therefore the correlation would be close to 0. For senior jobs such as managing directors there is a much stronger link and the correlation would be, say, +0.5 or +0.8. Interpreting a correlation coefficient is difficult as it depends to a certain extent on the size of the sample and the type of relationship between the variables.

Regression

Data with two variables such as pay and job size can be plotted as a scattergram (see Figure C.3). If the data is highly correlated then the data can be approximated by a (usually straight) line; this is known as a regression line. This is calculated by a complex formula, but one of the underlying assumptions is that the data are evenly distributed about the regression line. In most cases the dispersion in pay increases as the level of pay increases and so the underlying assumption is not valid. However, regression lines can be useful, especially over small variations in pay levels.

Multiple regression

This is similar to the linear regression outlined above but instead of relying on one explanatory variable it depends on two or more. For example, salary could be linked with age, experience and job size. It can be a helpful technique but the statistical assumption underlying it is that the explanatory variables are not correlated with each other. However, this is not always true (eg age and experience tend to go together) and therefore this method should only be used with great care.

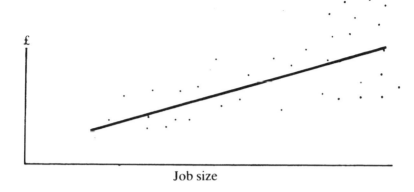

Figure C.3 Relationship between salary and job size

Examples of Role Profiles

The engineering job family

(The definition of the job family is based on specific aspects such a work type, customer base or technology requirements)

Engineering leader
Principal engineer
Senior engineer
Graduate engineer
Engineering technician

→ Individual role profile (see example)

Includes role purpose, accountabilities, knowledge and skills, performance indicators and behaviours.

A role profile – principal engineer

Role purpose statement
To lead and carry out complex engineering projects in area of specialism

Key accountabilities
- Ensure that all engineering procedures and schedules are implemented to agreed standards.
- Provide expert support and advice to junior colleagues.
- Lead and motivate specified engineering project teams.

Performance indicators
- Quality of engineering maintenance.
- Preventative maintenance carried out to schedule.
- Developing knowledge of rest of team.
- Full and appropriate resourcing of project team to meet project requirements.
- Clarity of project plans and timetables.
- Customer feedback on project planning process.
- Performance of team members against individual targets.

Competences
- Developing Others (2)
- Achievement Drive (3)
- Team Working (2)
- Commercial Awareness (2)

Knowledge, skills, experience
- Chartered Engineer
- Project management expertise
- Minimum 3 years in an appropriate engineering environment

Current performance objectives
- Implement new schedules in Watford plant.
- Reduce maintenance costs by 5%.
- ➡ Attain minimum 4 members of team at part-chartered level.

Development objectives
- Development of developing others' competency from level 2 to level 3.
- Broaden demonstration of teamworking to include cross-functional working (level 3).
- ➡ Complete stage 3 of in-house project management training programme.

Table D1.   A role definition in an engineering job family.

Table D.2 A role profile for an organizer.

Purpose
To provide an excellent operational delivery service to XYZ plc customers, within a geographic area or process, by planning and coordinating the activities of a team of technicians and third-party suppliers

Accountabilities	Performance measures
Coordinate the activities of a team of technicians within a geographical area or process to meet agreed performance targets of customer service delivery and recovery.	Composite Performance Index (CPI). Key Service Indicators (KSI). Performance of the team: – customer satisfaction (CSI); – speed of response; – first time fixes.
Plan and supervise specified project work, including on-site inspection, ensuring the delivery of appropriate service within time, cost and quality standards.	Service delivered to plan.
Organize and supervise third-party contractors and technicians to ensure all work carried out meets defined standards.	Number of failings. Customer satisfaction survey. Sampled quality of work.
Ensure that all plans and proposals meet the required standards and service levels.	Peer feedback. Successful implementation of plans.
Liaise and negotiate with customers, including ensuring access and compliance with the work, to ensure the required service can be delivered.	Customer satisfaction (CSI). Number of contacts under response failure. Number of aborted calls.
Provide a fault resolution service and an escalation point to the team of technicians to ensure service quality is maintained.	Composite Performance Index (CPI). Resolution time to service routines and regulatory requirements.
Produce estimates for large works, including design and pricing, to meet customer and corpoate requirements.	Cost recovery. Job delivered to cost.
Provide input into the development of business plans for own functional area or process.	Manager's feedback.

Experience/knowledge	Competencies
NVQ in subject relevant to job. City and Guilds. ONC/HNC in a relevant technical subject NRSWA. Three to five years' experience in a service environment. Project planning experience. Familiar with XYZ plc IT and systems, preferably gained through two years with XYZ plc. Knowledge of relevant legislation and regulatory requirements. IT literate.	Decision making 3. Influencing 3. Planning 3. Directing work through others 3. Achievement 4. Customer focus 3.

Table D.2

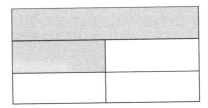

Role clarity – the combination of both the purpose statement and the key accountabilities gives the basis for ensuring a common understanding of what the job holder is required to achieve and why.

Table D.3

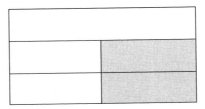

Performance management – the combination of performance measures and competencies help both the job holder and manager understand the 'how' as well as the 'what' of expected performance. They also provide a reference point for discussions about performance improvement (ie a basis for comparison with actual, current performance).

Table D.4

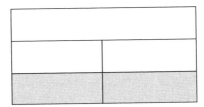

Development – the combination of experience/knowledge and competencies helps identify the critical skills and behaviours for a particular role and provides the basis for a discussion to highlight any skills/behavioural gaps and agree a development plan to close these gaps.

Appendix E

Examples of Job Evaluation Schemes and Systems

The job evaluation scheme described first in this appendix is the Hay Guide Chart Profile Method, which is by far the most frequently used of the 'proprietary' job evaluation schemes available in the UK. The appendix also describes the computerized approaches offered by Link Consultants and Pilat UK.

THE HAY GROUP GUIDE CHART – PROFILE METHOD OF JOB EVALUATION

History and development

The Hay Group Guide Chart Profile Method of Job Evaluation is the most widely used single job evaluation method in the world, being used by over 7,000 profit and non-profit organizations in some 40 countries. While it is perhaps best known for its application to management, professional and technical jobs, it is also extensively used for clerical and manual jobs, and when a single top-to-bottom evaluation method is required as the basis for integrated pay and grading structures.

It was initially conceived in the early 1950s, having its roots in factor comparison methods in which Edward N Hay was a pioneer, and has evolved by practical application into its present form.

Its widespread use, and the consistency of the job-size numbering scale used, enables it to provide the basis for valid pay comparisons between organizations, nationally and internationally. Comprehensive pay and benefits surveys, using job-size-based comparisons, are conducted by the Hay Group in over 35 countries.

The method can be applied by a wide variety of processes, both manual and computer assisted, tailored to the particular requirements of the user organization.

Basis of the method

The method is based upon the following principles and observations:

▌ While there are many factors which could be considered in developing a job evaluation scheme, these can be grouped into three broad factors: the knowledge and skills required to do the job; the kind of thinking needed to solve the problems commonly faced; and the responsibilities assigned to the job.

▌ This provides the basis of the three main factors of the Guide Chart Profile Method – Know-how, Problem Solving and Accountability – which are common to all jobs, and which are subdivided into several elements.

▌ For any given job, there will be a relationship between the three factors. Thus the output or end results expected from the job (the Accountability), will demand a certain level of input (Know-how), and processing of this Know-how (Problem Solving) to enable delivery of the output.

This can be represented by the simple model:

▌ Thus jobs can be characterized not only by the size or level of each factor, but also by the balance between the factors – the Profile – which reflects the 'shape' of the job. Thus, for example, a research job is likely to be heavily loaded towards Know-how and Problem Solving, whereas for a sales representative or production manager, the balance will be shifted towards Accountability. In addition to evaluating each factor, evaluators also assess the profile of the job, which provides an important check on consistency of treatment.

▌ The ability of evaluators to discern a difference between two jobs depends not only on the absolute difference, but on how big this difference is in relation to the size of the jobs themselves. Thus the numbering patterns used in the Guide Charts are based upon a geometric scale, each number being a constant percentage greater than the previous one. This percentage has been empirically determined at 15 per cent, as best representing the ability of experienced evaluators to discern a difference in any factor between two jobs. This 'step difference' concept provides the basic building block for the scales and for the comparisons between jobs, with one step representing a 'just discernible difference'.

▮ Jobs should not be evaluated in isolation, but viewed in their organizational context, so that working relationships both vertically and horizontally throughout the organization are taken into account.

▮ In order that the focus is on jobs, not the performance of job holders, 'standard acceptable performance' is assumed. Similarly, jobs are evaluated independent of any market-driven pay conditions which may pertain, recognizing that these require addressing explicitly as pay issues, not job-size considerations.

Components of the method

The method has three main factors and eight dimensions as follows.

Know-how

The sum of every kind of knowledge, skill and experience, however acquired, needed for acceptable job performance. Its three dimensions are requirements for:

1. Practice procedures, specialized techniques and knowledge within occupational fields, commercial functions, and professional or scientific disciplines.
2. Integrating and harmonizing the diverse elements involved in managerial situations. This involves, in some combination, skills in planning, organizing, executing, controlling and evaluating and may be exercised consultatively as well as executively.
3. Active, practising person-to-person skills in work with other people, within or outside the organization.

Problem Solving

The original, self-starting use of Know-how required by the job to identify, define, and resolve problems. 'You think with what you know.' This is true of even the most creative work. The raw material of any thinking is knowledge of facts, principles, and means. For that reason, Problem Solving is treated as a percentage of Know-how.

Problem Solving has two dimensions:

1. the environment in which thinking takes place;
2. the challenge presented by the thinking to be done.

Accountability

The answerability for action and for the consequences of that action. It is the measured effect of the job on end results of the organization. It has three dimensions in the following order of importance:

1. Freedom to act: the extent of personal, procedural, or systematic guidance or control of actions in relation to the primary emphasis of the job.
2. Job impact on end results: the extent to which the job can directly affect actions necessary to produce results within its primary emphasis.
3. Magnitude: the portion of the total organization encompassed by the primary emphasis of the job. Where possible, magnitude is expressed in annual financial figures representing the area of primary emphasis of the job.

Beyond these three factors of job content, additional scales can be used to assess factors relating to the context in which the job operates; for example, unpleasant working environment, hazards, physical demands, sensory attention, etc. When such factors are important for the jobs under consideration, scales are generated to enable their assessment within the context of the organization.

The Guide Charts

A Guide Chart for each factor (see Figures E.1, E.2 and E.3) contains semantic scales which reflect levels of each dimension. Each chart, except for Problem Solving, is expandable to reflect the size and complexity of the organization to which it is applied. The language of the scales, carefully evolved over many years and applied to literally millions of jobs of every kind, has remained fairly constant in recent years but is modified, as appropriate, to reflect the unique nature, character, and structure of any given organization or sector, eg local government, health, etc. The numbering pattern in each chart is based upon the 15 per cent difference concept noted above. To illustrate the use of the charts, consider the Know-how Chart (Figure C.1). If, for example, a job is considered to fall squarely into E Technical Know-how II Breadth of Management and 3 Human Relations Skills, then the chart indicates a Know-how value of 304 units. The 264 and 350 values are to allow for fine-tuning or shading when one of the elements is considered light or heavy compared with the basic definition or with comparator jobs.

The same total Know-how score of 304 units can of course be arrived at in a variety of ways. For example, F + I 2 304 indicates a job which is significantly more technical, but less demanding in terms of management and human relations skills – but on balance requiring the same total volume of knowledge and skills. In addition to their primary purpose of arriving at a job size, this illustrates the way that the Guide Charts are frequently used to provide a language in which jobs can be described and characterized in a consistent way.

Use of the other two Guide Charts is similar, though in the case of Problem Solving, the chart yields a percentage value which is applied to the Know-how score to give Problem Solving units. Total job size is the sum of three factor scores.

Consistency checks

▌ Profile: this is used as a powerful check for internal consistency within an evaluation. If, for example, the evaluation shows an Accountability score three 15 per cent steps higher than the Problem Solving score, it would be recorded as A3 (sometimes 'plus 3' or 'up to 3').

▌ Evaluators make a separate judgement on the profile expected for the job. Thus, typically, jobs in line functions would be expected to have strongly Accountability-orientated profiles, jobs in basic research would have strong Problem Solving orientation (P), while jobs in many staff functions like personnel, finance, etc, are likely to have the two more in balance. If the profile which emerges from the evaluation does not agree with the evaluators' view of the appropriate profile, it indicates an inconsistency of treatment between the factors, and causes the evaluators to reconsider the evaluation.

▌ Rank order: testing of rank order to identify anomalies is an important part of the process. It can be done at the level of total job size; by factor (eg total Know-how); or by individual dimension (eg freedom to act).

Application of the Guide Chart Profile Method

The basic measuring instrument of the Guide Charts can be applied through a wide variety of processes, both manual and computer assisted. The choice of a particular application process depends principally on the purpose for which the job evaluation is being undertaken, the size and diversity of the job population under consideration, and the time and resource constraints which exist. Thus traditional processes, based upon multi-functional evaluation committees, can provide great sensitivity to a wide diversity of jobs, and can generate valuable output in terms of organizational analysis and clarification, though they are demanding in terms of time and resources. Computer-assisted processes reduce the time and resource demands, particularly for large populations, but may reduce the opportunity for organizational debate and analysis. Hay consultants advise client organizations on the most appro-

HAY GUIDE CHARTS

Guide Chart for Evaluating KNOW-HOW

Know-How is the sum of every kind of knowledge, skill and experience required for standard acceptable job performance. It is the fund of knowledge (however acquired) which is necessary for meeting:

• The requirement for Know-How in practical procedures, specialised techniques and professional disciplines.

• ● The requirement for Know-How in integrating and harmonising the diverse elements involved in managerial situations. This Know-How may be exercised in an advisory capacity as well as executively. It involves combining to some degree the elements of planning, organising, directing, controlling and innovating and takes account of size, functional or organisational diversity, and time scale.

• ● ● The requirement for Know-How in working with and through people (within or outside the organisation).

MEASURING KNOW-HOW

Know-How has both breadth and depth. Thus, a job may require some knowledge about a few things. The total Know-How is the sum of breadth and depth. This concept makes practical the comparison and weighing of the total Know-How content of different jobs in terms of: "HOW MUCH KNOWLEDGE ABOUT HOW MANY THINGS".

BREADTH OF MANAGEMENT KNOW-HOW → □ ●●

DEPTH AND RANGE OF TECHNICAL KNOW-HOW ↓ □ ●

HUMAN RELATIONS SKILLS □ ●●●

Column groups:

- **O. TASK** — Performance of a task (or tasks) highly specific as to objective and content. Interaction with others is primarily concerned with receiving instructions.
- **I. ACTIVITY** — Performance or supervision of multiple activities, which are specific as to objective and content. There is a requirement to interact with co-workers and maintain an awareness of related activities.
- **II. RELATED** — Internal integration of operations or services which are generally related in nature and objective, and where there is a requirement for co-ordination with associated functions.
- **III. DIVERSE** — Operational or conceptual integration of functions which are diverse in nature and objective and/or strategically critical to the achievement of overall business goals.
- **IV. TOTAL**

Row descriptions:

- **A. PRIMARY:** Basic knowledge of simple instructions, facts and information necessary to perform straightforward tasks of a repetitive nature. Knowledge is generally acquired through a short period of instruction.
- **B. ELEMENTARY VOCATIONAL:** Knowledge of standardised work routines and methods, general facts and information and/or the use of simple equipment, machines and materials. Knowledge is generally acquired through training on the job.
- **C. VOCATIONAL:** Knowledge and insight are required for the application of practical methods and techniques, work procedures and/or proficiency in the specialized use of materials, equipment and tools. Knowledge is typically acquired through technical training.
- **D. ADVANCED VOCATIONAL:** Knowledge of the practical application of specialized (generally non-theoretical) methods, techniques and processes is required. Knowledge may be acquired through part professional qualification or by 'on the job' experience.
- **E. PROFESSIONAL:** The requirement is for sufficiency in a technical, scientific or specialized field built on an understanding of theoretical concepts and principles and their context. Knowledge is normally acquired through professional or academic qualification or through extensive practical experience.
- **F. SEASONED PROFESSIONAL:** Proficiency in a specialised field or a broad insight into the relationship between different fields. Knowledge is acquired through deep and/or broad experience built on concepts and principles.
- **G. PROFESSIONAL MASTERY:** Determinative mastery of concepts, principles and practices within a specialized field and/or authoritative insight into the relationships between multiple fields. Knowledge is gained through deep development in a specialized field or through comprehensive business experience.
- **H. EXCEPTIONAL MASTERY:** Externally recognized mastery of concepts and principles and their applications within a scientific field. This level would normally be associated with ongoing groundbreaking work.

	O. TASK 1	2	3	I. ACTIVITY 1	2	3	II. RELATED 1	2	3	III. DIVERSE 1	2	3	IV. TOTAL 1	2	3
A.1	38	43	50	50	57	66	66	76	87	87	100	115	115	132	152
A.2	43	50	57	57	66	76	76	87	100	100	115	132	132	152	175
A.3	50	57	66	66	76	87	87	100	115	115	132	152	152	175	200
B.1	50	57	66	66	76	87	87	100	115	115	132	152	152	175	200
B.2	57	66	76	76	87	100	100	115	132	132	152	175	175	200	230
B.3	66	76	87	87	100	115	115	132	152	152	175	200	200	230	264
C.1	66	76	87	87	100	115	115	132	152	152	175	200	200	230	264
C.2	76	87	100	100	115	132	132	152	175	175	200	230	230	264	304
C.3	87	100	115	115	132	152	152	175	200	200	230	264	264	304	350
D.1	87	100	115	115	132	152	152	175	200	200	230	264	264	304	350
D.2	100	115	132	132	152	175	175	200	230	230	264	304	304	350	400
D.3	115	132	152	152	175	200	200	230	264	264	304	350	350	400	460
E.1	115	132	152	152	175	200	200	230	264	264	304	350	350	400	460
E.2	132	152	175	175	200	230	230	264	304	304	350	400	400	460	528
E.3	152	175	200	200	230	264	264	304	350	350	400	460	460	528	608
F.1	152	175	200	200	230	264	264	304	350	350	400	460	460	528	608
F.2	175	200	230	230	264	304	304	350	400	400	460	528	528	608	700
F.3	200	230	264	264	304	350	350	400	460	460	528	608	608	700	800
G.1	200	230	264	264	304	350	350	400	460	460	528	608	608	700	800
G.2	230	264	304	304	350	400	400	460	528	528	608	700	700	800	
G.3	264	304	350	350	400	460	460	528	608	608	700	800	800		
H.1	264	304	350	350	400	460	460	528	608	608	700	800			
H.2	304	350	400	400	460	528	528	608	700	700	800				
H.3	350	400	460	460	528	608	608	700	800	800					

© 2003 Hay Group

Figure C.1 Part of the Hay Know-how Guide Chart

Guide Chart for Evaluating

PROBLEM SOLVING

Problem Solving is the "self starting" thinking required by the job for analysing, evaluating, creating, reasoning, arriving at and drawing conclusions. To the extent that thinking is circumscribed by standards or covered by precedents or referred to others, Problem Solving is diminished.

Problem Solving has two dimensions:

- The environment in which the thinking takes places.
- The challenge presented by the thinking to be done.

MEASURING PROBLEM SOLVING:

Problem Solving measures the intensity of the mental process which employs Know-How to (1) identify, (2) define, and (3) solve a problem. "You think with what you know." This is true of even the most creative work ... the raw material of any thinking is knowledge of facts, principles and means; ideas are put together from something already there. Therefore, Problem Solving is treated as percentage utilisation of Know-How. (The Problem Solving score can be readily derived from the conversion table printed above

THINKING CHALLENGE → THINKING ENVIRONMENT Freedom to Think →	1. REPETITIVE Identical situations requiring solution by simple choice of things learned.		2. PATTERNED Similar situations requiring solution by discriminating choice of things learned.		3. VARIABLE Differing situations requiring the identification and selection of solutions within the area of expertise and acquired knowledge.		4. ADAPTIVE Situations requiring q significant degree of evaluative judgement and innovative thinking to analyse, evaluate and arrive at conclusions.		5. UNCHARTED Pathfinding situations requiring creative thinking and the development of new concepts and imaginative approaches contributing significantly to the advancement of knowledge and thought.	
A. STRICT ROUTINE: Thinking within precise and detailed rules and instructions and/or rigid supervision (personal or system).	10%	12%	14%	16%	19%	22%	25%	29%	33%	38%
B. ROUTINE: Thinking within standard instructions and routines and/or continuous supervision.	12%	14%	16%	19%	22%	25%	29%	33%	38%	43%
C. SEMI-ROUTINE: Thinking within well defined, but somewhat diversified, procedures and precedents and/or subject to supervision.	14%	16%	19%	22%	25%	29%	33%	38%	43%	50%
D. STANDARDIZED: Thinking within substantially diversified, established procedures, standards and precedents; general supervised.	16%	19%	22%	25%	29%	33%	38%	43%	50%	57%
E. CLEARLY DEFINED: Thinking within clearly defined policies, principles and specific objectives, under readily available direction.	19%	22%	25%	29%	33%	38%	43%	50%	57%	66%
F. BROADLY DEFINED: Thinking within broadly defined polices and objectives, under general direction.	22%	25%	29%	33%	38%	43%	50%	57%	66%	76%
G. GENERALLY DEFINED: Thinking within general policies, principles and goals, under guidance.	25%	29%	33%	38%	43%	50%	57%	66%	76%	87%
H. ABSTRACTLY DEFINED: Thinking within business philosophy and cultural norms; subject to the general laws of nature and science.	29%	33%	38%	43%	50%	57%	66%		87%	

© 2003
Thesr
Kinr

Figure C.2 Part of the Hay Problem Solving Guide Chart

HAY GUIDE CHARTS

Guide Chart for Evaluating
ACCOUNTABILITY

Accountability is the answerability for action and for the consequences of that action. It is measures effect of the job on end results. It has three dimensions in the following order of importance:

- **Freedom to Act** – measured by the existence or absence of personal or procedural control and guidance as defined in the left hand column.
- •• **Job Impact on End Results** – as defined at upper right.
- ••• **Magnitude (Area of Impact)** – indicated by the general size of the area(s) most clearly affected by the job (measured on an annual money basis).

Nature of impact – magnitude 0 (Indeterminate)

A Minimal — Performance of simple and repetitive activities, with no direct relationship to other jobs.

B Limited — Performance of routine activities, such as the simple operation of tools and equipment and/or providing/recording information for use by others.

C Important — Performance of complex activities which require technical understanding and proficiency and/or administrative support services which are of a facilitating or interpretive nature.

D Critical — Provision of specialised advisory, diagnostic and/or operational services.

NATURE OF IMPACT – MAGNITUDE 1 LARGER

INDIRECT

R Remote — Providing information, record keeping and incidential services for use by others in the performance of their job.

C Contributory — Contributing interpretation, advice and facilitating support for use by others in making decisions and taking action.

DIRECT

S Shared — Explicit joint accountability with others for end results. (*N.B.: except own subordinates and superiors*).

P Prime — Decisive, controlling impact on end results. Shared accountability of others is of minor/secondary importance.

••• MAGNITUDE — Figures for uses in 1997/1998

FREEDOM TO ACT	(0) INDETERMINATE A	B	C	D	(1) VERY SMALL £37,500–£375,000 R	C	S	P	(2) SMALL £375,000–£3.75m R	C	S	P	(3) MEDIUM £3.75m–£37.5m R	C	S	P	(4) LARGE £37.5m–£375m R	C	S	P
A. PRESCRIBED: Subject to direct and detailed instructions, and closed supervision/immediate feedback. The nature of the tasks is totally confining.	8	10	14	19	10	14	19	25	14	19	25	33	19	25	33	43	25	33	43	57
	9	12	16	22	12	16	22	29	16	22	29	38	22	29	38	50	29	38	50	66
	10	14	19	25	14	19	25	33	19	25	33	43	25	33	43	57	33	43	57	76
B. CONTROLLED: Covered by instructions and established routines and closely supervised.	12	16	22	29	16	22	29	38	22	29	38	50	29	38	50	66	38	50	66	87
	14	19	25	33	19	25	33	43	25	33	43	57	33	43	57	76	43	57	76	100
	16	22	29	38	22	29	38	50	29	38	50	66	38	50	66	87	50	66	87	115
C. STANDARDISED: Subject to standardised work routines, practices and procedures and general work instructions. Supervision is of progress and results.	19	25	33	43	25	33	43	57	33	43	57	76	43	57	76	100	57	76	100	132
	22	29	38	50	29	38	50	66	38	50	66	87	50	66	87	115	66	87	115	152
	25	33	43	57	33	43	57	76	43	57	76	100	57	76	100	132	76	100	132	175
D. GENERALLY REGULATED: Covered by practices and procedures which have clear precedents and/or operational guidance. Subject to managerial control and review of results.	29	38	50	66	38	50	66	87	50	66	87	115	66	87	115	152	87	115	152	200
	33	43	57	76	43	57	76	100	57	76	100	132	76	100	132	175	100	132	175	230
	38	50	66	87	50	66	87	115	66	87	115	152	87	115	152	200	115	152	200	264
E. DIRECTED: Free to determine how to achieve clearly defined medium term (annual) objectives. Covered by functional precedents and policies and subject to magerial direction.	43	57	76	100	57	76	100	132	76	100	132	175	100	132	175	230	132	175	230	304
	50	66	87	115	66	87	115	152	87	115	152	200	115	152	200	264	152	200	264	350
	57	76	100	132	76	100	132	175	100	132	175	230	132	175	230	304	175	230	304	400
F. GENERALLY DIRECTED: Subject to general direction and broadly defined functional policy objectives.	66	87	115	152	87	115	152	200	115	152	200	264	152	200	264	350	200	264	350	460
	76	100	132	175	100	132	175	230	132	175	230	304	175	230	304	400	230	304	400	528
	87	115	152	200	115	152	200	264	152	200	264	350	200	264	350	460	264	350	460	608
G. GUIDED: By their nature or size these positions are subject only to guidance and broad direction on the orientation of policy.	100	132	175	230	132	175	230	304	175	230	304	400	230	304	400	528	304	400	528	
	115	152	200	264	152	200	264	350	200	264	350	460	264	350	460	608	350	460		
	132	175	230	304	175	230	304	400	230	304	400	528	304	400			40?			
H.	152		264	350	200	264	350	460	264											
	175			400	230			528												
	2??			460	264															

© 7

Figure C.3 Part of the Hay Accountability Guide Chart

priate process to meet particular needs and circumstances. The range of processes is illustrated in the following examples.

Committee-based process

In this, the most commonly applied traditional process, evaluation judgements are made by a committee (or committees), trained in the use of the Guide Charts, and using job information in the form of job descriptions.

The process usually starts with the selection of a benchmark of jobs, to reflect the range of job types and levels in the population, and to enable basic evaluation standards and interpretations to be set.

Job descriptions for the benchmark jobs may be prepared by trained analysts, by job holders or their managers – depending on circumstances. In most cases, approval of the final document by both job holder and manager is adopted, whoever has prepared the description. A variety of job description formats may be used, but an important feature of Hay job descriptions is an emphasis on the results expected from a job – the principal accountabilities – which assists clarity and conciseness, and can provide links into related processes such as organizational analysis and performance management.

The benchmark committee is selected, usually including members from a range of functions, not purely HR specialists, so as to provide a range of inputs and perspectives, and foster ownership of the results. Depending on the organization's needs, the committee may be a management group, or may include peer group members and/or trade union representatives.

The committee is trained and guided by a Hay consultant, and evaluates the benchmark sample to provide clear reference points, and standards and principles to assist evaluation of non-benchmark jobs.

An important component of this process is the establishment of evaluation interpretations which reflect the organization's values and emphases, within the Guide Chart framework.

For a small population or in a highly centralized organization, the same committee may proceed to evaluate the remaining jobs. Otherwise, additional committees are selected and trained (for example divisional committees in a diversified business), and processes established to ensure application of common standards.

Computer-based administrative support is available to assist this process, in many corporate e-HR systems. This enables recording and storage of job evaluation data, evaluation rationales and, if required, job descriptions, for rapid sorting and access when comparisons or rank order checks are being made.

Comparison and classification methods

The Guide Chart Profile Method can also be used to underpin job and career family models and a variety of comparison or classification approaches, particularly for large and relatively homogeneous populations.

These processes normally start with committee evaluation of a benchmark sample, using the Guide Charts in the conventional way.

Based on the results of this sampling and standard setting, a classification or 'slotting' framework can be established, to facilitate evaluation of remaining jobs by direct comparison. This can be presented in written 'workbook' form, or as a computer-based framework in HR software.

Such methods can achieve very rapid evaluation of large populations and provide for significant devolution of responsibility for evaluation, with relatively low training requirements.

Computer-assisted evaluation processes

In these processes, the use of job descriptions and committees for the bulk of the job population is replaced by structured questionnaires, processed by computer to generate evaluations directly, using an algorithm which has been established from full evaluation of a benchmark sample.

Where a single approach is required to cover all (or most) of the jobs in an organization, a single, comprehensive questionnaire is constructed. A benchmark sample of jobs is evaluated conventionally, using the Guide Charts, to provide the basic standards to underpin the process. The same jobs are also rated on the questionnaire and an algorithm built to replicate Hay job unit results from the questionnaire responses and programmed into specific software. For non-benchmark jobs, questionnaires are completed and processed through the computer (batch or interactive) to yield comparative evaluations. Quality checks are built in, both to the software and processes to ensure consistency.

An alternative approach, for a more tightly defined job group, is the job family questionnaire. This provides a shorter, more focused questionnaire that is typically developed in conjunction with members of the family in question to reflect quite explicitly the key differentiating factors which affect job size in that family, expressed in their language. It is often used when relationships between job evaluation, career development and competency analysis are important. The process for its implementation is similar to that described for the 'universal' questionnaire.

Mixed processes

Since all these application processes are underpinned by the same Guide Chart principles and numbering scales, they yield comparable results and so different processes can be applied to different job groups without loss of compatibility.

'LINK' – A COMPUTER-ASSISTED SYSTEM

One of the more widely used systems for general application (ie which can be used with any job evaluation scheme) is that available from Link Reward Consultants. The number of Link installations worldwide is in the hundreds, and the Link system was used to deliver the Equate method designed by KPMG and its health sector version MedEquate. More recently the software delivered the GLPC factor scheme developed for London local authorities. The Link system is outlined below.

Basis of the process

The basis on which the Link computer-assisted system operates is the analysis of answers provided to a comprehensive range of questions about each of the scheme factors in a structured questionnaire. This questionnaire can be produced in hard copy, for completion before the data are entered into the computer, or as an on-screen questionnaire. The former typically runs to 30 or 40 pages, hence the benefits of the on-screen version.

Establishing the 'rules'

Before any data can be entered, the evaluation 'rules' have to be determined and programmed into the software. These, in effect, determine what factor level is justified by all the answers given to the questions related to the factor concerned. They are developed from analyses of completed questionnaires related to test jobs that have already been ascribed factor levels, usually by a traditional evaluation panel approach. Client staff and union representatives are often involved directly in the development of these rules.

Evaluation

Job information is gathered via an on-screen job analysis questionnaire, usually input by an analyst or evaluator. Each question has online help and the ability to review which other reference jobs have answered it – an aid to ongoing consistency. As an option, the system will prompt for explanatory text to back up a response given.

The system performs a series of validation checks on the answers to different questions to identify any potential data inconsistencies. Checks are both internal (are the responses given consistent with each other?) and external to other jobs (are responses in line with other, similar positions?). When all questions have been answered and all checks completed, the score for the job is calculated by the system using the inbuilt 'rules', and added to the database of completed evaluations.

Openness

As explained by Link: 'the factors and weightings are usually made known to evaluators and job analysts and often extended to all interested parties. How the evaluation rules work behind the scenes to logically produce an appropriate factor level can be relatively sophisticated and this is less likely to be disclosed for the reasons of complexity rather than secrecy'.

Feedback to job holder

Job holders or line managers are normally informed of the evaluation result (score or grade), after an appropriate approval process.

'GAUGE' – AN 'INTERACTIVE' COMPUTER-ASSISTED SYSTEM

The Gauge software was specifically developed to promote the use of job evaluation by overcoming the principal disadvantages of traditional processes, ie:

▌ time-consuming, both in the overall evaluation process itself and in the elapsed time to get a job evaluated, and hence costly in management time;
▌ paper-intensive, in the necessary preparation of lengthy job descriptions and/or questionnaires, etc;
▌ open to subjective or inconsistent judgements;
▌ opaque in terms of how scores are determined – a criticism also levelled against computer-assisted systems;
▌ bureaucratic, and remote from job holders themselves, inevitably leading to 'appeals' against evaluation results.

Basis of the process

The Gauge process effectively replicates the tried-and-tested evaluation panel approach but needs neither job descriptions nor evaluation panels. The people who know most about the job (job holder and line manager) answer a series of logically interrelated questions on-screen, supported by a trained 'facilitator'. These questions will have been pre-loaded into the system in a series of logic trees (one for each factor) and will be the questions that a skilled job evaluation panel would ask in deciding what factor score to allocate to the job being evaluated.

Building the 'question trees'

Each factor has its own set of questions, each question having a number of pre-set answers. Client staff and/or their representatives will often be directly involved in the wording of these questions and answers, developed from the panel or project team deliberations recorded during the creation of the factor plan and its checking by evaluation of the test jobs.

Evaluation

Selecting one of the answers to a question (by simply 'clicking' on it) does three things. First, it identifies and presents the most logical follow-up question; second, if appropriate, it progresses the scoring process; and third it contributes to the Job Overview report.

Every job is presented with the same initial question in a factor but the logic tree format means that different jobs will take different routes through the other questions in that factor. This allows progressively more relevant questions to be asked and avoids, for example, senior managers being asked questions more relevant to clerical activities and vice versa. Any one job will normally be presented with about 20 per cent of the available questions, of which there are typically 400-500 in a completed system.

The scoring process is the predetermined 'elimination' of one or more of the possible factor levels from consideration. Questioning continues until every level except one has been logically eliminated. The remaining level is recorded as the 'correct' level for that factor and the questioning moves on to the next factor. Provided that there is reasonable agreement between job holder and manager about the job responsibilities and activities, the evaluation should take no more than one hour.

Openness

The identification of the correct factor level is a totally 'transparent' process in that the progressive elimination of the levels can be followed as each question is answered. (Even at a later time, the specific answer or sequence of answers that led to the elimination of a particular level can be demonstrated – a powerful tool in rebutting claims for higher scores.)

Feedback to job holder

At the end of an evaluation, the system displays a 'Job Overview', which presents the information provided through the question-and-answer process in a narrative format. Those involved in the evaluation can read this and, if anything appears incorrect, can return to the question that gave rise to the incorrect statement and reconsider the answer. Changing an answer will usually lead to a different set of follow-up questions but will not necessarily result in a different score, even though the Job Overview will have changed. It is normal practice to allow job holders and line managers a period of time following the evaluation to examine the Job Overview (on-screen or in hard copy) before 'sign-off'.

The Job Overview is thus the rationale for the score given, and a score cannot be changed without answering the questions in a different way (and even this may not change the score). Anyone wishing to challenge the score for a job must show that one or more of the statements on the Job Overview is incorrect. It is a key document for two main reasons:

1. An 'appeal' can only be lodged on the basis that there is an incorrect statement in the Job Overview (and evidence to support this claim would be required). As the job holder would have been a party to the acceptance of the Job Overview in the first place, the number of appeals is dramatically reduced.
2. As the Job Overview does not contain any reference to specific tasks carried out by the job holder, hard copy of a relevant Job Overview can be shown to holders of similar jobs for them to confirm that it is equally valid for their own particular post. If so, there is no need to evaluate these posts and, furthermore, the basis for role interchange-ability will have been established. Even if not, only the points of difference need to be evaluated for the new job – a substantial time saving.

Appendix F

Performance Management Documentation

PRESSURE TO SIMPLIFY AND INTEGRATE

Much of the focus over the last few years has been about reinforcing the importance of performance management as a business tool and at the same time simplifying what is recorded. Line management and employees alike generally seem to hate form filling and tend to associate their dislike of this with the process of performance management – usually to its detriment. Also, lengthy forms and the requirement for a significant evidence base for achievements are seen as rather low-trust and parent–child. The critical issue seems to be to record what is important and ensure there are sound links with business performance management, the development agenda and the reward system. Some organizations, even in the public service, are now insisting that the whole recording process takes up no more than two sides of paper – or the 'on screen' equivalent.

Increasingly, performance management is being managed through e-HR applications. Most providers of HR software have generic approaches and can produce bespoke applications as needed. Some are better than others: some still reflect a rather dated, top-down view of performance appraisal – as though the progress in this area of the last few years had never happened. A critical issue in bespoke or customized approaches is stakeholder involvement in design.

KEY HEADINGS FOR DOCUMENTS AND WEB-BASED APPROACHES

▌ Employee data: name, role, location, time in role.
▌ Performance plan, measures or outcomes agreed and review of achievements – often with a maximum number of targets (four to six is not unusual).
▌ Development plan and review of achievements – may be linked to a competency framework.
▌ Agreement/sign-off by individual and line manager.

Web-based approaches may provide for stakeholder input. Some approaches provide for 360-degree feedback inclusion. Countersigning manager or 'grandfather' sign-off may still occur in the public sector and where senior manager involvement in the talent management process is secured by this means.

Guidance and documentation on performance management should focus on the quality of the performance dialogue and ensuring that individuals and their line management have access to, and use, any support they need to help make sure performance management delivers on its promises.

Design of any documentation or Web-based approaches needs to be culturally sensitive and appropriate. This is one place to treat employees as customers and reflect their needs and visual standards in the paperwork and screens. Words and psychology matter – if most of your employees read the *Sun* or the *Daily Mail*, don't write performance management documentation in the language of the *Financial Times*. If bright colours appeal, use them. If prestige presentation matters, use that. The important thing is to imagine how and where the documentation will be used, how it will feel to use it (test this live) and how positively users will feel about a process designed to recognize success, agree priorities for change and secure organizational performance improvement.

Appendix G

An Example of a Long-term Incentive Programme for the Main Board Directors of a Public Company

The company is Compass Group, a FTSE 100 plc with turnover of £11 billion, operating globally. Compass operates a substantial long-term incentive programme, which is very highly geared to performance. The programme includes the following three elements.

- deferred bonus;
- share options;
- performance share plan (LTIP).

Compared to what long-term incentives in peer companies would deliver for equivalent levels of performance, the programme provides median rewards for good performance and upper-quartile rewards for excellent performance.

The design of each plan element is generally aligned with typical market practice. However, the performance conditions in the share option scheme are tougher than those used by many other listed companies.

We discuss the operation of each plan in detail below.

DEFERRED BONUS

Executives may volunteer to defer for three years up to 50 per cent of their annual bonuses; the deferred bonus is invested in company shares. If the executive remains with the company for the three-year deferral period, the company provides additional matching shares on a one-for-one basis.

SHARE OPTIONS

Annual grants are provided. The grant size is approximately three times salary for main board directors. Options vest after three years, subject to performance conditions. The options lapse if the performance conditions are not met after three years.

No options vest unless earnings per share (EPS) growth is at least 6 per cent per annum. The number of options vesting is determined on a sliding-scale basis with one-third vesting where EPS growth is 6 per cent per annum and all vesting where EPS growth is 12 per cent per annum.

PERFORMANCE SHARE PLAN (LTIP)

Main board directors receive an annual conditional award of shares equal to 75 per cent of salary. The number of shares vesting after three years depends on how Compass's total shareholder return (TSR) compares to that of the other companies that comprise the FTSE 100 at the start of the performance period.

At the end of the performance period, the companies are ranked in order of the TSR achieved. If Compass's TSR puts it into the bottom half of companies (ie below median), no shares vest. If it is in the top half, the number of shares vesting is determined on a sliding-scale basis, with 40 per cent vesting for median performance and 100 per cent vesting for upper-quartile performance or better.

There is a secondary performance condition that no shares will vest unless EPS has grown at least in line with the RPI.

A description of total shareholder return may be found in Chapter 23.

Appendix H

Using Excel for Managing Pay Reviews

IT IN SUPPORT OF IMPROVED DECISION-MAKING PROCESSES

The ever-evolving world of IT and electronic communications has changed how salary data are reviewed and managed quite radically in the last decade. Applications and data can now be accessed and assessed from almost anywhere in the world; organizations are making increasing use of the Internet, data are published on the Internet (for example, Hay Group's online application Hay Pay Net) and users can communicate at speed through e-mail.

In addition, the computers and the software are becoming more and more powerful and sophisticated. Hand in hand with this, HR and reward professionals are adapting to this changing environment to develop more efficient processes. It is now increasingly typical to manage pay reviews for an organization on an Excel spreadsheet, through which a number of alternative options can be tested.

Compensation managers now generally analyse the implications of new grade structures, cost pay review matrices and plan salary reviews such that any proposed options can rapidly be costed through simple changes on a spreadsheet. It also, very importantly in terms of improved local ownership and consistency of pay decisions, means that HR and reward professionals are able to carry out salary reviews for each operating division with the relevant line managers on-site using a laptop.

Most HR and reward consultancies can provide guidance and support in doing this and getting the best out of the links with the HR systems in use.

TYPICAL USES

The four main analyses that remuneration specialists undertake in using Excel spreadsheets for managing pay reviews are:

1. *Internal comparisons.* Pay practice can be analysed across divisions, functions, etc, within an organization.
2. *External comparisons.* Current practice can be analysed against salary and benefit survey market data.
3. *Policy development.* New pay and grading initiatives (eg new grade structures, pay progression rules and benefit costs) can be tested against the employee population to determine cost outcomes.
4. *Individual pay review modelling.* Once pay policies are agreed, reward specialists need to be able to allocate pay awards, based on factors such as market movements, performance, position in range, time in job and other influences on particular jobs.

Following this, results need to be communicated to managers for fine-tuning, through the production of reports showing the relevant facts about their staff. Again, spreadsheets that highlight the implications of their decisions are very useful for this.

Finally, when all pay movements have been agreed, employees need to be notified of the change. This can typically be produced through a standard letter or statement, using a mail-merge facility from the database. It is also straightforward to personalize pay review letters to recognize specific achievements or give differential performance messages (see Chapter 40).

EXAMPLES OF OUTPUT

The typical output for these four uses outlined above is generated via either tables or charts. Figures H.1 to H.4 and Tables H.1 and H.2 illustrate some examples of the analyses, and Figure H.5 shows an example of a computer-generated pay review letter.

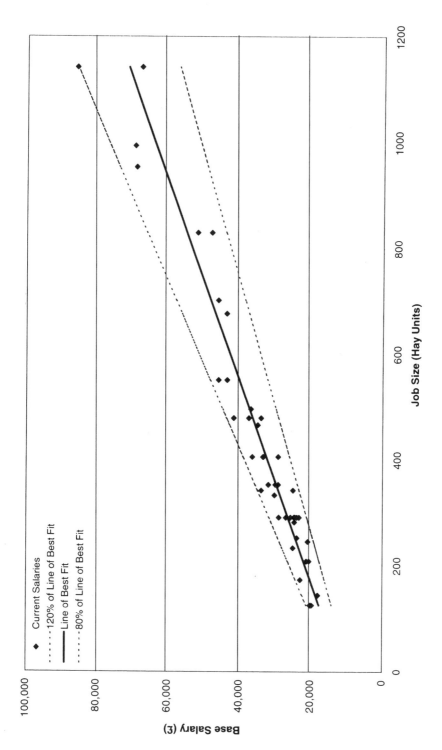

Figure H.1 Internal analysis of current pay of practice

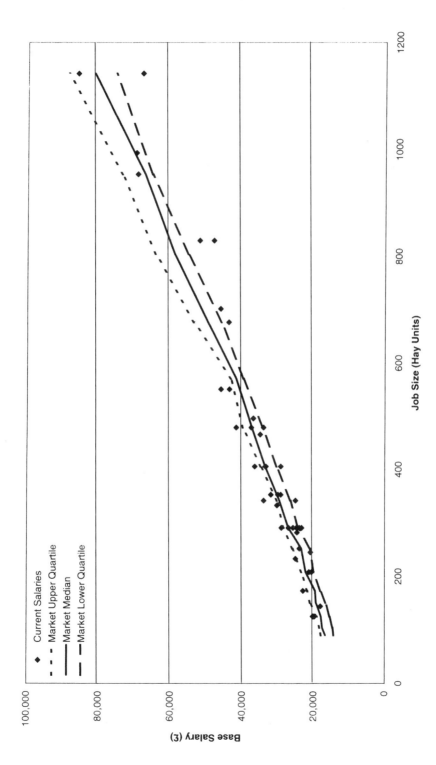

Figure H.2 Analysis of current pay practice compared to market data

Table H.1 Analysis of current pay practice compared to market data

Job title	Grade	Job size (Hay Units)	Current salary (£)	Salary market data (£)			Current salary as % of		
				Upper quartile	Median	Lower quartile	Upper quartile	Median	Lower quartile
Administrator	1	144	18,000	20,900	19,300	16,500	85%	93%	109%
Finance Manager	2	233	26,000	25,900	23,400	21,000	100%	111%	124%
Management Accountant	3	406	34,000	34,800	33,600	30,400	98%	101%	112%
Director or Communications	4	994	60,000	73,500	67,100	65,100	82%	89%	92%

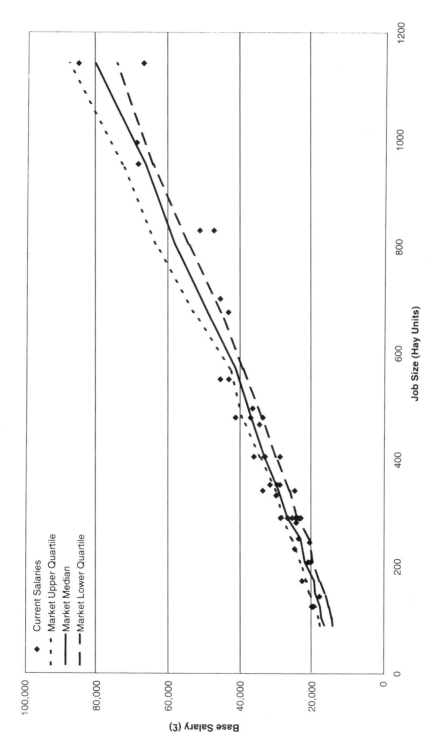

Figure H.2 Analysis of current pay practice compared to market data

Table H.1 Analysis of current pay practice compared to market data

Job title	Grade	Job size (Hay Units)	Current salary (£)	Salary market data (£)			Current salary as % of		
				Upper quartile	Median	Lower quartile	Upper quartile	Median	Lower quartile
Administrator	1	144	18,000	20,900	19,300	16,500	85%	93%	109%
Finance Manager	2	233	26,000	25,900	23,400	21,000	100%	111%	124%
Management Accountant	3	406	34,000	34,800	33,600	30,400	98%	101%	112%
Director or Communications	4	994	60,000	73,500	67,100	65,100	82%	89%	92%

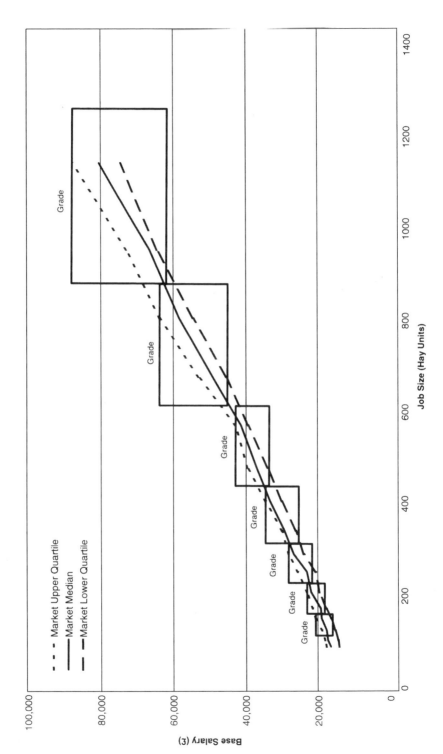

Figure H.3 Analysis of proposed grading structure compared to market data

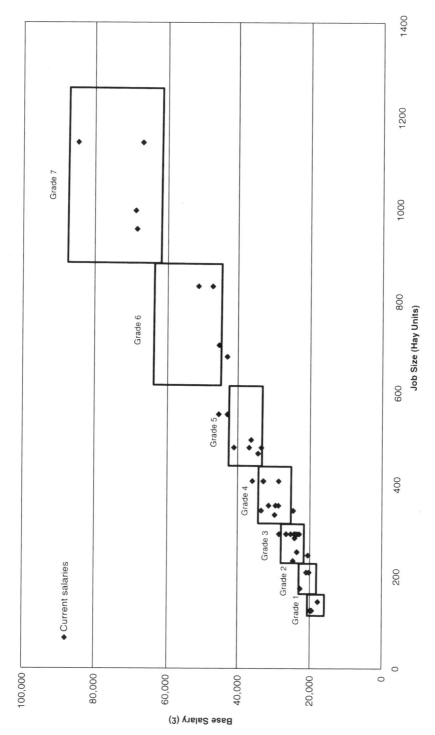

Figure H.4 Position of current salaries against proposed grading structure

Table H.2 Modelling of salary reviews

Job title	Grade	Current Salary (£)	Compa-ratio	Performance rating	Salary increase	New salary (£)	Cost (£)
Administrator	1	18,000	93%	3	2%	18,360	360
Finance Manager	2	26,000	111%	5	4%	27,040	1,040
Management Accountant	3	34,000	101%	2	0%	34,000	0
Director of Communications	4	60,000	89%	4	6%	63,600	3,600

16th January 2004

Private and Confidential
Mr Joe Bloggs
1 The Street
Anytown

Dear Joe

PAY REVIEW JANUARY 2004

Further to the pay review last July when cost of living increases only were applied, your salary has now been reviewed in accordance with our performance review scheme for staff. The scheme provides financial rewards in the form of increases to basic or lump sum bonuses linked to an assessment of your performance.

Consequently, I am pleased to confirm that from 1st January 2004 your salary is adjusted to £20,000 per annum. Please note that an additional 1.25% cost of living increase has been awarded.

In addition, you are to receive a lump sum bonus of £2,000.

Attached with this letter is a Total Remuneration Statement. This is a new feature which sets out the value of your total remuneration package.

XYZ plc recognise that the high reputation of our organisation is built on the commitment and skills of our employees.

As such, we believe that our employees deserve a high quality remuneration package. We also believe that there is a more to remuneration than just basic salary. Therefore, as an employee within the XYZ Group you also receive performance related pay and have access to a range of competitive benefits.

Surveys in other companies have shown that sometimes employees are not aware that they are entitled to certain benefits or realise how much the value of benefits adds to their package. Therefore, this statement outlines the benefits which make up your total remuneration package, including their value.

This statement has been prepared with assistance from Hay Group. They are a leading consultancy with extensive experience of employee benefits and are wholly independent of XYZ. Hay Group have used their standard actuarial methodology to value your benefits.

I hope that you find this statement useful. If you have any questions or comments contact the appropriate HR Manager for your business division or Head Office department.

On behalf of the company and its shareholders I would like to thank you for your efforts over the last year and look forward to your continued support in the future.

Yours sincerely

Joan Smith
Divisional Director

Figure H.5   Example of computer-generated pay review letter

XYZ PLC
TOTAL REMUNERATION STATEMENT

PERSONAL INFORMATION	EFFECTIVE DATE 1 JANUARY 2004
Employee Number: 99999999 Salary Band: 9	Employee Name: Joe Bloggs Company Start Date: 01/01/85

Summary of Remuneration Package

- ▬ Basic Pay (incl Allowances)
- ▬ Performance Related Pay
- ▬ Pension Scheme
- ▬ Company Car
- ▬ Healthcare
- Holiday

SALARY AND PERFORMANCE RELATED PAY	£ per annum
Basic salary as at 1 January 2004*:	20,000
Allowance at 1 January 2004:	0
Lump sum performance related pay, paid January 2004:	2,000
TOTAL VALUE OF SALARY AND PERFORMANCE RELATED PAY:	22,000

BENEFITS	£ per annum
Pension, death and ill-health benefits:	2,889
Car benefits (including vehicle incentive scheme):	3,620
Holiday (23 days);	1,538
Private Healthcare:	700
TOTAL VALUE OF BENEFITS:	8,747

TOTAL REMUNERATION:	£30,747

In addition you are eligible for the following benefits:

- – Accident Insurance
- – Special Leave
- – Long Service Awards

Notes

Every effort has been made to ensure the accuracy of your statement. If it is not consistent with your actual package, as outlined in your contract of employment, then the terms and conditions stated in that contract will prevail.

The valuation of your benefits (other than pay) has been carried out on your behalf by Hay Group. It is intended to illustrate the total value of your package; the figures should not be used for any other purpose. Please note that this statement does not take into account your individual family or financial circumstances.

Usage

All of these charts and tables can be produced fairly straightforwardly through Excel spreadsheets. The typical functions required are the chart wizard and lookup tables.

The most effective way of using Excel to carry out this work is by having a worksheet containing all the individual employee data and a 'master' worksheet containing the variables to be modelled.

For example, a table outlining pay increases in a matrix analysed by both current position in salary range and performance rating is shown in Table H.3, where 5 is the highest performance level. Using lookups for each individual from the table, his or her pay increase for the year can be determined and the total cost modelled. By adjusting any of the inputs in the table such as the percentage awarded by position in salary range, the change in cost can be seen immediately.

Table H.3 A pay matrix

| Performance rating | Position in salary range | | |
	<90%	90–110%	>110%
1	0%	0%	0%
2	2%	0%	0%
3	4%	2%	0%
4	6%	4%	2%
5	8%	6%	4%

Appendix I

Disclosure and Other Regulatory Requirements Relating to Remuneration

The annual report and accounts for all listed companies must disclose detailed information on their policies and practices concerning directors' remuneration. The required mechanisms, procedures and disclosures are set out in:

- the Combined Code on Corporate Governance;
- the UK Listing Authority's Listing Rules; and
- the Directors' Remuneration Report Regulations 2002.

The provisions cover the following areas:

- the remuneration committee;
- the report produced by that committee;
- remuneration policy, service contracts and compensation;
- share schemes and long-term incentives.

THE REMUNERATION COMMITTEE

A remuneration committee should be in place to advise on the policy governing executive directors' remuneration. They should advise on specific packages for each executive director, including pension rights and compensation payments. The Combined Code on Corporate Governance, section B2, sets out the role and responsibilities of the remuneration committee.

THE REMUNERATION COMMITTEE'S REPORT

The committee should produce a report containing certain basic information which should be disclosed in the annual report and accounts. The disclosures are set out in the Directors' Remuneration Report Regulations 2002, Schedule 7A, and the UK Listing Authority's Listing Rules, section 12.43A(c).

REMUNERATION POLICY, SERVICE CONTRACTS AND COMPENSATION

The provisions on directors' remuneration are broken down into four areas:

- the underlying principles;
- the remuneration policy of the company;
- the policy covering service contracts and compensation for loss of office;
- the prinicples supporting the company's procedures.

These are covered by the Combined Code on Corporate Governance, section B.

EMPLOYEES' SHARE SCHEMES AND LONG-TERM INCENTIVE SCHEMES

The requirements for companies introducing new and amending existing employees' share schemes and long-term incentive schemes are set out in The UK Listing Authority's Listing Rules, sections 13.13 to 13.17 and 13.30 to 13.32.

The types of new arrangements that require shareholders' approval are set out in sections 13.13 (certain arrangements are exempted by section 13.13A) and the contents of the circular to be put to shareholders with the request for their approval is set out in sections 13.14 to 13.16.

The contents of a circular to accompany a request to shareholders for the amendment of a scheme are set out in section 13.17.

Where (rarely) an employees' share scheme involves the issue of discounted options, the company must satisfy the additional requirements of section 13.30 (certain arrangements are exempted by section 13.31), and the additional contents of the circular to be put to shareholders with the request for their approval is set out in section 13.32.

SOURCE WEB ADDRESSES

The Combined Code on Corporate Governance,
www.frc.org.uk/combined.cfm
The UK Listing Authority's Listing Rules,
www.fsa.gov.uk/pubs/ukla/lr_chapters4
The Directors' Remuneration Report Regulations 2002,
www.hmso.gov.uk/si/si2002/20021986.htm

Appendix J

Examples of Incentive Schemes

Example A: an annual incentive scheme for the directors of a private company

> Author's Note: Health Warning!
> These case studies are based on real schemes in real companies. Each scheme was developed to suit a particular enterprise in a situation at a particular time. They are included to illustrate the decisions that need to be taken when designing a plan and some of the factors that will influence the decisions reached. They should therefore be read in conjunction with Chapters 22 and 35, which outline the design process and the issues to consider when developing a scheme.

The company

The company was a management buy-out in (MBO) June 1991 when the current chairman and chief executive and five other directors purchased the business. Institutional investors provided the equity finance and an organization provided the acquisition debt.

The business has grown rapidly since the MBO and it is likely to be floated or sold within the next few years.

The six executive directors have a significant equity stake but no annual bonus opportunity except for the company-wide plan for staff. This pays 2.5 per cent of salary if the company achieves its profit budget (this is considerably less than the norm for executive directors).

The equity interest held by the members of the team is considered to provide an appropriate linkage to medium term company performance and although this might need to be replaced following a change in ownership.

The aim of the bonus plan was to:

▌ provide a competitive remuneration package that is likely to remain broadly appropriate after flotation or a change of ownership (apart from medium/long term incentives);
▌ focus attention on key business objectives that are specified in the bonus plan targets;
▌ create a performance results orientated culture, ie pay for results not effort;
▌ add credibility to the budgeting/targeting process – targets are only acceptable to incentive participants if felt fair, since part of their pay is dependent on them;
▌ enhance its competitive position in attracting, motivating and retaining the highest calibre of management;
▌ motivate directors by providing the opportunity to earn bonus for the achievement of fair targets;
▌ increase the proportion of pay which is a variable cost; pay only for performance when it occurs – one-off, non-consolidated payments are made rather than adjustments to salary, which may have a higher cost in the longer term and after year one are not related to performance.

Size of payments

The following levels of payments were provided:

Performance Level	Bonus as a percentage of salary
Below threshold	NIL
Threshold	10
Target	20
Maximum	40

The 'threshold level' is the lowest performance that earns a bonus.

A sliding scale would apply between 'threshold' and 'target' and between 'target' and 'maximum' payment levels.

Form of payments

The plan pays out in cash only, as the directors already have significant shareholdings in the company.

Timing of payments

Payments are made annually after the company results have been audited.

Performance measures

The company reserves the right to vary the performance measures from year to year and their relative importance.

The key business objective is to improve profit before tax (PBT) and the cash generated from the business. Profit before tax is calculated after exceptional and extraordinary items.

The constituents of cash generated are:

1. profit
2. less increases in working capital
3. plus depreciation
4. less capital expenditure on fixed assets
5. less tax

Profit is already measured as the first measure of the incentive plan. Changes in working capital (which comprises stocks plus debtors less creditors) are crucial measures that management can and must control. Depreciation charges are a result of previous investment. It is essentially a known figure, so has minimal effect on the incentive outcome. Capital expenditure is managed via an agreed investment programme. It would be wrong to encourage (or reward!) holding back on investing. This is excluded.

Tax paid is in respect of the previous year. It is, in the long term, affected by management actions but is not appropriate for inclusion in an annual incentive plan.

The incentive focuses on working capital as the most controllable measure of cash generated. It takes account of the requirement for extra cash if turnover increases by measuring working capital as the ratio:

$$\frac{\text{working capital} \times 365}{\text{turnover}}$$

Individual measures

The roles and accountabilities of the directors are clear and the performance of each individual readily identifiable.

In these circumstances it was decided to have an individual element to the incentive. Participants will feel it is more equitable to reward those who contribute more than those who contribute less during the year to the group success.

Weighting of the Measures

The Directors should have the majority of their bonus weighted towards the overall group result:

	Bonus as percentage of Salary		
	Weighting	Target	Excellent
Profits	60	12	24
Working Capital	20	4	8
Individual Measures	20	4	8
Total	100	20	40

For the chairman and chief executive, there is no individual measure. His/her weighting would be 75 per cent profits and 25 per cent working capital.

Performance Criteria

The budget process is robust, and is subject to detailed, informed scrutiny by non-executive directors, prior to approval. This is important since the incentive scheme can become overly influenced by executive directors – such concerns are small in this organization.

An examination of recent results suggests that the recent history has been quite volatile. It would be extremely difficult to set a base figure by reference to the historical data. (Please note that many organizations will set the incentive target as, eg last year; or last year plus 10 per cent; or average of last three years plus inflation; etc. None of these simple formulae appears satisfactory for this company.)

On balance it was decided to use payments versus budget for the profit figure with a scale of payment starting at 90 per cent, with maximum reward for 130 per cent of target. For working capital a budget figure for a number of days was set.

Performance measurement period

The performance is measured annually over the accounting year.

Scales of Payment

Profits

The target was 90 per cent of budget. Payment for achieving this level is warranted as this threshold is tough. The excellent level of performance should be set at 120 per cent of budget. Historic results suggest that this is stretching but achievable.

Working Capital

The percentage of budget approach is not reliable over time for working capital, because we are taking percentages of small numbers. The threshold was set at an absolute level below the budget figure, ie five days, equal to about £882,000 of working capital.
   The excellent level was set at ten days (£1.76 million).

Example B – a retention bonus scheme for key contributors following a merger

Context

The announcement of the merger of two financial organizations has inevitably created temporary uncertainty among the senior executive cadre in one of the organizations. Some individuals would lose their main board positions; many roles will disappear in the next few months as operations are merged, but with no immediate clarity about which incumbents will be preferred; and other senior executives are likely to be needed to maintain the organization until the process is completed (ie for two years), but have no security beyond this. Retention is particularly important to the organization as there are many posts where successors are not immediately available.
   The organization has particular problems in retaining key contributors over the short and medium term. Several top executives are mobile, with little time invested in the organization, and thus no significant deferred rewards (such as pension) tied up in the firm. Others have very marketable skills and experience, for example in bank assurance integration and operations. It has also been the style of the organisation in the past to have additional lock-in schemes for key contributors – most of these have ended recently and the long-term incentive plan using restricted shares has been shelved as a result of the merger proposals.

In light of this situation, a bonus plan was introduced to assist in retention. Such plans were only part of a programme to retain the best talent from the organization.

Criteria for 'key contributor' treatment

A preliminary list of candidates for a key contributor retention plan was drawn up. From discussion of the individuals, it was possible to identify five groups of executives where there is an identified risk of loss and a perceived business need to safeguard retention:

▌ High performers who would quickly lose their current jobs but should be in line for key jobs in any new organization.
▌ Individuals with skills and experience which will be especially valuable in implementation of the strategy of the combined business.
▌ Individuals that are key to integration of the operations. It is to be expected that at some time in the future these people will be eligible for new roles in the integrated organization but there is unlikely to be clarity for some time.
▌ Individuals in roles that will continue to exist until the process is complete.
▌ Other executives in key jobs with high business impact and where there are no immediate successors.

A number of individuals fell into more than one group; but in combination these criteria define more than just an 'at risk' group. In effect they are the organization's identified key contributors.

General Principles of Retention Bonuses

The key general principles regarding retention bonuses were considered to be:

▌ They need offer the prospect of a sufficient payment at a date in advance to deter an executive from seeking alternative employment. The longer the period of retention the greater the sum needs to be. Obviously other deferred rewards such as share options and pension entitlements need to be taken into account. Much depends on an individual's situation, but as a general proposition, for the average mid-career executive who has marketable skills elsewhere, required for a period of two years, a sum of at least 50 per cent of salary, and, more probably, 75 per cent of salary to change behaviour in very uncertain conditions was considered necessary.
▌ The sum needs to be large enough to cause a potential employer who is head-hunting to think twice before making an offer. Obviously for

some really scarce skills even exceptionally high retention bonuses can be bought out, but in the case of the organization it would also be necessary to take into account other elements that a potential new employer would have to buy out, eg share options.

▌ Making them performance related (or share price related) reduces their effectiveness as retention vehicles, but ensures that they are only paid if the underlying performance justifies payment.

Plan Design

Taking the above design principles into account, and the reasons for considering a scheme, a key contributor plan was introduced which did not fit individual circumstances so well but which was simple and ensured equity within this key contributor group.

A key contributor programme

This was performance related, lasting a maximum of three years, when it is assumed that integration would be completed to the requirements of the current strategy.

The outline of the design is:

▌ *Participants*: all executives in both organizations who are identified as falling within the criteria identified above, following a review of all the executives of the combined organization.

▌ *Earnings potential*: a maximum of approximately 30 per cent of base salary per annum for the three years of the scheme, with accruals each year but payments only at the end of years two and three. This would be additional to payments under normal annual and long-term incentive arrangements.

▌ *Performance measures*: achievement of predetermined financial measures of performance for the relevant division or operating unit in which the individual works. The minimum expected earnings amounted to around 20 per cent of base salary per annum.

▌ *Payment currency*: cash.

The advantages of this scheme are its simplicity, avoidance of inequities and scope for aggressive relationship to performance. The disadvantages are the potential cost (not least in payments to those individuals who may be severed during the period), the duplication of payments made from other bonus plans, and the expectations such a scheme may engender for payments after the key retention period.

Example C: a bus company

Long-term incentives/rewards for senior executives

Annual awards, each to operate over a three-year performance period. Award level is 75 per cent of basic salary for executive directors, less for other participants:

- Executive Directors: 75 per cent
- Regional Directors, Group Financial Controller: 40 per cent
- Operating company MDs, selected senior managers: 25 per cent

Awards converted to a number of shares at (averaged) price prior to the share of the performance period. Performance measure is the bus company. EPS growth relative to EPS growth in FTSE 100.

Shares 'earned' at the end of the performance period are calculated as a percentage of those awarded, depending on the bus company's performance ranking compared to comparator companies:

Percentile Ranking	Percentage of shares earned
1–25	100%
26–49	Sliding scale
50	25%
51–100	Nil

Shares earned are released immediately.

Example D: annual incentive scheme for a financial services organization

Review of the current scheme

The current scheme was designed in 1993 and introduced for the financial year 1994/5.

It was based on the earlier scheme that had existed, but modified to make it more relevant to the business circumstances at the time and to eliminate some anomalies and ambiguities in the earlier scheme.

For three years prior to the introduction of the new scheme, the organization's profit performance was poor, and no bonuses had been paid on the old scheme – neither would they have been paid on the new scheme, had it been in place at the time.

However, since the start of 1994, profit performance has improved dramatically. As a result, the scheme paid approximately 18 per cent of salary in 1994/5, and is likely to pay out at the cap level of 30 per cent for the year just ended (1995/6). If planned performance for 1996/7 is achieved, it will also pay out at the cap level of 30 per cent.

Hence the scheme has done very much what it was intended to do – to provide significant reward to the executive directors to reflect the major profit improvements achieved.

However, in considering the appropriateness of the scheme in its present form for the next few years, there was a concern that it is not well geared to the levels of profit performance anticipated.

Over the four years remaining of the five-year plan period (ie starting January 1997), achievement of planned performance will generate payment at the cap level of 30 per cent in every year. In fact, the 'theoretical' payment which would be generated if the cap did not apply is significantly above the 30 per cent cap level every year, as shown in the following table.

Year	Pre-tax profit £m	Percentage ROSF	Capped Bonus as percentage	'Theoretical' [ercentage bonus if cap did not apply
07/8	49	35.08	30	39.15
98/9	55	33.45	30	36.20
99/0	67	345.55	30	38.19
00/0	75	32.47	30	34.45

This situation means that the existing scheme will not satisfy two basic criteria of good scheme design:

1 There is no 'upside' opportunity for increased earnings by achieving profit above the planned level.
2 Equally, the 'downside' risk of reduced payout if profit falls below planned level, is reduced. ROSF would need to fall by several percentage points below plan, before there would be any impact on incentive payment.

In other words, the payment will be largely insensitive to actual profit performance, and hence be largely predictable, except of course in the case of a severe downturn in profits.

The reason for this is the major change in profit expectation since the scheme was designed in 1993. At that time, the organization's business plan quoted 20 per cent ROSF as an overall objective, and the major emphasis was on generating sufficient profit to pay a dividend and maintain shareholder value, for which 15 per cent ROSF was needed. The cap level of 30 per cent ROSF was far removed from the performance at the time. In contrast, the year just ended has generated over 30 per cent ROSF and the five-year plan anticipates ROSF between 32 and 35 per cent every year up to 2001.

The scheme was, therefore, redesigned to reflect the new business situation and expectations, and hence maintain a genuine incentive content in the scheme.

Basis of the current scheme

Many features of the current scheme continue to provide a sound basis, irrespective of the actual level of performance anticipated, and were maintained in the redesign. Such features include:

- the use of a common measure of corporate performance rather than individual objectives or business unit targets, so as to reflect the nature of the Directors' roles and the strong requirement for teamwork;
- the use of ROSF as the measure of performance. This ratio is to a large degree 'self regulating', since improved profit performance builds reserves for the following year, hence raising the denominator in the ROSF calculation. Thus to maintain ROSF in percentage terms, the requirement is for continuing profit growth, which in turn builds shareholder value;
- the use of a threshold value of ROSF, to trigger payment;
- the use of a cap level of ROSF, above which no further payment is made;
- a simple straight line relationship between ROSF and payment, between the threshold level and the cap.

What was required is a recalibration to the levels of performance now expected, rather than a radical redesign.

Recalibration of the scheme

In examining possible recalibrations, there was regard for the following features of typical external practice regarding annual incentive schemes for Directors.

▌ The Median value for threshold payment is in the range 5-9 per cent The existing threshold payment of 7.5 per cent clearly aligns with this.

▌ The Median payment level for 'on target' achievement is 20 per cent of salary.

▌ The Median level at which schemes are capped is 40 per cent.

In the light of this, the current threshold payment of 7.5 per cent was maintained and the cap payment was increased to 40 per cent – though at a higher level of ROSF than in the existing scheme.

The issue of 'on target' calibration was more difficult. In the first instance, it was difficult to determine what 'on-target' actually means – though the plans for 1997–2001 indicate an expectation of ROSF in the region of 32-35 per cent.

However, if the scheme were recalibrated to pay around 20 per cent for achievement of this level, this would produce a significant drop in pay out from 30 per cent to 20 per cent for plan achievement, when compared with the current scheme. This could be demotivating for the directors, especially given the fact that plan achievement actually represents a steady and significant growth in profits each year.

The new scheme therefore aimed to produce a similar level of payment to the current scheme (ie 30 per cent) for achievement of ROSF in the planned region of 32–35 per cent, but with a potential of earning up to 40 per cent for significant over-achievement, and a higher ROSF threshold, so as to sharpen the decline in pay out if performance falls below planned levels.

This is based on the following parameters.

▌ The threshold ROSF at which the scheme pays out is raised from 17.5 per cent to 22.5 per cent.

▌ The actual threshold payment is maintained at 7.5 per cent.

▌ The scheme pays out 30 per cent of salary at an ROSF of 33.75 per cent, which is around the average level of planned ROSF for the four-year period 1997-2001.

▌ The scheme is capped at 40 per cent of salary, at an ROSF level of 38.75 per cent.

The formula for this is as follows (between threshold and cap).

$$\text{Payment as per cent of salary} = (ROSF \times 2) - 37.5$$

This compares with the current formula of:

$$\text{Payment} = (ROSF \times 1.8) - 24.$$

That is:

▌ The slope of the relationship is significantly steeper (2.0 compared with 1.8), giving a more sensitive response to changes in ROSF.
▌ The constant subtracted is much greater, to reflect the higher threshold.

The following table shows the payment that this scheme would generate in each of the four years 1997–2001.

Year	ROSF (per cent)	Current scheme payment (per cent)	Illustrative new scheme payment (per cent)
1997/8	35.08	30	32.7
1998/9	33.45	30	29.4
99/00	34.55	30	31.6
00/01	32.47	30	27.4

It thus satisfies the requirement of maintaining payment at around 30 per cent for plan achievement, thus avoiding demotivational effects.
    However, it is much more sensitive both to reduction and increase of ROSF performance, as illustrated in the following table.

ROSF	Current Scheme	Illustrative scheme payment (per cent)
17.50	7.50	0
20.00	12.00	0
22.50	16.50	7.50
25.00	21.00	12.50
27.50	25.50	17.509
30.00-	30.00	22.50
32.50	30.00	27.50
35.00	30.00	32.50
37.50	30.00	37.50
40.00	30.00	40.00 (capped)

(The 'breakeven' point at which the new scheme pays the same 30 per cent as the old scheme is at 33.75 per cent ROSF. Below this the old scheme pays more, above this the new scheme pays more.)

Index